BY DUMAS MALONE

JEFFERSON AND HIS TIME
(of which the following volumes have been published)

JEFFERSON THE VIRGINIAN

JEFFERSON AND THE RIGHTS OF MAN

JEFFERSON AND THE ORDEAL OF LIBERTY

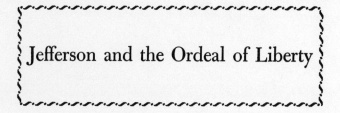

Jefferson and the Ordeal of Liberty

JEFFERSON AND HIS TIME

VOLUME THREE

Jefferson
and the Ordeal
of Liberty

BY DUMAS MALONE

BACK BAY BOOKS

LITTLE, BROWN AND COMPANY
BOSTON • NEW YORK • TORONTO • LONDON

This work as a whole is for
ELISABETH GIFFORD MALONE

This volume is for
MY FELLOW DIRECTORS
of the
THOMAS JEFFERSON
MEMORIAL FOUNDATION

Contents

Introduction

THIS volume is the third in the series which began with *Jefferson the Virginian* and was continued with *Jefferson and the Rights of Man*. Each volume is a unit in itself and can stand alone, which is fortunate in view of the years that have intervened between them. The lapse of time between the second of these books and the present one has turned out to be much greater than I had anticipated. No explanation of this delay need be given here beyond the statement that by force of circumstances I had to devote myself to other things for an unconscionable time, and that when I was enabled to concentrate on this work as my major task, it proved to be considerably more difficult than I had expected. The extraordinary man whose story I have been trying to tell is full of surprises even to those who flatter themselves that they know him rather well. By the same token, however, while bewildering at times, rarely if ever is he dull.

In the last volume we left him at the end of the year 1792, still secretary of state under George Washington, who had recently been unanimously re-elected President to nobody's surprise. In this book we carry him to his own election as President in February, 1801, after a tie vote with his running mate which was distinctly surprising. Thus, the present volume covers almost the same amount of time as its immediate predecessor; but since Jefferson was in retirement during more than three years of this period, and his own papers are less numerous than in the years covered by *Jefferson and the Rights of Man*, I not unnaturally assumed that this would be a shorter book. In fact, it is longer and has proved the most difficult of the three to write.

I hope that the unfolding story will not seem too long, and that the difficulties will appear to have been reasonably well overcome. The author of a book like this is supposed to build a road over which others may proceed less laboriously, and he would not want to discourage prospective travelers. Nor should he seek to anticipate their individual judgments, which may not and certainly need not coincide with his own. Yet he may be permitted to say something of the terrain over which he himself has passed with necessarily slow step, of the weather he encountered, and of the bearing of his distinguished companion. Much of this terrain proved rugged; there were violent storms and many cloudy spells, along with at least one considerable stretch of pleasant weather; and Mr. Jefferson, while not always like himself, generally managed to maintain his characteristic hopefulness and equanimity, adjusting himself skillfully if painfully to a succession of difficult situations.

The first two chapters of the book may be regarded as transitional between it and its predecessor, though I hope they are not without intrinsic interest. The rest of the chapters are divided into four parts, which are not equal as mere time goes. Had I followed the tentative outline I drew when making a preliminary survey of the period, the proportions of the narrative would have been different from what they now are. But a biographical year is not the same as a calendar year: its length depends on the actions of the central figure and on the importance of the events to which his life and career are related. By this standard the year 1793, with which the main narrative begins, was an inordinately long one. It may well have been the longest Jefferson ever spent: I thought I should never get him through it.

The unsuccessful attack on Hamilton which reached its climax in the Giles Resolutions may be described as the last phase of the battle on the fiscal front between the Secretary of the Treasury and his critics, especially the Virginians in Congress. Without entering here into the question of Jefferson's part in it — a moot question which is treated at some length in Chapter II — I will merely say that while he retained deep suspicions of his colleague's financial management, he could do nothing about this during the rest of the time that they served together. The issues that could be faced by him fell properly into his own department. While these had exceedingly important domestic implications, they may be accurately described as cosmic.

The first of the four main sections of the book covers the final and most crucial phase of his secretaryship of state in one of the most momentous years in the modern history of the Western world. The second deals with the period of his retirement, the third with the series of events culminating in his assumption of the leadership of the opposition party, and the fourth with the crisis during the half-war with France, when the very existence of political opposition was threatened at home and the basic freedom of individual human beings gravely imperiled. Only during his retirement from public life did he find the tranquillity he craved and the opportunity to be personally constructive — as the builder of a famous house and the restorer of wasted lands. In all the other sections of this book he was on the defensive, undergoing a succession of personal ordeals. Partisan considerations entered into his mind and affected his conduct increasingly as party lines were sharply drawn and as he came to identify the cause of genuine national independence and human freedom with the cause of his own party. To a greater extent than previously he reconciled himself to the exigencies of politics, but the best single explanation of his thought and actions in this highly controversial period is that he was seeking to preserve or restore what he called the "spirit of 1776," and that he viewed the ordeal of the decade as that of Liberty herself.

In the year 1793 the young American Republic, potentially a giant but as yet only a stripling among the Powers, had to find a *modus vivendi* in the midst of world war, revolution, and counter-revolution — and this at just the time that the voice of political opposition was gaining strength at home. We need not anticipate here the series of dilemmas with which the Secretary of State was confronted as a patriotic official concerned for the security of his country, as a republican who feared monarchical reaction, and as a sympathizer with the rising political opposition who himself could not yet be partisan. These can be best perceived as this responsible public servant faced and adjusted himself to them during this, the most crowded of his years thus far. On the world front the position the young Republic arrived at was the historic policy of neutrality: non-involvement in the affairs of Mother Europe. My own review of these events has enhanced my appreciation of the official American response to this world situation. The contrasts with the position of the giant Republic of the West in our own times are more striking than the parallels: our inescapable ordeal in the twentieth century has been that of leadership, not neutrality. But the similarities between that time and our own age of world war, revolution, and counter-revolution are sufficient to give us a certain feeling of familiarity and should help us to understand the difficulties that were then faced by the responsible leaders of the insecure Republic.

The policy they so wisely arrived at was the work of no single man but of an administration, and it was fortunate that different points of view were represented in the executive council. But the proclamation of a policy of non-involvement was far easier than the definition and implementation of it; and the day-to-day task of carrying it into effect fell chiefly on the Secretary of State. If we designate this as a policy of *fair* neutrality, as I think we should, it was chiefly worked out by Jefferson under the eye and with the continuing support of Washington. The narrative should show how painful the process was, and I hope it will also show that fair neutrality was no mere promise but an actual achievement. Others might shade this complicated story differently, but the net result of my study has been to increase my own admiration of Jefferson's high technical competence and diplomatic skill, his basic realism in international matters, and his extraordinary patience. In long retrospect he appears to have been far more successful in the final phase of his service as secretary of state than he himself realized either at the time, when he was so oppressed and agitated by his problems, or later in the decade, when the government was unable or unwilling to maintain fair neutrality. That failure, in my opinion, was the major cause of the diplomatic difficulties into which the country fell after he retired from office, as it was also of the extremes of partisanship to which the anti-Hamiltonians then went, less under Jefferson's leadership than has been commonly supposed but with his tacit approval.

I must confess that I shared Jefferson's feeling of relief when he completed his arduous tour of duty as secretary of state and retired to the quietude of Monticello. The three years and more that he spent there before assuming another office were in reality, and not merely in semblance, a period of withdrawal from public affairs. He was for the time a free man, able to realize on his individuality. Albemarle County, from which he strayed only once in this interim and then only as far as Richmond, offered no such sustenance for his inquiring mind as prerevolutionary Paris had done. Relatively little happened in what he called his remote canton, lovely though its hills and valleys were. But for the first and last time in his life he could really devote himself to farming, renewing his strength like Antaeus by contact with the soil; also, he could now proceed with long-cherished plans to remodel his house, availing himself of architectural ideas he had picked up abroad. Meanwhile he could strengthen the family ties which he valued beyond all else and could seek to repair his neglected finances. The pastoral symphony which he set out to compose remained unfinished, however. He did not have time to work out his full agricultural plans, he never really solved the financial problems he had inherited; and not during the period covered by this book did he complete his distinguished house. Thus the personal record of these years deepens the impression that besides being a man of incessant industry and amazing ingenuity, he was also one of dauntless faith and endless patience.

Developments on the public stage during the period of his retirement enter into this story not because of his direct influence on them, which was slight, but because of their effect on him and his subsequent career. He remained the most conspicuous symbol of republicanism: his services before he became secretary of state and the attacks of the Hamiltonians had made him that. In no active sense was he yet the leader of the opposition party, as his political critics claimed he was; but freed from the necessary restraints of public office, he became increasingly a partisan Republican. And, against rulers of all sorts, he based his hopes more than ever before on the sovereign people. The external political events which affected him most were two. The first was the denunciation of the Democratic societies by Washington, which indicated to him that the President was now a party man and marked the beginnings of divergence between him and the chief he had so long revered. He regarded this as an attack on the basic idea of political opposition, an idea which Washington never really accepted and which perhaps he himself had not fully perceived hitherto. The second was Jay's Treaty, which he regarded as an ignominious surrender of national independence to the British and an unwarranted departure from the policy of fair neutrality at which he himself had arrived so painfully in 1793 and which he and Washington had done so much to establish.

Some of his utterances as a private man were extreme and regrettable. They were not public pronouncements, however, and in this time of absorption in his personal affairs he did not determine party policy, though he went along with it. Individualist though he was in taste and philosophy, he was now convinced of the necessity of being a party man, and throughout the rest of this decade he was one. But even during the election of 1796, when the party of the opposition supported him for President, he played an essentially passive political part. That was the year, indeed, when he was busiest at home. Only in the summer of 1797, when he was back in Philadelphia as Vice President and Madison had retired to Orange County, did he recognize himself as the head of the Republican party. The story of how he came to be that is told in the third of my main sections, certain scientific adventures of his being thrown in to redress the balance.

The last section falls within one of the most intolerant periods in the whole of American history, though certain parallels with this can be readily perceived in the orgies of suspicious patriotism which accompanied and followed our two world wars. It was a time of foreign danger which was grossly exaggerated for domestic political purposes. Jefferson faced this challenge as a lifelong champion of individual freedom and as the most conspicuous figure in the party whose existence was threatened. Also, he was a sensitive human being who was now subjected as never before to personal abuse. His vice-presidential office gave him no power to affect the course of public affairs, but it made his position all the more precarious in a time of hysteria, when any sort of criticism of the administration might be labeled as traitorous. His public conduct hitherto had been marked by restraint, and he had already manifested his extreme distaste for personal controversy, but his political activities in this period were not only sharply restricted by force of circumstances; they were also the most secretive of his career thus far. He and his partisans were wholly on the defensive, and for long months there was little that they could do but wait for the abatement of the fever of the times. In the end they got powerful assistance from President John Adams, who was caught up in the madness at first but eventually did more than any other single man to remove the foreign question from domestic politics. The pity is that political circumstances kept him and Jefferson from getting together and removing it much sooner.

In many respects the issue between Jefferson and Adams was unreal, but between Jefferson and the High Federalists it was sharp, and in the end they defeated themselves by their own excesses. The most important thing that he did was to define this struggle as something more than one between parties, to emphasize the fact that human freedom itself was at stake. This he did in private, not public, and political considerations were mingled with philosophical in his own mind; but by encouraging his own followers to battle in the name of freedom he served both his party and his country well. The times called for the faith and patience with which he was so abundantly supplied. He remained a fitting symbol of republicanism, national independence, and individual liberties, for he embodied the "spirit of 1776" as well as any civilian could. Indeed, it may be contended that his importance as a party leader in these bitter years, as in those immediately preceding them, lay less in what he did than in what he was. It should be noted, however, that the image of him which the Federalists sought to impress on the public mind was far from a good likeness of the man himself.

The degree of his personal activity as a party leader in this period has been exaggerated by both his critics and his admirers. He unquestionably served as a rallying center, he promoted harmony, and he was at the same time a catalyst. His inveterate optimism was a positive quality which must have been contagious. But no small part of the success of this most unusual leader was owing to the fact that he did not meddle with local organization, that he was not officious, that he left other leaders to their own devices, that he was loyal to them even to the point of being uncritical, that he accepted counsel and did not merely give it. In important private letters he defined party policy, but in fact it represented a consensus of opinion. He pressed his own ideas chiefly when he believed the issue of freedom to be involved.

On specific questions the policy of the Republicans naturally reflected the fact that they constituted the opposition. One of the unfortunate results of the excesses of the High Federalists was that these drove their opponents into constitutional positions which now seem incompatible with an effective and balanced government. This was especially true with respect to the powers of the legislature vis-à-vis the executive and the rights of states as against the general government. In the former case Jefferson was in step with the Republicans in Congress, but in the latter he went beyond the most responsible leaders of his party. In connection with the Kentucky and Virginia Resolutions, in protest against the repressive Alien and Sedition Acts, he took the most extreme state-rights position of his entire life. This was in defense of human rights, however, and he was able to retire afterwards to the much more tenable position of Madison, since his own connection with these documents remained a secret. The episode of the Kentucky and Virginia Resolutions was perhaps the most difficult of any that I have attempted to describe in this volume, and I sincerely trust that I got the nuances right.

In an age of immoderation and scurrility Jefferson did not often lapse from his own high standards of propriety, and never consciously in public so far as I know. Furthermore, it would be hard to find another major personage who had comparable provocation. But in moments of desperation in these frustrating years he did avail himself of unworthy instruments and resort to dubious means to a greater degree than in any previous stage of his career. These occasions should be viewed in their full setting of time and circumstance, and I risk some distortion even by mentioning them here. While viewing him I do not forget the decline in the powers and judgment of Washington in this era, the vanity and indiscretion of John Adams, the ruthlessness of Hamilton, and the almost unendurable arrogance of the High Federalists as a group. Yet I must say that after living intimately in spirit with Jefferson in earlier periods of his life, I found him a rather different man in parts of this one. At Monticello and in the hall of the American

Philosophical Society he was wholly in character, but as a party leader he not infrequently seemed out of character. The struggle for political survival was costly and he did not come out of it without some scars. But as he emerged victorious he did not doubt that tyranny had been rebuked by his countrymen and counter-revolution halted. There might be, indeed there were sure to be, other ordeals, but he and his Goddess had survived a severe one.

Elsewhere I have made a number of grateful acknowledgments of the kindnesses shown me by particular persons in the course of the preparation of this book. Here I want to say that I hope to carry Mr. Jefferson through the remaining stages of his long journey with the continued help of such friends as these.

DUMAS MALONE

Alderman Library
University of Virginia
May, 1962

Chronology

1792

Aug. *10* Suspension of the French king, news of which reaches TJ in October.

20 Desertion of the French revolutionary cause by Lafayette, who is imprisoned by the Austrians.

Sept. 21–25 Creation of the French Republic, which becomes known in the U. S. in December.

Nov. *5* The second session of the Second Congress begins.

Dec. *27* A congressional resolution marks the beginning of an inquiry into Hamilton's administration of the Treasury.

1793

Jan. *3* TJ writes William Short about his attitude to the French Revolution ("Adam and Eve" letter).

4 TJ is re-elected vice president of the American Philosophical Society.
Hamilton submits a report on loans, following a congressional request.

9 Most of the stone for the foundations of TJ's remodeled house has been brought up the mountain.

21 Louis XVI is executed, a fact which becomes known in the U. S. in the latter part of March.

23 The first set of Giles Resolutions is introduced.

Feb. *7* TJ informs Washington he will continue as secretary of state for a time.

20 W. S. Smith reports to TJ on French affairs.

27 The second set of Giles Resolutions is introduced.

Mar. *2* The Giles Resolutions are defeated.

4 The second inauguration of Washington occurs.

24 On this date TJ writes one of several letters to American representatives abroad, anticipating neutrality in case of general war.

27 Washington leaves Philadelphia for Mount Vernon.

April *7* TJ informs Washington of the French declaration of war against England and Holland.

8 Genet lands at Charleston.

9 About this time TJ moves to a little house on the Schuylkill, shipping furniture and books to Virginia.

18   Washington, back in Philadelphia, submits 13 questions to his advisers.

22   Washington issues the Proclamation of Neutrality.

28   TJ sends Washington his opinion on the validity of the French treaties.

       He writes his daughter Martha about a scandal involving her sister-in-law.

May *8*   He writes Brissot.

16   Genet arrives in Philadelphia.

28   TJ's grave doubts about Genet are aroused about this time.

June *7*   TJ laments (to Madison) his sacrifices and sufferings as a public official.

14   TJ is presumably disillusioned about Genet by this time.

28   He writes a letter of introduction for Michaux.

29   The first of Hamilton's PACIFICUS letters appears.

30   TJ writes Carmichael and Short about relations with Spain.

July *3*   The Democratic Society of Pennsylvania adopts a constitution.

5   Genet informs TJ of his instructions to Michaux.

7   TJ urges Madison to answer the PACIFICUS letters.

       The *Little Democrat* episode approaches a crisis.

18   TJ, for the President, asks the Supreme Court to give counsel regarding the interpretation of laws and treaties (Jay declines Aug. 8).

31   TJ informs Washington of his determination to retire at the end of September.

       The first of Hamilton's No JACOBIN letters appears, revealing the threat of Genet to appeal from the President to the people.

Aug. *1–2*   The executive council agrees to ask Genet's recall.

5   Gideon Henfield is acquitted.

11   TJ agrees to remain till the end of the year.

       He advises Madison about Republican party policy.

12   In New York, Jay and King publicize Genet's threat.

23   TJ's letter about Genet is sent to France.

24   The first of Madison's HELVIDIUS letters appears.

29   TJ warns the Governor of Kentucky against Americans' joining an expedition against the Spanish.

       During the month, yellow fever appears in Philadelphia.

September   Yellow fever increases in Philadelphia.

10   President Washington leaves the city.

17   TJ leaves for home after informing Genet of the request for his recall.

Oct. *19*   TJ gives a letter of credit to his sister, Mrs. Marks.

25   He sets out from Monticello.

26   The last number of Freneau's *National Gazette* appears.

November   During the month Hamilton raises money to keep Fenno's *Gazette of the United States* alive.

1   TJ arrives in the temporary seat of government at Germantown.

8   He announces the three-mile limit.

30 He leaves Germantown for Philadelphia.

During the month, he works out arrangements whereby his son-in-law can save his Varina plantation.

December During the month Jay, King, Dallas, and Genet engage in controversy over what the Frenchman said.

5 Washington submits to Congress the message dealing with France and England which TJ has prepared.

16 TJ's report on foreign commerce is submitted to Congress.

His report on relations with Spain is presented in confidence.

Dec. 31 TJ formally resigns as secretary of state.

In the course of the year, a new stable is built at Monticello.

1794

Jan. 5 TJ leaves Philadelphia.

16 He arrives at Monticello.

April His correspondents bring him up to date about public affairs in Philadelphia.

May The first delivery is made from TJ's nailery.

12 John Jay sails on his mission to England.

14 TJ comments to Washington on the "degradation" of his lands.

27 Monroe informs TJ of his acceptance of the mission to France.

June 2–10 TJ makes a trip to Richmond and Eppington, the only one from home during his retirement.

August TMR, son-in-law of TJ, travels in the North in pursuit of health.

Toward the end of the month, TJ is visited by Madison.

September He suffers from rheumatism.

7 He declines the offer of the special mission to Spain.

15 James Madison and Dolly Payne Todd are married.

Oct. 24 TJ says he is living in a brick kiln.

In the course of the month, the Whiskey Rebellion is put down in western Pennsylvania.

Nov. 19 In his address to Congress, Washington associates this with the Democratic societies.

Dec. 16 TJ receives his first letter from Monroe about the situation in France.

24 He frees Bob Hemings.

28 He deplores Washington's denunciation of the Democratic societies.

29 He sums up his philosophy of crop rotation to John Taylor.

This month he sets out more than 1100 peach trees, chiefly between his fields.

1795

A harsh winter and excessively rainy summer are disadvantageous to TJ's crops, but conditions are favorable in the autumn.

January   The Randolphs are at Varina, while TJ's grandchildren and Maria are with him at Monticello.

June 24   Jay's Treaty is approved by the Senate.

July   This month, and later in the summer, the Randolphs are at "the Springs," TJ's grandchildren and many visitors at Monticello.

21   TJ receives a copy of Jay's Treaty.

August   Edmund Randolph resigns as secretary of state.

A meeting of protest against Jay's Treaty is held in Albemarle.

TJ expresses strong disapproval of the treaty in private letters.

Nov. 20–21   The Virginia General Assembly condemns the treaty, without implying censure of Washington.

Dec. 15   The Assembly proposes a constitutional amendment affirming the participation of the House of Representatives in the treaty-making process.

31   In a letter to Giles, TJ leaves no doubt that he regards a firm and decided party stand as necessary.

1796

Jan. 12   TJ sends his collection of old laws to a binder, from whom they are to go to George Wythe.

February   He begins his "demolitions" at Monticello.

5   He frees James Hemings by indenture.

26   Madison reports to Monroe that the Republicans will "push" TJ for the Presidency but that he fears his refusal.

29   Jay's Treaty is proclaimed by Washington.

Mar. 3   The treaty with Spain (Pinckney's) is approved by the Senate.

6   TJ hopes Gallatin will present a clear view of the country's finances.

24   He writes a private letter to Philip Mazzei which is to cause him much trouble afterwards.

Apr. 30   The House of Representatives finally votes to carry Jay's Treaty into effect.

May   Isaac Weld, Jr., visits Monticello.

June 17   TJ writes Washington.

22   La Rochefoucauld Liancourt begins a visit of a week to Monticello.

26   Volney leaves Monticello after a visit of about three weeks.

July 6   Washington writes TJ, ending their last exchange of letters.

10   TJ reports his finest wheat crop on record.

August   A threshing machine built on TJ's place begins to work.

The delayed arrival of Stephen Willis, brickmason, impedes construction at Monticello.

Sept. 19   Washington's Farewell Address is published in Philadelphia.

The active presidential campaign follows.

24   Adet in Boston urges support of TJ.

29   Madison says he has given TJ no chance to object to being embarked in the presidential contest.

October   The electoral campaign in Virginia and Pennsylvania reaches its height.

	17	The *Aurora* publishes the letter of Paine (July 30, 1796) to Washington.
Oct.	30	Ellen Wayles Randolph is born at Monticello.
November		Electors are chosen in various ways in the various states in the course of the month.
	15	Adet attacks the British treaty and announces the suspension of his own functions.
	28	Because of cold weather, work at Monticello is suspended before the walls are completed.
		TJ says he would rather have the second office than the first.
Dec.	5	The electors meet in their respective states and cast their votes for President and Vice President.
	28	TJ writes Adams a letter which Madison does not deliver.
	31	TJ learns from Madison that he will almost certainly run second to Adams and must prepare to assume the vice presidency.
		Adet comments on TJ to his own government.

1797

Jan.	8	TJ says he must resume tobacco culture in Albemarle.
	22	He inquires of George Wythe about parliamentary procedure.
Feb.	20	He leaves Monticello for Philadelphia.
Mar.	2	He arrives in Philadelphia.
	3	He is installed as president of the American Philosophical Society.
	4	His inauguration as Vice President of the U. S. is followed by that of John Adams as President.
	10	His memoir on Megalonyx is read before the American Philosophical Society.
	13	He leaves Philadelphia, arriving at home on Mar. 20.
	29	Luther Martin opens his attack on the Logan-Cresap episode in the *Notes on Virginia*.
May	5	TJ leaves Monticello for a special session of Congress.
	9	On the road he learns of the publication of his private letter to Mazzei (Mar. 24, 1796).
	11	He arrives in Philadelphia and during the weeks immediately thereafter assumes the leadership of the opposition party.
	13	He gives Elbridge Gerry his views on current public questions.
May	16	Adams reveals to Congress the deterioration of relations with France and recommends defense measures.
	31	By this date, TJ begins to seek information about the disputed episode in his *Notes on Virginia*.
June	17	He writes Aaron Burr.
	20	Adams completes the commission to France by nominating Elbridge Gerry to serve with C. C. Pinckney and John Marshall.
		TJ pays Callender $15.14 for the *History of the United States for 1796*.
	23	A supporter of Adams reports to him from memory TJ's letter

to Peregrine Fitzhugh, containing criticisms which Adams resents.

27   James Monroe, returned from France, reaches Philadelphia, where he confers with TJ, Gallatin, and Burr.

July *1*   TJ attends a party dinner to Monroe.

    6   He leaves Philadelphia.

The quarrel between Hamilton and Monroe, and the publication of the former's *Observations*, revealing the Reynolds affair, take place after that.

  11   TJ arrives at Monticello, after spending the previous night at Montpelier.

Aug. *3*   TJ explains to Madison his silence about the Mazzei letter.

He draws a petition to the Virginia House of Delegates in the case of Congressman Samuel J. Cabell.

Sept. *28*   Callender, who has fled Philadelphia for Virginia, asks aid of TJ.

Oct. *13*   Maria Jefferson is married to John Wayles Eppes at Monticello.

Nov. *18*   John Nicholas of Albemarle connects TJ with the Langhorne letter to Washington (Sept. 27), starting a chain of events that lead to a final breach.

Dec. *4*   TJ departs from Monticello, leaving his house tenantless for the winter.

  11   Luther Martin's best-known attack on TJ on account of the *Notes on Virginia* is written.

  12   TJ arrives in Philadelphia for the regular session of Congress, taking rooms at Francis's Hotel.

1798

January   TJ comments on the divisiveness of party animosities.

February   The Lyon-Griswold fracas enlivens the House of Representatives.

  28   A garbled version of the Mazzei letter is read in the House.

March *1*   Gallatin speaks on foreign intercourse and in effect defends the Mazzei letter.

   2   Congressman Robert Goodloe Harper attacks TJ.

   8   Washington's interpretation of the Langhorne episode marks a breach with TJ.

  19   Adams reports the failure of the mission to France and asks defense measures.

  21   TJ regards the President's message as insane, or almost so.

Apr. *3*   Adams communicates the XYZ dispatches at the request of the House.

  26   TJ reports an exodus of Republicans and the supremacy of the "war party."

May   Adams evinces ardent patriotism in his replies to addresses.

   4   A letter, describing TJ's "moldboard of least resistance," is read to the American Philosophical Society.

June *13*   Dr. George Logan sails for Europe on a personal peace mission.

18 A banquet is given John Marshall at Oeller's Hotel.
      The Naturalization Act is approved.

19 Secretary Wolcott is in New York, looking for treasonable correspondence.

21 Adams announces the end of negotiations with France and his determination to send no other minister unless assured of his respectful treatment.

25 The Alien Act is approved.

26 Senator James Lloyd's sedition bill has its first reading.

27 TJ leaves Philadelphia for home.

July 4 He arrives at Monticello, where he afterwards receives reports on later actions of Congress.

6 The Alien Enemies Act is approved.

14 The Sedition Act is approved.

26 A copy of letter from Joel Barlow to Abraham Baldwin is received by TJ.

      Most of the controversy among the Federalists over military rank occurs during the summer and autumn while TJ is at home and apparently uninformed about it.

Aug. 22 TJ writes Samuel Smith about his policy with respect to newspaper attacks.

      Meetings of protest against the Sedition Law are held in Virginia counties during the month.

September TJ drafts what came to be known as the Kentucky Resolutions of 1798, which appear not to have been seen by Madison.

Oct. 4 Wilson Cary Nicholas informs TJ he has given these resolutions to John Breckinridge.

9 Matthew Lyon of Vermont is convicted of seditious libel.
      Madison visits TJ late in the month.

Nov. 10 Breckinridge presents to the Kentucky House of Representatives a somewhat modified version of TJ's resolutions.

16 After their adoption by the legislature these are approved by the Governor of Kentucky.

22 TJ learns from Nathaniel Cutting about the more friendly attitude of the French government.

26 TJ tells John Taylor his "farming schemes are in abeyance."

29 TJ suggests changes in Madison's draft of resolutions for their own state, but these do not survive.

      In Philadelphia, during the month, the return of Dr. George Logan from France creates an uproar.

Dec. 18 TJ leaves Monticello.

21–24 Madison's resolutions (Virginia Resolutions of 1798) are adopted by the General Assembly.

25 TJ arrives in Philadelphia.

26 Debates leading to the passage of Logan's Law begin.

1799

Jan. 23 Address of the General Assembly to the people of Virginia is promulgated.

26   In a letter to Elbridge Gerry, TJ writes what amounts to a
party platform.

29   TJ urges Pendleton to address the public on current issues.

February   He causes political pamphlets to be distributed in Virginia
while decrying any appeal to force.

1   Washington sends Adams a letter from Joel Barlow.

18   Adams nominates William Vans Murray as minister to the
French Republic.

25   Under party pressure he names a commission of three.
In a debate in the House on the Alien and Sedition Acts, Republican spokesmen are drowned out.

Mar. 1   TJ leaves Philadelphia.
Most of the replies from the states to the Virginia Resolutions
are received after that.

8   TJ arrives at Monticello.

12   Adams issues a proclamation against the Fries rebellion in Pennsylvania, and he himself departs for Massachusetts soon thereafter.

29   John Nicholas of Albemarle charges the Virginia government
with rebellious purposes.

April   Apparently the entire house at Monticello is covered.

24   Elections in Virginia result in continued Republican control
of the legislature but of Federalist gains in Congress, including the election of John Marshall and Light-Horse Harry
Lee.

June 18   In a letter to William Munford, TJ gives one of the finest of
his expressions of faith in free intelligence.

Aug.–Sept.   TJ makes suggestions for the Kentucky and Virginia legislatures which are moderated by the influence of Madison.

Sept. 6   TJ subscribes to Callender's forthcoming work, *The Prospect
before Us.*

October   Adams, overriding his counselors, orders the departure of the
American commissioners to France.

November   The Kentucky Resolutions of 1799 are adopted.

Dec. 14   George Washington dies at Mount Vernon.

21   TJ leaves Monticello, omitting his customary stop at Montpelier on Monroe's advice.

26   By act of Congress, this is a day of formal mourning for Washington.

28   TJ arrives in Philadelphia.

1800

January   Madison's "Report" is adopted by the Virginia General Assembly.

17   TJ welcomes Du Pont de Nemours to America.

18   He asks Joseph Priestley's advice about the subjects to be
taught in a university.

Feb. 2   Philip Norborne Nicholas informs TJ of the party organization in Virginia.

4   TJ has learned of the death of Maria's infant and of his coach-
      man, Jupiter.

19 Duane publishes in the *Aurora* the text of the Ross electoral
      count bill, starting a controversy with the Senate which lasts
      through the session.

28 TJ explains to Wythe his purposes in compiling a parliamen-
      tary manual.

March He suffers a loss in the tobacco market and helps his son-in-law
         on a mortgage.

April He causes political pamphlets to be distributed in Virginia.
         The elections in Virginia are favorable to his party.

30 Thomas Cooper is convicted of seditious libel.

May TJ receives Priestley's "Hints concerning Public Education."
       Victory in the legislative elections in New York City assures
       Republican electors in the state.
       The Federalists in caucus agree to support Adams and C. C.
       Pinckney.

6   Secretary McHenry resigns at Adams's request.

7   Hamilton suggests that Governor Jay call the existing legisla-
      ture to revise the method of choosing electors in New York.

8   Before this date the first issue of the Appendix to the *Notes on
      Virginia* relative to the murder of Logan's family has been
      printed.

11 A Republican caucus agrees to support Burr for Vice President.

12 Pickering is dismissed by Adams.

15–29 TJ returns home by way of Richmond and Eppington, bring-
         ing Maria to Monticello for a visit.

June 3 Callender is convicted after his trial in Richmond.

30 A report of TJ's death is published in Baltimore and occasions
      alarm among his friends and supporters.

July 4 By this date he has harvested his best wheat crop.

26 He reports that he is in the best of health.
      He works on his parliamentary manual during the summer.

Aug. 13 He denies charges that he obtained his property by fraud and
           robbery but otherwise makes no answer to abusive attacks.
           He describes his "principles of government" to Gideon Granger
           of Connecticut.

24 He is sent Du Pont's work on national education in the United
      States.

Sept. 2 After this date he draws a private list of his public services.

23 In a letter to Benjamin Rush, after referring to clerical attacks
      on him, he affirms his eternal hostility to every form of
      tyranny over the human mind.

24 After visiting New England, Burr spreads favorable reports of
      Republican prospects in Rhode Island.

25 Gabriel, the leader of a slave revolt in Virginia, is captured.

Oct. 21 TJ is visited by Joseph Alston, later Burr's son-in-law.

22 Extracts from Hamilton's letter concerning the public conduct
      and character of Adams are published in the *Aurora*.

Nov. 1 About this time TJ visits Poplar Forest.

24 He leaves Monticello.

27 Arriving in Washington, he goes to the boarding-house of Conrad and McMunn.

   During the month electors are chosen in the various states in a variety of ways.

Dec. 3 The electors meet in their respective states and vote for President and Vice President.

12 TJ learns of the choice of Republican electors by the legislature of the crucial state of South Carolina and that he is expected to get one more electoral vote there than Burr.

14 He offers Robert R. Livingston the secretaryship of the navy.

15 He writes Burr.

16 By this date Hamilton is arguing that TJ is preferable to Burr.

18 TJ now thinks that an electoral tie between him and Burr is likely.

28 He knows that a tie is certain and that the election will be thrown into the House.

31 A letter from Burr to Samuel Smith, disclaiming competition with TJ, is published in the *National Intelligencer*.

1801

Jan. 1 TJ receives a reassuring letter from Burr (Dec. 23, 1800).

2 About this time he calls on Mrs. Washington at Mount Vernon.

4 Samuel Smith interviews Burr, who will not explicitly renounce his claims.

15 By this time the Federalist representatives, in caucus, have decided to support Burr.

16 In a letter to James A. Bayard, Hamilton gives a characterization of TJ which is destined to become famous.

27 The Senate consents to the nomination of John Marshall as chief justice.

Feb. 3 The Senate approves the Convention with France, with proviso.

11 Balloting for President begins in the House.

17 TJ is elected over Burr on the 36th ballot.

28 He delivers a farewell address to the Senate.

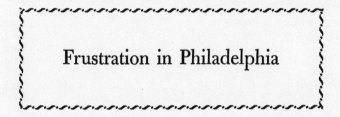

Frustration in Philadelphia

[I]

The Secretary of State Carries On

AT THE beginning of the year 1793, when he was approaching fifty, Thomas Jefferson was living in the house on the south side of High Street, often called Market, that he had occupied since his first weeks in Philadelphia as secretary of state, though he had told his landlord that he would vacate it before spring.[1] Besides five servants to take care of his household and his four horses, he still had with him as maître d'hôtel the invaluable Petit, whom he had induced to come from France. He gave a round of dinners before beginning to pack up his things and break up his establishment. No doubt these were delicious repasts at which the best of French wines stimulated the flow of universal conversation, but they were not official functions. The host styled himself "Th: Jefferson" on his cards of invitation, not the Secretary of State of the United States, and he had been chided by Hamiltonian pamphleteers for this "ridiculous affectation of simplicity." [2] Soon he expected to be wholly a private gentleman, for he had solemnly informed George Washington of his firm decision to retire at the end of the first term of this first President.[3] But that patient man was biding his time, keeping his peace, hoping against hope that he could retain his first assistant.

The General, now nearing sixty-one, was himself far from enthusiastic about remaining in office. He candidly admitted that he would have been chagrined if his re-election had not been by a "pretty respectable vote" and undoubtedly would have been disappointed if it had not been unanimous; but, as he wrote to one of his many well-

[1] To Thomas Leiper, Dec. 9, 1792, giving three months' notice (MHS).
[2] As by W. L. Smith in *Politicks and Views of a Certain Party, Displayed* (1792), p. 29. One of TJ's invitations is shown on the following page.
[3] To Washington, Sept. 9, 1792 (Ford, VI, 108). See also *Jefferson and the Rights of Man*, p. 485. NOTE. Explanations of the abbreviations used in the footnotes and further details concerning the works referred to may be found in "Symbols and Short Titles" and "Select Critical Bibliography" at the end of this book.

wishers, it would be a "departure from truth" to say that he felt pleasure in the prospect of commencing another tour of duty.[4] He had recently laid the cornerstone of the Executive Mansion in the new Federal City that was rising beside the Potomac and already bore his name, but the building would not be finished soon enough to do him any good. Meanwhile, he had to continue in the former residence of Robert Morris at 190 High Street (Market Street below Sixth), though his heart was really at Mount Vernon. He was planning to build a big new barn there, just as Jefferson was talking about agricultural and construction projects at Monticello, and he understood the restiveness of his first Secretary of State.

Th. Jefferson

presents his compliments to

and requests the favour of his company to dinner on   next at half after three oclock

The favour of an answer is requested

The Vice President, despite the officious urging of the Secretary of the Treasury that he come early,[5] had not arrived at the seat of government until the Senate had been a month in session; and, as the winter wore on, the thoughts of John Adams turned often to his snowy farm in New England, where his wife Abigail still was. Before the year was out he said that his country in its wisdom had contrived for him "the most insignificant office that ever the invention of man contrived or his imagination conceived."[6] Yet, because of his pride no doubt, he had wanted to be re-elected — even though he was unwilling to do anything about it. He probably got more unreserved support from the Hamiltonians in this instance than he ever did afterwards;

[4] Washington to Gov. Henry Lee, Jan. 20, 1793 (Fitzpatrick, XXXII, 310).
[5] Hamilton to Adams, Sept. 9, 1792, in the latter's *Works*, VIII, 514–515.
[6] Dec. 19, 1793 (*Works*, I, 460).

but, unlike the President, he received an electoral vote which was considerably less than unanimous. He got 77 votes to George Clinton's 50.[7] If he was not annoyed by the things that had been said about him in the course of the campaign, his wife surely was. Abigail Adams, who had amply demonstrated her heroic qualities during the American Revolution, was now fuming — less heroically but not unnaturally — about the "intrigue and falsehood" of the Clintonians, whom she identified with the Jacobins. Since she was not at the seat of government, there was no immediate question of social relations with her old friend Mr. Jefferson, who himself had received the four votes of Kentucky though he had not sought and did not want them. It is highly unlikely that Abigail understood his attitude toward her husband, but the latter gentleman himself may have surmised that, despite partisan and ideological differences, Jefferson really preferred him to George Clinton. Early in the new year Adams was elected a member of the American Philosophical Society, of which Jefferson had recently been re-elected first vice president, and they both attended the next meeting — at which the mathematician David Rittenhouse presided. Adams does not appear to have attended after that, but the Secretary of State nearly always did.[8] As a human being "John Yankee" could never be insignificant, but he was now receding into the background.

The Secretary of the Treasury, who was a dozen years younger than Jefferson, was in indifferent health in the month of January, but if Alexander Hamilton's personal vigor was weakened it was certainly not for long. He also lived on High Street, though he moved to a large house on Arch after a few months. There was no present indication that he had any thought of quitting the government, but he was no longer writing pieces against Jefferson for the newspapers. Hamilton was most engaged, during the winter, in drafting reports to Congress, but, as we shall see, these were defensive actions. Temporarily, the initiative had passed from his eager hands.

Jefferson's closest political friend, Congressman James Madison, still a bachelor, was living at Mrs. Mary House's at Fifth and High, as he had been since he first came to Philadelphia. That good lady went out like a candle in June, and her daughter, Mrs. Eliza Trist, did not continue the boarding-house, but it was the center of the political

[7] The certificates of the electors were received by Congress on Feb. 13, 1793. Washington had 132 votes; Adams 77; Clinton 50; Jefferson 4 (Ky.); and Aaron Burr 1 (*Annals*, 2 Cong., pp. 645–646).

[8] TJ was re-elected vice president Jan. 4, 1793; Adams, whose earlier election (1780) seems to have been overlooked, was elected a member on Jan. 18, and they both attended Feb. 1 (*Early Proceedings of the American Philosophical Society*, 1884, pp. 211–212).

conversations of the congressional Virginians until the session ended on Saturday, March 2.[9] Jefferson himself had stayed there in times past and he knew both these ladies well. He was also well acquainted with the other representatives and senators from his own state, but his official duties lay within the executive branch of the government and he claimed that they kept him there.

The mildness of the weather should have reconciled him somewhat to the prospect of remaining in this northern city through another winter. During the month of January the temperature rarely fell below the freezing point. This made things safer as well as more comfortable, for the local custom of washing the steps and sidewalks every Wednesday and Saturday morning, regardless of the weather, created the danger of breaking one's neck when ice had formed. A visiting Frenchman regarded this custom as insane.[10] Jefferson learned that the mild weather had tempted David Rittenhouse into indiscretion. The President of the American Philosophical Society, who was about Washington's age and rather feeble, complacently walked for an hour in the mud and contracted a violent cold. While packing his furniture, the Secretary of State had sent the astronomer a present which he described as useless, though Rittenhouse did not thus regard it. Acknowledging it gratefully, the older man said: "I shall ever remember with pleasure, whilst memory continues to perform its office, that I have counted the name of Mr. Jefferson in the very short list of my friends." [11]

The lanky Virginian was largely insusceptible to colds, much as he disliked cold weather, and the temperature was above freezing on the January day when he witnessed the greatest exploit of the season. The famous French aeronaut Jean-Pierre Blanchard made the first balloon ascent in the United States, taking off from the yard of the Walnut Street jail (at Sixth Street) in the presence of 40,000 excited people — according to the report of Dr. Benjamin Rush, who may have indulged in a degree of exaggeration. But Thomas Jefferson and his daughter Maria, aged fourteen, were surely there; and, besides paying a good price for a ticket, he made a substantial subscription. The daring airman is said to have worn a cocked hat with white feathers, and to have waved the tricolor of France and the American flag as he ascended in the spangled blue boat that hung beneath his balloon of varnished yellow silk. Jefferson must have heard the cheers of the

[9] TJ to Madison, June 2, 1793 (Ford, VI, 279); Irving Brant, *Madison*, III, 380.

[10] *Moreau de St. Méry's American Journey*, trans. and ed. by Kenneth Roberts (New York, 1947), p. 262.

[11] TJ to Rittenhouse, Jan. 7, 1793 (LC, 13965); Rittenhouse to TJ, Jan. 11, 1793 (LC, 13984). Rittenhouse was also Director of the Mint at this time.

incredulous crowd, the sound of the cannon, and the music of the band, but what this eighteenth-century prophet of scientific progress wrote home about was his own desire to fly. To his elder daughter in Virginia he said: "The security of the thing appeared so great, that everybody is wishing for a balloon to travel in. I wish for one sincerely, as instead of ten days I should be within five hours of home." [12]

In reality, Blanchard did not get very far and went in the wrong direction: he remained in the air forty-six minutes, traveled about fifteen miles, and descended in New Jersey. Furthermore, by the most sanguine calculations Jefferson was now at least two months away from Monticello. March was the month that Maria in Philadelphia and his family and friends in Albemarle County were looking forward to. Dr. George Gilmer wrote him from Pen Park, on the southwest slope of the Southwest Mountains, that his nerves began to vibrate more vigorously as the time of his neighbor's return approached, and that this was not owing to the use of auxiliary stimulants either, since he had foregone them.[13] But all these hopes were premature, and the Secretary was doomed to wear the shackles of office throughout the year.

It proved to be a momentous year in human history, and, except for his last one as governor of Virginia during the American Revolution, the most trying and discouraging that he had yet spent in public life. It was marked by the Terror in France and a scourge of yellow fever in Philadelphia. Abroad, it was a time of general war, of mad reaction against mad revolution; at home, it was a period of political fever from which not even the most scrupulous officials could remain wholly immune. The democratic movement in Europe assumed a more violent character which was communicated in some degree to America, involving Jefferson as a responsible minister in a whole series of dilemmas. His attempt to extricate himself from these is the major theme of a long section of this book. He never ceased to be an American patriot first of all, and this enemy of kings continued to designate himself as a republican, but he emerged from this year of conflict with a more democratic stamp upon him than he had ever worn before. The political issue in the United States remained uncertain,

[12] Account Book, Jan. 9, 1793 (date of the flight), Apr. 9, 1793, showing payments of five dollars for ticket and subscription of twenty dollars; TJ to Martha Jefferson Randolph, Jan. 14, 1793 (Randall, II, 191); Maria Jefferson to TMR, Jan. 13, 1793 (LC, 13997); passport to Blanchard from Washington, Jan. 9 (Fitzpatrick, XXXII, 296 and note); Benjamin Rush to Elizabeth G. Ferguson, Jan. 18, 1793 (Butterfield, *Letters of Benjamin Rush*, II, 627–629, and notes with references); colorful account of flight in J. T. Scharf and Thompson Westcott, *Hist. of Philadelphia*, I (1884), 471.
[13] George Gilmer to TJ, Jan. 26, 1793 (MHS).

but at the end of the year the advantage seemed to lie with Alexander Hamilton and his cohorts — who were certainly not democrats and in Jefferson's opinion not even republicans. They accused him of things that he did not do, but circumstances made it inevitable that both terms should be applied to him from this time forward, and that he should become more than ever a symbol. This was partly because of what he did but mostly because of what he stood for.

Though George Washington characteristically held his tongue, Jefferson himself could not wholly refrain from talking to intimates about his approaching retirement, and some comments on it crept into the newspapers. One admirer, calling himself MIRABEAU, addressed him as the "colossus" of republicanism in Benjamin Franklin Bache's extremely republican sheet, the *General Advertiser* (later the *Aurora*). "The *unity* of your conduct," said MIRABEAU; "your dignified and republican simplicity; your enmity to fastidious distance and reserve; your respect for the people, are subjects of affection and commendation, and ought to be of imitation to every man who is the friend of equality. . . . At present you appear to be the colossus of opposition to *monarchical deportment, monarchical arrogance, and monarchical splendor;* but were you withdrawn, monarchy and aristocracy, like an inundation, would overflow our country." [14] The Secretary of State himself was optimistic at this stage because of the reports he had of the recent congressional elections, though he did not think well of the Congress then in session and had lost none of his suspicions of the Secretary of the Treasury. The French minister, Ternant, believed that the talk of Jefferson's retirement was only a feint concerted with the leaders of the "popular party"; and staunch supporters of Hamilton wondered if it were not a trick to gain a few compliments. [15]

He got some from the American representatives in Europe. By this time, the letters that he had sent them in the fall had begun to reach their distant destinations and these men were expressing their regret at his avowed intentions, though their replies would be long in coming. David Humphreys in Portugal was hoping that Jefferson would be withheld from his "favorite retirement" a few years longer, and sent him wishes of "real friendship." Thomas Pinckney in England regarded his withdrawal as a public loss and spoke gratefully of his "kind

---

[14] Philadelphia *General Advertiser*, Jan. 5, 1793; unsigned reply, Jan. 12, 1793. See also Feb. 12, and Freneau's *National Gazette*, Jan. 12, 1793.

[15] Ternant to Minister of Foreign Affairs, Jan. 12, 1793 (*C.F.M.*, p. 168); Oliver Wolcott, Jr., to his father, Feb. 8, 1793 (Gibbs, I, 86).

attentions" and "friendly mode of conducting business." Even Gouverneur Morris in France, who viewed developments there quite differently from the Secretary of State, hoped that he would hold on until he could yield his official duties to a fit successor.[16] In the foreign service they recognized his high abilities and appreciated his unfailing kindness.

At the seat of government, the talk of his retirement continued to reflect partisan attitudes. John Fenno, Hamilton's chief journalistic henchman in Philadelphia, was sure that Jefferson would go out, since he had given up his house. In Fenno's unfriendly sheet it was asserted that the "Antifederal fleet" was commanded by "Commodore Pendulum" — referring to the author of the report on weights and measures — who was expected to resign as soon as he reached port, being dissatisfied with the service.[17] According to others, his retirement was ardently desired by the "consolidationists" but as ardently opposed by every real federalist and true republican.[18] This battle of terms and epithets was destined to continue; but there was an authoritative report, shortly after the inauguration, that the Secretary of State was remaining in the government.[19] If he himself is to be believed, he was carrying on reluctantly, without exaggerating his own importance, but also without abandoning any of the principles which he believed to be at issue at the time.

He informed the President of his decision on February 7. This was two days after the foreign intercourse bill passed the Senate, where he had feared it would be rejected. Some extreme advocates of isolation still opposed the policy of having regular ministers at foreign courts, and, in Jefferson's opinion, the Department of State would not have been worth administering if they had had their way. All that the provincially minded Congress finally agreed to was the extension of the old bill and the continuation of the modest foreign establishment for another year, but that was longer than Jefferson intended to remain in office: he had said, "perhaps till summer, perhaps autumn."[20]

Even by agreeing to continue for a few months this extremely domestic man was disrupting his personal affairs. He had given up his lease and was packing his furniture, which was no trivial chore in

[16] Humphreys to TJ, Jan. 8, 1793; Pinckney to TJ, Feb. 10, 1793; Morris to TJ, Feb. 13, 1793 (LC, 13977, 14113, 14135).

[17] Gazette of the U. S., Mar. 2, 6, 1793; for TJ's Report, see Jefferson and the Rights of Man, pp. 276–281.

[18] National Gazette, Mar. 6, 1793, quoting Boston Independent Chronicle.

[19] General Advertiser, Mar. 6, 1793.

[20] Annals, 2 Cong., pp. 639–640, 1411–1412; note of conversation with Washington, Feb. 7, 1793 (Ford, I, 214).

view of the amount of it he had brought from France, and he had to look for another house. Also, he had worked out plans of building at Monticello and operating his farms which would have to be largely postponed, since he could not ask anybody else, not even his son-in-law, to direct them. The immediate occasion for his decision, which had such annoying personal consequences, was not the world situation. He did not yet know how much that had worsened since the autumn and seems to have been relatively cheerful about it at this stage. The reasons which he gave were more personal and in their long-range implications more political, though they appear to have been based more on pride than on ambition. He had found among both his friends and his political enemies the belief that he was being driven from office "either from want of firmness or perhaps fear of investigation." His friends had prevailed upon him not to retire under fire and thus endanger his political reputation. He was extremely sensitive about that, though he gave no sign that he intended to exploit it in the future. Whether the postponement of his retirement would be for weeks or months, he could not now say. He wrote his son-in-law: "This must depend in some degree on the will of those who troubled the waters before. When they suffer them to get calm, I will go into port." [21] This seasoned observer could hardly have believed that the larger political waters would become smooth in the near future. He was referring specifically to the direct personal attacks that had been made on him in the fall by Hamilton. There was now reason to hope that these would not be repeated, since they had really failed of their purpose, and by continuing in the government he put the stamp of failure on them. [22]

He gave essentially the same reasons to the President as to his own family; and Washington, who had feared that his withdrawal would create further uneasiness in the public mind, and who had no replacement in sight, was much relieved by his announcement. The President was alarmed by the discontent, especially that in Virginia, and advanced his old arguments about effecting a "coalition" with Hamilton. His own actions in recent months had revealed no desire whatever to subordinate the Secretary of State to the Secretary of the Treasury, and this judicious executive had managed to keep the balance pretty even. By and large, Jefferson had had his way with him in foreign affairs and Hamilton in financial — which, to Washington's practical mind, was entirely proper.

The President was now consulting the department heads as a group

21 TJ to TMR, Feb. 3, 1793 (LC, 14088).
22 See *Jefferson and the Rights of Man*, ch. XXVII.

more frequently than hitherto, the Attorney General being included while the Vice President had dropped out. At the outset of his administration Washington's practice was to confer with his "assistants" individually, and to seek written opinions from the others when in doubt — as in the case of the constitutionality of the Bank. The practice of holding group conferences, which may be called meetings of the cabinet though Jefferson himself generally used the term executive council, arose from crises of general concern, such as Indian wars and dangerous foreign developments. Meetings were generally held in the President's house and from them joint policies emerged. Consultations of this sort became much more frequent during the rest of the year 1793, chiefly because of foreign developments, and thus it came about that policies for the administration as a whole were worked out first in connection with foreign affairs and Indian affairs, not domestic finance. By accident of circumstance as well as temperament, Hamilton's policies had been more distinctively his own in the first place; and never during Jefferson's secretaryship did they become administration policies in the sense that foreign policies had to be in a time of international crisis. The score was so written that this natural prima donna had many solo parts, while Jefferson was more often one of a quartet — or quintet if we include the President.

Jefferson's nature and habits led him to seek privacy for thought and personal labors, and he had worked out his political principles in considerable solitude, but in practical matters he liked to act in concert with his fellows. He had no trouble co-operating with the President. Washington was not a kindred spirit in the sense that Madison was, but he had a common interest with Jefferson in agriculture and a common birthright as a Virginian. Furthermore, Jefferson had lost none of his reverence for Washington's character and none of his respect for the older man's judgment. His attitude toward Hamilton was quite another matter, and in the discussions of international affairs during the winter of 1792-1793 the harmony between the two chief secretaries was considerably less than perfect. It happened not infrequently, however, that the two men, starting from opposite points, arrived at the same practical conclusion— for the simple reason that it was the most sensible one. The main difference at this stage was not in policies but in guiding principles; and with respect to the latter, in the field of foreign affairs, Washington was much closer to his Secretary of State than to his Secretary of the Treasury. So was Edmund Randolph, the handsome Attorney General, and Jefferson saw some signs that the huge Secretary of War, Henry Knox, was not following Hamilton blindly at this time. Everything considered, the joint discussions of foreign affairs were not working to Jefferson's disadvantage. His official situation was more than tolerable, and the course of events had permitted him to uphold certain principles which he regarded as exceedingly important.

The "coalition" with Hamilton, which the President suggested in February, Jefferson objected to chiefly on domestic grounds. He believed that a sacrifice of his "general system" by either man was impossible, and he renewed his allegations about improper influences on the legislative branch of the government. "My wish was to see both houses of Congress cleansed of all persons interested in the bank or public stocks," he said; "and that, a pure legislature being given us, I should always be ready to acquiesce under their determinations, even if contrary to my own opinions, for that I subscribe to the principle that the will of the majority honestly expressed should give law." Also, he confirmed the fears of his Chief about discontent among Southerners, attributing this to the sacrifice of their judgment and interests to those of the North, by means of a "corrupt squadron" in Congress under command of the Secretary of the Treasury.[23] Washington spoke again of the "extreme wretchedness" of his own existence while in public office, as though reproaching his assistant for reluctance in sharing it. A letter then reposing in the latter's files, from a resident of the Southwest Territory, would have brought comfort to both of them if it had been produced. This writer said: "In no era of the Universe, nor under no Constitution or form of government would I rather have lived than that of the United States of America, when principally administered by a Washington and a Jefferson." [24] The Secretary of State would have been out of character if he had communicated this laudatory passage, as the President would have been if he had attempted to answer the allegations about Hamilton's "improper" influence. Washington was loyal to both of his principal assistants in their respective spheres and still kept himself above the storms of partisanship.

Within a very short time, the high officials of the government were to learn of events abroad which, besides being momentous in world history, were destined to dominate the American political scene for months and years. The major task of the Secretary of State, working in conjunction with the President, was to adjust the policies of the young Republic to these developments. Difficult and delicate questions had already arisen in international relations, but during the winter

[23] Memo. of conversation, Feb. 7, 1793 (Ford, I, 214–216).
[24] David Campbell to TJ, Sept. 29, 1792, from Jefferson County, Southwest Territory (LC, 13396).

domestic affairs were more controversial. Therefore it seems desirable, before entering upon the main story of the year, to consider events in Congress where Alexander Hamilton was under fire. The struggle there constituted the last phase of the conflict over financial questions, before international matters usurped the center of the public stage.

[II]

An Attack that Failed: The Giles Resolutions

THE last session of the Second Congress, which began in the autumn of 1792 and ended with Washington's first term the following March, was marked by a continuing attack on the fiscal methods of the Secretary of the Treasury. The subject was highly technical, but the fight was extremely bitter. Since this attack followed Hamilton's on Jefferson in the newspapers it might be viewed as a retaliatory action. The purpose of Hamilton's ferocious assault on his colleague, as stated in one of the papers he wrote as CATULLUS, was to tear the veil from "the quiet, modest, retiring philosopher" and show him as "the intriguing incendiary, the aspiring turbulent competitor" he really was.[1] If the Secretary of the Treasury was trying to drive the Secretary of State from the government he defeated that purpose by his very excesses. His attempt to "expose" his colleague was also a failure, for Jefferson's anonymous defenders, of whom James Monroe was the chief one, gained at least a draw in this series of verbal encounters, if indeed they did not gain a clear-cut victory at the bar of enlightened opinion. When Hamilton retired from this particular field of battle he may not have realized that he had been repulsed, for it was not in his pugnacious nature to do that, but he was not slow to see that he himself had been challenged on another field. He now assumed a defensive role, though on ground with which he was thoroughly familiar.

His conduct of his office was first questioned and then assailed in Congress, and if the purpose of these legislative moves was not to drive *him* from the government, it was at least to administer a stinging rebuke. In the end the effort failed utterly, and this was another case in which excess defeated itself. The attack and counterattack were analogous in that respect, but there were important differences

[1] Sept. 29, 1792 (Lodge, VI, 353–354); see *Jefferson and the Rights of Man*, pp. 468–474.

between them. The inquiry into the conduct of the Treasury was made, not under a cloud of anonymity in the newspapers, but openly in the halls of Congress where it legitimately belonged; and the Secretary of State did not make it. The central gladiator was a representative from Virginia, William Branch Giles. Behind him, however, many later writers have seen Madison, and behind Madison they have sighted Jefferson.

This line of interpretation, which is based primarily on the writings of Hamilton himself and may be said to follow the official party line, is well drawn in a book by his son which long occupied a central place among the sacred Federalist writings:

> This machination originated with Jefferson. The mode of pro-
> ceeding was concerted between him and his useful friend. Madi-
> son obeyed Jefferson's behest, and prepared resolutions of inquiry
> into the conduct of the Treasury Department. Too timid to stand
> foremost as the antagonist of Hamilton, in a direct controversy,
> the introduction of the resolutions he confided to Giles. Not un-
> willing to be conspicuous, Giles undertook to play the cards put
> into his hand.[2]

This statement does violence to the characters of all three of the men mentioned, and it does not accord with the story of actual events as borne out by strictly contemporary documents. Jefferson thoroughly agreed with the severe criticisms of his colleague that were made in Congress, and he had occasion to say some of the same things to the President in his own official capacity. But there is no sufficient reason to suppose that he either instigated the attack or devised the tactics. This move can be best designated as Virginian. Though Jefferson fully sympathized with it and probably contributed to it, it was not at all dependent on him and might easily have occurred if he had retired to agricultural pursuits at Monticello a good deal earlier than he did. Furthermore, the legitimacy of a congressional inquiry into the conduct of fiscal affairs cannot be questioned, even if the tone of this one was objectionable.

The hostility among Virginians to the financial policies of the government, which had been marked from the time of the fight over the assumption of state debts, had shown no signs of diminution. Early in the new year, Fisher Ames wrote: "Virginia moves in a solid column, and the discipline of the party is as severe as the Prussian. Deserters are not spared. Madison is become a desperate party leader, and

---

[2] J. C. Hamilton, *History of the Republic . . . as Traced in the Writings of Alexander Hamilton*, V (1860), 173–174. This should not be confused with the *Works*, ed. by J. C. Hamilton, which is referred to as "J. C. H."

I am not sure of his stopping at any ordinary point of extremity." [3]
The most gifted orator among the Hamiltonians was hardly a fair
judge of Madison's desperation, and no doubt he overstated the case
with respect to the enforced unanimity of the Virginians, but many
others remarked on their spirit of opposition. Oliver Wolcott, Jr., second man in the Treasury and always loyal to his chief, believed that
this spirit could not be sufficiently explained on personal grounds and
attributed it to the pressure of their foreign debts on the Virginia
planters. "The effect of the treaty and of the constitution is to make
them responsible; at least, this is believed, though no decision of this
question has been made by the national judiciary. . . . They seem
determined to weaken the public force, so as to render the recovery of
these debts impossible." [4]

There was point in the observation, though Wolcott pressed it too
far. The planters were unquestionably restive under a burden of ancient debt, which, as they believed, the government was fastening on
them instead of doing something to lighten. That was an additional
reason for being disturbed by national policies which were imposing a
burden of debt on the whole country. In Jefferson's opinion, this was
greater than necessary and the Treasury really wanted to increase,
not reduce it. Fear of national debt was no discredit to the planters;
and at this stage their general grounds for discontent were still those
that had been stated in their official resolutions against assumption.
They feared that the creation and perpetuation of a "large monied
interest" would result in "the prostration of agriculture at the feet of
commerce." [5]

This was the language of Patrick Henry, whom Jefferson and Madison distrusted. They had a much higher opinion of George Mason,
another of the old opponents of the Constitution. Jefferson had
stopped for a night at Gunston Hall in the autumn, on his way to
Philadelphia, and had found this philosopher of human rights just
recovering, as was thought, from a dreadful attack of what he called
"colic." Actually, Mason died a week later. Jefferson could not let
the sick man talk as much as he wanted to, but he said some sharp
things which the Secretary of State recorded. "He said he considered
Hamilton as having done us more injury than Great Britain and all her

[3] Ames to Thomas Dwight, January 1793 (*Works,* ed. by Seth Ames [1854],
I, 127).
[4] Oliver Wolcott, Jr., to his father, Feb. 8, 1793 (Gibbs, I, 86).
[5] Resolutions of General Assembly, Dec. 16, 1790 (H. S. Commager, *Documents
of American History* [1948], I, 155). Julian P. Boyd has pointed out that the
planters feared not so much that they would have to pay their debts — many had
made arrangements to that end — as that they might have to pay all at once.

fleets and armies." Mason then set forth the plan by which he would have taken care of the national debt — by means which he deemed honorable and far more just and economical.[6] Jefferson and Madison had not retreated to the old antifederalist position, but they had reacted strongly against the financial policies of Hamilton as these had developed and were appalled by what they regarded as his irresponsibility. Jefferson was deeply suspicious of operations which he found mysterious. To Washington he described Hamilton as "the man who has the shuffling of millions backwards and forwards from paper into money and money into paper, from Europe to America, and America to Europe, the dealing out of Treasury-secrets among his friends in what time and measure he pleases, and who never slips an occasion of making friends with his means." [7] Things had been going on which seemed to call for explanation.

Yet Hamilton had not regarded it as incumbent on him to explain the conduct of the Treasury to Congress. His justly famous reports were made in response to specific congressional requests, and in fact were recommendations of positive legislative actions. Annual reports showing the precise condition and operations of the Treasury began under Jefferson's Secretary of the Treasury, Albert Gallatin, not under Hamilton. Certain people who had observed this imperious man in action believed that he was keeping things dark because of his arbitrary and contemptuous nature — or because there were things in the record which would not stand the light of day. The wisest policy on his part would have been to render full reports of his own volition, thus disarming all legitimate criticism. But the Secretary was an exceedingly busy man; he liked to do things his own way, never doubting that it was the right one; and, like many officials since, he wanted to be spared the trivial criticisms which so often accompany the important ones in American legislative bodies. At a later time he complained bitterly about the vexations and distracting labors which were imposed upon him by congressional requests, but he would have been well advised before now to spend more time compiling reports and less time in writing anonymous articles in the newspapers against his chief colleague.

That he would be called upon eventually to provide fuller information about transactions relating to matters pending in Congress was inevitable. The initiative in the last session of the Second Congress was taken by a young representative from Virginia, then only thirty years

[6] Memo. of TJ, Sept. 30, 1792 (Ford, I, 201–202); TJ to Madison, Oct. 1, 1792 (Ford, VI, 114). Mason died on Oct. 7.
[7] TJ to Washington, Sept. 9, 1792 (Ford, VI, 105).

old but already known as a fierce debater. William Branch Giles, like Madison, was a graduate of Princeton. He had studied law under Jefferson's old mentor, George Wythe; he had already achieved great success at the bar; and, strange though it might seem to Oliver Wolcott, he had served as counsel for British creditors in at least a hundred debt cases. He had written Jefferson, when the latter was preparing his reply to the British minister, George Hammond, that there was relatively little obstacle to the collection of just debts in Virginia, and he himself was certainly no repudiationist.[8] On the other hand, he had a particular antipathy to banks, with which he had had no experience in southside Virginia, and he voiced the sentiments of a predominantly agricultural society. He paid his compliments to the Secretary of the Treasury quite early in the season, remarking that some of the measures recommended by that official "discovered a princely ignorance of the country, for the wants and wishes of one part had been sacrificed to the interest of the other." [9] That was precisely what Jefferson told George Washington more than two months later, but he need not have picked up the idea from Giles any more than Giles need have picked it up from him. It was current among Virginians in this period. Giles was the sort of man who would speak his mind freely in public, and he needed no coaching. As time went on, however, he would be expected to confer about tactics with Madison, the acknowledged leader of the delegation.

It was the largest delegation in Congress. Jefferson's acquaintance and friendly relations with practically all the members of it may be taken for granted, though he may have been associating intimately with few of them at this time. Since the proceedings of the House were not secret like those of the Senate, he needed no special intermediary to find out what was going on. No doubt Madison kept him sufficiently supplied with inside information, and he had begun to pick up bits of gossip from John Beckley. Beckley, who is still a rather mysterious figure, was destined to play an important undercover role in the Republican politics of the decade. The son of an English knight, he had been educated at Eton and the College of William and Mary. He was clerk of the House until the Federalists displaced him in 1797, and from a political point of view he was probably more important than many actual members of the delegation. Jefferson recognized his limitations as a reporter. "Beckley is a man of perfect truth as to what he affirms of his own knowledge," said the Secretary of State, "but

---

[8] Giles to TJ, May 6, 1792 (*A.S.P.F.R.*, I, 234-235). D. R. Anderson, *William Branch Giles* (1914), is a good biography.
[9] Nov. 20, 1792 (*Annals*, 2 Cong., p. 706).

too credulous as to what he hears from others." Jefferson recorded a number of his gossipy reports, nonetheless, and these were consistently unfavorable to Hamilton.[10]

In the Senate, which played a quieter role than the House in this period, Jefferson had an intimate friend in James Monroe, who had so recently defended him with skill against the assaults of Hamilton. About the middle of December, Monroe was strongly reinforced by John Taylor of Caroline, lately appointed in place of Richard Henry Lee, who had resigned. He was tall and slender and had red hair as well as political principles in common with Jefferson. The latter did not bother to comment on such trivialities as the color of a statesman's hair, but at a later time he said that Taylor and he had "rarely, if ever, differed in any political principle of importance." In fact, the new Senator carried doctrines of state rights further than Jefferson did, and he may have detested Hamilton's financial system even more. It would not be surprising if some enterprising scholar should put him in the role of catalytic agent which has generally been assigned at this stage to Jefferson.[11]

The great congressional debate related specifically to the fiscal transactions of the government. This inevitably complicated subject, which the foes of Hamilton claimed he shrouded with mystery, was one that the Secretary of State had some knowledge of and interest in because of his official duties. To begin with, he was one of the commissioners of the Sinking Fund, which was designed to reduce the public debt by redeeming parts of it under specified conditions. The other commissioners besides Hamilton were the Vice President, the Chief Justice, and the Attorney General. John Adams had generally signed the formal reports that were submitted to Congress, but he was out of town when the session began in the autumn of 1792 and Jefferson signed the one presented at that time. Much the fullest report that had yet been made, it was more nearly the sort of thing the critics of the Treasury insisted on, whoever may have been responsible for its form.[12]

Besides being connected with the Sinking Fund, Jefferson as an

[10] Memoranda, Nov. 19, 1792; June 7, 1793 (Ford, I, 209, 233). On Beckley, see P. M. Marsh, in *Pa. Mag. Hist. & Biog.*, Jan. 1948, pp. 54–69; N. E. Cunningham, in *W. & M.*, Jan. 1956, pp. 41–52.

[11] Taylor took his seat Dec. 12, 1792. The best account of him is the *Life* (1932) by H. H. Simms, containing the description cited (p. 211). For TJ's comment, see letter to Thomas Ritchie, Dec. 25, 1820 (L. & B., XV, 296).

[12] Nov. 19, 1792 (*Am. State Papers, Finance* [1832], I, 162 ff.).

official was interested in payments on the foreign debt. Loans to provide for these had been made in Europe at an earlier stage through the agency of William Short, who negotiated in the Dutch market, but Jefferson does not appear to have concerned himself much with these transactions until the winter of 1792-1793, when the question of payments to France became acute.[13] He then learned of what was going on in Congress and studied the reports which Hamilton submitted to that body by request. But he had no more information than was publicly available, except in connection with the Sinking Fund, for Hamilton made no detailed fiscal reports to the President, and certainly not to his fellow secretaries. Jefferson could not have communicated inside information to his political friends. He did not have it.

The first serious skirmish, in a congressional battle which continued intermittently until the end of the session, occurred the day after Christmas, 1792. Jefferson heard about it that night, presumably from Madison who figured prominently in it, and he talked about it the next day with George Washington. In connection with a bill which included authorization of a loan of $2,000,000 to repay a loan from the United States Bank, two questions arose which were embarrassing to Hamilton. To begin with, there was a question why that large a sum should be borrowed when only $200,000 had to be paid the Bank in the near future. A motion to substitute $200,000 for $2,000,000 was defeated only by the vote of the Speaker. The Virginians were lined up on the losing side, but eventually they had their way in this particular matter, for the final decision was for the smaller figure. The bill "dropped from the hand of its patron," said Madison, attributing this to the light his colleague Giles had shed upon it.[14] Also, it came out in the debate that there was a large sum in the Treasury which had been drawn from abroad, though the money there was supposed to be used for the repayment of the foreign debt. This was part of the shuffling of funds from one continent to the other which Jefferson had previously mentioned to the President. This transfer of funds did not seem to fall within the provision of the original act of Congress, and apparently Washington did not like it.[15] Out of these circumstances came the congressional resolution of December 27, asking that the House be furnished with a particular account of loans and the disposition of them. This resolution is said to have been introduced by Giles and no doubt was regarded as partisan, but no one could properly have ob-

---

13 See below, pp. 41, 43–44. [Also, addition to Long Note, p. 528.]
14 *Annals*, 2 Cong., p. 935; see also pp. 758–760, 1452.
15 Memo. of Dec. 27, 1792 (Ford, I, 213).

jected to it.[16] Hamilton promptly presented a report which became available to Jefferson as well as Congress.[17]

The "most prominent suspicion" aroused in his mind by this report was that funds borrowed in Europe, which ought to have been applied to the debts there in order to save interest, had been drawn to the United States "and lodged in the bank, to extend the speculations and profits of that institution." Taking Hamilton's own figures, he arranged them in two accounts, European and American, thus serving in part to unscramble them. He felt a need for further information — about the government accounts with the Bank and about surplus revenues which might have been applied to the reduction of the public debt. Information of the sort he wanted was made available to the Senate by Hamilton about the middle of January, in response to a resolution of that body. The authorship of this was such that Jefferson could hardly have been accused of sponsoring it. He showed his own tables to Madison at some time, but they do not appear to be a necessary link in the chain of events in Congress.[18]

The resolutions, five in number, which were offered in the House by William Branch Giles on January 23 asked for the same information that the Senate had requested and a good deal more. Unlike the Senate resolution, they got into the papers, and they evoked a more spirited response from Hamilton because of the political circumstances. It has been said that Jefferson suggested these resolutions and that Madison drafted them.[19] There seems to be no contemporary record connecting Jefferson with them, though there is abundant reason for believing that he thought them a good idea. They were adopted by the House without a record vote, and the form of the resolutions themselves is far less important than their purport and what Giles said about them in his speech.[20]

The claim of the bellicose Virginian that he had been embarrassed in

16 *Annals*, 2 Cong., p. 761; Anderson, *Giles*, p. 20.

17 Dated Jan. 3, 1793, and submitted Jan. 4, *Am. State Papers, Finance*, I, 180–183; see also 185–186.

18 The Senate resolution of Jan. 15, 1793, was moved by Pierce Butler of S. C. and seconded by Stephen R. Bradley of Vermont; and Hamilton responded promptly (*Annals*, 2 Cong., pp. 629, 1187–1198). The sessions of the Senate were secret, and some of the documents submitted by Hamilton were account books, but TJ probably learned of the response through Monroe or John Taylor. See Long Note, below, following the Bibliography.

19 *Annals*, 2 Cong., pp. 835–840. Even the biographer of Giles, while denying that the latter was an automaton, accepts what he regards as the general opinion (Anderson, *Giles*, pp. 21–22, citing numerous writers in note 58).

20 Jan. 23, 1793 (*Annals*, 2 Cong., pp. 835–840; Lodge, II, 341–342).

his attempts to comprehend the report of Hamilton and the other financial papers can be readily appreciated by any layman who has struggled with these records. Hamilton had not deigned to give full information previously, and the obscurity of his proceedings was attested at a later time by another financial administrator who is rightly regarded as his peer, Albert Gallatin. Giles was not talking nonsense when he said that for some years they had been legislating "without competent official knowledge of the state of the Treasury, or revenues," even though they were engaged in the most important fiscal arrangements. His call for fuller and more systematic information may have been chiefly designed to embarrass Hamilton rather than to shed light on an inevitably complicated subject, but there can be no question of the right of Congress to seek more light. Giles frankly acknowledged that the impressions resulting from his inquiries, which his speech showed had been considerable, were "by no means favorable to the arrangements made by the gentleman at the head of the Treasury Department." That may have sounded like high treason to Hamilton's partisans, but Giles said he might be mistaken and was open to conviction. Probably his mind was really made up already, but it would have been the part of statesmanship to take him at his word.

As usual when under attack, Hamilton brought his heavy artillery into prompt action. He replied to these resolutions with a series of powerful reports.[21] The reason why his own partisans had not opposed the resolution, as he said in private, was to confound his critics "by giving a free course to investigation." That was undoubtedly the wise procedure, but he could not conceal his own impatience. He said in his first report:

> . . . The resolutions to which I am to answer, were not moved without a pretty copious display of the reasons on which they were founded. These reasons are before the public, through the channel of the press. They are of a nature to excite attention, to beget alarms, to inspire doubts. Deductions of a very extraordinary complexion may, without forcing the sense, be drawn from them.[22]

It is not an uncommon practice among public officials to belittle attacks on their conduct by characterizing them as partisan — as they

[21] To the House, Feb. 4, 13, 19, 1793. These can be seen in *Annals*, 2 Cong., pp. 1199 ff.; in Lodge, II, 342–356, 361–403, 417–452; and elsewhere. In the same period he made further reports to the Senate. On Feb. 1–4, he had an exchange with TJ regarding the fund for use with the Barbary pirates. This appears, however, to have been an unimportant detail in the larger struggle (LC, 14067, 14093–14094).

[22] Feb. 4, 1793 (*Annals*, 2 Cong., p. 1199).

very often are — but Hamilton himself made it more difficult to take these matters out of the realm of partisanship. In a private letter to William Short, who as the American agent in foreign financial transactions was unwittingly involved, he said: "The spirit of party has grown to maturity sooner in this country than perhaps was to have been counted upon. You will see a specimen of it in the inclosed speech of Mr. Giles, a member from Virginia." [23] In cold print that speech by itself does not seem a striking example of partisanship, and the resolutions could have been treated as a legitimate inquiry. While going to such pains to answer them, Hamilton would have been wiser to minimize rather than exaggerate their importance. It was about this time that Oliver Wolcott and Fisher Ames were shaking their heads over the incomprehensible Virginians.

After Hamilton submitted the third of his reports and before Giles introduced an even more famous set of resolutions, Madison expressed himself about the situation. Writing Edmund Pendleton about John Taylor of Caroline, whose talents had been "of such infinite service to the republican cause, and such a terror to its adversaries," he calmly summed matters up:

> You will have discovered from the Newspapers that a pretty interesting scrutiny has been started into the administration of the Treasury Department. The documents furnished shew that there has been at least a very blameable irregularity & secrecy in some particulars of it, and many appearances which at least require explanation. With some, suspicions are carried very far; others resolve the whole that is wrong with favoritism to the Bank, &c. whilst the partizans of the Fisc. either see nothing amiss, or are willing to ascribe everything that is so to venial, if not laudable motives.[24]

Jefferson was undoubtedly one of those who carried suspicions very far. Early in the month, when announcing to Washington that he would remain in office a little longer, he had referred to "a corrupt squadron of voters in Congress at the command of the Treasury." But he had also said that his personal attitude was less important than the President seemed to think, that he kept himself aloof from "all cabal and correspondence on the subject of the government" and saw and spoke with as few as he could.[25] There is nothing in the record to disprove the correctness of this statement at the time he made it.

[23] Hamilton to Short, Feb. 5, 1793 (Lodge, VIII, 292). At the same time he sent Short a printed copy of his own letter of Feb. 4, 1793, to the House, which constituted the first part of his answer to the resolutions.

[24] Madison to Pendleton, Feb. 23, 1793 (Hunt, VI, 124).

[25] Memo. of Feb. 7, 1793 (Ford, I, 215).

Before the controversy reached a decisive point, however, the fact was revealed that he, as a commissioner of the Sinking Fund, had not been wholly in accord with Hamilton. A resolution, requesting the commissioners to lay before the House a statement of their proceedings not hitherto furnished, was passed on February 19, though Hamilton's most loyal followers opposed it, regarding it as part of the attack on his official conduct. At the same time his critics were saying that he was delaying payment of the foreign debt, that is, payment to France, they were also saying that he was not doing all he was supposed to do in the matter of the domestic debt.[26]

The most important fresh document was the journal of the commissioners. Such disagreements as this disclosed had occurred in the previous spring, during the stock-market panic of that time, and they bore on the construction of the act under which the board was operating. Specifically, the question related to the price at which government securities might be bought in this process of debt reduction, and it was answered in Hamilton's favor by the voice of the Chief Justice, who held that under the act they might be purchased at more than the market price, up to their par value. The point is that Hamilton wanted to buy at par at that time, when securities were below par on the market. His major purpose, as he claimed, was to maintain the credit of the government, but numerous speculators, including his friend the notorious William Duer, had been caught in the sharp decline of securities.[27] Hamilton wanted to stay the panic, but to the mind of Jefferson he was purposely supporting the speculators. Furthermore, Jefferson believed that the purpose of the Sinking Fund was to retire the debt — as much of it as possible and under the most favorable conditions. He may not have sufficiently appreciated the positive functions of the Treasury in maintaining the level of public securities, but his simple philosophy was one that unsophisticated citizens could readily understand. Like him, they could not see why the government should pay more for its own securities than it had to, for the apparent advantage of men like Duer.

Even if it be granted that Hamilton's motives were primarily public, as he claimed, he had followed his own interpretation of the law before referring the question to John Jay and while the other four commissioners were evenly divided. He authorized purchases of certain stocks at par while the matter was pending, claiming that there

<hr />

[26] Resolution of Feb. 19, 1793 (*Annals*, 2 Cong., pp. 882–883); Journal, covering the period Aug. 26, 1790–Jan. 26, 1793, in *Am. State Papers, Finance*, I, 234–238 (submitted Feb. 25, 1793).

[27] See *Jefferson and the Rights of Man*, pp. 434–435.

was no difference of opinion among the commissioners.[28] If he regarded Jefferson as a legalistic quibbler in a time of financial stress, he himself was unquestionably high-handed in this instance and he appears to have been actually untruthful in private. Jefferson was not in a position to read his private letters, as we are, but he had ample grounds for believing that his colleague interpreted the law to suit himself and stretched his own powers to the limit. For that reason alone he could hardly have failed to sympathize with the congressional criticisms of Hamilton. In the end, however, these criticisms went too far. The Secretary of the Treasury tended to be irresponsible, but it could not be proved that he had been so in a vital matter, to the injury of the country.

The resolutions that Giles introduced on February 27, 1793, a week before the end of the congressional session, were nine in number, but three of them were promptly eliminated without extended discussion. The first two, asserting that laws making specific appropriations should be strictly observed by the administrator of the finances, and that a "violation" of an appropriation law was a violation of the Constitution, were dismissed from consideration by a rather close vote — chiefly on the ground that the time of the House should not be consumed by a discussion of such general questions. A difference of opinion with respect to the degree of legislative control of appropriations was clearly brought out, nonetheless. Hamilton and his partisans favored executive latitude, while his critics emphasized executive conformity to the letter of the law. But even the latter, including Madison and Jefferson himself, recognized the desirability of latitude in extreme cases. The difference was mainly one of shading, and but for Hamilton's high-handedness and imperious temper the issue might not have arisen at this time. Jefferson himself did not believe in legislative omnipotence and occasionally acted in financial matters without express authority, but in practice he had been far more scrupulous than his colleague and had shown much better manners toward the legislature.[29] The last resolution, calling for the transmission of all of them to the President, was defeated by an overwhelming vote. This could be interpreted as a request for Hamilton's dismissal. The House was quite unwilling to go that far, and said so promptly. Thus the issue re-

[28] Hamilton to William Seton, March 25, 1792 (J.C.H., V, 498-499). John Jay, to whom the question of interpretation of the law was referred on Mar. 26, during his absence in New York, replied on Mar. 31.

[29] This matter is discussed by L. D. White in *The Federalists* (1948), pp. 330-334, to the greater discredit of Hamilton's critics than is warranted, in my opinion.

solved itself into one of rebuking Hamilton rather than removing him.[30]

The other six resolutions were debated vigorously during the three remaining days of the session and well into the evenings. The chief specific allegation against Hamilton was that he had violated the Act of August 4, 1790, providing for the floating of a loan of $12,000,000 in Europe for the payment of the foreign debt, by withdrawing part of this to America. Another Act (August 12, 1790), providing for a loan of $2,000,000 for domestic purposes, was involved; and Hamilton himself stated that he had lumped the two together, admitting a technical violation of the law. But he himself was not disturbed by doubts that were suggested by a "pusillanimous caution," and he claimed that he exercised higher motives in the performance of his great trust.[31] It was further charged that the Secretary had deviated from the President's instructions, and that he had omitted to discharge an essential duty in failing to inform the House of his actions in withdrawing money from Europe. The latter charge, contained in the fifth resolution, received the largest vote, 15 to 33, which was less than a third of the total. The smallest vote of all was given the last one to be presented, declaring that the Secretary had been guilty of "indecorum" to the House, in undertaking to judge of its motives in making calls on him for information and in not giving all the necessary information in response to certain calls. The smallness of the vote for this resolution may be explained by the fact that the battle was now clearly lost, but, as had been true throughout the fight, nearly half of these votes were cast by the Virginians. Almost to a man they persisted in the attack, but there could be no possible doubt of their dismal failure.[32]

ii

The outcome of the bitter struggle during the last days of the congressional session was no proof that Hamilton's administration of the nation's finances was above criticism, or that his interpretation of the extent of his official authority was destined to prevail through the coming years. But it demonstrated that in this field at this time his

[30] The full resolutions are in *Annals*, 2 Cong., p. 900. The vote against the first two was 32 to 25, and only 14 voted in favor of the last (*ibid.*, p. 905).

[31] *Am. State Papers, Finance*, I, 204.

[32] The debates of Feb. 28–Mar. 2, 1793 (Thursday through Saturday) are in *Annals*, 2 Cong., pp. 900–963, the votes on the six resolutions on pp. 955–963. Giles and Madison led the fight throughout. Their most consistent supporters outside their own delegation were William Findley of Pennsylvania, John Francis Mercer of Maryland, Nathaniel W. Macon and John B. Ashe of North Carolina, and Abraham Baldwin of Georgia.

position was virtually impregnable. Since the fight over the last set of Giles resolutions served to strengthen rather than weaken that position, the introduction of these seems clearly to have been a grave political mistake on the part of his critics. One cannot help wondering, therefore, who ordered the final assault and for what reasons. The private comments of Jefferson immediately after the repulse are of sufficient interest in this connection to warrant extended quotation. Writing his son-in-law, to whom he might have been expected to speak frankly, he said:

> . . . You have for some time past seen a number of reports from the Secretary of the Treasury on enquiries instituted by the H. of representatives. When these were all come in, a number of resolutions were prepared by Mr. Giles, expressing the truths resulting from the reports. These resolns you will see in Fenno's paper. Mr. Giles & one or two others were sanguine enough to believe, that the palpableness of the truths rendered a negative of them impossible, & therefore forced them on. Others contemplating the character of the present house, one third of which is understood to be made up of bank directors & stock jobbers who would be voting on the case of their chief: and another third of persons blindly devoted to that party, of persons not comprehending the papers, or persons comprehending them but too indulgent to pass a vote of censure, foresaw that the resolutions would be negatived by a majority of two to one. Still they thought that the negative of palpable truth would be of service, as it would let the public see how desperate & abandoned were the hands in which their interests were placed. The vote turned out to be what was expected, not more than 3 or 4 varying from what had been conceived of them. The public will see from this the extent of their danger, and a full representation at the ensuing session will doubtless find occasion to revise the decision, and take measures for ensuring the authority of the laws over the corrupt manœuvres of the heads of departments under the pretext of exercising discretion in opposition to law.[33]

Not long after this, in a private memorandum, he made a list of "paper men" in Congress, saying that he got this from John Beckley.[34]

Certain conclusions emerge from these contemporary comments of his: (1) There is no possible doubt that he regarded the resolutions as justified, and that he attributed their defeat not to the merits of the case, but primarily to the votes of men who were attached to Hamilton

[33] TJ to TMR, Mar. 3, 1793 (Ford, VI, 194–195). This passage repeated in almost identical language his private memo. of Mar. 2, 1793 (Ford, I, 222–223).

[34] Mar. 23, 1793 (Ford, I, 223).

and his policies by ties of financial interest. Jefferson gave no intimation whatever that he himself thought the resolutions went too far. (2) Viewing the personnel of Congress as he did, it seems unlikely that he was one of the very few who were so sanguine as to believe the resolutions would pass and who forced them on. However, he may have been one of those who believed that the matter should be presented anyway, for the education of the public. (3) His reference to preliminary estimates of the vote suggests that he was informed of, if not a party to, discussions among the Virginians. He might have got the information from Madison or Beckley while holding himself personally aloof, or he might have been present at some small meeting when the matter was talked about. (4) He said that Giles "prepared" the resolutions, without suggesting that the Congressman got any help.

A few days after Jefferson wrote his son-in-law, John Taylor of Caroline published a pamphlet containing a much fuller contemporary account of these events than we have from the pen of any other major Virginian. It was entitled *An Examination of the Late Proceedings in Congress, respecting the Official Conduct of the Secretary of the Treasury* and showed that its author approved of the resolutions at all points.[35] In Taylor's opinion, the Secretary had clearly disregarded the law, had violated faith with France, and had acted without the knowledge of the President or the legislature. He spoke of the "very respectable and independent member" who had been most active in pressing the inquiry into Hamilton's conduct, obviously referring to Giles. Printing a list of "paper men" which was even longer than the one that Beckley had given Jefferson, he likewise attributed the defeat of the resolutions to them.[36]

To later readers it may seem that these charges of improper influences and a "corrupt squadron" should be dismissed as exaggerations of partisanship. But, as has been pointed out by one of the most distinguished students of the subject, public security holding bore a far larger ratio to investments in general at that time than it has since borne in the United States. Writing in 1915, Charles A. Beard said: "The situation would be more analogous to affairs today if we should put all of the railway and industrial securities in a single mass and make their value and their increment depend largely upon the measures enacted into law at Washington." He concluded that Hamilton's critics

---

[35] Mar. 8, 1793; reprinted Oct. 20, 1793. Beard analyzes it at length in *Economic Origins of Jeffersonian Democracy* (1915), ch. VII. TJ in a letter of May 5, 1793, to Monroe (Ford, VI, 238) showed that he had read it. He sent a copy to Madison.
[36] Beard gives this list, pp. 203-204.

correctly understood the enormous weight of the debt in politics.[37] It must be recognized that John Taylor and Jefferson were far from unrealistic. If they did not allow sufficiently for Hamilton's larger patriotism, they saw with clear eyes the grave dangers his policies had created and the vast power that lay in his hands. John Adams saw the same thing eventually. In later years he wrote: "The Funding system and Banking systems, which are the work of the Federalists, have introduced more corruption and injustice, for what I know, than any other cause." [38]

Taylor's praise of Giles and the few who stood with him was unqualified:

> To the manly efforts and disinterested patriotism of those who maintained the conflict, against such a combination of interests, and checked its rapid career, much praise is due. America is sensible of their services, and will remember their virtues. Thanks, illustrious patriots, your country . . . will enroll your names upon the immortal records of fame.[39]

The followers of Hamilton did not thus describe them, but with one accord heaped maledictions on them as parties to an infamous plot. A banker friend in New York expressed to Hamilton the hope that his health had not suffered from the work he had had to do in order "to get rid of these varlets." Elisha Boudinot, writing from Newark, congratulated him on his triumph over "the envious and malicious — enemies to the government as well as yourself," and assured him that the influence of these *"beings"* extended little beyond their own "selfish, narrow circle." [40] There was a contemptuous tone in these and other letters, they often spoke of the support of Hamilton by the "mercantile" interest, and they constantly referred to the opposition as localized. Quite clearly the Hamiltonians regarded this opposition as Southern and, more particularly, Virginian, but they do not appear to have blamed Jefferson for it to any considerable degree until after the fight was over.

This is somewhat surprising, in view of the party line which Hamilton himself had laid down in the previous year. He had then taken the position that his colleague in the executive branch of the govern-

---

[37] *Economic Origins of Jeffersonian Democracy*, pp. 219–220.

[38] Adams to Cunningham, Oct. 23, 1809 (*Correspondence . . . with William Cunningham* [1823], p. 181).

[39] *Examination*, pp. 27–28.

[40] William Seton to Hamilton, Mar. 5, 1793 (HP, 1 ser., 18:2846); Boudinot to Hamilton, Mar. 26, 1793 (J.C.H., V, 548).

ment was the focus of all the opposition to him, which to his mind amounted to opposition to the government itself. By so doing he actually built Jefferson up in the public mind, and it would have been the part of political wisdom to minimize his colleague's role, not to magnify it. This sort of negative wisdom was not characteristic of the aggressive Secretary of the Treasury, however, and the most plausible explanation of his relative indifference to Jefferson during the course of the congressional fight is that his attention was necessarily drawn to his immediate antagonists. Be that as it may, the strongest partisans of the Treasury began to talk about Jefferson after Congress had adjourned. From Connecticut the elder Oliver Wolcott wrote his son, the comptroller: "The pedagogue who is at the head of one of the departments is prominent in this business." [41] Even in Virginia, there was undercover talk about the Secretary of State which followed the lines of what was destined to be the enduring Federalist interpretation. By early summer the word seems to have got around.

According to a defender of Jefferson in a Virginia journal, the "paper dealers" in Richmond and Petersburg were taking two lines of argument: (1) that the inquiry into the Treasury did not arise from disinterested zeal for the public good, but from "personal dislike and a previously calculated system" against the Secretary; (2) that "Mr. Jefferson was the scourge of all opposition to the treasury administration, and the instigator of the inquiry from its inception to its maturation." [42] Saying that the stories smelled of slander and malice, this writer denied both aspersions. The inquiry was not premeditated but arose from unfolding circumstances, and the Secretary of State could not have instigated it. In his opinion, Jefferson had always conducted himself with "the most refined delicacy" respecting subjects of legislation; he rarely expressed his opinions on them; he did not impose his counsels on the delegation — in a word, he attended to his own business.

That was the claim he himself had made to the President early in February, when he said that he kept himself aloof from legislative matters which did not directly concern him, and there is no sufficient reason to doubt its correctness until that date. His representations to Washington bearing on the debt to France and the Sinking Fund were proper enough in view of his official position. The Virginia delegation required no prodding from him, and there was no need for him to put

[41] Oliver Wolcott, Sr. to Oliver Wolcott, Jr. (Gibbs, I, 91).
[42] FAIR PLAY, quoted from *Virginia Gazette* of July 11 in *National Gazette* of July 24, 1793.

speeches in anybody's mouth. If he showed Madison his own calculations, these were based on Treasury reports that were available to that statesman, and Madison or Giles could have made them for himself. His sympathy with the representatives of Virginia was complete, but the inception of the attack cannot be attributed to him in fairness, and if he provided direct aid to it this was unimportant — except, perhaps, at the very last. The only real question arises in connection with the last set of resolutions that were introduced by Giles. It has been claimed with considerable show of authority that Jefferson originally drafted these.

The basis for this claim is a "rough draft" which was supplied in the last decade of the nineteenth century by one of Jefferson's descendants to the editor of what was generally regarded until the middle of the twentieth century as the best collection of his writings. This document, which is said to have been in Jefferson's handwriting, though apparently without title or annotation, has not been discovered until the present time. We shall assume, nonetheless, that it was at some time among his voluminous papers. Conjectures based on unlabeled papers in anybody's files must be made with caution, but the similarity between this set of resolutions and the one presented by Giles is so close as to lead to the reasonable surmise that one was copied in considerable part from the other. The Congressman was wholly competent to draft his own resolutions, but they are actually milder than these, and it is a fair assumption that the stronger set came first in point of time, being modified on second thought and under circumstances of which we are uninformed.[43]

The chief differences between the two sets of resolutions appear at the very end. The supposed original draft had two final resolutions which were not offered to the House of Representatives. One of these called for the creation of a new officer, the treasurer, who was to be wholly independent of the Secretary; and the other called upon the President to remove the present Secretary of the Treasury because of maladministration. No doubt Jefferson would really have liked to go that far. The Giles version substituted for these two resolutions one

[43] Paul Leicester Ford says the "rough draft" was furnished by Sarah N. Randolph. He prints it (VI, 168–171) in parallel columns with the resolutions as introduced. He discusses it more fully in "The Authorship of Giles's Resolutions," in *Nation*, Sept. 5, 1895 (Vol. 61, pp. 164–165), speaking there of its being in TJ's handwriting. His arguments based on the assumption that Giles was incapable of drafting his resolutions, and that TJ was really the instigator of the whole fight, reflect the traditional Federalist interpretation and in my opinion are unsound. We are left, however, with the printed document itself.

that called for the submission of all the resolutions to the President (a proposal which was itself much too strong for Congress), but there is no way of knowing at whose instance the change was made. A good deal can happen between a first draft and a final one.

We must have recourse to sheer speculation in the effort to determine what actually happened. Possibly Giles or Madison or both of them asked Jefferson to draft some resolutions. Most of the ideas themselves had already been expressed in the debates, and the final version probably represented the opinions held in common by these Virginians. The most likely supposition is that the thought of presenting resolutions came in the first place from the fiery Giles, who had been the spearhead from the beginning. The modification of their tone, after the original essay, was more in the character of Madison, while Jefferson himself may well have agreed to it as a matter of policy.

If it be assumed that he participated in a private conference with Giles or Madison or both and actually drafted a set of resolutions, the question of the propriety of his conduct may be raised. These men were members of the legislative branch with which, in his announced opinion, members of the executive should not meddle, and they were moving against his fellow Secretary. By the standards of Hamilton such action can hardly be deemed improper, for he himself did that much and more. The Secretary of the Treasury not only conferred with legislators; he told them precisely what to do, and in times past had definitely lobbied against measures and policies favored by Jefferson. He had even intrigued with the British minister behind Jefferson's back. He had tried to drive his colleague from the government by anonymous attacks in newspapers.

If Jefferson is to be condemned, it must be in the light of his own higher standards and more scrupulous customary practice. Complete abstention from legislative matters was in fact an extreme and impractical policy, and nobody could have expected him not to talk freely with his intimate friend Madison. But the drafting of resolutions which either Madison or Giles could easily have drawn would have been better left wholly to them. In dealing with a man whom he thought unscrupulous, perhaps he overbore his own scruples to some extent about this time. Perhaps his anger against Hamilton clouded his judgment. He and his fellow Virginians showed bad judgment, at all events. They overreached themselves, just as Hamilton had in the autumn. Hamilton, who deserved to be questioned and even warned in this instance, though not to be dismissed or discredited, emerged triumphant; while the Secretary of State gained nothing by straying from the path of strict official propriety he had set for himself and which he generally pursued with care.[44]

If the rejection of the Giles Resolutions by an overwhelming vote confirmed for the moment the Hamilton position regarding administrative discretion, the lesson of his experience was not wholly lost — even upon his staunchest supporters. When Oliver Wolcott succeeded him nearly two years later, the new Secretary received from his own father the advice not to depart from established rules unless the necessity was "most urgent, important and apparent." [45] And if the outcome represented a sweeping victory over men whom admirers of the Secretary described as "Sons of Faction" and "persecutors," he himself was not so confident that he did not seek counsel and comfort. He had by no means crushed the hostile Virginians. Congressional elections were then held at different times, and the elections in Virginia occurred soon after these events. Writing Hamilton from South Carolina, Congressman William Loughton Smith reported that the mercantile interest in Charleston regarded his cause as their own, and that on his own recent visit to the back country of Georgia and South Carolina he spread the word that Freneau's paper was "stuffed with lies and propagated by the malicious party." Of Giles's state, however, he had no good report. He said:

. . . By the paper I find all the old members are re-elected in Virginia, except White, the only good one: it was what I apprehended; it was sufficient for him to have voted right once for them to have turned him out. When Col. Bland was the only good member in that Delegation he died; and now we have lost White! But what good can we hope from that quarter.[46]

Senator Monroe, now in his home state, viewed the local scene much more complacently. Writing Jefferson, he spoke for himself and Madison:

In every respect, so far as we have heard, we find the publick mind perfectly sound in regard to those objects of national policy, at present most interesting. Every member [of the Assembly] is either as he should be, or has gained his place by fraud & imposition.

[44] For other particular charges against him, see Long Note, below, following the Bibliography.

[45] Oliver Wolcott, Sr., to Oliver Wolcott, Jr., Feb. 16, 1795 (Gibbs, I, 180).

[46] Smith to Hamilton, Apr. 24, 1793 (HP, 19:2892) referring to Alexander White.

We find likewise the sentiment universal in favor of your continuance through the present crisis and of course that a contrary conduct would have proved a publick as well as a very serious private detriment to yourself.[47]

Congressman Madison gained the same impression when he went back to Orange County, and he made a similar report to Jefferson, who had necessarily remained in Philadelphia. "As far as I can learn," he said, "the people of this country [Virginia] continue to be united and firm in the political sentiments expressed by their Representatives. The re-election of all who were most decided in their sentiments is one of the proofs of the fact. The only individual discontinued, is the one who dissented most from his colleagues." He also suspected that the President himself was not wholly satisfied with the aspect under which certain parts of the fiscal administration had been left.[48]

In Virginia, Hamilton relied chiefly on Edward Carrington of Richmond, who at his instance got reports of the final proceedings of the House into the newspapers of such commercial centers as there were.[49] Apparently there was some talk of Hamilton's retirement from office, and some thought of it on his part. By summer he was writing Carrington that he would stay on till the end of the next session, and the latter was urging him to call for an inquiry into his conduct at that time, if his enemies did not.[50] That is precisely what the Secretary did at the next session.

Jefferson regarded the triumph of Hamilton in this particular battle as temporary and looked forward cheerfully to the next Congress. In the previous autumn, when only partial results were in, he had been confident of its favorable complexion and had hoped that nothing much would be done by the existing body, which contained so many "paper men." Later returns served to encourage him further. On the Sunday after the session ended, he wrote his son-in-law:

. . . The elections have been favorable to the republican candidates everywhere South of the Connecticut; and even in Massachusetts there is a probability that one republican will be sent who possesses the confidence of the men of that description in that state (& which forms the mass of the state) and who will fulfil the only object needed, that of carrying back to them faithful accounts of what is done here. . . .[51]

[47] Monroe to TJ, Mar. 27, 1793 (S.M.H., I, 250).
[48] Madison to TJ, Apr. 12, 1793 (MP, 16:1467–1469).
[49] Carrington to Hamilton, Mar. 26, 1793 (J.C.H., V, 549). Madison made the same report to TJ.
[50] Carrington to Hamilton, July 2, 1793 (HP, 1 ser., 20:3052–3053).
[51] TJ to TMR, Mar. 3, 1793 (Ford, VI, 195–196).

He expressed similar confidence a few weeks later in a more re-strained comment to the American minister in England, Thomas Pinckney, with whom his relations had remained extremely cordial. "I think it very certain that a decided majority of the next Congress will be actuated by a very different spirit from that which governed the two preceding Congresses," he said. "Public faith will be cherished equally, I would say more, because it will be on purer principles: and the tone & proceedings of the government will be brought back to the true spirit of the constitution, without disorganizing the machine in its essential parts." [52]

There had been a depression in public securities, owing to the fact that at this time cash was unusually scarce and there was a good deal of selling. But in Jefferson's opinion, this should not lessen the confidence of the holders of public paper. He wrote to a friend in England with whom he had had many financial dealings:

. . . There is not upon earth a more solid property; and tho' one party here affect to charge the other with unfriendly disposi-tions towards the public debt, yet I believe there is not a man scarcely in the United States who is not sacredly determined to pay it; & the only difference which I can see between the two parties is that the republican one wish it could be paid tomorrow, and the fiscal party wish it to be perpetual, because they find in it an engine for corrupting the legislature. Bank property stands on very different ground; as that institution is strongly conceived to be unauthorized by the constitution. It may therefore be subject to shocks. [53]

He still thought that his own objections to the Bank were valid, and he found it impossible to be unsuspicious where Hamilton was con-cerned. Soon after the session ended, he wrote William Short in cipher to be cautious in his letters to the Secretary of the Treasury, asserting that the latter had sacrificed Short in defending himself in the Senate regarding loans to Europe — by submitting, not pertinent extracts from Short's letters, but whole letters which contained strong expres-sions against the French republicans and were calculated to do Short harm in America. [54] A little later, Jefferson wrote Madison that William Duer, then in prison, was threatening that if he was not relieved by "certain persons," he would lay open to the world "such a scene of villainy" as would strike it with astonishment. [55] Long years later he

[52] TJ to Thomas Pinckney, Apr. 12, 1793 (Ford, VI, 214).
[53] TJ to A. Donald, Mar. 5, 1793 (LC, 14243).
[54] TJ to Short, Mar. 23, 1793 (Ford, VI, 207).
[55] TJ to Madison, Apr. 7, 1793 (Ford, VI, 213).

vouched for Hamilton's personal integrity, but he did not do so at this stage.

The scene of his next encounters with his colleague was not to be financial.[56] The echoes of congressional debate died away after the session ended, and fiscal operations were crowded out of the public mind by foreign affairs. These were already Jefferson's main concern and occupation, but he could not have been expected to foresee that he himself would be thrown on the defensive by what happened in the spring.

[56] For later events in the controversy between Hamilton and his congressional critics see below, pp. 181–182.

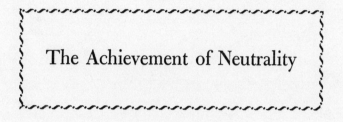

The Achievement of Neutrality

[III]

The Two Republics

1792–1793

AS MINISTER to France, Jefferson had observed the revolution
there in its most philosophical phase. A generation later, when
nearing seventy-five, he described the effect of these experiences
upon him. "I had left France in the first year of its revolution, in the
fervor of natural rights and zeal for reformation," he said in a tone of
nostalgia. "My conscientious devotion to these rights could not be
heightened, but it had been aroused and excited by daily exercise." [1]
This was a sincere statement, beyond a doubt, but it was not the whole
truth and did not claim to be. His attitude toward the French Revolution in its successive phases reflected to a notable degree the duality
of his political nature. On the one hand he was devoted to principles
which he regarded as timeless and universal; on the other he was an
experienced statesman, with a keen sense of practicality, who was
aware of the danger of pressing abstract principles too far in particular
situations when circumstances were unfavorable, and who not unnaturally perceived difficulties the more when he was himself in the
midst of them. Contemporary records show that when he was in Paris
the revolution moved faster than he expected or even desired, for he
believed that the French people were not yet ready for the liberty
and self-government they deserved. He used the term "reformation"
as long as he could, for that was what he actually preferred; and his
personal distaste for disorder and violence was unmistakably revealed
in the reports that he sent home.[2] The closer he was to scenes of bloodshed the less he liked them.

For upwards of two years as secretary of state he had viewed with

[1] In prefatory remarks to the Anas, dated Feb. 4, 1818 (Ford, I, 159).
[2] See *Jefferson and the Rights of Man*, ch. XII.

equanimity the course of events in France, but this was not wholly because of his distance from that country. Regarding the developments there as logical and relatively orderly, he rejoiced that they had led to the adoption of a constitution which was accepted by the King.[3] Gouverneur Morris, who was on the ground, thought this "good for nothing," and Jefferson himself did not approve of everything in it, but he never doubted that it represented a move toward fuller self-government. War broke out on the continent of Europe in the spring of 1792, and he showed his sympathy with the French from the first, believing that they were defending their liberties against foreign enemies of their revolution. He drew no distinction as yet between King and nation. In official communications he continued to refer to Louis XVI as the "best and greatest friend" of the United States. He was using symbolic language, to be sure, but the revolutionaries created considerable confusion in diplomatic circles when they erased the King as the symbol of France.

It was in August, 1792, while Alexander Hamilton was answering the objections to his "system" which Jefferson had made to George Washington, that Louis XVI was suspended by the Legislative Assembly; and it was in September, while the Secretary of State was being attacked by Hamilton as CATULLUS in Philadelphia, that the National Convention abolished the monarchy and created the first French Republic.[4] These were external facts of which the American government must eventually take cognizance, and there was an accompaniment of bloodshed in both these months which might have been expected to alarm the American public, though it does not appear to have done so very much. The trial of the dethroned Louis Capet began in December, and he was executed in January, 1793, but the latter event was not reported in the United States until after Washington's second inauguration.

In considering the American response to these fateful events, we must take into account the time-lag. As a rule, news of occurrences in Europe took from six to eight weeks to reach the United States, and it came first by way of England. Direct reports from France were much slower in coming, and official communications were generally the slowest of all. Early in November, 1792, the French minister, Ternant, who felt sadly neglected by his government, complained that no French boat had arrived in an American port in six months.[5] It

---

[3] The Constitution of 1791, communicated to the United States in February, 1792. See *Jefferson and the Rights of Man*, pp. 403–404.

[4] See *Jefferson and the Rights of Man*, ch. XXVII.

[5] Ternant to Minister of Foreign Affairs, Nov. 5, 1792 (*C.F.M.*, pp. 163–164).

would have been an enormous convenience to Jefferson, as well as to Ternant, if rapid and reliable means of communication had been available.

There were times when he had to take action on the basis of unauthoritative newspaper reports which both he and the French minister naturally suspected at first because of their English origin. Such a case arose when he heard, in October, 1792, of the suspension of Louis XVI a couple of months before, and of the calling of a National Convention. The practical question was that of payments on the American debt to France during the period that the Constitution of 1791 was suspended and there was no legitimate French government to receive the payments and give the United States an "unobjectionable acquittal." This was the subject of a "consultation" with the other high officers at the President's house, at which the decision was reached to suspend payment until further orders. Jefferson was in agreement with the decision and communicated it to Morris.[6] He made it clear, however, that the withholding of payments was to be regarded as temporary. He considered the National Convention a legitimate body, though he had not yet been officially informed that it had met. A difference had already appeared between him and Hamilton, who questioned the legitimacy of the Convention and doubted if the United States could safely make payments to a new government which omitted the King. The question related not merely to payments made in France, but also to those made to Ternant in America, in order to aid the French in Santo Domingo, and in this form it soon arose again.[7]

Meanwhile, Jefferson had received from Gouverneur Morris information about the bloody events in Paris in August. The American minister believed that matters had already resolved themselves into a simple question between absolute monarchy and a republic, all middle terms having been done away with. Morris was horrified by the actions of the Parisian populace and by no means sympathetic with the republicans, but he expected them to triumph for a time and asked for instructions respecting his line of conduct.[8] Jefferson's characteristically sympathetic and restrained reply was too late to serve any immediate purpose, as he knew, and he expressed the official American sentiments as a sanction of what the minister had probably done already. That is, he expected Morris to stay, unless proper concern for

[6] TJ to Morris, Oct. 15, 1792 (Ford, VI, 120–121). He must have been in error in his later note that the consultation occurred about Nov. 1 ("Anas" [Ford, I, 208, *n.* 2]).
[7] Memo. in Nov. 1792 (Ford, I, 208).
[8] Morris to TJ, Aug. 16, 1792 (*A.S.P.F.R.*, I, 333–334).

his personal safety should forbid, and to continue to do business with the French as well as he could under the circumstances. In reality, as Jefferson afterwards found out, relations between Morris and the French officials were severely strained and the American minister once went so far as to ask for his passport.

The principle which Jefferson now laid down, and which in fact Morris never contested despite his inability to conceal his detestation of the revolutionary government, is of genuine historic importance. Though soon questioned by Hamilton, it was destined to survive for generations as a foundation of American diplomatic practice. The Secretary of State said: "It accords with our principles to acknowledge any government to be rightful which is formed by the will of the nation substantially declared." [9] This statement may be regarded as an affirmation of the doctrine of the sovereignty of the people, but the expression "substantially declared" was important in his eyes, for he was a stickler for constitutional regularity. In his own state, in 1776, he had objected to the framing of a constitution by a legislative body, insisting that such a function should be performed only by a convention specially chosen for that purpose.[10] As time went on he concluded from newspaper reports that the French Convention was "invested with full powers by the nation to transact its affairs." Whereupon, with Washington's concurrence, he instructed Morris toward the end of the year to consider the suspension of payments as now taken off. At the same time, he laid down more emphatically what he called "the Catholic principle of republicanism." With Washington's express approbation, he stated it in almost identical language to Morris in France and Thomas Pinckney in England. Thus he wrote to the latter:

> . . . We certainly cannot deny to other nations that principle whereon our government is founded, that every nation has a right to govern itself internally under whatever forms it pleases, and to change these forms at its own will; and externally to transact business with other nations through whatever organ it

[9] TJ to Morris, Nov. 7, 1792 (Ford, VI, 131). Morris said virtually the same thing in a letter which TJ had not yet received: "I am bound to suppose that, if the great majority of the nation adhere to the new form, the United States will approve thereof, because, in the first place, we have no right to prescribe to this country the government they shall adopt, and next, because the basis of our own constitution is the indefeasible right of the people to establish it." (To TJ, Aug. 22, 1792; A.S.P.F.R., I, 336.) The subsequent failure of Morris to make his practices conform with his professions to the authorities at home can be attributed in part to the temper of the revolutionary officials with whom he had to deal, though he was not notable for his discretion.

[10] See *Jefferson the Virginian*, pp. 235–236.

chooses, whether that be a King, Convention, Assembly, Committee, President, or whatever it be. The only thing essential is the will of the nation. Taking this as your polar star, you can hardly err.[11]

Hamilton, who thought of a nation in terms of its rulers and not its people, would not have concurred in this "Catholic principle of republicanism" if it had been referred to him at this stage. It did not have to be, but financial questions did. During the fall, the Secretary of the Treasury had put himself on record with respect to Ternant's application for additional funds for the relief of Santo Domingo, on account of the American debt to France. He found the subject "extremely delicate and embarrassing" in view of the changes in the former monarchy and the possible restoration of the King — which he himself would unquestionably have liked. There was danger that the United States would not get credit for payments made to the existing government. He recognized, however, that aid to the colony of Santo Domingo, which had suffered under a severe insurrection, would be "so clearly an act of humanity and friendship" that it was very likely to be acknowledged. After mentioning a number of other difficulties, he concluded that nothing could be done without some risk to the United States. He recommended, therefore, that "*as little as possible* ought to be done," that whatever might be done should be "restricted to the single idea *of preserving the colony from destruction by famine*," and that care should be taken to avoid recognition of any political authority.[12]

This policy reflected Hamilton's lack of confidence in the future of the revolution in France, but there was commendable prudence in it. Jefferson's instincts were more generous and his fears were different, but regularity in forms also seemed important to him as an official. The United States had been helping Santo Domingo for months, on Ternant's application, without express sanction from France. Hence Jefferson's announcement to him that he would receive another payment was coupled with a polite warning that without more specific authorization from home he could expect little more. He did get more, a few weeks later, but Jefferson's attitude was strictly correct in this matter of aid to a French colony, just as it was with respect to the changed government in France.[13] He was as prudent as Hamilton in

[11] TJ to Pinckney, Dec. 30, 1792 (L. & B., IX, 7–8); TJ to Morris, in much the same language, Dec. 30, 1792 (Ford, VI, 149–150); memo. of Dec. 30, 1792 (Ford, I, 214); see also, Dec. 27, 1792 (Ford, I, 213). By this time TJ had received Morris's letter of Aug. 22, 1792.
[12] Hamilton to Washington, Nov. 19, 1792 (J.C.H., IV, 328–331).
[13] TJ to Ternant, Nov. 20, 1792, and Jan. 14, 1793 (Ford, VI, 136–137, 161–162).

this particular financial matter, and Ternant seemed no more grateful to him than to the Secretary of the Treasury.

Meanwhile, in this winter of 1792-1793, American public opinion was distinctly favorable to the newly established French Republic, despite the bloodshed, since it seemed to represent the overthrow of despotism. Ternant had reported in the first place that the news of it had caused general rejoicing, and Freneau was moving with, not against, the popular current of sentiment when he sounded a paean of triumph in the *National Gazette*, about a week before Christmas:

> Valour, at length, by Fortune led,
> The Rights of Man restores;
> And Gallia, now from bondage freed,
> Her rising sun adores:
> On Equal Rights, her fabric plann'd,
> Storms idly round it rave,
> No longer breathes in Gallic land
> A monarch, or a slave.[14]

At just this juncture Jefferson reported that the Republicans, rejoicing at French military successes, were assuming the name of "Jacobins" with pride, and Ternant wrote home that "the American public spirit appears to be in our favor everywhere." [15] This spirit was well reflected in a letter which came to James Madison from rural Virginia a little later. His correspondent said:

> The French Republic is in my opinion confirmed. . . . The Fate of human nature is involved in Europe at least in the Event of the French Revolution, & I do think that we may now without the Spirit of Prophecy predict, that the Reign of Despotism in whatever form it may appear in Europe will scarcely survive the 18th century. America may rejoice, & plume herself in the idea of having made the Rent in the great curtain that withheld the light from human nature — by her exertions she let the day & the Rights of Man become legible & intelligible to a Shakled World.[16]

This writer criticized the New Englanders for not having the spirit of 1776, and some unfavorable private comments were in fact emanating from the land of steady habits. There was enthusiasm in Boston,

---

14 *National Gazette*, Dec. 19, 1792.

15 TJ to J. F. Mercer, Dec. 19, 1792 (Ford, VI, 147); Ternant to Minister of Foreign Affairs, Dec. 20, 1792 (*C.F.M.*, p. 166). At this date, Americans could not have been expected to know about factions among the revolutionaries.

16 George de Turberville to Madison, from Richmond County, Jan. 28, 1793 (MP, vol. 15).

where the terms "citizen" and "citizess" (or "citess") had come into some vogue, but Chauncey Goodrich of Hartford would have no traffic with such foolishness, as he told Oliver Wolcott, Jr., the comptroller of the Treasury:

> . . . Our greatest danger is from the contagion of levelism; what folly is it that has set the world agog to be all equal to French barbers. It must have its run, and the anti-feds will catch at it to aid their mischievous purposes. . . . before long the authors of entire equality will shew the world the danger of their wild rant. We treat their Boston notions with derision, and the name of citizen and citess, are only epithets of fun and joke; . . . a noisy set of discontented demagogues make a rant, and it seems as if they were about breaking up the foundations, but the great body of men of property move slowly, but move with sure success.[17]

Such expressions were more characteristic of later opinion, however, than of the present spirit, even in New England.

Early in the new year, Jefferson, writing a private letter to William Short, now at The Hague, in the paternal tone which he had not yet laid aside, chided his former secretary for the "extreme warmth" with which the latter had censured the proceedings of the Jacobins in recent letters. He did this at the injunction of the President, he said, expressing the fear that if Short's criticisms became known they would injure him at home as well as abroad, since they would not be relished by his countrymen. This private letter contains as fervid comments as Jefferson ever made on the French Revolution, and it has been widely quoted by later writers for just that reason.[18]

Jefferson's proneness to express himself more vehemently in private letters and memoranda than in public papers and official communications does not make him unique among human beings. Other responsible officers besides him have let themselves go in private while weighing their public words, though the reverse has often been the case with campaign orators — of whom he was never one. Whether the measured judgments of a responsible statesman or the unrestrained private language of the same man should be regarded as the better index of his true sentiments is perhaps an unanswerable question, and both must be taken into account by anyone seeking to arrive at truth. A statesman must be judged at last by his public policies and official acts, which represent the results of his sober deliberation, but private

[17] Goodrich to Wolcott, Feb. 17, 1793 (Gibbs, I, 88).
[18] TJ to Short, Jan. 3, 1793 (Ford, VI, 153–157), replying to a batch of letters, including a private one of Sept. 15.

language affords an important clue to the state of his own mind and emotions. The contrast was unusually sharp in the case of Jefferson, who imposed extraordinary restraint on himself as a public man while revealing the fervor of his nature in intimate circles and in personal memoranda. To hostile interpreters this apparent contradiction has lent color to the charge of duplicity, but Jefferson himself resolved it by harnessing his emotions (which actually were an essential element in his leadership) to the realistic and reasoned conduct of public affairs (which was his business). His friends could not have been unaware of his proneness to exaggeration when blowing off steam in private; and the persons most aware of it should have been his *young* friends, who stood in the position of disciples to him, for, like a teacher among his pupils, he was least inhibited and most likely to indulge in hyperbole with them. No saying can be fully understood out of its specific setting, and some of the most vivid of Jefferson's were pedagogical in purpose. These would not have endured had they not contained kernels of eternal truth, but the specific language was owing to particular circumstance. This letter to Short is a case in point. The essential and abiding truth embedded in it is that all human progress is costly, especially progress toward liberty and democracy; but much of its imagery is such as poets would use — not mathematicians or coldly calculating statesmen.

Jefferson's defense of the Jacobins, as a political party in France, need not detain us. Owing to the time-lag, his information about groupings and objectives could not be up to date, and he naturally read back into current struggles the issues he himself had perceived when, as a personal spectator of the revolution, he was better informed of developments than he could ever hope to be again. To him the Jacobins were merely the republican element in the old party of the Patriots, and the Feuillants (who had been discredited by this time) were the monarchical. His friend Lafayette had belonged to the latter group and he himself had been far from unsympathetic with its immediate objectives.[19] In later years he reasserted, in its most essential points, his original opinion. He said in his late seventies:

> . . . I should have shut up the Queen in a Convent, putting harm out of her power, and placed the king in his station, investing him with limited powers, which I verily believe he would have honestly exercised, according to the measure of his understanding. In this way no void would have been created, courting the usurpation of a military adventurer [Bonaparte] nor occasion

[19] See *Jefferson and the Rights of Man*, ch. XII. Letters written him by Morris and giving fuller information about factional groupings had not yet been received.

given for those enormities which demoralized the nations of the world, and destroyed, and is yet to destroy, millions and millions of its inhabitants.[20]

But in the year 1793, when he was fifty, he believed that the experiment of retaining the hereditary executive, which he himself had favored at first, had failed completely and would have resulted in a return to despotism if it had been pursued. Thus he was now convinced that the "expunging" of the King had become an absolute necessity. By this he did not mean that the execution of Louis XVI was absolutely necessary, for at the time it had not occurred. What he did mean was that there was now an unavoidable choice between the revolution and the King. Gouverneur Morris had said practically the same thing, so the only real question was, which was preferable? Jefferson, who had never thought unkindly of this particular King and had given counsels of moderation to the Patriots while in France, had no possible doubt on that point. Being first of all a champion of liberty and popular sovereignty, he sympathized with this revolution, as he said ninety-nine one-hundredths of the American citizens did.

He was certainly not speaking with mathematical precision, but the celebrations of French military successes throughout the country that winter left no doubt that a large majority of the people did favor the Republic. Even Hamilton admitted this. He soon wrote to Short: "The popular tide in this country is strong in favor of the last revolution in France; and there are many who go, of course, with that tide, and endeavor always to turn it to account. For my own part I content myself with praying most sincerely that it may issue in the real happiness and advantage of the nation." [21] The Secretary of the Treasury harbored real doubts, but even he veiled them in noncommittal language.

In private conversation, as Jefferson noted, John Adams was more forthright and more pessimistic. Adams was convinced that the temporary accession to power of successive revolutionary groups would be marked by the destruction of their predecessors, and that in the end force would prevail. He was quite cynical about it, saying that neither virtue, prudence, wisdom, nor anything else was sufficient to restrain human passions, and that government could be maintained only by force.[22] Like Jefferson, Adams was prone to exaggerated statements, indulging in them in public as well as private to the confusion

[20] In autobiography (Ford, I, 141).

[21] Hamilton to Short, Feb. 5, 1793 (Lodge, VIII, 293). Because of the part played by Short in financial transactions in Europe, Hamilton had extensive correspondence with him.

[22] Note of conversation by TJ, Jan. 16, 1793 (LC, 13890).

of others regarding his actual philosophy of a balanced government, but he showed remarkable prevision regarding the course of events in France. Later developments there were to shake though never to destroy Jefferson's faith in the essential reasonableness of most men, and it is a notable fact that his faith lived on in times of greatest darkness. At the moment, however, he was in line with the predominant opinion of his countrymen. He indulged to some degree in what in our own day is called "rationalization," but he was on strong ground when he pointed out to Short that the logic of the events was inescapable.

Short needed comfort, however, more than logic. The personal cost of the revolution was mounting, and the human toll was being taken among the very people whom he and Jefferson had valued most during the latter's stay in France. Lafayette, who had abandoned the revolution, was now in custody, and the liberal-minded Duc de La Rochefoucauld had been snatched from his carriage and killed before the eyes of his old mother and young wife.[23] Of all the tragic events, it was this latter one that affected Short the most and that served most to embitter him. Jefferson did not yet have as full a tally of horrors as Short had, and he had been spared personal observation of them, but he was well aware of the general trend when he sought to bring philosophy to bear on these fearful developments.

> . . . In the struggle which was necessary [he said], many guilty persons fell without the forms of trial, and with them some innocent. These I deplore as much as any body, & shall deplore some of them to the day of my death. But I deplore them as I should have done had they fallen in battle. . . . *The liberty of the whole earth was depending on the issue of the contest, and was ever such a prize won with so little innocent blood?* My own affections have been deeply wounded by some of the martyrs to this cause, but rather than it should have failed, I would have seen half the earth desolated. Were there but an Adam & an Eve left in every country, & left free, it would be better than as it now is.[24]

23 See *Jefferson and the Rights of Man*, pp. 149–150, 210, 235, for the association of Short and Jefferson with this liberal nobleman and his family. It is not certain that TJ knew of his death when he wrote Short on Jan. 3, 1793. Morris reported it in a letter of Sept. 10, 1792, which TJ received Jan. 10, 1793. Short's failure to mention it in his letter of Sept. 15, 1792 (received Jan. 2, 1793) and in letters of Oct. 9 and 12, 1792 (actually received in December) suggests that he was avoiding the painful subject. It seems probable, nonetheless, that TJ had received this gruesome piece of news in some other way, and the tone of his letter strongly suggests that he had.

24 Ford, VI, 154, italics inserted.

In the last two sentences Jefferson indulged in hyperbole, and his words have inevitably been quoted, through the years since they have become known, because of their vividness. They are far more extravagant than the equally famous utterance of his to another young friend, William S. Smith, in a private letter relating to the Shays Rebellion in Massachusetts: "The tree of liberty must be refreshed from time to time with the blood of patriots and tyrants." [25] While that saying has been tortured by later interpreters who have quoted it out of context, its essential truthfulness cannot be questioned by anyone familiar with the course of human history. The expressions to Short are another matter. The annihilation of a large portion of the human race in order that the few survivors may have the full enjoyment of liberty cannot be justified on either historical or philosophical grounds; and the record of Jefferson's reasoned and disciplined life gives every ground to suppose that he himself would have recoiled from such a holocaust. He would certainly have said no such thing in public, and he could hardly have been expected to anticipate that private words of his would be quoted to schoolboys in later generations, seized upon by political partisans, or exploited by reckless demagogues.

In writing to one whom he regarded as a son he let his poetic imagery run away with him, while stating what he regarded as essential truth. The heart of his message lies in the sentence we have italicized: *"The liberty of the whole world was depending on the issue of the contest, and was ever such a prize won with so little innocent blood?"* In terms which should be understandable in any society threatened by any form of political absolutism, he was saying that despotism had been overthrown in France; that, therefore, it would eventually be overcome everywhere; and that in the light of this vast triumph for the cause of human liberty the losses must be regarded as slight. He afterwards had to revise the casualty lists upward, but he was prepared for that; and the abiding significance of his reflections lies in his frank recognition that the cost of liberty may be and frequently is exceedingly high. When the times were much less troubled he had written Lafayette: "we are not to expect to be translated from despotism to liberty in a feather-bed." [26] This lifelong champion of freedom could not lay first emphasis on security. The tragedy of French developments, as he later perceived it, lay less in their bloodiness, though that was bad enough, than in the fact that they led to

---

[25] Ford, IV, 467; see *Jefferson and the Rights of Man*, p. 166.
[26] Apr. 2, 1790 (Ford, V, 152).

new despotisms which seemed to confirm the pessimism of John Adams rather than his own optimism. But the counter-revolutionaries as well as the revolutionaries deserve blame for that, and at this stage the balance sheet seemed to show far more gain than loss.

At the moment, also, he was rejoicing that foreign developments were helping the cause of republicanism in his own country. He wrote Short that the triumph of republicanism in France had given the coup de grâce to the prospects of the monocrats in America. A few days later, he wrote his son-in-law that the outcome of the revolution in France was now little doubted, and that the sensation that had been created in the United States by the establishment of the Republic showed that the ultimate form of the American government depended far more on events in France than anybody had previously imagined.[27] By now he more clearly recognized the unity of the Atlantic world. Speaking of his own country, he said: "The tide which, after our former relaxed government [the Confederation], took a violent course towards the opposite extreme, and seemed ready to hang every thing around with the tassels and baubles of monarchy, is now getting back as we hope to a just mean, a government of laws addressed to the reason of the people, and not to their weaknesses." Thus he believed that the revolution in France had checked the incipient counter-revolution in America, which would have turned back the political clock.

As for Europe itself, he soon got from John Adams's son-in-law later and more encouraging reports than he had had from William Short and Gouverneur Morris. Writing him from New York, early in February, William S. Smith said:

> I left Paris on the 9th of November & have the satisfaction to inform you, that your friends there are well, and pursuing attentively the interests of that great & rising Republic, which notwithstanding the immense combination against them, I doubt not will be finally established, & the principles which gave it birth will expand and effect [sic] more or less every European state.[28]

When Smith came to Philadelphia, later in the month, he brought Jefferson fresh information about the hostile attitude of Gouverneur Morris toward the current French government.[29] The Secretary of State already knew a good deal about that. He had received from Morris himself copies of the latter's correspondence with the French Minister of Foreign Affairs, Le Brun, which indicated strained rela-

27 TJ to TMR, Jan. 7, 1793 (Ford, VI, 157).
28 W. S. Smith to TJ, Feb. 8, 1793 (LC, 14106).
29 Feb. 20, 1793 (Ford, I, 216–217).

tions; and the documents seemed so delicate that Jefferson, rather than let them go through the hands of a clerk, did the necessary translation himself before transmitting them to Washington, though the task took him nearly all day.[30] Philip Freneau, whose main business was editing the *National Gazette*, was still the translating clerk in the Department, but Jefferson kept these confidential documents out of his hands. He did not want the troubles between Morris and the French ministry to be bandied about in the American newspapers.

This correspondence showed that Morris had asked for his passport, because he did not like the tone of a letter from Le Brun to him. The manners of the present French officials were certainly not up to those of Vergennes and Montmorin, with whom Jefferson had dealt; they deserved a rebuke and treated Morris better after they got it. Furthermore, their importunity in this instance was definitely connected with financial matters with which, actually, Morris had nothing to do. These were being handled by William Short and events proved that he was not blamable. But the French minister described the situation in language which Jefferson undoubtedly approved. After reminding Morris that the French government had done business with and given aid to the Americans before the government of the latter had "any solid existence," Le Brun said:

> Before your Revolution, we had a Government which has always subsisted since. It is true, it has assumed another form; but liberty, the salvation of the country, have thus determined its creation. Besides, you, sir, who are born in the midst of a free people, should consider the affairs of France under another point of view than that of all the foreign ministers residing in Paris. *We support the same cause as that of your country: then our principles and yours should be the same*, and, by a series of natural consequences, no reason can be opposed to your residence at Paris.[31]

As he translated this passage, Jefferson's mind could hardly have failed to emphasize the words we have italicized, for they represented his own conviction. Morris himself had concluded that he would remain in France, though he wanted a passport into the interior, and he had told Le Brun what he had already told Jefferson. He said: "I have never doubted the right which every people have of forming, to themselves, such government as they please." [32]

---

[30] TJ to Washington, Jan. 13, 1793 (LC, 13985), sending correspondence between Morris and Le Brun, Aug. 30–Sept. 17, 1792 (*A.S.P.F.R.*, I, 338–340).
[31] Sept. 16, 1792; *A.S.P.F.R.*, I, 339, italics inserted.
[32] To Le Brun, Sept. 17, 1792 (*A.S.P.F.R.*, I, 340).

Being the representative of a government which had begun its existence in a revolt against a king, he could have consistently taken no other position, but there was no possible doubt of his strong personal dislike of the present French officials, and Jefferson soon learned more of their discontent with his conduct. Ternant turned over certain extracts from their correspondence with him and Jefferson left in his own files translations of these which he himself must have made.[33] One of these officials said of Morris: "His ill will is proved. It is vain that he conceals it under diplomatic forms, which cannot be admitted between two nations who will not submit their liberty to the dangers of Royalty. In this point of view, the Americans of the United States are our brothers, and their Minister . . . betrays them as well as us." Colonel William S. Smith, just back from France, had refused to serve as an official channel of complaint, but he told Jefferson privately that the French ministers had entirely shut their doors to Morris and would receive no further communications from him. It is not to be supposed that these revolutionists were reasonable, but, on his part, Morris was most undiplomatic. In the presence of company at his own table and in the hearing of servants he had cursed the French ministers as "a set of damned rascals" and said that the King would be restored. His own diary shows that he was conniving with the royalists, and he expected to be recalled, believing that the French had asked it.[34]

They had not asked his recall in so many words, but Washington himself did not see how Morris could be continued.[35] Perhaps he would not have been if the President had been able to make a more desirable arrangement. He raised sound objections to Jefferson's suggestion that Morris change places with Thomas Pinckney in London, believing that the French would not be satisfied by his transfer to that post. The President then suggested that if Jefferson was really determined to retire as secretary of state, the best possible arrangement would be for him to go to France for a year or two. The moment was important and, possessing the confidence of both sides, he might do great good. Jefferson would not hear of this, however. He was looking forward to real retirement, and he had no intention of ever crossing the

[33] Documents dated Sept. 13–19, 1792 (LC, 13376–13377).

[34] TJ's memo. of Feb. 20, 1793 (Ford, I, 216–218).

[35] M.D. Conway in *Edmund Randolph* (1888), p. 149, quotes the Attorney General as arguing (Feb. 22, 1793) against Morris's dismissal. Randolph's assertion that the charges against Morris had come in an "ambiguous form, half-private, half-public," must be harmonized with the extracts from Ternant in TJ's files. The charges were official enough; though, as Randolph said, there was a real question how far the French themselves intended to press them. Furthermore, the difficulties of Morris's position must not be minimized.

Atlantic again. He had been lucky on his past voyages but he was an exceedingly bad sailor. Furthermore, he said, there was a better chance for him to do good in America, since the French were sending a new minister, armed with sufficient powers. He knew from Smith that Edmond Charles Genet was coming to replace the unhappy Ternant; and, fortunately for his own peace of mind, Jefferson did not anticipate the vast trouble the new envoy would cause.

It was through Smith that Ternant himself first learned of his pending replacement. The news took the edge off the financial negotiations that this faithful public servant was carrying on. In February, on the receipt of instructions from home which he wished he had had sooner, Ternant applied for a payment of three million livres ($544,500, according to Jefferson) on the American debt to his country; the money was to be expended in the United States for provisions to be shipped to France.[36] In connection with this application, Jefferson expressed to Washington some of his doubts about the legality of Hamilton's fiscal operations to which we have already referred — particularly the diverting of the foreign fund to domestic uses.[37] He may have thought that Hamilton would claim that the necessary funds were unavailable, and, if so, he was prepared to ask why.

When the whole matter was referred to the executive council, however, it proved uncontroversial. The Secretary of the Treasury estimated that the arrears due France to the end of 1792 amounted to about $318,000, and he himself thought that no more than that should be furnished, though the law permitted the President to anticipate payments on the French debt if he saw fit. Hamilton stated that the whole sum could be provided, within periods that would answer the purposes of the application, without deranging the Treasury. Whereupon the others expressed the opinion that the whole amount should be furnished, and Washington accepted their judgment. Acting through Jefferson, he authorized Ternant to make the necessary arrangements with Hamilton. These were to comport with the state of the Treasury, however, and the times of payment were thus left in Hamilton's hands.[38] Ternant had to do his negotiating henceforth with the Secretary of the Treasury. He showed some vexation about the probable delays, but, judging from his official letters home, he did

---

[36] Ternant got his instructions Feb. 7, 1793, and made his request next day (*C.F.M.*, pp. 170, 173). He kept quiet about Morris at first, in order not to endanger his negotiations.

[37] Notes sent Washington, Feb. 12, 1793 (Ford, VI, 175–179); see ch. 2, above.

[38] Washington to TJ, Feb. 26, 1793 (Fitzpatrick, XXXII, 360); TJ to Ternant, Feb. 25, 1793 (LC, 14195); "Cabinet Opinion" of Feb. 25, 1793 (Ford, VI, 190).

not prefer Jefferson to Hamilton at this or any other time. As he had reported the attacks on the Treasury in Congress he had appeared sympathetic with Hamilton, rather than with what he called the "popular party." Within a month, Jefferson suspected that Ternant was a royalist at heart and that a "connection" between him and Hamilton was springing up.[39]

It is very likely that relations between the Secretary of the Treasury and the French envoy were more cordial now that the latter was out of favor with the revolutionary leaders at home, but on grounds of official policy toward France there was no serious rift within the administration as Washington's first term drew to a close. Friendship for the old monarchy had been transferred to the new republic in the Old World; and, up to this point, that friendship had been maintained.

[39] TJ to Madison, March, 1793 (Ford, VI, 193).

[IV]

Peaceful Intentions in a World of War

AS THE time approached when he must take the oath of office for a second time, the President, who had no precedent to guide him beyond the one he himself had set under rather different circumstances, was in doubt about the proper procedure. Therefore, late in February, 1793, he asked his department heads and the Attorney General to meet and give him their judgment. Hamilton was not there, but he had expressed the opinion that the oath should be administered in the President's own house. The Secretary of the Treasury, though the major champion of power in the government, was indifferent to mere trappings, and he regarded a private ceremony as safer. Randolph and Knox held that the oath should be taken in public, the big Secretary of War arguing for parade. Hamilton afterwards acceded, with some reluctance, to their recommendation that the ceremony take place in the Senate chamber and be open to the public. Jefferson concurred in Hamilton's original opinion, for reasons of his own.[1] If his colleague's fears of disorder and the instability of the government were extreme, his own reaction against pretentious formalities had carried him farther than there was any real need of going. The Secretary of State craved republicanism that was pure and unadorned. Only in his desire to house the new government in splendid public buildings, such as were being planned for the Federal City beside the Potomac, did Jefferson manifest any interest in impressive symbols. He did not want to surround the highest office with majesty, believing that George Washington did not need it and that the great man's successors might take advantage of unwise precedents. Monarchy had become a phobia with him in a time when France was un-

[1] Washington's letter of Feb. 27, 1793 and editor's note (Fitzpatrick, XXXII, 361); TJ's memo. of Feb. 28 (Ford, I, 221-222); Cabinet Opinions, Feb. 27, Mar. 1, 1793 (J.C.H., IV, 342-343).

doubtedly threatened with counter-revolution, and he appeared here as a doctrinaire formalist in reverse.

He had lost none of his faith in the American people, however, and none of his confidence in the unanimously re-elected President. He was now disposed to absolve Washington from responsibility for the levees, which he himself regarded as a silly and dangerous aping of foreign courts. About this time he recorded a story he had heard about the part played in the very first one by the President's pompous aide, David Humphreys. According to this, the doors were thrown open and Humphreys, in a loud voice, announced "the President of the United States" to the five or six gentlemen who had assembled. The General did not recover his composure throughout the levee, and afterwards he said: "Well, you have taken me in once, but by God you shall never take me in a second time." [2] Jefferson appears to have noted this episode because he found it reassuring, not because he thought it amusing.

Judging from contemporary accounts, the impressiveness of the second induction of the "beloved and venerable" George Washington on Monday, March 4, 1793, was owing to the innate dignity and characteristic elegance of the man himself, rather than to adventitious ceremony. He had convened the Senate in special session to attend to certain matters touching the public good, and he rode alone in his own carriage to its chamber in Congress Hall. There he took his seat in the chair usually occupied by the president of that body. John Adams was now seated at the right and in advance of him, while Justice William Cushing had a corresponding position on the left. Upon hearing the announcement of the Vice President that the Justice was present and ready to give the oath, Washington arose. It was afterwards said that he was dressed "in a full suit of black velvet, with black silk stockings and diamond knee-buckles," that he carried a cocked hat and wore a light dress sword. He was always fastidious in his dress but he did not dazzle this assembly very long. Besides taking the oath, he made a speech of four sentences, saying that he would make another on a more appropriate occasion.

The heads of departments were there, though Jefferson does not appear to have mentioned it, as were foreign ministers, such members of the House of Representatives as had remained in town, and as many spectators as could be accommodated in the hall. On his return, the President was preceded by the district marshal and the

[2] Memo. of Feb. 16, 1793 (Ford, I, 216), recording story of Edmund Randolph. This was confirmed years later by Madison, who was present (Journal of Jared Sparks, recounting visit in 1831, Harvard Univ. Lib.).

county sheriff with their deputies, who had been gathered to prevent disturbance and constituted the only physical protection that the great man had. It was an "extremely serene" day; for, as a newspaper said, "Providence has always smiled on the day of this man, and on the glorious cause which he has ever espoused, of LIBERTY and EQUALITY." The occasion may not have satisfied the Secretary of War, since there was so little parade, but it ought to have pleased the Secretary of the Treasury and the Secretary of State. The President was safe — still sacrosanct, and the bare ceremony had no splendor save that his presence gave it.[3] One spectator observed that the portraits of the King and Queen of France were covered. Trouble was coming to everybody from their direction, though the President does not appear to have anticipated this when he left Philadelphia for Mount Vernon toward the end of the month, taking with him three servants, including two postilions, and eight horses.[4]

According to Jefferson the rising of Congress was a joyful event, since it afforded some relaxation to everybody in the public business. Also, the unusual mildness of the season was pleasing to him, but he had to spend a vast lot of time catching up with his correspondence, and he viewed his situation with no satisfaction. Toward the end of March he wrote: "I am in truth worn down with drudgery, and while every circumstance relative to my private affairs calls imperiously for my return to them, not a single one exists which could render tolerable a continuation in public life." [5] He was going to continue for a time, nonetheless, and he had to find a place to live. He did not need a big one, for Maria who was in school, boarding with Mrs. Fullerton, was with him only on holidays. The state of her health disturbed him somewhat that spring. She was troubled with little fevers, nausea, and loss of appetite — from a weakness of the stomach, the doctor thought. It had been expected that her cousin Jack Eppes would go with the

---

[3] For the ceremony, see *Annals*, 2 Cong., pp. 666–667; W. S. Baker, *Washington after the Revolution* (1898), pp. 251–253, quoting *Dunlap's American Daily Advertiser*, Mar. 5, and a contemporary letter; Fitzpatrick, XXXII, 374–375. The more glowing account in Scharf & Westcott, *Hist. of Philadelphia*, I, 473, appears to be based on recollections. Washington made a longer speech to the 3rd Congress, Dec. 3, 1793.

[4] He left Philadelphia Mar. 27, 1793 (Fitzpatrick, XXXII, 404*n.*; see also 413–414). His nephew, George Augustine Washington, had died a few weeks before and he held funeral services in his memory while at home. As we shall see hereafter, he started back on April 13.

[5] TJ to Col. David, Mar. 22, 1793 (LC, 14384). His comments on the rising of Congress were made in a letter to Martha, Feb. 24, 1793 (Edgehill Randolph Papers, UVA). His Index to Letters for March shows that he wrote in that month almost a hundred of them.

American commissioners to the big Indian council, but the state of the finances of Francis Eppes dimmed that prospect and the boy went home instead. The main trouble was that an expected judgment in favor of the Wayles estate had not materialized and there was uncertainty whether there would be any ready cash from it anyway. This delay also embarrassed Jefferson, who had a share in the claim, and it was one of the complications in his personal affairs that made him wish that he could go home.[6]

The house he took was a little way in the country, on the Schuylkill near Gray's Ferry and within sight of Bartram's and Gray's Gardens on the other side of the river. He agreed with the owner, Moses Cox, to take it at the beginning of April, and he moved in a little before his fiftieth birthday.[7] He sent several loads of his books to the country, but shipped others to Virginia, along with his surplus furniture. Upwards of fifty packing cases were put aboard the good sloop Union, bound for Richmond, where he expected them to be stored temporarily in a warehouse. He figured that his goods would fill a room, and that the packages containing looking glasses would have to remain in Richmond until the next winter, since they must go thence to Albemarle by water. The season had been dry as well as mild, hence the rivers at the time were low.[8] Meanwhile, he had had certain repairs made in the house of Thomas Leiper which he was vacating, and just before he left he got the consent of the new tenant for his coachman's wife to remain a little longer. Happening to "lay in," she could not yet be removed with safety.[9]

He was not sure just how long he would stay on the banks of the Schuylkill, but he regarded the end of the summer as the outside limit and hoped to get away much earlier. In May he was "in readiness for flight" as soon as he could find "an apt occasion," and he tried to make it clear that when he did leave the government it would be for good. Writing his son-in-law, who had recently bought a horse for him, he said: "My next return to Monticello is the last long journey I shall ever

[6] TJ to Martha, Apr. 8, 1793 (copy, Edgehill Randolph Papers, UVA); Francis Eppes to TJ, Mar. 6, 1793 (ibid.); Account Book, Feb. 20, 1793, showing payment of $80 to Mrs. Fullerton for six months' board for Maria. The case was that of Cary's executor, which kept recurring in TJ's correspondence during the rest of his stay in Philadelphia.

[7] TJ to Cox, Mar. 12, 1793 (LC, 14287); see also TJ to Martha, Mar. 10 (Randall, II, 191); TJ to Cox, Mar. 7 (LC, 14252).

[8] Various items in Account Book, Apr. 6–9, 1793, show payments for "portage" of books and furniture. He wrote James Brown in Richmond about the shipment, Apr. 7 (copy, Edgehill Randolph Papers), and got a shipping receipt for 50 cases and 1 bbl. on Apr. 9 (LC, 14499).

[9] TJ to Thomas Leiper, Apr. 11, 1793 (LC, 14511).

take, except the last of all, for which I shall not want horses." [10] He did not get home as soon as he expected, but he got himself into the countryside anyway. Maria's health improved somewhat and she spent Sundays with him. When hot weather came he practically lived outdoors — eating, writing, reading, and receiving his company beneath the plane trees.[11]

In the middle of March the Secretary of State wrote his old friend, Dr. George Gilmer of Pen Park in Albemarle County, that there had been no news of France since the beginning of the King's trial.[12] He did not know that Louis XVI had been seven weeks dead. But he and Washington had enough knowledge of the plight of Lafayette to be deeply troubled about that, and before the President left for Mount Vernon they did what little they could for him.

The turn of events with respect to the Marquis was ironical in the extreme. Early in the previous summer, Jefferson, who had known him so intimately in Paris, had addressed him thus: "Behold you, then, my dear friend, at the head of a great army, establishing the liberties of your country against a foreign enemy. May heaven favor your cause, and make you the channel through which it may pour its favors." Employing the extravagance of language he allowed himself in private letters, he spoke of his old friend as "exterminating the monster aristocracy, and pulling out the teeth and fangs of its associate monarchy." This letter had not reached Lafayette when that liberal nobleman deserted the revolution and fled to Belgium, where he fell into the hands of the Austrians. In fact, he did not get it until after he emerged from prison some six years later.[13] Gouverneur Morris promptly reported that he had "taken refuge with the enemy," though this letter did not reach the Secretary of State much before the end of the year. "Thus his circle is completed," wrote the American minister. "He has spent his fortune on a revolution, and is now crushed by the wheel which he put in motion. He lasted longer than I expected." [14]

Early in 1793, Washington, without any solicitation, had deposited in Amsterdam 200 guineas to be subject to the orders of the Mar-

[10] TJ to TMR, May 19, 1793 (LC, 14864); TJ to J. W. Eppes, May 23, 1793 (Ford, VI, 264).

[11] TJ to Martha, May 26, July 7, 1793 (Ford, VI, 267; Randall, II, 191–192).

[12] Mar. 15, 1793 (Ford, VI, 202).

[13] To Lafayette, June 16, 1792 (Ford, VI, 78); from Lafayette, Nov. 20, 1800 (LC, 18846).

[14] Morris to TJ, Aug. 22, 1792 (A.S.P.F.R., I, 336). Lafayette deserted on Aug. 19, and TJ acknowledged this letter on Dec. 30, 1792.

quise — stating that he owed her husband at least that amount for services that had been rendered him but for which no account had ever been received.[15] Afterwards he heard from her and was somewhat reassured about her personal situation, though still at a loss about what, if anything, he could do for her imprisoned husband. At length Jefferson, on Washington's instructions, asked Morris to procure Lafayette's liberation by informal solicitations if possible, and to use formal ones if these should seem desirable. Also, he assumed the difficult and delicate task of drafting the letter which Washington sent to the Marquise. "My affection to his nation and to himself are unabated," said the President in the Secretary of State's language, "and notwithstanding the line of separation which has been unfortunately drawn between them I am confident that both have been led on by a pure love of liberty, and a desire to secure public happiness, and I shall deem that among the most consoling moments of my life which should see them reunited in the end, as they were in the beginning, of their virtuous enterprise."[16] The words were those of a friend of the man himself and also of the revolution which had engulfed him, and if they voiced the sentiments of Jefferson they were subscribed to by Washington. They had hardly been written when news reached Philadelphia that Louis XVI had been executed by the guillotine.

The death of the King was generally regretted by Americans, but the shading of opinion — between sorrow and anger — tended to conform to domestic political complexions. Jefferson noted this fact, but informed Madison that the execution had not produced as open condemnation from the "Monocrats" as he had expected. The ladies of the first social circle in Philadelphia were "all open-mouthed against the murderers of a sovereign" but their husbands were more cautious.[17] Even Oliver Wolcott, Jr., whom Jefferson placed on the extreme right wing, expressed himself with restraint. Sending his father a paper containing "an account of the fate of poor Louis," he mildly said: "It remains to see the result of the great experiment which the French are attempting." Chauncey Goodrich of Hartford spoke of the execution as "a wanton act of barbarity, disgraceful even to a Parisian mob," adding that it threatened the success of republicanism in France — a thing which he himself did not approve of. It

[15] Washington to the Marquise de Lafayette, Jan. 31, 1793 (Fitzpatrick, XXXII, 322).

[16] Washington to TJ, Mar. 13, 1793 (Fitzpatrick, XXXII, 385–386); TJ to Morris, Mar. 15, 1793 (Ford, VI, 202–203); draft of letter to Madame de Lafayette, Mar. 16, 1793 (Ford, VI, 203–204); letter as sent to Marquise de Lafayette, Mar. 16, 1793 (Fitzpatrick, XXXII, 389–390).

[17] TJ to Madison, March, 1793 (Ford, VI, 192–193).

might be expected to serve a good purpose in America, also — by checking "the passions of those who wish to embroil us in a desperate cause, and unhinge our government." [18]

At the other extreme was an anonymous writer in Freneau's *National Gazette* who entitled his article: "Louis Capet has lost his caput." This author said: "From my use of a pun it may seem that I think lightly of his fate. I certainly do. It affects me no more than the execution of another malefactor." [19] Jefferson himself would not have been in character if he had descended to such unbecoming levity, and, as a matter of fact, he left in the record very few contemporary comments on these events. In later years, while still declining to sit in historical judgment on the executioners of the King, he skillfully summed up their arguments and made clear his personal disagreement with them. Toward the end of his life he wrote:

> . . . I am not prepared to say that the first magistrate of a nation cannot commit treason against his country, or is unamenable to its punishment; nor yet that where there is no written law, no regulated tribunal, there is not a law in our hearts, and a power in our hands, given for righteous employment in maintaining right, and redressing wrong. Of those who judged the king, many thought him wilfully criminal, many that his existence would keep the nation in conflict with the horde of kings, who would war against a regeneration which might come home to themselves, and that it were better that one should die than all. *I should not have voted with this portion of the legislature.*[20]

At the moment, however, this peace-loving man who laid such store by orderly constitutional processes seems to have harbored no doubt that monarchs were "amenable to punishment like other criminals"; and, despite his generally charitable judgment of Louis XVI as a human being, he was wasting no sympathy on an ill-advised King, when more innocent men than he had died.[21] He might well have suffered a revulsion of feeling if he had been in France in early 1793, just as Thomas Paine did, but he still believed that the liberty of the whole earth depended on the issue of the contest. Nor was he any less aware than Alexander Hamilton of the possible repercussion of these events on the American public mind.

Reporting to him a little later about Virginia, James Monroe said: "I

---

[18] Oliver Wolcott, Jr., to Oliver Wolcott, Sr., Mar. 20, 1793; Chauncey Goodrich to Oliver Wolcott, Jr., Mar. 24, 1793 (Gibbs, I, 90). See also Oliver Wolcott, Sr., to his son, Mar. 25, 1793 (*ibid.*, p. 91).

[19] *National Gazette*, Apr. 20, 1793.

[20] In his autobiography (Ford, I, 141), italics inserted.

[21] To an unknown person, Mar. 18, 1793 (L. & B., IX, 45).

scarcely find a man unfriendly to the French revolution as now modified. Many regret the unhappy fate of the Marquis of Fayette, and likewise the execution of the King. But they seem to consider these events
as incidents to a much greater one, and which they wish to see accomplished." [22] These reassuring words really amounted to a summary
of Jefferson's own position. In its shading this judgment differed
from one that Edward Carrington, a man of different political persuasion, gave Hamilton about these same Virginians. He said: "I believe
the decapitation of the king is pretty generally considered as an act of
unprincipled cruelty, dictated by neither justice nor policy. In my
own mind, it was a horrible transaction in every view; and to an
American, who can yield to its propriety, it ought to be felt as a truly
sorrowful event." With respect to the cause of France, however, he
believed that the general wish was for its success.[23] Meanwhile in
Philadelphia, that friend of Thomas Jefferson and John Adams, Dr.
Benjamin Rush, while deploring the act and praising the King rather
more than he deserved, was saying that the noble cause in which
France was engaged, "though much disgraced by her rulers, must
finally prevail." [24]

About the time that George Washington went home to Mount
Vernon, the father of the comptroller of the Treasury wrote from
Hartford to his son: "I hope that the President will continually
superintend the conduct of the Secretary of State, so as not to suffer
by his indiscretion these states to be involved in the vortex of European politics." [25] Had this Connecticut Yankee been permitted to look
over the shoulder of the Secretary of State when the latter was writing American representatives abroad at this very juncture he should
have been reassured; though he would also have been deprived, at an
early stage, of one of the most important of the allegations of Hamilton and his partisans. Late in March, Jefferson wrote prophetically:

> . . . The scene in Europe is becoming very interesting.
> Amidst the confusion of a general war which seems to be threat-
> ening that quarter of the globe, we hope to be permitted to
> preserve the line of neutrality. *We wish not to meddle with the
> internal affairs of any country, nor with the general affairs of
> Europe.* Peace with all nations, and the right which that gives us
> with respect to all nations, are our object. It will be necessary for

[22] Monroe to TJ, May 8, 1793 (S.M.H., I, 252).
[23] Carrington to Hamilton, Apr. 26, 1793 (J.C.H., V, 555).
[24] To J. C. Lettson, *Letters of Benjamin Rush* (1951), ed. by L. H. Butterfield,
II, 635.
[25] Oliver Wolcott, Sr., to Oliver Wolcott, Jr., Mar. 25, 1793 (Gibbs, I, 91).

all our public agents to exert themselves with vigilance for securing to our vessels all the rights of neutrality, and from preventing the vessels of other nations from usurping our flag.[26]

Here is a major clue to the policy which Jefferson consistently pursued as Secretary of State, under much greater difficulties than he now anticipated, and here are some of the germs of the policy later pronounced by his disciple Monroe in his famous Doctrine. There is no point in arguing about the major credit for policies which were advocated by so many leaders in common, but these were wholly consistent with Jefferson's own past and represented a concern for the welfare of his own country which was relatively, if not wholly, independent of ideology. No one was more convinced than he that his country required peace and time to grow in. He had no thought of letting it be hitched to the war chariot of any other nation.

If there was any exception to his prevailingly peaceful intentions, it was with respect to Spain, the country that controlled the mouth of the Mississippi. He had instituted negotiations with the Spanish, but toward them he was not unwilling to sound bellicose.[27] At length his young friend William Short had joined William Carmichael in Madrid, where the two commissioners were destined to suffer long frustrations, and in the meantime new problems had arisen because of the activities of the Governor of Louisiana in connection with the Indians. When these were discussed in the executive council in the autumn of 1792, it was Hamilton who talked most of peace, and the Secretary of the Treasury even broached the matter of a British alliance. It was Jefferson who wanted to refer to Congress a recent Spanish communication, since the matter of declaring or not declaring war lay within their province. This is not to say that he himself wanted war, but he was prepared to consider it as a possibility. The Spanish letter was sent to Congress, and Jefferson wrote the American commissioners in Spain to make representations to the Spanish Court.[28]

Nothing came of this business, and it is mentioned here chiefly to illustrate Jefferson's attitude toward the Spanish. This was largely owing to his continuing concern for the navigation of the Mississippi and his consciousness that Spain was a waning power which could be challenged with relative safety by his own country, now growing

[26] TJ to C. W. F. Dumas, Mar. 24, 1793 (L. & B., IX, 56), italics inserted. He wrote in the same vein to others.

[27] See *Jefferson and the Rights of Man*, pp. 406–411.

[28] Memo. of Oct. 31, 1792 (Ford, I, 205–207); TJ to Carmichael and Short, Nov. 3, 1793 (Ford, VI, 129–130). The communication from the Spanish commissioners in America, Viar and Jaudenes, was sent to Congress on Nov. 7 (*A.S.P.F.R.*, I, 139). Short did not reach Madrid till Feb. 1, 1793.

rapidly in strength on the western waters. The further weakening of
Spain seemed so desirable to him that he welcomed later reports that
the French purposed to free the Spanish colonies, and he instructed
Carmichael and Short not to offer Spain any American guarantee of
these. Previously, he had been willing to guarantee her possessions
west of the Mississippi if she would cede those on the east, but the
situation was now changed. He had intimations that the French
would not object to the incorporation in the United States of the Spanish territories east of the great river, as he also had that the Spanish
and British were now acting in concert. That concert was to become
closer than he yet anticipated — for the old ally of Bourbon France
entered into a formal British alliance before summer, thus effecting a
diplomatic revolution, shifting the balance of power in the New
World as well as the Old, and causing the Spanish themselves to become more bellicose toward the Americans. This new alignment did
not endear them to Jefferson the more, and it gave him a new reason
for friendliness to France, but the point that calls for emphasis in the
early spring of 1793 is that Jefferson was most likely to be belligerent
on American questions — of which the security of the United States
on its own continent was a major one. As a responsible statesman he
had no thought of getting embroiled in European quarrels, regardless
of personal predilections and ideology. From the beginning to the end
he favored a policy of neutrality.[29]

Within ten days of the execution of Louis XVI the European war,
hitherto confined to the Continent, was extended to include Great
Britain, the news being received in Philadelphia early in April. At the
same time, Holland was drawn into it, as Spain was a few weeks
later.[30] It was now unquestionably a general war, and with the involvement of the colonial powers it embraced the entire Atlantic
world of which the United States of America was a part. The difficulties which the young Republic faced were not merely such as

[29] TJ learned of French designs against the Spanish colonies at least by Feb. 20,
1793, when he talked with W. S. Smith (memo. in Ford, I, 216-218). His change
in the instructions to Carmichael and Short was made Mar. 23 (Ford, VI, 206),
which was before he had heard of the beginning of war between France and
Great Britain and considerably before he heard of the declaration of war on Spain
by France. His intimations of the concert between Spain and Great Britain must
have been received earlier, perhaps from Smith. The treaty of alliance between
Spain and Great Britain (May 25) made the mission of Carmichael and Short
more futile than ever, for at this point or earlier Spanish fears for Louisiana temporarily disappeared. On June 23, 1793, TJ wrote Madison that Spain was trying
to pick a quarrel with the U. S. (Ford, VI, 316).

[30] France declared war on Great Britain and Holland on Feb. 1, 1793; and
against Spain on March 7.

would inevitably arise from conflicts on the seas where its commerce plied. The nation was allied by treaty with one of the contending powers, France, whose forces were now arrayed against the field. In the light of history, the conflict may be viewed as one between nations, for their respective advantages. It may also be described in terms of revolution and counter-revolution, for the countries opposing the French were trying to extinguish what threatened to become an all-consuming fire. Alexander Hamilton perceived this clearly from the start. Writing Washington, he said: "The present war, then, turns essentially on the point — What shall be the future government of France? Shall the royal authority be restored in the person of the successor to Louis, or shall a republic be constituted in exclusion of it?"[31] There could be no question where Hamilton stood in this conflict between legitimacy and revolution, between ancient authority and emerging democracy, and there can be no doubt where Jefferson stood. The irrepressible conflict between the two men and their philosophies was now being waged on a larger front.

While neither man could remain a mere spectator or a philosopher in a tower, it would be unjust to describe one of them as pro-French and the other as pro-British. That was the language of political partisanship in that day and it has found its way into many works of history, but fairness to both of these eminent Americans requires that such terms should not be loosely used.[32] Of the two, Hamilton had been much more indiscreet in his relations with British representatives, especially George Hammond, who was still in the United States, than Jefferson had been in his dealings with Ternant, the French minister. Judging from the past, therefore, Hamilton might have been expected to be less mindful of the proprieties and more reckless in his approach to the problems of the hour. In spirit he was far more the military man and less the civilian than his great rival, and there were grave dangers in the bellicosity of his nature, as Jefferson realized and John Adams afterwards found out. But his national patriotism was unquestionable, and the success of his financial policies was contingent on the maintenance of peace.

In public, though not always in private, Jefferson was much more controlled, and, as he told John Adams at a time when a rupture with Great Britain seemed much more imminent, he had been through one war and did not want to face another.[33] More clearly than Hamilton

[31] April, 1793 (J.C.H., IV, 365).
[32] This matter is well stated by C. M. Thomas, *American Neutrality in 1793* (1931), pp. 14–15. I have benefited greatly from reading this study.
[33] TJ to Adams, Apr. 25, 1794 (Ford, VI, 505).

he perceived that the victors are punished in war, as well as the vanquished; and certain efforts of his in later years to attain national ends by nonmilitary means led him to be described as a pacifist, though he certainly was not that. He was fully aware of the need of his growing country for peace, and he had said already that the only real gainers from war were the neutrals. Ever since his own stay in Europe he had believed that the United States stood to gain from the distress and vicissitudes of the nations of the Old World. There was astute calculation in his public policy, and history was destined to substantiate his major hopes.[34] But for the troubles in the Old World, the United States would hardly have picked up Louisiana and the Floridas so easily in later years. With respect to the interests of his own country, particularly its territorial interests, he was positively avaricious and at times sounded ruthless; but he relied on diplomatic methods and the assistance of external events even when, upon occasion, he rattled the saber or talked extravagantly behind the scenes. His benevolence toward the French cause at this stage may be assumed wholly apart from ideology, for he had long ago concluded — as indeed John Adams had — that France was the natural friend of the United States. This was true of the old monarchy and it seemed reasonable to suppose that it would be even truer of the new republic. Thus, unquestionably, he hoped for French victory. But he now believed that the United States could serve the French better as a neutral than as a belligerent. American armed might was small, but provisions were plentiful.

He regarded Great Britain as a natural competitor and rival and was deeply suspicious of a government which, in his American opinion, had deliberately violated the treaty of peace and had certainly ignored the elaborate representations he had made to George Hammond.[35] That minister had gained his impressions of the Secretary of State's position from Hamilton as well as from his own rather humbling experiences. Writing home to his government, he had expressed the opinion that the United States would not go to war with Great Britain, but was dubious about Jefferson, believing the latter to be "so blinded by his attachment to France, and his hatred of Great Britain . . . that he would without hesitation commit the immediate interests of his country in any measure which might equally gratify his predilections and his resentments." [36] There can be no possible doubt that Jefferson

---

[34] This point about TJ is strongly emphasized by S. F. Bemis in his writings.

[35] See *Jefferson and the Rights of Man*, pp. 417–420.

[36] Hammond to Grenville, Mar. 7, 1793, quoted from British State Papers by Thomas, p. 22*n*. This was before he had learned of the declaration of war.

resented the treatment that he and his country had received at the hands of the British government, but the zealous young minister's misinterpretation of him followed the Hamilton party line precisely and this fact could not have been wholly coincidental.

The President had first-hand knowledge of his Secretary of State. George Washington could hardly have been surprised, therefore, when Jefferson, in a letter announcing the extension of the European war, said that it was necessary "to take every justifiable measure for preserving our neutrality." About the same time Hamilton referred to "a continuance of the peace, the desire of which may be said to be both universal and ardent." [37] But peace and neutrality are very general terms, and within the broad area of agreement there was abundant ground for disagreement regarding specific actions. If the patient President, who viewed this conflict with fewer predilections than either of his chief advisers, did not realize this already, he found it out soon after he got back to Philadelphia.

[37] TJ to Washington, Apr. 7, 1793 (Ford, VI, 212); Hamilton to Washington, Apr. 8, 1793 (J.C.H., IV, 357).

[v]

Fair Neutrality in Theory and Practice

IF GEORGE WASHINGTON had any hopes of relaxing in the spring sunshine at Mount Vernon in early April, 1793, these were soon banished by the news from Europe. This was relayed by Hamilton as well as Jefferson; indeed, the ubiquitous Secretary of the Treasury wrote of the extension of the war a little sooner than his more prudent colleague.[1] Nobody had been caught napping, however, and the President, after replying to his two chief assistants in similar language on one day, set out for the seat of government on the next.[2] In both letters he used the expression "strict neutrality," and he referred to reports that American vessels were already being prepared as privateers. There lay the immediate danger of unneutral actions. Washington wanted his advisers to give thought to any measures which should be taken.

Back in Philadelphia within a week, he promptly submitted to the Heads of Department and the Attorney General a set of questions, thirteen in number, asking them to be prepared to discuss these at a meeting at his house the first thing next day. The questions were in the President's handwriting, but Jefferson and Randolph believed they were largely drawn by Hamilton, as they almost certainly were.[3] Because of patriotic or partisan zeal or both, the officious Secretary of the Treasury had seized the initiative in matters which directly

---

[1] Hamilton to Washington, Apr. 5, 8, 1793 (J.C.H., IV, 355-356); TJ to Washington, Apr. 7, 1793 (Ford, VI, 212).

[2] Both letters dated Apr. 12, 1793 (Fitzpatrick, XXXII, 415-416). In J.C.H., IV, 357, the letter to TJ is incorrectly designated as the one to Hamilton.

[3] Washington got back Apr. 17 and submitted the questions Apr. 18, 1793 (Fitzpatrick, XXXII, 419-421). See TJ's memo. dated Apr. 18 and written May 6 (Ford, I, 226-227). Thomas (pp. 28-30) thinks that Hamilton was responsible for at least 12 of the 13. He had already consulted John Jay and received from him a draft of a proclamation; Jay to Hamilton, Apr. 11, 1793 (J.C.H., V, 552-553, and draft in HP, 1 ser., 19:2877).

and more immediately concerned the Secretary of State. Also, he had caused some questions to be asked which, in Jefferson's opinion, should not have been raised at all.

Only two of the questions were answered at the first meeting at the President's house. It was unanimously agreed that a proclamation should be issued and that a minister from the French Republic should be received. The latter decision related to the newly appointed minister, Edmond Charles Genet, then en route, whom Washington, before he went away, had already decided to receive. Randolph and Hamilton had concurred in the decision, though the latter did so reluctantly.[4] Hamilton's present argument was that the outbreak of war had introduced a new element, but this consummate and inveterate politician may have thrown the question into the hopper merely for bargaining purposes. He now yielded to the judgment of the others, as Jefferson did in the matter of the proclamation, and the surprising thing is that either man should have demurred at all.

Since Jefferson had already made it abundantly clear to Washington and others that he favored a policy of neutrality, his doubts related wholly to the desirability of a *proclamation* and to its form and timing. His first objection was on the constitutional ground that a declaration of no war was as much beyond the competence of the executive as a declaration of war, which was clearly the prerogative of the legislative branch. In the light of Washington's later statement that "he never had an idea that he could bind Congress"[5] this sounds a good deal like legalistic quibbling. Jefferson soon agreed with his colleagues that the President should not summon Congress and thereby create alarm, but he suspected that Hamilton wanted to bind the future conduct of the country by executive act, pressing executive powers to their limit according to his custom.[6]

What he himself really wanted was a declaration that the country was in a state of peace, in which it was the duty of the citizens neither to aid nor injure any of the belligerents. This state of peace would properly be preserved by the Executive until the constitutional authorities (Congress) should determine otherwise. He said afterwards: "The declaration [by the President] of the disposition of the United States can hardly be called illegal, though it was certainly officious and

[4] TJ's memo. of Mar. 30, 1793, referring to earlier conversations (Ford, I, 224). Washington said he never had any doubts on the subject. He recommended that Genet should be received "not with too much warmth or cordiality," but TJ believed that this was a "small sacrifice" to the opinion of Hamilton.

[5] TJ's memo. of Nov. 18, 1793 (Ford, I, 266–267).

[6] His fears were largely borne out by Hamilton's PACIFICUS papers in the summer (Lodge, IV, 135–191); see below, pp. 110–111.

improper." [7] He also said: "The instrument was badly drawn, and made the P. go out of his line to declare things which, though true, it was not exactly his province to declare." [8] His objections were met at the time, supposedly, by the omission of the word "neutrality" from the document. He soon noted, however, that the word was widely used anyway; and it has seemed to many writers since his time that he was making a distinction where there was little or no real difference. The pressure of circumstances would not allow, it seemed, for this degree of constitutional purism.

His second line of objection was that a proclamation would be premature, since the warring nations, and especially the British, would be willing to buy American neutrality by the sort of concessions he had long been vainly seeking. He did not like to surrender his bargaining power, and he clung to the belief that he could have gained something. Some weeks later he wrote Madison: "I now think it extremely possible that Hammond might have been instructed to have asked it [neutrality], and to offer the *broadest neutral privileges*, as the price, which was exactly the price I wanted that we should contend for." Judging from Hammond's instructions, which we can read though Jefferson could not, such was not the case. No concessions of any sort were suggested in these, and the envoy was told to support the American friends of Great Britain, the chief of whom was unquestionably Hamilton.[9] Jefferson left no possible doubt of his own opinion of his colleagues's attitude. Before long he wrote James Monroe: "Hamilton is panic-struck if we refuse our breach to every kick which Great Britain may choose to give it. He is for proclaiming at once the most abject principles, such as would invite and merit habitual insults." [10]

Jefferson's initial wariness about the Proclamation cannot be separated from his inveterate and by no means unwarranted suspicions of the Secretary of the Treasury, and very likely there was in it an element of pique. But he fully recognized the necessity of warning American citizens against actions that were dangerous to them and to their country. For example, they must be told that they were not free to take sides with either belligerent and "enrich themselves by depredations on the commerce of the other." [11] He believed that, while the

7 To Madison, July 29, 1793 (Ford, VI, 328).

8 TJ to Madison, Aug. 11, 1793 (Ford, VI, 369). See also TJ to Monroe, July 14, 1793 (Ford, VI, 346).

9 TJ to Madison, June 29, 1793 (Ford, VI, 328); Grenville to Hammond, Feb. 8 and Mar. 12, 1793 (*I.B.M.*, pp. 35, 37).

10 TJ to Monroe, May 5, 1793 (Ford, VI, 238–239).

11 To Madison, Aug. 11, 1793 (Ford, VI, 368).

lure of easy profits was great, the desire for peace was practically universal. The day after the meeting at which he agreed to the issuance of a proclamation and two days before its signing, on April 22, he wrote to Gouverneur Morris in France:

> . . . No country perhaps was ever so thoroughly against war as ours. These dispositions pervade every description of its citizens, whether in or out of Office. They cannot perhaps suppress their affections, nor their wishes. But they will suppress the effects of them so as to preserve a fair neutrality.[12]

He himself did not hesitate to use the word "neutrality," for, indeed, there was no other so good to use. But he left no doubt of his own affections for France and his wishes with regard to the outcome of this conflict. In his opinion, the enemies of that country were "conspirators against human liberty."

The drafting of the proclamation was left to Edmund Randolph, with Jefferson's obvious consent. The instrument was communicated to him after it was drawn, but he said later that all he did was run his eye over it to see that it was not a "declaration of neutrality." [13] He was then engaged in drawing an elaborate opinion on the French treaties, in opposition to Hamilton, which he probably regarded as a more important piece of business at the moment. It has been alleged that he avoided direct responsibility for the proclamation in order that he might be free to criticize it afterwards.[14] He did speak slightingly of it in his intimate political circle, though apparently nowhere else. Within a week, when writing Madison, he referred to the "cold caution" of the government and he later spoke to this friend of the "milk and water views" of the proclamation, even terming it pusillanimous.[15]

In view of the fact that he, more than any other official, was charged with the enforcement of the policy of neutrality and that he was assiduous in his efforts throughout the rest of his term of office, this criticism seems to involve a contradiction. Here we have again a contrast between his public conduct and his private opinion. During the next few weeks this seems to have increased rather than diminished — as he learned more about the sentiment of the people and the views of his closest political friends, as he became increasingly im-

[12] Apr. 20, 1793 (Ford, VI, 217).
[13] TJ to Madison, Aug. 11, 1793 (Ford, VI, 369).
[14] Thomas, p. 45*n*.
[15] To Madison, Apr. 28, May 19, June 29, 1793 (Ford, VI, 232, 259, 328).

patient with Edmund Randolph and suspicious of Hamilton as an Anglophile. He regarded the policy as inevitable but regretted this damper on American enthusiasm for the cause of France. Very early he wrote Madison: "I fear that a fair neutrality will prove a disagreeable pill to our friends, though necessary to keep out of the calamities of a war." [16]

To his political intimates it did seem that a bitter pill was being administered. "Peace is no doubt to be preserved at any price that honor and good faith will permit," wrote Madison from Orange, but he feared "a secret Anglomany" behind the mask of neutrality.[17] A little later Madison spoke much more strongly:

> . . . I regret extremely the position into which the P. has been thrown. The unpopular cause of Anglomany is openly laying claim to him. His enemies masking themselves under the popular cause of France are playing off the most tremendous batteries on him. The proclamation was in truth a most unfortunate error. It wounds the national honor, by seeming to disregard the stipulated duties to France. It wounds the popular feelings by a seeming indifference to the cause of liberty. And it seems to violate the forms & spirit of the Constitution, by making the executive Magistrate the organ of the disposition, the duty and the interest of the Nation in relation to War & peace, subjects appropriated to other departments of the Government. It is mortifying to the real friends of the P. that his fame & his influence should have been unnecessarily made to depend in any degree on political events in a foreign quarter of the Globe; and particularly so that he should have anything to apprehend from the success of liberty in another country, since he owes his pre-eminence to the success of it in his own. If France triumphs, the ill-fated proclamation will be a millstone, which would sink any other character, and will force a struggle even on his.[18]

In comparison with such words as these, Jefferson's early private comments to Madison and Monroe seem mild. It would almost appear that he was justifying his own official conduct to them against the charge of being a traitor to their political cause and the cause of liberty. Also, the popular support of the French even surpassed his expectations. About six weeks after the issuing of the proclamation he wrote Monroe: "The war between France & England seems to be producing an effect not contemplated. All the old spirit of 1776 is re-

[16] Apr. 28, 1793 (Ford, VI, 232).
[17] May 8 and 27, 1793 (Hunt, VI, 128, 130).
[18] Madison to TJ, June 10, 1793 (Hunt, VI, 127–128n.).

kindling." [19] Though rejoicing in this revival of the spirit of liberty, he added: "I wish we may be able to repress the spirits of the people within the limits of a fair neutrality." He took no stock in the criticisms of George Washington. In his opinion, Hamilton, whom Knox supported, was for proclaiming "the most abject principles," Randolph was appallingly indecisive, and, in the councils of the government, every inch of ground had to be fought over desperately to maintain even a "sneaking neutrality." If this should be preserved, the country would be indebted to the President, not his counselors. He wrote Madison in May: "If anything prevents its being a mere English neutrality, it will be that the penchant of the P. is not that way, and above all, the ardent spirit of our constituents." [20]

There is no indication that he himself did anything to inflame the public mind in this time of reckless and irresponsible journalism, but up to a point he could and did rejoice at expressions of popular opinion which would deter the government from veering to the English side. Also, he observed to Madison that the alignment was much the same as on domestic issues. On the one side were (1) the fashionable circles of Philadelphia, New York, Boston, and Charleston, (2) merchants trading on British capital, and (3) "paper men." All the old Tories, he believed, were included in one of these three groups. On the other side were: (1) merchants trading on their own capital, (2) Irish merchants, (3) tradesmen, mechanics, farmers, and all other descriptions of citizens. These people believed, as he did, that the French were fighting the battle of democracy, whether or not they used that term, and many of them were more passionate partisans than his official responsibilities permitted him to be.

Following the unanimous and virtually inescapable decision on April 19 to issue a proclamation and to receive the new French minister, the executive council met again at the President's house next day to discuss the remaining questions he had submitted.[21] Practically all of these related directly or indirectly to the existing treaties with France, and American obligations under them.[22] The most disturbing obligation, in this time of general war, was the guarantee of French possessions in America, that is, in the West Indies. This guarantee was included in the treaty of alliance that was signed in 1778, when the United States

19 May 5, 1793 (Ford, VI, 238).
20 May 12, 1793 (Ford, VI, 251).
21 TJ's memo. in Ford, I, 226–227.
22 The question of summoning Congress, which was decided adversely by unanimous vote, was an exception. Also, there was a hypothetical question about the reception of the "future regent" of France.

had needed an ally so badly. Some also anticipated difficulty from the provision in the treaty of commerce of the same year whereby the United States agreed to admit to its ports French warships and privateers with their prizes, while denying this privilege to the enemies of France. All of these responsible leaders wanted to avoid any embarrassment to their country which the promises in the treaties might entail. There was a sharp difference of opinion, however, as to the degree and immediacy of danger and as to the policy which should now be pursued.

At the first meeting at Washington's house Jefferson gained the impression that Hamilton regarded the treaties with France as void, and at that time he made notes of his colleague's arguments.[23] He also noted that Knox supported Hamilton's position, "acknowledging at the same time, like a fool that he is, that he knew nothing about it." [24] He himself had no doubt whatever that the treaties were still valid, and he was supported by Edmund Randolph. At this juncture, however, Hamilton produced a quotation from an authority on the law of nations, Vattel, which seemed pertinent and which could not be countered at the moment since no copy of the latter's treatise was accessible. This led Randolph to agree to look into the matter further. The Attorney General announced that he would give a written opinion, whereupon Jefferson concluded that he would put his own ideas into written form. No opinion was ever offered by Knox, but Hamilton made up for this by writing two, with characteristic loquacity. Thus the private debate between the major antagonists was continued and concluded in writing. Neither Secretary appears to have seen what his colleague wrote. As in the case of the constitutionality of the Bank of the United States, the audience before which the two men debated consisted of George Washington and posterity, but Jefferson had much the better of it on this occasion.

In his written argument Hamilton did not go so far as to claim that the treaties were void, but spoke rather to the effect that they should be regarded as "temporarily and provisionally suspended." [25] He had backed down a little — perhaps as a result of the discussion in the executive council, perhaps on the advice of his friends. He had discussed matters with Chief Justice John Jay and Senator Rufus King. The latter wrote him: "The change which has happened will not, perhaps, justify us in saying 'the treaties are void' — and whether we may

23 Thomas, p. 60, cites LC, 14560, saying that TJ on the back of this slip of paper jotted down the principles he himself would use in replying to him.
24 Ford, I, 227.
25 J.C.H., IV, 363. His two opinions, dated April 1793 and May 2, 1793, are in that edn., IV, 362-390.

contend in favor of their suspension is a point of delicacy, and not quite free from doubt." [26] In these international matters Jefferson exercised a moderating influence on leading Republicans, while Hamilton's closest political friends were trying to moderate him.

In his opinions to Washington, Hamilton also made considerable concession both in regard to the right of a nation to change its own form of government and in regard to the binding effect of treaties regardless of change.[27] He argued, however, that no nation had the right to involve an ally absolutely and unconditionally in the effects of the changes it might make, holding that for "good and sufficient cause" that ally might renounce a treaty. The only real disagreement between him and Jefferson on this point lay in the meaning of "good and sufficient cause." He quoted Vattel as saying that an ally remained the ally of the state after the deposition of a king, but that, nevertheless, the alliance might be renounced when the change rendered it *"useless, dangerous, or disagreeable."* [28] From this Hamilton argued that there must also be the right to suspend the operations of a treaty in the midst of a revolution, while waiting to see what the results would be. It seemed to him that the admission that the treaties were still in operation was equivalent to taking the part of France. He wanted to be able to say to foreign powers: "In receiving the minister of France, we have not acknowledged ourselves its ally. We have reserved the point for future consideration." [29] Without delay he wanted to suspend the dangerous alliance. Also, he wanted to avoid the possible charge of support of the revolutionary group against the monarchy, with which the treaties had originally been made and which might be restored. Without avowing his own sympathy with the counter-revolutionaries he left no real doubt of it. He admitted that the United States was bound to pay the debt to France but saw no need to risk the resentment of other nations by recognizing any other obligations. The dangers of French resentment apparently did not at all disturb him.

He unequivocally took the position that this was an offensive war on the part of France. It was coupled, he said, "with a *general invitation* and *encouragement* to *revolution* and insurrection, under a promise of *fraternity* and *assistance*." [30] Thus it had ceased to be a war for the defense of French rights and liberties and had become one of

[26] Apr. 24, 1793 (J.C.H., V, 553). Edward Carrington wrote him moderately on Apr. 26 (*ibid.*, V, 556).
[27] J.C.H., IV, 365–367.
[28] *Ibid.*, IV, 371.
[29] *Ibid.*, IV, 380.
[30] *Ibid.*, IV, 386.

acquisition. Since the treaty of alliance with the United States was defensive, he concluded that the guarantee in it could not apply, even though the West Indian Islands were attacked.

This argument was in Hamilton's second paper, and does not appear to have entered into the oral opinion which Jefferson was answering. If it did not reflect representations which the British minister could easily have made to Hamilton by this time, it definitely followed the British line.[31] From the beginning Jefferson had presumed that the first declaration of war was on the part of France, but he also stated that previous British actions — such as their asking the French minister to retire — could be regarded as clear evidence of their intention to go to war. He did not believe that the guarantee would be asked of the United States anyway, and in this respect at least the British agreed with him.[32] So also did the French, as we now know, though their reasoning was quite different.[33]

By and large, Hamilton's two written opinions deserve the judgment that Jefferson passed on his colleague's oral one. The reasoning is ingenious, though not convincing. His own closely argued, well-organized paper gains by comparison with this rather confusing prolixity.[34] Since Washington told Jefferson that he had never doubted the validity of the treaties, the Secretary of State would not have needed to write at such length, and perhaps would not have needed to write at all, if the Secretary of the Treasury had not raised so many questions. In the "Opinion" that Jefferson gave the President he dealt convincingly with all of them that had not been answered already. More elevated in spirit than his powerful reply to Hammond, this reply to Hamilton is, altogether, one of the ablest of his papers. Because of Washington's acceptance of it, it became to all practical purposes the official statement of the American position.

Jefferson laid down certain basic "principles": that nations have the right to change their government as they like; that the people constitute the nation; that the treaties were not made between the United States and Louis Capet but between the two nations. Therefore, since the two nations remained in existence, though both of them had since changed their form of government, the treaties were still in effect. He recognized that the non-performance of contracts on the part of men

31 He took the same line later in his PACIFICUS papers.

32 TJ to Madison, Apr. 7, 1793 (Ford, VI, 212–213); Grenville to Hammond, Feb. 8, 1793 (I.B.M., p. 35). The British opinion was based on the ground that this was an "offensive" war.

33 Thomas, p. 63n., discusses this in the light of Genet's instructions.

34 April 28, 1793, with covering letter to Washington (Ford, VI, 218–231). See also TJ's memo. of that date (Ford, I, 227).

is sometimes excusable by circumstances — such as the impossibility or self-destructiveness of performance. Annulment is permissible under certain degrees of danger, "yet the danger must be imminent and the degree great." Thus the main difference between him and Hamilton appeared. He approached this problem in no absolutist frame of mind, but he inquired specifically what dangers might be apprehended from the French treaties, considering these one by one — on grounds of likelihood, not mere possibility. "If *possibilities* would avoid contracts," he said, "there never could be a valid contract. For possibilities hang over everything." [35] Some of Hamilton's fears were reducible to irrationality, if not to absurdity. Could it be that there was danger that the French government would issue in military despotism, and that the United States as an ally would thus be tainted with despotism? If so, the country would be back where it started, since the French government was a perfect despotism at the time the alliance was actually made. Could the peril be that it would issue in a republic and thus strengthen American republican principles? The great mass of the people hoped it would do just that. Or was it that the changes might "end in something we know not what and bring on us danger we known not whence?"

More importantly, he considered possible dangers under the specific promises in the treaties. Those relating to the admission of warships, privateers, and prizes of the French, while denying this privilege to their enemies, did not disturb him, for there were similar provisions in other treaties, including the last one between England and France. No one could object on this ground, he said, and events afterwards proved that the British did not. Then there was the prohibition to the enemies of France from fitting out privateers in American ports. "But," he said, "we are free to refuse the same thing to France, there being no stipulation to the contrary, and we ought to refuse it on principles of fair neutrality." [36] The danger here, as he soon found out, lay in French misinterpretation of the treaty; but he expressed at this early stage the policy by which the administration was to be guided.

The only danger with any semblance of reality, in his opinion, was connected with the guarantee of the French West Indies. He asked a dozen questions about it, thus giving a dozen reasons for believing that the country would never be called on to make it good. Obviously doubting that the United States could do anything effective it if were called on, he shrewdly suspected what was actually the fact, namely, that the French themselves had the same idea.

[35] Ford, VI, 222.
[36] Ford, VI, 223.

As for the reception of the French minister, which Hamilton wanted to couple with reservations, he regarded this as a recognition of the legitimacy of his government and nothing more. He believed that it had nothing to do with the treaties, being based only on the common usage of nations. Hamilton was making far too much of it. Furthermore, repudiation of the treaties would require positive action, while letting them go on required none, and such inaction could hardly be regarded as an infraction of neutrality. Nothing could deprive the United States of the right of noncompliance with the treaties when compliance would involve the country in "great and inevitable danger," but, as he believed, the present dangers existed chiefly in Hamilton's imagination. Or, to put it a little better, they arose from the conditions of war, not from the stipulations of the treaties. The renunciation of the treaties, as he rightly saw, would have been a real breach of neutrality, "by giving just cause of war to France."

This is probably the most devastating opinion that Jefferson ever directed against the arguments of his colleague. The most learned and by no means the least devastating part of it consisted of an examination of the quotation which Hamilton had extracted from Vattel, saying that an alliance may be renounced if a change in the form of government of one party made it "useless, dangerous, or disagreeable" to the other. Marshaling quotations from three other authorities (Grotius, Puffendorf, and Wolf), he set them impressively in parallel columns, and overwhelmed Vattel by sheer weight of numbers. Jefferson saw no reason for specifying "danger," recognizing that that exception existed in all cases, but he was outraged by the terms "useless" and "disagreeable," regarding this single quotation as distinctly unfair to Vattel himself. Among other quotations he produced from that writer was this: "No more security, no more commerce among men, if they think themselves not obliged to preserve faith, to keep their word. . . . he who does not observe a treaty is assuredly perfidious, since he violates his faith." [37] In view of the self-righteousness with which the Hamiltonians talked about money "contracts" of a much less formal nature, this was a fitting rebuke; and Jefferson was warranted in his indignation that "this scrap should have been culled, and made the hook whereon to hang such a chain of immoral consequences." [38] Madison was equally indignant, saying in a private letter: "The attempt to shuffle off the treaty altogether by quibbling on Vattel is equally contemptible for the meanness and folly of it. If

[37] Ford, VI, 229.
[38] Ford, VI, 230.

a change of government is an absolution from public engagements, why not from those of a domestic as well as of a foreign nature; and what then becomes of public debts &C&C." [39]

It was lucky for Hamilton that this controversy occurred wholly in private. Jefferson quoted, apparently from his notes, a reckless remark of his colleague's that the United States would not have allied itself with France under the latter's present form of government. Jefferson then asked: "Who is the American who can say with truth that he would not have allied himself to France if she had been a republic? or that a republic of any form would have been as *disagreeable* as her ancient despotism?" [40] If these papers had been used as a campaign document, instead of reposing in Washington's files, Hamilton could easily have been accused of being un-American on the strength of them. A more important observation can be made on this exchange of arguments, however: Jefferson demonstrated that, in these circumstances, the path of true neutrality was not only the way of honor but also that of common sense.

ii

Even more important than the Proclamation of Neutrality was the application and enforcement of the policy it embodied. While this task was shared by all the executive officers, it belonged primarily to the Secretary of State. The chief difficulties of that official came, not from the British of whom he was so suspicious, but from the irrepressible new minister of France, who was properly received without qualifications, as he had insisted. It was to Genet that he expressed the "twin principles" of neutrality: "that it is the *right* of every nation to prohibit acts of sovereignty from being exercised by any other within its limits; and the *duty* of a neutral nation to prohibit such as would injure one of the warring powers." [41] By emphasizing duties no less than rights he set the policy of the young American Republic on an unusually high plane.

It was the particular task of Jefferson to put into practice these twin principles which he pronounced. About the time he retired from office, the British attested to the success of the policy as it related to them. The Secretary of State for Foreign Affairs wrote in January, 1794: "With respect to the conduct of the present Government of America

[39] Madison to TJ, May 8, 1793 (Hunt, VI, 128).

[40] Ford, VI, 231.

[41] TJ to Genet, June 5, 1793 (Ford, VI, 283); well discussed by Thomas, pp. 92–93.

His Majesty's Ministers think that there appears to have prevailed in its general tenor a desire for the maintenance of a fair neutrality and even a disposition friendly towards this country." [42] Jefferson himself made no pretense of friendliness towards His Majesty's Ministers, but he cannot be justly denied major credit for the sincere and successful attempt of his government to be fair. A quarter of a century later, in the House of Commons, George Canning paid tribute to this policy. "If I wished for a guide in a system of neutrality," he said, "I should take that laid down by America in the days of the presidency of Washington and the secretaryship of Jefferson, in 1793." [43] The tribute to both men was deserved, but it is doubtful if any Britisher could have realized the agonies this Secretary suffered at a time when his emotions were in conflict with his reason and hardly anybody was in position to understand his difficulties.

His situation as the chief administrator of neutrality was precarious enough; but actually his position was never as anomalous as it appeared on the surface, and by painful effort he eventually resolved most of its seeming contradictions. He remained a devoted friend of the French cause, but his mind told him from the first that belligerency would be disastrous to the United States without being of any real benefit to France. The party line of the Hamiltonians was that just as they were the only true supporters of the Constitution and George Washington, so also they were the only genuine upholders of neutrality. Jefferson's conduct as a responsible minister, as shown in official records and his own public papers, comprises a sufficient rejoinder; but at the time there was much confusion about what neutrality really meant in practice. Referring to the numerous problems which had arisen, he said in midsummer: "These questions depend for their solution on the construction of our treaties, on the laws of nature and nations, and on the laws of the land." [44] His persistent effort to be fair to all the interested parties in this unending process of construction is written into the record, but he could not slough off his predilections readily and he gave vent to his personal feelings in private letters. Less than a week after the Proclamation, he wrote to his friend Madison: "Cases are now arising which will embarrass us a little till the line of neutrality be firmly understood by ourselves and the belligerent parties." [45] This was true enough, whether the pre-

[42] Grenville to Hammond, Jan. 1794 (*I.B.M.*, p. 44).

[43] Apr. 16, 1823 (quoted by Thomas, p. 13n.).

[44] To the Chief Justice, July 18, 1793 (Ford, VI, 351). This he said in connection with the request, which the Supreme Court denied, that particular questions be referred to that tribunal; see below, pp. 118–119.

[45] April 28, 1793 (Ford, VI, 232).

diction applied to the government or to his political friends; and even before the most disturbing actor, the new French minister, arrived on the scene in Philadelphia in mid-May, it proved to be an understatement as applied to Jefferson personally. He faced a real psychological problem as well as a vexatious administrative task from the very first.

The warship that bore Citizen Genet to America, the famous frigate *Embuscade*, came into the harbor at Philadelphia while the new and still unaccredited minister remained for purposes of his own in Charleston, where he had landed. The *Embuscade* brought with her a prize, as presumably she was entitled to do under the terms of the treaty, and it did not immediately come to light that the frigate had taken the British merchant ship *Grange* in Delaware Bay, that is, in American waters. Jefferson could not restrain his private delight at this French triumph and its electrifying effects on American opinion. He wrote his nephew Jack Eppes that thousands collected on the beaches when the prize came up, "and when they saw the British colors reversed and the French flag flying above them they rent the air with peals of exultation." Describing the scene to his son-in-law, he said that it was the "*yeomanry* of the city (not the fashionable part nor paper men)" who had showed this "prodigious joy." [46] Toward the end of the summer, when reviewing the course of events, he said that on the outbreak of war between France and Great Britain citizens of the United States were not in the first instant aware of the new duties resulting from their own new and unexperienced situation, and of the "restraints it would impose even *on their dispositions* toward the belligerent powers." [47] It appears that he himself was not fully sensible of new duties at the outset and put no such rein on his own dispositions as he did later.

When he said that the war was rekindling "the old spirit of 1776" he certainly meant the revival of enthusiasm for liberty — an abstraction which he always tended to personify and which he virtually invested with the attributes of divinity. In concrete terms he meant the revival of anti-British feeling, which seemed to him inevitable under the particular circumstances. Therefore, he rejoiced in the "furious Philippics" against England while hoping, at the same time, that the spirits of the people could be kept "within the limits of a fair neutrality." In view of the fact that he hewed to the line of fair neutrality in his official conduct with such success that ultimately the British acknowledged it, and that in his relations with the leaders of his own political

[46] TJ to J. W. Eppes, May 12, 1793 (MHS); to TMR, May 6, 1793 (Ford, VI, 241).
[47] To Gouverneur Morris, Aug. 16, 1793 (Ford, VI, 376).

group he exercised a moderating influence, he cannot be justly charged with hypocrisy. But no reader of his private correspondence can doubt that the problem of attaining and maintaining poise and balance in his own mind was difficult in the extreme.

About this time he despatched to France a letter which was ostensibly unneutral. In form it was a private letter of introduction, but it was addressed to Brissot de Warville, whom he supposed to be still a leader in the National Convention.[48] "We too have our aristocrats and monocrats," he said, "and as they float on the surface, they shew much, though they weigh little." For a more explicit description of characters, objects, and parties, he referred Brissot to the bearer of the letter. He told the latter it was important that these be well understood among the French, especially by their government. "Particular circumstances have generated suspicions among them that we are swerving from our republicanism," he said.[49] He was glad of the opportunity to remove these suspicions and of a safe occasion to put himself personally on record. He informed Brissot: "I continue eternally attached to the principles of your revolution. I hope it will end in the establishment of some firm government, friendly to liberty, & capable of maintaining it. If it does, the world will become inevitably free."

He wrote from deep conviction, and at the moment he was probably thinking more about the clash of ideas than of the struggle for power between nations, but he addressed to a supposed leader in a belligerent country a sympathetic letter. It was also an exceedingly ironical and a wholly futile one. Brissot and the Girondists associated with him were on the point of falling, and before this message could have reached him he was in prison, where he languished until his execution in the autumn. Jefferson could not have been expected to foresee the full course of events, and he was at a disadvantage because of the time-lag, but it now appears that he directed his friendly gesture to a most inappropriate person.[50] Brissot was the leading advocate of war in 1792, and in 1793 he presented the motion extending it to Great Britain and Holland.[51] At the bar of history he bears a terrible responsibility.

To Brissot this was "a war of the human race against its oppressors

---

[48] May 8, 1793 (Ford, VI, 248–249).

[49] To Dr. Enoch Edwards, May 8, 1793 (Ford, VI, 240).

[50] While in France, he had been consulted by Brissot about the book this journalist was writing with Étienne Clavière, De la France et des États-Unis (1787), and no doubt he remembered him as being notably pro-American (TJ to Brissot, August 16, 1786 (J.P., X, 261–264)). How much he knew of Brissot's career in the Legislative Assembly and the National Convention is difficult to determine.

[51] Eloise Ellery, Brissot de Warville (1915), p. 324.

. . . the most just, the most glorious war that had ever been known." [52] Gouverneur Morris, like Hamilton, took quite a different view of it. He reported to Jefferson in due course that one of the reasons for the declaration of the French was their hope to excite an insurrection in Austrian Flanders, and that their subsequent acquisitions of territory cast grave doubts on the sincerity of their protestations against conquest.[53] But Jefferson continued to view their actions as basically defensive, even when offensive in form, and the war had undoubtedly strengthened in his own mind the conviction that the democratic struggle was international. Also, he now realized that it had crystallized American parties. He wrote Monroe a few weeks later: "*The war has kindled and brought forward the two parties with an ardour which our own interests merely could never excite.*" [54] This created a real problem for one who shared the ardor but who, as a responsible official, could not publicly display it.

His official actions had to be taken on other grounds. The capture of the *Grange* occasioned protests from the British as well as exultation among the yeomanry of Philadelphia and private rejoicing on the part of the Secretary of State. Hammond, who had not yet transmitted a reply to the complaints Jefferson had submitted to him a year ago, showed the utmost promptness in presenting his own. He got speedy action on them. If this had happened in American waters the United States would not put up with it, Jefferson said; and the official opinion which Edmund Randolph gave him settled the matter. The Secretary asked Ternant, who was still the accredited French minister, to restore the ship and her cargo and release the prisoners. Hammond also wanted compensation for the detention of the vessel, but Jefferson was warranted in regarding this ruling as proof of the justice and impartiality of the United States to all parties. When Genet finally arrived, he acceded to it, though he afterwards seemed to think it more to his credit than Jefferson did.[55]

Hammond also objected to the action of the French consul in Charleston in condemning a captured British vessel. Jefferson agreed that this action was a legal nullity, since such a matter should have been handled by an American tribunal, and he described it as disrespect-

---

[52] *Ibid.*, p. 257, citing *Patriote Français*, April 21, 1792.

[53] Morris to TJ, June 10, 1792 (*A.S.P.F.R.*, I, 329), and Dec. 21, 1792 (*ibid.*, 347). The latter letter, speaking of the "adoption" of Savoy as a department, was not received until Apr. 22, 1793.

[54] June 4, 1793 (Ford, VI, 282), italics inserted.

[55] TJ to Hammond, May 3, 1793, and to Ternant that day (Ford, VI, 236–237); TJ to Hammond, May 15, 1793, and to Ternant May 15 (Ford, VI, 255); opinion of Randolph, May 14, 1793; Genet to TJ, May 27, 1793 (*A.S.P.F.R.*, I, 148–150).

ful to the United States. At the time the eloquent Genet asserted that the French republicans, enlightened on the rights of man, also had just ideas of the law of nations. So far as he was concerned there were already reasons to doubt this, for in Charleston he interpreted the Franco-American treaties to suit himself, but there was no question of Jefferson's attitude and intentions. In writing Ternant he stated that the government would apply impartially to both parties the principles on which it was proceeding; and he soon stated emphatically to Genet that as a neutral his country was concerned with its duties as well as its rights.

The *Grange* case fell within the area of American right, and it marked a step toward the determination of the limits within which the United States exercised legal authority. Other cases were not so simple, for many of them raised the question of the extent of jurisdiction beyond the coastline. The historic three-mile limit was not set until autumn. This, as Jefferson stated, was the smallest distance claimed by any nation, being the utmost range of a cannon ball, commonly given as one sea league, while the greatest was the extent of human sight, estimated at twenty miles or more. The lesser distance was decided on by the President, for practical reasons, and it proved acceptable to both the major belligerents. Jefferson himself would have preferred to claim wider jurisdiction, and he was strongly determined to maintain all just neutral rights.[56] More significant at this early stage, however, was his emphasis on neutral duties, and his worst headaches resulted from his attempt to perform these.

Working out the mechanics of enforcement was difficult, since no American precedents existed. As usual, the incessantly active Secretary of the Treasury had suggestions, and one that he made a couple of weeks after the issuing of the Proclamation aroused Jefferson's deep suspicions. Hamilton wanted to make particular use of the collectors of customs, who were responsible to him. After an inconclusive conference with him and Randolph, Jefferson wrote the latter at some length, believing that some of his own objections could be made with better grace by the Attorney General.[57]

Jefferson opposed the system of espionage which Hamilton wanted to set up, fearing that prosecution might be instituted on *"the secret information of a collector."* Believing that the acts of American citi-

[56] On the three-mile limit, see TJ to Washington, October 3, 1793 (Ford, VI, 433–435); TJ to Genet, Nov. 8, 1793 (Ford, VI, 440–441).

[57] See TJ's memo. of May 6, 1793 (Ford, I, 227–228), and his letter of May 8, 1793, to Randolph (Ford, VI, 244–246).

zens, as distinguished from foreigners, should fall under the ordinary system, he favored the substitution of grand juries and judges for customs collectors. Also, he wondered if the superintendence of neutrality and the preservation of peace with foreign nations could be properly assigned to the Treasury, which was supposed to deal with financial matters merely and was already "amply provided with business, patronage, and influence."

Randolph put himself on record in a long letter which Jefferson found disappointing.[58] He admitted certain current suspicions of Hamilton. "It was impossible not to have heard, that the revenue-officers have been suspected to be a corps, trained to the arts of spies, in the service of the Treasury," he said. But he had accepted Hamilton's assurances that he was not "prying into the conduct of individuals." Randolph regarded the customs collectors as suitable informants because of their closeness to the scene of probable violation. He stated, however, that Hamilton had accepted his suggestion that they should report to district attorneys. Thus he believed that Jefferson's main objection had been met, and he agreed with him that from that point on the normal legal machinery should operate. But he did not put himself on the side of his fellow Virginian in opposition to the entrance of the Treasury Department into this business. He took the position that something could be said on both sides and that the President must always decide in such matters. In Jefferson's opinion, this was a good example of fence-straddling.

The letter which Hamilton finally issued to the collectors ordered that information about violations of neutrality be referred to district attorneys and governors, and this partial modification was attributable to the Attorney General, no doubt.[59] But Jefferson had gained an impression of the latter's vacillation which he never lost. A few days after this exchange he wrote Madison that, because of the division of the council and the close vote, everything hung on the opinion of a single person [Randolph], "and that the most indecisive one I ever had to do business with. He always contrives to agree in principle with one but in conclusion with the other." [60] The vote was generally 2½ against 1½, he had told Monroe, thus dividing the Attorney General into halves; one of these supported Jefferson while the other went along with Hamilton and Knox.[61]

As a description of procedure in the executive council during that

[58] Randolph to TJ, May 9, 1783 (LC, 14757-14758).
[59] Aug. 4, 1793 (J.C.H., III, 574-576).
[60] TJ to Madison, May 12, 1793 (Ford, VI, 251).
[61] TJ to Monroe, May 5, 1793 (Ford, VI, 239).

trying summer this was inadequate, and the situation was not such a desperate one for Jefferson as he implied in these letters to intimates. Long years later, when arguing the advantages of a single over a plural executive, he wrote: "During the administration of our first President, his cabinet of four members was equally divided by as marked an opposition of principle as monarchism and republicanism could bring into conflict. Had that cabinet been a directory, like positive and negative quantities in algebra the opposing wills would have balanced each other and produced a state of absolute inaction. But the President heard with calmness the opinions and reasons of each, decided the course to be pursued, and kept the government steadily in it, unaffected by the agitation. The public knew well the dissensions of the cabinet, but never had an uneasy thought on their account, because they knew also they had provided a regulating power which would keep the machine in steady movement." [62] A survey of Jefferson's own contemporary memoranda for this year leads to the impression that the President, though tending to accept the judgment of a majority of his assistants in any matter presented to them as a group, followed no unvarying procedure. While by no means abdicating, he continued to serve as a balance wheel. He valued unanimity and got it more often than Jefferson's quoted comments imply.[63]

The Secretary of State did not exaggerate the difference between himself and the Secretary of the Treasury in world-view, and undoubtedly he believed that he must always be on guard against that aggressive colleague and his pro-British leanings, just as Hamilton believed he must be on guard in turn. But Jefferson would have found it hard to point out any major decision of the government affecting his own department in which he was overruled and to which in the end his mind did not consent.[64] The record which the administration made that summer was one on which it, and he, could stand with satisfaction. This amiable man of reason was always ill at ease in a quarrelsome atmosphere, however, and at first he may have been as distressed by the conflict in his own breast as by that within the administration.

His difficulties would have been great in any case. As he said a little later, the incidents to which the war had given rise filled the executive with business, "equally delicate, difficult, and disagreeable." Continuing, he said: "The course intended to be pursued being that

---

[62] To Destutt de Tracy, Jan. 26, 1811 (Ford, IX, 307).

[63] TJ's memoranda in the Anas, 1793 (Ford, I, 214–272).

[64] The negotiation of a new commercial treaty with France, as permitted by Genet's instructions, was a possible exception, but the course of events made this quite impracticable.

of a strict and impartial neutrality, decisions, rendered by the President rigorously on that principle, dissatisfy both parties, and draw complaints from both." [65] He was speaking particularly of the French and British ministers, but the generalization applied also to the domestic parties that were now assuming more definite form. He continued to rely on the wisdom of George Washington; but through force of circumstances foreign policy, along with other serious matters, was now superintended by the entire executive council. Hamilton's famous reports on the public credit had not had to undergo the advance scrutiny of his colleagues, but at this stage Jefferson's important letters were gone over by the others, sometimes paragraph by paragraph, sentence by sentence, and phrase by phrase. This must have been as galling to his spirit as the literary emendation of the Declaration of Independence by Congress, but there is reason to believe that the effects were good in both cases. In his earliest letters to Genet, while censuring that envoy's conduct, he inserted expressions of friendship to the French people which his colleagues struck out. He avoided these thereafter with the result, he said, that his letters were "as dry and husky as if written between the generals of two enemy nations." [66] This was disturbing to a polite man who still thought of the French as allies, but under existing circumstances it was just as well.

By and large, it was fortunate for the country that all the high executive officers were consulted about these crucial matters and the net result was a generally well-executed policy. But the difficulties which Jefferson faced as a diligent official, a loyal republican, a passionate advocate of human freedom, and a sensitive human being were enough to bear anybody down.

It is not surprising that these circumstances occasioned another informal debate between him and his closest political friend, Madison, regarding his own continuance in office. Writing him from his own sanctuary in Orange County, Virginia, Madison said: "I feel for your situation but you must bear it. Every consideration private as well as public requires a further sacrifice of your longings for the repose of Monticello." [67] Actually, Madison was laying chief emphasis on personal and partisan considerations. He said: "You must not make your final exit from public life till it will be marked with justifying circumstances which all good citizens will respect, and to which your

[65] TJ to Morris, June 13, 1793 (Ford, VI, 299–301).
[66] Memo. of Aug. 20, 1793 (Ford, I, 260–261).
[67] Madison to TJ, May 27, 1793 (Hunt, VI, 129).

friends can appeal. At the present crisis, what would the former think, what would the latter say?"

Jefferson's reply is one of the most moving of his many lamentations over the personal sacrifices incident to public office and one of his strongest disclaimers of personal ambition. Also, it describes vividly if extravagantly his longings and his sufferings as a human being at this time of stress and seeming frustration. Since no paraphrase can do justice to it, it must be quoted at some length.

> . . . To my fellow-citizens the debt of service has been fully & faithfully paid. I acknolege that such a debt exists, that a tour of duty, in whatever line he can be most useful to his country, is due from every individual. . . . I have now been in the public service four & twenty years; one half of which has been spent in total occupation with their affairs, & absence from my own. I have served my tour then. No positive engagement, by word or deed, binds me to their further service. . . . The motion of my blood no longer keeps time with the tumult of the world. It leads me to seek for happiness in the lap and love of my family, in the society of my neighbors & my books, in the wholesome occupations of my farm & my affairs, in an interest or affection in every bud that opens, in every breath that blows around me, in an entire freedom of rest or motion, of thought or incogitancy, owing account to myself alone of my hours & actions.

Against these prospects, this lover of home and books and nature set the circumstances of his present existence:

> . . . Worn down with labours from morning to night & day to day; knowing them as fruitless to others as they are vexatious to myself, committed singly in desperate & eternal contest against a host who are systematically undermining the public liberty & prosperity, even the rare hours of relaxation sacrificed to the society of persons in the same intentions, of whose hatred I am conscious even in those moments of conviviality when the heart wishes most to open itself to the effusions of friendship and confidence, cut off from my family & friends, my affairs abandoned to chaos & derangement, in short, giving everything I love, in exchange for everything I hate, and all this without a single gratification, in possession or prospect, in present enjoyment or future wish.[68]

The prospect was exceedingly doleful to George Washington, also. Jefferson reported that the President was not well; little lingering fevers hung over him and affected his looks remarkably. He was ex-

[68] TJ to Madison, June 9, 1793 (Ford, VI, 290–292).

tremely disturbed by the attacks made on him in the newspapers. The Secretary of State said: "I think he feels those things more than any person I ever met with. I am sincerely sorry to see them." [69] A little earlier, noting that the President was particularly incensed with Freneau, he had inferred that his own interposition with that editor was desired, perhaps the withdrawal of Freneau's appointment as translating clerk in the Department of State. To this Jefferson was quite unwilling, in view of Freneau's services in checking the "monocrats." He believed that the President, insensible to the designs of that party, had not with his usual good sense perceived that the good effects of this free journal outweighed the bad.[70] But Jefferson himself was again involved in a contradiction, for he believed that the newspaper attacks on his revered chief, though unfair in themselves, were planted on popular ground, on the love of the people for France and her cause, which he still regarded as that of all humanity.

The coming of Citizen Genet had stimulated these expressions of democratic ardor and, as Jefferson soon found out, caused the situation to become even more paradoxical. By his excesses of patriotic zeal this missionary of revolutionary democracy struck blows against that cause such as the Secretary of the Treasury could never have delivered, and these acutely embarrassed the policy of fair and strict neutrality. That in itself was a sufficient reason for Jefferson's unhappiness in office until he finally arrived at a distinction between the cause and its representative which brought him a measure of relief.

[69] Ford, VI, 293.
[70] Memo. of May 23, 1793 (Ford, I, 231).

[VI]

Impact of a Missionary: Citizen Genet

THE news of the arrival in the United States of the new minister of the French Republic, Edmond Charles Genet, who was to replace Ternant, an appointee of the monarchy, was received in Philadelphia on April 22, 1793, the day that the Proclamation of Neutrality was issued. Two weeks earlier he had landed in Charleston, a remote port as viewed from the seat of the federal government, and this news was surprising in itself. Jefferson expected him in Philadelphia in a few days, but actually he did not arrive until the middle of May. He was in the country about six weeks before even presenting his credentials, and it soon appeared that he was actively promoting the interests of his own nation before he was officially accredited as its representative. This irregularity of procedure might have been expected to ruffle the Secretary of State, a man who was notably scrupulous about official proprieties, and one wonders what he was expecting of Genet as he sat in his office on High Street or under the plane trees at his rented house beside the Schuylkill.

Jefferson was not in position to read Genet's instructions or his dispatches home, as we are, but he had some advance information from John Adams's son-in-law. Late in February, Colonel William S. Smith brought the encouraging report that Genet would be empowered to grant commercial privileges, especially in the French West Indies.[1]

[1] Anas, Feb. 20, 1793 (Ford, I, 216–217). Genet's instructions can be conveniently seen in *Correspondence of the French Ministers to the United States, 1791–1797*, edited by F. J. Turner; *Annual Report of the A.H.A., 1903*, II (1904), 201–211 (referred to as *C.F.M.*). I have greatly benefited from the analysis of these and of the mission as a whole by Albert H. Bowman, in "The Struggle for Neutrality: A History of Diplomatic Relations between the United States and France, 1790–1801" (Columbia University dissertation, 1953). Also, I have learned much from Maude H. Woodfin, "Citizen Genet and His Mission" (University of Chicago dissertation, 1928) and from other published and unpublished writings on the subject, to some of which I may not specifically refer.

Also, Jefferson heard Smith say that the French contemplated giving freedom to their own West Indian possessions and had plans to "emancipate" South America from the Spanish. Before Genet set out, as we now know, the French had given up the elaborate scheme which Miranda had talked them into, and were looking toward Florida and Louisiana. Almost any move against the Spanish, however, would have been viewed with sympathy by Jefferson.

Gouverneur Morris, in Paris, had not been consulted about Genet's appointment and he reported it to Washington rather than to Jefferson. If his descriptions of the envoy were passed on, Jefferson learned that Genet was a man of good parts and education and of an ardent temper. Morris thought him very much an opportunist and believed that the President would see in him immediately "the manner and look of an upstart." [2] Jefferson was disposed to discount Morris's unfavorable comments on the revolutionary upstarts, but by now he had received from this source better information about factional groupings than he possessed during the winter. He knew that there were differences between Brissot and his associates, known to later history as the Girondins, and the Jacobins, and that the former were in power at the time of Genet's appointment. He may have surmised that Brissot was responsible for this, as in fact he was, and that would have meant to Jefferson that the new minister was backed by a group professing great admiration and friendship for the United States.[3] He did not particularly associate Brissot and the Girondins with grandiose territorial ambitions and excessive zeal in propaganda, as historians now do.

Without specifying the Brissotines, Morris had issued timely warnings against the spirit of aggrandizement and propaganda among the revolutionists. He pointed out, in a letter received by Jefferson on the date of the Neutrality Proclamation, that their declaration that they would "erect the standard of liberty everywhere" had occasioned international alarm.[4] After the propaganda decrees of the autumn of 1792, Morris and others anticipated the attempt of the revolutionary leaders to surround their country with dependent states. Within a few weeks Jefferson himself, in private, became critical of French propagandist activities. He wrote his son-in-law: "The French have been guilty of great errors in their conduct towards other nations, not only in insulting uselessly all crowned heads, but endeavoring to force lib-

---

[2] Morris to Washington, Jan. 6, 1793 (*Diary*, II, 595). See also letter of Dec. 28, 1792, written before Morris met Genet (*A.S.P.F.R.*, I, 395). In a letter to TJ, Feb. 13, 1793, Morris complained that the members of the French diplomatic committee had slighted him by not consulting him (*ibid.*, I, 350).

[3] To Brissot, May 8, 1793 (Ford, VI, 248).

[4] Dec. 21, 1792 (*A.S.P.F.R.*, I, 347).

erty on their neighbors in their own form." [5] At first, however, he was disposed to accept their claim that their actions were defensive measures.

Practical questions bearing on Genet and his activities arose soon after his arrival on the South Atlantic coast. The actions of the French frigate *Embuscade* in Delaware Bay could hardly be dissociated from the new envoy, and reported events in Charleston certainly could not. The assumption of jurisdiction by the French consul there in prize proceedings in violation of American sovereignty was a case in point, since this action supposedly was taken on the instructions of Genet. Mangourit, the consul, whom he described as "an excellent patriot," was charged with arrangements for a projected expedition against East Florida, for which South Carolinians and Georgians were to be recruited, but it is doubtful that Jefferson knew about this. The vigilant British minister, George Hammond, informed him that French privateers were being fitted out in Charleston, and that these were manned for the most part by American citizens. This matter he referred to the federal district attorney in Philadelphia, asking him to take such measures to apprehend and prosecute citizens committing depredations on the property and commerce of nations at peace with the United States as were according to law.[6] He had already indicated his own unwillingness to permit the arming and equipment of privateers in American ports, though he did not make a decisive statement of the official position until after Genet reached Philadelphia.

Before he knew much about what was happening in Charleston, he wrote Madison that it seemed as if Genet's arrival in Philadelphia "would furnish occasion for the *people* to testify their affections without respect to the cold caution of their government." [7] Writing home, the missionary himself boasted that his journey northward through the interior was an uninterrupted succession of civic fetes and his entrance into Philadelphia a triumph for liberty. "The true Americans," he said, "are at the height of joy." [8] He was welcomed into towns by the roar of cannon and undoubtedly he attracted crowds, but, judging from the newspaper accounts, his journey was rather less triumphal than he supposed.[9] Congressman John Steele of North

[5] To TMR, June 24, 1793 (Ford, VI, 318).

[6] This led to the celebrated case of Gideon Henfield, which will be discussed hereafter. See Francis Wharton, *State Trials of the United States during the Administration of Washington and Adams* (1849), pp. 49–89. Hammond wrote TJ on May 8, 1793, and TJ wrote District Attorney Rawle on May 15.

[7] Apr. 28, 1793 (Ford, VI, 232).

[8] To Minister of Foreign Affairs, May 18, 1793 (*C.F.M.*, p. 215).

[9] Woodfin, ch. VI.

Carolina, whom time was to show as a rather moderate Federalist but who admitted that he feared "this citizen," described Genet as a man of good person and fine ruddy complexion who seemed always in a bustle.[10] From other accounts we learn that the new minister of the French Republic, who so announced himself to all comers, was thirty years old, of middling stature; that he had blue eyes and auburn hair; that he spoke English well; that his manners were engaging and he made a very favorable first impression. He had a quick temper, however, and showed little or no capacity to understand anybody who disagreed with him.

Genet arrived in Philadelphia on Thursday, May 16. Calculations about the number of people who were at Gray's Ferry to greet him varied with the sentiments of the reporters, but no doubt there would have been more if the emissary had not arrived sooner than expected and disrupted the original plans of certain citizens.[11] On that same day a group of merchants and traders of Philadelphia met and adopted an address to the President, approving the Neutrality Proclamation.[12] Jefferson, who regarded this group as pro-British, said that this address contained "much wisdom but no affection." He told Madison that the citizens, as distinguished from the merchants, perceived coldness in the Proclamation; and, suspecting that there was doubt in the minds of the President's counselors about receiving Genet, they determined to receive him and to draw up a counter-address. Apparently the Secretary of State perceived nothing unpatriotic in such action.

A body of these citizens held a meeting in the State House Yard that evening and appointed a drafting committee. Their leaders, though identified by Hamilton with the "enemies and disturbers" of the government, were men of importance and intelligence. Jefferson himself named the mathematician David Rittenhouse, president of the American Philosophical Society; the latter's son-in-law, Jonathan Dickinson Sergeant, a prominent lawyer; the popular physician Dr. James Hutchinson, who was interested in all things human and Republican; and Alexander James Dallas, secretary of the Commonwealth of Pennsylvania. The address was approved at a meeting at the same place the following evening, and a committee of thirty bore it to the City Tavern, two or three blocks away, where Genet was staying.

[10] Steele to Hamilton, April 30, 1793 (J.C.H., V, 561).

[11] For a newspaper account, see Philadelphia *General Advertiser*, May 17, 1793. Hamilton reported on Genet's reception during his first days in Philadelphia in an undated letter to an unnamed correspondent (Lodge, VIII, 300–303). Jefferson covered the same period in a letter to Madison, May 19 (Ford, VI, 259–261).

[12] Delivered May 17 and replied to that day by Washington (Fitzpatrick, XXXII, 460).

Even Hamilton admitted that a big crowd had been gathered by that time, and Jefferson described it as a "vast concourse." There is no reason to suppose, however, that he was a part of it.

A dinner was given Genet on Saturday night, about one hundred being present.[13] This was attended chiefly by French, whose numbers were being swollen by refugees from Santo Domingo, and by French-Americans. An ode by Citizen Pichon was read by Citizen Duponceau, and Citizen Freneau was requested to put this into English verse.[14] They sang the "Marseillaise," Genet himself rendered a song "replete with truly patriotic and republican sentiments," and somebody placed the cap of liberty on his head. To this group, however, these actions involved no derogation of the government of the United States and its head. One of the toasts was as follows: "The virtuous Washington; may heaven grant to France and to the United States many citizens that resemble him."

The newspapers of the time bear out Genet's boast to the Foreign Minister of his own country, two weeks after his arrival at the seat of government. "I live here in the midst of perpetual fetes," he said; "I receive addresses from all parts of the Continent." [15] The day after he wrote this sanguine letter the "citizens of Philadelphia" gave him "an elegant civic feast" at Oeller's Hotel, which had more room than any other place in town.[16] It is said that upwards of two hundred were present, including a number of state and federal officers who attended "in their capacity of private citizens — not as guests." Among these was Governor Thomas Mifflin, who gave a volunteer toast, but none of the accounts say that Thomas Jefferson was there. None of the fifteen regular toasts attacked the policy of neutrality or urged any direct participation of the United States in the war, but they left no possible doubt of this group's sympathies. Here are a few samples:

> The Republics of France and America — may they be forever united in the cause of liberty.

> The spirit of seventy-six and ninety-two — may the citizens of America and France, as they are equal in virtue, be equal in success.

---

[13] May 18, 1793 (General Advertiser, May 21, 1793).

[14] French version in General Advertiser, May 27; Freneau's on May 31. This was in 12 stanzas and was entitled "Ode to Liberty." It is not to be confused with Freneau's own ode which was sung June 1.

[15] Genet to Le Brun, May 31, 1793 (C.F.M., p. 216).

[16] June 1, 1793. Details drawn chiefly from National Gazette, June 5, 1793; see also General Advertiser, June 4, 1793. The account in the Hamiltonian Gazette of the U. S., June 5, though briefer, is not hostile in tone.

May the clarion of freedom, sounded by France, awaken the people of the world to their own happiness, and the tyrants of the earth be prostrated by its triumphant sounds.

All day the flags of the two republics had flown from the cupola of the hotel. They were also on the table, along with the cap of liberty. Following the regular toasts, this was placed on the head of Citizen Genet, "and in its revolution around the table, inspired every citizen with that enthusiasm and those feelings which baffle all description, which Freemen only can conceive, and of which slaves and despots have the most distant comprehension." [17] In the course of the evening, certain verses of Philip Freneau were sung to the tune of "God Save the King."

God save the Rights of Man!
Give us a heart to scan
Blessings so dear:
Let them be spread around
Wherever man is found,
And with the welcome sound
Ravish his ear.

Let us with France agree
And let the world be free
While tyrants fall.
Let the rude savage host
In their vast numbers boast
Freedom's almighty host
Laughs at them all.

There were four more stanzas identifying the cause of France with that of liberty. The last one ended:

Freedom will never want
Her WASHINGTON.

Other addresses to Genet and other dinners followed the elegant civic feast. Popular enthusiasm for him never approached universality as closely as he imagined, but it continued at a high pitch at least until midsummer, when the difficulties he had created in official circles began to be noised about. By that time the Republicans, whose zeal had been stimulated by his presence and who had embraced him too ardently, began to be embarrassed.

[17] *General Advertiser*, June 4, 1793.

Having fired the fraternal spirit of the American people all the way from Charleston to Philadelphia, as he believed, Genet delivered his credentials on May 17 and was presented to the President by the Secretary of State. He was now in position to act officially, and it was high time. He had not followed the wise counsel of the foreign minister of his own country. "Your mission requires of you very great activity," Le Brun had written, "but to be efficacious this ought to be hidden. The cold character of the Americans warms up only by degrees and indirect ways will be less useful than official steps." [18] Also, Le Brun assured him that he could have entire confidence in the sentiments of the President and the Secretary of State. Years later, when in a spiteful mood, he said that his reception by the President was "perfectly neutral and insignificant," [19] but Genet raised no objection in the first exuberant dispatches he sent home.

To his first ministerial conference with the Secretary of State, which occurred a few days later, he had looked forward with special confidence, knowing Jefferson's "principles, his experience, his talents, his devotion to the cause we defend." [20] Genet brought with him a letter from Condorcet, who, along with Lafayette and the Duc de La Rochefoucauld, had been Jefferson's guests at a parting dinner just before he left Paris in 1789.[21] The letter was six months old, and most of it was devoted to Lafayette, who, in Condorcet's eyes, had shown great folly in going over to the enemies of liberty. While vouching for Genet's zeal for liberty, Condorcet did not laud an envoy whose appointment he had actually opposed, as we now know, but he did glorify Franco-American friendship. "Our republic, founded like yours on reason, on the rights of nature, on equality, ought to be your true ally," he said; "we ought in some sort to form one people." The two republics, he continued, had the same interests, the same purpose to destroy all "anti-natural" constitutions, while the kings of Europe did not conceal their purpose to join forces to destroy liberty everywhere. These sentiments could hardly have failed to strike a responsive chord in Jefferson's breast. Genet presented himself, therefore, under favorable auspices.

Jefferson tended to be unsuspicious of persons who shared, or seemed to share, his general principles, being disposed to take them at

[18] Feb. 24, 1793 (*C.F.M.*, p. 215*n.*). This dispatch was one of those acknowledged by Genet on May 18, and he may have received it sooner.

[19] Genet to TJ, July 4, 1797, from Genet Papers (Woodfin, Appendix A).

[20] *C.F.M.*, p. 215.

[21] Condorcet to TJ, Dec. 21, 1792 (LC, 79:13778). This very difficult letter was deciphered for me by John J. dePorry of the Library of Congress. For the earlier association, see *Jefferson and the Rights of Man*, p. 235.

their own valuation as long as he could. The important principle in this instance was devotion to the universal cause of liberty, and Genet affirmed that with sufficient eloquence. Writing Madison shortly after his first conference with Genet, Jefferson did not commend the man himself but did say: "It is impossible for anything to be more affectionate, more magnanimous than the purport of his mission." [22] He told the President that the French were not calling on the United States for the guarantee of their West Indian islands, despite the treaty of alliance. This assurance vindicated his own judgment, and he was happy to be confirmed in his opinion of French friendliness. "Cherish your own peace and prosperity," Genet said, reporting at the same time that he was armed with full powers to make a more liberal treaty of commerce. Accordingly, it seemed to Jefferson that Genet offered everything and asked nothing. He doubted if the offers of negotiations would be accepted, however, and lamented to Madison that one or two at least of his colleagues (Hamilton and Knox) "under pretence of avoiding war on the one side have no great antipathy to run foul of it on the other, and to make part of the confederacy of princes against human liberty."

In this mood he probably was not appalled by the flamboyance of Genet's first written communications to him, though these were far different in tone from the formal diplomatic correspondence he had had with Vergennes and Montmorin and, more recently, with Ternant. The ebullient emissary referred to "innumerable hordes and tyrants" who were menacing the rising liberty of the French nation, and to "perfidious ministers of despotism" whom the citizens of the two allied republics must combat. These particular rhetorical flourishes were made in a covering letter to a decree of the French Convention, opening to United States vessels all ports of the French colonies on the same terms as French vessels.[23] Ostensibly the action was liberal, but its purpose can be readily surmised. The French wanted to avail themselves of American shipping, now that they were engaged in warfare with the British and likely to lose much of their own. The decree also proposed that the United States grant to French merchants "a like reduction of the duties granted by the present law to American merchants, and thereby more closely cement the benevolent ties which unite the two nations." The reference here was to provisions, already objected to by the French, favoring American vessels against those of all other countries in the matter of tonnage and

[22] May 19, 1793 (Ford, VI, 260).
[23] Decree of Feb. 19, 1793, enclosed in Genet to TJ, May 23, 1793 (A.S.P.F.R., I, 147).

import duties.[24] At the time Jefferson had thought the position of the French unwarranted on the ground of the existing treaty, but he was personally willing to relax provisions in their favor as an act of friendship in return for commercial favors already granted, or on the basis of a new reciprocal arrangement. He would have liked to work out such a reciprocal arrangement with the new envoy, whose professions of good will he did not yet doubt. In this particular matter Hamilton was nearer right than Jefferson was. He regarded Genet's offers as a snare into which he hoped the government would never fall, and Knox agreed with him.[25] We now know, as Jefferson did not, that in return for concessions, the French expected the United States to tighten its commercial and political ties with them to a degree that was incompatible with national independence. It appears, therefore, that he was fortunate in escaping commercial negotiations for a new treaty.[26]

The next two or three weeks, while Genet was cavorting with his Republican admirers in Philadelphia and Jefferson was still trying to take him at his face value as an evangel of freedom, were the period when the Secretary of State suffered his greatest emotional tension. There were signs of strain even in his relations with the President, whom he still revered and whose judgment he generally admired. The week after Genet's arrival he drafted at Washington's request a letter to the Provisory Executive Council of France regarding the recall of Ternant. In this Washington questioned his use of the expression "our republic," saying it was not in the customary official style. The document which was finally sent was very friendly in tone, but the words "our republic" were changed to "the United States." [27] This was not because of any lack of devotion on Washington's part to the republican form of government, which he regarded as safe in the United States. What he really was disturbed about was the threat of anarchy, which he scented in Freneau's newspaper.[28] This notably well-balanced man would not have liked the exuberance of the Republicans in any case,

---

[24] See *Jefferson and the Rights of Man*, pp. 328–331.

[25] TJ to Madison, May 27, 1793 (Ford, VI, 268–269).

[26] In a letter of June 2, 1793 to Madison (Ford, VI, 278) he said that the division of the executive council on the question of a new commercial treaty with France was 4 to 1 against it and that he proposed delaying that question until Randolph got back from a trip to Virginia, which he hoped would impress Randolph about public sentiment toward the French. The question was not afterwards taken up, ostensibly because the Senate was not in session.

[27] May 24, 1793 (Fitzpatrick, XXXII, 468–69). For TJ's account of his conversation with Washington, see Anas, May 23 (Ford, I, 230–31). His friendly letter to Ternant, dated May 22, is in Ford, VI, 263.

[28] See above, p. 89.

and some of their barbs were now being directed against him personally.

Jefferson had no sympathy with personal attacks on the President, but the fears he centered on the word "monarchy" amounted almost to an obsession. He expressed them rather more moderately than usual in a private letter to Harry Innes of Kentucky: "This summer is of immense importance to the future condition of mankind all over the earth, and not a little so to ours. For though its issue should not be marked by any direct change in our constitution, it will influence the tone and principles of its administration so as to lead it to something very different in the one event from what it would be in the other." [29] Driven by the logic of circumstances and the force of reason to the espousal of fair neutrality, he was determined that this policy should not weaken the cause of republicanism at home by injuring it abroad. Therefore, his own course lay between Scylla and Charybdis and it could not help being tortuous.

One question which Genet brought up very promptly was that of advances on the American debt to France, and on this Jefferson's stand was realistic and moderate.[30] The United States was under no obligation to anticipate payments, and the President was not authorized to do so unless this should seem advantageous. The executive officers were unanimously opposed to any change in the form of payments, and Jefferson spelled out a number of very practical objections to the French proposals.[31] He believed, however, that a refusal without assigning reasons, such as Hamilton favored, "would have a very dry and unpleasant aspect indeed." He himself saw no objection to anticipating the payments for the current year, if convenient for the Treasury, but beyond that he would not go. Beyond that the government did not go, and Washington accepted Jefferson's judgment regarding the form of communication.[32] The credit for forestalling certain of Genet's ventures by refusing to make advance payments on the debt belongs to the executive officers as a group. Only with respect to friendliness of tone toward France was this a real issue between the Secretary of the Treasury and the Secretary of State.

[29] May 23, 1793 (Ford, VI, 266).
[30] To TJ, May 22, 1793 (*A.S.P.F.R.*, I, 142). The debt question is well summed up by Thomas, Appendix II.
[31] To Washington, June 6, 1793 (Ford, VI, 287–289).
[32] The letters within the government can be conveniently seen in Lodge, IV, 121–131; Jefferson's letter of June 11, 1793, to Genet, enclosing a report from Hamilton, amended according to Washington's wishes, is in Ford, VI, 294–295. Genet brought up the same question later, but it need not further concern us here.

A more difficult question remained. What should be done about French privateers which had already been armed or outfitted in American harbors and the prizes they had taken? [33] Hammond, the British minister, argued that such prizes should be restored to their original owners. The case was argued over the *Little Sarah*, recently captured by the French. In a measured opinion Jefferson reaffirmed his conviction that the United States should not permit the French to arm or outfit privateers in American ports, "the treaty leaving us free to refuse, and the refusal being necessary to preserve fair and secure neutrality." [34] But, considering that this first case had arisen in a distant port before measures could be taken by the government, he believed that a very moderate apology ought to satisfy the British. He was opposed to restoring the prize to them. By the laws of war it belonged to the captors and could not be taken away except by force. The risks of antagonizing the French were great and he was undisposed to incur them. This line of reasoning appealed to Washington and still seems sensible.

The question was argued hotly in a Cabinet meeting a few days later. Judging from the outline he preserved in the Anas, Jefferson then took a position he did not afterwards maintain, and was very excited about it. [35] Hamilton and Knox favored the restoration of the prize; if that were not possible they favored the ordering away of both privateer and prize, or at least the privateer. Jefferson took the position that neither should be ordered away. He believed at the time that the privateers had been outfitted by Frenchmen at their own expense before they knew what the rules were. Randolph favored the ordering away of the privateer alone, and Washington approved that position. The matter was by no means settled, for Genet did not cooperate; and the *Little Sarah*, under the name *Little Democrat*, was afterwards involved in a much more notorious episode. Eventually, after a sufficient time had elapsed for the United States to make its position clear, Jefferson recognized that his government did have a responsibility for the prizes. Opposing the opinion of Hamilton that force should be applied, he held that the United States was responsible for indemnifying the owners, and that the indemnification should be charged against the debt to France. [36] His original position was owing to his determination to avoid a break with France, and perhaps it marks the high water mark of his efforts in her favor.

[33] Well discussed in Thomas, pp. 188–196.
[34] May 16, 1793 (Ford, VI, 257–259).
[35] May 20, 1793 (Ford, I, 229).
[36] Aug. 5, 1793 (Ford, VI, 370, wrongly dated as Aug. 15).

Jefferson's disillusionment with Genet was progressive, and there is no certainty just when it began. More than two weeks after he first met the effervescent missionary, he wrote James Monroe:

> ... France has explained herself generously. She does not mean to interrupt our prosperity by calling for our guarantee [of the West Indies]. On the contrary she wishes to promote it by giving us in all her possessions all the rights of her native citizens & to receive our vessels as her vessels. This is the language of her new minister. Great Britain holds back with the most sullen silence and reserve. She has never intimated to our Minister a wish that we would remain neutral. Our correspondence with her consists in *demands* where she is interested, & *delays* where we are.[37]

This was true enough as applied to George Hammond and his government, but by this time Jefferson had received most unreasonable demands from Genet. A question arises, therefore, about his gullibility. This cannot be answered decisively, for his personal records, good as they are, do not tell us what he was really thinking about Genet at this moment. It may be noted, however, that he was drawing a contrast between the friendliness of the French and the unfriendliness of the British government, and that insofar as he expressed approval of Genet this was only with respect to the latter's commercial proposals. His failure to mention difficulties which had already arisen does not mean that he was unaware of them.

On the basis of his official correspondence, one may assume that he began to be disillusioned with Genet toward the end of May, but that he continued until about the middle of June to hope that the irrepressible envoy would prove teachable and amenable to reason. This period of suspended judgment ended when Genet virtually challenged the official American position about the arming of privateers and threatened to appeal from the President to "higher authority." The flagrant challenge and more direct threat which brought about his downfall occurred three or four weeks later.[38] Not until the end of June does Jefferson appear to have intimated his disquietude even to intimates.[39] But considerably before then he faced the multiple problem of upholding American policy, moderating Genet, avoiding a breach with France, and limiting the unfavorable political effects of the envoy's recalcitrance. The isolation which he described in such

[37] June 4, 1793 (Ford, VI, 281).
[38] The terminal dates for the period, as thus defined, are May 28, 1793, when TJ got Genet's letter of May 27, and June 14, when he got the letters of June 8 and 14 (*A.S.P.F.R.*, I, 149–152).
[39] To Monroe, June 28, 1793 (Ford, VI, 323). See below, pp. 109, 114.

painful terms to Madison arose from the fact that nobody else in the government was concerned about all these things, and that some of them were better kept hidden from even his closest friends. The President nearly always supported his method of patient reasonableness, however, even when his own patience was sorely tried.

The first sharp difference between the new minister of the French Republic and the President and Secretary of State appeared when, after reading official communications to his predecessor, he gave his own interpretation of French rights under the treaty of commerce.[40] The particular points at issue had been raised by the British minister, and Genet said afterwards that Jefferson's communications needed only the name of Hammond to render them perfectly British.[41] Perhaps the most flagrant assertion in his own officious and egotistical letter was that the French had not only the right to bring their prizes into American ports, which was conceded, but also to do what they liked with them after they got there. That is, French consuls could set up prize courts, in disregard of American sovereignty. The question of the assumption of consular jurisdiction is one on which Genet never yielded, and it was not decisively settled until the late summer when the President summarily removed an offending consul.[42]

A more pressing question was that of the arming and manning of privateers. Admitting that several vessels had been armed at Charleston and that they had taken many prizes, Genet saw no reason why anybody but the English should be displeased. Governor Moultrie of South Carolina had agreed with him that no law prohibited this. He admitted also that Americans had been enlisted in the crews, but saw no legal reason why they should be denied the privilege of defending their French brothers, or, renouncing the immediate protection of their own government, the right of taking part with France.

Far from offering everything and asking nothing, Genet contested everything and conceded virtually nothing. Jefferson's reply was restrained and kind, but firm.[43] He properly spoke in the name of the President, but the very fact that he did so may have given a false impression to Genet, who was indifferent to diplomatic forms and grossly ignorant of American governmental organization. The firmness of the American stand against the arming and equipping of privateers reflected Jefferson's own conviction, however, as well as that of his chief and the other executive officers. Through the

---

[40] Genet to TJ, May 27, 1793 (*A.S.P.F.R.*, I, 149–150).

[41] Genet to TJ, July 4, 1797 (Woodfin, Appendix A, from Genet Papers).

[42] Consul Duplaine of Boston. This whole question is well discussed in Thomas, pp. 205–220.

[43] June 5, 1793 (*A.S.P.F.R.*, I, 150).

Secretary of State, the President politely requested that such illegally equipped vessels be kept out of the ports of the United States.

Genet was pained to learn that the President persisted in an erroneous interpretation of the treaty and did not hesitate to set his own against it.[44] He did not refer this disputed question to his own government, abiding by the American interpretation in the meantime. Some concession, which bypassed the crucial question of the arming of privateers, he was willing to make in the name of friendship. "I have instructed the consuls," he said, "not to grant *letters* but to the captains, who shall obligate themselves . . . to respect the territory of the United States, and the political opinions of their President, until the representatives of the sovereign shall have confirmed or rejected them." By this he meant Congress, which in his uninformed opinion could overrule the President.

The Secretary of State received this letter the same day as another, written later, which was worse.[45] In this Genet protested violently against the action of officials in New York who had stopped a vessel in that port; this he described as being "in contempt of treaties." Jefferson replied more elaborately this time, delivering a firm though friendly lecture on the laws of the land, the law of nature, and the usage of nations.

To enter fully into correspondence bordering on the interminable is unnecessary, but some of Genet's comments in letters home are of great interest in the present connection. While still in the honeymoon period among the Philadelphia Republicans, whose cordiality he grossly misinterpreted, he wrote Le Brun: "the voice of the People continues to neutralize the declaration of neutrality of President Washington." He was too busy fraternizing to write home often. In his next communication, three weeks later, he said that despite the glittering popularity with which he was surrounded, he was encountering obstacles without number. He had blocked the designs of the aristocrats by his mission to the people, and the true republicans were triumphing, but "Old Washington" forgave him none of his success. "He impedes my course in a thousand ways and forces me to urge secretly the calling of Congress, the majority of which . . . will be decidedly in our favor." [46] At the same time he called the attention of his superior to his ventures in the West, assuring him that these were full of brilliant promise.

[44] Genet to TJ, June 8, 1793 (*A.S.P.F.R.*, I, 151).
[45] Genet to TJ, June 14, 1793; TJ to Genet, June 17, 1793 (*A.S.P.F.R.*, I, 152, 154-155). See also Cabinet Opinion of June 17 (Ford, VI, 306-307).
[46] Letters of May 31, June 19, 1793 (*C.F.M.*, p. 216).

ii

"I excite the Canadians to free themselve from the yoke of England; I arm the Kentuckians, and I prepare by sea an expedition which will support their descent on New Orleans." Thus the vainglorious minister of the French Republic wrote home.[47] All this was still in the realm of talk, not deeds, but it reflected Genet's purpose to carry out what able historians have regarded as the most important part of his instructions. Jefferson had been forewarned of the plans of the French against the Spanish, but there seems to be no evidence that their representative spoke to him about these specifically until after he, at Genet's request, had addressed to the Governor of Kentucky a letter introducing André Michaux. Insofar as Jefferson let himself get involved in these schemes, and thus departed from the path of fair neutrality, it was in this connection. Michaux therefore becomes for the moment an important minor character.

He was a French botanist who had been sent to America by the royal government years earlier (1785) on an exploring expedition with a view to the introduction into France of American trees, shrubs, and plants. This industrious naturalist, who had made botanical explorations on much of the Atlantic seaboard, proposed to the American Philosophical Society in December, 1792, an expedition beyond the Mississippi, asking their support. This they agreed to give, and Jefferson was active in the negotiations, besides subscribing to the expenses.[48] The Michaux expedition, originally designed to reach the Pacific Sea, had no discernible political purpose at the outset. Soon after the arrival of the envoy in Philadelphia, however, the botanist addressed to him a memoir of observations about French settlements in North America and kindred matters; and shortly he presented an account of his own journeys and expenses.[49] By the last week in June he had been selected by Genet as the French agent in the West and was preparing for his journey. At this time Genet, after a vain at-

[47] Genet to Minister of Foreign Affairs, June 19, 1793 (*C.F.M.*, pp. 217-218). The essential documents relating to Genet's western ventures are in the "Correspondence of Clark and Genet," *Annual Report, A.H.A., 1896*, I (1897), 930-1107; and "Documents on the Relations of France to Louisiana, 1792-1795" (*A.H.R.*, III, 490-516). The basic story is told by F. J. Turner in "Origin of Genet's Projected Attack on Louisiana and the Floridas" (*A.H.R.*, III, 650-671).

[48] Portions of the Journal of Michaux, 1785-1796, with an account of him, are in *Proceedings of the American Philosophical Society*, XXVI (1889), 1-145. TJ recorded a contribution in his Account Book, April 28, 1793.

[49] First communication dated May 18, 1793 (*ibid.*, p. 90).

tempt to get Jefferson to authorize the appointment of Michaux as a French consul in Kentucky, asked the Secretary of State to give him a letter of introduction to Governor Isaac Shelby. Jefferson did this, describing Michaux as a botanist, but Genet wanted something more. He then drafted another letter saying also that Michaux had the confidence of the French Minister and was commended for that reason.[50]

A couple of weeks later, that minister communicated his plans more specifically — to "Mr.Jeff," he said, not to the Secretary of State. Genet then read "very rapidly" instructions he had prepared for Michaux and addresses to the inhabitants of Louisiana and Canada. What Jefferson heard may have differed in some respects from the rather long French document now in the record.[51] Genet may not have read the whole of this aloud, and he read rapidly. Our knowledge of what Jefferson knew can therefore be best gained from his own memorandum. From this it appears that two generals in Kentucky had proposed to take New Orleans if a sufficient sum (about £3000) were forthcoming. He did not give their names, but Genet mentioned George Rogers Clark and Benjamin Logan in the official instructions and Jefferson must have identified them. Though unwilling to advance this sum of money, Genet promised that much eventually for expenses. He proposed that officers be commissioned by French authority in Kentucky and Louisiana, that their forces rendezvous *out of the territory of the United States*, and that Louisiana, when taken by them, should be established as an independent state, connected with the United States and France by commerce.

Jefferson thus recorded his own response to this information: "I told him that his enticing officers and soldiers from Kentucky to go against Spain, was really putting a halter about their necks, for that they would assuredly be hung, if they commenced hostilities against a nation at peace with the United States. That leaving out that article I did not care what insurrections should be excited in Louisiana." This was not the language of formal diplomacy and fair neutrality, but the episode must be viewed in the light of the current international situation. Owing to the delay in communication in that slow-moving age, Jefferson could not have expected to know that Great Britain and Spain had signed a treaty of alliance (May 25, 1793). Had he known this, his fears of both powers would have been accentuated. But he

[50] Memo. of July 5, 1793, also describing events of about a fortnight earlier (Ford, I, 236–237). The letter that Michaux bore with him was dated June 28, 1793 (*A.H.A. Report, 1896*, I, 984).

[51] *A.H.A. Report, 1896*, I, 990–995.

had unquestionably perceived a "lowering disposition" in both countries and had abundant reason at this juncture to be concerned about
Spanish relations.[52]

Two days after he put Michaux's letter of introduction into
final form, he wrote a long letter to the United States Commissioners
in Spain for the benefit of the government there.[53] This followed the
receipt of a letter from the Spanish agents in Philadelphia in which
they said that in view of alleged proceedings of the United States
with respect to the Indians in the Southwest, especially the excitation
of the Chickasaws to war against the Creeks, they foresaw that peace
with the United States was very problematical in the future.[54] Jefferson
asked some very pointed questions. "The principal object of the letter
being *our* supposed excitements of the Chickasaws against the Creeks,
and *their* protection of the latter, are we to understand from this, that
if we arm to repulse the attacks of the Creeks on ourselves, it will disturb our peace with Spain? That if we will not fold our arms and let
them butcher us without resistance, Spain will consider it as a cause of
war?"[55] Jefferson continued: "Unmeddling with the affairs of other
nations, we had hoped that our distance and our dispositions would
have left us free, in the example and indulgence of peace with all the
world." Nevertheless, the government was resolute. "If we cannot
otherwise prevail on the Creeks to discontinue their depredations, we
will attack them in force. If Spain chooses to consider our defence
against savage butchery as a cause of war to her, we must meet her
also in war, with regret, but without fear; and we shall be happier, to
the last moment, to repair with her to the tribunal of peace and reason."[56] This was a spirited communication.

At the moment he would have undoubtedly preferred that New
Orleans be in French rather than Spanish hands, though quite the reverse was true a few years later and he had already expressed the
opinion that this vital port must eventually be American. His attitude at this time can be much better described as anti-Spanish than
pro-French. While maintaining official correctness by protesting to
Genet against the enlistment of Americans, he was doing nothing more
as yet to deter that gentleman. He did not withdraw the letter he had
already written for Michaux, nor did he yet send warnings to Kentucky. Maintaining contact with Genet, whom he already distrusted

[52] For a general account, see S. F. Bemis, *Pinckney's Treaty* (1926), pp. 210–214.
[53] To Carmichael and Short, June 30, 1793 (Ford, VI, 330–338).
[54] Jaudenes and Viar to Secretary of State, June 18, 1793 (*A.S.P.F.R.*, I, 264–
265). The Spanish had no minister in the U. S. at the time.
[55] Ford, VI, 337.
[56] Ford, VI, 338.

but from whom he still stood to learn much about French plans, he maintained a position of watchful waiting. Unless we assume unrealistic gullibility on his part toward the French, as Federalist critics were disposed to do, it was a shrewd policy; and if we condemn it we must do so, not because it fell below the level of contemporary diplomatic maneuvering, but on the ground that it did not comport with his own interpretation of fair neutrality.

Since Genet always put the best face on everything in his reports to his superiors at home, his interpretation of Jefferson's conduct and attitude cannot be safely taken at face value. He did not pass on the warning against enticing Americans to enlist against Spain, and he said that Jefferson put him in touch with several representatives of Kentucky. Among these was Senator John Brown, who recognized that his part of the country could never flourish without the free navigation of the Mississippi and, in Genet's words, "adopted our plans with as much enthusiasm as an American can show." [57] We can no more judge of Brown's motives from Genet's account than we can in the case of Jefferson, and it may be guessed that he also was anti-Spanish rather than pro-French, but the Senator wrote for Michaux letters of introduction to George Rogers Clark and Governor Shelby, telling the latter that the bearer stood high in the confidence of the Minister of France.[58]

On July 15, Michaux set out at 10 P.M., seeking to escape the heat of the day and to travel in the light of the moon. He bore numerous letters of introduction besides Jefferson's and Brown's, and his mission was still ostensibly scientific, though his elaborate instructions from Genet were political and military enough. By the time of his arrival in Kentucky in September, Genet's recall had been requested. Meanwhile, the Spanish agents in Philadelphia, getting wind that a move against Louisiana from Kentucky was up, had protested to the United States government. The Secretary of State then made a proper official response to the diplomatic representatives of a country with which, contrary to his earlier expectation, peace had been maintained. This action may be attributable to the President, in whose name the Secretary of State necessarily spoke, but there is no reason to doubt that it was wholly in line with Jefferson's own appraisal of the existing situation. He wrote the Governor of Kentucky before Michaux reached that state, charging him to be on his guard and to take the

[57] To Minister of Foreign Affairs, July 25, 1793 (*C.F.M.*, p. 221).
[58] June 24, 1793 (*A.H.A. Report, 1896*, I, 982–983). The fact that these letters bear an earlier date than TJ's of June 28 may be without significance, since his letter was a second draft.

necessary legal measures against any attempt to excite the inhabitants of Kentucky to join an enterprise against the Spanish dominions. Also, he reminded the Governor that the special interests of the state were involved, since these were under negotiation between Spain and the United States.[59] Whether or not his hopes of securing the free navigation of the Mississippi by diplomatic means had revived by this time, forceful action was now out of the question. Furthermore, he was done with Genet for any number of other reasons.

With the story of what Michaux did in Kentucky in the fall of 1793 and of the continuing unrest in the region we are not concerned here. The failure of Genet's particular western schemes was completed when his successor, Fauchet, revoked the military commissions he had handed out and forbade Frenchmen to violate American neutrality (March 6, 1794). Jefferson was in retirement at Monticello before then. A few weeks later Washington, still sensing danger, issued a proclamation against the proposed expedition.[60] After a couple of months, Congress passed a law making the enlistment of American citizens in such expeditions a crime.[61] Until then a number of people, including Governor Shelby, doubted if there was any legal obstacle to such participation. From these official actions and from numerous references in contemporary letters, one might assume that under somewhat more favorable circumstances Genet's project could actually have got under way. On the other hand, Hauterive, the French consul in New York, thought his schemes of conquest fantastic.[62] A sufficient reason for their failure is that they were not supported by the French government after the fall of the Girondins. He carried the burden of them alone.

His actions in this connection did not enter into the devastating indictment of him which Jefferson drew in August. One reason for this was that the United States government then based its case on his official letters and public utterances. The complaints of the Spanish were not presented until the indictment of him was already drawn. Jefferson could not have been expected to publish his own memoran-

[59] Aug. 29, 1793 (*A.S.P.F.R.*, I, 455). Shelby replied on Oct. 5, recognizing his responsibilities but expressing the opinion that no move against the Spanish was then in contemplation. Important later letters are: TJ to Shelby, Nov. 9, 1793, and Shelby to Jefferson, Jan. 13, 1794, mentioning George Rogers Clark (*ibid.*).

[60] March 24, 1794. It should be noted that the unsigned Cabinet Opinion bearing on this question which Ford prints under the date March 10, 1793 (Ford, VI, 198) should be dated March 10, 1794 (see Thomas, p. 181). In other words, TJ had nothing to do with it one way or the other.

[61] June, 1794.

[62] F. S. Childs, "The Hauterive Journal," *New-York Historical Quarterly*, April, 1949; see esp. pp. 71–72.

dum of a private conversation which would have undoubtedly have been used to his political disadvantage at the time. A few years later he was saying in another private memorandum that in the letter introducing Michaux at Genet's request, he described him as a botanist.[63] This was true as far as it went but was less than the whole truth. Later still, at the age of seventy, when connecting Michaux's expedition with that of Lewis and Clark, he gave the impression, wittingly or unwittingly, that it was wholly unpolitical.[64] In this particular context he did not need to describe the expedition fully, and others besides him observed that, after all, Michaux was essentially a scientist, more interested in a rare plant than in intrigue.[65] Nonetheless this appears to be an instance, albeit a minor one, of Jefferson's evasiveness with respect to unpleasant matters. This evasiveness arose in part from the sensitiveness to the opinions of others which was one of the major explanations of his political success, in part perhaps from the wish to escape twinges of conscience over departures from his own standards. But if the full record, including his own private memoranda and the letters of Genet, reveals him as rather less than candid it does not reflect on his patriotism or his skill as a diplomatist.

On the very day that Jefferson wrote the Governor of Kentucky, introducing Michaux as one who had the confidence of the French minister, he expressed his own qualms about that minister in private. His concern did not arise primarily or even importantly from his fears that, through Genet, the United States might become embroiled with Spain. He was trying to maintain a maneuverable position with respect to that power, being prepared to adjust himself to whatever situation might arise. He was much more disturbed by the prospect that Genet would injure the French cause in public opinion. He wrote James Monroe: "I fear he will enlarge the circle of those disaffected to his country. I am doing everything in my power to moderate the impetuosity of his movements, and to destroy the dangerous opinion that had been excited in him, that the people of the U.S. will disavow the acts of their government, and that he has an appeal from the Executive to Congress, and from both to the people." [66] To this intimate personal and political friend Jefferson reported that American sentiment was only for peace. "The Executive here have cherished it

[63] March 27, 1800 (Ford, I, 287).

[64] In his sketch of Meriwether Lewis, April 13, 1813 (L. & B., XVIII, 145).

[65] See the comment R. G. Thwaites in *Early Western Travels*, III (1904), 13.

[66] June 28, 1793 (Ford, VI, 323). No doubt he had in mind Genet's letter of June 22, 1793 (*A.S.P.F.R.*, I, 155–156), which was so insulting that he left it unanswered.

[peace] with equal and unanimous desire. We have differed perhaps as to the tone of conduct exactly adapted to securing it." At the moment he was stressing the basic unity of the government, not the divisions among its officers.

Against Genet he was a champion of the Constitution and the prerogatives of the Executive. It was therefore no small embarrassment to him, just at this juncture, that Hamilton, whom he thought he had unhorsed on the field of theory, re-entered the lists. Writing as PACIFICUS, his colleague assumed the role of public defender of executive prerogatives, pressing these further than Jefferson thought legitimate or safe. Also, he assumed the role of defender of the peace and the Constitution while reading into the Neutrality Proclamation more than Jefferson believed was there.

Hamilton's PACIFICUS papers began toward the end of June and appeared twice a week thereafter through most of July — at just the time that Genet became utterly insufferable.[67] Ostensibly, the writer, whose identity was promptly recognized, was answering objections to the Neutrality Proclamation. These had been urged "in a spirit of acrimony," he said; they indicated a design to weaken confidence in the President; they represented opposition to the government and a danger to the Constitution and the peace. Such published criticism of the Proclamation as Jefferson had seen up to this time seemed to him the work of "mere bunglers and brawlers." One that he had in mind was an intemperate piece by VERITAS which had appeared in Freneau's paper early in June and which he believed to have been written by a clerk in the Treasury Department with the purpose of drawing Washington to the side of the "fiscal party." Genet revealed his irresponsibility by telling his superiors at home that the Secretary of State wrote this.[68] Jefferson's own criticisms of the form and timing of the Proclamation had been made only in private; and he believed that Hamilton was merely amplifying the arguments already advanced by him in the executive council.

In the very first paper Jefferson detected "heresies" which he feared would pass unnoticed, and he soon urged Madison to take up his pen, select the most striking of these, and "cut him [Hamilton] to pieces in the face of the public." [69] Madison, rusticating in Orange County, thought himself at a disadvantage because of incomplete information and assumed this formidable task reluctantly. The first of

[67] June 29–July 20, 1793 in *Gazette of the U. S.* (Lodge, IV, 135–191).

[68] Anas, June 12, 1793 and July 18, 1793 (Ford, I, 235, 244); Genet to Minister of Foreign Affairs, Oct. 8, 1793 (*C.F.M.*, p. 245).

[69] TJ to Madison, July 7, 1793 (Ford, VI, 338). See also TJ to Madison, June 29, 1793 (Ford, VI, 327).

the papers that he wrote under the name HELVIDIUS appeared late in August and the fifth and last in mid-September.[70]

The historic debate between PACIFICUS and HELVIDIUS is chiefly significant as dealing with the question of the respective powers of the executive and legislative branches of the government in the realm of foreign affairs.[71] Hamilton sought to define the executive function as broadly as possible, perceiving no limitations to it beyond those expressly stated in the Constitution. He assigned the initiative in foreign affairs to the executive, recognizing that Congress was under no constitutional obligation to back the President but assuming that it would necessarily give weight to what he had done. In reply Madison, denying the "extraordinary doctrine" that the powers of making war and treaties were executive in nature, asserted that the determination of foreign policy rested with Congress, since that body alone could declare war. In his view the powers of the President in this field were instrumental.

Whatever the intentions of the Fathers may have been, or the predominant contemporary opinion, later trends were in the direction of Hamilton's interpretation. The Neutrality Act of 1794 showed that neutrality lay within the jurisdiction of Congress, but the tendency has been to increase the powers of the President in this field and to recognize increasingly that he is the fount of foreign policy, even though he can be checked by Congress. The dilemma created by the necessity for efficacious action on the one hand, and the desirability of popular control on the other, has never been fully resolved under the American system. Madison's more democratic view was probably closer to that of the electorate at the time than that of Hamilton, to whom democracy meant mob rule, and his presentation of the case attracted the enthusiastic approval of a very great Secretary of State, John Quincy Adams, a generation later.[72] The immediate implications of Hamilton's position were clearly perceived by Madison, who was also playing for political advantage. At the very outset he said that the PACIFICUS papers were applauded by "the foreigners and degenerate citizens among us, who hate our republican government and the French revolution." Furthermore, he charged that Hamilton had bor-

[70] Aug. 24–Sept. 18, 1793 (Hunt, VI, 138–188, with pertinent correspondence in the notes). Madison devoted himself almost wholly to the issues raised by Hamilton's first paper.

[71] An admirable brief discussion of it is in E. S. Corwin, *The President: Office and Powers* (1948 edn.), pp. 216–221.

[72] Adams said that Madison "scrutinized the doctrines of Pacificus with an acuteness of intellect never perhaps surpassed and with a severity scarcely congenial to his natural disposition and never on any other occasion indulged" (*Eulogy on James Madison*, 1836, p. 46, quoted by Corwin, p. 466, n. 34).

rowed his idea of executive powers from the British royal prerogatives, especially those of making treaties and declaring war.[73]

With these partisan sentiments Jefferson undoubtedly agreed, and he raised no objection to any of Madison's arguments. As a member of the executive branch, however, he had good reason to be aware of its necessary exercise of power in foreign affairs. He knew that the next House of Representatives would be Republican, but he had no sympathy whatever with Genet's threat to appeal to Congress. Speaking of the President to the uncomprehending Frenchman a few weeks later, he said: "He being the only channel of communication between this country and foreign nations, it is from him alone that foreign nations or their agents are to learn what is or has been the will of the nation." [74] Several years earlier he had said: "The transaction of business with foreign nations is executive altogether"; and he had gone to pains to uphold the presidential prerogative against the Senate.[75] In the exercise of his own functions as secretary of state, especially in his dealings with the Spanish, he had not been reluctant to take the initiative. Without consulting Congress he even engaged in warlike diplomatic talk. Thus his position as an official aware of practical exigencies, and as an apostle of liberty and popular government who perceived the dangers of Hamilton's position, was anomalous.

The particular "heresies" that he himself called to Madison's attention had direct and immediate bearing on the existing situation. He resented the assumption of Hamilton that the President had the right to declare that the United States was not bound to execute the guarantee of the American territory of France, and that the Proclamation was such a declaration. He himself favored no express recognition of this embarrassing obligation and believed that the guarantee would not be invoked. But he was not willing to slough off treaty obligations that lightly and could never agree that they had been removed by this particular proclamation. He resented Hamilton's claim that until the new government of France was recognized the treaties were "of course" suspended. To him, and as he thought to Washington, they were unaffected by any change in government. Also, he denied the assumed competence of the executive to declare that neutrality was the determined policy of the government. Neither he nor Washington believed that the executive had the right to bind Congress.

Madison, assuming an unwelcome task at Jefferson's behest, made

[73] Hunt, VI, 138–139, 150.
[74] Nov. 22, 1793 (Ford, VI, 451).
[75] Opinion on the Powers of the Senate, April 24, 1790 (Ford, V, 161).

some telling points against Hamilton's more extreme contentions, thus warning him not to press executive claims too far. But the learned little Congressman could not relieve the harassed Secretary of State of his most immediate and most pressing problem. Jefferson's immense difficulties with Genet reached and passed their climax before Madison was well started.

[VII]

"Liberty Warring on Herself": The Downfall of Genet

AT THE same time that Jefferson asked Madison to enter the lists against Hamilton on the field of theory, he revealed to this intimate friend that he had come to the end of his patience with Genet. "Never in my opinion," he said, "was so calamitous an appointment made, as that of the present Minister of France here. Hot headed, all imagination, no judgment, passionate, disrespectful and even indecent toward the P. in his written as well as verbal communications. . . . He renders my position immensely difficult." [1] By then he had had plenty of time to mull over the letter which Hamilton shortly described as "the most offensive paper perhaps that was ever offered by a foreign minister to a friendly power with which he resided." [2] Jefferson drafted a reply to this extraordinary communication but never sent it, no doubt concluding that such a tirade had best be ignored. Worse still, Genet was now threatening to defy the government in the matter of the *Little Democrat*, as the brigantine *Little Sarah* was renamed after her capture from the British.

A few days earlier, at a meeting of Jefferson, Hamilton, and Knox in the former's office, approval was given a letter from the Secretary of War to Governor Thomas Mifflin of Pennsylvania, asking him to make particular inquiry whether or not this vessel was arming.[3] The President and Attorney General were out of town, though the former was expected back in less than a week. On the following day, Saturday, July 6, the Governor reported that the ship had entered the

[1] July 7, 1793 (Ford, VI, 338).
[2] J.C.H., IV, 444, referring to Genet's letter to TJ, June 22, 1793 (*A.S.P.F.R.*, I, 155–156).
[3] Anas, July 5, 1793 (Ford, I, 235).

port with four guns and now had fourteen. The Secretary of the Commonwealth of Pennsylvania, Alexander James Dallas, heard that she was to sail next day. Dallas, who was one of the leaders of Pennsylvania Republicanism as well as Mifflin's administrative assistant, offered to call on Genet and did so towards midnight. He tried to persuade the envoy to delay the departure of the *Little Democrat* until after Washington got back but was rebuffed in extravagant language. On Sunday morning, when Jefferson was at his place on the Schuylkill, he was informed of the expected departure of the vessel. Going immediately to town, he conferred with Mifflin and Dallas; then, while waiting for Knox, who had also been summoned, he himself went to see Genet.[4]

Jefferson's own account of this meeting is more colorful than any summary of it can be. Stating that the government had learned that the vessel had been armed contrary to the President's decision, he asked Genet, as Dallas had, to detain her until Washington's return. The Frenchman then took up the subject "in a very high tone," going into "an immense field of declamation and complaint." Jefferson's own efforts to take part in the conversation were wholly ineffectual, as he said with more humor than he normally displayed. The sum and substance of Genet's torrent of complaints was that the United States had violated its treaty obligations, and that he had been thwarted and opposed in everything. He asserted that the President should have consulted Congress and that he himself would press for the convening of that body. Eventually he subsided long enough to listen to an explanation of the American governmental system and a statement that all the questions that had arisen thus far belonged wholly to the executive department. Genet expressed amazement that Congress was not sovereign in all things, including the execution of treaties, and manifested his own low opinion of such a system. Jefferson conceded that he had a right to his own interpretation of the treaties, but pointed out that when the highest authority in the United States had reached a decision his proper course was to acquiesce in it after making representations to his own government. He thought that Genet recognized the rightfulness of this, while not admitting it.

Genet claimed that all the guns added to the armament of the *Little Democrat* were French property, but Jefferson suggested that he present proof and afterwards found out that at least two of them were not. He informed the minister that it would be regarded as "a very

[4] Memo. submitted to Washington, dated July 10, 1793 (Ford, I, 237–241, printed from the fair copy from the Washington Papers rather than the abbreviated form TJ retained for the Anas).

serious offense" if the vessel should go away. While making no promise, Genet said she was not yet ready to go to sea, though she would drop down the river. Jefferson assumed that she would not put to sea until Washington's return, as actually she did not. Consulting afterwards with Dallas, he learned that Genet had declared that he would appeal from the President to the people. More than anything else, this threat damned him in the public mind. It was not made to Jefferson in just these words and he spoke of it only in private, but Dallas repeated it to the Governor and it could hardly have failed to get out even if Hamilton and his friends had not afterwards made sure that it did.

On Monday, July 8, the Secretaries of State, the Treasury, and War met in the office of Governor Mifflin in the State House. Washington had previously instructed the governors to stop vessels arming in American ports, even by military force. He said later that he assumed they would detect these projects in embryo and stop them with a small number of men.[5] The threat now raised by the *Little Democrat* had gone far beyond the embryonic stage, and since the chief ministers were accessible, Governor Mifflin asked them what steps he should now take. In the judgment of Hamilton and Knox, he might justifiably have employed military force without consultation, and they asserted that the advice they now gave him was fully conformable with the spirit of the President's instruction. It was that a battery be set up below the city at Mud Island, supported by a body of militia who should be directed to stop the *Little Democrat* by force if she should attempt to depart before the pleasure of the President should be made known. Jefferson dissented from this opinion, while agreeing that legal action be taken against such members of the crew of the vessel as were American citizens.[6]

He was confident that the *Little Democrat* would not be ordered to sea before Washington's arrival. He believed that the erection of such a battery would almost certainly lead to bloody consequences and noted the expected approach of a large French fleet which would carry on a conflict that had been once begun. Even if the vessel should depart, he thought the British would have no just cause for complaint in view of American diligence and obvious intentions, and in view of the fact that, by impressment, they had taken far more Americans into their service than the French had. The latter

[5] Anas, July 15, 1793 (Ford, I, 243).

[6] The Opinion, dated July 8, 1793, drawn by Hamilton but reported by TJ, is in Ford, VI, 339–340, and J.C.H., IV, 438–439. The Reasons of Hamilton and Knox are in J.C.H., IV, 443–448; those of TJ are in Ford, VI, 340–344. See his memo. of July 10, 1793 (Ford, I, 241).

consideration probably weighed far less with the British than the former, but later events proved the correctness of his judgment, since they did not complain. He distinguished between Genet's improper actions and the friendliness of his government, and his own policy was undoubtedly colored by his predilections, but on pragmatic grounds it made good sense at this moment.

Hamilton's position was colored by his predilections in the other direction, and it reflected his proclivity to rely on force. In view of all that had gone before, he believed that failure to take decisive action would prostrate the government. The President had forewarned the French minister and had assured the British that effectual measures would be taken against such abuses. The taking of them would not, in his opinion, be considered as an act of hostility by France; but if they were not taken the British would have just cause for complaint and even for attack. Events were to prove that the British did not think so. If war was to be hazarded, he preferred that it be risked with the insolent French rather than with the British, who in his eyes were inoffensive though they were hardly that. He made telling points against the French, while Jefferson made rather less telling ones against the British, and his fears were those of Jefferson in reverse. If, however, the main purpose of the government was to maintain neutrality and remain at peace he was the less realistic of the two inveterate antagonists. Jefferson kept his head better and charted a wiser course.

Any governor might have been hesitant to act in the face of such divided counsel, and considerably before the arrival of Washington, who alone was able to speak decisively, the view of Hamilton and Knox lost all practical significance. Whether or not news of their recommendation got out, the *Little Democrat* fell down the river to Chester, well below Mud Island and out of reach of any battery which might be set up there. This was all the more exasperating to the advocates of coercion because no valid objection could be made to this movement. Genet had said that something of the sort was likely and he could claim that it did not amount to departure. Hamilton would probably have liked to stop the vessel anyway, but the policy of inaction which Jefferson favored, and which he thought the less dangerous policy, won victory by default.

Washington generally kept his head better than any of his counselors, but when he arrived in Philadelphia on the morning of Thursday, July 11, he was temporarily shaken out of his characteristic equanimity. He found waiting for him papers from Jefferson marked "instant attention"; he also found that at this supposedly critical hour the Secretary of State had left the city for his place near Gray's

Ferry.[7] Not knowing that Jefferson had been suffering from fever, he dispatched a peremptory request for an opinion from him "before tomorrow" since the *Little Democrat* might be gone to sea by that time. On receiving an explanation, however, the President appears to have quickly quieted down. The Secretary of State had supposed that Hamilton and Knox would give him the opinion on the *Little Democrat* that Hamilton had drawn, and also the reasons with which they supported it. Finding, however, that Hamilton had been unable to prepare copies, he was sending Washington the copies they had given him, along with his own reasons for differing with them. In a covering letter, Jefferson stated that he had received assurance from Genet *that day* that the vessel would not put to sea before the President's decision.[8] Washington had all the pertinent documents in hand when his council met on Friday.

There was now no point in arguing about physical resistance at Mud Island. Jefferson gained the impression that Washington wished force had been used to stop the *Little Democrat*, though he himself would not have ordered it if he had been there. A few days later he expressed impatience with the request of Mifflin for cannon to be set up on Mud Island.[9] The implication is that these were set up, at this late hour, but they entered no further into the discussion of the crucial situation created by Genet. The policy of military inaction, coupled with verbal remonstrance, was victorious by force of circumstance, and the government now entered upon a delaying action while seeking to resolve some of its own internal conflicts. On certain questions, including the right to forbid the arming of vessels in American ports and the desirability of prosecuting American citizens who had joined in hostilities against nations with which the country was at peace, the members of the council were agreed. On other points — including the right of a foreign power to increase its armament by mounting its own guns, and the recruiting of its own citizens — there was sharp disagreement, Jefferson taking the affirmative and Hamilton and Knox the negative side.[10]

Since these questions hinged on the interpretation of treaties and laws, it was decided that they all be referred to "persons learned in the

[7] The papers, presumably, were TJ's memo. of July 10, 1793 (Ford, I, 237–241). The knowledge Washington indicated in his letter of July 11 to TJ (Fitzpatrick, XXXIII, 4) could have been gained from this.

[8] Ford, VI, 340–341n., citing an undated letter (LC, 15420), presumably written July 11.

[9] July 15, 1793 (Ford, I, 243).

[10] See TJ's recapitulation (Ford, I, 241–243). He committed this to writing on July 13, the day after the meeting, and no doubt it reflected both the agreement and disagreement on particular points which were manifest on July 12.

law" — that is, to the Supreme Court — and that in the meantime certain specified ships, both French and British, should not depart until the further order of the President. The *Little Democrat* was covered, as was the British ship *Jane*, alleged to be augmenting her force; to her the Governor of Pennsylvania was ordered to give particular attention. Jefferson, speaking for the President, informed Genet and Hammond of these actions in identical letters.[11] A little later, in the name of the President, he asked the Supreme Court if their opinion would be available and if particular questions might be referred to them.[12] More than anyone else, Jefferson had urged this procedure, partly because he was the member of the government most oppressed by these perplexities, but Hamilton actually drew most of the proposed questions.[13]

Except for clarifying the minds of the executive officers, these efforts were wasted, for the Court declined the proposed consultation, thus setting an important negative precedent.[14] Considering "the lines of separation drawn by the Constitution between the departments of the government," the Chief Justice and his associates deemed it improper to act in this matter. The immediate consequence of their refusal was that the executive branch had to reach its own decisions about these questions of legality. As though anticipating the rebuff of the Court, the council drew up a brief list of rules governing belligerents.[15] Meanwhile, three or four days after Genet was formally requested to detain the *Little Democrat*, the impatient Frenchman had sent her to sea in defiance of the United States government.

The efforts of the executive branch to ease its burdens by recourse to the courts were rebuffed by a jury in the noted case of Gideon Henfield, a citizen of the United States who took service in Charleston on the French privateer *Citizen Genet* and was apprehended when that vessel came to Philadelphia. On the complaint of Hammond, Jefferson had referred this case to the federal district attorney in Philadelphia, to take such action as was warranted by law. The Attorney

[11] TJ to Genet, July 12, 1793 (Ford, VI, 345).

[12] To the Chief Justice and Judges of the Supreme Court, July 18, 1793 (Ford, VI, 351–352). See also Washington to the Justices, July 23, 1793 (Fitzpatrick, XXXIII, 28).

[13] Entire list of 29 questions in Ford, VI, 352–354n.; 21 of these in J.C.H., IV, 450–453, as from Hamilton. The remaining 8 have generally been attributed to TJ, but he himself assigned the last one to Washington (LC, 15550–15554).

[14] Chief Justice Jay and Asso. Justices to Pres. Washington, Aug. 8, 1793 (*Correspondence and Public Papers of John Jay*, III, 488–489).

[15] Considered July 29–30, 1793; final form, Aug. 3, 1793 (Ford, VI, 358–360 and note).

General declared Henfield punishable, as did Chief Justice Jay and Justice James Wilson. On July 27, an indictment against him was returned by the Grand Jury of a Special Court of the United States for the Middle Circuit of Pennsylvania, and his trial quickly followed.[16] Edmund Randolph assisted the District Attorney in the prosecution, while Henfield was defended by three lawyers prominently identified with the Republican party — Peter S. Duponceau, Jared Ingersoll, and Jonathan Dickinson Sergeant, son-in-law of Rittenhouse. Thus the trial assumed a political coloration. Despite the charge of the judge and indisputable evidence, the jury returned a verdict of "not guilty." Reporting that this was joyfully acclaimed, Freneau's paper asserted that the right of a citizen of the United States to enter lawfully on board a French privateer was now established.[17]

This was not the interpretation placed on the verdict by Jefferson as an official. Speaking for the government, he took the position that "no citizen has a right to go to war of his own authority; and, for what he does without right, he ought to be punished." [18] The absolving of Henfield by the jury he attributed to the claim of the accused that he was "ignorant of the unlawfulness of his undertaking," accompanied by his manifestation of contrition and his avowal of national patriotism. In his opinion the verdict amounted to a pardon, such as might have been granted under constitutional authority. Later events did not warrant so charitable an interpretation of Henfield's conduct; accepting Genet's "protection," he avowed himself a citizen of France and set forth on another venture which led to his capture by the British.

Jefferson's position in this episode was complicated by Genet's vehement language with respect to it and by the espousal of Henfield's cause by leading Republicans, who no doubt regarded this as a case of "political" prosecution. Also, it was clouded by legal uncertainties in his own mind. Though the Attorney General and members of the Supreme Court made their pronouncements, there was no specific law forbidding such actions as Henfield's until the passage of the Neutrality Act of 1794, and, judging from his later record, he could not have been expected to accord common-law jurisdiction to federal courts. An expression in his first letter to Genet on the subject, suggesting uncertainty that Henfield was punishable, was altered at the instance of Randolph and finally dropped at that of Hamilton.[19] The

16 Full account in Wharton, *State Trials*, pp. 49–89. For a better understanding of this case I am indebted to Archibald F. Robertson, Jr.

17 *National Gazette*, Aug. 3, 1793.

18 To Gouverneur Morris, Aug. 16, 1793 (Ford, VI, 381). See also TJ to Madison, June 2, 1793 (Ford, VI, 277).

19 TJ to Genet, June 1, 1793 (Ford, VI, 273–274 and note).

emissary's vehemence continued. The crime charged against Henfield, he said, the crime which his mind could not conceive and which his pen almost refused to state, was "the serving of France, and defending with her children the common and glorious cause of liberty." He claimed that Henfield and others like him had gained the rights of French citizens if they had lost those of American, and peremptorily demanded their release.[20] A little later he wrote: "Do not punish the brave individuals of your nation who arrange themselves under our banner, knowing perfectly well that no law of the United States gives to the Government the sad power of arresting their zeal by acts of rigor. The Americans are free; . . . they may change their situation when they please."[21] Jefferson soon came to discount this revolutionary rhetoric, and if there was doubt about this case in his own mind it did not get into his official or even his private letters. He kept his official record clear and shared the discomfiture which the outcome of this case brought to the executive department.

Genet interpreted the verdict as further proof that the people were for him, even if the President and presidential advisers hated him. He still made an exception of Jefferson, although he claimed that the Secretary of State had the feebleness to sign opinions of his colleagues which he condemned.[22] At almost the same moment the French Minister of Foreign Affairs was roundly berating Genet for trying to deal with a portion of the people rather than with the government, but unfortunately this letter did not arrive soon enough to do the missionary any good.[23] He claimed that he had gained the esteem and good wishes of "all Republican Americans."[24] This was considerably more than the truth but there was enough truth in it to embarrass Jefferson, who now wrote Madison: "He will sink the republican interest if they do not abandon him."[25]

That Genet stimulated democratic ardor at first is unquestionable, and it is a notable fact that in political terminology the word "democrat" was now coming to be interchangeable with "republican." The establishment of democratic or republican societies was a significant feature of the period, and this was attributed by leading Hamiltonians, as it has been by many historians, to the influence of Genet. The descripton of these societies as virtual replicas of the Jacobin clubs of

[20] To TJ, June 1, 1793 (*A.S.P.F.R.*, I, 151).
[21] To TJ, June 22, 1793 (*A.S.P.F.R.*, I, 156).
[22] July 31, 1793 (*C.F.M.*, p. 232).
[23] July 30, 1793 (*C.F.M.*, p. 228).
[24] *Ibid.*, p. 233.
[25] Aug. 3, 1793 (Ford, VI, 361).

France is not precise, for they had their roots in previous societies in both England and America and were in the spirit of the American Revolution. Furthermore, Genet had little familiarity with the Jacobin clubs, and in strict terminology he himself was not a Jacobin but a Girondin.[26] Without question, however, these societies became centers of criticism of governmental policies. About forty of them were set up between 1793 and 1800, the most important being the Democratic Society of Pennsylvania. This has been aptly described as the mother society, not merely because of its central location in Philadelphia and the prominence of its members but also because it sent out a circular urging the organization of similar societies throughout the country. Its constitution, adopted on July 3, 1793, was the work of Alexander James Dallas, Secretary of Pennsylvania, and it had a highly distinguished list of members — including David Rittenhouse, Dr. George Logan, Dr. James Hutchinson, Charles Biddle (a prominent merchant), and others of comparable economic and social status. The line taken by Hamilton and Knox was that this society "was put in motion by Mr. Genet and would by their corresponding societies . . . draw the mass of the people, by dint of misinformation, into their vortex and overset the government." [27] Jefferson appears to have had no connection with the Philadelphia society or any of the others, but he never had any doubt of their legitimacy, and in the executive council he defended them against attack.

Genet was more than an intolerable liability to the Republican party; this firebrand had become a menace to the peace. Jefferson was slow to doubt the sincerity of his original declaration to the President that France did not want to draw the United States into war by invoking the clause of guarantee, a declaration which he afterwards several times repeated in private conversation. In the latter half of July, the Secretary of State saw some signs that Genet would reluctantly acquiesce in the President's decision against the arming of French vessels; and, now that a French fleet had arrived, escorting a host of refugees from Santo Domingo, that he would abandon the idea of further armament in American ports as a matter too small to be worthy of his attention.[28] Jefferson soon became convinced, however, that Genet, despite all his protestations, really wanted to embroil the United States

[26] On the entire subject, see E. P. Link, *Democratic-Republican Societies, 1790–1800* (1942).
[27] TJ to Madison, Aug. 11, 1793 (MP, 16:55).
[28] Note of TJ given Washington, July 26, 1793 (Ford, I, 248–250).

in the war.[29] He seems to have come to this opinion when Genet urged upon the lawyers defending Henfield that it was the *duty* of the nation and of individual Americans to fly to arms whether or not France chose to invoke the guarantee of her territories.

Following the departure of the *Little Democrat*, Genet was emboldened by the outcome of the Henfield case and the arrival of the fleet, and he was still intoxicated by his dreams of territorial expansion. Had Jefferson been able to read his dispatches, he could have gained full confirmation of his fears. At just the moment that the executive officers were sealing the minister's fate by agreeing to a course of action against him, he was writing home: "The American people, enlightened by our efforts [*soins*] as to their true interests, want war despite their tame government. . . . It is necessary that all the new world be free and that the Americans second us in this sublime design." [30] Having learned nothing from Jefferson's exposition of the forms and procedures of the government, he had written home: "My real political campaign will begin with the session of Congress, and it is then that you will be able to judge your agent." [31]

Jefferson perceived as clearly as Hamilton that if Genet's gross indiscretions and wild threats became widely known the result would be just the opposite of what the envoy expected. The people would rally round the President, hostility to the French cause would increase, and the United States might be drawn into world conflict on the British side. The threat to appeal from the President to the people was a bombshell, and its explosion could simultaneously wreck Republican fortunes and the country's neutrality.

That this incorrigible man had to go was obvious, and Jefferson's best hope lay in distinguishing between the agent and his country, giving as little offense as possible to the latter and making it as easy as possible for his government to disown him. At the same time, Jefferson sought to limit as much as he could the exploitation of Genet's words and actions by the Hamiltonians. Patriotic and partisan motives were commingled in his mind, and their relative importance cannot be precisely measured, but if the preservation of neutrality was the main desideratum of public policy the careful and dignified course he pursued was to the best interests of the country. His most intimate letters give no inkling that he was thinking of his personal political fortunes at this juncture. On the last day of July he informed Wash-

29 To Madison, Aug. 11, 1793 (MP, 16:55).
30 To Minister of Foreign Affairs, Aug. 2, 1793 (*C.F.M.*, p. 235).
31 July 31, 1793 (*ibid.*, p. 233).

ington of his determination to retire at the end of another quarter from scenes to which, as he was more and more convinced, neither his talents, his tone of mind, nor his time of life fitted him.[32] Meanwhile, to his family and closest friends he again stated that he meant this retirement to be permanent.

On the day that the executive officers reached their decision about the *Little Democrat* (July 12), Hamilton proposed that the French government be requested to recall Genet, and Knox added that he be suspended from his functions in the meantime.[33] It is a pity that Jefferson did not take the initiative, but at that time apparently he had not quite made up his mind. He proposed the submission of Genet's correspondence to his government with friendly observations. This may have been only a defensive move and delaying action. He was prepared to go further than that when the question came up for final settlement. A few years later, referring to the scenes of 1793, he described himself as descending daily into the arena like a gladiator and suffering martyrdom in every conflict.[34] There seems to be no contemporary evidence, however, that he disagreed, except in minor details, with the form the final decisions took, and these were much more in his spirit than in that of Hamilton. The decisive meetings of the executive council were on the first two days of August.[35] There was unanimous agreement from the outset that a full statement about Genet's conduct, with his correspondence, should be sent Gouverneur Morris to be communicated to the French authorities. It was also unanimously agreed that the minister's recall should be requested, the only difference of opinion being that Jefferson wanted to express the desire "with great delicacy," while the rest favored the use of "peremptory terms." He carried his point in this matter, with the support of Washington, who favored a "temperate but strong" presentation. Had the French been sharply challenged, as Hamilton desired, they might have been more disposed to support Genet. Hammond, who was kept informed of official proceedings by Hamilton, scented the strong likelihood of war in that case.[36] Only Knox now favored relieving Genet of his functions. It was decided to inform him of the

32 To Washington, July 31, 1793 (Ford, VI, 360).
33 Memo., committed to writing July 13, 1793 (Ford, I, 243).
34 To Madison, Jan. 22, 1797 (Ford, VII, 108).
35 Actions up to Aug. 23, 1793, are summed up in an opinion of that date (Ford, VI, 397; J.C.H., IV, 468–469). Outlines of discussion in Anas, July 23, Aug. 1, 2 (Ford, I, 247, 252–254).
36 Thomas, p. 229, citing Hammond to Grenville, Aug. 10, 1793.

request for his recall. Jefferson had opposed this, believing that it would make him all the more active and irresponsible and in due course he himself mitigated that danger by delaying to inform him until after the missive to Morris was well on its way.

There was no serious disagreement on any of these points, but heated argument followed Hamilton's proposal that Genet's correspondence be published, along with a statement of proceedings, "by way of appeal to the people." Jefferson noted that Hamilton made three speeches of three-quarters of an hour each on this topic, saying that he was "as inflammatory and declamatory as if he had been speaking to a jury." [37] In this entire matter Hamilton advocated a "tough" line and addressed himself more to Washington than to his colleagues. With his exhortations he coupled references to the Democratic Societies and to attacks on the President in the partisan press. Knox chimed in, citing certain wild comments on Washington which threw that restrained gentleman into one of his rare but terrifying passions. Jefferson thought the President much impressed by this dark picture.

Hamilton was manifestly motivated by partisan considerations, and so was Jefferson. He wrote Madison: "Hamilton and Knox have pressed an appeal to the people with an eagerness I never before saw in them." If there was any inconsistency in his own opposition to this, it may be noted that he favored calling Congress ahead of schedule while they opposed it, and that there were sound patriotic reasons for not inflaming the public at this critical juncture in international relations. They stressed the domestic danger of overthrowing the government, while he scouted it. On partisan grounds alone, however, he could have been expected to oppose this obvious maneuver to exploit Genet's indiscretions and implicate the Republicans. He told the President in the presence of his colleagues that "the intention was to dismount him from being the head of the nation, and make him the head of a party." This particular danger was obviated at the moment by a delaying action on the part of Randolph, who was wiser in his "half-way system" on this occasion than Jefferson gave him credit for. The postponement which he proposed and Washington acceded to was sagacious, for, as Jefferson himself believed, the expected demonstrations of popular support for the President would make an appeal to the people on his part quite unnecessary. No appeal was made, though the issue raised by Genet did get before the public, partly through his own continued indiscretion, partly through the efforts of Hamilton and friends; and in due course the correspondence got to Congress.

[37] Memo., Ford, I, 253-254; TJ to Madison, Aug. 11, 1793 (MP, 16:55).

For the better part of three weeks Jefferson worked on the letter to Gouverneur Morris. A draft of this was read at a Cabinet meeting on August 15; and it was considered again paragraph by paragraph on August 20, when it was agreed to. Changes in wording and detail were made at the instance of Jefferson's colleagues, but the basic form and tone of the famous communication was owing to him. It was one of the ablest and most skillful of all his diplomatic papers.[38]

He presented a mass of complicated materials with an effect which was more than convincing; it was overwhelming. The supreme merit of his presentation lay in the fact that by letting Genet himself do so much of the speaking he caused that emissary to convict himself. In his purpose to limit the indictment to what had actually passed between Genet and the American officials he was supported by Edmund Randolph. Hamilton would have liked to refer to Genet's unofficial actions and improper private conduct, but his official letters were more than enough to condemn him. Jefferson drew a sharp line of distinction between his conduct and the purposes of his government. French official records which are now available to us show that the main difference lay in the means employed by the envoy rather than in the ends he sought, but as a diplomat, and certainly as one who wanted to avoid a breach with France, the Secretary of State followed a wise course. It was proper to assume what he did until events had proved his assumption unwarranted. To have done otherwise would have been to risk contradiction and rebuff. The request for Genet's recall was in no sense peremptory, as Hamilton desired. Jefferson said that the United States was not suspending Genet's exercise of his functions and hoped it would not need to. For friendship's sake the French were expected to remove a representative who had proved so offensive.

While there are strong expressions of friendship for France in the letter, one that was favorable to the "general cause of liberty" was finally left out. According to Jefferson, this was the only thing on which there was not unanimity when the executive officers went over the letter paragraph by paragraph.[39] He had used the expression "liberty warring on herself" — meaning that such would be the case if the United States, a free nation, should be embroiled in war with the free nation of France. Hamilton objected to the identification of that country with the cause of liberty; and, although Washington agreed

[38] The executive officers decided that the letter should bear the date of the latest accompanying document, i.e., Aug. 16, 1793. In final form it is in Ford, VI, 371–393.

[39] Memo. of Aug. 20, 1793 (Ford, I, 259–260).

with Jefferson, the majority opinion was on the other side. In view of the trend toward despotic rule which had already appeared in the embattled French Republic, Hamilton's objection was far from pointless and this particular document was probably more effective without the expression. It had meaning, however, beyond what Jefferson himself now gave it, for the excesses of Genet and other revolutionaries not only injured the cause of France but the "general cause of liberty" as well. Jefferson did not yet escape, if indeed he ever did, from his tendency to endow abstract ideas with the attributes of personality; and his devotion to timeless causes, most of all that of human freedom, was a major element in his greatness; but as a responsible statesman he had to face painful realities and he would have been ineffective if he had not been educable. Genet, while intensifying his problems, contributed no little to his education.

Most of the policies which were set forth in this letter, in connection with the successive items in the indictment of Genet, had already been described to that minister in official communications as issues arose. No reference was made to his territorial designs, which did not enter into his official correspondence with the government. The most important of his offenses which had not been well covered by correspondence was his defiance of the authority of the United States government.[40] To say that he had assumed "a new and bolder line of conduct" than was customary in diplomatic representatives was an understatement, but Jefferson's bill of particulars against him was devastating enough. "When the government forbids their citizens to arm and engage in the war, he undertakes to arm and engage them. When they forbid vessels to be fitted in their ports for cruising on nations with whom they are at peace, he commissions them to fit and cruise. When they forbid an unceded jurisdiction to be exercised within their territory by foreign agents, he undertakes to uphold that exercise, and to avow it openly." The Secretary of State described in detail the episode of the *Little Democrat* as an instance of insult and defiance.

Besides all this, Genet had undertaken to direct the American government, presuming to pronounce what powers should be exercised by the executive and legislative branches and criticizing particular actions of the President. Nothing was said about the threat to appeal from him to the people, but an array of contemptuous expressions about him and the government, drawn from his official letters, was presented in French. As Jefferson said, these required no commentary.

[40] Section 6 in TJ's letter of Aug. 16, 1793 (Ford, VI, 388-391).

This masterly letter, which condemned Genet for all time out of his own mouth, ended with several paragraphs of restrained eloquence such as is not often met with in diplomatic documents. The references to Franco-American friendship and the desire for its continuance ought to have gratified all but the most rabid of Republicans. Hamilton could hardly have liked these, but he and his colleagues approved the letter. Posterity has approved it for reasons well expressed a generation later by John Quincy Adams. In this entire controversy with Genet, he said, Jefferson "triumphantly sustained and vindicated the administration of Washington without forfeiting the friendly professions of France." Adams, certainly one of the greatest of all secretaries of state, added this word of praise: "Mr. Jefferson's papers on that controversy present the most perfect model of diplomatic discussion and expostulation of modern times." [41]

Jefferson sent his long and unanswerable letter to Gouverneur Morris on August 23 by special messenger. Two or three weeks later he transmitted a copy of it to Genet, saying in his covering note that it was necessary to have in the United States a representative of France who was "disposed to respect the laws and authority of the country." [42] A regard for the interests of France, he said, induced the executive in the meantime to receive Genet's communications in writing and to admit the continuance of his functions so long as they should be "restrained within the limits of the law" as previously announced to him, or should be "of the tenor usually observed towards independent nations by the representatives of a friendly power residing among them." This sharp rebuke was accompanied by a statement that, since Genet had not restrained the proceedings of the French consuls, the President would do so by the authority of the country. If charges against the consul in Boston were proved, his exequatur would be revoked.[43]

Genet's intemperate reply showed that he had learned nothing about the constitutional framework of the government of the United States. To him the action of the President, in seeking the recall of a representative of the French people who had been recognized by the "sovereign People of the United States" even before diplomatic forms had been fulfilled, was utterly incomprehensible. This revolutionary pressed the doctrine of the sovereignty of the people to the uttermost

[41] *Parties in the United States* (1941 edn.), p. 17.

[42] The covering note in Ford, VI, 429–430, is assigned the date of Sept. 15, 1793. I find no record of it in TJ's Index to Letters, but Genet replied on Sept. 18.

[43] It was revoked Oct. 3, 1793, TJ to Duplaine (*A.S.P.F.R.*, I, 178).

point of absurdity. Professing adoration of the cause of liberty, which in his mind took precedence over all others, he again called for an appeal to Congress — defending in the meantime all of his official acts. This unrepentant letter was written in New York, where he was carrying on his mission at the moment, and under the abnormal circumstances of the yellow-fever epidemic Jefferson did not get it for two and a half months.[44] By then the President had decided to submit to Congress the correspondence between the French minister and the Secretary of State.

Had Jefferson received the letter in the customary time and shown it to Washington, it might well have increased the already strong pressure to suspend Genet's functions. During the intervening weeks, the emissary manifested his adoration of liberty and disregard of American constituted authority in words rather than deeds, but the "venom of his pen" in the letters actually received was so felt by Washington that the President himself raised the question of his dismissal in November.[45] Hamilton and Knox strongly favored this, while Randolph and Jefferson opposed it. The grounds taken by the Secretary of State were that France was still the only sincere friend of the United States, that according to precedent so harsh a measure would lead to war, that response to the request for Genet's recall could be expected shortly, that Congress was soon to meet. Speaking of Congress and identifying himself completely with the administration, he said: "They are with us now, probably, but such a step as this may carry many over to Genet's side." Randolph took the same position, and in the absence of unanimity Washington reluctantly left things as they were.

Official word was so slow in coming from France that Jefferson did not learn of the success of his own representations in the year 1793, while he was still secretary of state. Morris got his letter in about six weeks (on October 5); he sent it promptly to the French Minister of Foreign Affairs, and within two weeks (on October 19) he dispatched to America a letter from that official assuring him that Genet would be recalled.[46] This had not arrived when Jefferson left Philadel-

<hr />

[44] Genet's letter of Sept. 18, along with several others, was received at the Department of State when TJ, along with most officials of the government, was away from Philadelphia because of the yellow fever. Forwarded to Monticello, it missed him there and he got it only on Dec. 2 (*A.S.P.F.R.*, I, 172–174, with editorial note). The date is confirmed by TJ's Index.
[45] Notes of TJ on conference of Nov. 8, 1793 (Anas, Ford, I, 265–268).
[46] *A.S.P.F.R.*, I, 372, 374–375.

phia for Monticello early in January, 1794.[47] Not until Washington's birthday did Genet's successor, Fauchet, present his credentials. These circumstances called for patience and forbearance on the part of both Jefferson and Washington that was comparable in degree to the indiscretion of Genet.

What went on in French official circles Jefferson never fully knew. The Girondins had long since given way to the Jacobins, and Deforgues had replaced Le Brun in the Foreign Office. On the strength of Genet's own dispatches the Jacobin minister was much displeased with his procedure, viewing his disregard of the constituted authorities while appealing to the people as absurd, and his neglect of his instructions to get provisions from America as inexcusable.[48] Toward the end of September, before Jefferson's letter to Morris had been received, a report on Genet's conduct was drawn in the Foreign Office.[49] This very critical document declared that Genet, "carried away by indiscreet zeal, exceeded the powers which had been given him." Yet the report recognized that his intentions were very patriotic, and that the "infatuation" of the party with which he had identified himself could be useful. The party was described as consisting of the warmest Republicans, of those who were "truly devoted to France and ready to make every sacrifice for her." Therefore, in September it was judged unwise to recall Genet, though imperative to restrain his impetuosity and prescribe a more measured policy toward the government, so as to gain its confidence. The main criticism was of the means employed by him, not of the ends he sought, and much of his judgment about the degree of loyalty to France among Americans was accepted.

After receiving Jefferson's letter in October the French Foreign Minister wrote one containing the following passage: "The President of the United States has done justice to our sentiments in attributing the deviations of the citizen Genet to causes entirely foreign from his instructions, and . . . so far from having authorized the proceedings and criminal manoeuvres of citizen Genet, our only aim has been to maintain, between the two nations, the most perfect harmony."[50] This was disingenuous in view of Genet's actual instructions; before the year was out he published them in part, omitting sections dealing

47 On Feb. 26, 1794, it was submitted to the Senate as part of Morris's official correspondence (*ibid.*, p. 329). It had not been received by Jan. 10, when Edmund Randolph wrote Morris (*ibid.*, p. 402).

48 Especially letter of July 30, 1793 (*C.F.M.*, pp. 228–231).

49 *C.F.M.*, pp. 283–286.

50 Oct. 10, 1793 (*A.S.P.F.R.*, I, 375). It was this letter that Morris forwarded on Oct. 19 and which arrived after TJ left Philadelphia.

with his territorial projects.[51] Robespierre, attacking the foreign policy of the Girondins in a speech to the Convention a little later, denounced Genet more strongly; and his successor, Fauchet, was instructed to put him under arrest for return to France. (The American authorities refused to co-operate in this, and he was not arrested.) In their American policy, however, the Jacobins differed from the Girondins chiefly in their greater practicality.

It would appear, therefore, that Jefferson's interpretation of the attitude of the current group of revolutionary leaders was less realistic than his view of the total international situation. He erred little in his judgment of the British and the Spanish, who could be measured by traditional diplomatic standards. The French revolutionaries, Girondins or Jacobins, set their own standards. Their devotion to the sacred cause of liberty, while vociferous, was less pure than he supposed; and they did not yet regard the United States as a genuinely independent nation. Furthermore, they expected to continue their exploitation of republican zeal, and this policy continued to redound to the disadvantage of the Republican party. More immediately, that party suffered from the exploitation of Genet's indiscretions by the Hamiltonians. If Jefferson's own prestige suffered little diminution, it was because the course he followed, with only minor aberrations, was both wise and patriotic, and in the end he stood revealed as a patient but persistent upholder of fair neutrality.

[51] Louis-Guillaume Otto, "Considérations sur la conduite du Gouvernement américain envers la France," *Bulletin de l'Institut Français de Washington*, Dec., 1943, p. 23; Bowman, "Struggle for Neutrality," p. 112.

[VIII]

Politics and Yellow Fever

INFORMING the President of his determination to return to private life at the end of September, Jefferson said that he could now withdraw without exciting "disadvantageous opinions or conjectures." [1] The Secretary of the Treasury had not renewed the campaign against him in the newspapers but was directing his fire against critics of the Neutrality Proclamation and extreme partisans of France. It is true that some members of Hamilton's camp questioned the patriotism of the Secretary of State. On the very day that Jefferson wrote Washington about retiring, an anonymous citizen made a veiled attack on him in Fenno's paper, asking this question: "What punishment can and ought to be inflicted on a man, if such an one there be, who, holding an office of importance, prostitutes that office to the purposes of party; and thereby hazards the peace, happiness and prosperity of his country?" [2] Yet, during the summer, partisan writers found a much better target in Genet.

Washington took no stock in insinuations of this sort. On a visit to Jefferson at the latter's house in the country he said that his repentance at not having himself resigned was increased now that he was to be deserted by those he had counted on.[3] Hamilton had told him that he purposed to retire at the end of the next session of Congress — a thing which actually he did not do. Washington recognized the special difficulty presented by the secretaryship of state. For this office mere talents would not suffice, he said: it "required a person conversant in foreign affairs, perhaps acquainted with foreign courts." The troubles of the first President in manning his executive departments help to explain not only his reluctance to part with tested officials but also some

[1] To the President, July 31, 1793 (Ford, VI, 360).
[2] A CITIZEN OF THE UNITED STATES, in *Gazette of the U. S.*, July 31, 1793.
[3] TJ's memo. of Aug. 6, 1793 (Ford, I, 256).

of the unfortunate appointments of his last years in office. He hoped that Jefferson, like Hamilton, would stay through the next congressional session; then, having two appointments to make, he could consult the geographical situation as well as the talents of possible successors. Finally, he asked if Jefferson would remain another quarter, that is, until the end of the year; and, after a few days, Jefferson reluctantly consented to do so, on the understanding that he might make a visit home in the autumn.[4]

The discussion of the domestic political situation by these two men amounted to mutual reassurance. Jefferson was confident that the Republicans were loyal to the government and that they would abandon Genet as soon as they learned of his conduct. In his own opinion, "no crisis existed which threatened anything." Washington in turn reasserted his own opposition to monarchy, which Jefferson had never doubted, and declared that if there were those who wanted to abandon republicanism they were insane, since the public would never support them. The President thought that his Secretary of State exaggerated monarchical dangers, while Jefferson thought that Washington exaggerated those of public criticism, but their relations were grounded on mutual respect and understanding. There was nothing approximating a breach between them while they served together.

A load was taken off Jefferson's mind when a definite terminus was set for his official labors, even though it was farther off than he liked. His friend Madison was relieved to learn that he would remain through another quarter, believing this would be conducive to the maintenance of peace with France.[5] Monroe regretted his retirement more keenly and went to greater lengths in emphasizing the political value of his services. "I consider your situation the most important and interesting that can be conceived," he said. "Its importance is felt by the opposite party in such a degree that although in one view they would be gratified by your retreat, yet they fear greater injury to themselves from that event than your continuance, and therefore wish it. They know the solidity of your principles founded on reason and reflection, and in case the republican party should pass that boundary, count upon your restraining them; because they well know that that party repose an unlimited confidence in you."[6]

In interpreting the attitude of the Hamiltonians, Monroe may have

[4] TJ to Washington, Aug. 11, 1793 (Ford, VI, 366–367); Washington to TJ, Aug. 12, 1793 (Fitzpatrick, XXXIII, 45). Their discussion of possible successors will be referred to hereafter.
[5] Madison to TJ, Sept. 1, 1793 (Hunt, VI, 194).
[6] Monroe to TJ, Sept. 3, 1793 (S.M.H., I, 275–276).

engaged in wishful thinking, but as the Genet affair progressed the hostility of this group to Jefferson perceptibly declined. He told Washington that he had no communication with the Republican party in Philadelphia. To the President and others he lamented that he had to move in the circle of "aristocrats," merchants closely associated with England, and the holders of newly created paper fortunes, where his own views were most disliked. He had no part in the celebrations for Genet and the excesses of Freneau. His chief political influence at this juncture was exerted on his special friends in Virginia, whose conduct was directly affected by his counsel.

The party policy which he recommended is well described in a highly confidential letter he wrote Madison in the middle of August, telling him to reveal its contents only to Monroe.[7] His recommendations on fiscal matters represented a continuance, in spirit, of the attack on Hamilton in the last Congress. Since the Republican interest would be stronger in the new House of Representatives, he thought the time would be ripe for a division of the Treasury "between two equal chiefs of the Customs and Internal taxes." The main difficulty would lie with the Senate. He believed that a declaration of "the true sense of the Constitution" respecting the Bank, even if made by a single house, would suffice to divorce that institution from the government, and that the censurable actions admitted by Hamilton in his reports to the last Congress should be censured. Nothing of value came of these recommendations and they suggest that in advocating an attack on Hamilton on strictly fiscal grounds he was unrealistic.

Quite otherwise were his recommendations in regard to the policy of neutrality. Since the facts declared in the Proclamation were true, and the desire for neutrality was universal, he believed that the Republicans would appear in a very unfavorable light if they quibbled about small points of propriety. The conduct of Genet, he said, was exciting the indignation which was to be expected. "The towns are beginning generally to make known their disapprobation of any such opposition to their government by a foreigner, are declaring their firm adherence to their President, and the Proclamation is made the groundwork of these declarations." Even Philadelphia was going from him entirely. He summed up his recommendation thus: "So in Congress, I believe that it will be true wisdom in the Republican party to approve unequivocally of a state of neutrality, to avoid little cavils about who should declare it, to abandon Genet entirely, with expressions of strong friendship and adherence to his nation and confidence that he has acted

[7] Aug. 11, 1793 (MP, 16:55). Not to be confused with an earlier letter of the same date (Ford, VI, 367-371).

against their sense. In this way we shall keep the people on our side by keeping ourselves in the right." Here public and partisan interests undoubtedly coincided

In this letter, better than anywhere else, perhaps, Jefferson described the cruel dilemma in which Genet's conduct had placed him. "I adhered to him as long as I could have a hope of getting him right, because I knew what weight we should derive to our scale by keeping in it the love of the people for the French cause and nation, and how important it was to ward off from that cause and nation any just grounds of alienation. Finding at length that the man was absolutely incorrigible, I saw the necessity of quitting a wreck which could not but sink all who should cling to it." He then told Madison of the decision to ask Genet's recall, and of his own effort to prevent the airing of the whole business.

Before the middle of August the rumor of Genet's threat to appeal from the President to the people got into the newspapers. Hamilton mentioned it in the first of his communications as No Jacobin, and on August 12, in New York, John Jay and Rufus King gave it to the press.[8] The Chief Justice of the United States and the Senator from New York had picked up the report in Philadelphia. Apparently they felt safe in announcing it, but King wrote Hamilton for information, and the Secretary of the Treasury promptly gave them a full story.[9] This agrees in all essentials with Jefferson's own private records, but from the legal point of view it had one serious weakness: the information about the threat had come to Hamilton third hand, since Dallas, the only man who heard it, repeated it to Mifflin and Jefferson, and Hamilton could have learned of it only through them. He did not authorize King to use all the information he sent, but he marked certain passages as usable and these definitely involved Dallas, Mifflin, and Jefferson. Ten days later he was not fully determined whether a full story of the affair should be published, though he was inclined to think so, nor was he sure whether it was necessary to say to whom Dallas reported the conversation. If it should be necessary, he and Knox were willing to be witnesses.[10] He does not appear to have been much

[8] Hamilton's No Jacobin papers in Lodge, IV, 198–229, are inadequately dated. They appeared originally in Dunlap's *Daily Advertiser*, July 31–Aug. 23, 1793, and were reprinted in *Gazette of the U. S.*, beginning Aug. 31. The announcement of Jay and King was reprinted in *National Gazette*, Aug. 17, from New York *Diary*, Aug. 13. It is in King, *Life and Correspondence*, I, 459.

[9] Hamilton to King, Aug. 13, 1793 (King, I, 455–457). Later documents in the case follow, pp. 458–480.

[10] Hamilton to King, Aug. 23, 1793 (King, I, 457).

troubled by questions of official propriety, nor to have manifested any satisfaction in the governmental decisions already reached respecting the French envoy.

Not yet knowing that the American government was requesting his recall, Genet was as bumptious as ever. He was in New York and as soon as he saw in a newspaper there the announcement of Jay and King, he addressed a letter to the President, asking that dignitary to declare that Genet had never intimated to him any intention of appealing to the people. Jefferson replied to this, informing him that the President was to be addressed only through the Secretary of State and that he declined to interfere in this case. Genet, with customary effrontery and with indiscretion beyond his own high average, gave both letters to the press. Jefferson saw them in print on August 24.[11]

Commenting on these events to Madison, Jefferson said that, by throwing down the gauntlet to the President, Genet was "forcing that appeal to the public, and risking that disgust," which he himself was so anxious to avoid. In his own opinion, there were already sufficient indications that "the mass of the republican interest" disapproved of this "intermeddling by a foreigner, and the more readily as his object was evidently, contrary to his professions to force us into the war." This astute observer thought it not impossible however, that some of the "more furious republicans" would schismatize with him.[12] A little later, reflecting painfully on what all the papers were filled with, he lamented the fact that Genet's conduct had enabled "the enemies of liberty and of France" to show "a style of acrimony against that nation" which they would never before have dared to adopt.[13] Even Dr. Hutchinson and Dallas had given up Genet, and the former said that he had "totally overturned the republican interest in Philadelphia." As for his threat to appeal to the people, Jefferson assured Madison that it was a fact.

Certain correspondents of Freneau's paper, whom Jefferson would have designated as "furious Republicans" and whose identity he did not know, claimed that this appeal was rightful. One of these asked if the President was a *consecrated* character, so that an appeal from his decisions must be considered criminal, and if the *people* were in such a state of monarchical degradation that the talk of consulting them was an offense as it would have been under the old French system. Following Genet's line precisely, this writer claimed that the legislature of the

---

[11] Genet to Washington, Aug. 13, 1793; TJ to Genet, Aug. 16, 1793 (copied by Dunlap's *American Daily Advertiser*, Aug. 24, and by *National Gazette*, Aug. 28, from New York *Diary*, Aug. 21).

[12] To Madison, Aug. 25, 1793 (Ford, VI, 397-398).

[13] To Madison, Sept. 1, 1793 (Ford, VI, 401-402).

Union was but the People in Congress assembled, and that if there was a difference of opinion between the President and the French minister, the people should determine the question.[14] Other writers resorted to doggerel verse, of which the following is a sample:

> Let aristocrats say how wounded they feel,
> On hearing Genet's democratic *appeal*.
> But true sons of freedom their freaks shall deride,
> As founded alone on *monarchical* pride.
> Tho' *Jay, that great judge,* and the *senator King,*
> To join in their clamours, their evidence bring;
> Yet freemen will see how vain their attempt,
> And treat it as freemen with sovereign contempt.[15]

Freneau himself did not waver in his support of Genet. Early in September he reprinted the French Declaration of the Rights of Man and the Citizen, following it a few days later with the American Constitution.[16] He and some others, still living in a world of abstractions, emphasized the first of these documents over the second. They provided another instance of "Liberty warring on herself." At just this time the yellow fever which was raging in Philadelphia, and which soon distracted attention from all political questions, deprived the Republicans of their most beloved local leader. The death of Dr. James Hutchinson was attributed by Dr. Benjamin Rush, one of the few people who disliked him and that on professional grounds, to his "dining too heavily with Jefferson down at Gray's Ferry in the open air." [17] At all events, he was taken sick that night and died on September 6. Jefferson himself said: "It is difficult to say whether the republican interest has suffered more by his death or Genet's extravagance." [18]

About the middle of August, Jefferson wrote Madison that addresses in support of the Proclamation of Neutrality were becoming universal, "and as universal a rising in support of the President against Genet." [19] No valid objection could be raised by him or any other patriotic citizen to such resolutions upon their face, but he readily perceived their partisan implications. Promoted by what he regarded as the pro-British and monarchical faction, they were designed to exploit the Presi-

[14] JUBA, in *National Gazette,* Aug. 21, 1793. See also letter signed ALCANOR, *National Gazette,* Aug. 17, 1793.

[15] *National Gazette,* Sept. 28, 1793, from a Norfolk paper. See also the verses in *National Gazette,* Sept. 4, 1793, which may have been Freneau's own.

[16] *National Gazette,* Sept. 4, 7, 1793.

[17] J. H. Powell, *Bring Out Your Dead* (1949), p. 86.

[18] To Madison, Sept. 8, 1793 (Ford, VI, 419).

[19] Aug. 18, 1793 (Ford, VI, 394).

dent's popularity to the advantage of that faction and of Hamilton's interpretation of neutrality.[20] While Jefferson was demonstrating his own patriotism behind the scenes, in his representations to and about Genet, and was limiting his partisan activities to private letters to Madison and Monroe, Hamilton and his followers were incessantly active in promoting these patriotic resolutions, which were such an effective rejoinder to the over-enthusiastic addresses made a few weeks earlier to the French envoy.

The need to counter this campaign was impressed upon the Republican leaders of Virginia by the adoption in Richmond of resolutions similar to those emanating from Hamiltonian circles elsewhere. To their chagrin this meeting, in which John Marshall was active, was presided over by Jefferson's old law teacher, George Wythe, the purity of whose patriotism no man could question.[21] They would have been equally chagrined to learn that Washington asked Hamilton to draft a reply to this address, though they could hardly have found the reply exceptionable.[22] The plan devised by Madison and Monroe to meet this situation was to promote a series of meetings in Virginia counties, and the adoption of resolutions of a suggested type. While affirming devotion to the Constitution and loyalty to the President, these resolutions warned that attempts to alienate the American people "from the cause of liberty and republican government in France" would tend to weaken their affection toward the free principles of their own government. Also, they warned that a dissolution of the French connection would tend toward a British connection, and the form and spirit of the British monarchy.[23]

Madison and Monroe were reluctant to repudiate Genet as completely as Jefferson recommended. This was especially true of Monroe. Perceiving the extreme difficulty of keeping the popular feeling toward the minister distinct from that toward France, he could hardly prevail on himself, "absolutely and *openly*," to abandon him.[24] In the sample resolutions which Madison sent Jefferson, there was only a veiled reference to Genet in the recommendation that judgment regarding the conduct of particular individuals be suspended until full information became available. But Madison expected the suggestions

[20] Washington's answers to a number of these addresses are in Fitzpatrick, XXXIII.

[21] Meeting of Aug. 17. Madison to TJ, Aug. 27, 1793 (Hunt, VI, 179n.).

[22] Washington to Sec. Treasury, Aug. 27, 1793, and letter "To the Inhabitants of Richmond" (Fitzpatrick, XXXIII, 70–72).

[23] Suggestions sent by Madison to TJ as a sample, Sept. 2, 1793 (Hunt, VI, 192–193n.).

[24] Madison to TJ, Sept. 2, 1793 (Hunt, VI, 195).

to be modified "according to the state of information and the particular temper of the place."

Monroe wrote Jefferson that the latter's interpretation of Genet's conduct was confined to "a very narrow circle" of Republicans, and he believed that if it became current in the ranks it would create such despondency as to complete the triumph of the enemies of France and her cause.[25] The address which Monroe personally inspired at Staunton sought to put Jay and King on the same footing with the French minister as trouble-makers. Its concluding resolution follows:

> *Resolved*, finally, that we are attached to our own government — that we are attached to the President — that we are attached to peace, so long as it can be maintained upon honorable terms — that we are attached to the French nation, and the principles of their revolution — that we hate monarchy, and more intimate connections with it, as the worst of evils — and that we most ardently desire that the imprudence and indiscretion of a servant of France on the one hand, or an ill-judged interference of our own citizens (not in the executive department) on the other, may not disunite two nations, who have embraced the same principles of freedom, and who we believe esteem each other most ardently.[26]

Certain other Republican gatherings, while reiterating devotion to the French cause, were more explicit in condemnation of the methods of the French envoy. A group in Norfolk included in its resolutions a statement that foreign representatives should treat only with the government to which they were accredited and not appeal to the people. One of the resolutions that was adopted at a meeting in Caroline County over which the veteran Edmund Pendleton presided asked that the attempt to deal with people outside the regular channels of government be "treated with contempt." [27] Washington's reply to this was significant. Not only did he approve of the expressions of gratitude and affection toward the French people for past services; he also assured Pendleton of his own attachment to the principles of republican government, and his confidence that the good sense of his countrymen would counteract any attempt to weaken their devotion to these principles.[28] This letter was widely circulated by Republican leaders,

[25] To TJ, Sept. 3, 1793 (S.M.H., I, 275).

[26] Staunton resolutions of Sept. 3, 1793 (*National Gazette*, Sept. 18, 1793); Monroe to Madison, Sept. 25, 1793 (S.M.H., I, 276–277).

[27] Harry Ammon, "The Republican Party in Virginia, 1789–1824," p. 144, citing Norfolk *Virginia Chronicle*, Sept. 28, 1793; D. J. Mays, *Edmund Pendleton*, II, 308, citing *Virginia Gazette, and General Advertiser*, Sept. 21, 1793.

[28] To Pendleton, Sept. 23, 1793 (Fitzpatrick, XXXIII, 91–92); Mays, II, 309.

who regarded it as a rebuke to the Anglophiles and consolidationists and as a vindication of their patriotism by Washington himself. The President was maintaining his own balance and showing his customary good sense, but by and large the battle for public opinion was favorable to the Hamiltonians until the yellow fever brought about a virtual cessation of governmental operations and a lull in politics in Philadelphia while decimating Republican ranks and threatening the Secretary of the Treasury.

The fever raged for several weeks before Jefferson wrote home about it, and even then he played it down.[29] After a mild winter and early spring, unusually wet weather had been followed by the hottest and driest summer within memory. Streams dried up, insects swarmed, and sickness increased in the countryside as well as in crowded Philadelphia. The fever first appeared there on the water front; Jefferson said it started in the filth of the docks, and not unnaturally people attributed it to the refugees from Santo Domingo and the French sailors. It spread during August, when he and his colleagues were so occupied about Genet. One of the more sensible recommendations of the Fellows of the College of Physicians was that the tolling of bells be stopped. Handshaking ceased and everybody walked in the middle of the street to escape contamination. A more fearful enemy than monarchy or revolution had appeared.

In late August, Jefferson informed his son-in-law that he was busy packing his books, and that after sending off his furniture he would quit his house on the Schuylkill for private lodgings, "reserving nothing but a portmanteau of clothes." [30] This plan, which did not allow for the dangers of the plagued city and the desirability of remaining in the country, was not put into effect. According to the schedule then worked out, the President was to leave on September 10. Since Jefferson did not expect to go until October 1 and Washington would return before him, there would be little time when both would be away.

Long before October 1, however, panic seized upon the city. It did not seize upon Jefferson. Fearing that reports would be magnified by distance, he wrote Thomas Mann Randolph early in September, painting a picture which was not as dark as the circumstances warranted. He thought that the disease, while still spreading, was becoming less mortal. Everybody who could flee the city was doing so, and the country people were afraid to bring supplies to market, but he believed

---

[29] To TMR, Sept. 2, 1793 (Ford, VI, 406–407). J. H. Powell, *Bring Out Your Dead: The Great Plague of Yellow Fever in Philadelphia in 1793* (1949), is the fullest and most authoritative account.

[30] To TMR, Aug. 25, 1793 (LC, 15793).

there was more alarm than danger. His own imperturbability continued as the peril grew, and some of his comments on his colleagues were uncharitable. Washington calmly proceeded on his prearranged schedule. To Madison, Jefferson reported: "Knox then takes flight. Hamilton is ill of the fever, as is said."[31] Thinking Hamilton excessively alarmed, Jefferson made the nastiest remark of his about his inveterate foe that is on record: "A man as timid as he is on the water, as timid on horseback, as timid in sickness, would be a phenomenon if his courage of which he has the reputation in military circles were genuine." Actually, Hamilton had a mild attack and soon recovered. Jefferson's unkind remark perhaps serves to show that Hamilton brought out the worst in his own nature. Having stated that he himself would not leave until October 1, he wanted to avoid any appearance of panic; furthermore, he thought that some member of the administration should be at the seat of government. In official letters to consuls abroad he continued to minimize the danger.[32]

By the middle of the month, however, he decided that there was little point in remaining much longer.[33] All of his clerks had left, except one, and after the President's departure he ceased going to his office. He had brought Maria from the city to the Schuylkill and he wound up some official business there. At just this time he wrote Genet of his recall and sent him a copy of the enormous letter to Gouverneur Morris. He set out on September 17, stopped at Mount Vernon on the way, as he did again at Madison's Montpelier, and before the end of the month he was on his own hilltop in Albemarle County. He stayed at Monticello about a month, missing the height of the plague. When he resumed residence at the seat of government, it was in Germantown rather than Philadelphia, and he probably had no more personal belongings with him than "a portmanteau of clothes."

Two decades after these events, John Adams chided Jefferson for not giving due weight to the terrorism excited by Genet in Philadelphia, when, as he claimed, 10,000 people in the streets, day after day, threatened to drag Washington from his house and effect a revolution in the government—or force it to declare war in favor of the French Revolution. He expressed the opinion that nothing but the yellow fever, which carried off Genet's chief local adherents, could have saved the government.[34] This very extreme statement, which

---

[31] To Madison, Sept. 8, 1793 (Ford, VI, 419).
[32] Various letters of Sept. 11, 1793 (LC, 15944–15949).
[33] To TMR, Sept. 15, 1793 (LC, 15990), and other letters.
[34] To TJ, June 30, 1813 (*Adams-Jefferson Letters* [1959], II, 346–347). He ex-

cannot be matched in the contemporary comments of Adams, exaggerates both the political dangers of the time and the effects of the plague upon them. The fever was no respecter of persons or parties, but it did strike very heavy blows in Republican circles. Two leaders specifically mentioned by Adams were Dr. James Hutchinson and Jonathan Dickinson Sergeant. The latter, who had been notably active in succoring the victims of the plague, died in October, while Jefferson was at Monticello. In later years his sons sought to clear this respected citizen of the aspersions of Adams. Dr. Hutchinson had already abandoned Genet when he died, and his death was mourned in all ranks and both parties. A youthful exception was Rubens Peale, delicate son of the painter Charles Willson Peale, for whom Dr. Hutchinson had prescribed in times past very bad-tasting medicines and whom he had forbidden normal outdoor activities. While the rest of the Peales mourned the passing of the family physician, this boy ran and leaped about the house, hurled his medicines into the fire, and then rushed out into the open air.[35]

Another casualty was Freneau's paper. Jefferson noted the discontinuance of the *National Gazette* soon after his own return to Philadelphia, attributing this to lack of money.[36] The policy of this paper had long since diverged from his own, but he hoped it would be resumed and urged that subscribers send in their money. He paid up his own arrears and collected sums due from Madison and others. It was not resumed, however, and soon Jefferson learned that Freneau had resigned his translator's post in the Department of State.[37] On the other side of the fence Fenno was in serious financial trouble. He appealed to Hamilton, who asked Rufus King to raise $1,000 in New York while he did the same thing in Philadelphia, else they "must lose his services." [38] The *Gazette of the United States* continued.

The fever lulled party strife temporarily and relegated the Genet affair to relative unimportance. But the issue was really settled before the plague took its toll, and chief credit for this belongs to the wisdom of the government and the common sense of the people. Hamilton's assistant, Wolcott, wrote Noah Webster in August: "Let it be known that we can distinguish between an individual and a cause; that we are

pressed a similar opinion to William Cunningham, Oct. 15, 1808, while also stressing the part played by the writings of his son, John Quincy Adams (*Correspondence between the Hon. John Adams and the Late William Cunningham* [1823], p. 35–36).

35 C. C. Sellers, *Charles Willson Peale*, II, 39, 54.

36 To TMR, Nov. 2, 1793 (Ford, VI, 438); Account Book, Nov. 21, 1793.

37 Resignation dated Oct. 11, 1793; received Nov. 7 (LC, 16082).

38 John Fenno to Hamilton, Nov. 9, 1793 (King, I, 502).

competent to manage our own concerns, and that a foreign influence will not be permitted."[39] Jefferson was more disturbed about the British influence than the French, but that was just what he was saying. A few weeks later Wolcott wrote another staunch Hamiltonian: "The people of this country are too wise to suffer either kings or clubs to rule over them." While giving credit to the New Englanders, he used language which befitted any sort of patriot, and his judgment paralleled that of Washington.[40] Not until after Congress had assembled in December would representatives of the entire country know that Genet had been humbled, but there was no real issue left. The remaining danger was that past events would be improperly exploited for partisan advantage. In returning to the fray with Hamilton's support, as they did after the autumn frost had saved the plagued city of Philadelphia, Chief Justice Jay and Senator Rufus King were serving no real purpose beyond that of embarrassing the Republican interest.

To James Monroe the original announcement of Jay and King in New York had seemed a political trick, and certain less responsible Republican writers of doggerel verse made fun of it. The proud Chief Justice and the Senator from New York were undoubtedly annoyed by what they regarded as petty criticism, but they justified their reentrance into newspaper controversy on grounds of high patriotism, and on the further ground that Genet now denied having made to Alexander James Dallas or anybody else the statement that he would appeal from the President to the people. Supporting their own claim to truth and accuracy by a fresh document from Hamilton and Knox, they gave this to the press, along with their original announcement, at about the time that Congress was assembling.[41] Dallas remained the only actual witness, however. In a communication to the paper, dated December 7, he declined to affirm that he had reported the precise words attributed to Genet, and denied belief that the envoy had threatened any sort of appeal involving the incitation of insurrection and revolt. To Jay and King, Dallas was guilty of "apostasy," and unquestionably he was "foggily legalistic," as his biographer says.[42] Whatever subsequent doubts about the precise language had crept into his mind, perhaps impelled by Genet himself, there can be no doubt about what Dallas originally reported to the Secretary of State. Jefferson's own account to Washington was publicly quoted in connection

[39] Aug. 10, 1793 (Gibbs, I, 103).
[40] To Theodore Sedgwick, Sept. 5, 1793 (Gibbs, I, 108).
[41] "For the Daily Advertiser," Dec. 2, 1793; another statement dated Nov. 26; certificate from Hamilton and Knox dated Nov. 29. All in King, I, 458–462.
[42] King, I, 464–469; Raymond Walters, Jr., *Alexander James Dallas* (1943), p. 49.

with this controversy.[43] The use of this confidential official paper was of doubtful propriety, and information about its wording must have come from Hamilton or Knox. Jefferson himself refused to be drawn into the public quarrel, and thus was spared the necessity of reflecting on Dallas. He drew a paper on the question which he did not use.[44] This carries no more authority than any other discarded draft, but it shows that for a time at least he thought of giving to the public his entire report on the famous interview. There would have been impropriety in such action, however, unless Washington had authorized it, and he damned Genet sufficiently in other documents which were made public by official action. He could hardly have been expected to go out of his way to support the truthfulness of Jay and King, whose actions smacked of impropriety and officiousness all the way through and whose motives were manifestly partisan.

Rather more dubious was the disposition of a letter from Genet to the Attorney General in which he asked the prosecution of the Chief Justice and the Senator for libelous publications against him. Jefferson received a copy of this and laid it before the President. Then, at Washington's request, he referred the matter to Randolph for such action as seemed fitting.[45] This procedure struck Jay and King as so extraordinary that they addressed a strong letter to the President, in which both Randolph and Jefferson were "treated with much severity." This led to a later conference with Washington, after Jefferson had retired from office, and the burning of the letter along with the President's reply. With respect to this affair one is driven to supposition. It seems most unlikely that Washington ever expected any action to be taken against these prominent public men; but the Genet business was settled, except for the single question of the time when the troublesome fellow would be wholly relieved of his official functions, and at the end Washington felt sorry for him. He may well have thought the entire action of Jay and King unnecessary and improper — as even an encroachment on the executive — and thus may have wanted to administer to them an indirect rebuke. They were not on a like footing with Genet, as Monroe had claimed, but they were trouble-makers who, in the guise of patriotism, carried partisan politics too far.

[43] King, I, 471.

[44] Ford, VI, 432–433. The date October, 1793, assigned by the editor seems too early. Dallas wrote him on Dec. 4, 1793, asking how far he had authorized the use of Genet's alleged language (LC, 16304). Monroe wrote him about the matter the same day (S.M.H., I, 279). Political pressure was implicit in both letters.

[45] TJ to Attorney General, Dec. 18, 1793 (*Works*, Washington edn. [1854], IV, 97); this letter with statement by King (King, I, 476–479).

[IX]

End of a Tour of Duty

BECAUSE of the yellow fever the Secretary of State was away from the seat of government slightly more than six weeks. He spent more than a third of this time in the slow process of travel, and his month at Monticello was painfully short after an absence of a year, but he was able to give almost the whole of it to private matters. Within ten days of his arrival he got a batch of official correspondence from Benjamin Bankson, the one of his clerks who had remained in Philadelphia, and he had to take time out to attend to unfinished business. This included the revocation of the exequatur of the French vice consul in Boston, Antoine Duplaine, for forceful defiance of the law.[1] Also, he sent to Washington at Mount Vernon certain of the letters he had received and discussed various official matters with him.[2] He did not get another batch of letters from Bankson until the day before he left home and these he took with him on the road.

The President informed him that the executive officers were expected to forgather in Germantown on November 1, in ample time to prepare for the meeting of Congress in December. Washington was wondering just where that body could assemble and just what he could do about it. Jefferson took the position that the President had no constitutional authority to do anything with respect to the place of meeting, and reported that Madison, who rode over from Montpelier to see him, agreed with him. Since Congress had by its own action adjourned to Philadelphia, Jefferson believed that it would have to meet there, "even if it be in the open fields," and adjourn to some other place.[3] The other executive officers had fewer constitutional scruples but saw no reason for action, and in the end the Presi-

[1] To Duplaine, Oct. 3, 1793 (*A.S.P.F.R.*, I, 178); to Bankson, Oct. 3, 1793 (LC, 16034). Bankson affixed the seal to the letters patent.
[2] To the President, Oct. 3, 1793 (Ford, VI, 434–435).
[3] Washington to TJ, Oct. 7, 1793 (Fitzpatrick, XXXIII, 112–114), received Oct. 15; to Washington, Oct. 17, 1793 (Ford, VI, 436).

dent decided to do nothing beyond keeping his little official family at work in Germantown until Philadelphia seemed safe. That turned out to be a month.

Leaving Maria with her sister, Jefferson set out from Monticello on October 25. Sending back his horses from Fredericksburg, he proceeded to Baltimore by stage, accompanied by one servant. There he overtook the President and they went the rest of the way together in a hired conveyance at a cost which he regarded as excessive. He warned Madison to be on guard against the "harpies" who preyed on needy travelers. Besides being "fleeced" on this journey, he experienced "the extremes of heat, cold, dust and rain," he said.[4]

The great rains, after a long period of drought, were generally thought to have terminated the epidemic of yellow fever in Philadelphia, but when Jefferson arrived in Germantown on November 1 that place was so filled with refugees that he had to content himself with a bed in a corner of the public room of the King of Prussia tavern. The only alternative was to wrap himself in his cloak and sleep before the open fire. How many nights he had to endure this discomfort we do not know. At the King of Prussia his expenses included those of Thomas Lapsley, the "office keeper" and messenger of the State Department, who seems to have comprised his entire staff.[5] After a couple of weeks he procured rooms elsewhere for himself, Lapsley, and the Department.[6] He paid wages to his servant James, normally his cook, and recorded some small household expenses. The cost of the "hiccory" wood he bought was divided between him and the office. The latter probably contained little besides chairs, a table, and the official papers he brought with him; and only toward the end of the month did he have any clerical assistance in this makeshift establishment.

Meanwhile, the normal staff of the Department was being re-formed

4 TJ to Madison, Nov. 2, 1793 (Ford, VI, 438): to TMR, Nov. 2, 1793 (Ford, VI, 437). Account Book entry of Nov. 1 showed payment of $30 plus ferriage to Hartman Elliot for bringing him from Baltimore, and total traveling expenses of $77.65.

5 Also, he paid a dentist $4.66 for drawing a tooth. Perhaps it was a wisdom tooth which he did not count when he said years later that he had never lost a tooth from age (Account Book, Nov. 13, 1793; to Dr. Vine Utley, March 21, 1819 [Ford, X, 126]).

6 For an excellent account, see C. F. Jenkins, ed., *Jefferson's Germantown Letters* (1906), Introduction. This convenient volume contains, besides his correspondence from LC, his records of Cabinet meetings, his Account Book entries for the period, and other pertinent documents. He reserved a room for Madison and Monroe at the tavern on Nov. 9 and on Nov. 17 replaced this reservation with one in private lodgings. They did not avail themselves of it, but in December went straight to Philadelphia.

in Philadelphia. The chief clerk, George Taylor, brought his family back from New York about the middle of November. Jefferson sent him specific instructions about the assignment of clerical tasks. Because of the interruption of activities for a couple of months and the necessity of getting things ready for Congress, these were onerous and necessitated the temporary reinforcement of a staff which was small to begin with.[7] During the last third of the month three or four clerks were busily engaged in copying and translating in Philadelphia, in a freshly whitewashed office, and Jefferson apparently had one clerk helping him in his restricted quarters in Germantown.

Alone among the executive officers, he was continuously present at the temporary seat of the government. Hamilton, who was unwell throughout the month and feared that he had taken the fever again, missed at least one of their meetings. Both Knox and Randolph were away at times; and Washington made a trip of three or four days into the interior. In substance Jefferson's official letters were agreed to by his colleagues in advance, and he submitted rough drafts or fair copies for the approval of such of them as were available. This procedure was not followed in connection with the extremely interesting letter he wrote Eli Whitney about the latter's invention of a cotton gin, since this fell within his duties as head of the patent service.[8] It was followed, however, in such a noncontroversial matter as the announcement of the three-mile limit, which was made to the various diplomatic representatives and the district attorneys early in the month.[9] Jefferson had fully adjusted himself to the system whereby policies were determined in council meetings, and gave no sign that he resented submitting his letters for approval. One reason probably was that he would soon be out of all this, but another may well have been that, in the final period, his own views actually prevailed in the matters which most concerned him. Despite the inconvenience of his lodgings and makeshift office, and the loneliness of his state, a spirit of calm had settled on him. He suffered no such anguish of spirit as during the period of uncertainty about Genet.

It was at this time that Washington was inclined to order Genet

[7] Taylor to TJ from New York, Nov. 8, 1793, saying he would set off the first of the next week (*ibid.*, pp. 41-42); TJ to Taylor, Nov. 16, about finances, assigning tasks, and asking that one clerk come to Germantown (*ibid.*, pp. 91-92); Notes for Taylor, Nov. 18 (*ibid.*, pp. 99-100); Taylor to TJ, Nov. 18 (*ibid.*, pp. 101-102).

[8] To Whitney, Nov. 16, 1793 (Ford, VI, 448); also in Jenkins, pp. 90-91, with Whitney's reply of Nov. 24, 1793 (*ibid.*, pp. 111-115).

[9] Letters to the French and British ministers, Nov. 8, 1793 (Ford, VI, 440-442); also in Jenkins, pp. 42-46, with TJ's endorsement about approval.

from the country, since he continued to be so objectionable, but did nothing because of the division among his own counselors.[10] Jefferson thought it best to await the meeting of Congress, to which the documents in the case were to be submitted. These were to consist of the entire official correspondence, except for three or four letters bearing on the charges of John Jay and Rufus King that Genet had threatened an appeal from the President to the people. It was agreed that the President should not enter into that dispute.[11] Genet's letters continued to pour in. Jefferson drily referred to "new volumes" of them, and he had to keep on answering them, patiently but firmly, throughout his last weeks in office.

The executive officers always met at the President's, and after he got a more commodious house Washington sometimes, if not always, provided them with dinner. Their discussions now centered on "the subject of communication to Congress"; and the chief differences of opinion concerned the statements about the Neutrality Proclamation, which Randolph drew in the first place when drafting the President's speech, and about the messages on the subject of France and England, which Jefferson drew. Hamilton was well enough to raise vigorous objections but these were generally unavailing.

The discussion of the Proclamation followed the old lines.[12] Hamilton, arguing much as in his PACIFICUS papers, claimed that the Proclamation meant more than Randolph, and considerably more than Jefferson, thought it did, and he pressed his ideas of presidential power. Washington, while asserting that he never had any idea of binding Congress, let Hamilton make a draft. In the end he did not use this but contented himself with a factual and noncommittal statement which should have troubled nobody.[13] Jefferson was as convinced as ever that Hamilton would do everything in his power to shift the balance in the British direction, but neither he nor anybody else had reason to doubt Washington's desire to maintain *fair* neutrality under law regardless of his continued annoyance with Genet. The President, responding that month to an address from his own state, said that the Proclamation "neither cancelled nor weakened our obligation to the French nation"; and in another response he said that, while pursuing the obviously desirable policy of peace, it was the duty of Americans to remember the past services of the French nation and

10 Anas, Nov. 8, 1793 (Ford, I, 265–268). See above, p. 129.
11 Anas, Nov. 28, 1793 (Ford, I, 270).
12 Esp. Nov. 8, 21, 1793 (Anas, Ford, I, 266–269).
13 President's speech, Dec. 3, 1793 (*A.S.P.F.R.*, I, 21–23). For Hamilton's draft, see J.C.H., IV, 486–487.

to pursue the republican spirit of the Constitution.[14] These remarks were in the spirit of Jefferson, not Hamilton, and there were other signs that in the realm of foreign affairs Washington saw eye to eye with his first Secretary of State at the end of the latter's service.

He supported Jefferson's position both as to the form and content of the report to Congress with respect to international relations. It was agreed by the executive officers that, in view of pending negotiations with the government of Spain, communication regarding relations with that country should be delayed and kept confidential. In his draft of the President's message, Jefferson sought to balance the severe censure of Genet, whose proceedings had tended "to involve us in war abroad and discord and anarchy at home," with references to the general friendliness of the French government and to "favors ancient and recent." On Hamilton's objection he struck out the latter expression, though he could not agree that the dispositions of the American people toward France, which Hamilton seems to have regarded as still favorable, were to be viewed as a "serious calamity." [15]

Nor could he possibly agree that in matters of commerce the British had showed the United States more favors than France had, as Hamilton claimed. The contrast between Genet's conduct and the purposes of his government was not so great as Jefferson believed, but in the light of what had been reported to him he was warranted in drawing a contrast between French and British commercial actions. He toned this down somewhat as a result of Hamilton's protestation, and of his own accord he toned it further in the light of later information. A decree of the National Assembly (May 9, 1793) had subjected neutral vessels loaded with provisions to being carried into French ports, and made lawful prize of British goods in neutral vessels. American vessels had been formally exempted from this decree, but when reports came in that it had been extended to them in practice, Jefferson added to the President's message a passage describing the supposed situation.[16] His comments on the treatment of American commerce by the French, therefore, were eminently fair in the light of the known circumstances.

With respect to the British there was, in the first place, the old question of the infractions of the peace treaty, particularly the reten-

[14] To Nicholas Lewis, Nov. 16, 1793, replying to an address from Albemarle County; to Edward Stevens, Nov. 16, 1793, replying to one from Culpeper (Fitzpatrick, XXXIII, 153-154).

[15] Anas, Nov. 28, 1793 (Ford, I, 271).

[16] Draft of President's Message and note to Washington dated Nov. 30, 1793 (Ford, VI, 456-459, with footnotes).

tion of the posts in the Northwest, which Jefferson had discussed so powerfully in his letter to Hammond in May, 1792. To this no answer had yet been received. After the lapse of more than a year Jefferson inquired about the matter; and in reply Hammond, admitting that he had not yet received instructions from his home government about it, assigned as an excuse the absorption of the British ministers in more urgent events in Europe.[17] The question of a new demand for an answer was brought up by Washington, who was concerned about the posts at a time when the situation in the Northwest was becoming even more perilous.[18] The executive council agreed that unless word was received from England by the next packet, Jefferson should again inquire of Hammond just what had happened; and on November 13 he did so, only to receive the same old reply.[19] The net result of all this was to give Jefferson another item in the tale of British disregard to report to Congress.

A more recent grievance against the British arose from the Order-in-Council of June 8, 1793, generally referred to as the "Provision Order," news of which reached the United States in August. One article of this authorized naval commanders to stop and take to British ports all vessels laden with corn, flour, or meal bound to any French port. This was far more than an act of reprisal against the French decree regarding provisions, from which American vessels were excepted; it was part of the larger British policy of throttling all commerce with France, regardless of the effect on neutrals.[20] It may be regarded, also, as a major link in the chain of actions leading to the outburst of indignation against Britain in the United States after Jefferson left office. He wrote Thomas Pinckney, the American minister in London, in September about the Provision Order of June. This he did with the approval of his executive colleagues, except Hamilton who was absent from the meeting, and even Hamilton thought American protest necessary.[21] Jefferson's letter was not actually delivered to the British until December, by which time they had announced an even harsher policy. He had not learned of that when Congress met, but he had learned enough from Pinckney to be convinced that the rulers of the sea had no notion of backing down. He protested

[17] TJ to Hammond, June 19, 1793, and Hammond to TJ, June 20, 1793 (*A.S.P.F.R.*, I, 238). TJ's original letter of May 29, 1792, is in *A.S.P.F.R.*, I, 201-237; see *Jefferson and the Rights of Man*, pp. 412-417.
[18] Sept. 4, 7, 1793 (Ford, I, 265; VI, 412).
[19] TJ to Hammond, Nov. 13, 1793, and Hammond to TJ, Nov. 22, 1793 (*A.S.P.F.R.*, I, 238).
[20] Well discussed in S. F. Bemis, *Jay's Treaty*, pp. 154-157.
[21] Cabinet Decisions, Sept. 7, 1793 (Ford, VI, 412-416). On Hamilton's comments to Hammond, see Bemis, p. 156.

against the British action as contrary to the law of nations, since the specified provisions were not contraband and remained articles of free commerce. The British order, striking at the root of American agriculture, he said, tended to draw the country from the state of neutrality in which it wanted to remain, and if acceded to might draw the country into war. His able but temperate paper was still another item in the anti-British count.

At the last Cabinet meeting before Congress met, it looked for a time as though this item and others unfavorable to the British would not be presented to that body. Hamilton still disliked the references to the British in Jefferson's draft of the presidential message, though it is hard to see how he could have objected to these restrained factual statements.[22] He shifted his position by advocating that the matters relating to the British should be in a secret communication, since both the question of the inexecution of the treaty of 1783 and the restraining of the commerce in provisions to British ports and those of British friends were still pending. Knox supported him in both cases, and Randolph did in the second. Jefferson then became fearful lest all should be kept secret. In particular he urged that the President lay before the country what had passed about the inexecution of the treaty. He wanted the documents about the provision order to be presented also, but was less insistent with respect to these. He need not have been alarmed, for Washington now entered the discussion with unaccustomed vehemence and decided on the public submission of both sets of documents. In the case of the second, he joined with Jefferson and ruled against the three other members of his council, a thing which the Secretary of State could not remember that he had ever done before. To him this proved that Washington's feelings must have been very strong. The outcome marked a victory for impartiality, because the disagreeable things in relations with both the British and the French were to be revealed.

During the latter half of November the Chief Clerk of the Department of State had been busily engaged translating Genet's letters and other French documents, sending drafts periodically to Jefferson in Germantown, where he checked them against the originals. The other clerks were occupied in making copies of other documents, including Jefferson's own official letters and the entire exchange with Hammond. By December 1 Washington had returned to Philadelphia and Jefferson was comfortably lodged at the corner of Seventh and

[22] The draft, with indicated changes, is in Ford, VI, 456-459; for TJ's letter to Washington, Dec. 2, 1793, transmitting it, see Ford, VI, 460-462; for the discussion in the Cabinet, see Anas, Nov. 28, 1793 (Ford, I, 271-272).

Market.[23] At noon on December 3, the President, accompanied by the chief executive officers, went to the Senate Chamber and delivered the address which Randolph had prepared. Two days later he submitted the message dealing with France and England which Jefferson had drawn, along with the huge body of documentary material which the clerks of the State Department had made ready.[24]

The night before the presidential message on relations with France and Great Britain was sent to Congress, the Secretary of State called on his old friend Vice President John Adams and reported that "the whole budget of foreign affairs" would be presented. Writing to his wife Abigail, still in Massachusetts, Adams said: "He seems as little satisfied with the conduct of the French minister as any one." A couple of weeks later Adams wrote: "How a government can go on, publishing all their negotiations with foreign nations, I know not. To me it appears as dangerous and pernicious as it is novel; but upon this occasion it could not, perhaps, have been avoided." [25] The question was a proper one, and time was to show that such a policy of giving almost immediate publicity to diplomatic correspondence could not be indefinitely maintained. On the domestic political scene, however, the immediate effects were distinctly favorable to the President and the Secretary of State.

John Adams, remarking with pardonable if rather exaggerated paternal pride that the President viewed the conduct of Genet in virtually the same light as John Quincy Adams had in certain papers in the *Boston Centinel*, said that Washington had given the French envoy "a bolt of thunder."[26] He believed that the President stood as high as ever in the people's admiration and confidence, but feared that "many bitter and desperate enemies" would arise as a result of his "just judgment" of Genet. If anything, he himself thought that Washington had shown too much partiality for the French republicans, not realizing that the friendly tone toward the French nation, on which Jefferson had so insisted, provided the most effective answer to possible Republican discontent in America. Nor did he realize what influence the Secretary of State had exercised on the Virginian

---

[23] TJ to Martha, Dec. 1, 1793 (Edgehill Randolph Papers, UVA).
[24] Dec. 5, 1793 (*A.S.P.F.R.*, I, 141–243).
[25] Dec. 5, 19, 1793 (*Works*, I, 458, 459).
[26] Referring to J. Q. Adams's COLUMBUS papers; see S. F. Bemis, *John Quincy Adams and the Foundations of American Foreign Policy* (1949), pp. 37–38. That Washington needed the arguments of the younger Adams to show him his proper course is questionable, but they gave him a favorable impression of that able young man and prepared the way for his first diplomatic appointment.

leaders of the party, whose loyalty to Washington was genuine and deep, helping them to adjust themselves in advance to this situation in a spirit of discriminating patriotism.

An intimate friend and political supporter of Hamilton, though uninformed about what had been going on in Republican circles behind the scenes, sized things up judiciously. On Christmas day Robert Troup wrote Hamilton from New York:

> It is the general opinion of the friends of the government here that the President has never appeared to greater advantage than in his last speech to Congress & the communications which followed it. Genet is completely on his back and I cannot now hear of any person who attempts seriously to defend his conduct. Jefferson's letter to Gouverneur Morris has blotted all the sins of the former out of the book of our remembrance; and with the sentiments and temper Jefferson appears at present to possess we would much regret that he should quit his post until the clouds which threaten a storm be dispersed.[27]

Viewing these events in the next decade as the biographer of Washington, John Marshall said that the publication of Jefferson's correspondence with Genet "dissipated much of the prejudice which had been excited against him." In that correspondence, said Marshall, he "maintained with great ability the opinions embraced by the federalists on those points of difference which had arisen between the two republics."[28] The view that Jefferson had maintained, under force of necessity, a "Federalist" position of which he himself did not approve was adopted by other partisan writers and influenced historical interpretation for generations.[29] But the policy toward France as voiced by Jefferson was that of the administration, which was neither Federalist nor Republican at this time. Credit for it must be given all the executive officers, but in its final form it chiefly reflected the ideas of Jefferson and it was presented with Washington's full approval. If Hamilton had had his way the administration would have been much less conciliatory, much more peremptory, and might have provoked an open breach with France.

With the official presentation of British relations, Hamilton was unsympathetic and he definitely opposed making the official Anglo-

[27] HP, 21:2881.
[28] *Life of George Washington*, V, 488–489.
[29] That it was part of the official Hamiltonian "line" is suggested by the comments in J. C. Hamilton, *History of the Republic of the U.S.A.*, V (1860), 421, and elsewhere. That it reflected much contemporary opinion is suggested by the comment in *General Advertiser*, Jan. 6, 1794, that TJ's influence in the executive council was trivial.

American correspondence public. Hammond was much annoyed, both on the ground that the procedure was unconventional and because it contributed to the anti-British sentiment which became so strong early in the next year.[30] The common Hamiltonian allegation was that Jefferson's purposes in this instance were primarily those of a partisan politician, rather than a patriotic public servant. But the final responsibility for airing the correspondence with Hammond and reporting recent British actions injurious to American commerce was that of Washington, against whom no partisan motives could possibly be alleged and who was undoubtedly pleased with the total presentation of administration policy. The day before he addressed the new Congress he wrote his Secretary of State: "I am very well satisfied with the train things are in." [31] As for Jefferson's services in this connection, a descendant of John Adams summed them up in words which deserve the assent of the present-day historian. Charles Francis Adams said that the Secretary of State "very faithfully maintained the reputation of the country, equally well against the impertinent aggressiveness of M. Genet, the envoy of democratic France, and the supercilious arrogance of Mr. Hammond, the representative of British aristocracy." [32]

In the light of later events, it appeared that the report on commerce which Jefferson submitted to the House of Representatives in the middle of the month contributed to the rising anti-British spirit.[33] This report, made in the first session of the Third Congress, was actually in response to a resolution of the lower house of the First Congress, adopted toward the end of its final session.[34] Jefferson prepared a paper before the Second Congress had ended its first session (1791–1792); but, thinking there might be changes in the state of things, he informed the Speaker of the House that he would carry this over to the second session (1792–1793) unless it was desired sooner. In view of diplomatic negotiations at the time such delay seemed warranted. During this second session of the Second Congress he availed himself of the aid of Madison and Tench Coxe in compiling statistics, carried his figures to the end of 1792, and submitted to the representatives of Great Britain, France, Spain, and the United Netherlands the parts of

[30] Bemis, *Jay's Treaty*, p. 191.

[31] Dec. 2, 1793 (Fitzpatrick, XXXIII, 163).

[32] *Works of John Adams*, I (1865), 455.

[33] Report of the Secretary of State on the Privileges and Restrictions on the Commerce of the United States in Foreign Countries, Dec. 16, 1793 (*A.S.P.F.R.*, I, 300–304; Ford, VI, 470–484).

[34] Feb. 23, 1791. For the circumstances see *Jefferson and the Rights of Man*, p. 335.

the report bearing on their respective countries.[35] He made a few minor changes as a result of the replies. He told Washington that Hammond "kindled at the facts" presented by him, but that the British envoy gave him no ground for correcting his general statements.[36] About two weeks before the end of the session he informed the Speaker of the House that he was ready to deliver his report, but that there would be some advantage in retaining it until the next session. The House agreed not to call for it during the present session.[37] The chairman of the committee recommending the delay was William Branch Giles, whose resolutions against Hamilton were being so heatedly debated at just this time, but the followers of the Secretary of the Treasury brought no discernible pressure for early submission of the paper, which they would probably have been relieved to escape altogether.

Having delayed this long, Jefferson could not have failed to present his report in December, 1793, if he was going to present it at all. The paper embodied his thoughts over a long period about commerce and the economic development of the country, reflecting his wide experience since writing the *Notes on Virginia*. This was not the work of a mere theorist or an inexperienced provincial, for its author had had more direct contact with the problems of international trade than any other American in public life. During his five years abroad these problems had occupied more of his time as an official than any other; and they were never long absent from his mind as secretary of state, even though they seemed less urgent than the need to oust the British from the Northwest and to secure the free navigation of the Mississippi from the Spanish. No one realized more clearly than he that, in a world of closed commercial systems, the young Republic was still at a grave disadvantage, and that in the economic sphere it was still not far removed from a state of colonial subservience. In economics no less than in politics he wanted it to assume among the powers of the earth "the separate and equal Station to which the Laws of Nature and of Nature's God" entitled it. His major purpose as a public man, apart from the securing of human rights, was the completion and maintenance of national independence.

No doubt he still regarded tillers of the soil as the chosen people of

[35] Brant, *Madison*, III, 389; Coxe to TJ (LC, 14097); circular letter to Foreign Ministers, Feb. 13, 1793 (Ford, VI, 179–182 and note).

[36] TJ to the President, Feb. 16, 1793, to the British minister, Feb. 16, 1793; to the French minister, Feb. 17, 1793 (Ford, VI, 184, 186–189); to the Spanish agents, Feb. 17, 1793 (LC, 14160).

[37] TJ to Speaker of House, Feb. 20, 1793 (L & B, IX, 31); *Annals*, 2 Cong., p. 894.

God, but in this paper he laid no such relative emphasis on agriculture as in his *Notes on Virginia*. Commerce loomed large in his mind from the French period onward, not merely because of the necessity of getting agricultural products to market, but because of the value of commerce in itself as a branch of economic activity, a nursery of seamen, and a resource of defense. The views he presented here ought to have commended him to shipping interests in the Northeast, and perhaps were feared by Hamilton for just that reason, though in fact they did not. In the *Notes on Virginia* he said, too rhetorically, "let our workshops remain in Europe"; but he now recognized a need for manufacturing in the future economy of the country. His report is notably well balanced and distinctly national in spirit.

Jefferson referred only incidentally to restrictions growing out of the war. He described commerce in its prewar state, reducing complicated tables and statistics to relatively simple terms for the convenience of Congress. While considerably briefer than Hamilton's famous reports on banking and manufacturing, his paper can be properly compared to these as a source of factual information. Here one can learn that, among exports, breadstuff (grains and their products) easily stood first, followed by tobacco, and, considerably farther off, by rice, wood, salted fish, pot and pearl ash, salted meats, and indigo. More than half of the total exports were northern products. Great Britain and her dominions received far more of these than any other nation. France took about half as many as Great Britain, Spain and the United Netherlands less than half as many as France, Portugal less still, and Denmark and Sweden very little. The statistics about imports were even more striking, for these were overwhelmingly British, at the ratio of more than 7 to 1 over the French, and of more than 14 to 1 over the Dutch. As for the shipping engaged in this business, it appeared that the American tonnage from French ports was twice that from the United Netherlands, and more than twice that from Great Britain. That is, despite the far greater volume of trade with Great Britain, American ships played very little part in it.

Taking up these countries one by one, Jefferson described their treatment of American products and American shipping. All of them imposed disadvantageous restrictions of some sort which he would have liked to see removed, but on the whole, and certainly in view of the volume of trade with them, the British were most objectionable. This was true of the duties imposed on particular products — especially foodstuffs, whale oil, salted fish, and meat. It was also true that the British, alone of these nations except the United Netherlands, re-exported most of what they imported from America. To Jefferson this seemed wasteful and needlessly expensive, and he would have preferred direct trade with the countries of ultimate consumption. Worst of all, however, were the British restrictions on shipping, evincing their determination to dominate the carrying trade. American vessels could carry only American products to English ports, and that only on a year-to-year arrangement, while they were wholly excluded from the British West Indian trade, which they had entered into freely in colonial times.

The relative weight of the count against the British arose from the facts of the case, and in proposing remedies Jefferson did not single them out specifically. He stated his views in general terms, though the implications were unmistakable. Recognizing that the ideal situation of complete freedom of commerce did not and was not likely to exist, he saw as the best remedy the working out of friendly arrangements with particular countries. That is, he favored commercial treaties such as he, Franklin, and John Adams had vainly tried to negotiate in Europe during the days of the feeble Confederation. The United States already had a commercial treaty with the French, and he accepted their assurances that they would like to negotiate another, explaining that they had been prevented by internal disturbances. Their sincerity at this stage may well be doubted on the basis of present knowledge, but there could be no possible doubt of the indifference of the British, who saw no need for a treaty since they already had the bulk of American trade on their own terms. Failing friendly arrangements, Jefferson saw no choice but to protect American commerce by counter-prohibitions, duties, regulations, and the like.

To his mind principles founded on reciprocity could offer no reasonable ground for complaint. Where another nation imposed high duties on American products or prohibited them, the United States might do the same by theirs — first on products competing with American, and next on the more important manufactures which could be most readily supplied at home or from some other country. As an effect of such duties Jefferson foresaw the indirect encouragement of manufacturing in the United States. By implication he opposed direct aids such as the federal bounties Hamilton had suggested in his famous report on manufacturing.[38] Also, he stressed the encouragement by *states* of *household* manufacture, which he prized because of his emphasis on families and individuals. No doubt he still disliked large

[38] Lodge, III, 366–372.

workshops, fearing the effects on the workers which he described so vividly in his *Notes on Virginia*,[39] but he showed no animus against manufacturing as such, and he was advocating the raising of tariff duties on the protective principle. In effect, these would be levied on British goods and Hamilton opposed them for that reason, being fearful of any interference with existing trade and possible diminution in revenue. Thus Hamilton, in theory an ardent advocate of manufacturing and widely hailed in later years as the father of the American protective system, was actually opposing increased protection and this indirect stimulus to manufacturing. At the same time, Jefferson, while theoretically preferring free trade, was assuming the position of a moderate protectionist because of the actualities of the present situation. As between the two, it also appears that, apart from the creation of fluid capital and the development of banking facilities, which were basic in Hamilton's policy and the importance of which Jefferson did not fully grasp, the Virginian was more concerned with the total economic life and development of the country. With Hamilton, fiscal policy came first.

Jefferson recognized some inconveniences in the application of the policy of discrimination, especially the imposition of higher duties on imports from Great Britain, but believed these to be as nothing "when weighed against the loss of wealth and loss of force" which would follow perseverance in the present course of treating all nations alike, regardless of their treatment of the United States. "It is not to the moderation and justice of others we are to trust for fair and equal access to market with our productions, or for our due share in the transportation of them," he said; "but to our means of independence, and the firm will to use them." [40] As he noted, all the other nations practiced discrimination in one form or another. For the United States one distinction could be readily made: "That is to say, between nations who favor our productions and navigation, and those who do not favor them." Thus he came back to the proposals he had made earlier, which Madison had pressed in Congress in 1791, and which Hamilton had blocked on the ground that they would endanger relations with Great Britain.[41]

It is unfortunate that his broadly nationalistic and thoroughly patriotic policy with respect to commerce was never considered as a whole, and that its merit was never tested. It is unfortunate, also, that the term most commonly attached to it, at this time and there-

[39] Query XIX.
[40] Ford, VI, 483.
[41] See *Jefferson and the Rights of Man*, pp. 333-335.

after, was "discrimination" rather than "reciprocity." [42] Jefferson always thought of this policy as a means, as indeed the only available means, to the securing of commercial treaties on the basis of reciprocal advantage; and the actions of the British in 1791 and afterwards leave no doubt that the threat of retaliatory commercial legislation would have been an effective weapon in diplomacy. He could hardly have expected them to be amenable in the midst of world war, however; for, in what they regarded as a life-and-death struggle, they were less disposed than ever to yield any advantage they held as rulers of the sea. What, then, did he really hope to accomplish by making his proposals at this time?

The simplest answer is that he could no longer avoid making a report of some sort, that the facts themselves inevitably gave it an anti-British tone, and that his specific proposals reflected his continued conviction that no other action was possible in behalf of American commerce, short of war. A sympathetic scholar has suggested that his report was "a farewell declaration of his policy, which he no longer hoped to see carried into effect." [43] When he prepared and even when he presented it he may have had little hope that it would be adopted as a whole, but before the year ended, speaking of the rise of feeling against the British, he privately expressed the belief that Congress would impose high duties on their manufactures.[44] The rise of sentiment against them in the winter of 1793–1794 was occasioned by particular actions of theirs which were not covered in Jefferson's report and some of which even Hamilton recognized as indefensible. Undoubtedly Jefferson was aware that he was contributing to this sentiment, but his representations were by no means the main cause of American discontent, which would have arisen without them.

To the Hamiltonians, when they looked back, the combination of circumstances seemed more than accidental. On the strength of Jefferson's report, Madison, who had had a share in it, reintroduced in Congress, early in 1794, his resolutions of 1791.[45] As luck would have it, Jefferson's policy came nearest adoption soon after he retired from

[42] V. G. Setser, in *The Commercial Reciprocity Policy of the United States, 1774–1829* (1937), uses the latter term and is distinctly more favorable to the policy than the generality of American historians.

[43] Setser, p. 114.

[44] To Martha, Dec. 22, 1793 (Ford, VI, 489). He laid stress here on the "letting loose of the Algerines on us, which has been contrived by England." The reference was to the recent truce between Portugal and Algiers, instigated by British for other reasons, which had enabled the Barbary pirates to swarm into the Atlantic and prey on American commerce (described by Bemis, *American Secretaries of State*, II, 91–92).

[45] Well described by Brant, in *Madison*, III, ch. XXX.

the secretaryship of state. In retirement at Monticello he had nothing to do with the anti-British movement beyond exchanging letters with Madison and a few others. In these private communications, however, he was often vehement, showing much less restraint than in his public papers when in office. Out of office he became more partisan. But, considered in the setting of his secretaryship, his report on commerce was abundantly justified on broad grounds of statesmanship.

The presidential message about unsettled matters with Spain, which Jefferson wrote, was delivered in confidence on the same day as his report on commerce. With its documents, it was a very lengthy communication and it disclosed negotiations very close to his heart. These were fruitless while he was in office but highly successful when renewed under more favorable circumstances thereafter.[46] The negotiations of William Carmichael and William Short in Madrid, looking toward the free navigation of the Mississippi and a settlement of the southern boundary question, had not even got started when the international situation was drastically altered by the alignment of Spain with Great Britain against France. No longer fearful for her possessions on the continent of North America, Spain saw no need to treat with the United States and even adopted a bolder policy in the Southwest. Jefferson was sure that the Spanish officials were inciting the Indians against the Americans in that region, and made strong representations on this point, using more bellicose language than he employed in dealing with the British and the French.[47] These did not reach the American commissioners until September and nothing came of them while he was in office, though the Spanish agents in the United States moderated their language somewhat. On this question he had arrived at stalemate. What he revealed in confidence to Congress, therefore, was merely the policy he had followed. No doubt the ability and patriotic vehemence with which he presented his country's cause in his official letters contributed to his esteem in the minds of the representatives, especially the Westerners, but its value lay in the future. In the long view he had estimated the situation correctly, and historians have not failed to give him large credit for the success which was achieved by others, after Spain had withdrawn from her

[46] Message of Dec. 16, 1793, with documents (*A.S.P.F.R.*, I, 247–306). Ultimately these negotiations led to the Treaty of San Lorenzo, or Pinckney's Treaty, of 1795. In their earlier phases they are discussed in *Jefferson and the Rights of Man*, pp. 311–312, 406–407.

[47] To Carmichael and Short, June 30, 1793 (*A.S.P.F.R.*, I, 265–267).

alliances with Great Britain and was disposed to come to terms with the United States. He was the architect of policy toward Spain.[48]

A few days before Christmas, the President made his "last set" at Jefferson to continue in office, and shortly thereafter the first Secretary of State started his remaining books and furniture homeward by placing them on a sloop bound for Richmond, only to discover a little later that the loaded vessel loitered until the river froze and would be held up till spring.[49] On the last day of the year he submitted to the President his formal resignation.[50] "I carry into my retirement a lively sense of your goodness, and shall continue gratefully to remember it," he said. Washington's expression of regret was more than perfunctory. "I cannot suffer you to leave your Station, without assuring you, that the opinion, which I had formed, of your integrity and talents, and which dictated your original nomination, has been confirmed by the fullest experience; and that both have been eminently displayed in the discharge of your duties." [51] There is clear evidence of his strong approval of Jefferson's official conduct, and of genuine friendliness between them when they parted.

Washington had been deeply concerned over the problem of finding a fit successor to his first Secretary of State. His first choice would have been Madison, he said. That appointment would have kept the office on a higher intellectual plane than it actually rested on during the remaining years of the decade, but the President knew Madison would not accept it. Jefferson himself suggested as a possibility Thomas Johnson, former governor of Maryland who served briefly as Associate Justice of the Supreme Court. Though Washington's first thought was that in foreign affairs Johnson would be a fish out of water, he offered him the place — only to have it refused, probably on grounds of health.[52] Jefferson also suggested the *ad interim* appointment of Edmund Randolph, of whose capabilities both he and Washington were uncertain and of whose private financial difficulties he was fully aware. Perhaps Jefferson, who had so sharply criticized Randolph in private for vacillation, came to think of him

---

[48] This matter is well described by S. F. Bemis in *American Secretaries of State*, II, 57–58, and *Pinckney's Treaty* (1926), p. 335, and elsewhere.

[49] To Martha, Dec. 22, 1793 (Ford, VI, 488); to TMR, Dec. 30, 1793 (LC, 16425).

[50] Dec. 31, 1793 (Ford, VI, 496).

[51] Jan. 1, 1794 (Fitzpatrick, XXXIII, 231).

[52] Anas, Aug. 6, 1793 (Ford, I, 258); TJ to Madison, Nov. 2, 1793 (Ford, VI, 439).

rather more favorably toward the end of the year, and quite obviously neither he nor Washington could think of anybody better who was eligible. The President appointed Randolph after failing in the "last set" at Jefferson, and there is good reason to believe that he was still trying to maintain balance in the government.

One of the very last of Jefferson's official letters was to Genet. In this he read that irrepressible though discredited envoy a final lesson in official manners, returning to him certain documents which he had requested the President to lay before Congress and reminding him that as missionary of a foreign nation he could deal only with the executive.[53] The other members of the executive council read and signed this letter. Thus Jefferson ended his career as secretary of state on a note of official correctness.

He was pleased with the political situation at the moment. "This session of Congress is the most interesting one I have ever seen," he said, "and I have great confidence that their measures will be wise." He regarded this body, in which the republican interest was greatly strengthened, as more representative of the country than its predecessor.[54] Also, it was fully informed about foreign relations. He saw some possibility of war, but no nation had striven more, he said, "to merit the peace of all by the most rigorous impartiality to all."

That he had faithfully sought to maintain fair neutrality, despite his original and continuing conviction that the British government was hostile to American interests and that French victory would be to the American advantage, no reader of the huge documentary record that he submitted to Congress could justly deny, nor could anyone fairly question his competence. While unsympathetic with Jefferson as a party man, John Quincy Adams at a later time spoke of his "consummate ability."[55] Even John Marshall recognized that on retirement "he stood particularly high in the esteem of his countrymen"; at the time the hostility of his enemies was "considerably lessened without a corresponding diminution of the attachment of his friends."[56] One of the closest of his political friends, James Monroe, writing him from Philadelphia a couple of months after his retirement and predicting that he would find tranquillity and contentment in private life, added this observation: "And yours will be the greater because you

[53] Dec. 31, 1793 (Ford, VI, 495–496); draft in LC, 16446. The particular documents were translations of Genet's instructions, and the circulation of these aroused severe criticism of him in French circles.

[54] To Col. Gamble, Dec. 22, 1793 (LC, 16395); to Dr. Enoch Edwards, Dec. 30, 1793 (Ford, VI, 494–495).

[55] *Parties in the U. S.*, pp. 12–13.

[56] *Life of George Washington*, V, 488–489.

carry to it, notwithstanding the important and even turbulent scenes you have passed through, not only the approbation of your own heart, and of your countrymen generally, but the silence and of course the constrained approbation of your enemies." [57]

[57] Monroe to TJ, Mar. 3, 1794 (S.M.H., I, 281).

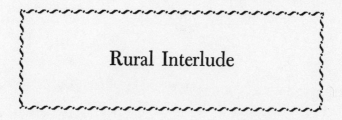

Rural Interlude

[x]

Escape to Domesticity

EARLY in January, 1794, the former Secretary of State left Philadelphia — for good, as he believed. Of the numerous financial transactions he recorded with exactitude in his ever-present account book while winding up his affairs, one of the most interesting and most moving was his settlement with Adrien Petit. For several years he had been in considerable debt to the maître d'hôtel who had served him in France and whom he had induced to return to his service in America.[1] Most of this debt, presumably, represented accumulated household expenses which Petit bore and Jefferson had not wholly repaid. It now stood at $753.72, though Jefferson did not write it thus since he did not yet use the dollar mark. He commonly used the letter *D*, through which he was beginning to run horizontal lines after the analogy of the symbol for the British pound. He now transferred to Petit a large note he had just received from somebody else, adding a small one of his own. Apparently the thrifty Frenchman did not need the cash, and no doubt he was glad to get the interest Jefferson paid him, but the episode illustrates the reliance on credit, the constant borrowing and lending, which were characteristic of the day-to-day financial operations of Jefferson and doubtless of others at the time. His salary of $3500 was payable quarterly, not in advance, and he often had to anticipate it. This particular episode is most significant, however, as marking the close of a chapter in his domestic life. As a farmer at Monticello he did not need Petit, and his fare henceforth might be expected to be more Virginian and less French.

He paid up small debts at Mrs. Fullerton's that Maria had left behind her in September, settled with Joseph Major for five weeks' board, handed out gratuities with his customary openhandedness, and

[1] See *Jefferson and the Rights of Man*, pp. 67, 257, 391. Final settlement in Account Book, Jan. 5, 1794.

boarded the stage for Baltimore, which he reached on the fourth day. At his stopping places he generally patronized a barber when he could find one, to spare himself the unwelcome task of shaving. From Baltimore to Fredericksburg he was driven in a private conveyance, and to Georgetown he had a companion who shared the expense.[2] At Fredericksburg, by prearrangement, he was met by horses of his own, brought by his servant Bob, and after a pause there, he proceeded to Monticello, arriving on January 16. He had escaped to the hills and finally come home to the red-clay country.

He did not complain of the rigors of this journey of some ten days in which he covered less than three hundred miles, for it was made in the right direction. He expected to do little further traveling. Soon he was to write: "The length of my tether is now fixed for life between Monticello and Richmond."[3] The prophecy was accurate for three years anyway. Until February, 1797, when he went back to Philadelphia to be inaugurated as vice president, he made no journey of any length except a single trip to Richmond in the spring after he came home. All the rest of the time he was on his grounds or in their neighborhood. He was beginning a period of rustication, and beyond a doubt he liked it. Choosing a specially good moment, John Adams in April congratulated him "on the charming opening of the spring." The Vice President, writing from Philadelphia, wished that he too could enjoy it out of the "din of politics and the rumors of war." From Monticello, Jefferson responded that the only mistake he had made about his retirement was in postponing it four years too long.[4]

His family, his farms, and his books called him irresistibly, he had said, and he was impatient to rebuild his house. In the autumn he wrote his old teacher George Wythe that he would like to gratify that learned gentleman's taste for books by introducing him to a collection "now certainly the best in America."[5] But months passed before he reassembled his precious tomes, and, despite his collector's pride, he spent little time reading them after they came. He could hardly have been expected to turn to them when he could ride about this countryside — and least of all in the sweetness of the spring or when the haze was on the blue hills in October. This first winter would have been a more fitting season. Soon after his return the weather turned cold. For six weeks the temperature was below freezing about half the time,

[2] He left Philadelphia on Jan. 5, was in Baltimore by the night of Jan. 8, and in Fredericksburg on Jan. 12. He designated his traveling companion as Mr. Brent.

[3] To Horatio Gates, Feb. 3, 1794 (LC, 16571).

[4] Adams to TJ, Apr. 4, 1794, and TJ to Adams, Apr. 25, 1794 (*Adams-Jefferson Letters* [1959], I, 253–254).

[5] Oct. 23, 1794 (LC, 16747).

and there were two snows that lay longer than usual. Because of the unusual wetness of the ground, plowing had never been so backward, he lamented, and obviously he faced immediate frustrations as a farmer and a builder.[6] But if he did not yet have his books back and could not set about planting his crops, restoring his wasted lands, and remodeling his house, he had his full family at the very beginning. At a later time, writing his absent son-in-law and speaking for all the others, he said: "We are fully satisfied that the most solid of all earthly happiness is of the domestic kind, in a well-assorted family, all the members of which set a just value on each other, and are disposed to make the happiness of each other their first object." [7]

The family of six at Monticello in the winter of 1794 lacked a grandmother, for Jefferson, who would be fifty-one in the spring, had been a widower for almost a dozen years, but otherwise it was well distributed among the generations. His daughter Martha or Patsy, though only a little past twenty-one, had been married nearly four years to her cousin Thomas Mann Randolph, Jr., and was the mother of two children. These were Anne Cary Randolph, now approaching three, and a baby boy now started on his second year, Thomas Jefferson Randolph, who was known as Jefferson. His adoring grandfather seems never to have called him "Jeffy," though his mother sometimes did. Martha's husband was twenty-five, and Maria, known in childhood as Polly, turned sixteen that summer.

Jefferson's manner toward the different members of his little family, while always marked by generosity and solicitude, varied with their ages. This was normal enough but was pronounced in his case. While his motherless daughters were growing up he often assumed toward them a didactic tone which they must have found disquieting. He addressed homilies to Martha up to her marriage but after that ceased to do so, treating her thereafter as wholly grown-up, just as he treated her young husband as a peer. In that century the fact that he addressed the latter as "Dear Sir" in letters and referred to him as "Mr. Randolph" even within the family may have meant no more than adherence to convention, but it undoubtedly reflected his attitude. One reason for his unusual appeal to young men, as had been shown so conspicuously in Paris, was that he gave to them and their opinions the respect that is accorded to an equal.

Maria, the member of the family he had seen the most of while an official in Philadelphia, was still under tutelage and subject to parental injunction. In boarding school, first at Mrs. Pine's and then at Mrs.

[6] Details about weather in letter to Monroe, Mar. 11, 1794 (Ford, VI, 500–501).
[7] Aug. 7, 1794 (LC, 16667).

Fullerton's, she had been regularly in her father's house only on holidays. But she was spared the necessity of exchanging letters with "Dear Papa," whose pen was so much more facile than hers. She disliked writing and was often chided by him for not keeping up her end in correspondence. This difficulty was of long standing, and actually he issued his most terrifying threats before Polly was in her teens. Writing her from New York as a "vagrant father" when she was staying at Eppington with her mother's sister, he had suggested that she might be deprived of her dinner until she wrote. It is most unlikely that her Aunt Eppes, a more understanding adult, would have imposed such a heavy penalty; and at a later time Jefferson contented himself with suggesting the somewhat milder punishment of writing her next letter in French. Nowhere else, perhaps, does her generous father appear more exacting than in his earlier letters to the less articulate of his two daughters. In one of these, when he was in New York and she at Eppington, he demanded answers to a whole series of embarrassing questions: whether she got up every day at sunrise, how many pages she read daily in *Don Quixote*, whether she was continuing her music, whether she yet knew how to make a pudding, cut out a beefsteak, sow spinach, or set a hen. This was followed by an exhortation to cultivate all the virtues which was undoubtedly irksome to a girl of twelve and would doubtless have been disturbing at any age.[8] Her father seemed quite humorless at this stage; he did not lecture her so much after she emerged from childhood, but he did not relax his standards. While in school in Philadelphia, Maria was often unwell, and her father implied that she was lazy. She tried to be a dutiful and affectionate daughter, but she must have found him wearing, and his efforts to be both father and mother to her were less successful than with Patsy. Her devotion was more spontaneous to her Aunt Eppes, who had been her second mother before she went to France. Also, she much preferred sheer domesticity to book learning.

Her life at Monticello in this nonofficial interlude in her father's life was uneventful. Apparently he required her to subject herself to no further formal education, though it is hard to believe he did not continue to counsel her about her reading. Not unnaturally, she preferred her sister's two babies to his books. "My sweet Anne grows prettier every day," she had written a few weeks after that young lady's birth.[9]

---

[8] Apr. 11, 1790; *Domestic Life*, p. 181. This is perhaps the most didactic and hopelessly mature of any of TJ's letters to his little daughter. The story of the general relationship through the years is told in my article, "Polly Jefferson and Her Father," *Va. Quart. Rev.*, Jan. 1931.

[9] July 10, 1791 (*Domestic Life*, p. 205).

She continued to stand in some awe of her prodigious father, whom she resembled much less than Martha did, but, back in the country, she could watch the babies grow while she herself was budding into beauty beyond that of her more articulate and more robust sister.

Absorbed though she was in her cares as wife and mother, Martha had heeded her father's injunctions; she and her husband had been in regular communication with him all the time he had been away. The mails were often delayed, however, and in the spring of 1793 he was so disturbed by them that he wrote the Postmaster General.[10] The mail to and from Albemarle County went by way of Richmond, and the post rider was extremely unpunctual, sometimes not going as far as Charlottesville for three weeks. Jefferson stated that the road was always practicable on horseback, and generally for carriages. He and his family exchanged "weekly notices of health" which he did not want interrupted. There were frequent references to the health of the babies in these letters, and Jefferson, though not officious, did not hesitate to give his counsel. Some of it sounds modern, even now. Once, when little Anne was suffering from recurring illness, he wrote her father: "Having little confidence myself in medicine, and especially in the case of infants, and a great deal in the efforts of nature, I direct my hopes towards them. Her mother was so much lower for 6 months, and was recovered almost instantaneously by a good breast of milk, that it learnt me to confide in some good turn of nature in these cases." [11]

Some of Jefferson's most illuminating comments on public affairs can be drawn from his letters to Thomas Mann Randolph, Jr., and Martha, but during his absence they had discussed with him family troubles other than those of health. The most serious of these bore on the relations of the young husband to his own father and close kindred, and one of the most important results was an increase in the debt of gratitude to his father-in-law. Thomas Mann Randolph, Sr., who can be more conveniently designated as Colonel Randolph of Tuckahoe, had taken unto himself a second and very young wife soon after his son was married to Martha Jefferson, and this action created inevitable complications. Jefferson told his daughter at the time that the Colonel's marriage might have been expected: since all his amusements depended on society, he could not live alone. Martha's father

[10] To Timothy Pickering, April 1, 1793 (Edgehill Randolph Papers, UVA). This official was not yet a department head and did not attend meetings of the Executive Council.

[11] Oct. 19, 1792 (LC, 13465).

thus described him, while sagaciously urging her to maintain affectionate relations: "He is an excellent, good man, to whose temper nothing can be objected, but too much facility, too much milk." [12]

It was soon after this that Jefferson effected an agreement with the
father to sell to the son Edgehill in Albermarle County. The Varina
plantation in Henrico County, which had been conveyed to the
younger Randolph when he married, did not seem a good place to live
and there were strong personal reasons for the young couple to be
near Monticello. But the Colonel soon objected to the sale agreement
and infuriated his son by trying to get out of it. The latter, who had
plenty of fire in his own temper, did not now find "too much facility,
too much milk" in his father's. Temporarily he abandoned his hopes to
acquire Edgehill, but at length his father, who had been trying to
safeguard the younger children and wanted better terms, reopened
the negotiations. Early in 1792 an agreement was reached, and the
property was formally taken over in the spring of 1793. After conveying 400 acres of the tract to John Harvie, grandfather of his young
wife, the Colonel sold the residue of some 1500 acres to his son, along
with the slaves on it, for $2000. This was not as good a deal as the
latter originally counted on, but the cost was less than the assessed
value of the property.[13] Before Jefferson came home Randolph had
begun to put into operation at Edgehill his plan of crop rotation, but
not until 1799 did he and his family begin to live there. Meanwhile,
they had headquarters either at Monticello or Varina.

Discord arose in the Colonel's branch of the mighty Randolph clan
after his marriage to a wife who was younger than his own older children and who soon bore him another son. This was in marked contrast
to the concord among the descendants of Peter Jefferson which
Thomas Jefferson went to such pains to maintain throughout his life.
He also did all he could to ease the discord among the Randolphs,
with whom he was so closely related by birth and so closely connected
by his daughter's marriage. He could not influence the course of events
outside his own immediate circle, however, nor do more than counsel

[12] July 17, 1790 (*Domestic Life*, p. 187). The circumstances are briefly described
in *Jefferson and the Rights of Man*, p. 252.

[13] Negotiations and transaction described by William H. Gaines, Jr., in his dissertation, "Thomas Mann Randolph of Edgehill" (UVA, 1950), pp. 64-67. The
following letters and others bearing on this topic are in the Edgehill Randolph
Papers, UVA: TJ to TMR, Jr., Oct. 22, 1790; TMR, Jr., to TJ, Nov. 11, 1790,
Aug. 21, 1791; MJR to TJ, Feb. 20, 1792. For tax purposes the property was valued
at $2390.45.

charity when, under circumstances which have never been fully explained, the greatest scandal arose that ever touched this proud family.

Finding things uncomfortable at Tuckahoe, Nancy Randolph, then unmarried, went to live with her sister Judith and the latter's husband (and cousin), Richard Randolph, brother of John of Roanoke. This was on the Bizarre plantation on the Appomattox River in Cumberland County in Southside Virginia. Early in the autumn of 1792, Richard, Judith, and Nancy were guests at Glynlyvar in Cumberland County. The story was that Nancy was there delivered of a child, or had a miscarriage, and that Richard Randolph, alleged to have been the father, removed the physical evidence. He was formally charged with infanticide. In the sensational trial which ensued in the spring of 1793, he was defended by Patrick Henry and John Marshall and pronounced not guilty.[14] That ended the matter so far as the law went, and there would be no need to enter into it here if Jefferson and his daughter had not discussed it.

Before the trial he heard rumors of the affair and saw something in a paper. Knowing how distressed she must be by this scandal connected with her sister-in-law, he wrote her a wise and comforting letter. It should be remembered that in the generally charitable society of his state and class the utmost propriety was required of women, that his own standards in this respect were rigid, and that his indulgence in the risqué went no farther than joking about the married state with married people. He thought it nothing amiss to tell George Washington that his own daughter was "in the straw" when she was about to have a baby, but he positively blushed when he heard a shady story. Also, according to his code of chivalry, women were to be shielded — always being given the benefit of doubt while blame was placed on the offending male. Mentioning no names in writing his own daughter, he showed a delicacy befitting a gentleman of his school when he talked of delicate subjects to a woman.[15] After assuring her that she and her husband need have no uneasiness about the effect this scandal would have on the world's opinion of them, he manifested his sympathy for the "pitiable victim, whether it be of error or of slander." He hoped that Martha would deal out comfort and commiseration to her in full measure. "Never throw off the best affections of na-

[14] Full story in W. C. Bruce, *John Randolph of Roanoke* (1922), I, 106–123; II, 273–295.

[15] Randall, II, 221, in printing part of TJ's letter shows even greater delicacy, omitting the date and name of the newspaper which TJ mentioned. From Martha's reply of May 16, 1793 (Edgehill Randolph Papers, UVA), we know that the date was April 28, the day before the trial started.

ture in the moment when they become most precious to their object," he said; "nor fear to extend your hand to save another lest you sink yourself."

His daughter's reply showed that for months she and her husband had been deeply troubled, and at times painfully embarrassed. She reported that by following the dictates of her own heart she had stumbled on the affectionate course of conduct he had suggested. She reported, also, that the divisions in the Randolph family were increasing, and that the Colonel made matters worse by his childish passions. She herself regarded the decision of the court as unconvincing, obviously thinking this a case of error. Her father, dismissing his doubts, accepted the interpretation that it was a case of slander.[16] That was to put the best face upon the matter, and also to follow a chivalric and kindly course.

Colonel Randolph of Tuckahoe, though only a couple of years older than Jefferson, was in failing health and no longer able to attend to business. Under these circumstances his son learned that the state of affairs was much worse than he had expected with respect to the Varina plantation. When this was conveyed to him by his father at the time of his marriage there was a mortgage of about £500 on the property — to Herman Leroy, a merchant living in New York — and the Colonel had obligated himself to pay this off. In the fall of 1793, while Jefferson was in Germantown, he learned that this had not been done, that the property was further encumbered, and that a suit had been instituted which would have led to the loss of it. While the Colonel was at death's door, Jefferson worked out with Leroy an arrangement whereby his son-in-law would set aside all the profits from Varina to pay off the mortgage and add another plantation of young Randolph's, Dover, to the security. The latter had suggested Edgehill but Jefferson caused him to follow a course which did not endanger the property in Albemarle. Though saved for the present, Varina continued to be insecure. Seven years later Jefferson once more came to the rescue, making a large remittance from his own resources and again saving the place.[17]

The Colonel died soon after the arrangement was made with Leroy. Jefferson mourned the passing of one whom he had known with the

[16] To St. George Tucker, stepfather of Richard Randolph, Sept. 10, 1793 (Ford, VI, 425).

[17] Among letters in Edgehill Randolph Papers, UVA, dealing with the episode are: TJ to Herman Leroy, Nov. 11, 1793; and Nov. 17, 1793 (also in Jenkins, pp. 94–95, where the episode is incorrectly described); TJ to TMR, Jr., Nov. 24, 1793 (Jenkins, pp. 118–119). Gaines describes these and later events, pp. 71–72, 81–83.

intimacy and affection of a brother since he was five or six years old.[18] He was fully apprised, however, of disquieting circumstances. Young Randolph, who did not get to Tuckahoe in time to have a hand in the drawing of his father's will, reported that this was done by Mr. Harvie at a time when the dying man was virtually insensible. Good provision was made for the younger children, he said. Oddly enough, one of these, a son of the second marriage, had also been given the name Thomas Mann Randolph, so that before the Colonel's death there were three persons who bore it. If this did not annoy Martha's husband it unquestionably added to the genealogical confusion. Old debts were not well provided for, he said, and he and his brother William, though appointed executors, were not named guardians of the children. He regarded this as an "unaccountable and mortifying omission." [19] The failure to make adequate provision for his father's old debts should have disturbed him more, for these were to be a burden on the estate and on him for many years.

Jefferson, scrupulously avoiding reflection on Colonel Randolph, Colonel Harvie, or anybody else connected with the family of his son-in-law, served the latter well as a sympathetic counselor. Also, he manifested his generosity in many lesser ways — as in the case of the horse Tarquin. On his last visit to Monticello before retiring he left that steed behind him, asking that he be sold because of his awkwardness in going downhill. When Randolph offered to take him for himself at the suggested price Jefferson insisted that he take him for nothing.[20] In the year after the older man came home Randolph's prowess as a horseman was attested by his appointment as a captain of cavalry in the militia, while his increased prominence as a citizen was shown by his appointment as a Justice of the Peace of Albemarle County.[21] But the Captain was not destined to cut much of a figure in local affairs as yet, for reasons of health if for no other. Precisely what was the matter with him nobody knew, but in the summer of 1794 he went traveling in the North in pursuit of health, sailing first to Boston — or, as his little son said, to "Bossum" — and proceeding to New York.[22] These travels had no curative effect and, low in spirits, he went to the springs in Augusta County in 1795 and 1796, finally making a complete recovery. Perhaps his depression was connected with the troubles which had beset him as a Randolph, and quite clearly this was a time

[18] To TMR, Jr., Dec. 8, 1793 (LC, 16334).
[19] To TJ, Nov. 30, 1793 (Edgehill Randolph Papers, UVA).
[20] TMR to TJ, Nov. 14, 1793, and TJ to TMR, Dec. 30, 1793 (Edgehill Randolph Papers, UVA).
[21] Gaines, pp. 74–75.
[22] TJ to TMR, Aug. 7, 1794 (LC, 11667); Gaines, pp. 76–77.

when patience as well as tireless kindness was required of his father-in-law.

The unfailing interest of the master of Monticello in the members of the family in which he himself had grown up is abundantly illustrated by his relations with his nephews Peter and Dabney Carr, sons of his sister Martha, who lived in his vicinity, in whose education he directly shared, and who were habitués of the house on the mountain for many years.[23] Peter lived there for a time in this period. Perhaps the most striking illustration of his solicitude, however, was provided by his relations with his youngest sister, Anna Scott Marks, who had married late and unimpressively and was now in need. Learning of her plight when on his brief visit home in the autumn of 1793, he wrote her tactfully: "I have thought it might not always be possible for you to command supplies of those comforts which habits and constitution may have rendered necessary to you." Accordingly, he sent for her a letter of credit effective for six months but without limit of amount. He hoped that she would make free use of this as proof of her affection and that she would visit Monticello after his return there in the new year.[24] There is no reason to suppose that he regarded this action as one of generosity, for he thought it only right and proper that he meet family obligations when he could. Instances of aid rendered by him to other persons to whom he was under no particular obligation could be easily multiplied, however, and some of these led to other requests and consequent embarrassment. He was often gullible in such cases, but he thought niggardliness worse than gullibility. The reputation he gained through the years is suggested by a letter he got shortly before he was elected President. The writer, in far-distant New York, described himself as a student though he had not made much progress in his spelling. "I take this opportunity to let you know that I am verry much in want of a little money," he said. "*I have heard that you are very good to the nedy.*"[25]

It must not be assumed that when Jefferson retired from office in his fifty-first year his financial situation was favorable. For two decades he had borne a heavy burden of debt to British houses, though he was

---

[23] See E. D. Coleman, "Peter Carr of Carr's-Brook," in *Papers Albemarle County Hist. Soc.*, IV (1944).

[24] To Mrs. Anna S. Marks, Oct. 19, 1793, and bill of credit of same date (LC, 16093–94). The latter was sent to his sister Martha Carr, and she was to put it in the hands of some storekeeper or other person who could provide the needed supplies. TJ was unacquainted with the neighborhood in which Mrs. Marks lived.

[25] James Henry to TJ, Nov. 8, 1800 (MHS).

not personally blamable for this. He acquired most of it along with his wife's inheritance when the estate of her father, John Wayles, was divided two years before the Declaration of Independence.[26] Shortly thereafter Jefferson sold lands, later described by him as worth £5000 and sufficient to meet his share in the debt, but the British creditors declined to accept the bonds of the purchasers. He was afterwards paid in depreciated currency and stated that he had to pay the Wayles debt all over again. "It consequently cripples all my wishes and endeavors to be useful to others," he said, "and obliges me to carry on everything starvingly." [27]

In the year 1794, following his retirement, this methodical man drew up a Balance Account which shows the chief items in this old debt.[28] Much the larger part of it was to the British firm of Farell & Jones. He and his two brothers-in-law, Francis Eppes and Henry Skipwith, had reached an agreement with Richard Hanson, a representative of the surviving member of that house, early in 1790, shortly before he went to New York to become Secretary of State. As he recorded it, the total assumed by him was upwards of £4500, more than a third of which was for interest although no charge was made for interest in the war years. Jefferson gave Hanson seven bonds, payable 1791–1797, and throughout those years he was struggling to pay these off. In the midst of his secretaryship of state he wrote a fellow Virginian that he was "haunted nightly by the form of our friend Hanson"; and his correspondent described the latter "as one of the worst of all the human race." [29]

Hanson's vigor in suing the debtors of his firm in the state did not endear him to the planters, and the sentiments of Jefferson's correspondent at this juncture were a less sophisticated reflection of his own, for at just this time he was framing his reply to George Hammond about the British infractions of the peace treaty.[30] His friend, writing from Richmond, expressed suspicions that there was too much British sentiment in the Cabinet, saying that "to subject our citizens to pay the British debts without having the treaty fully complied with on their part, makes them pay this debt doubly, for sure I am, many who owes those debts have lost more Negroes than would amply make

[26] On the Wayles inheritance and his debts see the Long Note toward the end of this volume, after the Bibliography.

[27] To Mr. Carr, May 8, 1791 (MHS).

[28] Fee Book, HEH, Photostat, UVA.

[29] D. L. Hylton to TJ, Mar. 25, 1792 (MHS), quoting TJ's letter of Mar. 17. The first of the bonds were assigned to J. Dobson, with whom TJ had some painful correspondence.

[30] See *Jefferson and the Rights of Man*, pp. 412–417.

them compensation." In Jefferson's own mind, the main desideratum was that the British surrender the Northwest posts, rather than that they make compensation for slaves they had carried off, but he had estimated that his own losses to the enemy in the Revolution were greater than his entire debt to his chief creditor.[31] And no doubt he shared the fear of his friend that, in their distress, the Virginians would become enemies to "a government fraught with injustice to them," that is, to the new federal government. At the same time he was doing everything in his power to meet his own obligations and his correspondence with Hanson shows that he had the full respect of that aggressive collector.

The other major debt was to the Glasgow firm of Henderson, Mc-Caul & Co., represented by James Lyle, with whom Jefferson's correspondence was consistently cordial. This amounted to upwards of £2000, of which more than one third was for interest. Some of this went back to the estate of his mother.[32] None of it may have been directly chargeable to John Wayles, but TJ could have paid off this debt if he had not had the other larger one. His total accumulated debt, most if not all of it inherited, was over £6500, a very large sum for those days. Before his period of retirement ended, £700 or £800 was to be added to this, following a court judgment in favor of Farell & Jones and against the three Wayles executors.[33]

Toward meeting this longstanding debt and its ever-increasing interest, Jefferson had allocated all the income from his farms when he went to France, striving thereafter to live wholly on his salary. This he appears to have done through 1793, except that he fell behind £400 or £500 because of continuing expenses in his Paris house after he left it and because of the heavy cost of shipping his books and furnishings to America. How much of a dent he managed to make in his major debt from the proceeds of his farms is uncertain, but obviously such a total as the one given above required the sale of capital assets, of which he had only land and slaves. By the time of his retirement he had sold more of his outlying lands, the last of those in Cumberland and also Elkhill, after a sad experience in renting that place. The renters were in full arrears for everything, including the Negro la-

[31] D. L. Hylton to TJ, Mar. 25, 1792 (MHS); TJ to William Jones, Jan. 5, 1787 (Ford, IV, 354). See Jefferson the Virginian, pp. 445-446.
[32] James Lyle to TJ, Aug. 11, 1792 (MHS).
[33] The suit, decided in 1795, grew out of a bond for which Wayles was held to have been security, and is generally referred to by the name of Wayles's surviving partner, Richard Randolph. Another suit, involving a much larger sum and relating to the slave ship Prince of Wales, was decided in favor of the Wayles executors in 1798 (J.P., XV, 647-648).

borers Jefferson had sold them. The slaves he sold, besides those at Elkhill who were expected to stay there, were chiefly from his lands in Bedford County, whence most of his tobacco came. He sought to keep the families of these slaves intact and to safeguard the aged, but he found slave-selling unpalatable and while in public office tried to keep his name out of the papers in connection with the sale of any property.[34]

In the debt-ridden Virginia economy of this time virtually all transactions of any size were on a credit basis and payments were slow and uncertain. Bonds were signed and passed from hand to hand in a vicious circle. Jefferson himself was a large creditor. Besides the bonds he got for his slaves, he had others from debtors to the Wayles estate and from various friends and relatives of the best social standing. This paper he passed on to his own creditors, insofar as they were willing to accept it, and his own troubles were compounded when collections failed or were deferred. On paper, he provided adequately for his major debts by or during the period of his retirement, but for one reason or another he fell behind on some of his own bonds, none of which were backed by any security. Before the period ended, in order to cover these, along with a loan from a Dutch banking house which apparently was necessitated by building operations at Monticello, he mortgaged a very large number of slaves. That is, he assigned them as security, believing that they need not be delivered to his creditors in the foreseeable future.[35] Not until this period had he ever mortgaged anything and he took this action now with a view to putting his affairs in order. This was a few months before he returned to public office as vice president, with duties which were relatively unexacting, and again drew a regular salary.

He could not have been expected to anticipate all these developments when he got back to Monticello in 1794. The year before, writing from Philadelphia, he had said: "My business here is of such a nature as to oblige me for long intervals to put aside all my private matters, and only to take them up at times when I have a little glimmering of leisure. Hence an almost total abandonment of my pecuniary interests, in cases often of real magnitude." [36] Other years had been less demanding than his last one as secretary of state, but it was undeniably true that now for the first time in nearly a decade he could give his personal affairs the attention they sorely needed.

---

[34] To Bolling Clark, Sept. 21, 1792, and to Randolph Jefferson, Sept. 25, 1792 (LC, 13389, 13391). This particular sale seems to have been on account of his debt to Farell & Jones.

[35] See Long Note on his debts, below, after the Bibliography.

[36] To Col. Bell, Apr. 14, 1793 (MHS).

⌈XI⌉

Political Bystander

1794–1795

THE master of Monticello did not learn for weeks what happened to the unfinished public business he had left behind him in Philadelphia. About a month after he got home he wrote Madison: "We are here in a state of great quiet, having no public news to agitate us." [1] He had seen no Philadelphia paper, and only through courthouse rumor had he heard that Genet was to be recalled. If the rest of the country was as ignorant as Albemarle County about what was going on in the capital, he reflected, the people were "not in a condition either to approve or disapprove of their government, nor consequently influence it." He had repeated to his successor the saying that ignorance is the softest pillow on which any head can lie but apparently he found more ignorance of national affairs than he had expected, just as he found in his home country more stagnation in business and a greater shortage of cash.[2] Happy as he was to be rid of the responsibilities of office, and relieved though he may have been at escaping newspapers, he manifested some impatience that letters from Philadelphia were so slow in coming. It may have been tedious at Monticello when the cold kept him housed and the ground was too wet for plowing.

At first his friends were slow in writing because they were waiting upon events. Then an epidemic of smallpox in Richmond stopped the post rider altogether. For three months Jefferson had no choice but to let his political mind lie fallow. By April, however, the jam was broken, as though by the thaw of spring. At almost the same time he got half

[1] Feb. 15, 1794 (Ford, VI, 499). A few weeks later he wrote Monroe that no printed copy of his correspondence with Hammond had reached Richmond, though he had heard of one in Staunton; Mar. 11, 1794 (Ford, VI, 500).
[2] To Edmund Randolph, Feb. 3, 1794 (Ford, VI, 498).

a dozen informative and illuminating letters from Congressman James Madison and Senator James Monroe. They brought him up to date about public affairs and until Congress recessed in June kept him posted about all the important happenings, including some "behind the curtain" which did not get into the formal record. He wrote them less often, for his hillside was now in blossom and he was following the farmer's habit of leaving letter writing to a rainy day, but, out of office, he was quite uninhibited and said just what was on his mind.

He learned of the course of the investigation of Hamilton's conduct of the Treasury. This had been resumed at that gentleman's request in the hope of finally silencing the criticisms which had persisted after the defeat of the Giles Resolutions of the last Congress. The committee appointed by the House after Jefferson's departure, containing Giles among its members, finally gave the Secretary what has been commonly interpreted as a complete vindication.[3] Peering "behind the curtain," Jefferson's informants thought otherwise. The major question was whether or not Hamilton had exceeded his authority in withdrawing from Europe certain funds which had been designated for use there. Seeking to justify himself when pressed by the committee, Hamilton brought Washington into the business, with results which were embarrassing to both. In short, the President had to admit his own forgetfulness; and, while stating that undoubtedly he had approved measures proposed from time to time by Hamilton for disposing of the foreign loans, he said he had done so upon the condition that Hamilton's actions should be "agreeable to the laws."[4] This was not the unqualified support Hamilton was seeking, but censure of him would have involved Washington to some extent by implication and none was now recommended even by the Republicans. Before the report was rendered, Madison wrote Jefferson: "The letter from the President is inexpressibly mortifying to his [Hamilton's] friends, and makes his position to be precisely what you always described it to be."[5] Jefferson left no doubt as to what he thought this position was when he wrote Monroe that Hamilton had lately brought the President forward "with manifestations that the business of the treasury had got beyond the limits of his comprehension."[6]

He himself carried into retirement the same ideas about Hamilton's fiscal operations that he had held at the time of the Giles Resolutions.

[3] May 22, 1794; *American State Papers, Finance* (1832), I, 281–301, Report 68. See above, ch. II.

[4] Washington to Hamilton, Apr. 8, 1794 (Fitzpatrick, XXXIII, 18). Discussed by Brant, *Madison*, III, 397.

[5] Apr. 14, 1794 (MP, 17:51).

[6] Apr. 24, 1794 (Ford, VI, 504).

He continued to refer to the "fiscal party," and in the very first letter he wrote back to Philadelphia, while announcing his determination to be a stranger to everything political, he made one exception. "I indulge myself on one political topic only," he said, "that is, in declaring to my countrymen the shameless corruption of a portion of the representatives of the 1st and 2d Congresses and their implicit devotion to the treasury. I think I do good in this, because it may produce exertions to reform the evil, on the success of which the form of our government is to depend." [7] A further reason may have arisen from his immediate concern over the sad state of business in Virginia and his own long-neglected finances. His correspondence with John Taylor of Caroline in this period, though chiefly devoted to agriculture, and his flattering references to that implacable foe of Hamilton's fiscal policies show that these had again become prominent in his own mind, after months of necessary absorption in foreign affairs. He was sure that disgrace and public execration must finally fall on the creator of a national debt which he regarded as excessively large and as an instrument of corruption.[8] Actually, the sentiment against Hamilton in Congress at about this time was so strong that certain partisans of his were talking about the probable dissolution of the Union, asserting that Easterners and Southerners could not live in the same government.[9] But foreign issues crowded out domestic, and to all practical purposes the fiscal battle ended when the Hamiltonians created a diversion in the foreign field.

From Jefferson's point of view the first reports about foreign affairs that reached him were good, but these were soon followed by bad news. He learned that Fauchet had succeeded Genet, and that the new French envoy was behaving himself. His own policies with respect to France thus appeared to be vindicated. Before Jefferson left Philadelphia, Madison had presented a set of resolutions in line with his report on commerce, but action on these was delayed. His position was attacked by Congressman William Smith of South Carolina in a speech which Madison sent him and in which he immediately recognized the hand of Hamilton. Actually, the Secretary of the Treasury wrote

[7] To Edmund Randolph, Feb. 3, 1794 (Ford, VI, 498).

[8] To Monroe, Apr. 24, 1794 (Ford, VI, 504).

[9] Memo. of John Taylor, *Disunion Sentiment in Congress in 1794* (1905), ed. by Gaillard Hunt. Rufus King and Oliver Ellsworth talked with Taylor, and financial questions were emphasized on both sides. This memo. of May 11, 1794, was sent to Madison confidentially, and one can hardly believe that TJ did not eventually learn of it.

the speech.[10] Jefferson's own opinion was that his report was fully justified. It was not debated on its merits, however, and it had virtually no support from the shipping interests it was designed to aid. The Hamiltonians attacked it as a pro-French document, emphasizing the immediate value of commerce with Great Britain and the danger that the policies recommended by Jefferson and proposed by Madison would provoke war. Defenders of the British were increasingly at a disadvantage, however, as word spread of further high-handed actions of theirs on the seas and of their encouragement of Indians on the land. Jefferson's proposals were already outdated. Madison reported to him: "The progress of the evils which they were to remedy having called for more active medicine, it has not been deemed prudent to force them on the attention of the House during more critical discussions." [11]

The former Secretary of State expressed himself on this point in a letter to the President which was devoted chiefly to agriculture: "My opinion of the British government is that nothing will force them to do justice but the loud voice of their people, and that this can never be excited but by distressing their commerce." [12] He added that he cherished tranquillity too much to let political things enter his mind at all, but he was more anti-British than ever, and, when relieved of official responsibility, seemed less averse to war. He noted with apparent satisfaction that in his own region the "ancient hatred" of Great Britain was very much alive. He wrote Monroe: "Some few very quiet people, not suffering themselves to be inflamed as others are by the kicks and cuffs Great Britain has been giving us, express a wish to remain in peace. But the mass of thinking men seem to be of opinion that we . . . invite eternal insults in future should not a very spirited conduct be now assumed." [13] He himself was for peace, he said, if it could be preserved with honor, and he wrote John Adams that, while his countrymen were groaning under the insults of the British, he himself had seen enough of one war never to want to see another.[14] Rarely did he sound so bellicose, however, and he favored "very spirited conduct" at all events.

He viewed with consternation the move to send a special envoy to

[10] Madison to TJ, Mar. 2, 1794 (MP, 17:28), received Mar. 31; TJ to Madison, Apr. 3, 1794 (Ford, VI, 501–502); sympathetic accounts of debate in Brant, *Madison*, III, ch. XXX, and Setser, pp. 116–117.
[11] Mar. 26, 1794 (Hunt, VI, 210).
[12] May 14, 1794 (Ford, VI, 510).
[13] Apr. 24, 1794 (Ford, VI, 503–504).
[14] Apr. 25, 1794 (Ford, VI, 505).

England, wondering why the regular minister, Thomas Pinckney, was being ignored. He was appalled by the possibility that Hamilton might be the missionary, and whatever he may have thought of John Jay's appointment he gained satisfaction no doubt from Madison's report that Hamilton had been laid aside "to his great mortification." He accepted without question the interpretation his confidants gave this entire move as a partisan maneuver. In judging of its political effects he had to rely on what they told him. The action was executive, designed to remove British relations from the consideration of Congress, and Madison, reporting that the democratic societies were attacking it, saw in it "the most powerful blow ever suffered by the popularity of the President." [15] But its immediate effect, while blocking further action in Congress, was to damage greatly the Republican cause in that body. Madison himself summed the matter up after a couple of weeks: "The influence of the Executive on events, the use made of them, and the public confidence in the P. are an overmatch for all the efforts Republicanism can make. The party of that sentiment in the Senate is compleatly wrecked; and in the House of Representatives in a much worse condition than at an earlier period of the session." [16]

Whatever may be said about the wisdom or unwisdom of the executive decision to send John Jay to England to negotiate, there can be no doubt that the action was owing to Hamilton's influence. From this time on he was in effectual control of foreign policy, as of domestic. Such a position of dominance he could hardly have assumed if Jefferson had remained in office. What precise steps Washington would have taken under the advice of the first Secretary of State is a matter of sheer speculation, but it cannot be doubted that in Jefferson's absence the President found it increasingly difficult to follow the course of fair neutrality which his government had charted and maintained when his executive council was better balanced.

That Washington himself wanted to avoid trouble with France as well as Great Britain was shown by his appointment of Monroe to replace Gouverneur Morris as minister to France, shortly before Congress recessed. The recall of the latter, at the behest of the French government, was not engineered by Jefferson, though he had long had qualms about Morris and undoubtedly approved the President's determination to send "a republican character" to that nation. After both Madison and Robert R. Livingston had declined appointment, Monroe, following a conference with Madison and other friends, decided to

---

[15] To TJ, May 11, 1794 (MP, 17:64).

[16] To TJ, May 25, 1794 (Hunt, VI, 217). Monroe spoke to the same effect to TJ, May 26, 1794 (S.M.H., I, 297).

accept it because of "the necessity of cultivating France, and the uncertainty of the person upon whom it might otherwise fall." [17] The procedure was typical of the Virginia Republican leaders, and Jefferson would undoubtedly have been drawn into the conference if he had been available. Monroe did not have time to return to his home in Albemarle County before sailing or to receive any sort of counsel from Monticello. Though his departure marked no severance of his political ties with Jefferson and Madison, it reduced the active members of the trio on the domestic scene to one, and Madison's political activities were soon reduced temporarily, when at the age of forty-five he got married and became involved in more intimate domestic matters. The seas now separated Jefferson from the political confidant he trusted most after Madison. As a foreign correspondent, however, the new minister provided him with firsthand information about the course of affairs in France, a subject on which he needed enlightenment.

The condemnation he had heaped upon Genet was sharply distinguished in his own mind from his attitude toward the French government and the course of the revolution and the war. He knew that there had been sweeping changes in personnel. When Tobias Lear, former secretary of the President, went abroad in the fall of 1793, Jefferson gave his friend a number of letters, but none to political leaders in Paris, because, as he said rather plaintively, "all my friends there have been turned adrift in the different stages of the progression of their Revolution." [18] He still had a few correspondents in France, including Thomas Paine and Joel Barlow, but their long-delayed letters were generally outdated before he got them. Still rejecting all interpretations of the war which did not accord with his own predilections, he continued to regard the French as crusaders for human liberty. During his first months of retirement his comments on the continuing international struggle were in sharp contrast to the balanced judgment which had generally characterized his official conduct, and nearly always his public utterances. Regarding the guarantee of French possessions in the western hemisphere, he went so far as to say in a letter to Madison that, while uncertain about the best time, he had no doubt that at a proper time the United States should declare that these islands must remain French and that it would "make common cause" with the French for that object.[19] As secretary of state he had regarded such actions as entirely impractical, and his offhand suggestion implied that his "ancient hatred" of Great Britian had been so accentuated as

[17] Monroe to TJ, May 27, 1794 (S.M.H., I, 300).
[18] To Lear, Nov. 5, 1793 (Jenkins, p. 37).
[19] Apr. 3, 1794 (Ford, VI, 502).

to mar his judgment. A little later, seizing upon comforting news about French affairs, he made, in another private letter, one of the most extreme of all his statements about the international conflict. To Tench Coxe, who had told him just what he wanted to hear, he wrote:

> Over the foreign powers I am convinced they [the French] will triumph completely, & I cannot but hope that that triumph, & the consequent disgrace of the invading tyrants, is destined, in the order of events, to kindle the wrath of the people of Europe against those who have dared to embroil them in such wickedness, and to bring at length, kings, nobles, & priests to the scaffolds they have been so long deluging with human blood. I am still warm whenever I think of these scoundrels tho I do it as seldom as I can, preferring infinitely to contemplate the tranquil growth of my lucerne & potatoes.[20]

He made no such bloodthirsty remarks when he was viewing kings, nobles, and mobs with his own eyes. And one wonders how he had managed to overlook the Reign of Terror. He must have made it a practice to discount the stories he heard and what he read in the papers, attributing their gruesome details to the British. He was anti-British for other than ideological reasons, and he probably would have favored the French on balance in any case, but as a private citizen he was less judicious, less realistic, than he had been in public office.

He should have been disillusioned to some extent by what he had heard by now from Thomas Paine. After observing that the Jacobins acted with neither prudence nor morality, the author of *The Rights of Man* had written: "Had this revolution been conducted consistently with its principles, there was once a good prospect of extending liberty through the greatest part of Europe; but I now relinquish that hope." [21] Later he wrote that there was now no prospect either that France could carry revolutions into Europe, or that her combined foes could defeat her.[22] It seems that Jefferson, in this period of retirement, voiced no criticism of the French, even in private, until after he had heard from Monroe, who was optimistic enough about the future but who recognized that in the past some things had been very wrong. To get ahead of the story somewhat, for letters were slow in transit, Monroe in his first to Jefferson observed that the execution of Robespierre was hailed with universal joy as "a deliverance from a terrible oppression" that per-

---

[20] May 1, 1794 (Ford, VI, 507–508).

[21] Paine to TJ, Apr. 20, 1793, received Sept. 9, 1793 (*Writings*, III, 132–133).

[22] To TJ, Oct. 20, 1793 (*Writings*, III, 134). In this and another letter he urged the sending of American commissioners to Europe to bring about a termination of the war. These judgments Jefferson does not appear to have acceded to, even in private.

vaded the entire republic. The list of these repressions, he said, would *amaze* Jefferson.[23] Now, and possibly for the first time, that champion of human freedom had to recognize that the atrocity stories had not been fabricated, and that cruel practices had accompanied noble professions. In the second spring of his retirement he summed things up rather more judiciously than had been his wont. Writing to a Frenchman who had had to quit his country, he said: "Being myself a warm zealot for the attainment and enjoyment by all mankind of as much liberty, as each may exercise without injury to the equal liberty of his fellow citizens, I have lamented that in France the endeavours to obtain this have been attended with the diffusion of so much blood." He knew the leading characters of 1789 and those of the Brissotine party, and he always believed that these men were upright. He was doubtful about those who followed, that is, the Jacobins, but he saw many signs of "good sense, moderation and virtue" in the present government.[24]

Toward the end of August "the great little Madison," who had just been accepted by the widow Dolly Payne Todd, made a hasty visit to Monticello before his marriage in mid-September. Believing in domesticity as he did, Jefferson heartily approved this alliance, destined to become famous, but inevitably his chief political friend and ally was more than commonly occupied with private matters that fall, and to Jefferson's dismay he was thinking of retiring from Congress.[25] About the time of Madison's visit the older man suffered an attack of rheumatism which continued in acute form for about two months and which, as he believed, marked the breaking of his health. He had been in bed for ten days in "constant torment" when he got, through his successor as Secretary of State, an invitation from the President to go as a special envoy to Spain.

Edmund Randolph, who was perhaps more astute in this than in any other important episode while in office, correctly concluded that the Spanish were now ready to treat. But they wanted to deal with a more important and impressive personage than Carmichael or Short, who had been waiting so long in the anterooms of the haughty Spanish court; and in this situation Jefferson, who had briefed these representatives so well and who had already shown himself to be an astute negotiator, appeared an ideal choice. The opportune moment for which he

[23] Monroe to TJ, Sept. 7, 1794, received Dec. 16, 1794 (S.M.H., II, 49–50).
[24] To Demeunier, Apr. 29, 1795 (Ford, VII, 13).
[25] TJ's first mention of Madison's wedded state in writing appears to have been in his letter of Oct. 30, 1794, in which he wished the couple "joys perpetual." The marriage was very private and Madison was reticent about it (see Brant, III, 410–411).

had long been hoping had arrived, and it would have been eminently fitting if he had completed in person the negotiations he had set on foot.[26] If he had done so, Pinckney's Treaty (1795) would have been known as Jefferson's Treaty and major public credit for the chief diplomatic achievement of the Washington administration would have been his. To say this is no discredit to Thomas Pinckney, who handled himself with dignity and skill when he assumed the task.[27] The fruit of his own thought and labors was not to be Jefferson's, however. While expressing pleasure that he still enjoyed the President's esteem and approbation, he categorically declined the invitation. The state of his health would have provided a sufficient excuse, but he went far beyond mention of that in his brief reply. Writing Randolph immediately, despite his "paroxysm of rheumatism," he closed the door completely when he said: "No circumstances, my dear Sir, will ever more tempt me to engage in anything public. I thought myself perfectly fixed in this determination when I left Philadelphia, but every day and hour since has added to its inflexibility." [28]

While Jefferson was nursing his rheumatism at home and "the great little Madison" was in the first weeks of his happy marriage, some 12,000 militiamen from four states, accompanied by Alexander Hamilton, were crossing Pennsylvania to Pittsburgh to put down the revolt against the excise tax which is known to history as the Whiskey Rebellion.[29] At the end of October, 1794, after he had "crept out a little on horseback," he was wondering how "such an armament against people at their ploughs" would be represented.[30] It was represented by the government as a sign of the majesty of the law, and Hamilton's interpretation of it as a timely manifestation of the power of the young federal government was taken up by his partisans and afterwards commanded wide acceptance among historians. Since no opposition was encountered, this ostentatious military display now appears disproportionate if not ridiculous, and modern students of this episode can

[26] See above, p. 63, and *Jefferson and the Rights of Man*, pp. 409–411.

[27] Pinckney's Treaty, or the Treaty of San Lorenzo, gained for the United States recognition of the southern boundary at the 31st parallel, free navigation of the Mississippi and right of deposit at New Orleans for a term of years, with the promise of renewal, along with agreements looking to the end of the Indian menace and recognition of the historic policy of the United States with respect to commerce on the high seas.

[28] Sept. 7, 1794 (Ford, VI, 512). Randolph's letter of Aug. 28, 1794 (LC, 16675–16676), reached him that day.

[29] Well described by L. D. Baldwin in *Whiskey Rebels: The Story of a Frontier Uprising* (1939).

[30] To Madison, Oct. 30, 1794 (MP, 17:89).

readily perceive the pathos of the situation of the small farmers in the transmontane country, faced with a hated tax on what was their only marketable product and virtually their medium of exchange. Jefferson was more sympathetic with them than most people east of the mountains: he described this as an "infernal tax," and he thought the conduct of the "rebels" no worse than riotous. A few months later, reviewing the affair in a letter to Monroe, he said that "an insurrection was announced and proclaimed and armed against, but could never be found." [31]

He and Madison promptly perceived the political implications of the episode. They believed that Hamilton seized on an opportunity to gain glory for himself while demonstrating governmental power, and sought to put the Republicans on the defensive by identifying them with lawlessness and disorder. More particularly, the administration blamed the rebellion on the democratic societies. Resentment was very great in the Monongahela country considerably before two democratic societies were established there in 1794, but these were undoubtedly centers of discontent. Washington much disliked these voluntary political organizations, associating them with feverish supporters of Genet and critics of the appointment of John Jay. He would have condemned them earlier but for Jefferson, who warned him that by doing so he would abandon his role as the President of all the people and become the President of a party.[32] Washington, who was excessively sensitive to criticism and who, while by no means averse to differences of opinion within the government, never recognized the value and certainly not the necessity of political opposition, now followed the course Hamilton had always favored. In his annual address to Congress he associated the resistance to the laws in Pennsylvania with certain "self-created societies." [33] Since he spoke in even stronger and more specific terms in private than in this public paper there can be no doubt of his state of mind. Writing John Jay a little earlier, he said that the "self-created societies" which had spread over the country had been "labouring incessantly to sow the seeds of distrust, jealousy, and of course discontent, thereby hoping to effect some revolution in the government," and that undoubtedly they had been the "fomenters" of the disturbance in the West.[34] He had wholly come over to Hamilton's position. The Republicans were therefore in a most unenviable situation: if they raised their voices in defense of the democratic societies

[31] To Monroe, May 26, 1795 (Ford, VII, 16); see also TJ to Madison, Dec. 28, 1794 (Ford, VI, 516–519).
[32] See above, p. 125.
[33] Nov. 19, 1794 (Fitzpatrick, XXXIV, 29).
[34] Nov. 1, 1794 (Fitzpatrick, XXXIV, 17).

they could be charged with patronizing them, abetting lawlessness, and opposing the revered President.

Madison in Congress perceived the dilemma and reported it to his rheumatic friend on the little mountain.[35] All he felt able to do in Congress was to use his position as a member of the committee which drafted a reply to the President's address to prevent a blanket reprobation of the societies. The arguments for reprobation, as he told Jefferson, "fell with equal weight on the press and every mode of animadverting on public men and measures." It seemed to him that the "most sacred principle" of the Constitution had been attacked. He saw the President as menacing the citadel of the people's liberties and implied in his words of lamentation that Jefferson was needed.[36]

Jefferson was entering no public discussion; he was not even writing many private letters and he preferred to talk about the rotation of his crops. But he regarded this issue as one of major importance and his comments on it are important as a revelation of his thoughts. "The denunciation of the democratic societies," he wrote Madison, "is one of the extraordinary acts of boldness of which we have seen so many from the fraction of monocrats. It is wonderful indeed, that the President should have permitted himself to be the organ of such an attack on the freedom of discussion, the freedom of writing, printing and publishing." [37] He wondered what modification of these rights would be proposed and how a line could be drawn between the democratical societies, whose avowed purpose was "the nourishment of the republican principles of our Constitution," and the *self-created* Society of the Cincinnati, which sought to establish hereditary distinctions and undermine the Constitution. He was emphasizing the *abstract* attack on rights, rather than the particular actions — that is, the occurrences in Pennsylvania — which had given occasion to it. But he expressed concern over the present detestation of the government in the invaded region and the consequent increase in the danger of separation from the country, which the "rebels" were charged with threatening. And he thought it strange that the government should be so patient under the "kicks and scoffs" of the country's enemies (meaning the British) and should rise "at a feather" against friends. If one need pick the pre-

35 To TJ, Nov. 30, 1794 (MP, 17:108, received Dec. 16). On the same day TJ got a letter from W. B. Giles, dated Dec. 7, and stating that the sensation had somewhat subsided (LC, 16726–16727).

36 In a letter of Dec. 21, 1794 (MP, 17:119) he was rather more cheerful, believing that "the attack on the essential and constitutional right of the citizen" did not seem to have had the intended effect. Meanwhile, the societies themselves were protesting.

37 To Madison, Dec. 28, 1794 (Ford, VI, 516–519).

cise point at which he began to question the wisdom of Washington, whose judgment he so generally respected, this seems to be it.

He tried to encourage Madison to hold on. No, he must not retire "unless to a more splendid and more efficacious post." That is, he hoped to see Madison President, a thing which he seems not to have talked with this friend about before. He admitted that it was rather inconsistent to do so at this time, in view of his concern for Madison's happiness, for he was also saying, "I would not give up my own retirement for the empire of the universe."

No other public question particularly exercised him in the second winter of his retirement, and from the public scene he became increasingly remote. He did not yet know the precise results of Jay's negotiations in England, though Madison told him the preliminary reports were not encouraging. He learned that Hamilton was leaving office, and, in Madison's words, that Knox "as the shadow follows the substance." [38] He probably did not anticipate that the retired Secretary of the Treasury would continue to dominate the Cabinet. Madison told his friend that Hamilton had written "an arrogant valedictory report," offering a plan for the reduction of the debt which would require thirty years of uninterrupted operation.[39] If Jefferson got this report there is no sign that he now read it, and perhaps he had humor enough to chuckle over the remark of John Adams that Republicans, who delighted in rotations in office, ought to be gratified that all the ablest men in the nation were being "roted out." [40] It was a hard winter and he gave some signs of loneliness, for his daughter Martha and her husband were at Varina, but Maria and the two grandchildren were with him and he gave no indication whatever of discontent.

Describing his situation and state of mind to a European that winter, he wrote: "It is now more than a year that I have withdrawn myself from public affairs, which I never liked in my life, but was drawn into by emergencies which threatened our country with slavery, but ended in establishing it free." [41] He had returned "with infinite appetite" to the enjoyment of his family, his farm, and his books, determined to meddle with nothing beyond them. This he said in connection with a slight departure from his resolution. He referred to a member of the state legislature the "splendid project" of Francois D'Ivernois to transfer to Virginia from the political turmoil of Europe the entire Geneva

[38] To TJ, Dec. 21, 1794 (Hunt, VI, 229–230).
[39] Feb. 15, 1795 (MP, 18:24).
[40] Adams to TJ, Feb. 5, 1795 (*A-J Letters*, I, 256).
[41] To Francois D'Ivernois, Feb. 6, 1795 (Ford, VII, 2). This fascinating letter deserves fuller description than I can give it here.

Academy.[42] The project was deemed impracticable, as he seems to have expected, but it appealed to his imagination and evoked glowing reference to his "attachments to science and freedom, the first-born daughter of science." He had not relinquished his interest in things of the mind, as his letter to this disturbed Genevan scholar and various letters to John Adams at the time and later clearly show. But he was giving no more attention to public matters than he could help, and when the weather permitted him to live on horseback he had little time for books. He had returned to the land. "The earth is grateful," Adams wrote him enviously, adding that he wished they both could say the same of its inhabitants.[43] "Tranquillity becomes daily more and more the object of my life," said the Squire of Monticello, "and of this I certainly find more in my present pursuits than in those of any other part of my life." [44] On the affirmative side the explanation lay in his engrossing present pursuits, on the negative in "a total abstraction from everything political." Accepting the happy and largely irresponsible role of an elderly grandfather, he was leaving public questions to those who would live longer.

Under these circumstances the belated response to his private suggestion of Madison for President was most disturbing. It came just as spring was starting.[45] After a long pause, Congressman Madison briefly answered from Philadelphia "that reasons of *every* kind, and some of them of the most *insuperable* as well as *obvious* kind shut my mind against the admission of any idea such as you may seem to glance at." The obliqueness of both his and Jefferson's references to the Presidency reflected their unvoiced feeling that this office should not be directly sought — least of all by a gentleman reared in the Virginia tradition. At the outset of his public career Jefferson had "stood" for the House of Burgesses, but at no time had he "run" for anything. Madison, asserting that nothing more need be said about himself and that the many other things that needed saying had better be reserved for private conversation, proceeded to issue a warning: "You ought to be preparing yourself however to hear truths which no inflexibility will be able to withstand."

Jefferson's reponse to this friendly but alarming admonition was less emotional than the one he made, a couple of years earlier, to the re-

[42] TJ to W. C. Nicholas, Nov. 22, 1794 (Ford, VI, 513–515); see also correspondence with John Adams in *A-J Letters*, I, 255–259.

[43] Nov. 21, 1794 (*A-J Letters*, I, 255).

[44] To Adams, Feb. 6, 1795 (*A-J Letters*, I, 257).

[45] Madison to TJ, Mar. 23, 1795 (MP, 18:35), replying to TJ's letter of Dec. 28, 1794.

quest that he remain in the secretaryship of state.[46] Then he said that his debt of service to his fellow citizens had been fully and faithfully paid, that he was worn down with fruitless labors, that the motion of his blood no longer kept time with the tumult of the world. A free man now, he was more composed though just as firm.[47] He admitted that the subject of the Presidency, which he still did not refer to by name, had been forced upon his mind by "continual insinuations" in the papers while he was in office. Since he recognized these as hostile in origin and purpose, he gives the historian ground for saying that the well-known practice of impugning the motives of public men by charging them with presidential ambitions goes back to the first administration. Also his testimony gives further ground for believing that he was first "built up" in the public mind by the attacks of his enemies.[48] Though the idea came in the form of hostile insinuation rather than friendly suggestion, he had to face and examine it for his own peace of mind, he said; and he concluded at the time that every reason which had determined him to retire from the secretaryship of state operated even more strongly against the higher office.

To the general considerations which moved him then and still applied, he added certain special ones. His health was entirely broken down, he said, and his age required that he put his affairs in order; these were "sound if taken care of, but capable of considerable dangers if longer neglected." Most important of all were the delights he now felt in his family life and agricultural pursuits. "The little spice of ambition which I had in my younger days has long since evaporated," he said, "and I set still less store by posthumous than present fame." With him, therefore, the question was "forever closed."

It remained closed for another year at any rate, while the ardent farmer proceeded "with a slow but sure step" in his agricultural plans, eschewing things political.

[46] To Madison, June 9, 1793 (Ford, VI, 290–292). See above, p. 88.
[47] To Madison, Apr. 27, 1795 (Ford, VII, 8–11).
[48] See *Jefferson and the Rights of Man*, p. 477.

[XII]

The Ardent Farmer

1794–1797

"THE most ardent farmer in the state" — thus Jefferson described himself during his retirement. He reported to John Adams and others that he had returned to farming with an ardor beyond that of his youth and found it more engrossing than he had ever thought possible. We are in no position to compare the agricultural activities of his youth with those of his fifties, for the former are unrecorded. At the age of twenty-three he began to keep his Garden Book, where he noted the blooming of the hyacinth and narcissus and the planting of asparagus and peas, but not until he came into his wife's inheritance of land and slaves at thirty-one (1774) did he begin to keep his Farm Book. In the aggregate his agricultural records, including his pertinent correspondence, are richer and fuller than those left by any other American of his generation, not excepting George Washington and John Taylor of Caroline. While generally interesting, these become most detailed and most fascinating in the middle of his life.[1]

In the twenty years intervening between 1774 and his retirement from the secretaryship of state, Jefferson gave abundant evidence of his zeal for agriculture, even though he was chiefly concerned with public matters. In his *Notes on Virginia* he sang an unforgettable hymn of praise for the farmer's life, in Europe he was more concerned to observe and report on the agriculture than anything else, and he manifested nostalgia for the countryside in any number of personal letters throughout his service in New York and Philadelphia. But at no time

[1] The admirable editions of E. M. Betts, *Thomas Jefferson's Garden Book* (1944) and *Thomas Jefferson's Farm Book* (1953), contain very numerous extracts from letters and other records. My references to the facsimile of the Farm Book itself are in italics. It is quite impossible to do full justice to these materials here.

in these two decades was he able to devote himself to agricultural operations as he did in this period of retirement, which actually came to only a little more than three years. Nor indeed was he ever again in like position to do so.

This tyro in agriculture, as he called himself, talked of himself as an old man even now and he continued to be self-depreciatory. A couple of years after he got back to Monticello he wrote: "I am but a learner; an eager one indeed but yet desperate, being too old now to learn a new art. However, I am as much delighted and occupied with it as if I was the greatest adept." [2] The Duc de La Rochefoucauld Liancourt, a visitor to Monticello in 1796 who left one of the best accounts of Jefferson's situation, said that his host had drawn the principles of agriculture "either from works which treat on this subject or from conversation." He then remarked that while knowledge thus acquired may be misleading and is insufficient in itself, it is preferable to "mere practical knowledge" in a country where bad practice prevails. That bad farming practice was all too prevalent in Virginia was obvious to this visitor, as it was to a sagacious and forward-looking planter like George Washington. The conclusion of the Frenchman, therefore, was a proper one: "Above all, much good may be expected, if a contemplative mind, like that of Mr. Jefferson, which takes the theory for its guide, watches its application with discernment, and rectifies it according to the peculiar circumstances and nature of the country, climate, and soil, and conformably to the experience which he daily acquires." [3]

While recognizing Jefferson's inexperience in the day-to-day operations of a farm, such as had been under the direction of his overseers, we should be careful not to exaggerate the contrast between theory and practice. His mind was bold and imaginative in this field as in others, but he was not floating on the clouds over Monticello. His purpose to restore and improve his farms was an eminently practical one, and his basic ideas about the lines of agricultural progress could hardly be called visionary. His disapproval of absentee ownership and of crops that wasted the land, his advocacy of crop rotation, and the best available implements, his tireless quest of more useful plants — these were quite in accord with the best agricultural thought of England and America. He was in touch with that thought and continued to be throughout his active years, as his correspondence shows unmistakably. Fresh in mind and perennially experimental in spirit, he sought workable ideas everywhere, applying them with varying de-

[2] To W. B. Giles, Apr. 27, 1795 (Ford, VII, 12).
[3] *Travels Through the U. S. of North America*, quoted by Randall, II, 303.

grees of success but with characteristic enthusiasm and individuality. With respect to specific practices, plants, and implements he probably got more suggestions from conversation and correspondence with contemporaries than from any formal treatises, and he was as aware as George Washington that conditions on the American land were very different from those in England.

While secretary of state, Jefferson prepared some notes on agriculture at Washington's request in partial answer to certain queries of Arthur Young, the best-known English writer on agricultural matters in his generation. For the first time he sought to calculate the profits of capital invested in Virginia agriculture — a thing which, as one who had inherited both his lands and slaves, he had not previously thought of doing, any more than his fellow planters had. Young had reckoned slave labor as dearer than labor in England, while Jefferson, entering into what has remained until this day a highly controversial statistical problem, essayed the opinion that Negro slave labor was cheaper, everything considered. In his estimate he allowed something for the greater productivity of free white labor, which he conceded. After calculation, he estimated the return on total capital investment in Virginia agriculture as a theoretical 14 per cent. Young challenged some of these figures, especially those relating to the increase in value of slaves and land, and got the theoretical profit down to 8 per cent.[4]

Jefferson offered no particular objection to the criticisms of his essay in statistics, regarding it "rather as a mode of calculating the profits of a Virginia estate than as an operation which was to be ultimately relied on," and promising at a later time a calculation based on real experience. Young appreciated it, and he took greatest exception to certain details which, as a matter of fact, pointed to important differences between agricultural conditions in England and Virginia. He could not understand the suggested ratio between wheat on the one hand and sheep and cattle on the other; to his mind, there was relatively too much of the former and not enough of the latter. "Arable land can yield wheat only by means of cattle and sheep," he said; "it is not dung that is wanted so much as a change in products: repose under grasses is the soul of management."

Jefferson profited from this exchange with Arthur Young. He took the hint to give more consideration to sheep, he said. In Virginia, however, sheep faced dangers from wolves and dogs such as they did not meet in England; and cattle roamed the uncleared and abandoned land

[4] TJ's notes went with Washington's letter of June 18, 1792, to Young, and his comments on Young's criticisms are in his letter of June 28, 1793 (Ford, VI, 81–87). See also Fitzpatrick, XXXII, 64–72.

instead of pasturing serenely in green meadows. Manure did not enter into good husbandry in his home country, Jefferson said, "because we can buy an acre of new land cheaper than we can manure an old one." Young was unacquainted with virgin soil, as he was with an economy based on abundance of land and scarcity of labor. "Good husbandry with us," Jefferson said, "consists in abandoning Indian corn and tobacco: tending small grain, some red clover, fallowing, and endeavoring to have, while the lands are at rest, a spontaneous cover of white clover. I do not present this as a culture judicious in itself, but as good, in comparison with what most people there pursue." He was glad to note that in his own highland country farmers were turning to small grain, after sixty years of successive cropping of tobacco followed by Indian corn, four or five years' rest of the land, and then a return to the old exhausting cycle.

He quoted Arthur Young in his Farm Book many times thereafter, but more immediately he looked not to England but to Pennsylvania, where both he and George Washington specially admired the farming — not to Young but to Dr. George Logan of Stenton near Philadelphia, whom he described as the best farmer in that state and who, besides that, was an ardent Republican. He even turned to Logan for advice about the one of Young's voluminous writings which would be best to buy, though he eventually bought several. And, with respect to the rotation of crops, which he took to be "the most important of all the questions a farmer has to decide," he informed his son-in-law that he had learned more from Dr. Logan than from all others put together.[5] In order to gain further benefit from the farming practice in the same part of the country, he engaged an overseer from the head of Elk, Samuel Biddle by name.[6] This overseer proved disappointing and lasted only a year, but the selection of him was one of many signs of the direction in which his employer was looking.

By precept and example Jefferson was an outstanding leader of the movement, which gained considerable headway in his region in the 1790's, against the staple agriculture which had characterized the economy of Virginia since colonial days and toward the more diversified and self-sufficient farming to the north of him. That the movement was sensible and conducive to economic and social health can hardly be doubted. His services to agriculture in his own region and in the nation as a whole cannot be measured merely in terms of his operations

[5] To TMR, July 28, 1793 (Garden Book, p. 199); to Logan, July 1, 1793 (ibid., p. 196).

[6] Agreement of June 18, 1793 (Farm Book, p. 152, from MHS); also TJ to Biddle, Dec. 12, 1792 (Papers, MHS, pp. 43-46).

on his own acres under his particular circumstances. By stimulating and inspiriting others throughout his long life he served his country better than he served himself.

The degree of his success in working out his own problems is very difficult to measure. He met greater practical obstacles than he had expected and was deflected from his chosen course before he could make much progress on it. He kept unusually detailed records, without clerical assistance, but seems never to have drawn for the benefit of Arthur Young the fresh calculation he had promised. Some enterprising scholar of today may be able to estimate what rate of profit his farms actually returned on capital investment at this and other times, but apparently he himself did not do so, nor did he clearly separate farm income and outgo from other financial operations. Toward the end of his presidency, as though forgetting the years of his retirement, he remarked regretfully to his son-in-law that he had "only very general ideas of the theory of agriculture, without actual experience." [7] In the light of his contemporary records, he did not do justice to his diligence, intelligence, and ingenuity during the time when he devoted himself wholeheartedly to his farms, but obviously his success fell far short of his aspirations. In the last year of his life, when beset with troubles not of his own making, he summed things up to James Monroe: "A Virginia estate managed rigorously well yields a comfortable subsistence to its owner living on it, but nothing more." [8] He had found that it ran the owner into debt if he was absent from it and if he was forced to deal on credit. By that time he might have added that its proceeds could not be expected to pay off heavy debts already existing, or to finance extensive construction projects, or to provide for the failures of others.

In the year 1794 Jefferson had upwards of ten thousand acres of land, as indeed he did for the rest of his life.[9] Roughly half of this was in Albemarle County and half elsewhere, chiefly at Poplar Forest in Bed-

[7] To TMR, Jan. 31, 1809 (*Papers, MHS*), p. 134.

[8] Feb. 22, 1826 (Ford, X, 379).

[9] His land roll of 1794 is in *Farm Book*, pp. 32, 324–325. See also *Jefferson the Virginian*, app. II. Precisely, he had 5591⅔ acres in Albemarle, 5101½ in Bedford and Campbell, and 157 in Rockbridge (Natural Bridge), making a total of 10,850⅙. He himself made it 10,647, presumably because he changed individual items without changing the total. He used the name Poplar Forest as the overall designation of his Bedford lands, though actually there were two other plantations, Bear Creek and Tomahawk. In 1810, when he drew another land roll he had about 800 acres less, altogether, chiefly because of gifts of land to his children. Except for Pouncey's, which was woodland, and Limestone in the south of the county, his Albemarle holdings were contiguous.

ford County. The latter plantation, which was a few miles southwest of Lynchburg and about eighty miles from Monticello by the roads he traveled, knew him only as a periodic visitor, and not until old age did he make long visits there. His personal supervision of agricultural operations, therefore, was confined to the lands in Albemarle where he himself lived. These were divided into two parts by the Rivanna River. The part below the stream, including the plantations of Monticello and Tufton, was somewhat larger than the part above it, including Shadwell and Lego. Less than a fourth of these Albemarle lands were under cultivation — between 1100 and 1200 acres — the cultivated areas being about the same size on the two sides of the little river. Crossing was by the ford at Shadwell and by the Secretary's Ford farther upstream. There were no bridges.

Jefferson, who always loved his home country, went so far as to say in an enthusiastic moment that "these mountains are the Eden of the United States for soil, climate, navigation, and health." [10] The range of mountains around which his fields clustered was low, and his occasional reference to himself as a mountaineer was of course an exaggeration. So also to many minds was his praise of the local climate. He always described it as moderate, and to one who hated the cold as much as he did it probably seemed so, especially at elevated Monticello, but the heat of the low hills and valleys was often oppressive and the summer sun baked the open fields. There could be no doubt that, in comparison with the tidewater region and, indeed, with a low-lying city like Philadelphia, this piedmont country was healthful.

As for navigation, that was provided by the Rivanna, often referred to in earlier days as the north branch of the James. This shallow stream, now so unimpressive, played a highly important part in Jefferson's personal history. His first public service of note was the initiation of a project to clear it so that canoes and bateaux could use it safely and thus provide transportation to and from Richmond.[11] By this route his own farm products went to market and his books and furniture finally arrived from Philadelphia. At the head of navigation of the Rivanna the village of Milton had sprung up; this was about three miles below Monticello and six below the village of Charlottesville. The roads in this hilly country were often little more than trails, but Jefferson had a short haul to Milton.

The little river was indispensable to him, but it did him harm as well as good. He involved himself in enormous trouble and huge expense

[10] To Volney, Apr. 9, 1797 (Gilbert Chinard, *Volney et L'Amérique* [1923], p. 80).

[11] See *Jefferson the Virginian*, pp. 115-116.

in his efforts to restore the gristmill at Shadwell which had been swept away, along with its dam, by the "great fresh" of 1771. Seeking to avoid building another dam, he determined to dig a new canal which would take in the water three-quarters of a mile further upstream, above a ledge of rocks. Work on this unwise project was begun in the year of the Declaration of Independence and continued at intervals until he went to France, requiring in that time more than seven thousand man-days of labor. During the latter part of his secretaryship of state he was impatient to resume operations; he talked of its being finished in the summer of 1793 and even went so far as to seek a tenant for the mill he intended building. He did not actually resume this costly undertaking until 1796, and his gristmill did not begin to operate until his first term as President.[12] During his period of active farming, therefore, his canal and gristmill, along with the dam he eventually had to build and the manufacturing mill he was already planning, fell in the category of unfinished business. More immediately he directed his attention to his farms.

As Jefferson said, the land below the mountains was in "large waving hills" and of a dark red color. In its native state he thought it good, especially the bottom land — excellent for wheat and rye, though poor for oats and only middling for Indian corn.[13] It had been subjected, however, to what he regarded as very slovenly husbandry. He reported to George Washington in 1794 that, on more minute examination of his own lands than he had been able to make on previous short visits, he found that a ten years' "abandonment of them to the unprincipled ravages of overseers" had brought them "to a degree of degradation" far beyond his expectation.[14] John Breckinridge of Kentucky, of whom he had requested some clover seed, suggested that he be sent soil as well, to make sure that the seed would grow. Writing from the bluegrass country, this friend said he wished that a thousand acres of that fertile land could be spread around Jefferson, who could then "really farm with both pleasure and profit." [15] A little later the ardent farmer at Monticello lamented to Washington: "never had any reformer so barbarous a state of things to encounter as I have. It will be the work of years before the eye will find any satisfaction in my

[12] The basic document, bearing the title "Grounds for estimating the value of the Shadwell Mills," and covering the years 1771–1806, is in LC, 42029. Most of this is in *Farm Book*, pp. 363–365. The editorial comment in that work on the river, the mills, the canal, and the dam (beginning on p. 341), and the extracts of correspondence that follow this, cover the entire subject.

[13] Comment in 1791 (*Farm Book*, pp. 328–329).

[14] May 14, 1794 (Ford, VI, 509).

[15] To TJ, July 25, 1795 (quoted from LC in *Garden Book*, p. 237).

fields." [16] After the unremitting efforts of more than two years to restore them, he said: "My hills are too rough ever to please the eye, and as yet unreclaimed from the barbarous state in which the slovenly business of tobacco making has left them." [17]

Quotations could be multiplied to demonstrate Jefferson's aversion to tobacco culture. The best-known of these is in his *Notes on Virginia*, written more than a decade earlier: "It is a culture productive of infinite wretchedness. Those employed in it are in a continued state of exertion beyond the powers of nature to support. Little food of any kind is raised by them; so that the men and animals on these farms are badly fed, and the earth is rapidly impoverished." [18] By contrast, he said, the culture of wheat clothed the earth with herbage, preserved the fertility of the soil, fed the laborers well while requiring less toil of them, raised animals for food and service, and diffused plenty and happiness throughout the economy. He favored wheat, therefore, on social and moral as well as economic grounds.

In local usage the cultivator of tobacco was a planter, while the man who raised small grains was a farmer. Planting, in this sense, had largely given way to farming in Albemarle by the time Jefferson came home to stay, though the change proved to be only partial. He described himself as a farmer but continued to raise tobacco at Poplar Forest, depending on it for his major cash income. The Bedford tobacco, after being prized or packed into hogsheads by slaves who were often careless, was taken by wagons to Lynchburg, loaded there on bateaux, and floated down the James River to Richmond, where as a rule it was sold. Jefferson had to give attention to the perennial problem of marketing, but he appears never to have concerned himself personally with the tedious processes of planting, cultivating, harvesting, and curing tobacco. He wanted to abandon this plant rather than reform its culture, and in Albemarle he turned to wheat as a substitute cash crop, showing deep interest in it from the plowing to the harvest.

Personally, he would have liked to get away not only from tobacco but also from Indian corn, with which, as Washington said, the overseers would have filled the land if left to their own discretion. [19] The President fully agreed with his fellow Virginian about its destructiveness as a crop. Jefferson did not care for corn as food and would have liked to substitute potatoes, but it was basic in the plantation ration for both men and beasts. He had to allow for it in all his plans, and

[16] Sept. 12, 1795 (quoted from LC in *Garden Book*, p. 238).
[17] To Francis Willis, July 15, 1796 (*Farm Book*, p. 266).
[18] William Peden edn. (1955), pp. 166–167.
[19] To TJ, Oct. 4, 1795 (Fitzpatrick, XXXIV, 323).

at times he even had to purchase it from some neighbor. His greatest enthusiasm was for cover crops, especially clover; his dominating purpose was to rest and renew his tried lands. This called for long-range planning and, as Washington said, the adoption of the motto "slow but sure."

The specific programs of crop rotation that Jefferson outlined in letters, shortly before and during his relatively brief period of actual farming, together with the detailed charts and tables he drew, reveal his characteristic patience and constructiveness as a reformer.[20] He also made careful note of the plans of others, especially George Washington and Dr. Logan.[21] Neither of these forward-looking men scoffed at his program as doctrinaire, nor did his son-in-law, who had one that was even more elaborate; but John Taylor was dubious of rotation schemes, and Jefferson's noble French visitor, with whom he undoubtedly discussed his plans at great length in 1796, was no better than noncommittal. The Duc de La Rochefoucauld Liancourt said: "His system is entirely confined to himself; it is censured by some of his neighbors, who are also employed in improving their culture with ability and skill, but he adheres to it, and thinks it founded on just observations." [22] The student of today, who is in position to compare Jefferson's rotation with those of George Washington and other contemporaries, is less disposed to question his particular choices than to wonder, when poring over these old papers, if farming could have been expected to be as mathematical in practice as it appears to have been in Jefferson's mind.

To provide for a seven-year rotation he proposed to divide each of his four Albemarle farms into seven fields of forty acres each, furnishing each with four men and four women laborers, four horses and four oxen.[23] The fields were to be supposed equal and were to go through the same succession of crops — beginning at different points in the cycle. Thus, year by year, the total acreage would be the same in wheat, corn, clover, field peas, or potatoes as the case might be. By-products and minor variations resulting from the addition of new fields were allowed for, but this paper scheme seems rigid. We do not know to what extent its author put it into operation. As a working

20 See, e.g., the correspondence with TMR in 1793 in *Garden Book*, pp. 194–203, and with John Taylor and Washington in 1794 (*ibid.*, pp. 217–223); also commentary and extracts in *Farm Book*, pp. 310–317. The best account of his plans by a contemporary that I have seen is that of the Duc de La Rochefoucauld Liancourt in 1796 (quoted in Randall, II, 303–306, and *Garden Book*, pp. 241–244).

21 *Farm Book*, p. 97.

22 Randall, II, 305.

23 This description is largely based on the undated documents in *Farm Book*, pp. 314–317, but many of the same ideas and details are in contemporary letters.

farmer he got through only about half the cycle, so he could not have carried it into full effect. Also, we know from his own records that his course was deflected by fluctuations in prices and by the vagaries of the weather. Some relatively conspicuous things he did do that may have seemed to his neighbors theoretical, unnecessary, and even wasteful. He divided his farms into fields, which he himself surveyed at some time and to which he gave names.[24] In 1794 he separated his Albemarle fields, or most of them, not by fences but by rows of peach trees with a road between them. In December of that year he set out nearly 900 trees for that purpose, at the same time that he planted 263 in his north orchard.[25] His motives, as he himself described them, were less esthetic than utilitarian. The cross fences that had been between the fields were removed and the rails used for outer fences, thus protecting all the fields from pasturage. A distinctive feature of his program was that his fields were not to be trodden by grazing animals. Another was that the ground while resting between "extractor" crops like wheat and corn must be covered, mostly by clover, and not be baked hard by the southern sun.

The philosophy on which he proceeded is well summed up in a letter to John Taylor of Caroline:

> . . . I am sensible of the truth of your observations that the atmosphere is the great storehouse of matter for recruiting our lands, that tho' efficacious, it is slow in its operation, and we must therefore give them time instead of the loads of quicker manure given them in other countries, that for this purpose we must avail ourselves of the great quantities of land we possess in proportion to our labour, and that while putting them to nurse with the atmosphere, we must protect them from the bite & tread of animals, which are nearly a counterpoise for the benefits of the atmosphere. . . . And though I observe your strictures on rotation of crops, yet it appears that in this I differ from you only in words. You keep half your lands in culture, the other half at nurse; so I propose to do. . . . My years of rest, however, are employed, two of them in producing clover, yours in volunteer herbage. . . . I think that the important improvement for which the world is indebted to Young is the substitution of clover crops for unproductive fallows . . .[26]

[24] His various fields are listed by Betts in *Farm Book*, p. 336. The names varied from year to year, and the total pattern is not that of seven fields per farm, suggesting that he did not long maintain a rigid scheme. His surveys of the fields at Shadwell, Monticello, Tufton, and Tomahawk (Bedford County), as shown there, reflect no geometrical uniformity.

[25] *Garden Book*, p. 212. Presumably this was at Monticello and Lego.

[26] Dec. 29, 1794 (*Garden Book*, p. 220).

Jefferson regarded himself as definitely successful with red clover, which not only protected his lands while they were "at nurse" but also was used for stock feed, as were other "ameliorative" crops. Besides horses, mules, and oxen he had cattle and hogs and was beginning to breed sheep, but he did not raise animals for sale.[27] There was no market for them in a society where virtually everybody raised them. Except for wheat, therefore, all the products of his fields were for human or animal consumption on his own farms. He did all he could to make his agricultural principality self-sufficient, but it was never wholly so, even in food. Furthermore, a man of his tastes and debts needed a considerable cash income. The fate of his personal venture in farming in Albemarle and of his system of crop rotation, therefore, was inseparable from the fortunes of his wheatfields.

His record of sales is more fragmentary in the case of his wheat than of his tobacco, but clearly he did not turn all of his crop into cash; relatively little wheat was consumed as food, but some of it was used locally for barter. The rest of it was sold in Richmond, a market which was relatively accessible to him. His unprocessed grain was taken by wagons to Milton and there was loaded on bateaux to be floated downstream. The details of his marketing procedure are far from clear, but in these years of active farming he did not complain about prices or suggest any inability to sell his product, which he himself judged to be of high quality. Nor does he appear to have suffered grievously from the pests which so commonly plagued wheat — especially the weevil. In this period, however, he had major difficulties created by the farmer's fickle friend — the weather.

He raised winter wheat, and the winter of 1794–1795 was so harsh on it that, giving up all thought of a great crop, he even doubted if he would make a good one.[28] In the summer of 1795 his lands, in an area particularly susceptible to erosion, suffered terribly from excessive rains. "I imagine we never lost more soil than this summer," he said. "It is moderately estimated at a year's rent." [29] The chief damage in Albemarle was to the corn crop, in Bedford to the tobacco. During

[27] TJ's own records in his *Farm Book* (esp. pp. *33, 44*) show that early in 1794 his workhorses, mules, broodmares, colts, yearlings, two- and three-year-olds, together with his 8 riding horses, totaled about 75. He had about the same number of steers (including work oxen), bulls, cows, calves, and beeves. There were very few of the latter, while there were about 200 hogs and pigs, which were relied on for plantation food much more than beef was. At the beginning of the year he had no sheep but he got some later. He showed considerable interest in breeding sheep in his later years, but apparently had none in breeding cattle. Throughout life he was enormously interested in horses.

[28] To Tench Coxe, June 1, 1795 (Ford, VII, 22).

[29] To TMR, Aug. 18, 1795 (*Garden Book*, p. 238).

the late summer and early fall some three hundred acres of wheat were sown on the two sides of the river. Happily the autumn weather was admirable for the sprouting grain, and in 1796 he had the finest harvest on record.[30] From this high point he plunged into deep trouble. Between the middle of October and the middle of December of that year there was not enough rain to lay the dust; virtually no grain sprouted before severe cold came, and he apprehended that he would have no wheat crop. In January of 1797, a couple of months before he returned to public life as vice president of the United States, he wrote James Madison: "Much as I am an enemy of tobacco, I shall endeavor to make some for taxes and clothes." [31] He had never ceased making it in Bedford, and he now planned to use for this purpose some newly cleared lands in Albemarle.

He was not wholly withdrawing from active farming as yet; in fact his public duties required him to be away from Monticello only a few months that year, and as vice president he spent far more time at home than as secretary of state. Nor had he ceased to believe in his rotation system; he wrote about it enthusiastically to an English agriculturist early in the next year.[32] Toward the end of 1798, however, when public affairs were really pressing, he announced an agricultural retreat. He wrote John Taylor that the high price of tobacco, which seemed likely to continue, had tempted him to go entirely into that culture. In the meantime, he said, "my farming schemes are in abeyance, and my farming fields at nurse against the time of my resuming them." [33] Under pressure of practical necessity, the master of Monticello had again become a tobacco planter in his home country.

Never again was he an absentee owner in the sense that he had been during his years in France, but he took a long step away from personal control when he began to lease portions of his farm. This was in the latter half of his vice presidency. He had thought of doing this a good deal earlier, hoping to gain personal relief and a dependable cash income at the same time.[34] One feature of the arrangements he made in 1799 and 1800 is of particular interest here. In his Farm Book, under the heading "Tenants," he wrote this: "Tie them up to some rotation of crops which shall include meliorating years to counterbalance at least the exhausting ones." [35] In his effort to carry out that policy he stipulated that each field be rested two of every five years, clover being

[30] To Monroe, July 10, 1796 (Ford, VII, 89).
[31] Jan. 8, 1797 (Ford, VII, 104); also to TMR, Jan. 9, 1797 (*Farm Book,* p. 266).
[32] To William Strickland, Mar. 23, 1798 (*Garden Book,* pp. 262-263).
[33] Nov. 26, 1798 (*Garden Book,* p. 260).
[34] See letters, extracts of 1787-1793, in *Farm Book,* pp. 161-166.
[35] *Farm Book,* p. 119.

permitted, and that no field be put in Indian corn more than one year in this cycle.[36] He was standing by his theories and protecting his lands as best he could on paper, whatever failure there may have been on his tenants' part in practice.

[36] Indenture of Oct. 1, 1799 with Craven Peyton, and Heads of Agreement with John H. Craven, Aug. 22, 1800 (*ibid.*, pp. 167–169). In later agreements he stipulated a more precise rotation.

[XIII]

Slaves, Plows, and Nails

PERIODICALLY, Jefferson listed his slaves by name, showing their location. In the year 1794 he had about a hundred and fifty, of whom roughly two-thirds were in Albemarle and one-third in Bedford.[1] This figure represented a reduction of about fifty from the number he had listed a decade earlier, the difference being chiefly attributable to sales. This sort of traffic was repugnant to him whenever it involved the removal of slaves from the land on which they had been living, but the prime purpose of his sales, both of lands and slaves, was to pay off the old Wayles debt. Most of this, he said, was originally contracted by his father-in-law for the purchase of slaves, and nearly all of the ones he sold could be regarded as part of the Wayles inheritance.

His desire to make these transactions as humane as possible is shown by his stipulations for the sale of eleven Negroes from Bedford in 1792.[2] A family of four was to be kept intact, and an old couple were to go with their two sons if they wished — no charge being made for them. It seems that old Will and Judy chose not to go, preferring to remain at Poplar Forest in honorable retirement. In other cases he bought or sold individuals in order to unite families; and in general, under circumstances of necessity, he made the best he could of an institution which he deplored far more than the slovenly culture of tobacco.

His personal activities against the institution of slavery were greatest in the period of the American Revolution, when he vainly proposed a plan of gradual emancipation for his own commonwealth.[3] He re-

[1] Roll of Negroes, Nov. 1794, and location for 1795 (*Farm Book*, p. *30*. His roll for 1783 is on p. *20*).
[2] To Bowling Clarke, Sept. 21, 1792 (*Farm Book*, p. *13*, from LC).
[3] See *Jefferson the Virginian*, pp. 264–269.

flected that the public mind was not ready for this, and he had wondered how his fellows would take the strictures on slavery in his *Notes on Virginia*. While in France, however, he expressed the hope that his state would "begin the redress of this enormity," his reliance being on the young men, who had "sucked in the principles of liberty as it were with their mother's milk." [4] More recently, events in Santo Domingo had caused his mind to revert to this question. The massacre of whites on that island, and the flight of others to the United States, occasioned his reflection that eventually the people of color would expel all the whites from the West Indies and wholly take over. The percentage of whites was much higher south of the Potomac, but, anticipating that there would be bloody scenes there some day, he told his friend Monroe and his son-in-law that something should be done to prevent these. "What is to take place in our Southern states will depend on the timely wisdom and liberality of their legislatures," he said. [5]

Meanwhile, he had to consider his own obligations as a private person. A score of years later, when the public was still apathetic, he summed up the working philosophy by which he had long sought to guide his feet: "My opinion has ever been that, until more can be done for them [the slaves], we should endeavor, with those whom fortune has thrown into our hands, to feed and clothe them well, protect them from ill usage, require such reasonable labor only as is performed voluntarily by freemen, and be led by no repugnancies to abdicate them, and our duties to them." [6] It was a realistic and humane philosophy.

To have emancipated the whole body of his slaves, depriving himself thereby of his entire labor force and a large part of his property while turning them loose in an inhospitable world, would have been neither practicable nor kind. When he freed a particular slave, that individual was prepared for freedom in his opinion, and had a good place to go to. In this period he emancipated two members of the Hemings family of mulattoes which was so prominent at Monticello. Bob Hemings, now thirty-two, seems to have bought his own freedom, at a valuation of £60. His future employer advanced the money. [7] The case

[4] To Richard Price, Aug. 7, 1785 (*J.P.*, VIII, 356–357); see *Jefferson and the Rights of Man*, pp. 95–96.

[5] To TMR, July 14, 1793 (LC, 15506–15507); to James Monroe, July 14, 1793 (Ford, VI, 349).

[6] To Edward Coles, Aug. 25, 1814 (*Farm Book*, p. 39). See also his letter to W. A. Burwell, Jan. 28, 1805 (*ibid.*, p. 20).

[7] Indenture of Dec. 24, 1794, freeing Robert Hemings (*Farm Book*, p. 15; Account Book, Dec. 24, 1794). TJ said "Straus" advanced the money, while Isaac Jefferson in *Memoirs of a Monticello Slave* (1955), p. 10, identified him as "old Dr. Strauss" of Richmond, adding that Bob afterwards had the misfortune of having his hand blown off by a blunderbuss.

of James Hemings was different. Jefferson had had him with him in Paris and Philadelphia and had had him taught "the art of cookery" at great expense. Before leaving Philadelphia, where James probably wanted to stay, Jefferson signed an agreement to free him after he had returned to Monticello and stayed there long enough to teach somebody else how to cook — presumably in the French manner. In due course, when James reached the age of thirty, Jefferson freed him and gave him $30 to bear his expenses to Philadelphia, undoubtedly hoping that he would live happily ever afterward. His culinary duties seem to have been taken over by his brother Peter, though there was another cook, named Lucy.[8]

The roll of Negroes for 1794 begins with Jupiter the coachman, who was born in the same year as Jefferson and had accompanied him on many a trip, starting with his days as a law student, always enjoying his full confidence; it ends with old Will and Judy at Poplar Forest. Within a couple of years Jefferson sold a considerable number of slaves from Bedford, in the unending process of providing for his major debts, and during these years he did not keep up with the Negroes there as he did with those in Albemarle, who were "his people" in a special sense. In his Farm Book he drew careful and detailed lists, showing the distribution of blankets, food, and clothing in successive years. These are not merely the records of an unusually systematic man, but of a notably just and humane master who, in the absence of a wife, was trying to take care of all the colored members of his large family. They were not merely his workers but his dependents.

Since Jefferson noted the years of his slaves' birth, grouped them in families, and often designated their particular occupations, his rolls are susceptible of rough statistical analysis. Almost half of his hundred-odd slaves in Albemarle in this period were under sixteen years of age, and about thirty were under ten. Supplementing his more formal records are items about human productivity that are interspersed with agricultural references in his farm diary, as in the year 1796:

> May 1. The first blossom I see of red clover.
> 5. Began to cut clover to feed.
> 6. Iris lays in with a boy Joyce.
> 10. Began to sow peas.
> June 1. Lucy lies in with a boy. Zachary.
> 6. Began to cut clover for hay.
> 14. Finished cutting clover.

[8] Agreement of Sept. 15, 1793, indenture of Feb. 5, 1796, and Account Book entry of Feb. 26, 1796 (*Farm Book*, pp. 15–16).

> Ned's Jenny lies in with a boy. James.
> 23.   The White pea beginning to blossom.[9]

In his Farm Book he wrote out certain practical suggestions about the disposition of "his people" with special reference to their age:

> Build the Negro houses near together that the fewer nurses may serve and that the children may be more easily attended by the super-annuated women.
>
> Children till 10 years old to serve as nurse. From 10 to 16 the boys make nails, the girls spin. At 16 go into the ground or learn trades.[10]

There were always servants who were retired from labor because of age or infirmity, and a very considerable portion of the plantation population consisted of economically unproductive children. Jefferson had a relatively large number of artisans or tradesmen, as he called them, for a vast number of things were made at Monticello and building was nearly always going on. In 1794 he listed six carpenters and he had three smiths: Great George and the latter's two sons George and Isaac, children of Ursula, who had been Martha Jefferson's nurse. This highly esteemed family group was almost wiped out in 1799 and 1800, when all but one died of the same malady. Isaac Jefferson lived on to give posterity his unique recollections. To him we are indebted for the following description:

> Mr. Jefferson always singing when ridin or walkin: hardly see him anywhar out doors but what he was a-singin; had a fine clear voice, sung minnits [minuets] and sich: fiddled in the parlor. Old Master very kind to servants." [11]

The house servants are not specifically designated as such on Old Master's lists, but many of them come alive in other references. A goodly number of them were children of Betty Hemings, who had come with the Wayles inheritance and was about sixty at this time. According to Isaac, who was very black, she was of a "bright" color, and her children were noted for their looks as well as their intelligence.[12] As for looks, this was particularly true of Sally, now twenty-

[9] *Garden Book*, p. 246, capitals inserted.
[10] *Farm Book*, p. 77, capitals and some punctuation inserted.
[11] *Memoirs of a Monticello Slave*, p. 30.
[12] There is a chart of the Hemings family in the notes to *Memoirs of a Monticello Slave*, pp. 56–57. TJ's solicitude for this family was a ground for later charges of immorality on his part. Since these charges were political in purpose and do not appear to have been made until his presidency, they need not be lugged into the narrative at this point. Suffice it to say here that I regard them as wholly unwarranted.

one, who had accompanied Polly Jefferson to Paris. Betty's son John, now nineteen, afterwards became the best carpenter among the slaves. She herself, along with Ursula, is said to have been in the room when Mrs. Jefferson died.

It is uncertain how many besides the house servants lived on Monticello mountain. There were only five servants' houses on Mulberry Row, all log cabins, but very likely there were others within easy reach. Probably most of the artisans lived nearby. It is doubtful if many of the laborers in the ground did, for the cultivated fields were below the mountain. The house of the overseer on that side of the river was half a mile away.

The field workers numbered less than a third of the total slave population. Jefferson told Samuel Biddle that he would have from twelve to fifteen workers under him; and in 1796 he himself listed sixteen laborers on each side of the river. These may well have included slaves hired from others, of whom he generally had about a dozen. He had to have carters and other auxiliaries, and the figures varied from year to year, but probably there were not more than thirty field hands most of the time. In the harvest season, however, he mobilized virtually the entire force, male and female, first on one side of the river and then on the other. At that time practically everybody except the aged, the children under ten, and the most favored house servants and artisans took to the fields. The total reached sixty-five in 1795, besides the master himself and the two overseers.

One reason why Jefferson got a new overseer at Monticello was that he regarded the previous one as unkind to the workers. This difficulty he hoped to obviate by bringing from the vicinity of Elkton to "overlook" his fields below the Rivanna a man who knew how to manage Negroes, though "not in a very harsh manner." [13] Writing Samuel Biddle about the laborers who would be under him, the master said: "They will be well clothed, and as well fed as your management of the farm will enable us, for it is chiefly with a view to place them on the comfortable footing of the laborers of other countries [states], that I come into another country [state] to seek an overlooker for them, as also to have my lands a little more taken care." [14] The same thoughts were in his mind a year later, no doubt, when he got Eli Alexander from the same region as overseer at Shadwell. Neither lasted very long, however, and in the end their employer got his best

[13] Jacob Hollingsworth to TJ, Dec. 9, 1792 (*Garden Book*, p. 182).

[14] To Biddle, Dec. 12, 1792 (*Papers, MHS*, p. 44). In writing TMR, he gave his impression that the previous overseer, Clarkson, was not kind enough (Ford, VI, 317).

results with overseers from his own locality.[15] How harsh or lenient they were, in comparison with the practices on other plantations, it is impossible to say, but if the master himself erred he did so on the side of leniency. "I love industry and abhor severity," he said.[16]

Jefferson, who was nothing if not systematic and might have qualified as an efficiency expert in another age, hoped to increase the effectiveness of his labor force by better planning. Among his surviving memoranda are calendars of work in which the activities of laborers, horses, and oxen are outlined month by month in a sort of ideal pattern.[17] It is uncertain to what extent he ever sought to put these into practice. Since he did not copy them in his Farm Book they may have been only tentative in his mind. More revealing of his hopes and experiences in this period are entries in his farm diaries for 1795 and 1796.[18]

The accounts of the grain harvests are of special interest. On June 27, 1795, they began to cut the wheat on the Shadwell side with a force of 17 cradlers, 5 reapers, 7 stackers, and 36 gatherers (women and boys). On July 3 they began to cut on the Monticello side, finishing the wheat on July 6 and the rye next day. Then they began to tread out the wheat at Monticello with 7 horses, following the traditional method. The treading at Shadwell, long delayed by heavy rains, was not finished until September. Immediate threshing was, in Jefferson's opinion, the only safeguard against the weevil in Virginia, but in this instance the delay had no ill effects.[19] By another year he was using a threshing machine.

Meanwhile, he reflected on the harvest and jotted down suggested improvements in procedure. One of these was that the treading floor should be laid down before the harvest, and another that spare scythes should be made ready, but perhaps the most interesting was the following:

> Great George with tools & a grindstone mounted in the single
> mule cart, should be constantly employed in mending cradles &

[15] Betts gives a list of overseers in the *Farm Book*, p. 149. Biddle was succeeded on Nov. 18, 1794, by Hugh Petit; and Alexander on Nov. 24, 1795, by William Page, who came from the locality and seems to have been diligent in the performance of his duties. Edmund Bacon, who served Jefferson so long and well in later years, was a native of Albemarle.

[16] To John Strode, June 5, 1805 (*Garden Book*, p. 303).

[17] Several of these, which are undated, are printed in the Betts edn. of the *Farm Book*, pp. 318-323.

[18] In original *Farm Book*, pp. 45-48, 54; printed in *Garden Book*, pp. 227-231, 245-247.

[19] TJ to Thomas Pinckney, Apr. 12, 1793 (*Farm Book*, p. 70, from LC).

grinding scythes. The same cart would carry about the liquor, moving from tree to tree as the work advanced.

Jefferson fell in with the custom of providing whiskey on the gala occasion of the harvest, though as a rule he frowned on the use of spirits by his workmen. Special cooks were provided, and the food — including molasses, "middling," fresh meat, and peas — surpassed the normal ration. He recorded his hope that his "whole machine" would move in exact equilibrium another year, that the plowmen would not all need to be called into service, and that thus an even smaller force could harvest his 300-odd acres of wheat in six days. Virtually, that would have been to cut the time in half. The harvest of 1796 took just as long, however, and the plowmen had to be summoned, though there was satisfaction in the thought that this was the finest of his harvests.

This single illustration does not prove that Jefferson's personal efforts to increase the effectiveness of his labor force by more careful planning were futile. His presence on the scene and his continued attempt to keep his "whole machine" in useful activity throughout the year could hardly have been wholly vain. Nor should we lay too much stress on his statement of a few years later, "I find that I am not fit to be a farmer with the kind of labor we have," for by then he had withdrawn from his fields for other reasons.[20] Yet his personal experiences and observations may have disposed him to question his earlier statement to Arthur Young that on the whole slave labor was cheaper than free.

Nothing was more characteristic of him than his enthusiasm for labor-saving implements, and his threshing machine calls for special mention.[21] While secretary of state he went with George Washington to look at a threshing machine on a farm near Philadelphia, and he saw in Arthur Young's writings an account of another. He got a model of the latter through Thomas Pinckney, minister of the United States in England, and had a machine constructed on his own place. This was such a slow process that his machine did not get to work until late August, 1796. It was made, he said, on the Scotch model; it was operated by horse power, and it could be taken from field to field in a wagon.[22] Along with the practice of dividing his farms into fields, he was following one of building in each field a barn sufficiently large to store its produce. Each barn consisted of two rooms with a passage be-

[20] To S. T. Mason, Oct. 27, 1799 (Ford, VII, 396).
[21] The story is admirably told in the commentary and extracts of correspondence, 1791–1798 in *Farm Book*, pp. 68–76.
[22] *Garden Book*, pp. 242–243.

tween them, and it was in this that the threshing machine operated. Jefferson liked his machine but was constantly seeking to improve it. He was also enormously interested in drills, but his most noteworthy personal efforts to improve the implements of husbandry had to do with the plow. This, as he said later, was to the farmer what the wand was to the sorcerer.[23]

If he had had his way plowing would have been going on somewhere on his farms every day of the year, when the weather permitted. He noted in his farm diary of 1795 that in the previous fall, despite fine weather, it fell behind — partly through the negligence of the overseers, partly because of shortage of horses, partly because he himself was incapacitated by rheumatism.[24] The winter, cold and snowy, was "unfriendly to the labors of the field," and the following summer was twice as wet as usual — nothing like it had been seen within human memory, he said. Nevertheless, adding things up at the end of the year 1795, he figured that there had been 220 plowing days. He had hired one new overseer in the meantime and bought five more horses. In the spring four plows were going on each side of the river, and he sought to keep the number of workhorses up to sixteen. The large plows were drawn by two horses, though he also used mules as soon as he had accumulated a stock of them. At the end of the year there were at Shadwell and Lego six large plows and tackle and seven single plows.[25] Presumably there were about that many on the Monticello side. By this time he had at least one that utilized the moldboard "of least resistance" he had designed several years before he became a full-time farmer. He could not have failed to hope that it would turn the stiff red clay of Albemarle some day, but when he first thought of it he was looking at the soil of France and thinking of agricultural progress in general.

Just when he first came to regard the plow as "the most useful of the instruments known to man" is uncertain, but it was while he was minister to the court of Louis XVI that he first recorded his thoughts about improving it. Until his century plows were little more than hoes pulled through the ground. A great step forward came with the development of the moldboard, sometimes described as the breast of the plow, which turned the soil after the coulter had cut and the plowshare had penetrated it. On his trip back to Paris from Strasbourg in the spring that he was forty-five, after a tour of Holland and the Rhine

23 To C. W. Peale, Apr. 17, 1813; quoted in *Farm Book*, p. 47.
24 *Farm Book*, p. 45; *Garden Book*, p. 227.
25 *Farm Book*, p. 47.

Valley, watching the peasants plowing with oxen not far from Nancy, he was struck with the awkwardness of their moldboards and considered just what the shape of these ought to be. "The offices of the moldboard," as he noted in his memorandum, "are to receive the sod after the share has cut under it, to raise it gradually and reverse it." [26] The form, therefore, should be determined by the function. "The fore end of it then should be horizontal to enter under the sod, and the hind end perpendicular to throw it over, the intermediate surface changing gradually from the horizontal to the perpendicular." The two drawings he put in the margin of his memorandum, to show just how he would make such a logical moldboard, look like something from a schoolbook in solid geometry. Starting with a block of wood, he showed how it might be divided with a saw and adz so as to achieve the transition, fore to aft, from the horizontal to the vertical.[27]

All this was on paper until after his return to the United States. While he was Secretary of State he showed his drawings to David Rittenhouse, who vouched for their mathematical correctness, as did Professor David Patterson of the University of Pennsylvania a few years later. He sent a small model to his son-in-law from New York in 1790. We do not know who made this but later, at Monticello, he made one with his own hands for the English agriculturist, William Strickland. In 1794 he was boasting to John Taylor that he had invented a perfect moldboard. By that year he had had this constructed for trial on his own farms, and he used it for five years "with entire approbation." [28] At this stage it was made of wood, and if it worked and lasted in that soil it survived a severe test by any reckoning. He said later that he used it with the common bar-share plow, changing nothing but the moldboard; and that the same horses made a furrow two inches deeper than with the customary moldboard, "owing to the difference of resistance." [29] He did not displace all the common moldboards at Monticello and Shadwell, but he himself became convinced, during his own brief period of active farming, that he had reduced theory to practice. Professor Patterson, after saying that the "doctrine of resistance" was little understood, complimented him by a statement based on his own observation of moldboards variously fashioned by

[26] Memo. dated April 19, 1788 (*J.P.*, XIII, 27; also in *Farm Book*, p. 49).

[27] For his preliminary sketches, see *J.P.*, XIII, illustration opp. p. 16; for a model actually made by him at a later time, see *Farm Book*, illustration opp. p. 56. The whole story of this improvement can be reconstructed from the materials in the latter, pp. 47–64, though there was not space there for all the letters.

[28] To John Taylor, June 4, 1798 (*Papers, MHS*, p. 61).

[29] To Harry Innes, June 20, 1806 (*Farm Book*, p. 55, from LC).

carpenters: namely, that by the friction of the soil they eventually assumed a figure "exactly resembling" that of Jefferson's models.[30]

He had no thought of patenting his improvement; as one of his correspondents correctly surmised, his object was to be "extensively useful." [31] His description of it, about a year after he became Vice President of the United States, in a letter to Sir John Sinclair, first president of the National Board of Agriculture at London, was read to the American Philosophical Society a few weeks later and duly published in that learned society's *Transactions*.[32] This may be regarded as his formal presentation of it to the scientific world. He spoke modestly of his "improvement" of the plow, drawing on the Scriptures to say that only the mite was expected of the widow, that he had contributed according to his poverty, and that others would contribute from their abundance. At the same time he said: "The combination of a *theory* which may satisfy the learned, with a practice intelligible to the most unlettered labourer, will be acceptable to the two most useful classes in society." To him the savants and the working farmers were the hope of the earth. He addressed the former while hoping and believing that the latter could make moldboards like his with their own saws and adzes.

The later history of his improvement, extending to almost the end of his life, belongs to the larger story of his relations with the fraternity of scientists and his patronage of agriculture. Afterwards he gave his moldboard a sharp toe instead of a blunt one, and when he was really an old man and finally retired from public life he had it cast, a thing he had been asked to do much sooner.[33] Then, if not before, he had the pleasure of seeing it extensively used on his own acres. Meanwhile, it had found a place in a *Domestic Encyclopedia*, as a machine deserving particular notice.[34] Also, it gained for him a gold medal from the Société d'agriculture du département de la Seine.[35] Among other recipients of similar medals was a simple cultivator, who was honored for perfecting the plow he himself used and thus stood beside the President of the United States. About this time that high offi-

---

[30] Robert Patterson to TJ, Mar. 29, 1798 (*Farm Book*, pp. 50–51, from MHS).

[31] H. B. Latrobe to TJ, Sept. 22, 1798 (*Farm Book*, p. 53, from LC).

[32] Letter of Mar. 23, 1798, read to Am. Philos. Soc., May 4, 1798 (*Transactions*, IV, no. XXXVIII [1799], 313–322). He was president of the Society at the time, and was also a Foreign Honorary Member of the National Board of Agriculture (Certificate, dated June 20, 1797, MHS).

[33] From James Mease, Mar. 28, 1804 (*Farm Book*, p. 53); to John Staples, May 4, 1814 (*ibid.*, p. 62).

[34] James Mease's *Domestic Encyclopedia* (1803), IV, 288–292; see *Farm Book*, p. 53.

[35] *Mémoires*, VII (1805), pp. xlix–lviii.

cial, explaining his pride in his own invention, wrote sagaciously: "Nothing is so common as to see men value themselves most for what they know least about. In truth ignorance is always the parent of vanity." [36] But advanced agriculturists of his day thought he knew a great deal about that prosaic but indispensable instrument of husbandry, the plow. Since he did not patent or manufacture his moldboard, no one can say for sure how many used it. Anybody who wanted to could copy it, wholly or in part, without even mentioning his name. The extent of its influence cannot be measured with any confidence, but modern historians of agriculture have recognized its contemporary significance. One of them described it as "the last great fundamental development in the series of wooden plows, the product of the family farm." [37] It represented Jefferson's attempt to meet the needs of his own situation, and if more powerful metal plows outmoded it in the ante-bellum era he would not have minded that. It is doubtful, however, if he would have been happy if he had foreseen the ultimate eclipse of the family farm which the improvement of agricultural machinery actually did so much to accelerate in later years.

"What with my farming and my nail manufactory I have my hands full. I am on horseback half the day, and counting and measuring nails the other half." [38] Thus Jefferson wrote John Adams in the second year of his retirement, referring to activities which provide one of the most interesting minor examples of his virtuosity. He set up his nailery early in 1794, attaching it to the blacksmith shop he had moved from the Shadwell Branch to a newly constructed wooden building on Mulberry Row, to the southeast of his mansion and overlooking his garden. This operated virtually without interruption for nearly a score of years, and intermittently until almost the end of his life.[39]

In a letter to a Frenchman to whom he had previously given much information about America, he put this venture in its social and philosophical setting. "There is no such thing in this country as what would be called wealth in Europe," he said. "The richest are but a little at ease, and obliged to pay the most rigorous attention to their affairs to keep them together. . . . In our private pursuits it is a great

[36] To John Strode, March 11, 1805 (*Farm Book*, p. 54, from LC).
[37] M. L. Wilson, "Thomas Jefferson — Farmer," in *Procs. Am. Philos. Soc.*, LXXXVII (July 1943), 220.
[38] To Adams, May 27, 1795 (*A-J Letters*, I, 258).
[39] The first delivery of nails was in May 1794. Betts gives an admirable sketch of the nailery, with extracts from many letters, in *Farm Book*, pp. 426-453. See also J. A. Bear, Jr., "Mr. Jefferson's Nails," in *Magazine of Albemarle County History*, XVI (1958), 47-52.

advantage that every honest employment is deemed honorable. . . . My new trade of nail-making is to me in this country what an additional title of nobility or the ensigns of a new order are in Europe." [40] This honorable occupation he assumed because it required little capital and promised to bring a much-needed cash return. Another advantage was that he could employ in it his Negro boys between ten and sixteen, who were not yet ready for heavy labor and might easily fall into mischief if not engaged.

He used about a dozen of them at first, overseeing their operations himself, he said. Judging from his detailed description of the making of a hand-wrought nail, he understood these operations very thoroughly. [41] In 1796 he got a nail-cutting machine, and thereafter his manufactory employed both methods. His close personal supervision may have continued until his assumption of the vice presidency, but the blacksmiths were always nearby and Great George may have been foreman all along, as he was later. The long illness of that much-respected servant, from what his master diagnosed as dropsy, ending with his death in 1799, slowed down the nail-making after Jefferson returned to public life. His nailrod was shipped by water from Philadelphia to Richmond, and then up the James and Rivanna to Milton. Starting with one fire in his nailery, he got up to three in 1796, expecting to increase his output of a ton a month to a ton and a half. By then he was using charcoal made from wood on his own place. [42]

During the first two years, at least, this venture looked like a distinct financial success. After about a year's operation, Jefferson figured that he made enough nails in a fortnight to cover the cost of his groceries for a quarter. [43] By "groceries" he meant coffee, chocolate, tea, sugar, molasses, rice, rum or French brandy — all of which he had been ordering quarterly from Philadelphia and which cost him $400 to $500 a year. He inquired whether a Richmond merchant would be willing to take payment in nails at the wholesale price, in which case he would transfer his business from Philadelphia. Whatever the result of this particular query may have been, Jefferson had arrangements whereby his nails were credited against his accounts with certain local merchants (such as Fleming & McLanahan in Milton and Colonel Bell in Charlottesville), and in the summer of 1795 he wrote one of his major creditors that his nailery provided completely for the mainte-

[40] To Jean-Nicolas Démeunier, Apr. 29, 1795 (Ford, VII, 13–14). For TJ's previous service of information to him see *Jefferson and the Rights of Man*, p. 107.
[41] *Farm Book*, pp. 427–428.
[42] *Farm Book*, p. 454.
[43] To William Temple, Apr. 26, 1795 (MHS); extract in *Farm Book*, p. 429.

nance of his family.[44] He was forced to engage in barter because of the great difficulty of getting cash for anything in Virginia.

Just when he was increasing his output he encountered competition from a deluge of British nails. Importing merchants declined to take his product, he said, on the principle of "suppressing every effort towards domestic manufacture," and local merchants under their influence took foreign nails from them along with other goods.[45] For these reasons Jefferson, who had avoided retailing, started a consignment business in Milton, Charlottesville, and Staunton. Since he charged Richmond wholesale prices plus a small commission, he was convinced that he could outsell his foreign competitors in the upper country. He had to tie up his own money in nailrod, however, and to assume all the risks. He himself got three months' credit in Philadelphia, but his own debtors took much longer than that to pay him and often did not pay at all.

He was harassed by the problem of collection after his return to public life, when he had less time to spare. On occasion he dispatched his trusty servant Jupiter across the Blue Ridge to Staunton to pick up cash payments. Late in 1798 he wrote his son-in-law that extreme disappointments in receiving money for the nails of the last year had painfully embarrassed him, since he had long relied on his nail money to meet particular bills. Later still he was driven to the expedient of proposing to one specially dilatory debtor in Staunton that he take payment in goose feathers, which he would soon be needing in quantity for making beds. It is a pity that this interesting and unusual offer to swap nails for feathers was not taken up, because of scarcity of the latter.[46]

Difficulties about production increased after Jefferson ceased to spend the entire year in Albemarle. He gave the nailery his personal attention when he was there, however, and he had no intention of giving it up, despite the trouble it caused him. In the year that he became President of the United States he was planning a stone building for it, and that year he employed a skillful white smith who was also a nailer. This capable workman turned out to be intemperate and something of a madman, but he stayed for some years and nail-making on

[44] To James Lyle, July 10, 1795 (MHS); extract in *Farm Book*, p. 430.

[45] To Archibald Stuart, Jan. 3, 1796, and to TMR, Jan. 11, 1796 (*Farm Book*, pp. 431–432). Presumably the "importing merchants" to whom he referred were chiefly in Richmond. Some local merchants, like Fleming & McLanahan in Milton, continued to sell his nails, as his Account Book shows.

[46] To John McDowell, Feb. 1, 1800, and from McDowell, Feb. 14, 1800 (*Farm Book*, pp. 441–442).

the mountain was not suspended until the War of 1812 made the shipment of nailrod impracticable.[47]

Apart from Jefferson's absences from home, beginning in 1797, the main reason why the nail business was so much less successful than it had promised to be was the extreme difficulty of collecting money in a region enslaved by the credit system. It is doubtful, however, that he regarded this venture in domestic manufacture as a failure. He needed nails in large quantity for his own building operations, he sold them to trustworthy friends like James Madison, and he used them for barter with neighbors like George Divers. Even now, his nails are performing the useful function of holding things together at places like Monticello, Montpelier, and Farmington.[48]

[47] On the smith, William Stewart, see *Farm Book,* pp. 424–426, 443.
[48] The Farmington house was built later, but the generalization holds.

[XIV]

A Noble Spirit of Building

DURING most of the long generation he was in public life Jefferson was building or rebuilding his mansion on the little mountain. He began work on it the year he entered the House of Burgesses, when he was a bachelor of twenty-six, but not until the end of his presidency forty years later did he complete it in its enduring form. Except perhaps for the payment of his inherited debt, this was the most important item of his unfinished private business throughout his most active years.

He actually built two houses, though the second grew out of the first and largely incorporated it. The Chevalier de Chastellux (later Marquis) visited and described the earlier building at the end of the American Revolution, in the spring of 1782, and the wife of the host died there that same year before the leaves fell.[1] Of his master plan for Monticello, Jefferson had then completed little besides the dwelling house and the southeast pavilion to which he had brought his bride. All future plans were suspended after he lost her, then he sought to submerge private grief in public service, and, after a bit, he put the seas between himself and the scene of his misery, abandoning his home for the longest absence of his life.[2] Though his love for Monticello revived and was in fact unquenchable, he did little about the place for a decade. He probably began to think about remodeling his house when in France, he definitely planned to do so while secretary of state, and he set to work on it after his retirement, starting a process of rebuilding which lasted a dozen years and more. "He is a very long time maturing his projects," a visitor to the still unfinished house remarked early in his presidency.[3] The history of Monticello shows him

[1] See *Jefferson the Virginian*, Chs. XI, XXVII.
[2] The reference is to his mission in France, 1784–1789; see *Jefferson and the Rights of Man*.
[3] Comment of Mrs. William Thornton, Sept. 22, 1802, in her Diaries (LC).

as a man of extraordinary patience and tenacity and also of rare vision, but it raises some doubts as to whether he was wholly a man of reason. In his time in Virginia a man of his standing was open to no criticism for building an impressive house, but in his particular circumstances there were grounds for charges of impracticality.

The story abounds in anomalies and is shot through with tragedy. Jefferson began the house of his dreams when he was a bachelor with no immediate prospects of marriage and before he himself may have recognized his inveterate domesticity. Since he did not finish it in its first form until his wife's last year, if he did so even then, she lived amid scenes of construction during virtually all of her life with him. He began to remodel his house when he was a widower with one married daughter; his other daughter was marriageable and actually became a wife long before the work of reconstruction approached completion. He wanted more room for guests, but presumably he had a fair amount of it already and one may argue that there were insufficient practical grounds for his drastic actions. There were long periods when his house was scarcely habitable, though he probably never anticipated these. Finally, the parlous state of his finances might have been expected to argue powerfully against extensive and costly building operations from which there could be no monetary return.

Jefferson is reputed to have said to a visitor in his old age that he hoped Monticello would remain in a state of re-edification while he lived, "as architecture is my delight, and putting up and pulling down one of my favorite amusements." [4] His lifelong zest for construction is indisputable, but this was something more than indulgence in expensive amusement. When he started rebuilding his house he told friends that he was more concerned about conveniences than he had been in his youth, and he found place for many of them in his second version of the mansion, but he would hardly have been led into such an elaborate operation for reasons of mere comfort. It is best to think of his building activities in terms of self-expression. Few men in history, and even fewer who were eminent in public life, ever found more outlets for superabundant intellectual energy, but perhaps the most gratifying that he ever found as a private man was in architecture, where beauty and utility join hands. In building and perfecting his own dwelling place he found self-expression in its most satisfying form. He was impelled to remodel his home because his earlier venture in brick and stone no longer reflected his taste and personality;

[4] B. L. Rayner, *Sketches of the Life, Writings, and Opinions of Thomas Jefferson* (1832), p. 524.

and in fashioning a fitting habitation for his own spirit he minimized difficulties and was relatively unmindful of the costs.

Though he was not the sort of man to speak above a whisper about anything so sacred, memories of his ever-lamented wife were sure to linger at Monticello despite any changes he might make; and this deeply domestic man expected to hear there, very frequently through the years, the voices of his daughters and the prattle of their children. Yet there never was any doubt in their minds or any other that this was *his* house in the fullest sense. He planned it in its successive phases, he directed its construction, he selected its furnishings, through the years he developed the design of its grounds. It was his home, his body, the center of his personal universe. Also, on this entrancing spot he erected what was to prove an enduring monument. He was painfully long in doing it, and at the end he was aware that it was not beyond just criticism on purely architectural grounds, as indeed it was not on grounds of mere utility; but as the reflection of the mind, the taste, the individuality of a great man, Monticello remains unique.

Visitors from the Old World applied the term "elegant" to his first house, and described it as being in the "Italian style." [5] One of the young Hessian officers who saw it during the Revolution spoke of Jefferson's "noble spirit of building," and obviously the place had distinction.[6] The statement of the Duc de La Rochefoucauld Liancourt, who visited it in 1796, that "Monticello, according to its first plan, was infinitely superior to all other houses in America in point of taste and convenience," may well be questioned; but this French aristocrat was correct in saying that, when he first designed his mansion, "Mr. Jefferson had studied taste and the fine arts in books only," and that his travels in Europe had supplied him with models.[7] He may have begun to be dissatisfied with his house before he visited the Old World, but beyond much doubt his observations there caused him to plan its improvement.

Architectural writers have described him as a Palladian and a neo-classicist, but on his one brief trip to Italy, which was predominantly agricultural in purpose, he saw none of the extant buildings of Palladio; and, going no farther than Turin, Milan, and Genoa, he scarcely got into classical ground.[8] He never visited Palladio's Vicenza or saw

[5] Baron Von Closen, in Feb. 1782 (*W. & M.*, April 1953, p. 220); Chastellux, a little later that spring (Randall, I, 373).

[6] See *Jefferson the Virginian*, p. 296.

[7] Randall, II, 302.

[8] On his Italian trip in 1787, see *J.P.*, XI, 433-442, and *Jefferson and the Rights*

on a hillock in its outskirts the Villa Rotonda. On this building he based the design for the President's House in the new federal city of Washington which he submitted anonymously when secretary of state. The knowledge he had gained of it from Palladio's own description was sufficient for his purposes.[9] Despite its dome and porticoes, this bold building bears no close resemblance to the central dwelling house that Jefferson finally erected at Monticello, and it was not the source of his ideas about the layout on his mountain-top. Since La Rotonda was so close to town, Palladio did not include it in his country houses, but Jefferson could have studied the descriptions of these to equally good effect before ever he went abroad.[10] One of the plates of the famous Italian architect shows an arrangement of dependencies very much like the one the Virginia planter adopted as a young man and finally effected as a grandfather.[11] He did not have to go to Europe to see this, and nothing that he saw in the Old World caused him to alter his master plan. Schooled as he already was in Palladio, there was relatively little that he *had* to learn in that master's country.

It seems a pity, nonetheless, that he did not get into Treviso, where the loveliest of Palladio's surviving country houses — Villa Barbaro at Maser and Emo at Fanzolo — stretch against the Asolo Hills. There is no way of knowing whether he had read the Master's brief descriptions of these or had looked at the plates, but they would have interested him.[12] These villas were of the "winged block" rather than the temple type and thus invite comparison with the grouping at Monticello. In his master plan, Jefferson had adopted the basic idea of a central building connected by arcades with lesser structures.[13] But he did not follow a straight line as Palladio did in the two beautiful villas that still stand in the foothills of northeast Italy. He turned the ends inward so as to get a rectangle open at one side, or, to put the matter somewhat differently, his master plan called for a central house with two L-shaped blocks of rooms, each terminating in an outbuilding.

---

of Man, pp. 122–124. His letter of Sept. 16, 1787, to George Wythe (J.P., XII, 127) is of particular interest.

[9] His drawings show a dome and hexastyle porticoes on all four sides, as in the original. He increased the dimensions while maintaining the proportions. See Fiske Kimball, *Thomas Jefferson, Architect* (1916), p. 53 and figures 125–129; and *Jefferson and the Rights of Man,* p. 384. The building is described in *Architecture of A. Palladio* (1742), I, Second Book, p. 48, Plates XIV, XV. On it and other villas mentioned here see the beautifully illustrated book of Giuseppe Mazzotti, *Palladian and Other Venetian Villas* (1958), pp. 105–161.

[10] Book II, Chs. XII–XIII.

[11] Book II, Plate XLI.

[12] Palladio describes these villas in Book II, pp. 59, 61, and they appear on Plates XXXVI and XL.

[13] See *Jefferson the Virginian,* pp. 148-149, and illustration opposite p. 131.

While following a Palladian scheme, he wisely adjusted it to his particular situation.

Other differences strike the eye of the modern visitor. The most obvious one relates to the materials employed in the construction. If Palladio's rusticated stonework ever appealed to Jefferson, he had no ready access to suitable building stone, and it is doubtful if he would have had recourse to yellow stucco even had he seen it in all its present beauty in this Italian setting.[14] Naturally and fortunately he turned to brick, as produced in his own region, thus maintaining the historic tie with the antecedent architecture of Virginia, however little he may have liked the Georgian. Even more interesting are the differences that arose from functional considerations. Palladio's country houses were summer places, not year-round seats; they were designed for show and pleasure in a sense that a planter's permanent home could not rightly be. Thus the departures of Jefferson from the Palladian norm were less in the arrangement of the dependencies and outlying buildings than in his design for the central structure. This was his major problem as he thought things over when in Europe; and, while never ceasing to consult and honor Palladio, he found his more immediate inspiration elsewhere.

He did not need to go to Rome to be converted to classical columns, and he could continue to work out their proportions according to the specifications of Palladio. From this source, also, even before he acquired the plates of Piranesi, he might have gained more precise knowledge of the measurements of the Pantheon, which he regarded as the finest example of spherical architecture, than he could have from an examination of that famous structure on the spot. He had already gone to school to the Italy of classical antiquity, but it is a pity that he did not see the glorious Doric columns at Paestum, golden yellow in the sunshine. They were in an even more ancient tradition than the one to which he turned.

Though he might have added no notable architectural ideas to those he had already, he could have found stimulation in Italy had he been there longer. It is doubtful if he got much of that on his brief visit to England.[15] Such work of the English Palladians as he saw and commented on he did not much like, and it now appears that except for Inigo Jones, who belonged in an earlier century, and James Gibbs, who had his own individuality and is not chiefly notable for his country houses, they followed the Italian master much more slavishly than

[14] There is rustication in wood, in imitation of stone, in the wall of the East portico at Monticello, but this is far from the rough stone used in Italy.
[15] See *Jefferson and the Rights of Man*, ch. 4.

he did and with nothing like such good effect.[16] Lord Burlington's Chiswick, inspired by the Villa Rotonda, did not impress him. He thought well of Leoni's Moor Park in Hertfordshire, which must have looked better then than it does today, but his enthusiasm for English country places was virtually confined to their gardens.[17] He might have been expected to admire Russborough in County Wicklow, Ireland, a villa in the best Palladian manner if a little heavy for his taste, but he never got that far and seems to have known nothing of it. Throughout life he made much use of English architectural books and manuals, but the particular buildings that his eye most feasted on during his immensely stimulating years abroad were in the country across the Channel where he stayed so long and where he found the intellectual and esthetic atmosphere so congenial. He picked up ideas about building in Holland and almost everywhere else he traveled, but as an architect he was most impressed and most affected by the structures that he saw in France. These were his fresh "models."

The one he talked about most eloquently was the Maison Carrée at Nîmes, on which he gazed "like a lover at his mistress" and which he described as "one of the most beautiful, if not the most beautiful and precious morsel of architecture left us by antiquity." This he regarded as the best example of the cubical style, as the Pantheon was of the spherical. Using it as a model for the state capitol of Virginia, he introduced the temple form into American public architecture.[18] Also, he was "violently smitten" with the Hôtel de Salm in Paris, now the Palace of the Legion of Honor, across the Seine from the Louvre. He went to look at this from the Tuileries almost every day, he said, sitting on a parapet and twisting around until he had a stiff neck.[19] Perhaps this one-story town house with a dome was more in his mind than any other when he set out to remodel his own mansion.[20] Follow-

---

[16] See, in particular, John Summerson, *Architecture in Britain, 1530 to 1830* (1953), ch. 20. I have profited from reading the dissertation of Hanna Lerski, "The British Antecedents of Thomas Jefferson's Architecture" (The Johns Hopkins Univ., 1955), which contains a very detailed account of TJ's English tour and full description of buildings he saw or may have seen in England. I cannot agree with this author, however, that Monticello and its dome were inspired by Lord Burlington's Chiswick. On the dome, see note 25, below.

[17] B. S. Allen, *Tides in English Taste* (1937), I, Fig. 6 shows Moor Park as a central building with wings and connecting colonnades. When TJ was there they were taking down the wings. Deprived of colonnades and dependencies, the central building, now used as a golf clubhouse, looks like a big white box.

[18] See *Jefferson and the Rights of Man*, p. 89.

[19] To Madame de Tessé, Mar. 20, 1787 (J.P., XI, 226). It was built in 1786 while he was in Paris. For comment, see Kimball, *Jefferson, Architect*, p. 57.

[20] F. D. Nichols, in *Thomas Jefferson's Architectural Drawings* (1960), p. 6,

ing the excavations at Pompeii which did so much to stimulate the new classicism, it marked a trend toward the sort of houses the Romans were now believed to have lived in — that is, houses with only one story or with a mezzanine. The atrium courtyards of Pompeii were not for him, but he was deeply sympathetic with the neoclassicism of this period, which was drawing upon archaeological discoveries unavailable to Palladio. Though he by no means abandoned his Italian teacher, in a real sense he had outgrown him. He himself was disposed to be more eclectic and less rigid in domestic architecture than in public, but he remained a classicist in both fields. In France his classicism was revitalized, as he caught up with the fashion.

Some years later, drawing on his European experiences when writing a friend who had asked for architectural suggestions, he argued the case for the single-story house on more practical grounds:

> . . . The method of building houses 2, 3, or 4 stories high, first adopted in cities where ground is scarce, and thence without reason copied in the country, where ground abounds, has for these 20 or 30 years been abandoned in Europe in all good houses newly built in the country, & very often even in the cities. That is of the height of 16 or 18 f. generally, & the whole of it given to the rooms of entertainment; but in the parts where there are bedrooms they have two tiers of them of from 8 to 10 f. high, with a small private staircase. By these means great staircases are avoided, which are expensive & occupy a space which would make a good room in every story. Nor is the single storied house as expensive as those higher, when you credit them for the cellars & offices below & saving of partition walls, & charge the higher ones the thickening of the walls below, the expense of mounting materials so high, space for chimneys, great staircases, &C.[21]

In this letter he recapitulated arguments he had already addressed to himself and suggested the plan he himself was following. A distinguished student of his architecture has said that this plan "resulted naturally . . . from the form of the old house and from the general requirements." After he had carried it into effect he himself expressed regret that his essay in architecture had been "so much subordinated to the law of convenience, and affected also by the circumstance of

---

refers also to the Hotel Beaugeon (1781) which he must have seen and may have studied.

[21] To John Brown, Apr. 5, 1797 (LC, 101:17350). The plan TJ sent him arrived too late, and the completed house in Frankfort, Ky., was a two-story Georgian structure.

change in the original design." [22] The law of convenience did not require him to erect a dome, and his desire to approximate a one-story house arose in very considerable part from artistic reasons, but he could not start *de novo* since he already had a house on his chosen site.

It is difficult if not impossible to determine just what the first house looked like. There were porticoes on both fronts, but he may never have erected the set of Ionic columns which are shown as superimposed on the lower Doric in an elevation that he drew before the American Revolution.[23] Nor can we be sure just when he put on the octagonal bays at the two ends of the building; visitors during the Revolution did not mention them, though they were surely there by 1796 and may have been much sooner.[24] The main feature of the first floor was the large, lofty salon or parlor, projecting as an octagon on the west, one of the most distinguished rooms in Virginia. The dining room, on one wing, opened into the north bow room, while the south wing consisted of a dressing room and an octagonal bedroom. Apparently these constituted Jefferson's own quarters in the old house as they did in the new. To the left of the east entrance was a small stairway. The plan of the second floor can only be conjectured. It is known that the library was upstairs in the central portion and that the space above the two wings was designated as attic. There must have been bedrooms also.

The plan at which Jefferson finally arrived, in his effort to increase both convenience and beauty, called for doubling the width of what was at the outset a rather shallow house, lowering the central second story, and placing an octagonal dome over the salon. Long years later he said this was built on precisely the same principles as the dome of the Halle aux Bleds in Paris, though much smaller.[25] On the west he attained a one-story effect, and it is from this view that his house looks most Palladian.[26] On the east front he pushed the portico forward and added the hall into which so many thousands of visitors to

---

[22] Comment of Kimball in *Jefferson, Architect*, p. 30; TJ to B. H. Latrobe, Oct. 10, 1809 (*Garden Book*, p. 416).

[23] Shown in J. A. Bear, Jr., *Old Pictures of Monticello* (1957), p. 6, as the west front, and followed there by a drawing by Milton Grigg, showing the supposed upper columns.

[24] They appear on the drawing made by TJ to accompany an insurance declaration; this also shows the buildings on Mulberry Row in 1796. It can be conveniently seen in *Farm Book*, p. 6. For the final plan of the first floor in the original building, see Nichols, *Thomas Jefferson's Architectural Drawings* (1960), No. 4; Kimball, *Jefferson, Architect*, Fig. 24.

[25] To Thomas Munro, Mar. 4, 1815 (Bixby, p. 219).

[26] See the elevation of this front by Mills, reproduced in this volume. Final version of first-floor plan in Nichols, No. 15; Kimball, Fig. 150, notes on p. 164.

Monticello have been ushered. On each side of this hall he placed a square room and a bay or bow room, corresponding to the two he had already. One of these new bay rooms, generally called the cabinet in later years and containing books and writing apparatus, was to form part of his own quarters, but he stood to gain three bedrooms on the east side for other members of the family and guests. These new rooms opened on a north and south passage, off which he set a pair of staircases; these had merit in his eyes in that they were inconspicuous, but they were narrower and steeper than Palladio recommended.

Instead of a central second story and two attic wings, he now planned a mezzanine floor the whole length of the house, containing four bedrooms that corresponded to the new rooms below. The windows on the east front were placed with a mind to external effect rather than internal convenience, and not unfittingly this is the view of the house that is most familiar to the public. They were included in the casings with those of the rooms below, so as to give unity to the façade and accentuate the impression of a low building, but viewed from within they are only a few inches above floor level. Still another bedroom on the mezzanine was provided above the southeast octagon; and on a higher floor, wholly invisible from the outside, were three bedrooms with skylights only. The space under the dome, at this same level, was called the sky room, but nobody seems to know just what its purpose was. On the main floor the two bay rooms at each end were connected at some time by arcaded loggias which partially nullified the octagons; one of them was closed and the other left open. In virtually all the bedrooms Jefferson allowed for bed-alcoves, such as he had seen and used in France.

Many details he worked out as he went along, and matters of ornament need not concern us here. The same can be said of revised domestic arrangements in his enlarged establishment, for it was to be a good many years before he made them. The house he planned was much bigger than it looked, and much bigger than anyone would have supposed he needed. As an architectural design it is inferior to Poplar Forest, which he built in Bedford County a decade later; there he did not have to adjust his plan to what was already built. At Monticello, while showing great ingenuity, he did not achieve such unity; the various components do not hang together. Had he started afresh he could have treated the ends rather differently. He could have made less labored and more convenient arrangements above the first floor. Unquestionably he achieved pleasing and impressive results downstairs and outside. He wrote Latrobe after his retirement from the presidency, "what nature had done for us is sublime and beautiful and

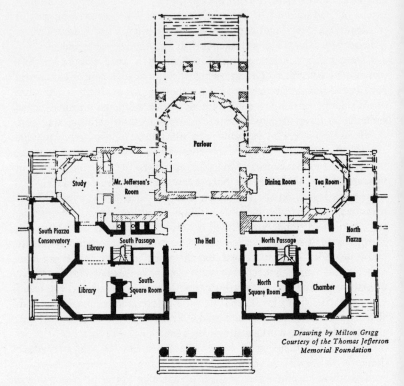

MONTICELLO

Plan of the first floor of the remodeled house.
Newly built portions shown in black.

unique." [27] Any house in such a place could perhaps be regarded as a *tour de force*, but by lowering the height of his dwelling, and contriving to make it look even lower than it was, he caused it to rest snugly on the hilltop as though it belonged there. The red brick arise naturally from the soil of which they are made, while the carefully proportioned columns and white woodwork impart dignity and serenity.

L'Enfant, the gifted but vainglorious planner of the federal city of Washington, when referring to certain ideas of the Secretary of State, used the expression "tiresome and insipid" and spoke of "cool imagination wanting a sense of the real grand and truly beautiful." [28] Jefferson was more aware of practicalities than L'Enfant and tried to curb that architect's exuberance. He was characteristically restrained in all his own architecture, but the house he designed for himself was both noble and elegant, and like him it was endlessly interesting. In certain respects it must have been inconvenient, and one wonders how he could have borne to give up his large library on the second floor, except perhaps out of consideration of his rheumatism. He undoubtedly increased domestic ease by putting so many bedrooms on the first floor, and eventually he added numerous conveniences, including a private toilet off his own room. Considering his times, he went far toward attaining *confort moderne*. In another respect this inveterate classicist showed himself to be very modern in spirit; by the use of long windows and French doors, besides supplementary skylights in the dining room and his own quarters, he suffused the first floor of his gracious house with brightness. It was a fitting habitation for a lavish dispenser of hospitality who sought for himself both spaciousness and privacy and who believed that light and liberty go together.

[27] Oct. 10, 1809 (*Garden Book*, p. 416).
[28] See *Jefferson and the Rights of Man*, p. 375.

[XV]

Monticello in Transition

1793–1800

THE story of the reconstruction of the dwelling house at Monticello is one of hopes long deferred, of close attention on the master's part to workmen, materials, and building operations through many years, and of very considerable personal inconvenience. Few things that Jefferson ever did manifested so impressively his unquenchable optimism and his infinite capacity for taking pains, but in this important enterprise he met more·delays and tribulations than he bargained for. Precisely when he made his working drawings we do not know, but his purposes had crystallized by 1792, when he informed Washington that he would remain in office only during the President's first term, that is, until March, 1793.[1] During the autumn of 1792, after he had reaffirmed this determination, he sought to put things "in train," hoping to dig his new foundations the following spring, then to do the stonework, and to start on the brickwork before another winter. Accordingly, he described his purposes to a master mason whom he hoped to engage to lay the brick. He ordered some special window sashes from abroad, tried to find in Scotland a skilled stonemason, to whom he would give employment for five years, ordered Bohemian window glass from a Philadelphia importer to be delivered by midsummer, and sent detailed instructions to his son-in-law about assembling building materials from his own place.[2] Nothing if not forehanded, he corresponded with his old clerk, Henry

---

[1] Feb. 28, 1792 (Ford, I, 174–178) and Sept. 9, 1792 (Ford, VI, 108); see *Jefferson and the Rights of Man*, pp. 404, 431–433.

[2] Among letters and instructions the most important are TJ to Stephen Willis, Nov. 12, 1792 (*Garden Book*, p. 173); to A. Donald, Nov. 11, 1792 (MHS); to Jos. Donath, Nov. 16, 1792 (MHS), and Account Book, Nov. 27; instructions about timbers, etc., Nov. 1792 (LC, 13723).

Remsen, Jr., in New York about a fresco painter to whom he would like to give about six months' employment divided between the three years 1794, 1795, and 1796.[3]

His instructions were carried out with sufficient expedition at Monticello, if nowhere else. About two-thirds of the stone he required for the foundations had been brought up the mountain by early January, 1793.[4] This local stone, a variety of gneiss, is often called greenstone though little of it is green. Jupiter was "raising" limestone, presumably to be crushed and used in making mortar, and before summer most of the timber Jefferson had ordered for sleepers, rafters, scantlings, and sheeting was hewn and ready for the saw.[5] Included in his plans was a new stable at the northeast end of Mulberry Row. Work on this was begun early in 1793, during his absence, and it appears to have been finished that year. This building was 105 feet in length, which was longer than the first version of his mansion.

His decision to remain in office a little longer disrupted his major building schedule, which was too optimistic in the first place, and from April onward he was too busy with affairs of state to give much time to anything personal. Before facing the problems of neutrality, however, he put his mind on brick. He first calculated that he would get about 60,000 of these from the demolition of the walls he would first take down, and, with 20,000 new brick he had on hand, he figured he would have enough for the new construction in 1793, that is, for about half that he had in mind. His revised plan (March, 1793) was to make in the spring and summer of 1794 from 60,000 to 80,000, and to have the entire lot laid before winter.[6] He delayed his demolition, but in the autumn of 1794, the first year of his retirement, he wrote his old friend George Wythe: "We are now living in a brick-kiln, for my house, in its present state, is nothing better."[7] One has visions of the mountain-top cluttered with brick piles, as indeed it may have been though the kiln was some distance from the house. It was beside a spring to the southeast, just below the present entrance to the grounds, and its product may not have been brought up the mountain until actually required.[8]

At all events, Jefferson's workmen made his brick on his own place

[3] To Remsen, Nov. 13, 1792 (LC, 13623); from Remsen, Nov. 19, 1792 (LC, 13664); to Remsen, Nov. 25, 1792 (LC, 13701).
[4] From TMR, Jan. 9, 1793 (MHS).
[5] To Randolph, Jan. 21, 1793, and from Randolph, June 19, 1793 (Monticello Construction File).
[6] To Stephen Willis, Mar. 3, 1793 (Monticello Construction File from LC).
[7] Oct. 24, 1794 (LC, 16749).
[8] There may have been another kiln on the other side, but we are sure of this one.

out of the clay of his native region. He had ordered Bohemian glass, he owned French furniture, and he was nothing loath to ransack the earth for curiosities and artistic treasures, but, like most other builders of the past, he got his basic materials from his own locality. Because of the color of the soil of Albemarle, his bricks were of a deeper red than those of Tidewater, and a good many of them were over-fired. They differ in shade from the salmon-colored brick in Williamsburg, and in general are of rather inferior quality to the ones used later at the University of Virginia, when Jefferson was more experienced. He was of the opinion that better brick was made in the neighborhood of Philadelphia, whose workmen he particularly admired, and upon examination today a good many of his seem too porous. But these walls have a pleasing texture, nonetheless, and it is all the more to the credit of Jefferson that he achieved his results with materials which were considerably less than perfect.

Brick-making got started in 1794, the first year of his retirement, continuing many months thereafter, but the work of demolition and construction did not begin that year or even in the next, though he was on the ground to direct it. Perhaps he could not yet assemble proper workmen; perhaps he wanted more time to collect materials. In 1795 he had some interesting correspondence about glass with the importer in Philadelphia — where he was also having sashes made. On account of the winds on the mountain he specified glass of the thickness of $1\frac{1}{2}$, and he later rejected some because it was of only the normal thickness.[9] His delay can be better explained, however, by the presence of nails than the absence of glass. The year 1795 was an important one in his nail business. During the course of it he told John Adams that he was on horseback half the day, and counting and measuring nails the other half. His nailery probably required so much of his ready cash that he had little to spend for other purposes. Before another year went by, he negotiated a loan from the Dutch banking firm of Van Staphorsts and Hubbard, securing this and other heavier obligations by a mortgage on slaves.[10] Without this, he probably would have been unable to pursue his ambitious plans.

At all events, 1796 was the year in which he began to push his building project. In February he began his demolitions, starting with the portico on the east. Taking down the columns proved relatively easy, but the walls offered difficulties. It is uncertain whether or not,

9 To Josiah Donath, Aug. 12, Sept. 16, 1795; Dec. 4, 1796 (Monticello Construction File from UVA).
10 See Long Note on his debts, following the Bibliography, below.

at this stage, they took down any walls besides those of the antechamber and those surrounding the staircase, but the confusion was dreadful and the work unexpectedly tedious.[11] They found rotten timbers, which bore out his statement that his old house was in bad condition, but the walls were so solid that seven men got down only 3000 or 4000 bricks a day. He reflected that new ones could be made that fast. The tumbling brickbats kept them in constant danger, but he informed his son-in-law two days before his own fifty-third birthday in April that as yet only one workman had been knocked down.[12] If, as he said, he enjoyed pulling down as well as putting up, he had much pleasure that spring, but not until late summer or early fall did he witness much construction. He reported in April that he had 140 men on the job — a figure which must have included most of his own slaves of working age and perhaps included men digging his canal, an operation which was resumed that year. But he lacked brickmasons and could not get started on his new walls. His old house still had its roof on, but it had a gaping wound instead of a stately entrance.

His son-in-law, who had been so useful in collecting materials while he himself had to remain in Philadelphia, was now absent from the Monticello scene. Young Randolph and his wife Martha went to Varina the previous winter (1794-1795), leaving the two little children, Anne Cary and Thomas Jefferson, with their grandfather and Maria.[13] Though solicitous of the children's health, the grandfather, who relied more on nature than on medicines, delighted in the hardihood of his namesake. The little boy, when in his third year, persisted in going barefoot in the dead of an unusually cold winter and was only circumvented by the use of laced moccasins which he could not take off.[14] In the summer of 1795 the grown-up Randolphs set out for the springs in Augusta County to see if these could restore the young husband's "nearly hopeless" health. The death of their third child, an infant named Eleanor, occurred while they were there. The grandfather sent to the Valley for the little body and had it interred at Monticello. Sad episodes of this sort had been all too frequent in his life,

[11] He did not speak of unroofing the old house until considerably later, but one wonders how anybody got upstairs from this time forward.

[12] To TMR, Apr. 11, 1796 (LC, 17121).

[13] Martha sometimes referred to her first son as "Jeff" and, in order to avoid confusion, we shall sometimes call him that even though his grandfather seems never to have done so.

[14] TJ to Martha, Jan. 22, 1795 (Edgehill Randolph Papers, UVA). There are many pleasant domestic items in the correspondence of these years.

but his prolific elder daughter was to be luckier than most. He reported to her that Anne and Jeff were remarkably well but that the house was "a mere hospital of sick friends." Two of his sisters were there, along with sick servants, while others had stopped on their way to the springs, so that every corner of every room was occupied. It was fortunate for this horde of relatives and friends that he had not yet begun to take down his walls.[15]

The Randolphs went back to Varina for the winter of 1795-1796, and there Maria and one or both of the children joined them in February. Thus the younger members of the family avoided the menace of flying brickbats. In August, 1796, about the time Jefferson was so impatient for brickmasons, Randolph set off again for the healing waters — with good results this time, for he was soon recovered from the malady nobody could diagnose. During his absence Martha was at Monticello, as Maria was. Peter Carr, who had been staying there, took rooms in Charlottesville; and, the "chamber being dismantled," Patsy was relegated to the "out-chamber" — presumably the southeast pavilion. It must have been there that her third surviving child, Ellen Wayles, was born at the end of October.[16] She and her husband returned to Varina for still another winter (1796-1797), though the two older children remained at Monticello, where they could see anything that might be going on.[17]

To one friend who wanted to visit him in 1796 Jefferson wrote: "We shall have the eye of a brick-kiln to poke you into, or an Octagon to air you in." To another he said that during the summer they would live under "the tent of heaven."[18] As we have seen, he did not take the roof off the old part of his house until another year, and the fact that he had guests shows that the place was still habitable. He wrote one of these, the French writer Volney: "The noise, confusion and discomfort of the scene will require all philosophy and patience." Nonetheless, Volney came in the month of June and remained three weeks. An

---

15 TJ to Madison, July 15, 1795 (LC, 16888); TJ to TMR, July 26, 1795 (LC, 16892); Account Book entries of that date; TJ to Martha, July 31, 1795 (Pierpont Morgan Library, N. Y. City, courtesy of the Curator of Monticello).

16 TJ to TMR, at Sweet Springs, Aug. 19, 1796 (LC, 17198). Ellen Wayles Randolph, who was destined to marry Joseph Coolidge, Jr., of Boston, was born at Monticello on Oct. 30, 1796.

17 The Randolphs were all at Monticello in the summer of 1797. After that they lived for a couple of years at Belmont, about 6 miles away. Not until 1799 did they begin to live at Edgehill.

18 To W. B. Giles, Mar. 19, 1796 (Ford, VII, 67); to Benj. Hawkins, Mar. 22, 1796 (LC, 17094).

even earlier visitor was Isaac Weld, Jr., an Irishman in his early twenties whose popular account of his travels in North America contains a brief description of Monticello.[19] Undoubtedly his host explained to him his building plans, as he did soon thereafter to the Duc de La Rochefoucauld Liancourt, who left a better-known description.[20] William Branch Giles came visiting in the summer, by which time Maria must have been back. According to the slave Isaac, he was courting her without success.[21]

During the summer of 1796 the work was impeded by persistent rains and by the late arrival of the brickmason Stephen Willis, on whom Jefferson had depended but who was delayed by "the fever and ague." [22] The net result was that he did not get his new walls up before work had to be suspended in an unusually cold November. He told his son-in-law late in the month that the thermometer had dropped to 12°, and that the ink froze on the point of his pen. He wrote Madison that eight more days would have sufficed to complete his walls and permitted him to cover in, an estimate which later events showed to be much too sanguine.[23] By now he realized that with the coming of another spring he would again be in a public station — whether in the first place in the nation or the second he did not yet know, though he insisted that he preferred the latter. One advantage it seemed to offer: it would require him to spend less time than the first at the seat of government. During his four years as vice president he was actually at home just about as long as he was away, and his absences always included the winter months, which were not suitable for building operations. Yet, except perhaps for the year 1797 when he was at home two-thirds of the time, he was now only secondarily a builder. In the course of that year of transition from private to public life, his second daughter was married; and at its end his unfinished house was closed for the first of a long series of winters.

In late February, 1797, the newly elected Vice President of the United States set out for Philadelphia to be inaugurated and he was

[19] G. Chinard, *Volney et L'Amérique* (1923), pp. 38-40; Weld, *Travels Through the States of North America* (2 edn., London, 1799), I, 206-208.

[20] Randall, II, 302-307. We have already quoted him at some length in connection with TJ's agriculture.

[21] *Memoirs of a Monticello Slave*, pp. 38-39.

[22] Willis had not arrived on Aug. 19, 1796. The first payment to him that I have noted in the Account Book was Oct. 2, though there are somewhat earlier references to Mrs. Willis.

[23] To TMR, Nov. 28, 1796 (*Papers, MHS*, p. 55); to Madison, Dec. 17, 1796 (Ford, VII, 92).

away from the mountain for a month. On his return he found the cherry and peach trees in blossom, but, as he wrote Martha at Varina, the bloom of Monticello was chilled by his solitude.[24] He had written Maria that she should remain with her sister until the weather became disagreeable — that is, hot. There was not much society for her in the Monticello neighborhood, he said, and as a matter of fact he himself had to go back to Philadelphia in May for a special session of Congress.[25] Meanwhile, he was disappointed in his expectations of a visit from his son-in-law. Young Randolph, who had become a Justice of the Peace in Albemarle three years before and was an officer in the local militia, was a candidate for one of the two seats for the county in the Virginia House of Delegates, but he wrecked his chances by not appearing on election day. His excuse was that he stayed at Varina to help nurse the children, who had been recently inoculated for smallpox. Jefferson, after apologizing for his absence in a circular letter, chided him for the uneasiness and embarrassment he had caused his friends.[26]

The solitary master of Monticello found the spring season delicious, nonetheless, and he was now able to resume building. About the time of his fifty-fourth birthday the bricklayers set to work, and by June, when he was back in Philadelphia, all the walls were done except those of the hall, which were being raised. The Randolphs and Maria and arrived for the summer and the latter did the reporting.[27] Home again in July to remain until the fall session of Congress, he was soon talking about unroofing the old part of the house, an operation which would require the family to seek shelter elsewhere. Hoping for a visit from James and Dolly Madison before this happened, he told his friend in Orange County that he had had both the Shadwell and the Secretary's Ford well cleared and gave him precise directions how to proceed up the mountain after crossing.[28] The Madisons did not come, but the roof must have still been there when Maria was married to her cousin John Wayles Eppes in October. This was an exceedingly important domestic event, though the father of the bride said very little about the ceremony. In his Account Book, on Oct. 13, 1797, he wrote: "My daughter Maria married this day."

24 To Martha, Mar. 27, 1797 (Randall, II, 338).

25 TJ to Maria, Mar. 11, 1797 (UVA). Check this letter.

26 TJ to TMR, Mar. 23, 1797 (LC, 17328) and Apr. 9, 1797 (LC, 17358); Gaines, in "Thomas Mann Randolph of Edgehill," p. 77, saying that Wilson Cary Nicholas and Francis Walker were elected.

27 TJ to Volney, Apr. 9, 1797 (Chinard, *Volney*, p. 80); Maria to TJ, June 12, 1797 (MHS). He was away May 5–July 11.

28 July 24, 1797 (Ford, VII, 157).

The Vice President had learned of the engagement of his second daughter in June, while he was in Philadelphia, and it served him right that he got the news, not from her, but from her sister. Maria, who besides being a dilatory correspondent was always disposed to compare herself unfavorably with Martha, had delighted him with the tenderness of a letter she wrote him from Varina in the spring. Her tenderness was probably increased by her thoughts of Jack Eppes, but she soon lapsed into silence.[29] Apparently she had not consulted him about the vital matter of her engagement, and when it came to pass she hesitated to write him about it, being in considerable awe of her exacting parent.

She could have had no doubt of his approval of her future mate. John Wayles Eppes was the son of Francis and Elizabeth Wayles Eppes, half sister of Maria's mother and virtually the girl's own mother when she lived at Eppington before her father had her brought, against her childish desire, to join him in Paris at the age of nine.[30] Jack, who was six years older than Maria, had lived with Jefferson in Philadelphia part of the time while the latter was secretary of state and was much liked by him. On no other grounds except closeness of kinship could that reserved but sentimental gentleman have possibly objected to this alliance. Relieved to learn that Maria had found a life partner, he said with all sincerity that if he had had the whole earth to choose from he could not have picked a better. Reading between the lines, however, one can see that this marriage imposed a psychological difficulty precisely the reverse of the one created by Martha's.

It may be doubted if Jefferson's elder daughter ever ceased to give him the first place in her affections, and circumstances combined to make her and her husband continuously dependent on his unfailing generosity. Such was not the case with Maria, whose ties with Eppington were so close and who may be said to have been an Eppes in spirit before she became one in name. Sincerely devoted to her father though she was, she gave first place in her heart to her husband from this time forward. Furthermore, he and she were less dependent on the master of Monticello than the young Randolphs were. Her father settled on them some eight hundred acres at Pantops, adjoining Shadwell, but they never came there to live as he hoped they would. While gaining a son whom he always liked, Jefferson now had lost first claim on

[29] TJ to Maria, Mar. 11, 1797 (UVA); to Martha, June 8, 1797 (Randall, II, 358). His Index to Letters shows that he wrote Maria June 14, and received from her on June 20 a letter of June 12. Apparently he had no correspondence with Jack Eppes before returning to Monticello, though he received on July 3 a letter from Francis Eppes, dated June 21.

[30] See *Jefferson and the Rights of Man*, pp. 134–137.

a daughter. He could not refrain from writing her a didactic letter in the first months of her marriage, giving some excellent advice about the maintenance of domestic harmony, but afterwards he treated her as an adult.[31] Henceforth he referred to Jack as "Mr. Eppes" and addressed him as "Dear Sir" in letters.

They were launched on an independent career, but for a time the young couple remained at Monticello amid the confusion. Their stay was prolonged because Maria, who earlier in the year had tumbled through the floor into the cellar without hurt, now fell out of a door, suffering a sprain which incapacitated her for travel.[32] This accident, together with a bad cold and incessant rains, caused the Vice President himself to delay his departure for Philadelphia several weeks after the beginning of the Senate session. By December 4, 1797, when at length he set out, Maria had gone with her husband to Eppington, and the Randolphs had taken up quarters at Belmont, about six miles away from Monticello, leaving the house there tenantless for the winter.

A couple of months later he urged his elder daughter, who had found Belmont unhealthy and was living over a cellar full of water, to bring her family back, telling her that, besides the south pavilion, the parlor and study could be occupied.[33] She did not come, but it thus appears that two rooms had not been unroofed. Except for these, everything was open all winter, and Jefferson was now bemoaning his "houseless situation." Apparently no roofing whatever was done before he got back on July 4, chiefly because of the failure of the man who had promised to get sheeting and shingles.[34] Despite the fact that most of the house was open to the sky, Martha was at Monticello before he arrived and presumably spent the summer of 1798 there with the children, though her husband remained at Belmont. Jefferson expected Maria, also. Until he had word that she was ill and could not make the journey he imagined that every sound he heard was that of her approaching carriage.[35]

His workmen could not proceed an hour without him, he said, and they do not seem to have moved very fast when he was there. Some

[31] To Maria, Jan. 7, 1798 (*Domestic Life*, pp. 246-248).

[32] She was still there on Nov. 16, 1797, when Jefferson gave her some money, perhaps preparatory to her setting out (Account Book), and was certainly gone by Dec. 2, when he wrote her (Randall, II, 358). The earlier accident is referred to in TJ to TMR, Jan. 22, 1797 (LC, 17292).

[33] To Martha, Feb. 8, 1798, and to Maria, Mar. 7, 1798 (Randall, II, 405-406).

[34] In his letters to his son-in-law there are several references to Davenport, who had provided 3000 chestnut shingles by Apr. 29 but was generally disappointing.

[35] To Maria, July 13, 14, 1798 (Randall, II, 409-410).

roofing was done before December, when he set out again for Philadelphia, and he was then hoping that the house would be covered in
three or four weeks more, but at the north end it was open for a second
winter.[36] Because of the short session of Congress, he got home in
March, 1799, to find that hardly a stroke of work had been done toward covering the house. He wrote Maria: "It seems as if I should
never get it inhabitable." [37] The Randolphs moved in from Belmont,
nonetheless; they were giving up that place, preparatory to settling at
Edgehill in a house designed by Jefferson and now being completed.
In April, 1799, he paid off a roofer, and one would assume that by
then his entire house was covered.

It is uncertain just when the dome was done. When he was in his
seventies Jefferson said that James Dinsmore built it for him.[38] This
workman, whom Jefferson described as a house joiner of the first
order, began his ten years' service at Monticello in the autumn of
1798, when he arrived from Philadelphia.[39] At the seat of government
Jefferson was tapping the skilled-labor market. Another workman he
particularly relied on in this period was Richard Richardson, a native
of Albemarle who began at Monticello as a bricklayer. During Jefferson's first winter as Vice President, Richardson, with his encouragement, betook himself to Philadelphia to learn stone-cutting and plastering, and he returned to Monticello much improved. He was still
there in 1800, serving as a sort of overseer, though he chiefly oversaw
building and digging rather than the production of crops. Despite
Jefferson's avowed policy of discouraging drinking among his workmen, he provided whiskey regularly for Mr. Dinsmore and Mr. Richardson, each of whom consumed it at the rate of nearly half a pint
per day without discernible ill effects.[40]

Throughout his long stay at Monticello, Dinsmore was chiefly occupied on the interior woodwork. Of more immediate importance,
after the roofing of the house, was the laying of the floors, which
Jefferson said could not be done except when he himself was there.
In 1799, fortunately, he was at home from March to December, and
most of the rooms had some sort of flooring before he went off again
for a six-months' absence. It is impossible to say just how much of the

[36] Statement in Account Book, Nov. 8, 1798: "McGee begins to work on the
North end of the roof." TJ to Maria, Dec. 8, 1798 (UVA).
[37] Mar. 8, 1799 (UVA).
[38] To Thomas Munro, Mar. 4, 1815 (Bixby, pp. 218–219).
[39] Account Book, Oct. 24, 1798, noting payment of his expenses; see also June 13,
1798.
[40] Account Book, Sept. 30, 1799.

house was then usable, but it is safe to mention some things that had *not* been done. Even on the exterior, the structure was still incomplete when the eighteenth century passed into the nineteenth. Part of the cornice, the balustrade above it, and the Chippendale lattice beneath the dome and at the bottoms of the long windows on the west were not put up until Jefferson's presidency. Early in 1801, his son-in-law wrote him that they had erected one of the columns, only to find that it was not perpendicular; and no information has come to light to show when all were placed. Inside the house Dinsmore worked continuously on arches, moldings, and cabinets; and not until the owner's first presidential term had run half its course was the major work of plastering completed. He was in his second term when his granddaughter wrote him that the house looked much better, now that it had been painted.[41]

The insurance policies he took out in 1800 showed no increase in buildings beyond those he had described in his application four years earlier, though the dwelling house was now of a different size and shape.[42] The southeast pavilion was still unconnected with the central structure, while its counterpart on the southwest was not started. On Mulberry Row he was soon to build a new nailery, but, except for the stable at one end and perhaps an additional shed or two, this plantation street was much as it had been when he ceased to be secretary of state. During his retirement he had had a road built to Secretary's Ford, the descent being one foot in ten.[43] He had finished the third of his roundabouts and begun the fourth. He had made the place more accessible but had had little time as yet to do much about his grounds, though Bailey had been his gardener for half a dozen years, living in a house below the orchard.[44] Some years earlier, trees had been planted round the main house but these were not yet full-grown, and this scene of construction must have been rather bare and raw.

At the turn of the century, when he was entering a new phase of his public life and soon to occupy the most eminent of his stations, the mansion of his dreams was far from finished. His plans were taking physical form, however, after disappointment and frustration, and with the passage of slow time this indomitable man of vision would witness their fulfillment.

41 From Anne Cary Randolph, July 11, 1805 (Monticello file from MHS).
42 MHS, under date of August, 1800.
43 *Garden Book*, p. 239.
44 *Ibid.*, p. 224.

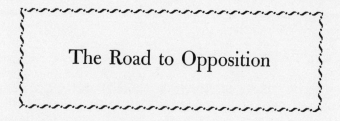

The Road to Opposition

[XVI]

Distant View of Jay's Treaty

1795–1796

LATE in the summer of 1795, in the second year of his retirement, Jefferson said that he had forbidden himself the reading of newspapers, and thinking or saying anything on public questions beyond what he was drawn into by the conversation of his neighbors.[1] This may not have been strictly true, but beyond a doubt his deep immersion in the operations of his farms and nailery, and his absorption in building plans, left him little time for serious thought on national affairs. Most of his information about the outside world came from interested friends and the papers they sent him. As the most important news that obtruded on his privacy during the first year of his retirement was that of the Whiskey Rebellion and the attack on the Democratic societies, the most important of his second year related to Jay's Treaty with Great Britain. A former Secretary of State whose anti-British sentiments had increased rather than diminished since he left office could not fail to be dismayed by this. Receiving a copy of the document in midsummer from Senator Henry Tazewell of his state, he quickly concluded that he was against it, just as Tazewell and the other Virginia senator, Stevens Thomson Mason, were.[2]

By this time the treaty had been approved by the Senate, without a vote to spare, on condition that one specially unpalatable article be partially suspended.[3] It had not yet been ratified by the United States

---

[1] To Tench Coxe, Sept. 10, 1795 (Ford, VII, 30).

[2] Tazewell, writing him from Philadelphia, July 1, 1795, said that he was able to send a copy, now that the treaty had found its way into the press (LC, 16885, endorsed as received July 21). Mason was responsible for the publication of a document which was supposed to remain secret. TJ replied to Tazewell on Sept. 13, 1795 (Ford, VII, 30–31). The standard account is S. F. Bemis, *Jay's Treaty* (1924).

[3] Article XII. The Senate approved June 24, 1795.

— that is, signed by the President — or by the British, to whom the Senate's amendment would have to be referred. Not until late in the following winter was it proclaimed, and even then it had to run the gauntlet of the House of Representatives, since it could not be carried into effect without appropriations.[4] Jefferson's friends, chiefly Madison, kept him informed of the prolonged struggle as it proceeded. No other public controversy during his retirement aroused him to the same degree, and he denounced the treaty strongly, even violently, in private letters, but in no other sense was he a participant in the campaign of protest and opposition.

Writing to persons whose sentiments were like his own, he felt no compulsion to analyze the terms of an agreement which he regarded as an ignominious surrender. The only merit claimed for it by its most zealous defenders, he said, was that it prevented war, but on his part he held to "the eternal truth that acquiescence under insult is not the way to escape war." [5] At long last the British agreed to withdraw from the Northwest posts, thus recognizing the sovereignty of the United States in that region, though they made no promise to restrain the Indians. The provision for a commission to which Americans could appeal for compensation for shipping losses turned out to be more of a gain than he probably expected. The establishment of the principle of settling such questions and boundary disputes by recourse to commissions was, in fact, the most constructive part of the entire treaty, but this was a long-range benefit which he does not appear to have appreciated at the time. In practically all other respects the agreement amounted to a complete surrender of what Jefferson had advocated in his negotiation with George Hammond and in the reports he submitted at the end of his secretaryship. No compensation was offered for the slaves carried off by the British, and the United States assumed the private debts to the collection of which legal obstacles had been imposed — despite the fact that the courts were open and that the whole trend of American decisions was to uphold the British merchants against the Virginia planters and other debtors. The United States, besides virtually accepting the British interpretation of international law, gave a ten-year guarantee against tariff and tonnage discriminations such as Jefferson and Madison had so strongly favored; and, finally, the whole instrument was so pointedly in favor of the

[4] Ratified by the U. S., Aug. 14, 1795, though this fact was not known to TJ until after Sept. 6; ratified by Great Britain, Oct. 28, 1795; proclaimed, Feb. 29, 1796.

[5] To Henry Tazewell, Sept. 13, 1795 (Ford, VII, 31); to Monroe, Mar. 2, 1796 (Ford, VII, 58).

British that it was almost certain to cause trouble with the French.

With due allowance for contemporary partisan exaggeration, this treaty signalized a departure from the policy of fair neutrality which the administration had successfully pursued under such difficult circumstances when Jefferson was in office. To him it also appeared as a diabolically clever partisan maneuver. Two months after he first saw it he wrote Madison: "A bolder party-stroke was never struck. For it certainly is an attempt of a party, which finds they have lost their majority in one branch of the legislature, to make a law by the aid of the other branch and of the executive, under color of a treaty, which shall bind up the hands of the adverse branch from ever restraining the commerce of their patron-nation." [6] The essential correctness of this political judgment need not be discounted because of the extravagant language Jefferson employed in his private letters. To his son-in-law he described the treaty as a "monument of folly or venality"; and, in writing to another, this man of the hills employed an exaggerated nautical metaphor. Speaking of the people in his own neighborhood, he reported: "They say that while all hands were below deck mending sails, splicing ropes, and every one at his own business, and the captain in his cabin attending to his log book and chart, a rogue of a pilot has run them into an enemy's port." [7]

Neither then nor thereafter did he know, as modern scholars do, the full extent to which Hamilton issued the sailing orders. He did not say that this treaty could be more aptly given the name of Hamilton than Jay.[8] Beyond a doubt, however, he had his former colleague in mind when framing his private indictment. "I do not believe with the Rochefoucaulds and Montaignes, that fourteen out of fifteen men are rogues," he said: "I believe a great abatement from that proportion may be made in favor of general honesty. But I have always found that rogues would be uppermost, and I do not know that the proportion is too strong for the higher orders, and for those who, rising above the swinish multitide, always contrive to nestle themselves into the places of power and profit. These rogues set out with stealing the people's good opinion, and then steal from them the right of with-

[6] Sept. 21, 1795 (Ford, VII, 33).

[7] To TMR, Aug. 11, 1795 (LC, 15702); to Mann Page, Aug. 30, 1795 (Ford, VII, 25). TJ does not appear to have discussed the terms of the treaty in detail in any letter of this period. He came nearest to summing things up in his letters to Monroe in France, but not even in these was he explicit except about political developments; see Sept. 6, 1795 (Ford, VII, 27–28); Mar. 2, 1796 (Ford, VII, 58–59).

[8] Bemis, Jay's Treaty, p. 271.

drawing it, by contriving laws and associations against the power of the people themselves." [9] One kernel of truth in this rhetorical passage is that Jefferson was convinced that the treaty was against the public interest and in defiance of popular opinion. He was likewise convinced that its major advocates, exclusive of George Washington, were perfectly willing to hoodwink the people and apply any handy constitutional device to maintain their power. This judgment may now seem harsh but in its historical setting it is entirely understandable.

Once news of the treaty got out, opposition to it was spontaneous wherever anti-British sentiment was pronounced and the "republican interest" strong. Jefferson himself exercised no leadership in this connection and did not need to. In Philadelphia, viewed by many as the center of "Gallomania," there was a meeting in the State House Yard. In this, according to Secretary of the Treasury Wolcott, the "ignorant and violent class of the community" did the voting, while Dr. William Shippen, Alexander James Dallas, Judge Thomas McKean, and other "ostensible leaders" sat on the stage. Then the treaty was placed on a pole, borne to the house of the French minister (said to have conducted himself with propriety) and finally burned before the house of the British minister, George Hammond.[10] Jefferson may not yet have heard of this performance when he learned of recent events in New York from someone just arrived from points north. He reported to Madison in Orange County that Hamilton defended the treaty at a meeting and carried the session. "But," as he added with apparent relish, "the Livingstonians appealed to stones and clubs and beat him and his party off the ground." [11] In August, he believed that support of the treaty was confined to "English merchants," but by September he had concluded that other merchants, as open-mouthed against the treaty as anybody at first, having become alarmed by "the general expression of indignation," had decided "to tack about and support both treaty and government, rather than risk the government." [12] The violence of the opposition in a few cities played into the hands of the treaty's supporters, who assumed the role of defenders of public order and the government itself. Fisher Ames of Massachusetts predicted: "The treaty will go in spite of mobs." [13] Without

[9] To Mann Page, Aug. 30, 1795 (Ford, VII, 24). The term "swinish multitude" was from Burke. Judging from other letters of the period, the references to "profit" relate particularly to merchants engaged in business with England and to the special beneficiaries of Hamilton's financial policies.

[10] Oliver Wolcott, Jr., to Washington, July, 1795 (Gibbs, I, 217–218).

[11] Aug. 3, 1795 (Ford, VII, 23).

[12] To Madison, Sept. 21, 1795 (Ford, VII, 32–33).

[13] To Thomas Dwight, Aug. 24, 1795 (*Works*, I, 173).

explicitly deploring the violence he had done nothing to incite but fearing a revulsion in public sentiment, Jefferson urged Madison to enter the field of argument by taking up his pen in reply to Hamilton, who was defending the treaty under the name CAMILLUS.

At this time the former Secretary of State paid one of his most famous tributes to the prowess of his late antagonist. "Hamilton is really a colossus to the anti-republican party," he wrote. "Without numbers, he is an host within himself. They have got themselves into a defile, where they might be finished; but too much security on the republican part will give time to his talents and indefatigableness to extricate them. We have had only middling performances to oppose to him. In truth, when he comes forward, there is nobody but yourself who can meet him." [14] This suggestion Madison did not accept, choosing to have his say in the more familiar forum of the House of Representatives when that body should reassemble. Jefferson himself refrained from writing for the newspapers either when in or out of office. In the aggregate his private letters bearing on this topic were relatively few, and they were generally in reply to ones received from particular friends. No full or systematic critique of the treaty of Hamilton and Jay came from his facile pen, but he summed it up privately as an "infamous act, which is nothing more than a treaty of alliance between England and the Anglomen of this country against the legislature and people of the United States." [15]

While following the path of privacy, he may be charged with a departure from that of strict propriety in one case. Replying to a letter from the French minister, Adet, which had covered a communication from a Genevan savant, he went beyond the requirements of politeness. In view of his experiences with Genet, he may have been warranted in expressing the wish that his period of service in Philadelphia had overlapped that of the present French minister, but he said more than that:

> . . . The interests of our two republics also could not but have been promoted by the harmony of their servants. Two people whose interests, whose principles, whose habits of attachment, founded on fellowship in war and mutual kindnesses, have so many points of union, cannot but be easily kept together. I hope you have accordingly been sensible, Sir, of the general interest which my countrymen take in all the successes of your republic.

[14] To Madison, Sept. 21, 1795 (Ford, VII, 32–33). Hamilton was not writing under the name of CURTIUS as TJ supposed.
[15] To Edward Rutledge, Nov. 30, 1795 (Ford, VII, 40).

In this no one joins with more enthusiasm than myself, an enthusiasm kindled by my love of liberty, by my gratitude to your nation who helped us to acquire it, by my wishes to see it extended to all men, and first to those whom we love most. I am now a private man, free to express my feelings, & their expression will be estimated at neither more or less than they weigh, to wit, the expressions of a private man. Your struggles for liberty keep alive the only sparks of sensation which public affairs now excite in me. As to the concerns of my own country, I leave them willingly and safely to those who will have a longer interest in cherishing them.[16]

Since he ceased to be a private man by the end of another year and this minister was charged with participation in the effort to elect him President, this letter could have been very damaging if brought to light. There is no sufficient reason, however to attribute it to any personal political ambition.

In Virginia, late in the summer of 1795, there was a concerted campaign of opposition to the treaty. This took the form of a succession of meetings, which appear to have been orderly. Jefferson described to his son-in-law the plan of a meeting of protest in Albemarle, to be followed by the appointment of a committee from this and adjoining counties to draw an address to the President.[17] Very likely he was consulted about this gathering, but there is no indication that he participated in it. He certainly did not attend the others, though he was pleased with reports of them, especially of the one in Richmond over which his old friend George Wythe presided. In his own state, opposition to the treaty was overwhelming at this stage. After the signing of it by Washington became known there was a lull in the campaign, but this was resumed at the next session of the General Assembly in November. By a vote of two to one the House then adopted a resolution, to which the Senate agreed, approving the conduct of Senators Tazewell and Mason in opposing the treaty. A resolution commending the integrity and patriotism of the President and stating that the earlier resolution implied no censure of his motives was adopted by a closer vote. Jefferson, whose son-in-law was in Richmond at the time and gave him a firsthand account of these events, strongly approved of the first of these actions and did not object to

---

[16] To Adet, Oct. 14, 1795 (LC, 16948–16949), replying to letter of Sept. 9 (LC, 16918), received Sept. 22.

[17] Ammon, "Republican Party in Virginia," pp. 149–150; TJ to TMR, Aug. 11, 1795 (LC, 15702).

the second.[18] In writing Madison he used strong partisan language, referring to the "bigots and passive obedience men" who had allied themselves with the merchant group of Alexandria. Also, he gave one of the earliest of his unfavorable characterizations of John Marshall, who, as he believed, would do less mischief now that he had thrown off the "mask of Republicanism" and "come forth in the plenitude of his English principles." But the Squire of Monticello was merely a spirited commentator on events in which he had no personal share.

The continuing conflict centering on the treaty related to the powers, or lack of powers, of the federal House of Representatives with respect to it. This raised an important constitutional question which had immediate political implications, since the Republicans controlled that body and saw in it the only hope of a staying action against the detested treaty. Hamilton in his CAMILLUS letters, and the Federalists in Congress, took the position that the lower House had no choice but to enact whatever enabling legislation was necessary, now that the Senate had approved the treaty and the President had signed it. They regarded it as a *fait accompli*, as the supreme law of the land to which the House must bow. To the Republicans the constitutional issue did not seem that clear and simple. Not only did the treaty by its specific terms limit the powers of Congress in matters of commerce, tariff duties, and the like; it required the appropriation of money to carry certain of its terms into effect (setting up the commissions, for example), and, according to the Constitution, Congress controlled the purse strings.

Madison and Albert Gallatin had to think through this problem before making elaborate speeches in the House, as they did late in the winter. Jefferson in his retirement drew no paper on it. Viewing the treaty as a barefaced attempt to override the public will, he might have been expected to magnify the powers of the Republican House of Representatives in this connection, as he did. Most of his comments on the question were incidental, and they were probably not the result of systematic thought. Writing Monroe a few weeks after he first saw the treaty, he said that, if the President had signed it, many believed that the House would oppose it as "constitutionally void" — implying that the President had no right to sign it without consulting the House.[19] He used the term "unconstitutional" later when writing

[18] *General Assembly of Virginia: Journal of the House of Delegates*, Nov. 20, 21, 1795; TJ to Madison, Nov. 26, 1795, enclosing extract of a letter of Nov. 22 from Randolph and asking that it be communicated to Giles (Ford, VII, 36–39 and note). Madison said that this report corroborated news he already had (Dec. 6, 1795 [MP, 18:86]).

[19] Sept. 6, 1795 (Ford, VII, 28).

Madison, taking the position that all matters in the treaty normally requiring the concurrence of the two legislative branches and the President should be referred to the House; and that the House might reject these, either by explicit action or by refusing to pass acts carrying them into effect. He preferred explicit rejection.[20] The practical consequence of such action would have been the severe limitation of the treaty-making powers of the President and the Senate.

So far as the record shows, he bore no responsibility for a resolution of the Virginia General Assembly in December embodying this idea. It appears to have been widely current in the state at the time, and, impracticable as it now seems, it raised the continuing question of the democratic control of foreign relations, or at least participation in them.[21] The legislature of Jefferson's state called upon its senators and representatives to use their utmost exertions to obtain certain amendments to the Constitution. The first of these read as follows:

> That no treaty containing any stipulation upon the subject of the powers vested in Congress by the eighth section of the first article, shall become the supreme law of the land, until it shall have been approved in these particulars, by a majority in the House of Representatives; and the President, before he shall ratify any such treaty, shall submit the same to the House of Representatives.[22]

Other resolutions called for the institution of some other tribunal than the Senate for the trial of impeachments and for the reduction of the Senate term to three years, and forbade the holding of any other office or appointment by any United States judge. Writing Monroe in March about this set of resolutions, Jefferson said: "Their reception by some of the other assemblies has been such as to call for the sacrifice of all feeling rather than ruffle the harmony so necessary for the public good." [23] Only in the far South and in Kentucky were they well received; elsewhere the judgment was unfavorable, and all the more because the reference to impeachments could be interpreted as a threat against the President himself.[24] The Virginia Republicans were

[20] To Madison, Nov. 26, 1795 (Ford, VII, 38). His son-in-law had informed him that Marshall had conceded that the whole commercial part of the treaty rested with the House.

[21] Well discussed, in relation to the twentieth century, by A. N. Holcombe, *Our More Perfect Union* (1950), pp. 280–283, 424–429.

[22] *General Assembly of Virginia: Journal of the House of Delegates*, p. 91 (Dec. 12, 1795). This resolution along with 3 others was adopted by a vote of 88 to 32. The Senate agreed on Dec. 15.

[23] Mar. 2, 1796 (Ford, VII, 60).

[24] The best account of this that I have seen is in S. G. Kurtz, *The Presidency*

not such "disorganizers" as Fisher Ames asserted when commenting contemptuously on their "desperate innovation" and "revolutionary amendments," but in their fury against the Jay Treaty they had over-reached themselves.[25] Jefferson gave no sign of disapproval, but, busily occupied on his mountain-top, he was personally aloof from this campaign.

During this winter of political discontent he gave serene attention to certain matters which might be described as antiquarian. While the season would not permit building operations he concerned himself with what he called "precious monuments" of the past. His services in safeguarding some of these deserve remembrance. Beginning in his early manhood to collect all the existing laws of his native province that he could lay hands on, he preserved many which otherwise might have ended up as waste paper. His collection of printed laws was still unbound, and when he got home from Philadelphia it was in such a chaotic state that he did not have the courage to tackle it. Stimulated, however, by his old law teacher, George Wythe, who wanted to see some of these old laws, he finally brought himself to arrange them. Early in the year 1796, before the spring thaw could swell the streams beyond passage, he put his "whole precious collection" of printed laws in a box, and sent them by wagon to his son-in-law at Varina. They were then to go to Wythe, whom he would trust with anything he had in the world he said, but before they were used he wanted them bound, as he had long intended they should be. He gave explicit instructions which were eventually carried out. The unhurried binder required about three years.[26]

Besides the printed laws, Jefferson also had a number of rarer items

of John Adams (1957), ch. 1, though the title of the chapter and certain quotations from Federalist sources create what I regard as an erroneous impression. This was far more a Republican-party and anti-treaty than a pro-Jefferson campaign, and I find no evidence that he had any personal part in it. Madison was aware that the first resolution, or something like it, would be submitted, and he may be presumed to have discussed it with Joseph Jones (Jones to Madison, Oct. 29, 1795; Madison to Jones, and to his father, Nov. 8, 1795, in MP, 18:74–76). But I find no evidence that Madison told TJ of this, or that Jones saw or wrote him before the action of the Assembly (Jones to Madison, Nov. 22, 1795 in MP, 18:80; Dec. 19, 1795, in MP, 18:91).

[25] Ames to Thomas Dwight, Feb. 11, 16, 1795 (_Works_, I, 186–187).

[26] See E. M. Sowerby, _The Library of Thomas Jefferson_, II (1953), 246–254, for an account of the collection and extracts from pertinent letters. TJ dispatched 7 vols. on Jan. 12, 1796, and additional laws soon thereafter. An 8th vol. was to consist of the collection of the year 1794, which TMR was to procure. One of Miss Sowerby's illustrations shows five of these handsome and historic volumes, with "Monticello Library" stamped on them. Apparently the binding was not finished until 1799.

in manuscript, some of which were in danger of disintegration. In order to protect these he wrapped and sewed them into oiled cloth. To Wythe he sent a list, not only of the printed laws, but also of all others that he possessed or knew of. This beautifully written general statement is an admirable example of what he could do when he turned scholar, just as the letter to his old friend with which he sent it is a classic statement of the desirability of preserving historic documents. While political storms were raging in Richmond and Philadelphia he was not only overlooking his quiet acres; he was calmly striving to preserve for future generations of Americans what he regarded as priceless morsels of their heritage.[27]

The open battle within the federal government over the treaty did not ensue until Washington proclaimed it on Feb. 29, 1796, and transmitted it to the members of the two branches of Congress next day. He had already submitted to the Senate the treaty with Spain, which was promptly approved without a dissenting vote. Oddly enough, Jefferson expressed dissatisfaction with this, asserting that at an earlier time the Spanish would have conceded more, particularly with respect to commerce with the West Indies.[28] But everybody else thought well of it, including the members of the House, who voted the necessary appropriations in due course without demur. Dr. Benjamin Rush reported from Philadelphia that this treaty had revived Jefferson's name among his republican friends; they attributed Pinckney's success as a negotiator to information and instructions provided at a time when his influence was felt in the government. At almost the same time Thomas Pinckney himself wrote him, as one planter to another, sending observations on Spanish agriculture and showing a very friendly spirit.[29] Dr. Rush, a fellow signer of the Declaration of Independence, said that thousands wished and prayed that the draftsman of that act would live to realize it, by giving them "the principles and happiness of an *independent* people."

Jefferson's basic objection to Jay's treaty was just that it restricted national independence by drawing the young republic back into the British system from which it had so painfully emerged. His interest

27 TJ to Wythe, Jan. 16, 1796 (Ford, VII, 52–55). The recipient's copy of the statement, dated Jan. 13, 1796, is in MP, 19:5; press copies, with legislative acts, in LC, 17009–17020. For the use afterwards made of TJ's MSS in connection with W. W. Hening's *Statutes at Large* (1809 and thereafter) see Sowerby, II, 255 ff.

28 To Madison, Mar. 6, 1796 (Ford, VII, 63).

29 Rush to TJ, Mar. 1, 1796 (Butterfield, II, 771–772); Pinckney to TJ, Mar. 16, 1796 (LC, 17072–17074), received June 3.

in current public affairs was unquestionably quickened by this dread prospect. He was now reading some newspapers and asked Madison to give him a weekly history of what was happening in government "behind the curtain." While not promising to do that, the busy little Congressman sent him brief reports approximately that often throughout the late winter and early spring. About this time Jefferson was saying that he was never "so hard run with business." [30] The brickbats were now falling at Monticello, and this was the spring when he said he had 140 workmen on the place. The net result was that, while he made sharp comments on public affairs during this period of intense political conflict, he made relatively few and addressed these to few people — rarely to anybody in Philadelphia except Madison and Giles, whom he did not need to convert to his way of thinking.

He viewed with enthusiasm the emergence of another gladiator, Albert Gallatin, who had taken up arms against Hamilton's financial system with a skill no other Republican could match. At Gallatin's instance in December of that year, two weeks after the former Genevan took his seat as a representative from Pennsylvania, the House set up the ways and means committee, thus moving toward a closer supervision of fiscal affairs. Reporting to Jefferson some of the early findings of that committee, Madison asked: "Who could have supposed that Hamilton could have gone off in the triumph he assumed with such a condition of the finances behind him?" [31] Jefferson's response, in effect, was "I told you so." He asserted that Hamilton's object had been to throw the finances of the country into "utterly undecipherable forms," that the Secretary himself had not understood them, and that his own opinion was that the debt had been increasing over a million dollars a year. "If Mr. Gallatin would undertake to reduce this chaos to order, present us with a clear view of our finances, and put them into a form as simple as they will admit, he will merit immortal honor. The accounts of the United States ought to be, and may be made as simple as those of a common farmer, and capable of being understood by common farmers." [32] Whether or not this suggestion was directly responsible for Gallatin's *Sketches of the Finances of the United States*, which appeared in November, it appears to have been the most important of the very few suggestions Jefferson made in connection with the political campaign of 1796. Gallatin's exhaustive study bore out Jefferson's rough calculation about the increase in the

[30] Madison to TJ, Feb. 7, 1796 (MP, 19:20); TJ to John Harvie, Feb. 22, 1796 (MHS).
[31] Jan. 31, 1796 (MP, 19:15).
[32] To Madison, Mar. 6, 1796 (Ford, VII, 61–62).

national debt.[33] He must have wished that Gallatin had come to the House sooner, and that Hamilton's financial policy had been attacked earlier with such authority at its most vulnerable point, its unnecessary expensiveness. Meanwhile, the financial issue had been blanketed by foreign questions.

Immured at Monticello, Jefferson appears to have made no proposal of consequence in connection with the controversy over the treaty which raged in the House of Representatives during March and April, 1796, though his private letters leave no doubt of his moral support of Madison, Gallatin, and the other speakers on the side of the opposition. Having occasion to write Monroe, he stated the position which had become orthodox among them. "On the precedent now to be set will depend the future construction of our constitution," he said, "and whether the powers of legislation shall be transferred from the P, Senate and H. of R. to the P, Senate and Piarningo or any other Indian, Algerine or other chief. It is fortunate that the first decision is to be in a case so palpably atrocious as to have been predetermined by all America." [34]

Gallatin asserted that if the Federalist doctrine were carried to its logical conclusion the President and Senate could legislate under the forms of treaty-making wholly without regard to the House. His speech so enchanted Jefferson, who read it in the *Aurora*, that he described it to Madison as "worthy of being printed at the end of the Federalist, as the only rational commentary on the part of the constitution to which it relates." [35] He recognized that difficult objections could be raised to the doctrine of Gallatin, but did not say just what these were. He contented himself with asserting that they could be more easily swallowed than those arising from Federalist arguments which in fact annihilated the legislative powers of the popularly elected branch of Congress. Regardless of his own very extensive experience as a negotiator, he now saw little harm in "annihilating the whole treaty-making power, except for making peace." Such a stripping of the executive power in foreign affairs he could hardly have welcomed when himself in executive office. On the basis of past actions, however, it could have been assumed that if he had been in authority

---

[33] Raymond Walters, Jr., *Albert Gallatin* (1957), p. 91.

[34] Mar. 21, 1796 (Ford, VII, 68).

[35] To Madison, Mar. 27, 1796 (Ford, VII, 68), referring to *Aurora* of March 14. He was replying to a letter of Mar. 13, which he received on Mar. 25, and it seems unlikely that he had read Gallatin's speech before writing Monroe. Gallatin's argument is discussed by Henry Adams, who terms it irresistible and says it was never answered (*Life of Albert Gallatin*, 1943 edn., pp. 161–162); and by Raymond Walters, Jr. (*Albert Gallatin*, p. 98).

he would have been far more mindful of opinion in the country and in the lower House than those responsible for this treaty had been. He resolved the constitutional dilemma by going over to what he was sure was the people's side. Indeed, these events perceptibly quickened the course of this gentleman of Virginia in the democratic direction.[36]

He was in full agreement with the position of the Republican spokesmen that the House had a right to see the official papers relating to Jay's mission, except such as pending negotiations would make it improper to disclose. The resolution calling for them was adopted on March 24, 1796, by a vote of 62 to 37.[37] Washington's statement, in denying this request, that the full disclosure of papers bearing on foreign negotiations would be "extremely impolitic" commands respect and sympathy. But it could have been made with comparable appropriateness in December, 1793, when there was an extraordinarily full disclosure of papers bearing on negotiations with foreign powers.[38] John Adams had wondered about the wisdom of that action at that time, while Hamilton, who objected to it in the case of the British though favoring it in the case of the French, had been overruled by Washington. The President was prudent in not submitting Jay's instructions, however, for, as Hamilton pointed out, these were "a crude mass which will do no credit to the administration." [39] The President contended that to admit the *right* of the House to demand all the papers bearing on a foreign negotiation would create a dangerous precedent, and undoubtedly it would have created a troublesome one, but the phraseology of the present request offered a loophole, and in any event the refusal was too peremptory.[40] The most galling thing

[36] Note the comments of Henry Adams on the conflict over democracy between Jefferson and Hamilton, and the final breaking of the partial truce on the arrival of Jay's Treaty (*Gallatin*, p. 159).

[37] *Annals*, 4 Cong., 1 sess., pp. 759, 760. It should be noted that these documents were submitted to the Senate, June 8, 1795 (*A.S.P.F.R.*, I, 470 ff.). At some time they were seen by TJ. A list of the documents, summaries of some of them, and the full text of a few are in his papers in his own handwriting (LC, 16629-16632). Presumably some senator turned over copies of the documents to him, and he copied them in turn. Also in his papers on a single small sheet are "Heads of information given me by E. Randolph" (LC, 16747, no date). His contemporary correspondence does not suggest that he had these materials while the treaty fight was going on. If Randolph's information was accurate, the President held back some papers from the Senate, since they would reflect on Jay. He also reported that the President, speaking with him "on the hypothesis of a separation of the Union into Northern and Southern, said he had made up his mind to move and be of the Northern."

[38] See above, pp. 152-154.

[39] To Washington, Mar. 28, 1796 (Lodge, VIII, 387).

[40] Henry Adams, among others, pointed out that, in connection with the pur-

about it was the assertion that the inspection of these papers could relate to no purpose "under the cognizance of the House, except that of an impeachment." Since men like Madison and Gallatin were not dreaming of impeaching him, the President was actually taking words out of the mouths of the Federalist extremists.

Washington supported his position by a reference to his own membership in the Federal Convention and his understanding from the first that the treaty-making power was vested *exclusively* in the President, with the advice and consent of the Senate.[41] According to Fisher Ames, who viewed the Republican spokesmen as modern Catilines, Madison was "deeply implicated" by Washington's appeal to the proceedings of the Federal Convention and thought by most persons to be "irrevocably disgraced, as a man void of sincerity and fairness." On his own part, writing to Jefferson, Madison described the tone and temper of the President's message as "improper and indelicate." [42] As he remembered, the journal of the convention had been deposited with the President "to be kept sacred until called for by some competent authority," and he did not see how Washington's use of it could be reconciled with this. Though he wanted to avoid "an overt rencontre with the Executive," he asked Jefferson to look at the notes on the Convention which he had left in his friend's hands. Jefferson sent a verbatim copy of an extract from these, saying that the President of the Convention (Washington) should retain the journals and other papers "subject to the orders of the Congress, if ever formed under the Constitution." [43] From his own papers Jefferson turned up a few items showing that the President had not always taken the position he did in his recent message. With regard to the ransom of American citizens from the Algerian pirates, an action recommended by the Senate but calling for an appropriation, he did not think he could enter into *absolute* arrangements without previous authority from *both branches* of the legislature.

This minor research on his own part served no immediate purpose.[44] Before Jefferson wrote this letter, Madison had drawn resolutions as-

---

chase of Alaska a couple of generations later, the administration took a wholly different attitude, with results which were not disastrous (*Gallatin*, p. 161).

[41] His message, dated Mar. 30, 1796, is in Fitzpatrick, XXXV, 2–5.

[42] Ames to G. R. Minot, Apr. 2, 1796 (*Works*, I, 191); Madison to TJ, Apr. 4, 1796 (Hunt, VI, 265n.).

[43] To Madison, Apr. 17, 1796 (Ford, VII, 70). The Secretary of State received the Convention papers into his keeping from the President on Mar. 19, 1796 (Farrand, *Records of the Federal Convention* [1911], III, 370).

[44] Kurtz, in *Presidency of John Adams*, p. 44, while denying the statement of Bowers that TJ made no effort to influence the outcome of the debate, says that this was "virtually the only part he played in the campaign of 1796."

serting the constitutional rights of the House as he and Gallatin were presenting them, and the House had adopted these by a vote of 57 to 35.[45] On the constitutional question the popularly elected branch of the legislature put itself on record without Jefferson's assistance. These resolutions claimed no agency in making treaties, but they asserted the right and duty of the House, before passing any enabling legislation, to discuss a treaty on its merits. Furthermore, they claimed that the House, in the exercise of its constitutional functions, had the right to apply to the Executive for information without specifying precise purposes. Jefferson, in his remoteness, fully agreed with this.

On April 30, after an impassioned plea by Fisher Ames, the representatives finally voted, 51 to 48, to carry into effect a treaty which a majority of them still greatly disliked. Madison kept Jefferson informed of events, writing him every week until the issue was settled — and, indeed, until Congress rose. In interpreting the final acceptance of the treaty he detested, the former Secretary of State was much impressed, we may be sure, by what he learned from this trusted friend who spoke from "behind the curtain." Recognizing that sentiment in the country toward the treaty had changed, Madison told Jefferson that the people had been made to believe that the object of the House of Representatives was *war*, and that they had listened to the summons "to follow where Washington leads." The New England states, as he believed, had been ready to rise in mass against the House.[46] In the light of this judgment, it is not hard to understand why certain Republicans — even though they may have believed that Jay should never have signed such a treaty, or the Senate have approved it, or the President have ratified and proclaimed it — concluded that they had better accept it than run the risk of disrupting the government, or of being charged with doing so. As Madison saw the political results, however, they were bad. He wrote Jefferson: "A crisis which ought to have been so managed as to fortify the Republican cause, has left it in a very crippled condition; from which its recovery will be the more difficult as the elections in N. Y., Massachusetts and other states, where the prospects were favorable, have taken a wrong turn under the impressions of the moment. Nothing but auspicious contingencies abroad or at home can regain the lost ground."[47]

That the foreign situation was inauspicious, information he had re-

[45] The resolutions, drawn by Madison though presented by another, and adopted Apr. 7, 1796, are in Hunt, VI, 264n.
[46] May 9, 1796 (MP, 17:63).
[47] May 22, 1796 (MP, 19:58), received June 3.

ceived from James Monroe in France, and now passed on to Jefferson in cipher, showed very clearly. That minister had learned that the French foreign office considered that the treaty of the United States with Great Britain had annulled the treaty of alliance with France. They said they would rather have an open enemy than a perifidious friend, and that they were resolved to send to the United States an envoy extraordinary whose powers would expire with the execution of his trust — that is, that diplomatic relations would then be severed. Monroe had succeeded in stopping this move and reported it to the executive in his own country. As Jefferson deciphered this passage he could not have failed to reflect that time and circumstance had made wreckage of foreign policies he had nurtured patiently while in office. Though he had not renounced neutrality, his attitude toward the French at this stage may be assumed to have been still friendly. There can be no possible doubt of his continuing anti-British feeling, or of his belief that his country had needlessly bartered away part of its independence.

[XVII]

A Little Spice of Fanaticism:
Jefferson and Washington

THE effectiveness of the campaign of the pro-treaty forces lay in their appeal on the one hand to fear of war and disruption of the government, and to loyalty to the President on the other. That Jefferson scouted the idea of war with the British and minimized the dangers of public criticism of the government may be stated categorically, but the question of his attitude toward the executive authority, and toward Washington in particular, calls for further consideration and comment. During the next few years political foes often asserted that he was an avowed enemy of executive power and a secret enemy of the first President. But Hamilton correctly perceived when they were in office together, and afterwards stated at a crucial moment, that he was by no means disposed to compound all authority in the legislature.[1] He had cried out against legislative omnipotence such as prevailed in his own state when he was governor during the Revolution and such as characterized the Confederation. Fears of the extension of executive power were present in his mind while he was secretary of state, but these were chiefly aroused by Hamilton and were very considerably though not wholly allayed by his confidence in Washington.

His respect and admiration for the President bordered on reverence during most of his own service with him. The two Virginia planters parted on the best of terms, and their mutual enthusiasm for agriculture was a continuing bond between them. While working with Washington, Jefferson's private criticisms of him were relatively minor, generally boiling down to regret that he was so sensitive and

[1] Hamilton to J. A. Bayard, Jan. 16, 1801, giving reasons for his preference of TJ to Burr (Lodge, VIII, 502).

that he did not sufficiently exercise his own fine judgment but leaned too much on that of others. He never intimated that the President was pro-British.

While secretary of state, Jefferson thought of Washington as no figurehead, and actually the persons who, through the years, contributed most to that erroneous impression were admirers of Hamilton who exaggerated his influence during the time when Washington was striving with no inconsiderable success to maintain balance in the government. Jefferson at this time did regard his chief as a necessary symbol of Union and expected him to be President of the nation, standing above parties. The first important sign, as Jefferson perceived it, that Washington was ceasing to achieve this was given when he denounced the democratic societies in connection with the Whiskey Rebellion.[2] He spoke in the name of law and order, without distinguishing between resistance to the government and criticism of its policies. That fine line was not yet perceived by many leaders as it was by Jefferson and Madison, who defended the societies without condoning the rebellion, but the immediate implications of the President's action were obvious. In effect he condemned the Republican partisans and aligned himself with the Federal party, as its leaders called it while identifying it with the government and the Constitution. The course of later events served to tighten this identification in Washington's own mind. The fight against the treaty was marked by violence at the beginning, and by the challenge to executive authority in the name of the Republican House of Representatives at the end. It was also marked by verbal attacks on the sensitive President surpassing those he had endured in the time of Genet. In reality he took an unfavorable view of the treaty in the first place and was basically nonpartisan, but circumstances combined to impel him into the Federalist camp and to isolate him from old friends like Jefferson and Madison among the Republicans.

These circumstances were skillfully exploited by Federalists who were far less moderate than Washington was and by whom, in the end, he was completely surrounded. The Hamiltonian point of view was clearly ascendant in the executive counsels from the time of Jefferson's retirement and was strongly reflected in the treaty. It became dominant after the resignation of Edmund Randolph as secretary of state in August, 1795. Randolph, who had been largely ignored by Jay and Hamilton during the negotiation of the treaty, tried to delay its ratification by Washington, after the Senate had approved it, until the British should revoke a recent order to seize American vessels

[2] See above, pp. 189–191.

bearing provisions.[3] The circumstances under which Secretary of War Pickering and Secretary of the Treasury Wolcott induced Washington to sign the treaty without delay, and caused the Secretary of State to resign under unwarranted suspicions of treason with the French, have been clarified only in our own day.[4] Randolph did himself little good by the confused *Vindication* which he published shortly and which Jefferson read with care. The latter does not seem to have been fully aware of the political *coup* that Pickering and Wolcott effected.

Randolph's political status was anomalous, but he was hardly a Hamiltonian. He himself wrote Madison of a "conspiracy" to destroy the "republican force" in the country. Washington, whom he had revered all his life, he charged with "the profound hypocrisy of Tiberious, and the injustice of an assassin."[5] While confident of his successor's innocence, Jefferson, who had a low opinion of his competence and steadfastness, did not blame Washington for his plight. In the course of time, after several persons had declined the secretaryship of state, Pickering got the place, virtually by default. James McHenry, a protegé of Hamilton, took over Pickering's former post; and, following the death of Attorney General Bradford, Charles Lee was appointed in his stead. "Through what official interstice can a ray of republican truths now penetrate to the P," asked Madison of Jefferson.[6] The chances are that Washington would have eventually signed the treaty if there had been no "conspiracy" against Randolph, and after signing it he saw no turning back, but through force of circumstances he came to be surrounded by men who viewed all opponents and critics of the treaty as Jacobins and disorganizers. If, along with Hamilton, they did not determine the course of the government, they can hardly have failed to heighten the tone of arrogance and self-righteousness in its proceedings.

Jefferson saw signs of vanity in some of Washington's communications to Congress, and, in one of the letters printed by Randolph, a

[3] Even Hamilton took the position that ratification should not be formally exchanged until the order was rescinded; to Wolcott, Aug. 10, 1795 (Lodge, VIII, 355).

[4] By Irving Brant, in "Edmund Randolph, Not Guilty!" *W.&M.*, April 1950, pp. 180–198. The story centered on an intercepted dispatch from the French minister, Fauchet, containing allusions to the Whiskey Rebellion and veiled references to patriots who were for sale. This was turned over to Wolcott by the British minister, who thus intervened in American affairs. Part of the false impression it created arose from faulty translation.

[5] Randolph to Madison, Nov. 1, 1795 (MP, 18:71). It is hardly likely that Madison did not inform TJ of this at some time.

[6] Feb. 7, 1796 (MP, 19:20), referring also to judicial appointees.

"most infatuated blindness" on the President's part to the true character of the partisans of France, whom he regarded as *"partisans of
war and confusion."* Nonetheless, commenting on the answer of the
House to Washington's address on the opening of Congress, he
expressed pleasure that it was respectful toward the President, who,
he said, "errs as other men do, but errs with integrity." [7] He never
took that back, but a little later, under conditions of greater stress, he
sounded much more critical.

The degree of his own party feeling at this stage is revealed by his
severe comments on the past conduct of Emund Randolph, whom he
regarded as a trimmer. If parties in America were divided by mere
greed for office as in England, he said, it was unworthy of a man of
morality and reason to take the part of either. But, he continued,
"where the principle of difference is as substantial and as strongly
pronounced as between the republicans and Monocrats of our country, I hold it as honorable to take a firm and decided part, and as immoral to pursue a middle line, as between the parties of honest men
and rogues, into which every country is divided." [8] This sounds more
like a stump speech than the calm utterance of a retired statesman. In
private letters to the faithful, Jefferson not infrequently indulged in
partisan exaggeration which may and often should be discounted. His
allegations cannot be lightly dismissed, however, for to him unquestionably the issues were basic and very real.

Some months earlier, John Taylor of Caroline had written him:
"There is a spice of fanaticism in my nature upon two subjects —
agriculture and republicanism." [9] Jefferson could have said that about
himself, despite the fact that he had been notably patient and realistic
in the actual conduct of public business. When in office he did not
often tilt at windmills. The republicanism he was now championing
so ardently in moments not devoted to his lands and house he did not
define precisely, though he left no possible doubt as to whom he regarded as its enemies. No systematic statement of his political philosophy can be found in the occasional private writings of these years of
retirement, or anywhere else for that matter. But at times he summed
things up and gave significant expression to his ideas about the
government of his country from the Revolution onward, and
about attitudes toward it.[10]

---

[7] This quotation and the others in the paragraph are from a letter to W. B.
Giles, Dec. 31, 1795 (Ford, VII, 41–44), in which he commented extensively on
Randolph's pamphlet in vindication of himself.

[8] Ford, VII, 43.

[9] Letter of May 5, 1795 (LC, 16819–16822).

[10] Of particular interest in this connection are certain notes of his (Ford, VII,

Generally avoiding the words "federalist" and "anti-federalist," he used the terms "republican" and "anti-republican," commonly but not invariably employing the lower case. This circumstance may be attributed to his dislike of capital letters, but one of its results is that we are left uncertain as to when he was and when he was not referring to a party. He also used the term "monocrat," and one wonders just what he meant by it, or by the "monarchical" features of the Constitution. If he meant these to be precise terms he used them too loosely for them to be thus regarded. They can best be understood as symbolic words. To him the American Revolution meant not merely independence from British rule but also escape from the British system of government into republicanism. Thus the "spirit of 1776," which he so loved to refer to, had a double meaning. By the same token, the "Anglomen" represented to him a domestic as well as a foreign danger; in his opinion they were looking back longingly toward the forms and practices of the British government.

Jefferson said nothing about "monocrats" in a letter he wrote John Adams in the winter of the fight over Jay's treaty. Indeed, having occasion to refer to a book from France, he expressed strong disapproval of the French idea of an executive council and strong approval of the American presidency, embodying the principle of unity in the executive. If this was a "monarchical" feature, he certainly did not reject it. What he really favored most and feared most is well expressed in the following passage:

> . . . This I hope will be the age of experiments in government, and that their basis will be founded on principles of honesty, not of mere force. . . . Either force or corruption has been the principle of every modern government, unless the Dutch perhaps be excepted, . . . If ever the morals of a people could be made the basis of their own government, it is our case; . . . I am sure, from the honesty of your heart, you join me in detestation of the corruption of the English government, and that no man on earth is more incapable than yourself of seeing that copied among us, willingly. I have been among those who have feared the design to introduce it here, and it has been a strong reason with me for

44-49), on a letter of July 30, 1795, from Professor Christoph Daniel Ebeling of Hamburg, who was writing a book relating to the U. S. (LC, 16898-16901, received Oct. 15, 1795). I have found no letter to Ebeling, and in view of the fact that TJ's "notes" as preserved in his papers are original in form rather than a copy, I think it unlikely that these notes were actually sent. The book was *Erdbeschreibung und Geschichte von Amerika. Die Vereinten Staaten von Nord-Amerika* (7 vols., Hamburg, 1793-1816), which TJ seems never to have owned.

wishing there was an ocean of fire between that island and us. . . .[11]

Parliamentary corruption in England had declined somewhat since the days of Lord North, but there was still enough of it to relieve Jefferson of the charge of exaggeration with respect to that country. Thus, even if his fears of the "corruption" of the American government were extreme, his fear of the domestic consequences of a political rapprochement with Great Britain at this stage was justifiable. In his judgment of the French he had not yet fully escaped from what a later generation would have termed wishful thinking. About the British, however, he was realistic enough, and his total record shows unmistakably that his goal for his country was that of genuine, not nominal, independence. The domestic controversy that had arisen in connection with foreign policy had served to clarify and accentuate in his mind the basic issue of popular government and the sovereignty of the people. He greatly magnified the danger of monarchy, as George Washington undoubtedly believed, and he rarely used the word "democracy," which still had for many members of his generation the connotation of mob rule. But, in sharp contrast to Hamilton, who scorned the people, and even to Washington, who became increasingly fearful of disorder and criticism, Jefferson on his detached mountain-top was staking his hopes as never before on a genuinely democratic republic.

He blamed the Jay treaty on the "machinations" of a "faction," conspiring with "the enemies of their country" and defying the will of the people. The acquiescence of Washington, whose honesty he did not question and whose judgment he had long admired, he described as incomprehensible. While the question was still pending in the House he wrote Madison: "I wish that his honesty and his political errors may not furnish a second occasion to exclaim, 'curse on his virtues, they've undone his country.' "[12] This quotation implied no thought that Washington was or desired to be a tyrant, such as Cato thought Caesar was, for Jefferson never intimated that. It did suggest, however, that the great and good man was being used by others as a "front."

In the mood of vexation and helplessness induced by the developments of the winter and early spring, Jefferson wrote a private letter

[11] Feb. 28, 1796 (*A-J Letters*, I, 259–260). Adams replied Apr. 6 (I, 261–262).

[12] March 27, 1796 (Ford, VII, 69). This is from Joseph Addison's *Cato* (first performed in 1713), Act IV, sc. 4.

to a friend abroad which got into print some months later and upon which the contemporary allegation of his secret hostility to George Washington was chiefly based. Its political repercussions were not felt until the spring of 1797, when he was back in the public eye as vice president, but it deserves mention here because of its revelation of his state of mind in the spring of 1796, when he was personally remote from politics. It was addressed to the Florentine Philip Mazzei, then living in Pisa, a neighbor of his in the early years of the American Revolution whose first wife was buried at Monticello, and it dealt primarily with Mazzei's personal affairs, which, through the years, required a disproportionate amount of Jefferson's attention and sometimes taxed his patience.[13] Its incidental though rather extended political comments, addressed to a politically sympathetic person who had been long absent from the American scene, were couched in the language of extravagance.

> The aspect of our politics has wonderfully changed since you left us. In place of that noble love of liberty, & republican government which carried us triumphantly thro' the war, an Anglican monarchical, & aristocratical party has sprung up, whose avowed object is to draw over us the substance, as they have already done the forms of the British government. The main body of our citizens, however, remain true to their republican principle; the whole landed interest is republican, and so is a great mass of talents. Against us are the Executive, the Judiciary, two out of three branches of the legislature [that is, the Senate and the President], all the officers of the government, all who want to be officers, all timid men who prefer the calm of despotism to the boisterous sea of liberty, British merchants & Americans trading on British capitals, speculators & holders in the banks & public funds, a contrivance invented for the purposes of corruption, & for assimilating us in all things to the rotten as well as the sound parts of the British model.

As a political analysis this passage has value, despite its clichés and denunciatory rhetoric. But it was the next passage, alleged to contain a veiled reference to Washington, which aroused most unfavorable comment in later months and years:

> It would give you a fever were I to name to you the apostates who have gone over to these heresies, men who were Samsons in the field & Solomons in the council, but who have had their heads

---

[13] Apr. 24, 1796 (Ford, VII, 72–78). For earlier associations of Mazzei with TJ, see *Jefferson the Virginian*, pp. 164–165; *Jefferson and the Rights of Man*, pp. 109–110, 212.

shorn by the harlot England. In short, we are likely to preserve the liberty we have obtained only by unremitting labors & perils. But we shall preserve them; and our mass of weight & wealth on the good side is so great, as to leave no danger that force will ever be attempted against us. We have only to awake and snap the Lilliputian cords with which they have been entangling us during the first sleep which succeeded our labors.

This burning indictment may be cited as a sample of what its author might have produced through the years if he had employed his potential talents as a pamphleteer. The imagery may be regarded as a sign of his literary imagination or as an instance of bad taste. As Madison sagaciously remarked many years later, allowances "ought to be made for a habit in Mr. Jefferson as in others of great genius of expressing in strong and round terms, impressions of the moment." [14] This was a blanket indictment, too broadly and too loosely drawn. Nowhere else did he describe the President as an apostate or charge him personally with subservience to the British, and it is most unlikely that he meant to do that now, even though his opinion of George Washington had reached its historical nadir. He unquestionably believed that a party which was false to the historic ideals of the American Republic had annexed the nation's hero and was exploiting his prestige. And Jefferson left no doubt of his conviction that the degree of uncritical deference which was accorded Washington was incompatible with genuine self-government. Writing Monroe after the treaty fight was over, he said: "Congress has risen. You will have seen by their proceedings the truth of what I always observed to you, that one man outweighs them all in influence over the people, who have supported his judgment against their own and that of their representatives. Republicanism must lie on its oars, resign the vessel to its pilot, and themselves to the course he thinks best for them." [15]

In his opinion this situation smacked of monarchy, and, irrespective of the fortunes of a particular political party, he was warranted in regarding it as unhealthy. He consoled himself with the reflection that it was temporary. On sober later thought, recurring to his normal long-range optimism, he concluded that the triumph of the "Anglomen" over the "cause of republicanism" had been costly to them. Writing Monroe again, he said that they would be glad to be back where they stood before Jay was sent abroad. "They see that nothing can support them but the Colossus of the President's merits with the

14 To N. P. Trist, May, 1832 (Hunt, IX, 479).
15 June 12, 1796 (Ford, VII, 80).

people, and the moment he retires, that his successor, if a Monocrat, will be overborne by the republican sense of his constituents, if a republican he will of course give fair play to that sense, and lead things into the channel of harmony between the governors and governed. In the meantime, patience." [16] His mood of resentment had given way to one of hopeful resignation.

Meanwhile, he had written a long letter to the President and received a lengthy reply. [17] In what turned out to be their last written exchange, each man characteristically lapsed into agricultural talk before he finished. Jefferson's initial purpose was to assure Washington that certain confidential information recently publicized in the *Aurora* did not come from him. [18] His action, while certainly not improper, turned out to be unnecessary, since Washington denied harboring any suspicion that he had revealed official secrets. The President's conjectures pointed toward Edmund Randolph, though he did not say that in so many words. [19] Jefferson's protestations were probably welcome, nonetheless, as his reiterated statement that he did not write for the papers doubtless was. But, having said that much, he should have hastened to talk of his peas and clover.

He would have been more consistent with his own policy of silence under attack if he had not referred to malicious charges against him by an unnamed person, readily identifiable as Henry (Light-Horse Harry) Lee. [20] This person, he said, had tried to sow tares between him and Washington by representing him as "still engaged in the battle of politics, and in turbulence and intrigue against the government." Since these charges were quite untrue according to his lights, he described the supposed informer as a "miserable tergiversator." At the same time, while claiming that he avoided political conversation as much as he could without affectation, he admitted that he had never conceived that the fact that he had once been in public required him

[16] To Monroe, July 10, 1796 (Ford, VII, 89).

[17] To Washington, June 17, 1796 (Ford, VII, 81–85); from Washington, July 6, 1796 (Fitzpatrick, XXXV, 118–122; received July 16).

[18] In the issue of June 9, 1796, a paper signed PAULDING gave the 13 queries propounded by the President to his department heads before the neutrality proclamation was decided on.

[19] This is the opinion of J. A. Carroll and M. W. Ashworth, in *Washington*, VII (1957), 392n. (in continuation of D. S. Freeman). Washington, seemingly better informed on this matter than TJ was, stated specifically that copies of the questions were in the hands of Representatives Josiah Parker and W. B. Giles of Virginia early in the past session of Congress.

[20] A generation later, Henry Lee, Jr., quoted the entire letter and vigorously defended his father in *Observations on the Writings of Thomas Jefferson* (1832), Letter I.

to belie or conceal his opinions when urged by others to express them. This attempt to prevent the deterioration of personal relations with Washington while maintaining his own political independence was hardly a happy one.

His suspicions of Lee were warranted. About two years earlier, when that erratic Virginian was governor of his state, he had passed on a secondhand report of Jefferson's dinner-table conversation. This related to the President's advisers and pro-British tendencies. Washington regarded it as deregatory but rejected it, and soon thereafter he showed his continued confidence in his former Secretary of State by offering him the mission to Spain.[21] Now that Jefferson himself had opened up the subject, Washington, without intimating the source, admitted that he had heard something. This was that Jefferson had described him to "particular friends and connections," and they in turn had "denounced" him, as "a person under a dangerous influence," the claim being that all would be well if he listened to "some other opinions." Particular friends very probably had said something like that, but they did not need to get from Jefferson the idea that the President had suffered from bad counsel. There were differences of opinion among Republicans as to how "dangerous" it was, but Jefferson was certainly not the only one who deeply distrusted Hamilton. Moreover, the assertion that the President had been badly advised could not be fairly construed as a manifestation of disloyalty to him, even though he thought so.

Washington's own reply implied that he expected more than he had a right to, but it was an impressive statement, even a noble one:

> . . . My answer invariably has been, that I have never discovered any thing in the conduct of Mr. Jefferson to raise suspicions, in my mind, of his insincerity; that if he would retrace my public conduct while he was in the Administration, abundant proofs would occur to him, that truth and right decisions, were the sole objects of my pursuit; that there were as many instances within his own knowledge of my having decided against, as in favor of the opinions of the person evidently alluded to; and moreover, that I was no believer in the infallibility of the politics, or measures of any man living. In short, that I was no party man myself, and the first wish of my heart was, if parties did exist, to reconcile them.

[21] Henry Lee to Washington, Aug. 17, 1794; Washington to Lee, Aug. 26, 1794 (Fitzpatrick, XXXIII, 474–479 and note). On the offer, see above, pp. 187–188. Lee, who had been critical of the administration, became favorably disposed toward it after participating in the campaign against the Whiskey Rebellion. In 1796, TJ could give no reason for Lee's hostility to him except that he had de-

This is an admirable description of his position while Jefferson was in office with him, and it is a sufficient answer to the unwarranted claim, sometimes advanced by admirers of Hamilton, that the Secretary of the Treasury was then the master of the administration. But it did not allow for the changed situation, as the moving passage that followed it clearly showed. Not until the last year or two, he said — that is, not until the departure of Jefferson had upset the balance of the government — had he conceived to what lengths parties would go. And not until very lately — that is, until the fight over Jay's Treaty — could he have believed that he would be charged with being an enemy to one country (France) and under the influence of another (Great Britain), or that he would witness such gross misrepresentations of his administration. These were described, he said, "in such exaggerated and indecent terms as could scarcely be applied to a Nero, a notorious defaulter, or even to a common pickpocket."

Jefferson must have been touched by these words, for no one was more aware than he of Washington's extreme sensitiveness. He could appreciate it the more because he himself found personal differences almost intolerable and could hardly bear to be misunderstood. He was not above employing devious devices to avoid wounding one he had admired so much. Yet, his rather inept attempt to smooth things over, while asserting at the same time his right to voice private opinions which could be assumed to be critical of the administration, was an inevitable failure under the existing facts of political life, which Washington was still unable to understand.

Jefferson made very few references to the President in correspondence during the latter's remaining months in office. One of these was after his own election to high position justified him in discussing party policy. "Such is the popularity of the President," he said, "that the people will support him in whatever he will or will not do, without appealing to their own reason or to anything but their feelings toward him. His mind has been so long used to unlimited applause that it could not brook contradiction, or even advice offered unasked. To advice, when asked, he is very open. I have long thought therefore it was best for the republican interest to soothe him by flattering where they could approve his measures, and to be silent where they disapprove, that they may not render him desperate as to their affections, and entirely indifferent to their wishes, in short to lie on their oars while he remains at the helm, and let the bark drift as his will and a

---

clined to share that General's confidences. D. S. Freeman says that TJ seems always to have mistrusted him (*R. E. Lee*, I [1934], pp. 7–8).

superintending providence shall direct." [22] This was astute political counsel rather than full-bodied personal appraisal, but it may be coupled with a reference Jefferson made soon thereafter to "the preponderant popularity of a *particularly great character*." [23]

The actual breach between the two men did not occur until after Washington had retired.[24] Many years after that, when this storm of controversy had wholly subsided, Jefferson gave a measured judgment of George Washington which is one of the best that was ever written about the one man who was utterly indispensable in the founding of the Republic.[25] Never for any considerable period did he really question Washington's greatness or the uniqueness of his public service. In this election year, however, rightly perceiving that this legendary hero had finished the essential task which could have been performed by no one else, he concluded that it was well for the country, as it was for the man himself, that he retire from the public scene.

[22] To Archibald Stuart, Jan. 4, 1797 (Ford, VII, 101–102). This was in response to a query whether or not it would be advisable to address the President on the subject of war against France. TJ thought him anxious to maintain peace.
[23] To James Sullivan, Feb. 9, 1797 (Ford, VII, 118), italics inserted.
[24] See ch. XIX, below.
[25] TJ to Dr. Walter Jones, Jan. 2, 1814 (Ford, IX, 448–449).

[XVIII]

The Election of 1796

THE presidential election of 1796 lacked little of projecting Jefferson into the first office in the Republic and did project him into the second, but the simple truth is that he had nothing to do with it. The evidence leaves no room for doubt that this supposed principal in a national contest was actually a nonparticipant; and his personal indifference at this time appears to have been genuine. The reasons for his desire to stay out of public office have already been set forth sufficiently, but something further should be said about the way this particular election was conducted. His policy of silence and inaction can be better understood in the light of existing circumstances.

When devising the electoral system the framers of the Constitution did not allow for parties, and in 1796 the two-party system to which English-speaking peoples afterwards became so accustomed was not fully recognized as legitimate. Party lines had been sharpened by the fight over Jay's Treaty, but this fight had taken place in Congress. No mechanism for the nomination of presidential candidates was yet developed; in the strict sense no candidacy was avowed, and by the same token anyone who said in public that he was *not* a candidate might be charged with presumption. Silence was clearly the proper course unless one were asked point blank. What we call "nominations," for lack of a better term, were in fact informal agreements made by small groups of leaders regarding the persons whom their party should support. Two "candidates" had to be recommended, for each elector voted for two men without distinguishing between his choice for President and Vice President. In the case of the administration party, or as historians say the Federalists, the inner group consisted of Hamilton and such others as he chose to consult. In the case of the Republicans, this was the congressional group centering on Madison and Gallatin in the House, where the last fight against Jay's Treaty was waged, and including Aaron Burr, who had been conspicuous in the earlier struggle in the Senate and had become a power in Republican circles in New York.

In the minds of these congressional leaders there was no doubt whatever about their best candidate for President. Late in February, 1796, Madison reported to Monroe in France that they intended to "push" Jefferson, the only person with whom they could hope to succeed. He greatly feared, however, that their friend would "mar the project" and insure the victory of their political foes by "a peremptory and public protest." [1] At this time no decision had been reached about the other man for whom the Republican electors should be asked to vote. Indeed, that question was never answered decisively, though by summer it was generally supposed that Aaron Burr would be supported. In choosing their major candidate the Republican leaders naturally turned to Virginia, the state with the largest vote and the one most identified with opposition to the policies of the administration. On practical grounds the best alternative to Jefferson would have been Madison, for Gallatin's foreign birth would have been an insuperable political handicap, and even if he had attained impressive national stature by now it is doubtful if any of the others had. Ever since his first divergence from Hamilton over fiscal policy, Madison had been the chief organizer of the opposition and its field commander at the seat of government, but the very fact that he had so long been in the center of the public fight was a political disadvantage, just as intimate association with the unpopular treaty was a political handicap to John Jay. Madison himself, along with many others, believed that the "British party" really preferred Jay, but settled on John Adams as a political necessity. They could hardly have ditched the Vice President anyway, in view of his distinguished Revolutionary services and his strong personal following in New England. Their major concern, therefore, was to join with him somebody who could split the Southern vote, and they eventually agreed on Thomas Pinckney of South Carolina.

No Republican could have been expected to stand up to Adams except Jefferson. He also had been a notable Revolutionary Patriot and had served at a foreign court and in Washington's official family with a distinction which could not be denied. His direct service to the Republican party until this time had been considerably less than that of Madison and far less than his political enemies alleged. At the

---

[1] Madison to Monroe, Feb. 26, 1796 (MP, 19:30). Commenting on this, Irving Brant (*Madison*, III, 433) lists Blount, Butler, Baldwin, Dearborn, and the Livingstons along with Madison, Gallatin, and Burr.

time of Genet he had helped save the party by wise counsel which was transmitted through Madison and Monroe. An avowed partisan in the treaty fight, he may have communicated some of his ardor to his close political friends, but he had exercised no particular influence on the course of events and had kept out of sight. His preferred status among the Republicans was owing far less to what he had done for them than to their belief in the firmness of his convictions and their confidence in his political sagacity. That his name was the greatest among them was also owing in no small degree to the advertisement his enemies had given him. No other man did more to build him up and turn him into a symbol than Hamilton did by extreme and unwarranted attacks. The party line which Hamilton laid down was followed thenceforth by his followers. They coupled Jefferson's name with those of Madison and Gallatin when he was quietly tilling his red soil in Albemarle, attributing to him leadership which he neither exercised nor claimed. Any disclaimers of his they may have heard of they attributed to insincerity.

Madison, who knew more about the state of his friend's mind than any of the other leaders, told him nothing about their sentiments but wisely let well enough alone. There was no need to rush things, for there could be no open campaign for the presidency until the unwillingness of Washington to continue in office became a matter of public knowledge. This was not until September 19, 1796, when he published his Farewell Address in a Philadelphia newspaper. Madison had correctly discerned his purpose in the previous February, and the leaders of both parties assumed it by May, but doubts arose in a good many minds thereafter, and, out of deference to him if for no other reason, they kept political activity "behind the curtain" until fall.

Jefferson, in his "remote canton," was largely oblivious of politics that summer, but he had some report of what was going on in the other camp. In July he wrote Monroe in France that if the "Anglomen" thought they could count on Patrick Henry they would run him for Vice President, their first object being to produce a schism in Virginia. "As it is they will run Mr. Pinckney, in which they regard his southern position rather than his principles. Mr. J [Jay] and his advocate Camillus are completely treaty-foundered." [2] Apparently he found little fault at this time with the "principles" of Thomas Pinckney, who had carried through the negotiations with Spain so successfully and had written him so amicably about the agriculture of that country. As for John Adams, he had carried on an intermittent but entirely friendly correspondence with this old friend during his

[2] To Monroe, July 10, 1796 (Ford, VII, 89–90).

own retirement and had connected him in no particular way with the detested treaty. In his own mind he could never dissociate John Adams wholly from the Declaration of Independence and the "spirit of '76," nor could he have forgotten how the two of them had been snubbed at the British court when they were abroad on diplomatic missions.[3] If not impossible, it must have been exceedingly difficult for him to think of John Adams as an "Angloman." His entire avoidance of reference to the Republican candidates when writing a political intimate like Monroe may suggest that he had heard some rumors about himself, but there was nothing definite for him to affirm or deny. A sufficient reason for Madison's not driving over from Orange County to see his friend in Albemarle that summer was provided by the building operations at Monticello, but no doubt he was glad to avoid a meeting. Late in September, the little Congressman wrote Monroe: "I have not seen Jefferson and have thought it best to present him no opportunity of protesting to his friends against being embarked in the contest." [4] This was after Washington's public announcement that he would retire.

The newspapers were not so restrained. A week before the Farewell Address appeared in print, an editorial paragraph in the *Aurora* said:

> It requires no talent at divination to decide who will be candidates for the chair. THOMAS JEFFERSON & JOHN ADAMS will be the men, & whether we shall have at the head of our executive a steadfast friend to the Rights of the People, or an advocate for hereditary power and distinctions, the people of the United States are soon to decide.[5]

If the master builder of Monticello was still in blissful ignorance, which seems unlikely, he could hardly have remained so much longer. But the political ardor which he had manifested sporadically during the treaty fight had waned thereafter and he had been counseling patience. If his political ambition was not wholly dead, unquestionably it was slumbering, and there was no clear issue to arouse him. He accepted no "nomination," but, in a fatalistic mood, he silently acquiesced in a judgment which the leaders of his party regarded as inevitable.

Since they had sedulously avoided telling Jefferson that he would be "pushed," they would hardly have consulted him about the other man whom they expected to support. During the previous year, early in the autumn, Aaron Burr had made a brief visit to Monti-

---

[3] See *Jefferson and the Rights of Man*, ch. 4.
[4] Sept. 29, 1796 (MP, 19:91a); quoted by Brant, III, 444.
[5] Sept. 13, 1796.

cello.[6] In the campaign of 1796, Leven Powell, who turned out to be the only successful Federalist candidate for elector in Virginia, tried to make political capital out of this meeting. Describing Burr as a man of "considerable talents" who was one of the most violent opponents of the present government in America, he said that several Virginians of equally violent politics met with him at Jefferson's house, and that there the "rash and violent measures" of the last session of Congress were planned. He claimed that Jefferson not only approved but wrote to different Southern members urging them to persevere "in the line of conduct there agreed to." [7] This charge got into newspapers and campaign pamphlets as far away as Boston. Soon after it was noised in Albemarle, two neighbors of Jefferson made a deposition, certifying that no other "political character" was at Monticello at the time. They relied not only on their personal knowledge as neighbors, they said, but also on positive testimony that only the gentlemen of his family and a couple of personal friends were there. The testimony had to come from somebody at Monticello, and the deposition finally got into Jefferson's papers.[8] There is no necessity to believe that he inspired it but he did not repudiate it, and in fact it stated what was true. Perhaps his friends wanted to demonstrate his aloofness from politics. Perhaps they wanted to dissociate him from Burr, who enjoyed no popularity in Virginia. If they made any political use of the deposition, this probably consisted of spreading report of it by word of mouth.

Actually it is still uncertain just what agreement there was among the leading Republicans about backing Burr for Vice President. In mid-October, when supposedly the campaign was under way, Oliver Wolcott, Jr., reported to his father that the "antis" did not expect Burr to succeed and secretly wished that John Adams would run second to Jefferson, believing that he would then resign.[9] William Smith

[6] In late September, 1795, Burr had been visiting in Washington, whence he wrote his daughter, saying he would be there until Oct. 10 and expected to be home on Oct. 24 (M. L. Davis, *Memoirs of Aaron Burr* [1858], I, 389–390). TJ wrote Wilson Nicholas, Oct. 19, 1795 (MHS), that Burr left two or three days before after one day's stay.

[7] Richmond *Virginia Gazette, and General Advertiser,* Oct. 12, 1796, printing from *Alexandria Gazette* an address of Leven Powell to Freeholders of Loudoun and Fauquier Counties. For this reference I am indebted to Noble E. Cunningham, who also refers to the matter in *Jeffersonian Republicans* (1957), pp. 86–87, citing a campaign pamphlet.

[8] Deposition of J. J. Monroe and Thos. Bell, Oct. 17, 1796, partially quoted by Cunningham, is in LC, 17228. I have found no reference to it in newspapers, though that does not preclude the possibility that it appeared somewhere. There is no documentary evidence that TJ wrote the letters, as alleged.

[9] Oct. 17, 1796 (Gibbs, I, 387).

of South Carolina, who was the most vociferous Federalist from that state, understood that Burr was to run on the ticket with Jefferson "in some of the states." He had been told that the Republican plan was for their electors to vote for Jefferson and anybody else but Adams or Pinckney.[10] Whether or not instructions to that effect went out, the final vote shows that Burr was not pressed everywhere. In Virginia he got only one electoral vote to Jefferson's 20, Samuel Adams getting 15 by way of compliment.

It should be borne in mind that, according to the Constitution, the electors were chosen in whatever way the legislature of a particular state might prescribe, and that there was no uniformity of practice as yet. In roughly half of the states they were still chosen by the legislatures, which were themselves elected at different times. Virginia was one of the states where they were elected by districts, Pennsylvania one of those where they were on a general ticket.[11] With the rise of party spirit, the tendency of electors to declare themselves in advance had grown. In Virginia individual Republican candidates for elector pledged themselves to Jefferson, though not to Burr, while in the crucial state of Pennsylvania there was a Republican slate and equal support for Burr was urged. Since the final determination was in the hands of the electors, however, the whole process was clouded with uncertainty, as it was infested with intrigue.

Hamilton would have been pleased if Pinckney had run ahead of Adams, and he would have if the Federalist electors in the North had supported the two equally, as Hamilton desired. He was far stronger than Adams in the South, while Jefferson had little strength north and east of Pennsylvania. There was no danger of Burr's running ahead of Jefferson, but the latter's supporters in Virginia went to particular pains that Pinckney should not get any votes from Republican electors.[12] Under the law, no elector could vote for two persons from his

---

[10] William [Loughton] Smith from Philadelphia to Ralph Izard at Charleston, Nov. 8, 1796 (*A.H.R.*, XIV, July, 1909, p. 785). Cunningham says that Smith's observation was not far wrong.

[11] See table in C. O. Paullin, *Atlas of the Historical Geography of the U. S.* (1932), p. 89. Methods were considerably determined by the exigencies of politics, the party in control of a legislature being disposed to adopt the procedure most advantageous to it. For this reason, choice by the legislature was more common in 1800 than in 1796. According to the Act of 1792, electors had to be appointed in each state within 34 days preceding the first Wednesday in December, when they were to meet and vote in their respective states (Act printed in Edward Stanwood, *History of the Presidency* [1898], I, 36–38). That is, they were chosen at some time in November.

[12] Joseph Jones to Madison, Dec. 8, 1796 (*M.H.S. Proceedings*, 2 ser., XV [1902], 157).

own state. Therefore, Patrick Henry was a danger. Talk of him as a presidential possibility did not die down in Virginia until he publicly declared his fixed intention of declining the office in the remote chance of his election.[13] How much Jefferson knew at the time about all this maneuvering it is impossible to say, for he himself said virtually nothing until the electoral votes were being reported in the newspapers.

Even though he may not have closely followed the course of the campaign while he was struggling to get his walls up so that he could cover his house before winter, he must have been aware of the general state of affairs in his own commonwealth and of particular developments bearing on his own reputation. In Virginia, where the Republicans had overreached themselves in their struggle against the Jay treaty, the political contest of 1796 was tepid. Criticism of Washington, which had previously gone so far that it provoked a reaction, was now wisely muted. Many Republicans, indeed, went out of their way to praise him. Adams, who had long been unpopular in the region, was attacked chiefly on the ground of the "monarchical" views which had been attributed to him. Little or nothing was said against Pinckney, there or elsewhere. During the summer Fisher Ames made a visit to the state in the course of which he must have been well fed since he gained seven pounds. "I saw Virginia, and it is not in a state to brag of," he wrote; "the land is good, but the inhabitants scattered, and as bad farmers as politicians." [14] To do the inhabitants justice, however, the eloquent champion of the British treaty said that many of them loved the President, the Constitution, and the Union, and would support them against the "Jacobins"; he did not believe that Jefferson would get *all* their votes.

Actually, the contest in Virginia largely resolved itself into one between rival candidates for elector in the various districts. The "Feds" waged battle most vigorously in the northern counties, especially in the districts where Leven Powell of Loudoun and Charles Simms of Alexandria were their candidates. From thence charges against Jefferson emerged which could not have failed to make him wince. His supporters afterwards accorded to Simms the dubious distinction of reopening, after the passage of fifteen years, the question of his conduct as governor during the Revolution, and of adding charges that were

[13] Nov. 2, 1796; statement printed in *Va. Gazette and Gen. Advertiser*, Nov. 9, 1796. Two weeks later (Nov. 25), the General Assembly, in a grateful mood no doubt, proceeded to elect him governor, an office which he also declined.

[14] To Jeremiah Smith, Sept. 4, 1796 (*Works*, I, 198).

not made in 1781, but Powell and others said much the same thing at virtually the same time. In Virginia this appears to have been seized upon as the most effective line of attack on him.[15] Although he had acquitted himself to the apparent satisfaction of his contemporaries at the time, the care with which he preserved his records of the most painful experience of his public life suggests that he himself had recognized the possibility that this matter would be reopened by persons opposed to him on other grounds.

In addresses to the freeholders of their respective districts, both Powell and Simms denounced Jefferson for twice abandoning his trust — first by his "resignation" as governor at the height of the British invasion, and later by quitting his post as secretary of state in a time of international crisis.[16] "These instances," said Colonel Simms, "shew him to want firmness; and a man who shall once have abandoned his helm in the hour of danger, or at the appearance of a tempest, seems not to be trusted in better times, for no one can know how soon or from whence a storm may come." The second allegation of lack of "firmness" probably impressed few and appears to have been short-lived, but the first persisted until almost the end of Jefferson's public career. It was interpreted as showing lack of "fortitude," a charge which could not have been made appropriately in 1781, since the legislators, including the redoubtable Patrick Henry, fled before Tarleton's cavalry far more precipitately than the Governor, and it gave ground for the argument that Jefferson was not qualified for executive position.

Hostile writers, commenting that charges of lack of firmness and personal fortitude were serious, asserted that if Jefferson could justify these "desertions" he should come forward boldly in his own name. This he did not do; indeed, he is not known to have made any reference whatever to these charges at this time. The candidate for elector against Simms — Daniel C. Brent, who was pledged to Jefferson — concluded that *he* had to answer them. He delayed his address to the freeholders, in fact, until he could collect authentic information about

[15] Beginning his series, "Vindication of Mr. Jefferson" (*Richmond Enquirer*, Aug. 23, 1805), in answer to charges against TJ as governor which had been renewed, Thomas Ritchie blamed Simms for commencing these charges in 1796. For the entire episode of 1781, see *Jefferson the Virginian*, pp. 358-359.

[16] Powell, on Sept. 27, 1796, in the address already referred to (copied in *Va. Gazette & Gen. Advertiser*, Oct. 12, 1796); Simms, about the same time, in address copied from an Alexandria paper by *Maryland Journal*, and from thence by Philadelphia *New World*, Oct. 28, 1796. Similar charges by A FREEHOLDER, dated Sept. 8, 1796, were published in *Va. Gazette & Gen. Advertiser*, Oct. 12, 1796; these were addressed to John Mayo, candidate for elector in the district including James City County.

the events under dispute.[17] His solicitation and the interest of others elicited several communications or depositions bearing on Jefferson's governorship which are of genuine historical interest. Among these was a letter from John Taylor of Caroline, who had served in both the Assembly and the militia at the time, who had strongly approved of the Governor's conduct then, and who now unhesitatingly characterized the charges of Simms as groundless. Brent did not publish this with his address — perhaps because he did not get it soon enough, perhaps because it was much too long. At some time it found its way into Jefferson's papers, as did the depositions of other friends of his who had been in position to observe his conduct during the British invasion and who saw in him no lack of personal courage. The latter documents, if they reached Brent at all, probably did not get to him in time.[18]

Brent did print from the journals of the General Assembly the important resolutions. His position was that, far from resigning, Jefferson finished out his term, and that, because of "mistaken resentment" at the time, he could not have been re-elected. He claimed, however, that the later resolutions of the Assembly showed how short-lived this resentment was. He concluded that in the awful period "which tried men's souls," Jefferson's conduct and achievements, including the Declaration of Independence, would "enroll him in the annals of fame, among the most distinguished patriots of America." With this judgment the historian can agree, perceiving also the force of the local argument which this candidate described as secondary but raised nevertheless — namely, that Jefferson might be expected to support the interests of northern Virginia and see that the capital was really located on the Potomac.

When Federalist writers outside Virginia exploited these charges, others took up their pens to defend him in the newspapers. One of his public defenders, signing himself Cassius, did him no good by conceding that he "resigned the government of Virginia, because he felt himself unfit for war." Cassius played into the hands of Jefferson's

---

[17] Address, dated Oct. 17, 1796, from *Alexandria Gazette* (published in *Va. Gazette & Gen. Advertiser*, Nov. 9, 1796, "by desire"). The address of Albert Russell, who was opposing Leven Powell, dated Sept. 16, 1796, did not refer to the charges, presumably because they had not yet been made public (*ibid.*, Oct. 12, 1796, from *Alexandria Gazette*). As things turned out, he was defeated while Brent was elected.

[18] Taylor to Brent, Oct. 7, 1796 (LC, 17217–17218; printed in *Branch Historical Papers*, II, June 1908, pp. 263–268). Depositions of A. Blair and D. L. Hylton, Oct. 12, 1796, and of James Currie, supposedly about the same time, are printed in *J.P.*, IV, 271–273, from LC. They are followed by similar documents from 1805, when Thomas Ritchie published his "Vindication of Mr. Jefferson."

critics when he said: "Not educated amid the din of arms, he had devoted his fine talents to the elegant pursuits of calm philosophy. It was laudable in him to retire from a station which a fiercer genius could fill better." [19] This writer argued that Jefferson's "constant and ardent attachment to virtuous principles" demonstrated his firmness, but John Beckley, who had actually been on the Virginia scene, was more skillful in his presentation of this disputed matter. Pointing out as Brent had that the term "resignation" was improper, he called attention to the fact that no lack of firmness on Jefferson's part was alleged in the resolution of the Assembly which vindicated and commended him. This resolution could now be read in a number of newspapers.[20]

John Beckley, clerk of the federal House of Representatives and chief organizer of the Republican campaign in Pennsylvania, was replying particularly to William [Loughton] Smith, Congressman from South Carolina, who wrote a series of pieces under the name PHOCION. Soon published as a pamphlet under the title, *The Pretensions of Thomas Jefferson to the Presidency Examined*, this campaign document was afterwards described as famous. Intended as a full-bodied attack, it was by no means limited to Jefferson's conduct as governor. Smith, who had long been hand in glove with Hamilton and had Wolcott's assistance in this instance, devoted much attention to Jefferson's actions as secretary of state. The *Aurora* charged that this pamphlet was deliberately published at so late a date that it could not possibly be refuted before the election.[21] As for its effects on public opinion, probably nothing in it was so damaging to the reputation of the man it attacked as the references to his conduct as governor, connected as these were with comments on his merits as a philosopher. While ridiculing Jefferson's claims to that title, Smith said there would be no real harm in admitting them, for "of all beings, a philosopher makes the worst politician"; when confronted with practical problems he shows timidity, whimsicalness, indecisiveness.

[19] "To the People of the U. S.," in Philadelphia *New World*, Oct. 28, 1796. While weak on this particular point, CASSIUS made a strong defense on the whole.
[20] The resolution of Dec. 12, 1781, was reprinted in the *Aurora*, Oct. 24, 1796; see also that paper, Oct. 28, 1796, reprinting a letter about Simms and Powell. Beckley's letter, signed A SUBSCRIBER, appeared in the *Gazette of the U. S.*, Oct. 29; it is printed in the note by Philip Marsh, "Jefferson and the Invasion of Va." (*Va. Mag.*, LVII, 1949, pp. 322–326); see also *J.P.*, IV, 273, confirming his authorship.
[21] *Aurora*, Nov. 1, 1796. Tench Coxe's pamphlet *The Federalist* (Nov. 1796), which was chiefly a criticism of John Adams, contained "some strictures" on Smith's pamphlet, but its author said that no correction of the "errors" of PHOCION could possibly reach the distant electors in time. Smith was replying to HAMPDEN in a Virginia paper, and dealt with the various "pretensions" of TJ in the order that this writer presented them.

After the election another South Carolina Federalist spoke to the same effect, while making rather more generous admissions about Jefferson's scientific knowledge and literary abilities. Robert Goodloe Harper went so far as to say that he had been greatly, and in some degree justly, commended for his diplomatic writings, but this Congressman took him to be "a weak, wavering, indecisive character" in his public conduct. "I might think him fit to be a professor in a College, President of a Philosophical Society, or even Secretary of State; but certainly not the first magistrate of a great nation." [22] From this line of attack Jefferson was not to be spared during the rest of his public life.

The political effectiveness of the references to Jefferson's conduct as governor lay in the undeniable fact that circumstances had combined to make him seem unheroic and that in the minds of an uninformed public these charges of weakness were hard to down. So far as past events were concerned, the charges were manifestly cruel and unjust, but Jefferson himself admitted, almost too readily, that his temperament demanded quietude and peace. Toward the end of this election year, in a mood of self-depreciation, he wrote a friend of Revolutionary days: "I have no ambition to govern men; no passion which would lead me to delight to ride in a storm. Flumina amo, sylvasque, inglorius." [23] His executive abilities had not been really tested, for under existing law and circumstance he was doomed to impotence as a wartime governor, and, having once been badly burned, he may well have dreaded the fire too much. If he had denied his friends, who were "pushing" him for an office he said he did not want, he would have been spared the personal attacks he loathed and need not have been reminded by political foes of the episode in his public life he most wanted to forget.

In the course of this campaign he was attacked for his religious views, and even charged with plagiarism in his famous report on weights and measures.[24] It is doubtful, however, if any words of his were tortured as the writings of John Adams were. The lowest point of absurdity was reached when a Republican handbill pointed out that this "avowed friend of monarchy" had sons who might try to succeed him — on the throne, no doubt — while Jefferson had only daughters.[25] Though this was primarily a campaign of abuse, the fa-

22 R. G. Harper, in letter to his constituents, Jan. 5, 1797 (*A.H.A. Report, 1913,* II [1915]), 25.

23 To Edward Rutledge, Dec. 27, 1796 (Ford, VII, 94).

24 *Aurora,* Aug. 8, 17, 1796. Smith also argued to this effect. For the report, see *Jefferson and the Rights of Man,* pp. 276–281.

25 Handbill dated Oct. 3, 1796, in Cunningham, p. 99.

vorite of the Republicans was also showered with lavish praise. One enthusiastic admirer not only credited him with the Declaration of Independence and the Neutrality Proclamation, but also described him as the "first prime minister" under the federal government — an office to which he was appointed by "the patriot Washington." [26] In Philadelphia, by order of a Republican mass meeting, it was proclaimed in three languages that "a man of such enlightened views, such pure patriotism, such unsullied integrity, and such zeal for human happiness" as the "great Jefferson" could "alone make our country flourishing, tranquil and happy." Describing him as of no party but "the great party of human benefactors," this address optimistically predicted that he would "allay the fears of our country, heal its divisions, and calm the boisterous elements of political controversy." [27]

During October, the "friends of Jefferson" were thus described in a handbill circulated in the counties of western Pennsylvania: "decided republicans, respectable yeomen, opposers of perverse systems of finance, enemies of monarchical trumpery and parade, enemies of peculation, such as wish to reduce the debts of the nation instead of increasing them, men of science and lovers of literature." This characterization of his supporters he would almost certainly have liked better than the partisan adulation of himself. Long years later he agreed with Adams that they were "the passive subjects of public discussion." [28] He had no share in the political activities in Pennsylvania which John Beckley organized so skillfully. Nor did he have anything to do with the unwise efforts of the French minister, Pierre Adet, in his behalf.

The deterioration of relations with France as a result of Jay's Treaty had been anticipated by the recent Secretary of State. Although the letter he wrote Adet as a private citizen in the autumn of 1795 was occasioned by something else, it may be interpreted as an attempt to stay this process in some degree by reminding that minister that the French cause still had friends.[29] This momentary and rather incidental departure from his policy of silence and propriety is hardly comparable to Hamilton's more numerous and more explicit assurances to the British minister when he was secretary of the treasury, but it may be assumed to have had an unfortunate effect upon Adet. The French

[26] *Aurora*, Nov. 18, 1796.
[27] *Aurora*, Nov. 1, 1796.
[28] To Adams, June 27, 1813 (*A-J Letters*, p. 336); the handbill, said to have been distributed in October, was published in Philadelphia *New World*, Nov. 11, 1796, as just received.
[29] See above, pp. 249–250.

authorities were not warranted in doubting Jefferson's devotion to the policy of fair neutrality, as borne out by his official conduct, but in this instance he probably contributed to the false impression they already had about what Republican sympathy for their cause really meant. Monroe, who was having so much trouble explaining to the authorities in France the treaty he himself deplored, also contributed to this exaggerated impression, being much more blamable since he was an official of the United States, not a private citizen. Early in 1796, when trying to prevent an open breach, he was so indiscreet as to say to a French official: "Left to ourselves, everything will I think be satisfactorily arranged, and perhaps in the course of the present year." [30] The French not unnaturally interpreted this as referring to the presidential election of that year. Though the Washington government decided late in the summer to recall Monroe, without yet making the news public, the President did not know of this highly improper utterance. There is no way that Jefferson could have learned of it unless Monroe told him about it upon that envoy's return home in 1797, long after the election. He undoubtedly sympathized with Monroe in his difficult position, and he afterwards loyally defended him, but he was in no way responsible for the indiscretions of his overzealous friend; and there is no reason whatever to believe that he or Madison had any idea that the Directory would adopt the reckless and ultimately self-defeating policy of trying to intervene in American domestic affairs. Genet had done that with direful political results they well remembered.

Before summer Adet concluded that the Republicans would support Jefferson and Burr, while the other party — which he generally described as the "British faction" — would back Adams and Pinckney.[31] Writing home, he referred to "our friends" and those "devoted to us." They would gain strength, he said, from learning the Directory's unfavorable opinion of the conduct of the federal government, and from assurances that silence proved neither feebleness nor indifference on the part of France. More adroit than Genet, he believed that official silence should be broken only at an opportune moment. His instructions allowed him leeway as to timing, and actually he did not come

[30] To Minister of Foreign Affairs, Feb. 17, 1796; quoted by S. F. Bemis, in *A.H.R.*, XXXIX (Jan. 1934), 258. The article of Bemis, "Washington's Farewell Address: A Foreign Policy of Independence" (*ibid.*, pp. 250–268), is important in this connection, as is that of Alexander De Conde, "Washington's Farewell, the French Alliance, and the Election of 1796" (*Miss. Valley Hist. Rev.*, XLIII, March, 1957, pp. 641–658). Some differences of interpretation between both of these scholars and myself will appear in the course of this narrative.

[31] To Minister of Foreign Relations, June 9, 1796 (*C.F.M.*, p. 920).

into the open until autumn. In late September, on a visit to Boston, he sought to encourage "nos amis" by telling them of French indignation over the treaty and assuring them that the Directory would not abandon them to the pleasure of the British.[32] He informed his superiors that he had revived the lagging spirits of the friends of France in Massachusetts Bay and gained their promise to work actively for the election of Jefferson. In this letter he indicated his current opinion of that gentleman when he said that it was necessary to place at the head of the government a man whose known character inspired the confidence of the French Republic, and who could be expected to play the role of "mediator" between it and the United States. Meanwhile, Washington in his Farewell Address had warned his fellow citizens against "the insidious wiles of foreign influence." Since he said that the "jealousy of a free people" against these must be impartial and denied infidelity to "existing engagements" — which included the treaty of alliance with France — his words at this moment need not be interpreted as referring to French influence any more than British. But the actions of Adet thereafter made it difficult to be both a friend of France and a free and loyal American.

The week before the election in Pennsylvania, while Washington was away, the minister transmitted to Secretary of State Pickering a resolution of the Directory stating that henceforth the French would treat neutral vessels in the same manner as these permitted the British to treat them.[33] Upon its face the resolution may not seem unreasonable, but Adet's accompanying note undoubtedly does. Expecting his action to be regarded as a threat, he stated that he would cause this note to be published, and this he did in the *Aurora*, with the result that it was available to the public before it was submitted to Washington.[34] Pickering properly objected to this presumption and asked for an explanation of the minister's allegations. About two weeks later, speaking in a long and violent letter for a government "terrible to its enemies, but generous to its allies," Adet charged that the treaty of 1778 had been violated by the United States and that the recent American treaty with Great Britain was equivalent to an alliance. At the same time he announced the suspension of his own functions, saying that this should not be regarded as a "rupture" between the two countries, but "as a mark of just discontent, which is to last until the Government of the United States returns to sentiments, and to measures,

[32] To Minister of Foreign Relations, Sept. 24, 1796 (*C.F.M.*, p. 948). On the same date George Cabot commented to Rufus King on this visit (King, II, 91).

[33] Oct. 27, 1796, communicating resolution of July 2 (*A.S.P.F.R.*, I, 576–577).

[34] William Smith to Ralph Izard, Nov. 3, 1796 (*A.H.R.*, XIV, 781). A good general account is in Kurtz, *Presidency of Adams*, pp. 127–134.

more comfortable to the interests of the alliance, and the sworn friendship between the two nations." [35]

In taking this drastic action Adet was carrying out the considered policy of the Directory. He did not regard himself as engaging in "a momentary intrigue," though he did hope and believe that by publicizing his official actions he would have great influence on the election.[36] Later commentators have remarked upon the shrewdness of his timing, but he gave out the news of the suspension of his functions too late to exert much influence on the choice of electors anywhere. He may have hoped to intimidate some of the electors themselves before they cast their votes in December, but there is no indication that he did. His first note, accompanying the resolution about sterner maritime policy, was published on the eve of the election in Pennsylvania and a few High Federalists thought it influential in Philadelphia and vicinity. William Smith asserted that it created "momentary alarm" among the Quakers, who conceived that France was about to declare war and that Jefferson could conciliate that country.[37] In view of the narrow margin of Republican victory in that state, the claim would be important if it could be substantiated, but this seems unlikely because of the scantiness and partisan nature of the testimony. Apparently no serious claim was made then or thereafter that Adet's actions were helpful to the Republican cause anywhere else, and there is considerable contemporary testimony that they were harmful.[38] Their immediate effect is not measurable, and because of the facts of chronology it would have been difficult if not impossible to make them the chief issue in the campaign. Hamilton, aware of the delicacy of the diplomatic situation and more mindful of proprieties than he had been in Genet's time, was critical of Pickering for entering into a newspaper controversy with Adet and disliked the sharpness of his tone.[39] He advised Washington that it was all-important "if possible to avoid rupture with France," and, if that could not be, "to evince to the people that there has been an unequivocal disposition to avoid it."

---

[35] Nov. 15, 1796 (*A.S.P.F.R.*, I, 579–583, followed by notes). A brief outline of this in English was published in the *Aurora* Nov. 18, 1796, before the State Department could translate the original. A brief note in French, signed by Adet and described by the *Aurora* as a "notification," appeared in that paper on Nov. 16.

[36] See particularly his two letters to the Minister of Foreign Affairs on and about Nov. 22, 1796 (*C.F.M.*, pp. 972, 975).

[37] Smith to Ralph Izard, Nov. 8, 1796 (*A.H.R.*, XIV, 784). Wolcott also regarded Adet's actions as decisive in Pennsylvania (Gibbs, I, 396–397).

[38] Kurtz, p. 134, sees no favorable effects outside Pennsylvania, and J. C. Miller, in *Alexander Hamilton* (1959), p. 450, says the contemporary opinion was that they were not favorable even there.

[39] Letters to Washington and Wolcott, Nov. 5–22, 1796 (Lodge, VIII, 423–433).

In assuming this statesmanlike position he was not denying himself the partisan use of this episode after Congress had met and the election campaign was over, but he was counting on public revulsion against Adet rather than any immediate political exploitation of the Frenchman's grave indiscretions.

Whatever the effects of Adet's actions on the outcome of the election may have been, in the longer view they unquestionably redounded to Republican disadvantage. They provided a ready handle of attack on the patriotism of the party and the candidate he had hoped to benefit. Before Secretary of the Treasury Wolcott knew just what the vote was, he wrote his father that Jefferson's election would be "fatal to our independence, now that the interference of a foreign nation in our affairs is no longer disguised." About the same time his father in Connecticut, asserting that the northern people would never submit to French domination, pointed to a separation of the Union as a desirable alternative. "Of all policies which ever existed among mankind, the French is the worst," he said. After the returns were nearly all in, Congressman Chauncey Goodrich spoke with less perturbation: "Adet's note has not done them [the Republicans] the service they intended, and they are apprehensive the spirit of the country will not bear it." [40]

Saying nothing about British influence in the government, these gentlemen implied that the leaders of the other party were hand in glove with the Frenchman. That Benjamin Franklin Bache of the *Aurora* supported him and echoed his arguments can hardly be doubted, but, back among their own rural constituents, Gallatin and Madison had no share in these connivings that anybody has been able to discover. Soon after his return to Philadelphia, Madison expressed himself on this subject to his remote friend Jefferson. "Adet's note, which you have seen, is working all the evil with which it is pregnant. Those who rejoice at its indiscretions and are taking advantage of them, have the impudence to pretend that it is an electioneering maneuvre, and that the French Government have been led to it by the opponents of the British Treaty." [41] He feared that it would lead to "a perpetual alienation of the two countries by the secret enemies of both." This, indeed, was a major danger, for, as Hamilton quickly perceived, the French themselves had opened the door of escape from the alliance and he was by no means disposed to close it, though he was still asserting

[40] Oliver Wolcott, Jr., to Oliver Wolcott, Sr., Nov. 19, 1796, and the latter to the former, Nov. 21, 1796 (Gibbs, I, 397); Goodrich to the elder Wolcott, Dec. 17, 1796 (Gibbs, I, 413).

[41] Madison to TJ, Dec. 5, 1796 (MP, 19:104), received Dec. 16.

the need for peace.[42] It seems safer to date the concerted move against the alliance from this letter than from Washington's Farewell Address, the general terms of which could be applied equally to the French and the British.

Students of a later time, with access to once-secret diplomatic documents, are in better position than the contemporaries of Jefferson were to assert that the French authorities and Adet himself were wholly responsible for his actions. Also, they have a far better opportunity to read his mind. The suspension of his functions was not contingent on the outcome of the election but was to occur in any case. He interpreted it as a sort of "shock treatment." If Adams should be elected, his withdrawal would show the dissatisfaction of France and would awaken the solicitude of the People and her friends. If Jefferson should become President, it would show that the Directory would not be content with mere words but counted on positive effects. What he specifically hoped for, in this event, was the negotiation of an arrangement which would terminate the differences between the two countries, but this would be only after he had returned home and consulted his superiors, as he intended to do at the end of the present session of Congress.[43] While he, like Genet, falsely interpreted the attitude of the American friends of France, he was a far better reporter of actual events and situations. In his comments on particular men he showed considerable discrimination and, at times, surprising penetration. Perceiving that the Hamiltonians really preferred Pinckney to Adams, he predicted that the personality of the President-elect was such that he would follow the counsels of no man, least of all those of Hamilton, whom he detested.[44]

With notable perspicacity, on the last day of the year, Adet commented on the candidate whom he and his country had favored:

> . . . I do not know if, as I am assured, we shall always find in him a man wholly devoted to our interests. Mr. Jefferson likes us because he detests England; he seeks to draw near to us because he fears us less than Great Britain; but he might change his opinion of us tomorrow, if tomorrow Great Britain should cease to inspire his fears. Jefferson, although a friend of liberty and learning, although an admirer of the efforts we have made to break our bonds and dispel the cloud of ignorance which weighs down the human race, Jefferson, I say, is American and, as such,

---

[42] To Wolcott, Nov. 25, 1796 (Lodge, VIII, 433).

[43] See especially his letter of Nov. 22, 1796 (*C.F.M.*, pp. 974–975).

[44] Dec. 15, 1796 (*C.F.M.*, pp. 978–980), containing much more extended comments than can be mentioned here.

he cannot be sincerely our friend. An American is the born enemy
of all the European peoples.[45]

Except for the substitution of "European governments" for "European peoples," this descriptive passage can scarcely be improved
upon. One cannot help wishing that Jefferson's contemporaries, both
Republican and Federalist, could have read it.

In his remoteness Jefferson did not become reasonably sure of the
outcome of the election until the end of the year. On the very last
day of 1796 he got a letter from Madison saying that he must prepare
himself for a summons to the place now occupied by John Adams.[46]
Even when Madison wrote, returns from the two northernmost and
the two southernmost states had not yet reached the seat of government, but he was virtually certain that Adams would be first and believed that Jefferson would be ahead of Pinckney. Such proved to be
the case, for the official tally was: Adams 71, Jefferson 68, Pinckney
59, and Burr 30, the rest of the votes being scattered.[47]
So far as one can judge from the records of his scanty correspondence during the autumn, he did not refer to the election in writing until the end of November, when acknowledging a paper his son-in-law
sent him from Richmond.[48] By this time he could not have failed to
learn that electors pledged to him had carried 20 out of the 21 Virginia districts, and he now had from young Randolph a favorable report about the balloting in Pennsylvania though he was not yet ready
to accept it. The electors, who were chosen in such a variety of ways,
had not yet met in their respective states when he added a few political comments to his remarks to his son-in-law about the coldest November on record, the necessary cessation of his building operations,
and a good sale on wheat from his place in Bedford. Regarding the
election he said: "Few will believe the true dispositions of my mind
on that subject. It is not the less true, however, that I do sincerely

[45] Dec. 31, 1796 (*C.F.M.*, p. 983). Most of this passage, differing in translation
only slightly from the above, is in the article by Bemis in *A.H.R.*, XXXIX, 267.

[46] Madison to TJ, Dec. 19, 1796 (Hunt, VI, 296–302), received Dec. 31. Judging
from his letter of Dec. 27 to Edward Rutledge (Ford, VII, 93–94), he was practically certain by that date, perhaps having received news from the southward.

[47] He got no votes north and east of the Delaware River and said he expected
none.

[48] To TMR, Nov. 28, 1796 (LC, 16280). Complete silence on his part, of course,
cannot be proved, but his Index to Letters shows that virtually his entire correspondence from September through November was personal or relating to business
matters. Among those to whom he wrote there appears to have been no one of
immediate political consequence. Almost the same thing can be said of those who
wrote him, the name of Madison being conspicuously absent until December.

wish to be the second on that vote rather than the first. The considerations which induce this preference are solid, whether viewed with relation to interest, happiness, or reputation. Ambition is long since dead in my mind. Yet even a well-weighed ambition would take the same side."

It is an odd fact that both his friends and political enemies, while assuming that he had made up his mind to accept the first place if he should be called to it, had been wondering if he would be willing to take the second. Madison, after he began to make periodic reports to him in December, argued that he *must* not refuse the lesser station if this should prove to be his lot.[49] Madison, who had not seen his fellow Virginian for months, would have been spared considerable trouble if he had known what in due course he found out — that the chief Republican "candidate" regarded the vice presidency as the lesser evil. For Jefferson to have said this earlier would have been disheartening to his supporters and would certainly have seemed improper to him, but he seized the first decent opportunity to make his feelings known. This was when Madison sent him a preliminary and very uncertain report on the electoral prospects. Now feeling at liberty to talk about a subject on which he had long been silent, Jefferson repeated the wish that Madison had been proposed for the administration of the government. As for himself, he said that he anxiously hoped that his name would come in second or third. In the one case he would be home two-thirds of the year, in the other all year.[50] By this time he had concluded, however, that Pinckney's chances were not so good as Madison supposed, and that the issue really lay between Adams and himself. On the basis of his own calculations, indeed, he thought it possible that they would be tied and the decision referred to the House. In that event, he prayed and authorized Madison to urge that Adams, his senior in public life, be preferred for the higher honor.[51]

Word of this got out somehow with the result that he was charged in High Federalist circles with hypocrisy and deep design "to cajole and deceive the public," as well as Adams.[52] But this private statement

---

[49] Especially in his letters of Dec. 10, 1796 (MP, 19:106) and Dec. 19 (Hunt, VI, 296–302), both of which crossed TJ's letter of Dec. 17 (Ford, VII, 91–92) in the mail. It was generally assumed that Adams would not take the second place in any case.

[50] Madison to TJ, Dec. 5, 1796 (MP, 19:104), received Dec. 16; TJ to Madison, Dec. 17, 1796 (Ford, VII, 91–92).

[51] He thought a tie in the House also possible. In view of Adams's actual margin of only 3 votes, and of what happened in the election of 1800, the possibilities which TJ foresaw were by no means remote.

[52] Fisher Ames to Thos. Dwight, Jan. 5, 1797 (*Works,* I, 213). Theodore Sedg-

was fully consistent with sentiments he expressed later to Madison and others. His respect for Adams was genuine, and his friendliness toward him sincere. After he was confident that he had escaped the presidency, he wrote an old acquaintance of '76, Edward Rutledge of South Carolina:

> . . . I know well that no man will ever bring out of that office the reputation which carries him into it. The honey moon would be as short in that case as in any other, & its moments of extasy would be ransomed by years of torment & hatred. I shall highly value, indeed, the share which I may have had in the late vote, as an evidence of the share I hold in the esteem of my countrymen. But in this point of view, a few votes more or less will be little sensible, and in every other, the minor will be preferred by me to the major vote.[53]

Denying ambition to govern men and delight in riding a storm, and referring as he did so often to the joys of farm and home, he added a very solid consideration: "This is certainly no time to covet the helm." This farmer who loathed the sea often had recourse to nautical metaphors which would have come more appropriately from the mouth of an Adams of New England. He told Madison that the only possible reason for his going into the presidency for a while would have been "to put our vessel on her republican tack before she should be thrown too much to leeward of her true principles."[54] His judgment of the prospects of a successful voyage, however, was expressed in a comment about foreign affairs to this same friend which he repeated in almost the same words to others. "I think they never wore so gloomy an aspect since the year 83," he said. "Let those come to the helm who think they can steer clear of the difficulties. I have no confidence in myself for the undertaking."[55] It may be added that the Adet episode would have been a special embarrassment to him in the conduct of foreign relations, and that his position as a national leader might have been precarious in view of his lack of support in the Northeast and the threats of disunion in the event of his election which were being voiced there. Unquestionably, this would have been a bad time for him to be elected President and his escape was fully as lucky as he thought it.

---

wick wrote Rufus King, Mar. 12, 1797, that the letter was shown *in confidence* (King, II, 156).
[53] Dec. 27, 1796 (Ford, VII, 93–94).
[54] Jan. 1, 1797 (Ford, VII, 98).
[55] Dec. 17, 1796 (Ford, VII, 92).

It was to his credit as a gentleman and a patriot that he wanted to send some word of congratulation to Adams, but he had no precedent to guide him since this was the first contested presidential election. Furthermore, since neither he nor his major rival had publicly avowed himself to be a candidate, since neither had been defeated and both had been elected, the whole situation was anomalous, as it is without modern parallel. The gist of what he wanted to say was that he had expected no other outcome and really wished no other. He wondered, however, if Adams would believe him. He drafted a letter but was so doubtful of its wisdom that he sent it to Madison in Philadelphia, to be delivered or not at that friend's discretion.[56] Madison decided to withhold the letter, which he apparently regarded as rather labored and undoubtedly thought unnecessary, since Adams had already given signs that he was convinced of the personal friendliness of his recent rival. Some of Jefferson's well-meant phrases might have irritated a man of such ticklish temper instead of conciliating him, and it seemed the part of wisdom not to borrow trouble. Jefferson had interjected an ironical reference to Adams's "arch-friend" from New York, which, besides being in doubtful taste, was quite superfluous. As Madison pointed out, the President-elect was already informed of Hamilton's intrigue. Finally, Jefferson should not run the risk of minimizing the efforts of his own supporters, or tie his own hands in the future by a formal expression of confidence in Adams.

A formal statement of any kind would almost certainly have been suspect, but the sincerity of Jefferson's attitude is abundantly demonstrated by comments he made in private letters to Madison in which there was no need for him to be self-conscious or deceitful.[57] He believed that Adams had deviated from the republican line of the Patriots in the American Revolution and had become biased to the English constitution. To express matters in more modern terms, he thought his old friend insufficiently democratic. He was not much disturbed about Adams's attitude in foreign affairs, however, and knew that on financial questions he did not see eye-to-eye with Hamilton. Since Adams was, perhaps, "the only sure barrier against Hamilton's getting in," some sort of future understanding between him and the Republican leaders was not unthinkable. Jefferson's most important desire at the moment, however, was that Adams should not think that he minded serving under him in the second place or that the heated ex-

---

[56] To Adams, Dec. 28, 1796, enclosed in letter of Jan. 1, 1797 to Madison (Ford, VII, 95–100). Madison replied Jan. 15, giving reasons for withholding it (Hunt, VI, 302–305).

[57] Especially Jan. 1, 22, 30, 1797 (Ford, VII, 99, 109, 115).

pressions of others in a political campaign had really marred an old personal friendship.

Indirect means were wiser than direct ones in making his feelings known. Having occasion to reply to Senator John Langdon of New Hampshire, who had written him about his election to the vice presidency, he said things which would be "grateful" to Adams and which he supposed would be reported to him. Even this discreet letter was unnecessary, for Adams had learned of Jefferson's sentiments by word of mouth; he said he was not surprised and apparently he was pleased.[58] It is even more significant that Abigail Adams still described Jefferson as a friend, saying that, while there had been some disagreement between him and her husband, there never was any public or private animosity between them.[59] The first contested presidential election did not mark the end of the longstanding friendship between the two major "candidates," and this widely heralded fact aroused considerable concern among the High Federalists. After what was in fact an inconclusive election, the second man basked in the sunshine of amicability while he could, hoping that his nominal official duties would not prevent him from spending most of his time above the storms at Monticello.

[58] TJ to Langdon, Jan. 22, 1797 (Ford, VII, 111–112, see also 115); remarks of Adams to Tristam Dalton, Jan. 19, 1797 (quoted in Ford, VII, 108*n*.).

[59] Abigail Adams to Elbridge Gerry, Dec. 31, 1796 (J. T. Austin, *Life of Elbridge Gerry* [1828–1829], II, 144).

[XIX]

Status of the Vice President

1797–1798

JEFFERSON saw no necessity to go to Philadelphia to take the oath of office as Vice President, since he assumed that any senator could administer it to him at Monticello or anywhere else. Furthermore, such a trip in February would be a "tremendous undertaking" for one who had not been seven miles from home since the first months of his "resettlement." He quickly decided to go, nonetheless, out of respect to the public and especially to silence the reports that he considered the second office beneath his acceptance. Following his own suggestion that he be notified of his election without formality and with the least inconvenience — that is, by post — he had learned that he could be advised at any place on the journey and thus escape "disagreeably ceremonious notification." In order to spare his horses he sent Jupiter back with them from Dumfries, going the rest of the way by stage and hoping to be unnoticed. "I shall escape into the city as covertly as possible," he wrote Madison. "If Governor Mifflin should show any symptoms of ceremony, pray contrive to parry them." [1] Either by post or messenger he got his certificate of election in Alexandria without disagreeable ceremony, but he did not wholly escape fanfare in Philadelphia. Arriving on March 2 after a journey of ten days, this "tried Patriot" was met by a company of artillery and welcomed by a discharge of sixteen rounds from two twelve-pounders. A flag was displayed bearing the device JEFFERSON THE FRIEND OF THE PEOPLE.[2]

---

[1] To Madison, Jan. 30, 1797 (Ford, VII, 116); see also Jan. 22, 1797 (Ford, VII, 107); to TMR, Jan. 22, 1797 (LC, 17292); to Senator Henry Tazewell, Jan. 6, 1797 (Ford, VII, 106-107); from Tazewell, Feb. 1, 1797 (LC, 17308); certificate of election dated Feb. 11, 1797, received Feb. 24 (LC, 17316; see also 17317-17318).

[2] Philadelphia *Minerva*, Mar. 4, 1797. The item in this small weekly literary paper is the only one I have seen, though something of the sort must have appeared elsewhere.

His entrance was less covert than he desired but it was unspectacular. He lodged the first night with the Madisons, then went to Francis's Hotel on Fourth Street, remaining there until he started home again ten days later. His total stay in Philadelphia was little longer than the time he took to get there.[3]

The first thing he did on his arrival was to call on John Adams. Returning the visit the next day, while Jefferson was still at the Madisons', the President-elect entered immediately into a discussion of relations with France.[4] Before Jefferson left home he had heard that the report of the refusal of the French to receive Charles Cotesworth Pinckney, who had been sent to relieve Monroe, had increased apprehensions of war.[5] Adams said that the first wish of his heart was to have Jefferson undertake a mission to France but that he supposed this out of the question. The Vice President-elect promptly agreed that it was, on grounds both of impropriety and personal disinclination. Adams had already decided to send a dignified commission of three men, broadly representative of the geographical divisions of the country. His present wish was to join to Pinckney of South Carolina, who had remained abroad, his friend Elbridge Gerry of Massachusetts and James Madison. Jefferson said he saw no hope of gaining the latter's consent but agreed to ask him. He was anxious to maintain peace and gave no sign that he opposed the idea of a commission. Thus, on the eve of the inauguration, the two recent rivals parted without apparent strain.[6]

The exercises of the inauguration itself, on Saturday, March 4, were pervaded by an equally amicable and sportsmanlike spirit. Jefferson's brief speech in the Senate chamber, following his taking of the oath some time after 10 A.M., was characteristically felicitous.[7] In view of his historic reputation as a parliamentarian, later readers can find particular interest in his modest statement about his probable insufficiency as a presiding officer, after his long absence from legislative

[3] Account Book, Mar. 3–13, 1797.

[4] Anas, Mar. 2–6, 1797 (Ford, I, 272–273). This entry, part of which was made later, is in LC, 17461.

[5] Senator Tazewell's letter of Feb. 1, which mentioned this, reached him Feb. 10 (LC, 17308).

[6] I find no grounds for the intimation of C. F. Adams, in his biography of his grandfather (in the latter's *Works*, I, 508), that TJ was less cordial towards the "proposition" of John Adams than he should have been and that he was blamable for the rejection of a promising "overture."

[7] See *Annals*, 4 Cong., 2 sess., pp. 1579–1586, for proceedings of special Senate session of Mar. 4, 1797, with speech of the Vice President, followed by a brief account of the inauguration of Adams, with his speech.

halls, but his hearers were probably most impressed by his remarks about the sharp limitation of his official functions and his disclaimer of higher ambitions. Since his political foes had said so much to the contrary, there was polite irony in his declaration that he was zealously attached to the Constitution and that he regarded the Union of the states as the first of blessings.

His praise of John Adams may have been regarded by some of these foes as insincere, but it was quite in accord with his private utterances. He meant what he said when he spoke of the "eminent character" whose talents and integrity had been known and revered by him for many years and with whom he had enjoyed "a cordial and uninterrupted friendship." A sympathetic writer soon said in a newspaper: "A man of an enlarged and scientific mind is alone capable of doing such justice to a competitor." [8] In fact, he was often ungenerous in his judgment of those who disagreed with him on issues he deemed fundamental. But, at the moment, there appeared to be no grave political differences between him and Adams, and few public men ever set higher store on personal friendship or tried harder to keep it above the strife.

After the modest performance in the Senate chamber on the second floor of Congress Hall, the new Vice President and the senators descended to the larger chamber of the House of Representatives, where the major ceremonies began at high noon. It is said that he wore a long blue frockcoat, single-breasted and buttoned to the waist, that his lightly powdered hair was in a queue, tied with a black ribbon, that this tall man was straight as an arrow, that his countenance was benign. Adams, in light drab or pearl-colored cloth and wearing a sword and cockade, was more resplendent. Washington wore a black suit, and his hair, like that of Adams, was well powdered.[9] A modern observer would have been struck by the fact that no member of the family of either Adams or Jefferson was present, and that the former delivered his speech before taking the oath.[10]

Adams wrote his wife that he had had no sleep the night before

[8] Copied from N. Y. *Argus* by *Aurora*, Mar. 11, 1797.

[9] Reminiscences of William McKay, quoted in J. T. Scharf and Thompson Westcott, *History of Philadelphia* (1884), I, 488n. See Carroll & Ashworth, *George Washington*, VII, 436–437.

[10] Three Philadelphia papers carried precisely the same story of the inauguration: *Claypoole's American Daily Advertiser*, and the *New World*, Mar. 6, 1797; *Gales's Independent Gazeteer*, Mar. 7. An independent account, containing the erroneous statement that Adams took the oath before speaking, is in *Porcupine's Gazette*, Mar. 6. Adams's speech can be conveniently seen in his *Works*, IX, 105–111. For the comments of his grandson, C. F. Adams, see *Works*, I, 506.

and feared that he would faint in the sight of the world, but quite obviously he enjoyed this hour of glory.[11] One passage in his speech, actually a single sentence that occupies about two pages in print, was admitted by his grandson to be elaborate; it must have been written without consciousness of auditors. But, while characteristically ponderous, this was a dignified, able, and moderate speech which should have satisfied any reasonable person that he properly respected the Constitution. He had never objected to it, he said, on the ground that the Executive and the Senate were not more permanent. While he sounded at one point as though he doubted the desirability of parties, he made no such direct and unfavorable reference to them as Washington did in his Farewell Address. He spoke of foreign influence in elections but again was not specific. He expressed an "inflexible determination" to maintain peace and good faith with all nations and to uphold "the system of neutrality and impartiality among the belligerent powers of Europe" which the government had adopted. Though he approved of Jay's Treaty, this was the speech of no Anglophile. He spoke of his personal esteem for the French, based on his years of life among them, in a way that the bitterly anti-Gallican Pickering whom he had inherited as secretary of state would scarcely have done, and he expressed a sincere desire to maintain friendship with them. Adet, who did not depart until several weeks later, wrote home that the new President was a disappointment to the "English faction." [12]

Hamilton afterwards described this speech as equivocal and temporizing, saying that it "had the air of a lure for the favor of his opponents at the expense of his sincerity." [13] Adams's words now sound like those of a man who wanted to unite the country behind him in the face of a common danger. At the moment he may have relieved the fears of the Republicans more than he aroused the hopes of the High Federalists. While still in a mood of exaltation, after he had acted the major role in his most affecting and overpowering scene, he wrote his wife that Stevens Thomson Mason, who had roused Federalist ire by publishing Jay's Treaty, was reported to have said that he never heard such a speech in his life. Later, at a time of emotional reaction, he lamented to her: "All the Federalists seem to be afraid to approve anybody but Washington. The Jacobin papers damn with faint praise, and undermine with misrepresentation and insinuation." [14] At the mo-

---

[11] Mar. 17, 1797 (*Letters to His Wife*, II [1841], 251).

[12] Mar. 10, 1797 (*C.F.M.*, p. 993).

[13] In his famous letter on Adams in 1800 (Lodge, VI, 410).

[14] Mar. 5, 1797 (quoted in *Works*, I, 507); Mar. 17, 1797 (*Letters to His Wife*, II, 251–252).

ment, however, he thought he had done well and rightly so. Jefferson appears to have made no particular comment on his initial performance but could hardly have found it displeasing.

The two men met a couple of days later at a dinner given by the old President, who had punctiliously yielded to both Adams and Jefferson when they left Congress Hall and was wholly in character in seeking to maintain amicability and manifesting good will. Afterwards, when they walked a little way together, Jefferson took his first chance to report to the new President that Madison was unwilling to go to France, just as he had anticipated. Adams then told him in some embarrassment that certain unexpected objections had been raised to this nomination anyway. His conclusion was that, in the enthusiasm of the inauguration time, Adams "forgot party sentiments, and as he never acted on any system, but was always governed by the feeling of the moment, he thought, for a moment, to steer impartially between the parties." The systematic Vice President might have couched this memorandum in more generous language, but his judgment that Adams was soon diverted by his Cabinet members is borne out by what that impulsive gentleman himself said. Completing his own record of the episode at some undetermined later time, Jefferson noted that never afterwards was he himself consulted "as to any measures of the government." [15] Adams said much the same thing long after his own retirement: "We parted as good friends as we had always lived; but we consulted very little together afterwards. Party violence soon rendered it impracticable, or at least useless, and this party violence was excited by Hamilton more than any other man." [16]

Adams's later reflections were far more unfavorable to Hamilton than to Jefferson, but there are contemporary indications that he was not long in repenting his generous first thought of sending the Vice President abroad, and this despite the fact that the suggestion continued to be made by Federalists of high standing. In private letters Adams was less complimentary of his old friend and recent rival than when talking or writing to the man himself, but what impressed him most, as he reflected on it, was the impropriety of this appointment. The "circumstance of rank" was too much, he wrote Henry Knox; the Vice President, as "the first prince of the country, and the heir apparent to the sovereign authority," could not be sent on such a mission without degradation.[17] The President was equally vainglorious in

[15] Ford, I, 273.

[16] In the correspondence originally published in the Boston *Patriot* in 1809 (*Works*, IX, 285). He said that Wolcott threatened to resign. See also his letter to Benjamin Rush, Aug. 23, 1805 (*Old Family Letters*, p. 76).

[17] Adams to Knox, Mar. 30, 1797 (*Works*, VIII, 536).

what he wrote Elbridge Gerry, whom he eventually appointed: "The nation must hold itself very cheap, that can choose a man one day to hold its second office, and the next send him to Europe, to dance attendance at levees and drawing rooms, among the common major-generals, simple bishops, earls, and barons, but especially among the common trash of ambassadors, envoys, and ministers plenipotentiary." [18] Such expressions would have occasioned much ridicule of "His Rotundity" if they had been made public. Fortunately they were not, though the impression was already widespread that this strong, honest, and deeply patriotic man was obsessed with vanity.

Jefferson undoubtedly hoped that Adams would be "detached" from Hamilton and the "British faction," and he correctly perceived that the new President's views about international affairs were closer to his own than to those of the High Federalists. But if what he said to his most intimate correspondents is to be believed, both duty and inclination forbade his direct participation in the deliberations of the executive. His constitutional duties, as he saw them, were sharply limited to the legislative department.[19] "A more tranquil and unoffending station could not have been found for me," he wrote his friend Dr. Benjamin Rush before the inauguration.[20] He had little occasion to change his mind about it during his brief and predominantly ceremonial stay in Philadelphia, when gratified comments on his cordial relations with Adams were appearing in the papers, especially the Republican papers. It is true that the harmony of the inaugural period was sadly marred by the violent "nunc dimittis" pronounced on George Washington by the *Aurora* on the very day he had Adams and Jefferson to dinner.[21] No doubt there were High Federalists who saw the hand of the latter in this, but at the time the recent recluse of Monticello was largely absorbed in social matters. He said he received "a thousand visits of ceremony and some of sincerity." [22] Also, as a countryman come to town, he attended to various matters of personal business. Now that he was again a salaried official, he could count on a regular income not subject to the vagaries of the weather or contingent on the state of the market. As secretary of state he had been paid $3500 annually; as vice president he got $5000, but he was still paid in quarterly installments. Expecting to be in Philadelphia little during the current year, he gave John Barnes power of attorney to receive his salary,

[18] Apr. 6, 1797 (*Works*, VIII, 538–539).
[19] To Madison, Jan. 22, 1797 (Ford, VII, 108); to TMR, Jan. 22, 1797 (LC, 17292).
[20] To Rush, Jan. 22, 1797 (Ford, VII, 114).
[21] *Aurora*, Mar. 6, 1797. This diatribe will be referred to hereafter.
[22] To Volney, Apr. 9, 1797 (Chinard, *Volney*, p. 79).

meanwhile drawing on Barnes as seemed desirable. Since it was now incumbent on him to keep well informed about public affairs, he paid for subscriptions to the *Aurora* and other papers. Also, he paid a tailor for a cloth coat and fleecy waistcoat, and took out enough time to see an elephant.[23] He assumed the presidency of the American Philosophical Society, but no grave burdens of state oppressed him during these ten days, and he found the social atmosphere pleasant in comparison with what he found when, after a brief stay at home, he returned to Philadelphia in May for a special session of Congress.[24]

In the midst of that session he said that political passions had reached such a point that men now crossed the street to avoid meeting men with whom they had long been intimate, and turned their heads the other way lest they be obliged to touch their hats.[25] During the amicable inauguration period he had been visited by everybody in town who knew him, as well as by many who did not, he said. Now he determined to stand on the ceremony of the first visit for the first time in his life, thus being enabled to sift out those who chose to be separated from him.[26] In the summer of 1797 he seems to have suffered a degree of social ostracism. He attributed the situation to the "war fever" following further reports of French actions. Though he was not always fair in his ascription of belligerent motives to particular individuals and appears to have been unduly alarmed over the immediate danger of war, he did not exaggerate the political effect of the increased anti-French feeling. Through most of the remaining course of the Adams administration, and more next year than this, the perfervid patriotism of the ruling group made any and all criticism of the policy of the government exceedingly difficult, since this could be readily labeled as pro-French and un-American. Though the judgment of Adams, a sincerely patriotic man, was likely to be clouded by his vanity, he admitted the inevitability of divisions and parties in a free country without liking them or being much of a party man himself.[27] But the High Federalists, whose captive he somewhat unwittingly became, regarded almost any form of political opposition as suspect and were not averse to designating it as treasonable. Thus the "war

---

[23] Various items in Account Book, Mar. 4–13, 1797.
[24] He was at Monticello, Mar. 20–May 5, arriving back in Philadelphia May 11. For his relations with the American Philosophical Society, see ch. XXII, below.
[25] To Edward Rutledge, June 24, 1797 (Ford, VII, 155).
[26] To William Hamilton, Apr. 22, 1800 (LC, 18265), referring to the situation in 1797.
[27] Adams to Elbridge Gerry, July 8, 1797 (*Works*, VIII, 548).

scare" already cast over the Republicans a cloud which was destined to grow darker.

There were other developments affecting Jefferson's own status — one in particular. A few days before he set out from Monticello the private letter he wrote Philip Mazzei more than a year before, describing in extravagant terms the supporters of the Jay treaty, appeared in Noah Webster's *Minerva* in New York. Mazzei had indiscreetly given it to a Florentine paper, after putting it into Italian; the Paris *Moniteur* had turned it into French; and the *Minerva* had published an English translation of the French version. This was promptly copied by papers in Philadelphia and elsewhere.[28] The Vice President himself first learned of this *contretemps* at Bladensburg, where he breakfasted on May 9, and at the moment he thought he must "take the field of the public papers." [29] By the time he reached the seat of government two days later the letter had been under heated discussion for a week.

William Cobbett, or PETER PORCUPINE, who had now assumed the role of chief castigator of all critics of the government, claimed that it had created much confusion among the "democratic printers," who had both denied and admitted that it was from Jefferson. Benjamin Franklin Bache of the *Aurora*, however, had promptly voiced agreement with the opinions expressed in it, regardless of its authorship, and had sharply challenged the assertion of Noah Webster that these were treasonable.[30] He replied at length to the author of the most popular American spelling book, defining treason for Webster's benefit and stating that, if the latter's view was correct, every page of the *Aurora* for several years had been treasonable. The High Federalists would certainly not have contested that.

How many times Jefferson had the doubtful pleasure of seeing the Mazzei letter in the papers, after his return to Philadelphia, would be hard to say. Within less than a month it appeared twice more in the ultra-Federalist *Porcupine's Gazette*, once in English and once in French. This was in connection with a communication calling upon

[28] N. Y. *Minerva*, May 2, 1797, translated from Paris *Moniteur* of Jan. 25, 1797; copied in Philadelphia by *Porcupine's Gazette*, May 4, and *Aurora*, May 5. The original letter of Apr. 24, 1796, is in Ford, VII, 72–78, the *Minerva* version of the political portion and comments from the *Moniteur* being given in a note which contains several factual errors. The text of Mazzei's translation into Italian, taken from his *Memoire*, is in R. C. Garlick, Jr., *Philip Mazzei, Friend of Jefferson* (1933), pp. 135–136. For an account of the letter at the time of its writing, see above, pp. 267–268.

[29] To Madison, Aug. 3, 1797 (Ford, VII, 165); Account Book, May 9, 1797.

[30] *Porcupine's Gazette*, May 5, 1797; *Aurora*, May 8, 1797, replying particularly to editorial note in N. Y. *Minerva*, May 3.

him either to avow or disavow it, and another stating that his authorship of the "abominable letter" could no longer be doubted.[31] Rumors soon spread that he admitted he had written it, while saying that it had been garbled in translation. One staunch Federalist remarked that it put this "jesuitical friend of the people" under a cloud.[32] The rumors were not far from right, though he followed a wholly private course — for reasons he gave his friend Madison later.

He could not avow the letter as it stood, he said, for, after its successive translations, it now varied from its original language. One change in particular he regarded as a serious misrepresentation. In the first instance he wrote that an object of the "Anglican, monarchical, and aristocratical party" was "to draw over us the substance, as they have already done the forms of the British government." By "forms" he meant "the birthdays, levees, processions to parliament, inauguration pomposities, etc." In the American newspaper version the word appeared as "form," implying that the government itself was already on the British model and that he himself was opposed to it — that is, to the Constitution. Since Federalist papers were saying just that, on the strength of the letter, he was not engaged in mere verbal quibbling. But he saw no way to make the necessary distinction between "forms" and "form" without "bringing on a difference" with Washington, a thing which nothing else had done. The only point at issue between himself and Washington that he stressed was this matter of ceremonies.[33]

Other explanations would be necessary, also, if he publicly avowed the letter, and proofs would be called for. He would have to go into the secret transactions of the Washington administration, he said, and could not avoid embroiling himself with many prominent individuals. It may be noted that the allegations in his letter, while they now seem extravagant, were general rather than specific. He had not called names — as Hamilton had in direct attacks on him in anonymous public and numerous private letters, and as the High Federalists did repeatedly in correspondence. Whether his characteristic policy was motivated primarily by modesty or by prudence or by propriety, the

[31] *Porcupine's Gazette*, May 22, June 2, 1797, communications signed A Fellow Citizen. Comments from the *Moniteur* were quoted extensively in the latter.

[32] Chauncey Goodrich to Oliver Wolcott, Sr., May 20, 1797 (Gibbs, I, 535).

[33] The best if not the only contemporary explanation that he gave in writing is in his letter of Aug. 3, 1797 to Madison (Ford, VII, 164–167). The fullest later explanation that I have seen is in his long letter of June 29, 1824, to Martin Van Buren (Ford, X, 308–316). At the age of 81 he interpreted his relations with Washington more favorably than he was warranted in doing a quarter of a century earlier and in certain details he showed a lapse of memory, but in their emphasis on ceremonies the two accounts are in agreement.

fact is that he had kept out of the papers and still wanted to do so. He soon decided to follow his customary policy of silence in the face of newspaper attack. Several friends in Philadelphia approved of this decision, and he did not mention the matter to Madison when he stopped at Montpelier on his way home from Philadelphia in July — either because he had dismissed the episode from his mind or, more likely, because he simply did not want to talk about it.[34] Not until Monroe urged him to avow the letter did he consult Madison about it.

Monroe, back from France and temporarily in New York, apparently gave his counsel without any solicitation:

> I think you should acknowledge your letter to Mazzei stating that it was a private one and brought to public view without your knowledge or design; that the man to whom it was addressed had lived long as your neighbour & was now in Pisa whither it was addressed: that you do think that the principles of our Revolution and of Republican government have been substantially swerved from of late in many respects; have often expressed this sentiment which as a free man you had a right to express in your public places & in the walks of private life &c. according to the letter: That you declined saying anything about it till you got home to examine how correct the letter was. This brings the question before the public & raises the spirits of the honest part of the community.[35]

Monroe suggested that by not denying the letter Jefferson had "all the odium of having written it and yet without taking a bold attitude which is necessary to encourage friends."

Jefferson himself recognized that failure to disavow would be in effect an avowal, since the general sentiments of the letter were such as he was well known to hold. But, despite the distinction he tried so hard to maintain between personal correspondence and public disputation, he showed no inclination to defend himself on the ground that, while he himself was in private life, he had addressed a private letter to a distant person who had imprudently publicized it. Though he was careful not to sign his next letter to Mazzei, he cast no reproaches on that troublesome but rather pathetic man. He did not suggest, as any historian of today honestly can, that major contemporaries of his could have been deeply embarrassed if some of their private letters had been displayed for all the world to see. He simply took the pragmatic position that little good and probably more harm would be done by ex-

[34] This brief visit was on July 10, 1797. Madison had not stood for re-election to Congress.
[35] July 12, 1797 (S.M.H., III, 69-70).

planations, and that he would tend to perpetuate a controversy indefinitely.

Madison saw things much as he did. "I consider it, moreover, as a ticklish experiment to say publicly yes or no to the interrogatories of party spirit," wrote the sagacious former Congressman. "It may bring on dilemmas, not to be particularly foreseen, of disagreeable explanations, or of tacit confessions." Furthermore, he said that the trend of precedent was the other way.[36] Jefferson not only maintained the policy of silence at the time; as far as the written record goes, he appears not to have departed from it until he was a very old man, and merely in a private letter even then.[37]

The assertion that the letter spoke the truth was the predominant Republican contention from the time that Jefferson's authorship was tacitly recognized, and apart from verbal errors this appears to have been Jefferson's own unchangeable opinion. In his papers is a copy in his own handwriting of a paragraph by Judge Hugh Henry Brackenridge in a newspaper of two or three years later.[38] Besides commenting on the confidential nature of this letter to a friend in a distant country, Judge Brackenridge said that the "truths" contained in it were not generally perceived at the time, and therefore seemed harsh to some. But, in his opinion, the existence and the grounds of the party division, which Jefferson discovered earlier than his fellow citizens at large, became generally recognized. This prominent Republican believed that the letter deserved "to be inscribed on a pillar of marble, as the testimony of a wise man against degenerate times." Regarding it as "a faithful portrait of things as they are," he republished it. In contrast to this may be cited the words of John Marshall at a crucial hour in 1801: "The morals of the author of the letter to Mazzei cannot be pure." [39]

The tone of high morality in the face of criticism was typical of the Federalists, among whom in fact Marshall was relatively moderate in this era, but the predominant character of contemporary judgments on the Mazzei letter, both pro and con, was that of partisanship. If there had been a transient mood of national unity, it was now begin-

---

[36] Madison to TJ, Aug. 5, 1797 (*Letters and Other Writings of James Madison*, 1884, II, 118). With his letter of Aug. 3, TJ had sent Madison that of July 12 from Monroe to him. The latter saw him a little later at Monticello, though Madison did not visit him as he had hoped.

[37] To Martin Van Buren, June 29, 1824 (Ford, X, 308–316).

[38] LC, 18567. From internal evidence this was published during TJ's vice presidency, presumably toward the end of it. Brackenridge, to whom he gave the title of Judge, was appointed justice of the supreme court of Pennsylvania in December, 1799.

[39] Marshall to Hamilton, Jan. 1, 1801 (J.C.H., VI, 502), referring to the relative claims of Jefferson and Burr to the presidency.

ning to dissolve. And if Jefferson had traced the line of division between parties with no inconsiderable discernment, the extravagance of his language and his sweeping ascription of ulterior motives stamped him in the public mind irrevocably, not as the personally disinterested public servant he had so generally been while in office, but as a political partisan. In this time of international trouble, also, the circumstances inevitably rendered him suspect on patriotic grounds. The letter had been taken from a French paper, and some of the remarks which accompanied it in the *Moniteur* could hardly have failed to give offense to a great body of Americans, though he himself was in no sense responsible for these. From a country with which diplomatic relations were virtually broken Americans were told that they were ungrateful children. The actions of the French government in breaking off communication with "an ungrateful and faithless ally" were approved on grounds of justice and sound policy, and the confident hope was expressed that the resulting discussions would lead to the triumph of "the party of good republicans, the friends of France." [40] Had national patriotism been as fervid as it became a few months later, such words might have amounted to the kiss of death.

Inevitably, certain expressions in the letter were interpreted as applying to Washington, whether or not they were intended to. The most striking of these was the reference, cruder in the American newspaper version than in the original, to "men who were Solomons in the council, and Sampsons [sic] in combat, but whose hair had been cut off by the whore England." Even in its more polite original form, this sort of language was not characteristic of Jefferson, who was prudish if anything; though often stilted, he was rarely vulgar. At the time he wisely refrained from any attempt to explain away the unfortunate metaphor, but long years later he claimed that Washington understood perfectly that the reference to "Samsons" was to members of the Society of the Cincinnati. He had discussed this "aristocratical" military organization with the General, who undoubtedly knew just how he felt about it.[41] There is no reason to believe that he associated Washington with the things he most disliked about the Cincinnati, nor need it be supposed that he had Washington specifically in mind in this particular reference. Just what he did think is borne out by other letters of

[40] Ford, VII, 74–77n. The comments of the American editor, P. L. Ford, are open to considerable exception in my opinion; and it should be noted that the American translation from the French contains a final sentence not in either the English original or Mazzei's translation into Italian. (Garlick, p. 136, note 9, refers to this. He also says, however, that despite the three translations, the final version is surprisingly like the original.)

[41] Ford, X, 311–312.

the period, as we have already shown. At the worst, this was that the great man himself had reached the point that he could take no criticism, and that latterly he had been hoodwinked by advisers who were exploiting "the preponderant popularity of a particularly great character." [42] Nonetheless, Jefferson had not excepted Washington from the sweeping indictment he had drawn of the pro-treaty party in a mood of intense resentment, and not unnaturally he was now identified in the public mind with critics of the retired hero who were far less discriminating and far more abusive than he, even in his darkest moments. The two most notorious of these were Thomas Paine and Benjamin Franklin Bache of the *Aurora*.

In the summer of 1796, no longer in prison in Paris but still smarting under the alleged neglect of one whom he had hailed as the major symbol of human freedom, Paine wrote a letter to Washington which was published in the *Aurora* in the autumn. "And as to you, Sir," he had said, "treacherous in private friendship (for so you have been to me, and that in the day of danger) and a hypocrite in public life, the world will be puzzled to decide whether you are an apostate or an impostor; whether you have abandoned good principles, or whether you ever had any." [43]

Equally infamous in the history of abuse, though without comparable excuse on grounds of personal suffering, was the valedictory that the *Aurora* published on the second day after the retirement of the first President.[44] In what was perhaps the most extreme condemnation of Washington ever published he was not merely charged with having been a shield for political iniquity and legalized corruption. Viewing his administration as a whole, this utterly partisan writer asserted that a single individual had "cankered the principles of republicanism in an enlightened people" and had jeopardized the very existence of public liberty. Thus the day of his reduction to a level with his fellows ought to be hailed as one of jubilee.

That Jefferson, who made such a point of official propriety and of personal friendship, should have been associated in the public mind with such diatribes, though obviously unfair, was little short of inevitable. Actually, he had maintained contact with Paine, and he read this letter when it appeared, apparently without indicating any disapproval even in private. Also, he had some personal contacts with Bache

[42] See above, pp. 268, 272. The statement of the editor in Ford, VII, 77*n.*, about the severity of his private comments about this time gives a false impression, in my opinion.

[43] Dated July 30, 1796 (M. D. Conway, ed., *Writings of Thomas Paine* [1885], III, 252; whole letter, 213–252); *Aurora*, Oct. 17, 1796.

[44] *Aurora*, March 6, 1797, dated March 4.

— partly, he said, because of his grandfather — and he encouraged many to take the *Aurora*. There is no reason to believe that he had the slightest personal connection with these particular attacks on Washington. At the same time, there appears to be no record that he expressed any regret over their excesses. When in responsible office he had expressed sympathy for Washington under attack, but he had continued to support Freneau even when that journalist took a more extreme position than he did. He was not disposed to discourage any of the relatively few Republican papers. At this particular time, when the government was controlled by men he distrusted, he saw little hope that the Republicans could affect public policy except through the pressure of public opinion. Not until he himself became President did he become thoroughly aware of the dangers that lie in the abuse of freedom of the press.

After Washington's retirement to Mount Vernon he and Jefferson never met again, nor did they correspond on any subject whatsoever — not even agriculture. On the Mazzei letter, described in High Federalist circles as "infamous," he appears to have been wholly silent, even in private.[45] The full alienation of the two men can be better dated from another letter, for which he was led to believe that Jefferson was responsible. On this he commented with asperity. The John Langhorne episode has been aptly designated as a "cobweb conspiracy," but it was this cobweb that broke the camel's back.[46]

Early in the autumn of 1797, Washington received from Warren, Albemarle County, Virginia, a rhetorical letter. The writer, who signed himself John Langhorne, speaking with deep sympathy of the "unmerited calumny" of Washington and of "villainous machinations" against him, sought to "administer some comfort to a mind eminently just and virtuous." The recipient's reply to this gratuitous proffer of sympathy and comfort was noncommittal; he thought a pedant was trying to show

[45] Carroll and Ashworth, *George Washington*, VII, 476, say that he "had not deigned to comment, even confidentially."

[46] The expression "cobweb conspiracies" is that of Randall, II, 373*n*. He discusses this episode with good sense and good taste (II, 371–373). A more recent and fuller account is that of Manning Dauer, in "The Two John Nicholases," *A.H.R.*, XLV, 338–353 (Jan., 1940), correcting errors in the article "John Nicholas" in *D.A.B.* These corrections Carroll and Ashworth seem to have overlooked (*George Washington*, VII, 483*n.*). In the introduction to the Anas, Feb. 4, 1818 (Ford, I, 168), TJ attributes the alienation to his own opposition to Jay's treaty and the copious diet of falsehoods provided Washington by "a malignant neighbor," meaning in this instance Nicholas, not Light-Horse Harry Lee as Ford supposes. An authoritative account of his earlier relations with Nicholas is in *J.P.*, XVI, 139–145.

off.[47] There the matter might have ended but for the fact that John Nicholas, county clerk of Albemarle, an ardent Federalist and busybody, took it upon himself to inform Washington that the writer, who was using a fictitious name, was closely associated with some of his "greatest and bitterest enemies" and was employing a hypocritical device to ensnare him. Nicholas said that, living as he did "in cannon shot of the very headquarters of Jacobinism," he himself knew that Washington had been deceived by professions of friendship and wanted to put him on his guard. Washington might have suspected that his informant was a troublemaker and have dropped the whole matter as inconsequential. It need not be assumed that he confused this John Nicholas with the congressman of that name, who was a strong Republican, but he had good reason to be impressed with the distinguished surname that the county clerk of Albemarle bore. At all events he sent Nicholas copies of the original Langhorne letter and his own reply, on the chance that they might be a means to detect some "nefarious plan" of persons assailing the government. If they would serve no purpose, the papers could be burned.[48] Nicholas was not the sort of man to destroy political ammunition. Instead, he used these and other papers to prove conclusively that the author was no less a person than Peter Carr, nephew of Washington's *"very sincere friend"* Jefferson. Receiving no reply to a report he regarded as startling, he wrote again about this "very extraordinary" and "even infamous" affair. He dilated on the "vile hypocrisy of *that man's* professions of friendship" to Washington, as proved by the Mazzei letter, and referred to other controversial matters, including Monroe's defense of his conduct in France — which Washington could not have been expected to like. In reply to this letter Washington exploded.

He wrote Nicholas: "Nothing short of the evidence you have adduced, corroborative of intimations which I had received long before, through another channel, could have shaken my belief in the sincerity of a friendship, which I had *conceived* was possessed by me, *by the person* to whom you allude." [49] Thus he attributed to the insinuations of the Clerk of Albemarle, following those of Light-Horse Harry Lee,

[47] John Langhorne to Washington, Sept. 27, 1797 (Jared Sparks, ed., *Writings of George Washington* [1855], XI, 501–502); Washington to Langhorne, Oct. 15, 1797 (Fitzpatrick, XXXVI, 52–53).

[48] Nicholas to Washington, Nov. 18, 1797 (printed by Dauer in *A.H.R.*, XLV, 348–349); Washington to Nicholas, Nov. 30, 1797 (Fitzpatrick, XXXVI, 81–82).

[49] Mar. 8, 1798 (Fitzpatrick, XXXVI, 182), after letters of Dec. 9, 1797, and Feb. 22, 1798, from Nicholas (*A.H.R.*, XLV, 349–353). For the earlier "intimations" from Light-Horse Harry Lee, see above, pp. 269–270.

the cessation of a long-standing personal friendship. By swallowing the suspicions of the former that Jefferson was the author or inspirer of a silly letter, and that this cloaked a nefarious design, he showed a higher degree of gullibility and more tendency to hysteria than when the two men were associated in public office. In perspective the occasion of the breach seems trivial indeed, and further explanation must be sought elsewhere. It may be surmised that, while Washington had been disposed to give Jefferson the benefit of the doubt following the latter's retirement, the course of events had brought him almost to the point of lumping the Vice President with Paine, Bache, and all other critics of him and the policies of the government. The gossamer Langhorne episode sufficed to tip the balance.

Actually, Jefferson had never attacked his character or motives, even in private, but the prevalent atmosphere of suspicion was not conducive to discrimination. Furthermore, Washington never comprehended the role of political opposition in a self-governing society but viewed attacks on public policy as attacks on the government itself. Apparently he had now come to full acceptance of the High Federalist contention that Jefferson was the fountainhead of all Republican criticism and activity. Taking the words out of the mouth of an informer, he referred to his former Secretary of State as *that man* and said he knew not in what form the next insidious actions would appear. "But," he continued, "as the attempts to explain away the Constitution and weaken the government are now become so open; and the desire of placing the affairs of this country under the influence and control of a foreign nation is so apparent and strong, it is hardly to be expected that a resort to covert means to effect these objects will be longer regarded."

Nicholas, wanting to publish a statement regarding the fictitious John Langhorne, approached Bushrod Washington some months later with that purpose in view. Washington himself told his nephew that if Jefferson was the real author or abettor "it would be a pity not to expose him to public execration, for attempting, in this dishonorable way, to obtain a disclosure of sentiments of which some advantage could be taken." [50] He believed that if "a trick so dirty and shabby" could be proved beyond doubt, the effects would be good; but if not, the result would be the reverse. He virtually put the matter up to his nephew and Nicholas, but nothing came of it.

No scintilla of evidence has ever been produced to show that Jefferson had anything to do with the episode which so rankled in Washington's mind. If Peter Carr thought to play a prank, as he may have done

[50] To Bushrod Washington, Aug. 12, 1798 (Fitzpatrick, XXXVI, 408).

though he was twenty-seven at the time, it was an exceedingly stupid one. If he sought political ends one cannot help wondering what they possibly could have been.[51] Unwittingly he provided the occasion for the irreparable breach between his kindly uncle and Washington, thus offering another illustration of the embarrassments Jefferson's friends and relatives brought him — embarrassments which "the great man on the hill," as Nicholas sarcastically described him, characteristically overlooked. There can be little doubt, however, that the unhappy episode was the occasion of the breach rather than its cause, and that this might have been expected to develop anyway in view of the political situation and Washington's inability to distinguish between the government and the governors.

Anyone who would draw a balance sheet of the relations between the two greatest Virginians of this generation must record some debits on each side. The harshest of Washington's recorded comments on Jefferson are those in his letters to the marplot Nicholas, and in the perspective of history these are manifestly unfair. His former assistant had no thought of destroying the Constitution or of bringing his country under the control of France. Nor did the Vice President greatly overstate the case when he wrote another old associate: "I can say with truth, and with great comfort to my own heart, that I never deserted a friend for difference of opinion in politics, in religion, in physics; for I place all these differences on a footing. But great numbers have deserted me." [52] These words, directed to General Henry Knox after partisanship had grown even hotter, suggest what this champion of freedom of opinion had to endure from the time he again became a conspicuous public man.

[51] Elizabeth D. Coleman, in "Peter Carr of Carr's-Brook," *Papers Albemarle County Hist. Soc.*, IV (1944), 17, reaches no definite conclusion. Randall, without calling Carr by name, dismisses the letter as a thoughtless prank. He and Dauer leave no doubt whatever of the character of Nicholas, who fawned on TJ in later years and sought to demonstrate the latter's friendliness toward Washington.

[52] TJ to Gen. Henry Knox, Apr. 8, 1800 (LC, 106:18251).

[XX]

The Assumption of Party Leadership

BELIEVING that under Adams the government and its policies would be better balanced than they had been recently, Jefferson had looked forward to "a pretty rapid return of general harmony." Convinced that the great body of citizens were republican in sentiment, he had hoped before the inauguration to see them moving together "in the paths of regular liberty, order, and a sacrosanct adherence to the Constitution." Such would be the case, he thought, if war with France could be avoided.[1] Adet talked with him soon after the inauguration, but the Frenchman described his conversation as circumspect and thought his views on foreign affairs much the same as those of Adams. When the Vice President got back to Philadelphia in May, he found waiting for him a letter from the departed envoy. His political enemies would probably have seen this as another sign of collusion if they had got hold of it, but, besides manifesting personal goodwill, it did little more than express a desire for peace which Jefferson probably accepted as sincere. If he himself did not deserve as much credit as Adet gave him for the avoidance of war between the two republics, unquestionably his major concern now was for the maintenance of peace. Regardless of what he thought of the French cause at this time, he rightly anticipated that the involvement of his own country in war would slow down and might defeat the American experiment in self-government, while perpetuating the rule of the "Anglomen."[2]

Nowhere did he state better the foreign policy he himself favored

[1] To James Sullivan, Feb. 9, 1797 (Ford, VII, 118).

[2] Adet to Minister of Foreign Affairs, Mar. 10, 1797 (*C.F.M.*, pp. 993–995); Adet to TJ, May 4, 1797 (LC, 17374), received May 13, a faded letter in French which was deciphered and translated for me by John J. de Porry. Adet said he was replying to a friendly letter from TJ, but this I have not found. He made a final call on Adams, who described it as inconsequential (*Works*, VIII, 532n.).

than in a letter he wrote Elbridge Gerry after he had returned to Philadelphia in May and before Congress had yet assembled. He had sufficient reason to write, in reply to a couple of friendly letters, but he knew from Adams of the possibility of Gerry's appointment as one of the commissioners to France.[3] Writing with care to one whom he regarded as a moderate and who undoubtedly regarded him as the chief Republican, he put himself on record. "I do sincerely wish with you," he said, "that we could take our stand on a ground perfectly neutral and independent towards all nations." He claimed — with sufficient justification so far as his official actions showed — that this had been his constant object throughout his public life. He had expressed himself too often to the British for them to doubt his views, "if they would be content with equality." *That* was the rub. "But they have wished a monopoly of commerce and influence with us," he said; "and they have in fact obtained it." Then he drew a devastating bill of particulars — referring to industry, commerce, finance, their alliance with "the most influential characters in and out of office," and their demonstrated ability to direct the policy of the United States. Through the control of the press, they and their adherents had fixed on those who wished "merely to recover self-government the charge of subserving one foreign influence, because they resist submission to another." For all these reasons, he thought it impossible for Americans to say they now stood on independent ground.

If toned down a little, most of his allegations of fact were indisputable. They could have been countered only by the contention that, under existing conditions, full national independence was impossible, and that the conduct of the French was more insufferable than that of the British. Avoiding all defense of the Directory, he covered himself well in a later letter to Gerry. He then said: "The insults and injuries committed on us by both the belligerent parties, from the beginning of 1793 to this day, and still continuing, cannot now be wiped off by engaging in war with one of them." [4] To this correspondent, and also to others in this period, he advocated a policy wholly in accord with the Neutrality Proclamation and Washington's Farewell Address. "Our countrymen have divided themselves by such strong affections to the French and the English," he said, "that nothing will secure us internally but a divorce from both nations; and this must be the object

[3] To Gerry, May 13, 1797 (Ford, VII, 119-124). An incomplete draft (LC, 17371) shows much editing. Since this was before the address of Adams to Congress which TJ objected to, his complimentary references to the President need not be regarded as insincere.

[4] To Gerry, June 21, 1797 (Ford, VII, 149); to Edward Rutledge, June 24, 1797 (Ford, VII, 154).

of every real American, and its attainment is practicable without much self-denial. But for this, peace is necessary." Speaking of the European nations he said to another: "As to everything except commerce, we ought to divorce ourselves from them all." [5]

Not only did he put himself on record at the beginning of the administration as an advocate of genuine independence and a partisan of peace. He also wrote Gerry that whatever follies the country might be led into with respect to foreign nations, he would never give up the Union, "the last anchor of our hope" which alone could prevent "this heavenly country" from becoming a gladiatorial arena. Much as he abhorred war, the greatest scourge of mankind, and anxious as he was to keep out of the broils of Europe, he would yet go with his brethren into these rather than separate from them. Addressed to a citizen of Massachusetts these words of a Virginian should have been reassuring. But, since they came from one whom the French minister had intrigued to elect, they would have been viewed by the High Federalists with skepticism.

During the five days between his arrival at Francis's Hotel and Adams's address to the two houses of Congress on May 16, the Vice President, who had virtually nothing else to do, did a good deal of listening, and it may be safely assumed that the voices he heard were primarily Republican. As he read the signs of the time, these pointed to the maintenance of peace. Summing things up to Madison, who had not stood for re-election to Congress and was rusticating in Orange County, he reported: that the administration — meaning Adams and his Cabinet — had been much excited by the dispatches in which Charles Cotesworth Pinckney described his rejection by the French; that after numerous council meetings they had fixed on war; that the tone of the Federalist party continued high until news came of the troubles of the Bank of England; that after this the war spirit cooled and the Executive repented of having called Congress.[6]

It may reasonably be supposed that financial difficulties in England and French military successes on the Continent dampened whatever war spirit there may have been, but Jefferson carried his suspicions too far in the first place, especially with respect to Adams. The President had never departed from his intention to negotiate further; and,

[5] To Gerry, May 13, 1797 (Ford, VII, 122).

[6] TJ to Madison, May 18, 1797 (Ford, VII, 124). The suspension of specie payments by the Bank of England and the danger of national bankruptcy were reported by the American minister, Rufus King, to Pickering, Mar. 5, 1797 (King, II, 150–152), letter received Apr. 26, and were referred to in later communications. TJ thought King's pacific admonitions influential.

although the High Federalist counselors he had inherited from Washington opposed the sending of a commission at first, they agreed to it after Hamilton advised them to do so. A principal object of it, according to the power behind the Cabinet, was "the silencing of Jacobin criticism and promoting union among ourselves." [7] At this juncture he wanted to maintain the peace. Jefferson's distrust of the ultimate purposes of Hamilton and his followers would not have been removed by a reading of their letters, had these been available to him, but actually the danger of a complete breach with France was not immediate. His vigilance as a sentinel of freedom and independence was a major ground of his public reputation and enduring fame, and his warnings might have been less effective if they had been hedged about with qualifications. At times, however, he became alarmed prematurely, and in this instance he would have been fairer to give the benefit of the doubt to Adams. In the light of present knowledge, it seems that he judged the President's address to Congress too harshly, though in this he reflected the opinion of the Republican spokesmen in general and of a large number of moderate Federalists. [8]

Adams reported in considerable detail the refusal of the French to receive Pinckney and their written request that he leave their country, submitting soon thereafter the dispatches received from him. [9] What was more disturbing to Jefferson and the Republicans, he commented on the words addressed to the departing Monroe as evincing a disposition on the part of the French "to separate the people of the United States from the government." Furthermore, he recommended measures to protect commerce, strengthen the navy, and reorganize the militia which Jefferson thought unnecessary and provocative. Since Congress adopted hardly any of them at this special session, the Vice President wondered why that body had been summoned at all. He was not one to lay much stress on defense measures, since he regarded the commerce of the country as its most powerful weapon, but he would have been more just to Adams if he had surmised that the President, besides being genuinely desirous of developing the navy as a matter of general policy, was chiefly concerned to strengthen the bargaining position of the United States. At the moment Jefferson,

[7] Hamilton to Pickering, May 11, 1797 (Lodge, VIII, 466); see also letter of Mar. 22, in which he specifically suggested policies (Lodge, VIII, 452-454). The starting of the Adams administration is well described and discussed by Dauer, ch. 8.

[8] His immediate reaction is well shown in his letter of May 18, 1797 to Madison (Ford, VII, 124-127). See comments of Dauer, p. 129.

[9] Speech in Adams, *Works*, IX, 111-119; documents, as submitted May 19, 1797, in *A.S.P.F.R.*, II, 5-18.

along with other leading Republicans, concluded that Adams had gone over to the ultras, and believed that this speech was likely to reduce the prospects of peace rather than increase them. Perhaps it was, since events showed that the French resented it, and at least it gave them another talking point. In any case, Jefferson deplored it, and if he had not already turned decisively against Adams he now did so.

With the commissioners to France he was sufficiently satisfied, when, following the declination of Francis Dana of Massachusetts, Elbridge Gerry was appointed as the third man, to serve with Pinckney and John Marshall. Gerry, who had been opposed within the Cabinet, was solidly supported by the Republican senators, while half a dozen Federalists voted against his confirmation. Saying that this appointment brought "infinite joy" to him, Jefferson urged Gerry to accept it. His letter was too effusive, but it can be explained on grounds of patriotism as well as partisanship.[10] More surprising is his statement that he was now assured that there would be a preponderance in the commission, sincerely disposed to be at peace with France. The most likely explanation is that he thought C. C. Pinckney (commonly referred to as General) not unfriendly to the French. Writing Thomas Pinckney, with whom his relations had remained amicable, he said that the conduct of General Pinckney had met with "universal approbation" and suggested that the French had been misinformed about his real attitude toward them." [11] Jefferson's cultivation of men whom he thought moderate was rather too obvious, his language too cajoling. He was trying to bring influence to bear on the commissioners in behalf of peace. Precisely what he wanted them to do he did not say. To Gerry and others he expressed the belief that the war would not last much longer, an opinion in which he did not stand alone, and that the United States ought to "rub through" this year. As secretary of state he had actually yielded very little to the French, but in this period he did not sound as though he would have made many demands of them. There was, indeed, an almost hysterical quality in his passionate pleas for peace.[12]

---

[10] Letter of June 21, 1797 (Ford, VII, 149–151), to which we have already referred.

[11] TJ to Thomas Pinckney, May 29, 1797 (Ford, VII, 129). He appears to have thought of both Pinckneys as relatively moderate, though in his letter of June 1 to Madison (Ford, VII, 133) he reported that he had just heard things about the attitude of Thomas, and by implication about that of the General, toward the Jay treaty which much disturbed him. Hamilton, while trusting Pinckney's "integrity and federal attachments," thought him a sort of "middle character" with some French leanings (to Pickering, May 11, 1797 [Lodge, VIII, 466–467]).

[12] See, e.g., the passage in his letter of May 29, 1797, to T. Pinckney in which

His goals and fears for the country are clear enough, but something further should be asked about the means he employed while occupying what he had expected to find a "tranquil and unannoying station." What precisely did he do? How and why did he do it? The best short answer is that he rarely did as much of a partisan nature as his political enemies claimed, and that, in keeping as much as possible out of sight, he followed not only the dictates of his own nature but also those of the existing situation.

High Federalist leaders had viewed with dismay the prospect of Jefferson's presence in the government as vice president. Fisher Ames had issued a doleful prophecy:

> . . . In a Senate that will bring him into no scrapes, as he will have no casting votes to give, responsible for no measures, acting in none that are public, he may go on affecting zeal for the people; combining the *antis*, and standing at their head, he will balance the power of the chief magistrate by his own. Two Presidents, like two suns in the meridian, would meet and jostle for four years, and then Vice would be first.[13]

Another had written in somewhat less concern: "We must expect him to be the nucleus of a faction, and if it will give him some greater advantages for mischief, it draws him more from his covert." The image of Jefferson as a secret intriguer had long since been planted in many minds by Hamilton's assertions and insinuations. Even Elbridge Gerry, who would have liked to cast an electoral vote for him had that been possible without injuring Adams's chances, thought him "not entirely free from a disposition to intrigue."[14] In reality his past conduct provided insufficient ground for this reputation, but it is a proper question whether his actions did after he became vice president.

As presiding officer of the Senate he was virtually powerless to control the course of events; and, actually having very little to do, he fretted over his enforced idleness. Early in the year he asked George Wythe, an authority on parliamentary procedure, for any notes he might have on the subject, but he had a discouraging reply from his

---

he anticipated the burning of seaports, havoc on the frontiers, etc. (Ford, VII, 128).

[13] To Christopher Gore, Dec. 17, 1796 (*Works*, I, 211).

[14] Chauncey Goodrich to Oliver Wolcott, Sr., Dec. 17, 1796 (Gibbs, I, 411–412); Gerry to Abigail Adams, Jan. 7, 1797, quoted by Dauer from Gerry MSS in *Adams Federalists*, p. 114.

old mentor. Throughout his term he worked intermittently on the manual he finally left to his successors as a legacy, but at first he probably contented himself with the rules adopted by the Senate in its first session and those subsequently added to these.[15] Before his term ended, the Senate chamber on the second floor of Congress Hall was so well fitted up that a young English observer described the furniture and arrangements as much superior to those of the House of Lords.[16] Each senator had a large red morocco chair with a desk before it, and the chair of the vice president was elevated and had steps leading up to it. In 1797 this was a place where one could be sufficiently comfortable while doing nothing in particular. The most stirring occurrence of the session, the expulsion of William Blount of Tennessee on charges of conspiracy to conquer Spanish territory with British aid, was at the very end, after the bored Vice President had left for home and while a President pro tempore was in the chair. This affair dragged on indecisively for several years, until impeachment charges were finally dismissed on grounds of lack of jurisdiction. In its political implications it was extremely confusing, since Blount was a *Republican* senator who had been conniving with the British, not the French. Jefferson, who called it "Liston's plot" from the current British minister, commented on it from time to time, but at the moment he did not think the business important enough to prevent his returning home in time for the county court in Albemarle.[17]

Immobilized as an official, Jefferson occupied himself considerably as a reporter — especially to Madison, with whom he had exchanged roles. He knew what happened in the Senate and easily found out from participants what happened in the House — either from conversations in or near Congress Hall or at Francis's Hotel, where, as an unsympathetic observer put it, he lodged with "a knot of Jacobins." [18] Much that he wrote was mere party chatter. In the Senate the Republican body was weak, he said, numbering ten who could be relied on, while there were eighteen on the other side with two waverers and

---

[15] To Wythe, Jan. 22, 1797 (Ford, VII, 110); from Wythe, Feb. 1, 1797 (LC, 17307). His own *Manual of Parliamentary Practice* was first published in 1801. It will be discussed hereafter.

[16] Description of Jan. 1, 1799, by D. M. Erskine (*W. & M.*, 3 ser., VI, 265–266).

[17] The whole case is well described by Morton Borden, in *The Federalism of James A. Bayard* (1955), ch. 5. TJ left on July 6, and Blount was expelled July 8. The insinuation that he went early to get away from the Blount case seems farfetched (comment in *Aurora*, July 21, 1797).

[18] Wm. Smith to Ralph Izard, May 23, 1797 (*A.H.R.*, XIV, 787). He named Baldwin (Ga.), Sumter (S. C.), Varnum (Mass.), Brown (Ky.), and Skinner (Mass.), saying they also had Henry (Md.), whom he feared they would corrupt. Brown and Henry were senators.

two absentees. The House was much more closely divided. John Beckley, whom he described as the ablest clerk in the country, was defeated for re-election by one vote on opening day, when there were numerous absentees. He blamed the decline of Republican strength in the House chiefly on absentees and on the separation of three Virginians from their brethren. He described these three to Madison as "renegadoes," leaving no doubt that he himself was a good party man, rarely critical of any except the indolent or disloyal.[19] This was a basic reason for the loyalty of the party to him.

Obviously the outstanding Republican of the country by virtue of an electoral vote which had lacked little of making him President, he could have been expected to assume, under the sheer force of circumstances, a more active role in party affairs than he had ever played before. Madison had withdrawn from the Philadelphia scene, leaving Gallatin as the Republican leader in the House. There, however, the Genevan devoted himself chiefly to financial questions, believing that his birth was a disadvantage to him in connection with foreign matters. He needed no urging from Jefferson to oppose expenditures for the navy and he was strongly set against any trend toward war. The strategy of the Republicans in Congress was to counter this trend and to safeguard their own existence as a party; the tactics were to oppose Adams's recommendations except for the commission to France. All this was in full accord with Jefferson's ideas, but there was probably little need for him to advise it. No doubt he heartened the faithful and stimulated the laggards by his very presence in Congress Hall and Francis's Hotel, but there is virtually no record of his activities at this stage except in the form of letters.

In the aggregate he did not write many in this brief period, and rarely did he write except in response to those he had received. Seizing upon opportunities as they were afforded, he sought to influence men he regarded as moderates — like Gerry, Edward Rutledge, and even Thomas Pinckney — and to inform, reassure, and stimulate persons already of his own persuasion. Hardly any letter dealt with public affairs alone, and in discussing these he was merely following his long-established practice, which he had considerably restricted while secretary of state. As vice president he was in an anomalous position, but he thought of himself as no part of the administration and felt free to criticize it as he saw fit. Out of regard to the proprieties, however, and because of his extreme aversion to public controversy, he chose to avail himself of private channels only.

[19] Information from various letters, chiefly to Madison, in May and June (Ford, VII, 124 ff.).

Also, he sought to impose certain safeguards. In view of what had happened to his letter to Mazzei, and the proneness of the Federalists to characterize all critical comments on governmental policy as contemptible and subversive, it was not unnatural that he should have cautioned certain of his correspondents not to let his letters get out of their hands and into the newspapers. But when word of this got out, along with garbled versions of some of the things he wrote, it was all the easier for Federalist partisans to describe him as a secret intriguer with dangerous intent.

As an example of the way rumors spread in those days, the story of a letter of his which bore directly on his relations with Adams is of particular interest. Written to Peregrine Fitzhugh, a political supporter in Washington County, Maryland, in response to a letter from that gentleman about agricultural and public matters, it has added interest because it contains Jefferson's earliest recorded reference to the attack which the "Federal Bull-dog," Luther Martin of Maryland, had launched against him because of certain statements in the *Notes on Virginia*.[20] Somewhat more than half of this long communication consisted of comments on public affairs. The recipient said later that the wisdom of the words of caution with which it ended was proved by what happened. According to his account, he communicated its contents to his father, who was of the decided opinion that Jefferson did not want to keep his sentiments from his Republican friends but merely to keep out of the papers, as indeed may have been the case. Afterwards, in the company of warm admirers of the Vice President, Peregrine Fitzhugh mentioned the contents of the letter, affording them much satisfaction. One of these gentlemen repeated part of the substance, so that it got to the ears of one of the opposite party, who then forwarded the report in exaggerated form to Frederick and Georgetown, the two "hotbeds of aristocracy" in the state. He himself afterwards heard it in the latter place and sought to correct the exaggerations — going so far as to show the letter to a relative of his in the other party and mentioning the substance of it to a couple of other "aristocrats." Later still he found that a garbled report had got into a Frederick paper; this, presumably, was what he sent to Jefferson. He mentioned his relative, General Uriah Forrest, with whom he often exchanged political squibs, but if he knew that that gentleman had

---

[20] TJ to Fitzhugh, June 4, 1797 (Ford, VII, 134–138), replying to a letter of May 19 (LC, 17386–17387). The attack of Martin, which is referred to in ch. XXII, related to certain statements about the share that his father-in-law, Col. Cresap, had in the murder of Logan's family. TJ asked Fitzhugh to send information about Cresap, who had lived in his part of the country.

communicated the substance of the letter to John Adams, he did not say so.[21]

One passage in the original which might have been expected to displease Adams was the following:

> . . . I consider the calling of Congress so out of season an experiment of the new administration to see how far & on what lines they could count on its support. Nothing new had intervened between the late separation & the summons, for Pinckney's non-reception was then known.[22]

This statement was less than accurate and therefore misleading, for certain dispatches from Pinckney, including the one reporting the official request that he leave France, had not been received when the old Congress ended. Adams was not then President anyway.

Jefferson also made some questionable value-judgments:

> . . . It is possible from the complexion of the President's speech that he was disposed or perhaps advised to proceed on a line which would endanger the peace of our country: . . . The nomination of the envoys for France does not prove a thorough conversion to the pacific system.

After reading these and other passages, Forrest wrote down the substance of the letter from memory. He claimed that he exaggerated nothing and actually performed something of a feat, but at all the crucial points his statement was stronger than the original and more explicit in the reference to warlike intentions which were abandoned because of insufficient congressional support. While recognizing the impropriety of violating the confidence of his kinsman, he was persuaded that he was doing his patriotic duty in apprising Adams of the contents of the letter. Its "disgraceful insinuations, barefaced assertions and dangerous principles" ought to be made known so that the President could be on guard. He hoped, however, that no other use would be made of his communication. One may assume that he might have found his relations with his kinsman embarrassing if it had been published.

Adams would not have liked the original and the version he got was worse, but it was hardly sufficient to justify his characterization of his recent rival and old friend. Thanking Forrest for his letters, the President said:

---

[21] Peregrine Fitzhugh to TJ, Oct. 15, 1797 (LC, 17498–17499), received Nov. 10; Uriah Forrest, from Georgetown, June 23, 1797, to Adams with enclosure (Adams Papers, MHS, microfilm UVA).
[22] Ford, VII, 136.

. . . The paper inclosed in it is a serious thing. It will be a motive, in addition to many others, for me to be upon my guard. It is evidence of a mind, soured, yet seeking for popularity, and eaten to a honeycomb with ambition, yet weak, confused, uninformed, and ignorant. I have been long convinced that this ambition is so inconsiderate as to be capable of going great lengths. I shall carefully keep the secret, as far as it may compromise characters and names.[23]

There is no evidence that Jefferson knew anything about this private outburst, which so sharply marked the cessation of personal friendliness on Adams's part. It was some weeks after this that he got from Fitzhugh a report of the "perversion" of his expression. In his own delayed reply he said:

. . . I have been for some time used as the property of the newspapers, a fair mark for every man's dirt. Some, too, have indulged themselves in this exercise who would not have done it, had they known me otherwise than thro these impure and injurious channels. It is hard treatment, and for a singular kind of offence, that of having obtained by the labors of a life the indulgent opinions of a part of one's fellow citizens. However, these moral evils must be submitted to, like the physical scourges of tempest, fire, &c.[24]

His tone was loftier than the circumstances justified, for he had made unprovable assertions and voiced unwarranted suspicions so far as Adams was concerned. Unquestionably he engaged in exaggeration when communicating his fears to the faithful, and as a partisan he was often injudicious. But Adams had not taken him into his confidence or implied any difference between President and Cabinet. It may be noted, also, that Jefferson neither belittled his old friend's intelligence nor questioned his character; his concern was with issues. He was wholly right in claiming that he would never have been attacked as he was but for his status as a Republican. He might have complained, though apparently he did not, that much of his suffering was occasioned by the indiscretion of his friends.

If any single action marked Jefferson's assumption of the leadership of the Republican party as an organization, insofar as that term was warranted at this stage, it was the writing of a letter to Aaron Burr after Congress had been about a month in session. Hitherto he had

---

[23] Adams to Forrest, with the obviously erroneous date of June 20, 1797 (*Works*, VIII, 546–547).
[24] To Peregrine Fitzhugh, Feb. 23, 1798 (Ford, VII, 208–209).

been his party's chief symbol, as in fact he continued to be, and had concerned himself with issues, a thing he by no means ceased to do. Insofar as he had influenced particular party policies and activities he had done so through persons in the legislative branch who had consulted him. His actions in this respect, prior to his vice presidency at least, were greatly exaggerated by the Hamiltonians, as they have often been by later admiring writers.[25] The further role he now assumed can be more fittingly described as that of mobilizer than that of organizer. If anybody was in command it was he, but as a commander he was disposed to make suggestions rather than issue orders, and, outside his own state, he did not concern himself as a rule with local activities. But he was in better position than congressmen and senators to view the whole field and see where there was special need or prospect of energizing the forces of republicanism. It was not at all surprising, therefore, that his thoughts should turn to Burr, who was now back in New York, since the Federalist Assembly of that state had replaced him in the Senate by Hamilton's father-in-law, Philip Schuyler, and who, as a newly elected member of that Assembly, was operating effectively at the local level.

A conciliatory gesture to Burr was definitely in order, after the scant notice paid him by the electors of Virginia and other states where Jefferson was strongest. There is no way of knowing just what the Vice President thought of the New Yorker at this time. The best guess is that he regarded him as a necessary evil. We must not assume, however, that Burr's reputation was as unsavory as it afterwards became. In view of the moral lapse to which Hamilton soon publicly confessed, he was under a darker cloud than Burr at this juncture. In any case, Jefferson recognized that the cooperation of the most promising Republican politician beyond Pennsylvania was a virtual necessity for the future success of the party in the country as a whole. The alliance with Burr which had been initiated by others had been weakened by the events of the election, and he set out to restore it. He may have expressed more personal esteem for Burr than he actually had, but as a political performance his letter was unexceptionable.[26]

Writing Burr in much the way that he wrote Madison, and thus recognizing him as a member of the inner band of leaders, Jefferson lucidly described the political situation in Philadelphia as he saw it and ably set forth the issues as he perceived them. The basic issues

[25] Notably Claude G. Bowers; see Merrill Peterson, *The Jefferson Image in the American Mind* (1960), pp. 347–350.

[26] June 17, 1797 (Ford, VII, 145–149). For a later statement that he always distrusted Burr, see memo. of Jan. 26, 1804 (Ford, I, 304).

were "the preservation of our republican government," the equilibrium of which had in his opinion been upset by executive encroachments in disregard of popular opinion, and the preservation of the Republic itself at a time when war was threatened with an ancient ally. He called for a return to the "spirit of 1776." The great political need as he saw it was to awaken the eastern states, and he inquired of Burr if his newly kindled hopes of New York were vain.

The effectiveness of his letter was shown by the prompt and grateful reply, in which Burr manifested full agreement with Jefferson about the issues. "The moment requires free communication among those who adhere to the principles of our revolution," he said. But, since that had best be made in person rather than in writing, he hoped to see the Vice President very soon in Philadelphia.[27] He did more than fulfill that promise; he was in the city when Monroe arrived from France, and, along with Jefferson and Gallatin, spent two hours with the displaced envoy.[28] The inner Republican circle had been re-formed, though Madison was not physically present and Jefferson, because of his prestige if for no other reason, was the focal center in a sense that his friend from Orange County had not been when in Philadelphia.

These men undoubtedly talked about Monroe, who was a storm center from the moment of his landing. Gallatin, gaining a strong impression of "integrity superior to all the attacks of malignity," concluded that as minister he had conducted himself with "irreproachable honor and the most dignified sense of duty." The party policy was to defend him on all counts, just as Jefferson was impelled to do as a loyal friend. Testifying to their approbation of his conduct, his fellow Republicans gave a dinner to him at Oeller's Hotel on July 1. Anticipating that Jefferson, Judge Thomas McKean, the Governor of Pennsylvania, and about fifty members of Congress would be there, Gallatin wrote his wife: "I expect the Administration, Porcupine & Co. will soundly abuse us." [29] They received sarcastic treatment from *Porcupine's Gazette*. That extreme Federalist sheet, listing the major guests, called each of them "Monsieur," and it termed Monroe's speech "Citizen's Reply." [30] The first of the volunteer toasts, after the Vice President had retired, was to "The Man of the People, Thomas Jefferson." In the meantime, however, PHOCION's campaign pamphlet, exposing his "pretensions" to the presidency, was placed on sale. An advertisement of it in Porcupine's paper said: "Mr. Jefferson's ac-

27 Burr to TJ, June 21, 1797 (LC, 17438), received June 23.
28 Gallatin to his wife, June 28, 1797 (Adams, *Life of Gallatin*, p. 186).
29 Letter of June 30, 1797 (*ibid.*, p. 187).
30 *Porcupine's Gazette*, July 5, 1797.

knowledged *Letter to Mazzei* having rent the veil that concealed from the partial and prejudiced many of his political deformities, the PRESENT CRISIS demands that they should now be exposed without reserve." [31]

Actually, there was no public crisis when the Vice President set out for home on July 6. The country was at peace and he thought it would stay so. The storm of partisan controversy kept on raging, but he escaped for a time to the fringe of it, while it centered on his old foe Hamilton and involved his old friend Monroe.

[31] *Porcupine's Gazette*, July 3, 1797, and earlier. For the pamphlet by PHOCION, or William Loughton Smith, see ch. XVIII, above.

[XXI]

Hamilton, Monroe, and Others

THE political conflict of the late summer and autumn of 1797 may be described as an intermittent series of minor actions. It consisted chiefly of attacks on public characters and the defense of them. Jefferson, in his mountain fastness, did not directly participate in these, but he staunchly supported the partisans of Republicanism while remaining alert as a sentinel of freedom.

It was ironical that Alexander Hamilton should have been a particular object of partisan attack at just this time, for actually he had been giving counsels of moderation to Adams's Cabinet. This attack, however, bore upon the past of the "prime mover" of the Federal party. In a work entitled *The History of the United States for 1796* (originally a series of pamphlets), documents appeared that exposed to public gaze the unsavory Reynolds episode, hitherto known to only a few.[1] Hamilton, in order to quiet the suspicions of a trio of Republican members of Congress, including James Monroe, with respect to allegedly improper actions of his as secretary of the treasury, had revealed to them in December, 1792, his illicit relations with Mrs. Reynolds and the blackmailing operations of her husband James. The documents in the case were supposed to have been kept secret as a matter of honor, the assumption being that the gentlemen in question were satisfied that Hamilton had cleared himself as a public man by this humiliating personal disclosure.

The unsigned publication which exposed them was the work of James Thomson Callender, a free-lance pamphleteer and hack writer, but early rumor attributed it to John Beckley, who was said to have written it in revenge after the failure of the House of Representa-

[1] The preface of the full work was dated July 19, 1797, but Nos. V and VI, which bore on this episode, appeared several weeks earlier.

tives to re-elect him as clerk.[2] The denial of this rumor in the preface of the *History*, when after appearing in parts it was issued as a whole, seems to have diverted suspicions from Beckley, who, according to Monroe's later private statement, was actually responsible for the release of the confidential documents to Callender.[3] The author of the pamphlet emphasized Monroe's connection with the original episode, saying that partisan attacks on him were ungrateful in view of the leniency he had displayed toward Hamilton.[4] Not unnaturally, therefore, the latter blamed him for the "leak."

Virtually all of the resulting correspondence, and the heated interviews between Hamilton and Monroe in New York and Philadelphia, occurred after Jefferson had gone home to Monticello, where no doubt he received a full oral report from his friend and neighbor a little later. He already knew about the meetings between the legislative trio and Hamilton in December, 1792, having made a brief memorandum about them at the time.[5] Hamilton's private confession had immediately followed his series of vicious newspaper attacks on his colleague, then secretary of state, under such pseudonyms as AN AMERICAN, CATULLUS, and SCOURGE — attacks which showed him at one of the highest, or lowest, points of his arrogance as a censor of the conduct of others. Furthermore, his blackmailer, James Reynolds, had been previously involved in buying up, at a fraction of their value, the claims of old soldiers to arrears of pay before the veterans knew how much they were entitled to. His actions led directly to congressional resolutions in 1790, seeking to protect the veterans against speculators, which Hamilton opposed and Jefferson favored in the first important clash between these historic antagonists. Jefferson was sure there had been fraud in this instance, based on advance information which could have been procured only from somebody in the Treasury Department, and obviously Hamilton was taking the part of the speculators against the former soldiers. Jefferson's memorandum of December, 1792, was

---

[2] T. Sedgwick to R. King, June 24, 1797 (King, II, 193), referring to an advertisement which related to No. V.

[3] Monroe to Burr, Dec. 1, 1797 (quoted by P. M. Marsh in "Hamilton and Monroe," in *Miss. Valley Hist. Rev.*, XXXIV [Dec. 1947], 467). Monroe said that copies of the documents were made by Beckley's own clerk in the first place, and that Beckley informed Hamilton that he regarded himself as under no obligation of secrecy. W. P. Cresson, in *James Monroe* (1946), ch. 15, gives an excellent account of the Reynolds affair, blaming Beckley though he did not know about this letter. He involves TJ to a greater degree than seems warranted.

[4] Hamilton referred to this statement in his letter of July 5, 1797, to Monroe (Lodge, VI, 510).

[5] Dec. 17, 1792 (Ford, I, 212); see *Jefferson and the Rights of Man*, p. 476.

factual and noncommittal, but he never ceased to believe that Hamilton countenanced speculation and collusion, whether personally a party to it or not, and this judgment he could hardly have failed to communicate to his friend Monroe.[6]

In the light of these original doubts it is not surprising that, when the episode of 1792 was made public in 1797, Monroe conducted himself in a way not wholly satisfactory to Hamilton. The recent envoy to France, who was so severely castigated by Federalist critics, signed a statement that he had no agency in or knowledge of the publication of the papers. On this count he may be said to have cleared himself at the bar of history, but he did not implicate Beckley at the time and never did so publicly. Also, Hamilton learned from Callender's pamphlet that, after his own confession, Monroe and the two other legislators had listened to Jacob Klingman, an associate of Reynolds, and that Monroe had left a signed statement of this man's charge that Hamilton was covering up official misconduct with a fabricated personal story. That the account of these amours was trumped up seems most unlikely, and Hamilton's indignation that Monroe had listened to an insignificant man with a grievance, instead of taking his own word as final, is understandable. While declining to say either that he believed or disbelieved Klingman's story, Monroe stuck to his right to consider it, thus implying that he still harbored some suspicions. The altercation between him and Hamilton lacked little of issuing in a duel — in which Burr would have been his second — but neither man was willing to assume the role of aggressor. Hamilton had to content himself with the publication of the entire correspondence, along with other papers.

He gave an elaborate account of the Reynolds affair and the various negotiations in his well-known *Observations*, consisting of more than thirty printed pages of text and more than fifty of appended documents.[7] It would be easy to dwell on the unsavory details of this shocking confession — the protracted amours, illiterate letters from Maria

[6] The controversy over the resolutions concerning arrearages in soldiers' pay, and the cabinet opinions of Hamilton (May 28, 1790) and TJ (June 3, 1790), are fully dealt with in *J.P.*, XVI, 455–470, and in an appendix on the facts in the case which is to be published in the next volume. The editor believes that the Reynolds affair and the later Glaubeck episode need to be re-examined in the light of fresh evidence. My own opinion, on reconsidering the matter, is that neither TJ nor Monroe was convinced that Hamilton had *fully* cleared himself in 1792 of the charges against the conduct of his public office.

[7] The precise title is: *Observations on Certain Documents contained in Nos. V. and VI. of "The History of the United States for the Year 1796," in which the Charge of Speculation against Alexander Hamilton, late Secretary of the Treasury, is fully refuted* (Philadelphia, 1797; text dated July, 1797). See Lodge, VI, 449–535.

Reynolds, letters to her husband which were admittedly in a disguised hand, records of repeated payments of money under duress. By his startling admissions, first in private and then in print, Hamilton showed the extent to which he would go in vindication of his public honor. This publication may also be cited as a conspicuous example of his audacity. But one may question the need for him to go to such lengths unless the threat to his reputation as an official was greater than appeared upon the surface. And he made it all the more difficult to draw a line between public and private morals by attributing all criticism of himself to nefarious designs against the national interest. He blamed everything on the "spirit of Jacobinism," which in his opinion threatened greater mischiefs to the world than had previously flowed from war, pestilence, and famine; it threatened, indeed, the complete overthrow of the political and moral world, of which he obviously regarded himself as a mainstay. A major instrument of this spirit was slander of upright men. From what appeared to be "a conspiracy of vice against virtue" he could not hope to escape. To him, then, this was but another instance of the excessive calumny and persecution to which he had been subjected by the "Jacobin Scandal-Club."

There seems to be no record of any comment on Hamilton's *Observations* by Jefferson, any more than there is on the episode which occasioned it, but we do have one that Madison made to him:

> . . . The publication, under all its characters, is a curious specimen of the ingenious folly of its author. Next to the error of publishing it at all, is that of forgetting that simplicity and candour are the only dress which prudence would put on innocence. Here we see every rhetorical artifice employed to excite the spirit of party to prop up his sinking reputation; and whilst the most exaggerated complaints are uttered against the unfair and virulent persecutions of himself, he deals out in every page the most malignant insinuations against others. The one against you is a masterpiece of folly, because its impotence is in exact proportion to its venom.[8]

The "insinuation" against Jefferson related to his alleged friendliness toward a former clerk in the Treasury, Andrew G. Fraunces. Several years earlier this "worthless man" had accused Hamilton of misconduct in connection with the purchase of the pension of Baron de Glaubeck at a reduced figure in behalf of the widow of General Nathanael Greene, to whom Glaubeck was indebted. A committee of the House exonerated Hamilton on this charge early in 1794, but let-

[8] Madison to TJ, Oct. 20, 1797 (*Letters and Other Writings*, 1884, II, 119).

ters of his suggest that the transaction, while made in behalf of a deserving person, was of the kind that speculators were carrying on and smacked of the sort of collusion with Treasury officials that had been charged in the Reynolds case.[9] In the appendix to his pamphlet Hamilton included two recent letters to Fraunces from Jefferson, without saying just how he got hold of them.[10] The Vice President, after denying with more civility than may have been necessary a request from Fraunces for financial aid, had declined to give him a certificate of character, on the ground that he had seen him only on the occasion of one call, when he himself was secretary of state. What infuriated Hamilton, no doubt, was the additional statement that the inability of the former clerk to get one from the Treasury might be attributed to his "particular misunderstanding" with his principals. The words of the former Secretary of the Treasury could be interpreted as insinuating that Fraunces had been encouraged by Jefferson to bring charges in the first place and had some claim on him. These letters offer no proof of that, though they do show that he had some sympathy for an obscure man who had fallen on evil days and might be viewed as the object of Hamiltonian "persecution." They also imply that he was by no means undisposed to give a hearing to critics of the public conduct of his inveterate antagonist.

The emphasis with him was on *public* conduct, not personal morals. According to his code the latter were a private matter, like religion. He issued numerous moral exhortations to the junior members of his own family but hardly any to anybody else; and, despite the strict standards he applied to himself, he was characteristically tolerant of human frailty. The lurid comments on Hamilton's private conduct in later letters of John Adams — including references to "the profligacy of his life; his fornications, adulteries and his incests" — cannot be matched in those of Jefferson, who appears to have referred to them little, if at all.[11] In the long run, Hamilton did John Adams more injury than he did Jefferson, but the latter had abundant reason to dislike Hamilton personally, in view of his colleague's overt and covert attempts to undermine him while they were in office together.

[9] For Hamilton's reference to this matter in his *Observations* of 1797, see Lodge, VI, 454–455; for two letters of his about it, dated Sept. 3, 1793, see J.C.H., V, 583–585. The editor of Jefferson's *Papers* believes that this transaction merits reexamination, along with the Reynolds affair.

[10] Appendix, Nos. XLIV, XLV (Lodge, VI, 528).

[11] Specially pungent comments from Adams are to be found in his letters to Benjamin Rush, such as the above, Sept. 1807 (*Old Family Letters*, p. 163). It will be recalled that it was Adams who termed Hamilton the "bastard brat of a Scotch peddler."

At this stage of his life there was no one he detested more, but rarely did he give vent to his personal resentment. He did so most notably to Washington, when Hamilton was attacking him anonymously, but that was the exception, not the rule.[12] His basic objection to Hamilton always was the belief that "his system flowed from principles adverse to liberty," and that he regarded corruption, along with force, as a necessary instrument of government.

It is a fair supposition, therefore, that he agreed with the contention of Callender that the Reynolds affair bore on something more than private morals — that Hamilton's official character was involved. So far as the record shows, he neither deplored nor commended the publicizing of Hamilton's confessed amours, but he purchased copies of Callender's pamphlet. Furthermore, this action marked the beginning of his connection with a man who turned out to be the most unscrupulous of the Republican pamphleteers and the most notorious scandalmonger of the era. Deeply embarrassed by it in later years, he did not refer to it in public and never explained it adequately in private.

Jefferson first learned of Callender as the author of a tract, *The Political Progress of Britain, or An Impartial History of Abuses in the Government of the British Empire*, first published in London in 1792. On its republication in the United States, he read it with great satisfaction and learned that its author was "a fugitive from prosecution" on account of it. Having described Parliament as "a phalanx of mercenaries" and the English constitution as "a conspiracy of the rich against the poor," besides loosing barbs against the King, Callender was indicted in Edinburgh for sedition, but managed to escape before his trial.[13] In the second American edition of this work appeared the following passage:

> . . . In Britain, authors and editors of pamphlets have long conducted the van of every revolution. They compose a kind of forlorn hope on the skirts of battle; and though they may often want experience, or influence, to marshal the main body, they yet

[12] See, especially, his letter of Sept. 9, 1792 (Ford, VI, 101–109) and *Jefferson and the Rights of Man*, ch. XXVII.

[13] Proceedings in T. B. and T. J. Howell, *A Complete Collection of State Trials* (1817), XXIII, 79–84. TJ commented on the work in essentially the same terms in two letters to Monroe, May 29, 1801, and July 15, 1802 (Ford, VIII, 61, 164–167), which give an account of his relations with Callender. W. C. Ford, in *Thomas Jefferson and James Thomson Callender* (1897; originally in *N.-Eng. Hist. and Genealog. Register*, 1896–1897), gives a brief sketch of Callender and prints the correspondence between the two men. A longer recent account is C. A. Jellison, "That Scoundrel Callender" (*Va. Mag.*, July 1959, pp. 295–306).

enjoy the honour and danger of the first rank, in storming the rampants of oppression.[14]

When pamphleteers were attacking abuses and restrictions that he himself deplored, Jefferson no doubt regarded them as brave sharp-shooters, and he appears to have allowed insufficiently for the reck-lessness of their aim. He was not at all critical of critics of British government and policy; almost instinctively he sympathized with any man who was suffering because of the expression of free opinions; and he was notoriously generous to almost any needy person who approached him. According to his later statement, he expressed will-ingness to help Callender on first learning of his plight.

Nothing was more certain about this fugitive writer than that he was needy. He had regular work as a reporter of congressional de-bates for a time, but, managing to displease both sides, he lost it. He appealed to Madison to help him find a place as a schoolteacher, but throughout his American career he supported his family precariously by the irregular returns from his pen. Jefferson afterwards said that none of his later works fulfilled the promise of the first, but on June 20, 1797, he paid Callender $15.14 for the *History of the United States for 1796*, which was not yet complete.[15] Apparently this was on the occasion of a visit to him at his lodgings. The sum was hardly sufficient to be characterized as a subsidy, but was considerably more than the price of a single copy. Jefferson probably was cloaking an act of charity with the form of a purchase, though it is difficult to see how he arrived at this precise figure. He could scarcely have failed to know by this date that in part the work was an attack on Hamilton.[16] There is no ground for believing that he had instigated it, and at this stage he probably could not have stopped it even if he had wanted to. It may be assumed that Callender was importunate, and few things were harder for Jefferson than to deny anybody who was on the Re-publican side.

The help he gave the needy writer served to encourage further im-portunity, though this was not great at first. During the summer of 1797, after the Vice President had gone home to Monticello, Callender

---

[14] Advertisement, dated Nov. 14, 1794, and prefixed to edn. of 1795. The author said that one cause of the appearance of the American edn. was the encouragement of Jefferson and other gentlemen. He quotes TJ as saying that the work contained "the most astonishing concentration of abuses that he had ever heard of in any government." William Cobbett remarked that the word "abuses" should have been "abuse."

[15] Account Book.

[16] Hamilton's friends knew this by June 24 or earlier.

said that two leading Republicans "handsomely" gave him "most effectual" financial assistance while he was preparing another work. These were Thomas Leiper, a prominent merchant and Jefferson's former landlord, and Alexander James Dallas, who was still secretary of the Commonwealth of Pennsylvania. But, while the city was again plagued with yellow fever, the author wrote Jefferson, asking for five or ten dollars as an advance. This is the first letter known to have passed between them.[17] According to him, Jefferson, at Francis's Hotel, had dropped a word about giving him financial assistance on his finishing his next volume. Something of the sort the Vice President may well have said through excess of kindness or partisan zeal, but he made no known response to this plea. He did not take up the suggestion that he draw a draft or check in favor of a third person, Callender's own name "not being very proper to appear."[18] When he got back to Philadelphia in the winter, however, he made him several payments for pamphlets and books for himself and others, totaling somewhat more than ten dollars, presumably doing so in person.[19] His former landlord Leiper appears to have done most to urge Callender's claims upon him. A few weeks later he paid Leiper five dollars for five copies of *Sketches of the History of America* (1798). In the spring he gave the same Republican sixteen dollars for Callender, and paid the writer himself a total of eight dollars for books. His entire payments to and for Callender in 1797 and the first half of 1798 came to slightly more than fifty dollars — most of the money being ostensibly for the purchase of books. Later, when Callender was a fugitive from American "persecution," he contributed more substantial sums — to the amount of one hundred and fifty dollars altogether before his presidency.[20]

The extent of this financial aid, which Jefferson afterwards described as charity, was not enough at this early stage to warrant the pamphleteer's rather effusive thanks.[21] But it could readily be interpreted as an encouragement and as an approval of his writings in general, though not necessarily in detail. The time had not yet come when Jefferson

[17] Callender to TJ, Sept. 28, 1797 (LC, 17492). The letter can be conveniently seen in Sowerby, III, 420–421.
[18] TJ's surviving financial records are remarkably full with respect to cash transactions. Since few if any of his contemporaries left comparable records, there is no real way of knowing what gifts they may or may not have made to partisan journalists and pamphleteers, but it may be assumed that they made a good many. There is no doubt that John Fenno received contributions from Hamilton and others. Furthermore, administration papers were given government printing.
[19] Account Book, Dec. 14, 17, 23, 1797.
[20] Account Book, Jan. 9, Mar. 23, May 23, May 29, 1798; Sept. 6, 1799; Oct. 22, 1800; TJ to S. T. Mason, Oct. 11, 1798 (Ford, VII, 282).
[21] To TJ, Mar. 21, 1798 (*N.-Eng. Hist. & Gen. Reg.*, 327–328).

wanted to stop this pen. As a party leader, believing that the political war against him and what he believed in was relentless, he was countenancing a supporter whose venom was not fully revealed but whom as a private man he could have been expected to find offensive. He may have fully agreed with Callender's comment on Hamilton's pamphlet about the Reynolds affair, but as a high-minded and punctilious gentleman he should have found this disquieting. "If you have not seen it," wrote Callender gleefully, "no anticipation can equal the infamy of this piece. It is worth all that fifty of the best pens in America could have said against him, and the most pitiful part of the whole is his notice of you." [22] Callender's *Sketches of the History of America*, of whose large and quick sale the author boasted, contained numerous favorable references to Jefferson. That gentleman had not suggested them, and certainly he never thought of himself as paying for them, but his enemies could have claimed it and he should have given them no ground for such a charge. The price he really paid for encouraging this irresponsible pen was not to be shown till later. He was to have abundant reason to regret this instance of letting a great end — the attainment and preservation of popular representative government — justify what he must have known were dubious means.

In the stormy period of his career on which Jefferson entered when he accepted the role of leader of the Republican party — that is, in the summer of 1797 — the partisanship which he justified on patriotic and philosophical grounds entered into his political judgments and colored his actions to a degree which was unparalleled in his earlier public service. In a minor episode in his own state, however, he was in character as a sentinel of freedom, a foe of federal encroachment, a defender of genuinely representative government, and a champion of the liberties of individuals. His actions in the so-called Cabell case, which actually never came up for trial, may also be regarded as prophetic.

Samuel J. Cabell, representative in Congress for the district that included Albemarle County, had voiced certain criticisms of the federal government in circular letters to his constituents. The grand jury of the federal circuit court in Richmond drew a presentment against him (May 22, 1797), charging him with endeavoring at a time of public danger "to disseminate unfounded calumnies against the happy government of the United States" and to increase or produce a ruinous foreign influence. [23] In Republican quarters it was claimed that British

22 Letter of Sept. 28, 1797.
23 Episode described by Adrienne Koch and Harry Ammon in *W. & M.*, April

influence, in the persons of jurymen of British birth and interests, entered into the assertion that Cabell promoted French interests. Referring to this presentment shortly after he heard about it, Jefferson said that federal judges, in their charges to grand juries, had for some time been inviting them "to become inquisitors on the freedom of speech, of writing and of principle of their fellow citizens." Thus the grand jury was threatened with perversion from a legal to a political institution.[24] Meanwhile, Cabell himself had accused the federal judges of becoming a band of "political preachers." [25]

After his return home Jefferson drew a lengthy paper on this subject in the form of a petition to the Virginia House of Delegates from the inhabitants of the congressional district.[26] His strong constitutional argument, upholding the freedom of legislators from the cognizance or coercion of the judicial and executive branches of the federal government, and their right to communicate freely with their constituents, could have been regarded as sufficient to justify Cabell. Jefferson's prime concern, however, was with Cabell's constituents. Independently of constitutional considerations, he upheld the right of free correspondence between citizens as a natural right which had not been alienated by the adoption of the Constitution or any other action.

Regarding the presentment of the grand jury as an attack on representative government and individual liberty, he described it as a crime "of the highest and most alarming nature" which called for extraordinary action. Seeing no power to deal with it except what inhered in the Commonwealth of Virginia, he addressed the petition to the House of Delegates. It requested that body to institute such proceedings for impeaching and punishing the grand jurors as would secure the inhabitants of the state in their constitutional rights. With this emphasis on the authority of the state and the rights of individuals he coupled an appeal to nativist feeling which did him little credit. He suggested that jury service henceforth be restricted to native citizens, or such as were citizens at the end of the American Revolution. In making this uncharacteristic proposal he was really taking the position of the High Federalists, who were declaiming against French influences.

Jefferson submitted this document to Madison, who made minor suggestions, and to Monroe, who raised the important question whether a state legislature could enter into the relations between a

---

1948, pp. 152–153; and Koch, *Jefferson and Madison*, pp. 182–184. Presentment of May 22, 1797, quoted from Norfolk, Va., *Herald*, May 29.
[24] To Peregrine Fitzhugh, June 4, 1797 (Ford, VII, 138). This was the letter of which Adams was informed, see above, pp. 320–322.
[25] J. M. Smith, *Freedom's Fetters* (1956), p. 184, quoting *Aurora*, May 31, 1797.
[26] Ford, VII, 158–164.

citizen and his representative. Monroe was disposed to think the petition would be more properly addressed to Congress.[27] Jefferson recognized that the rights of Cabell as a representative fell within the jurisdiction of Congress. As to the rights of citizens, he believed that to petition Congress in their behalf would be to invite rebuff, and that the authority of the state in a matter between citizens could be maintained. He wanted to appeal to it in any case. He wrote Monroe:

> Were the question even doubtful, it is no reason for abandoning it. The system of the General government, is to seize all doubtful ground. We must join in the scramble, or get nothing. Where first occupancy is to give a right, he who lies still loses all. Besides, it is not right for those who are only to act in a preliminary form, to let their own doubts preclude the judgment of the court of ultimate decision. We ought to let it go to the Ho[use] of delegates for their consideration, & they, unless the contrary be palpable, ought to let it go to the General court, who are ultimately to decide on it.
>
> It is of immense consequence that the States retain as complete authority as possible over their own citizens. . . .[28]

His idea was that Peter Carr or somebody else should present the petition to the counties at their general muster and that it should then go to the House of Delegates, his own name having been wholly kept out of the business. It followed that course, and the lower house of the legislature passed a resolution which embodied Jefferson's theoretical position: it referred to the presentment of the grand jury as "a violation of the fundamental principles of representation," as a "usurpation of power," and "a subjection of a natural right of speaking and writing freely." [29] No punitive measures were adopted, however, and the whole question of the means of redress remained unanswered. It was not answered effectively by Jefferson or anybody else in connection with the more serious federal encroachments on individual rights which followed a few months later. Before the Sedition Act, however, there were clear indications of the tack he was taking in both thought and procedure:

(1) At this stage, when both the executive and judicial branches of the federal government were manned by persons whom he regarded as inimical or indifferent to the freedom of individuals, and when the legislative branch was at best uncertain, he saw no recourse except to

27 Monroe to TJ, Sept. 5, 1797 (S.M.H., III, 85).
28 TJ to Monroe, Sept. 7, 1797 (Ford, VII, 173).
29 Koch & Peden, *W. & M.*, April 1948, p. 153, citing *Journals of the House of Delegates . . . for 1797*, pp. 55-58, Dec. 28, 1797.

the states. Accordingly, he emphasized the powers of states to a degree that he had not done hitherto.

(2) He himself was uncertain about specific means of redress, beyond the adoption of resolutions of protest against infringements.

(3) His own procedure was to draft or inspire resolutions which were presented by others, while he kept out of sight.

(4) Though he was motivated by philosophical considerations that had been central in this thinking since the time of the American Revolution, he was also influenced by partisan considerations, as his reference to natives and foreign-born implied and many of his actions clearly showed.

His wholehearted support of James Monroe and his uncritical acceptance of the late envoy's defense of his conduct in France are a case in point, though his own attitude was to be expected on grounds of friendship and personal loyalty. His intimacy with Monroe dated from the last years of the American Revolution, when as governor of Virginia he had befriended and counseled the younger man, to the latter's undying gratitude.[30] Monroe had moved in 1789 to Albemarle County, where he occupied a house afterwards on the grounds of the University of Virginia. He bought land nearer Monticello, and, while Jefferson was in France, had some correspondence with him about building a house there. Nothing came of the plans they wrote about, and not until 1799 did Monroe get into the house he finally built in that place, but, according to standards in Virginia, one was a fairly close neighbor when no more than three or four miles away. The personal relations of the two men were intimate long before there was any special political tie between them. During his student days Jefferson wrote in a notebook a quotation from Euripides which aptly described his continuing judgment of Monroe: "Nothing is better than a reliable friend, not riches, not absolute sovereignty." [31] In this period political differences were sharply limiting his own practice of friendship as a fine art, but there was no difficulty of that sort in this case.

While Monroe was in France he had corresponded with him chiefly as a reporter. He himself was out of office, and such political advice as he might send across the Atlantic would arrive too late to do any good. Jefferson was not disposed to give specific advice to his political intimates anyway; that they agreed with him in general policy was enough. He himself was in full agreement with Monroe's desire to preserve friendship with France, but, giving no specific advice, he

---

[30] See *Jefferson the Virginian*, pp. 324–325.
[31] *Literary Bible*, p. 94; see *Jefferson the Virginian*, p. 85.

was not responsible for particular words or actions. Smarting under his recall, Monroe sought explanations from the Secretary of State after his return. An impasse was inescapable, however, since Washington had recalled him and Adams was now President. There was the same Secretary of State, to be sure, but Timothy Pickering regarded official explanation as improper in any case. He gave one, in effect, nonetheless; and what it boiled down to was divergence in policy between the minister and the government. The attempt at bipartisanship in foreign policy ended with the retirement of Edmund Randolph and the accession of Pickering; and henceforth the administration stood on Jay's Treaty. Regardless of any impropriety or unwisdom on the part of Monroe, his recall was inevitable under the circumstances. What really was at issue was the foreign policy of the government.

Rebuffed by Pickering, Monroe saw no choice but to present his case to the public for vindication. In Republican circles at least there was no objection to this procedure on grounds of propriety. As printed by Benjamin Franklin Bache, Monroe's apologia came to somewhat more than fifty pages of text and more than four hundred pages of documents.[32] Jefferson remarked sympathetically on his friend's labors on it in the late summer and early fall and probably talked with him about it, but the record shows only that he gave advice, upon request, about the title and the exclusion of certain documents. He preferred a title that would not inculpate the Executive, but Monroe did not accept this suggestion.[33] His own references to the published work were wholly complimentary. After he had returned to Philadelphia in December he wrote the author: "Your book was later coming than was to have been wished: however it works irresistibly. It would be very gratifying to you to hear the unqualified eulogies both on the matter and manner by all who are not hostile to it from principle." [34] The gist of the matter was in the last sentence. Jefferson approved of Monroe's conduct and view of foreign affairs *in principle,* and by the same token approved of his criticism of the policy of the administration. Also, he had complete confidence in Monroe's integrity. He was critical at no point because, both as a Republican and friend, he was completely loyal.

During the autumn of 1797, when he saw his daughter Maria mar-

32 *A View of the Conduct of the Executive in the Foreign Affairs of the United States, Connected with the Mission to the French Republic during the Years 1794, 5 & 6,* by James Monroe, Late Minister Plenipotentiary to the Said Republic (1797).

33 Monroe to TJ, Oct. 15, 1797, enclosing two proposed titles (S.M.H., III, 86–88); TJ to Monroe, Oct. 25, 1797 (Ford, VII, 177–179).

34 To Monroe, Dec. 27, 1797 (Ford, VII, 183)

ried, and the ensuing winter, when his house was unroofed and ten-antless, he remained hopeful of the foreign situation and the mainte-nance of friendship with France. Not until spring did he learn that events in that country had rendered Republican criticism of the for-eign policy of the administration obsolete, played into the hands of the extreme Federalists, and provided the occasion for an increase rather than a diminution of the influence of the supposedly discredited Hamilton. Before turning to the crisis' the leader of the opposition then faced, we may pause to consider what befell him in the field of science, into which partisanship is not supposed to enter.

⌈XXII⌉

Honors and Embarrassments of a Scientist

1797—1800

JEFFERSON had anticipated that the "tranquil and unoffending station" to which he was called would give him "philosophical evenings in the winter and rural days in the summer." He said this in a letter to Dr. Benjamin Rush, who had congratulated him on his election as Vice President of the United States and his *escape* from the office of President.[1] With respect to the winter he was thinking particularly of the American Philosophical Society, of which he had been a diligent member for upwards of fifteen years. During his retirement he had undoubtedly missed its meetings and his personal contacts with its members. Word now came that, on his welcome return to Philadelphia, he was to become president of this notable organization in succession to the mathematician David Rittenhouse, who had succeeded Benjamin Franklin.[2]

The formal letter of notification of his election included the statement that, in the same chair from which two philosophers had instructed the Society and the world, a third would now be seated "by whose genius and knowledge, our national name will preserve a distinguished place in the annals of science." No trace of jealousy of his predecessors marred Jefferson's pride in his succession to them. At this time his chief title to fame as a scientist in his own right was his author-

[1] TJ to Rush, Jan. 22, 1797 (Ford, VII, 114), replying to letter of Jan. 4 from Rush (Butterfield, II, 784).

[2] Rittenhouse died June 26, 1796. TJ's relations with the Society are sketched by Gilbert Chinard in "Jefferson and the American Philosophical Society," (*Proc. A.P.S.*, vol. 87 [1944], pp. 263-276). No. 3 of that volume, dated July 14, 1943, consists of papers read in April of that year in celebration of the Jefferson Bicentennial. Rush reported TJ's election of Jan. 6, 1797, somewhat in advance. Formal notice, dated Jan. 7, and TJ's reply of Jan. 28 are in *Transactions*, IV (1799), xi-xiii.

ship of the *Notes on Virginia*, a work which his fellows in learning highly regarded. More indubitably, his election attested his national eminence as a patron of science — in the broad sense that he used the term, that is, as embracing all knowledge. This honor from a body which, in his opinion, comprehended whatever distinction the American world had in philosophy and science, he described as the most flattering incident of his life. In his letter of acceptance he said: "I feel no qualification for this distinguished post but a sincere zeal for all the objects of our institution, and an ardent desire to see knowledge so disseminated through the mass of mankind, that it may at length reach even the extremes of society, beggars and kings." Apart from any other consideration, the zeal which he himself regarded as his chief contribution was so highly valued by these savants that they kept him in this post until 1815, when he had relinquished other titles which loomed larger in the minds of most men but which he himself probably cherished less than this one.

The evening before he became Vice President of the United States he was installed as president of the society that Franklin had fathered, but the scientific proceedings were deferred a week; then, while he was in the chair, the Secretary read a communication from him. Describing the fossil remains of a huge animal, recently found in a cave in Greenbrier County in his state, he fired the "signal gun of American paleontology."[3] His communication on the subject of what he called the Megalonyx or Great Claw had in it elements of embarrassment, however, and its story is not without humor. Besides reflecting his extraordinary zeal, the episode shows him as a man of bold imagination. In his opinion, science recognized no political or national boundary lines, but in this case patriotism affected his scientific judgment, as indeed it did that of others who had somewhat better claim to the title of professional. Altogether, it is a tale very much worth telling.[4]

Jefferson could hardly wait to describe this find to his fellow philosophers. During the previous year his friends John and Archibald Stuart, sure of his interest, had reported the discovery of certain bones of a gigantic animal of the "clawed kind." Promptly describing the creature as being very like a lion, they told some tall stories in the course of their correspondence. On a rock near the confluence of the Great Kanawha was a perfect figure of a lion, of which this or some

[3] *Science*, Apr. 19, 1929, p. 411.
[4] It has been best told by J. P. Boyd in "The Megalonyx, the Megatherium, and Thomas Jefferson's Lapse of Memory," *Procs. A.P.S.*, vol. 102, pp. 420-435 (Oct. 1958). See also illustrations in *J.P.*, XIV, facing pp. 40-41, and editorial notes on these, pp. xxv-xxxiv.

similar animal was presumably the model. Since hunters, a decade or so earlier, had heard roaring that surpassed all thunder, it even seemed likely that the species was not extinct. Jefferson, enchanted by the bones that were sent him and exhilarated by these superlative reports, proceeded to name the beast Megalonyx or Great Claw. Concluding that it was as pre-eminent in size over the lion as the mammoth was over the elephant, he thought this "too victorious an evidence against the pretended degeneracy of animal nature" in North America to be neglected.[5] Here was far more powerful physical evidence than he had previously presented in vindication of things American against the contentions of the French scientist Buffon and others who, for patriotic reasons of their own, had belittled them.[6] With excitement such as he rarely if ever displayed in matters political, he reported the amazing discovery to Rittenhouse, unknowing that the revered mathematician was dead. The bones were to go to the Society, of course. He also told the editor of the Society's *Transactions* that he wanted an account of the find to appear in the next volume.[7]

As finally procured by him the fossil remains consisted of the lower extremity of the femur or thighbone, a perfect radius, an ulna or forearm broken in two, three claws, and a number of other foot bones. Unfortunately there were no teeth. Measuring them with a piece of paper and comparing them with Daubenton's measurements of the lion as given by Buffon, he concluded that the megalonyx was more than three times the size of the king of beasts and probably a formidable antagonist of the mammoth. In the memoir he prepared for the Society he reported numerous traditions about lionlike animals in early America, including those he had picked up from the Stuarts; he referred to terrible roars and eyes like balls of fire. Also, he recalled past efforts of his own to convince Buffon of the size of American animals. For example, he had delivered to the French scientist the skeleton of the palmated elk or moose, seven feet high above the shoulders, whereas the European elk was not more than two-thirds that size. He did not claim that nature had "formed the larger animals of America, like its lakes, its rivers, and mountains, on a greater and prouder scale than in the other hemisphere" — though he seems to have believed

---

[5] Quotations from letters from and to John and Archibald Stuart and to David Rittenhouse in 1796 are given by Boyd. TJ's letters of Nov. 10, 1796, to John Stuart and of Jan. 22, 1797, to Rush are in Ford, VII, 90–91, 113–114.

[6] His own evidence was chiefly in the *Notes on Virginia* and in the specimens he had sent to France. See *Jefferson and the Rights of Man*, pp. 98–102.

[7] His letters of July 3, 1796, to Rittenhouse, who had been dead a week, and to B. S. Barton, Aug. 1, 1796, are quoted by Boyd in *Procs. A.P.S.*, vol. 102, pp. 422–423.

it had. All he insisted on was that scientific systems be built on facts.[8] He was not yet aware that in his own speculations he had ventured into the realm of fancy.

His friend Rush, with whom he had discussed this discovery most enthusiastically, saw in it something of a parable. Such stupendous animals, once probably tyrants of the forest, had perhaps been extirpated by a confederacy of lesser beasts. In like manner might not kings be extirpated by "a general insurrection of the reason and virtue of man," leaving behind them crowns and scepters, like the claws and bones of extinct animals, as the only proof that such cannibals ever existed. Also, giving an indication of his own scientific imagination, this eminent physician was preparing for the Society a paper seeking to prove that the blackness of the Negroes was actually the effect of a skin disease of the leprous kind.[9]

After Jefferson prepared his paper for the American Philosophical Society but before he presented it, by chance which must be described as lucky, he received a shock. He read in an English magazine an account by a young French scientist later to become eminent, Georges Cuvier, of a skeleton discovered in Paraguay and mounted in Madrid.[10] Though Cuvier had only an incomplete report, he correctly identified this large clawed animal as a relative of the sloth, naming it Megatherium. Since it lacked cutting teeth it could not well be carnivorous. Jefferson had no way of knowing what sort of teeth the megalonyx had, but he quickly perceived that in other respects it closely resembled the megatherium. Accordingly, he hastily modified his communication by removing sentences and phrases that unequivocally identified it with lions and tigers and substituting a more general reference to animals of the "clawed kind." [11] Also, he added a postscript about the remains from Paraguay, saying that comparison of them with the megalonyx was difficult, since so few of the latter's bones — and none of its teeth — were available. Meanwhile, he thought that the question of identification should be left open and the distinctive names maintained. He could not alter the trend of his whole argument but he could and did render it more tentative, showing himself as not only prudent but also open-minded.

[8] His memorial of Mar. 10, 1797, is in *Transactions*, IV, 246–260; the quotation is from p. 258.

[9] Rush to TJ, Feb. 4, 1797 (Butterfield, II, 785–786). His paper on this subject was read July 14.

[10] Boyd, pp. 425–426, referring to the *Monthly Magazine, and British Register for 1796*, Sept. 1796, and giving the illustration TJ saw. It is among those in *J.P.*, vol. XIV. Boyd thinks this was between Mar. 3 and 10.

[11] Boyd, pp. 427–428, reproduces the manuscript, showing alterations.

Ironically enough, an early description and crude drawing of the megatherium, which he had been sent eight years earlier in Paris before Cuvier knew about it, was reposing at the moment in his papers.[12] He was under injunction not to make this public at the time he received it; and, without giving it much attention, he may have filed it hastily among the papers he had already packed up to take home to Virginia. At all events, he appears to have forgotten all about it in the intervening years, when he was giving far more thought to other things than to fossils. Had he remembered it, he might have got ahead of Cuvier, and undoubtedly he would have spared himself embarrassment.

For further description, the bones that Jefferson had presented to the Society were submitted to Dr. Caspar Wistar, adjunct professor of anatomy in the University of Pennsylvania. His report, drawn some months later and based on fuller information, was published in the same volume of the *Transactions*.[13] After measuring these bones with dividers, Wistar pointed out resemblances between the animal's foot and that of the sloth; but he saw some differences, and, in the absence of a complete account of the skeleton found in Paraguay, was disposed to reserve final judgment. In fact, the scientific status of the megalonyx and the megatherium remained unsettled for some years. Spanish scientists, resenting Cuvier's coup, tending to minimize him, and questioning his classification, urged caution.[14] Even as late as 1803, a critic of Cuvier, applying the term megalonyx to both animals, designated this as "*un genre particulier.*"[15]

Jefferson himself seems never to have questioned Cuvier's classification of the megatherium, and early in his presidency of the United States if not sooner he came round to the opinion that the megalonyx was probably the same sort of animal. He had to abandon exciting thoughts of its leonine roars and phosphoric eyes in the North American wilderness. Cuvier, in a section on the megalonyx in a classic work that appeared when Jefferson was eighty, left no doubt that he regarded as puerile the arguments based on oral traditions and the figure of a lion upon a rock. But, while decisively classifying the ancient beast as belonging with the *édentés* (anteaters, sloths, armadillos), he gave

12 Enclosure with letter of Jan. 26, 1789, from William Carmichael in Madrid (*J.P.*, XIV, 504–505, with drawing, facing p. 40).

13 Vol. IV (1799), No. LXXVI, pp. 526–531.

14 As in an account of the Paraguayan animal by José Garriga, published in Madrid in 1796, which TJ saw in Philadelphia in the summer of 1797 (*J.P.*, XIV, xxx–xxxi).

15 B. Faujas-St-Fond, *Essai de Géologie*, I, Ch. X, "Du Mégalonix ou de l'animal inconnu du Paraguay."

Jefferson full credit for making this fossil animal known.[16] Also he said that Jefferson, besides the superior qualities he had manifested in government, had "an enlightened love and extensive knowledge of the sciences," to which he had "procured notable increases." The statement was accurate and the tribute well deserved.

Before the life of the Sage of Monticello ended, specialization had gone considerably beyond anything he had observed in the eighteenth century, and by the same token technical competence had increased. Since his day, some scholars have compared his procedure in this particular matter unfavorably with that of Caspar Wistar, who was unquestionably a better technician. But, besides the enterprise and enthusiasm with which Jefferson has been rightly credited, he showed in this instance notable receptiveness and adaptability. A modern scientist has said: "Like all daring thinkers and workers in the pioneer days of so many of the sciences, Jefferson went off the deep end a few times." Noting that the misadventures were actually few as compared with the successes, this commentator continued: "He had, as they say, pretty nearly everything. In the field of natural philosophy he had caution and daring, inquisitiveness and a willingness to change his mind in the light of new facts or as a result of further thought. What we would now call proper scientific methods appeared to be instinctive with him." [17]

In the judgment that he had "pretty nearly everything" his colleagues in the Society in this relatively unspecialized age would have readily concurred. At the beginning of his second year as president of the organization, that is, the year after he presented his paper on the megalonyx, he received a letter from the secretary reminding him that the regular meeting would be at the usual hour, six in the evening. The scribe continued: "It is a matter of sincerest pleasure to every well-wisher of science that one deep in its researches, and distinguished for its diffusion, is to honour its chair again in this city, invited thereto by an unanimous suffrage." [18] He was not very deep in researches at the moment or soon thereafter, but he continued to play a notable part in the diffusion of light and learning. That year he presented to the Society "a bone of the mammoth, some time ago found in Virginia," and a hand-operated threshing machine invented in his state.[19] In May the letter to the president of the National Board of Agriculture at London in which he described his moldboard of a plow was

[16] *Recherches sur les Ossemens Fossiles* (Paris, 1823), V, Part I, pp. 160–173.

[17] Harlow Shapley, in "Notes on Thomas Jefferson as a Natural Philosopher," *Procs. A.P.S.*, vol. 87 (1944), pp. 234, 237.

[18] Jan. 19, 1798 (MHS).

[19] *Transactions*, IV, xxxiv–xxxv.

read; published in the same volume of the *Transactions* with his communication on the megalonyx, it showed that his interest ranged from fossil bones to the turning of a furrow.[20] There is no reason to believe that his scientific ardor waned during the rest of his vice presidency, but increasingly he had to devote his attention to public matters and politics. Meanwhile, he had fallen heir to a controversy which was personal and political in origin but which bore, at the same time, upon his standing as a seeker after truth. By challenging something he had said in his *Notes on Virginia*, Luther Martin of Maryland struck at the base of his reputation as a scholar.

When Jefferson, in his early thirties, first became acquainted with the speech of the Mingo chief Logan, addressed to Lord Dunmore at the end of what was known as Lord Dunmore's War, it seemed to him to match the eloquence of Demosthenes and Cicero. For that reason he inserted it in the *Notes on Virginia*, when defending the American Indians against the aspersions of Buffon. In this speech Logan charged Colonel Cresap with the murder of all his relations; and Jefferson, introducing it, described this frontiersman as "a man infamous for the many murders he had committed" on these much-injured Indian people.[21] Jefferson had no personal knowledge of the man but was undoubtedly aware that this conflict also went by the name of Cresap's War. According to him, the speech was declaimed by schoolboys long before he printed it. The inclusion of the Logan story in the "readings and recitations" of James Fennell in Philadelphia in the winter of 1796-1797 ostensibly provided the occasion for Luther Martin, who had married the daughter of Michael Cresap some years after the latter's death, to protest against the speech as a fiction and the allegations as a groundless calumny. He held Jefferson responsible by giving currency to these in the *Notes*.

The letter he wrote the obscure entertainer a few weeks after the inauguration, when Jefferson was back at Monticello, was an open one. He sent it to the editor of *Porcupine's Gazette,* saying that the propriety of publishing it would be evident, as it was to William Cobbett, and inviting editors elsewhere to copy it.[22] This was no dignified

---

[20] On the moldboard, see ch. XIII, above.

[21] The speech and passage can be conveniently seen in Ford, III, 155-157; the speech in William Peden's edn. of the *Notes* (1955, referred to hereafter as Peden), p. 63, and the introductory statement, which TJ afterwards modified, *ibid.,* pp. 274-275, note 96. For a discussion of the passage as originally written by TJ and his purposes, see *Jefferson the Virginian,* pp. 386-387; *Jefferson and the Rights of Man,* pp. 101-102. In the present treatment I am less favorable to Cresap than in my earlier references to him.

[22] Martin to James Fennell (spelling the name Fennel), Mar. 29, 1797, in *Por-*

protest against historical injustice; it was a direct attack on Jefferson which was at the same time a masterpiece of innuendo. Mr. Jefferson was a philosopher, the writer said with obvious scorn, who like all other philosophers had his hypothesis to establish. Continuing, he said contemptuously:

> When we see him employed in weighing the rats and mice of the two worlds, to prove that those of the new are not exceeded by those of the old — when, to establish that the body of the American savage is not inferior in form or in vigor to the body of an European, we find him examining minutely every part of their frame, and hear him declare that, though the wrist and the hand of the former are smaller than those parts of the latter, yet, "*les organes de generation ne sont plus faibles ou plus petits;*" — and that he hath not only as many hairs on his body, but that the same parts which are productive of hair in the one, if left to themselves, are equally productive of hair in the other: — when we see him so zealous to establish an equality in such trifles, and to prove the body of his savage to be formed on the same modula with the "*Homo sapiens Europoeus,*" how much more solicitous may we suppose him to have been to prove that the mind of this savage was also formed on the same modula.[23]

He said that Jefferson, picking up any story he could without scrutinizing it, had calumniated a noble man. He himself declared without hesitation that "no such specimen of Indian oratory was ever exhibited." While admitting that Cresap had engaged actively in conflicts with the Indians, he flatly denied that he had any part in the extinction of Logan's family or that he killed any friendly Indians. Also, he lugged in an inexact and irrelevant reference to Governor Jefferson's precipitate flight before the British invaders of Virginia. The writer of this open letter was no exemplar of the disinterested quest for historic or scientific truth. This ruthless and pertinacious slugger was out to do all the damage he could to the entire reputation of the author of the *Notes on Virginia*.

Luther Martin, attorney general of Maryland for many years and in the eyes of his contemporaries a fabulous lawyer, was a notoriously intemperate and slovenly man in whose family life unhappiness verged into tragedy. He claimed to be most concerned to clear the name of

---

cupine's Gazette, Apr. 3, 1797. It may be seen also in a publication called *The Olden Time* (Pittsburgh, 1848; repr. Cincinnati, 1876), II, 51–54. Fennell's reply of Apr. 3, assuring Martin that he had used the speech only as "a specimen of natural eloquence," that he brought in the story of Logan only as an introduction, and that he would not again offend, appeared in *Porcupine's Gazette*, Apr. 5, 1797.

23 *The Olden Time*, II, 51.

the father of his dead wife and the grandfather of his two daughters, though in fact he served to advertise further the ill repute of this man. He did not take up the subject until some years after his wife's death, and in Jefferson's opinion he had merely seized upon a pretext. Conjoined with his political animus against the chief Republican, however, was an intense personal animus which set him apart from many who applauded him on political grounds. His own political record was by no means consistent, for he had opposed the Constitution. He may have been an opportunist, and unquestionably he timed his charges well, but this bizarre character cannot be properly termed the mere catspaw of a party, as he was by Jefferson.[24] The man whom he described, when President, as "this unprincipled and impudent federal bull-dog," probably acted on his own initiative.[25]

That Jefferson was duly apprised of Martin's public letter to Fennell and quickly recognized the dangers in it is shown by the fact that he speedily began to seek pertinent information. He wrote General John Gibson, now in Pittsburgh, who as Lord Dunmore's emissary had heard and translated Logan's speech and whose prompt reply confirmed his opinion of its authenticity.[26] The only error in it seeming to require correction was the reference to Cresap as Colonel rather than Captain. In a letter to a supporter in Maryland in which he inquired about the character of the latter in his own locality, he said that he did not desire to enter into newspaper controversy with Martin, but that if any injury had been done Cresap in his own statement it would certainly be corrected in the next edition of the *Notes*. "I have given it as I have received it," he said. He was probably less desirous of procuring information from this correspondent than of letting his purposes become known in Martin's state.[27]

A few weeks later, when he was back at Monticello from the special session of Congress, Martin addressed a letter to him: that is, after giving this to the press he sent him a printed copy.[28] The belligerent law-

[24] To Harry Innes, Mar. 21, 1800 (Sowerby, III, 314).

[25] TJ to George Hay, June 19, 1807, in connection with the Burr trial (Ford, IX, 58). Any interpretation of Martin is difficult because his extant papers are so sparse — a fact to which the lack of a good biography of him may be attributed.

[26] TJ to Gen. Gibson, May 31, 1797 (LC, 17408). According to his Index to Letters, he received a letter of June 17 from Gibson. This I have not seen, but he spoke of it in his letter of Dec. 31, 1797 to Gov. John Henry of Maryland, to which reference will be made shortly, and it may be presumed to have been in line with Gibson's later deposition.

[27] To Peregrine Fitzhugh, June 4, 1797 (Ford, VII, 137). It was from this letter that comments of his on the administration also got out.

[28] Dated June 24, 1797, it appeared in *Porcupine's Gazette*, July 17. In a letter to the editor, Martin said this was a copy of a letter which would be delivered to TJ immediately after the rising of Congress. The Vice President left sooner than

yer now asked answers to specific questions. Also, he stated that, in the process of effacing the calumny on whichever one of the Cresaps had been referred to, he would send the letters already written, and all he should later address to Jefferson, to every other author known to have copied the Logan speech from the *Notes on Virginia*.

The author of this work said afterwards that he read only the first of Martin's letters, and that only sufficiently to get the style, having determined at once "not to gratify him by reading what he wrote to give me pain." [29] In that case he did not read the one addressed to him after he came back to Philadelphia and Congress in the winter, though it seems to have been the one that created the greatest stir.[30] In this the Attorney General of Maryland charged that, by maintaining "obstinate, stubborn silence," Jefferson had pursued a dishonorable course. "For your silence the public expects a reason. — It already condemns you," he said. He announced his determination to continue correspondence through the medium of the newspapers until he had effaced from the name of Cresap the stain Jefferson had tried to fix on it; he would leave the world to determine whether he sullied that of Jefferson in the process. Twitting his enemy for the confusion of the Colonel with the Captain, he said that the former, though more than a hundred years old when the British invaded Virginia, would not have fled if he had been governor. It should be noted, however, that the best estimate of the age of the Colonel is that he was only approaching eighty at the time.[31]

Not unnaturally, the controversy the Attorney General was trying to engender was a particular topic of conversation in the capital of Maryland. The governor of the state was John Henry, who had recently resigned his seat in the United States Senate to accept unanimous election by the Assembly to this post. A moderate Federalist who had been a fellow lodger of the Vice President's at Francis's Hotel, he had formed a high opinion of Jefferson's private and public conduct and found his virtues "endearing." A few days after his election, an incident occurred which made him wonder if he was not in Turkey rather than Annapolis. Entering into a discussion of Mar-

---

he expected. TJ noted in his Index to Letters that on July 31 he received one from Martin dated July 20. Judging from later remarks, he may have first seen Martin's letter in a Baltimore paper.

[29] To Gen. John Gibson, Mar. 21, 1800 (Sowerby, III, 314).

[30] Dec. 11, 1797 (LC, 17515–17516). Sowerby, III, 304–314, gives this and most of the other pertinent correspondence. In the absence of other references for particular letters and documents in this connection, the reader may assume that I am referring to this collection. For the letters and depositions published by TJ in 1800, see the Appendix attached to the *Notes on Virginia* (Peden, pp. 226–258).

[31] Sketch in *D.A.B.*

tin's letters, he expressed admiration for Jefferson, lamented the "disgraceful calumnies" circulated to his injury, and warned against the "wicked and malicious reports" circulated by "unprincipled men." This conversation, as he afterwards reported, "kindled a flame which flew through all the boarding houses" and so violently agitated a majority in the legislature that he believed they would have displaced him if they had had the power.[32] To this incident he and others attributed the election of James Lloyd as his successor in the Senate — a man whose later actions showed his desire to stamp the members of the Republican opposition as traitors.[33] Martin's efforts were achieving political results.

Governor Henry, who had perhaps expostulated more violently than he afterwards thought prudent but who gave the impression of a sincere desire to lessen the animosity to Jefferson, heard his side of the story from Martin, whom he described as his friend, and then approached Senator Henry Tazewell of Virginia. He asked his recent colleague "to press upon the mind of Mr. Jefferson the propriety of not adding unnecessarily to the number of his enemies," who, as God knew, were already numerous and bitter enough. He saw no good reason why Jefferson should not give speedy assurance to Martin that a correction would be made in the references to Cresap. He was sure, however, that whatever Jefferson did in this matter would be "strongly marked with that sincerity, candor and simplicity" which had "so eminently distinguished his character." [34]

This friendly intermediation gave the author of the *Notes on Virginia* an opportunity to state his position which he promptly seized upon. Writing the Governor, he said that if Luther Martin had made a proper inquiry he would have felt obliged to heed it.[35] "But he chose to step at once into the newspapers and . . . adopted a style which forbade the respect of an answer." He himself had instituted inquiries, however, and promised that the results would be printed in the next

[32] The incident described above is from a letter of Gov. Henry to Senator Henry Tazewell, Mar. 13, 1798 (LC, 17641–17642).

[33] This was in connection with the successive sedition bills; he was the author of the more extreme one, and joint author of the Sedition Act of 1798. On his election over Winder, the Governor's brother-in-law, see Wm. Hindman to R. King, Apr. 12, 1798 (King, II, 314); and Wm. Hindman to Wm. Hensley, Jr., Dec. 3, 1797 (King, II, 249). He won by a single vote.

[34] Dec. 24, 1797, without designation, but almost certainly addressed to Tazewell (Sowerby, pp. 305–306, from LC).

[35] His letter of Dec. 31 to Gov. Henry, which he afterwards placed at the beginning of the appendix to the *Notes*, is in Sowerby, III, 306–307; and Peden, pp. 226–229.

edition of the *Notes* or separately as an appendix. After giving a rather full account of his own receipt and use of the Logan story, he said:

> . . . If it shall appear on enquiry that Logan has been wrong in charging Cresap with the murder of his family, I will do justice to the memory of Cresap, as far as I have contributed to the injury by believing & repeating what others have believed & repeated before me. If, on the other hand, I find that Logan was right in his charge, I will vindicate as far as my suffrage may go, the truth of a Chief, whose talents & misfortunes have attached to him the respect & commiseration of the world.

To anyone genuinely concerned to arrive at truth and justice this statement should have been sufficient. Quite clearly, however, he was by no means convinced that an undeserved stain had been placed on Cresap's memory. Yielding nothing to those who believed that the only good Indian was a dead one, he had not gone over from Logan's side. He was quite willing for Governor Henry to use the communication in any way he might think proper, except to let it get into a newspaper. He would enter into no contest in that field.

Governor Henry, who promised to make use of this letter as occasion offered, continued to be appalled by the malignity with which Jefferson's enemies had reviewed all the incidents of his life. Never in his own experience, he said, had partisan misrepresentation gone so far.[36] Jefferson himself, quoting the well-known prayer — "Oh! that mine enemy would write a book!" — wrote a western friend in March: "I had written a book, and it has furnished matter of abuse for want of something better."[37] He said that the attack continued, and there is evidence that it found some support in Virginia. In *Porcupine's Gazette* he could have seen a communication from Francis Corbin, a man of some prominence, saying to Martin that the public approved his position and that Jefferson would have to render satisfaction. One of the latter's friends reported to him from Fredericksburg that the "furious invective" of Martin had been "publicly applauded" by Corbin in their own state.[38]

He himself said that he received every day bitter proofs of the violence of party passions — from people who knew of him only through

[36] To Tazewell, Mar. 13, 1798.
[37] To Dr. Samuel Brown, Mar. 25, 1798 (Ford, VII, 222–223).
[38] *Porcupine's Gazette*, Mar. 28, 1798; communication to Fenno in TJ's behalf by David Riddick (LC, 17688), and Riddick to TJ, Apr. 19, 1798 (LC, 17727); James Lewis, Jr., to TJ, May 4, 1798 (Sowerby, III, 310–311); TJ to Lewis, May 9, 1798 (Ford, VII, 249–250; partly in Sowerby).

Porcupine and Fenno. He believed, however, that the fever would not last. The Logan-Cresap episode had furnished the occasion for an attempt to write him down, but he correctly perceived that those who rejoiced in it did so on other grounds. While its echoes did not soon die away, if indeed they ever did, by the summer of 1798 the public was far more excited by other things and this became a minor episode.[39] Meanwhile, his friends rallied to him, especially in Virginia and Kentucky. One of the oldest of them thought that more should be done in his defense. John Page wrote him: "I admire your philosophical contempt of the malicious tales which party-spirit has indefatigably propagated respecting you, but I much doubt whether that philosophical disposition ought to be so much indulged, when the public good requires that the calumnies of a dangerous faction should be exposed in their true colours to the public view." He believed that if Jefferson's friends advised him not to defend himself, they should come forward and defend him.[40] From the West, however, he received words of approval for the policy of "silent contempt" of Martin, along with assurances that he had lost no support in that part of the country.[41]

The statements he made in private letters, chiefly to persons from whom he was seeking information, constituted his immediate efforts in his own defense. He had a few printed copies made of one letter of general explanation, and these he distributed carefully to persons on whom he could depend not to let them get into the papers.[42] For him this was a considerable indiscretion. In the whole matter he went much further than was customary with him when under attack. During the next two years he assiduously collected information from the relatively few living persons who were competent to speak about these events. By the time he was in a position to fulfill his promise to issue an appendix to the *Notes*, that is, early in 1800, he had come to definite conclusions about the matters in controversy. These he gave in several letters, and, in somewhat more measured language, in his appendix.[43]

[39] Martin himself was writing Gibson in 1800, as the latter told TJ on Mar. 14.

[40] Page to TJ, June 21, 1798 (LC, 17806–17808), referring to this attack and others.

[41] Dr. Samuel Brown to TJ, Sept. 4, 1798 (LC, 17861–17862).

[42] He referred to these in writing Dr. Samuel Brown, Mar. 25, 1798, and to others. I have not seen this printed statement, but it may be safely assumed that if it was not the letter to Gov. Henry it was something like it.

[43] Especially in letter of Mar. 14, 1800, to Gen. John Gibson. The entire appendix of 1800, including documents, is in Peden, pp. 226–258; TJ's historical statement with substitute passage is on pp. 250–254.

The authenticity of Logan's speech he had never questioned, but the testimony of General John Gibson, the original reporter of it, confirmed this to his entire satisfaction. Nor had he ever doubted that the allegations against Cresap which he had repeated were made by Logan in the first instance. The documents he collected, particularly one he got from Judge Harry Innes, fully supported him in this. With respect to the actual "murders," he found that common report had blended four incidents. Upon examination he concluded that Cresap was directly responsible for the first two of the killings, and that relatives of Logan were among his victims. He found that in the most notorious of them, the one at Yellow Creek (off the Ohio) and its immediate aftermath, constituting the third and fourth of the grim series, Daniel Greathouse was the leader, Cresap not being present. In Jefferson's opinion, however, the massacre at Yellow Creek was a direct consequence of the earlier actions and all of them were of a piece. While saying that the public could now judge for itself whether Cresap was innocent, he left no doubt of his own belief that the frontier Captain well deserved Logan's sad reproaches.

The letters, depositions, and other documents he printed in his appendix, though at variance in certain details, amply substantiated his position. In some of them the absence of Cresap from Yellow Creek was emphasized more strongly than in Jefferson's own statement; he probably regarded this physical fact as relatively unimportant in the entire chain of circumstances. After the first printing of the appendix, however, he promptly ordered another one, so as to include a recently received declaration which seemed to go further than any of the other documents in exculpating Cresap. John Sappington declared not only that the Captain had had no part in the Yellow Creek affair, but also that he hated the Greathouse family for it.[44] With this declaration, however, was printed a certified statement by the man who attested it, reporting other things Sappington had said which showed Cresap in a less favorable light. More important, in the eyes of some later scholars, is a fact which came out long afterward, namely, that Jefferson did not publish a letter from George Rogers Clark. Seizing upon this, some have claimed that he deliberately suppressed evidence favorable to Luther Martin's father-in-law.[45]

This letter was from the famous frontier soldier to Dr. Samuel Brown, who sent it to Jefferson from Lexington, Kentucky, and ad-

[44] Peden, pp. 255–257.
[45] Brantz Mayer made this charge in *Tah-Gah-Jute; or Logan and Cresap* (1867). In an earlier version of this, published under virtually the same title by the Md. Hist. Soc. in 1851, he included Clark's letter to Dr. Brown but did not then know that TJ had received it.

vised its publication.[46] While supporting the authenticity of Logan's speech and confirming the judgment that the Chief *thought* Cresap responsible for the most notorious killing, which Dr. Brown assumed were all that Jefferson wanted to establish, Clark virtually exculpated Cresap from blame for any in the series and gave him a good character. The reasons for the nonpublication of this letter can only be surmised. Jefferson wrote Dr. Brown: "Your brother has explained to you what was thought best about General Clark's deposition." [47] The brother in question almost certainly was Senator John Brown of Kentucky, a fellow lodger at Francis's Hotel with whom Jefferson could have easily talked in Philadelphia. A suggestion as to why the Vice President and the Senator thought the publication of Clark's letter unwise may be gained from a passage in the covering letter from Dr. Brown. In this the latter passed on with apparent approval the comment of another in regard to the existence of two parties in the region where these events occurred, as in most frontiers. "By the one Capt. Cresap was considered as a wanton violator of treaties [and] as a man of cruel and inhuman disposition; by the other he was esteemed as an intrepid warrior and a just avenger of savage barbarities." Adding that Clark joined Cresap on the warpath, Dr. Brown implied that the General belonged to the latter party.[48] Jefferson may well have concluded that this frontier hero, who was personally involved in all this business, was trying to apply a coat of whitewash to it. Since this letter did not alter his own judgment, we may assume that he regarded the testimony of Clark as unreliable. If he thought it discreditable he may have withheld it in order to shield one whose past deeds had been notable but whose conduct required considerable indulgence of judgment in later years. Viewing Cresap as Jefferson did, he would not have wanted to associate Clark with him in the public mind. And it would have been embarrassing to him to publish the document while repudiating its testimony. The old General was seeking to condone the barbarities of frontier warfare and Jefferson could not be a party to that.

It now seems, after the passing of these many years, that historical evidence supports Jefferson's judgment of Cresap rather than that of Clark and later defenders of the frontier Captain. Clark's letter is discredited by contemporary documents; and, entirely apart from Logan,

[46] Clark to Dr. Brown, June 17, 1798 (LC, 17801–17804; partly in Sowerby, III, 310); Brown to TJ, Sept. 4, 1798 (Sowerby, III, 309–310); both letters in Mayer.

[47] May 10, 1800 (Sowerby, III, 314). Actually it was a letter, not a deposition, and TJ spelt his name "Clarke," showing a degree of inaccuracy in minor matters.

[48] Sept. 4, 1798 (Sowerby, III, 309–310). By implication, also, TJ in Williamsburg was sympathetic with the former. Mayer omits this part of Brown's letter as irrelevant (p. 159).

contemporary opinion laid the major blame for the series of killings on Cresap, who seems unquestionably to have committed some of the "murders." He was reported at the time to have threatened to kill every Indian on the river and to attack the village at Yellow Creek if he could get enough men together. If anything, Jefferson seems to have understated the case against him.[49]

Also, it appears that the historian who first gave currency to the charge of the deliberate suppression of Clark's letter because it absolved Cresap, himself distorted or disregarded evidence on the other side.[50] A generation after the death of the author of the *Notes on Virginia*, this critic of him said: "It is not improbable that party feeling — then quite as venomous as in later days — may have swayed Jefferson's mind from the justice which should govern historians in regard to even the humblest of whom they write." He described Jefferson's unwillingness to grant Cresap full exculpation as "a sad picture of the infirmity of a nature which was not proof against political passion, and was known to be ambitious, at least of seeming to be never mistaken." [51] The man who was thus described did not like to admit himself in error but unquestionably he had done so in part, a thing which could not be said of Luther Martin. He had displayed far less venomous passions than his political enemies. Present-day scholars may regret that he did not publish *all* the documents, but they can hardly fail to recognize his shrewdness in assaying evidence and would have difficulty in proving that he did not render essential justice.

Perhaps the most valid criticism of him as a scholar to which this episode gives ground is that, while realistic about the barbarities of the frontier, he continued to view the Indians through a considerable haze of sentimentality.[52] His determination to uphold the honor and dignity of the American aborigines was shown in other ways at just the time he was completing his appendix. Accepting an offer of two Indian busts of stone found on the Cumberland, he went to great pains to get them delivered by way of New Orleans. Such monuments

[49] Irving Brant, who deals with the entire episode in *Madison*, I, 281–291, has gone into the contemporary evidence with care.

[50] It seems to me that Brant presents convincing evidence in support of this severe charge.

[51] Mayer, pp. vi, vii.

[52] His scientific friend Benjamin S. Barton afterwards (1806) expressed grave doubts that Logan's speech had ever been delivered (title of pamphlet of that year and correspondence with TJ in Sowerby, III, 357). These doubts were inspired by Barton's reading a version of the speech of one "Lonan" in the *Travels* of the Abbé Robin. This speech, which Mayer claimed was the first version of Logan's, has been described as a caricature by Brant, who shows that the first version was given out by Madison and was very like the one TJ used (*Madison*, I, 285).

of the state of the arts among the Indians, he believed, would furnish new and strong proofs of how far the patience and perseverance of the Indian artist made up for his limited means of execution.[53] Also he continued to seek and acquire Indian vocabularies. That year one of his correspondents who had previously sent him Creek and Chickasaw words sent him words of the Choctaws.[54] His interest was not merely that of an enthusiastic student of language and ethnology, though he was that; he was deeply concerned to do justice to those who, in his opinion, received less of it than the frontiersman. If against Cresap, he was *for* Logan. And he was never so likely to overreach himself as when defending things which he regarded as distinctively American.

[53] TJ to Morgan Brown, Jan. 16, 1800 (LC, 18133) and to Gen. James Wilkinson on that date (LC, 18132).

[54] Benj. Hawkins to TJ, Nov. 6, 1800 (LC, 18434), and other letters.

The Crisis of
Republican Freedom

[XXIII]

A Desperate Holding Operation

1798

AT ALMOST the end of his days Jefferson described his services to his country and party during the second session of the Fifth Congress as among the most important he ever performed.[1] They seemed that in long retrospect, but he did not forget that to him both as a patriot and a party leader this period was one of the gloomiest and most frustrating of his entire public career. Midway in the course of what is sometimes designated as the XYZ Congress, events in France played into the hands of the extreme Federalists so that they attained a dominance in the government such as they had never had before. They maintained this until the last year of the administration, when honest John Adams, finally sensing that he had been held captive by men whose views went far beyond his own, shook off their control. In the year 1798, however, he appeared to be the beneficiary of the hysterical patriotism which the actions of the French engendered, riding on a higher tide of popularity than at any previous time, while this same tide threatened to engulf Jefferson and the opposition. Therefore, the service the Vice President performed was that of holding on. Its importance depends on the value which may be set on the survival of a party of opposition in a self-governing society, and on what this particular party and its leader did for the country in later years. He properly recognized that Albert Gallatin should share any credit that might be given him; and no historian need hesitate to say that if the survival of Republicanism at the seat of government did not depend on these two men, it very nearly did.[2]

[1] February, 1826, in what is probably the most moving account of his services (Ford, X, 368–369).
[2] Note the comments of Henry Adams, *Gallatin*, p. 206.

Actually, Jefferson did not endure the whole of this painful session of Congress, for he arrived about a month late and left several weeks before the end.[3] His delay in arriving was caused in the first place by an accident to Maria: before her departure from Monticello with her newly wedded husband, Jack Eppes, she fell out of a door. In the second place, he was taken with one of his rare colds during a period of uncommonly bad weather, which also rendered the rivers unfordable.[4] He rightly anticipated that as vice president he would have very little to do anyway. When he got to Philadelphia his official duties left him plenty of time to read Luther Martin's letter about Captain Michael Cresap if he wanted to.[5] Congress itself could do little but await word from the envoys extraordinary to France; and if the news was favorable to peace, as he sanguinely expected it would be, he saw no reason why they should not all go home. But when official news came in March, it proved to be far from favorable.

The only home he had in Philadelphia was at Francis's Hotel, where he had rooms. This was about three blocks from Congress Hall in State House Square. His social life appears to have been as restricted as it was the previous summer, if not more so. A few weeks after his arrival he wrote a nostalgic letter to Angelica Church, whom he had known so well abroad before ever he came into conflict with her brother-in-law, Alexander Hamilton. In this he said: "Party animosities here have raised a wall of separation between those who differ in political sentiments." [6] Apart from his fellows in the American Philosophical Society, many of whom were in fact Republicans, he associated with public men of his own persuasion. Every day he dined with a group of congressmen and senators, engaging in familiar conversation which was largely political, no doubt.[7]

A Federalist congressman had supposed that the "Antis" would reach no decisions until Jefferson and Giles arrived, but the latter, who had been married the previous spring, did not get there until February.[8] In the absence of Madison, Gallatin stood without a peer among the Republicans in the House and if any single man was re-

[3] The session lasted from Nov. 13, 1797 to July 16, 1798; he was there from Dec. 12, 1797 to June 27, 1798.
[4] TJ to Senator Henry Tazewell, Nov. 28, 1797, explaining the circumstances (LC, 17509).
[5] Dec. 11, 1797; see previous chapter, note 30.
[6] TJ to Mrs. Church, Jan. 11, 1798 (LC, 17553). Ford (VI, 115) wrongly dates this letter Oct. 1792. TJ also wrote an affectionate letter on Jan. 11 to Kitty Church, telling her about her friends Maria and Martha (LC, 17552).
[7] To John Wise, Feb. 12, 1798 (A.H.R., III, 488-489).
[8] W. Hindman to W. Hensley, Jr., Dec. 3, 1797 (King, II, 250); Anderson, Giles, p. 57.

sponsible for the formulation of policy there it was he. The part that Jefferson played in this is virtually impossible to discover since his activities in this connection were not of the sort that are reflected in written records. In his letters to Madison, Monroe, and other old friends he sounds more like a reporter than a participant. The best guess is that, while frequently consulted by Republicans, he left tactics to the men actually on the field of battle, remaining a symbol and rallying center. That he and Gallatin were in full agreement in all basic matters may be assumed, though of the two he tended to be the more sanguine.

Republican absentees were a continuing problem to the party leaders, and Gallatin reported to his wife that there was a shortage of good speakers on his side of the House.[9] John Nicholas, a Virginian but not to be confused with the Clerk of Albemarle County who was writing insinuating letters to George Washington, was one of the best. Judging from the early votes, Jefferson concluded that, despite the absentees, the Republicans were stronger than the Federalists in the House on all "strong questions" by a majority of about half a dozen.[10] Later, he revised his estimate downward, figuring that the "whigs" were in a minority of four.[11] Others agreed with him that the margin was small, one way or the other; and it became apparent in these early months that no obviously warlike measure could command a majority. The main purpose of the opposition party was to prevent anything much from happening; and, with the aid of moderate Federalists, they were generally successful until bad news came from France.[12]

Of the body over which he himself presided Jefferson expected nothing good, since the Federalists had a majority of more than two to one. The question of the impeachment of William Blount, who was expelled from the Senate in the previous summer after Jefferson himself had gone home, came up early in the year.[13] After the House had drawn articles, the next move had to be made in the Senate, where, as he put it, many knotty problems arose. The proceedings did not really begin until another year, but his attitude at this time is of interest, especially in view of the impeachments during his own presidency in another decade under quite different circumstances. Though party attitudes on this particular question continued to be confused, and in his opinion the anti-republicans would have liked to get out of it, his

[9] Feb. 18, 1798 (Adams, *Gallatin*, p. 193).
[10] To Monroe, Dec. 27, 1797 (Ford, VII, 183).
[11] He judged by the vote on the foreign intercourse question; to Monroe, Mar. 8, 1798 (Ford, VII, 215).
[12] The legend of votes in Dauer, *Adams Federalists*, p. 304, shows this.
[13] See above, ch. XX, note 17.

own sympathies were now with Blount — who, although charged with conniving with the British, was after all a Republican and might be regarded in some sense as an object of persecution. In private Jefferson supported the position of Senator Tazewell of his state that Blount should be given a jury trial. He based his opinion on the amendment to the Constitution in the bill of rights which provided that there should be jury trials in all cases of criminal prosecution.[14] He sent Tazewell legal references which he spent an evening digging up, to show that impeachment even for a misdemeanor was a criminal prosecution. He mentioned this matter in several letters to Madison, revealing his fears as he viewed a body in which the party division was 22 to 10 without prospect of change. "I see nothing in the mode of proceeding by impeachment but the most formidable weapon for the purposes of a dominant faction that ever was contrived," he said. "It would be the most effectual one for getting rid of any man whom they consider as dangerous to their views, and I do not know that we could count on one third on an emergency." [15]

Madison did not go along with Jefferson's constitutional argument. Neither did the Senate, though in the end that body declared Blount unimpeachable. The Vice President's concern at this time and throughout the rest of this administration was for the protection of minorities and individuals. Also, he deeply distrusted this body of men, chosen for long terms which Adams had told him should be even longer so that they might bear up against "all popular storms and passions." They consider themselves as the "bulwarks of the government," Jefferson said, "and will be rendering that the more secure, in proportion as they can assume greater powers." [16] This was no popularly elected body carrying out a mandate of the sovereign people; the Senate, as he was well aware, had consistently done the bidding of Hamilton.

Certain minor episodes which enlivened these weeks of waiting for news from the distant envoys were learned of by Jefferson second-hand and reported only briefly to his absent friends. There was, for example, the ball on February 22 in honor of George Washington which faced the Federalists with a ceremonial dilemma, since some, including Abigail Adams, thought this a reflection on her husband the

[14] Using the enumeration of the amendments as introduced he cited the Eighth, meaning the Sixth as adopted. To Tazewell, Jan. 27, 1798 (Ford, VII, 194–195), with attached references (LC, 17563–17566).

[15] To Madison, Feb. 15, 1798 (Ford, VII, 202); and also Jan. 24, Feb. 8, 22, 1798 (Ford, VII, 192–193, 195–196, 207–208); to Monroe, Feb. 8, 1798 (Ford, VII, 198–199); from Madison, Mar. 4, 1798 (MP, 20:90).

[16] Ford, VII, 208.

President. Using a mixed agricultural metaphor, Jefferson remarked that it had "sown tares among the exclusive federals" and had also "winnowed the grain from the chaff." The sincere Adamites did not go, he said, while the Washingtonians went religiously and viewed the "secession" of the others with "high dudgeon." About all one can be sure of from his report is that he rejoiced in any sort of dissension among the "federals" and that he approved of the attendance of the "whigs" (not including himself) as showing that the celebration was of the man, not the office. That is, they took no stock in ceremonialism that smacked of royalty.[17] Madison, whose comments on Adams at this stage were more extensive and more critical than Jefferson's and who contrasted him unfavorably with Washington, stressed the "hypocritical professions of attachment" to the latter.[18]

There was a degree of humor in this episode which the Vice President seems to have missed, and there was comedy in the fracas in the House of Representatives between Matthew Lyon of Vermont and Roger Griswold of Connecticut which would not be suspected from such comments as he left. Lyon was a rough example of democracy, and the Connecticut gentlemen, according to Gallatin and others, had got into the habit of saying hard things, making a particular target of one whom they regarded as a "low-life fellow." Griswold charged him with cowardice when they were in a group talking at the back of the House chamber, and Lyon retaliated for the insult by spitting in Griswold's face. The episode, which was made to order for the lampoonist, reverberated in the House. The motion to expel the rude representative from Vermont commanded a majority vote but lacked the necessary two-thirds. When his colleagues failed to avenge him Griswold took matters into his own hands. Finding Lyon in his seat a few days later (this was after prayers but before the Speaker had called the House to order), he attacked him with a cane, somewhat as Congressman Brooks of South Carolina attacked Senator Charles Sumner of Massachusetts more than a half century later, though the parallel was imperfect. Lyon (whose name led to innumerable puns) escaped from his desk and defended himself with fire tongs. Since the honors were now approximately even, it was moved that both men be reprimanded. The nays had it, however, by one vote.[19] Jefferson, who was habitually polite, spoke of the "disgusting proceedings," but

[17] To Madison, Mar. 2, 1798 (Ford, VII, 211–212). On the celebration see Dauer, p. 140. Adams himself declined and Gallatin did not attend.

[18] To Jefferson, Mar. 12, 1798 (MP, 20:92); for an extended contrast of Washington and Adams, see his letter of Feb. 1798 (Hunt, VI, 310).

[19] The incident is well described in Adams, *Gallatin*, pp. 191–192; and from the Federalist point of view by James A. Bayard, in *A.H.A. Report, 1913*, II, 148.

what he had particularly in mind was the effort to expel Lyon; the main object of this, in his opinion, was to get rid of this Republican's vote. There is no recorded intimation that he saw anything comic in the situation. Madison regarded the whole affair as "extremely disgraceful," and beyond a doubt there was plenty of disgrace to go around.[20]

What Jefferson thought of the party situation at the time, and more particularly the political terminology, is well stated in a letter he wrote in February. This was not to a political intimate who already knew the state of his mind and needed from him no measured and balanced judgment, but was in response to a polite request for explanation from one whom he supposed to be on the other side. John Wise of his own state, hearing that in conversation at Francis's Hotel the Vice President had spoken of him as being "of Tory politics," wanted to know just what he meant. If Wise was trying to embarrass Jefferson the latter gentleman does not appear to have thought so. His own reply, while candid, was a model of good manners and good taste.[21] Why his relatively unguarded expression, in familiar conversation with gentlemen who ate with him every day, should have been repeated, he said that he did not know or ask. It was intended as no personal reflection on Wise, at any rate, and was based indeed on secondhand information which might have been incorrect. If it was correct, however, Wise was entitled to his own political convictions. In other words, the two of them could differ as free men and gentlemen. This was to put political disagreement on a higher plane than it currently occupied in the halls of Congress.

That there was a sharp difference in the country, however, he frankly recognized, and he thought it could be best designated by the terms whig and tory. He did not here speak of the "spirit of 1776," as he so often did in this period, but obviously it was on his mind.

> . . . It is now well understood [he said] that two political Sects have arisen within the U. S. the one believing that the executive is the branch of our government which the most needs support; the other that like the analogous branch in the English Government, it is already too strong for the republican parts of the constitution; and therefore in equivocal cases they incline to the legislative powers: the former of these are called federalists, sometimes aristocrats or monocrats, and sometimes tories, after

[20] TJ to Madison, Feb. 15, 1798 (Ford, VII, 202); Madison to TJ, Mar. 4, 1798 (MP, 20:90).
[21] To John Wise, Feb. 12, 1798 (*A.H.R.*, III, 488–489), replying to a letter of Jan. 28 (Bixby, pp. 69–70).

the corresponding sect in the English Government of exactly the same definition: the latter are stiled republicans, whigs, jacobins, disorganizers &C. . . . both parties claim to be federalists and republicans, and I believe with truth as to the great mass of them: these appelations therefore designate neither exclusively, and all the others are slanders, except those of whig and tory which alone characterize the distinguishing principles of the two Sects as I have before explained them: . . .

The thought that virtually all were federalists (that is, supporters of the Constitution and its basic principle), and virtually all republicans (that is, believers in a republic rather than a monarchy) reappeared in classic phrase in his first inaugural address three years later. That it was his conviction, or at least his faith, with respect to the people generally can hardly be doubted, but he judged certain leaders quite differently and in indiscreet or unguarded private utterances he used some of the appellations that he here described as slanderous. He did not do so in public, however, and not even in his wildest moments did he describe the monarchical-aristocratic faction as anything but small. Even in the Mazzei letter he was castigating leaders, but those whom he called tories said that was just what a patriotic citizen should not do. As the leader of the unrecognized opposition he himself was perhaps the chief sufferer of the time in this regard.

The asperity of partisan conflict in Congress, which was physically demonstrated in the Lyon-Griswold episode, is attested by many comments. Early in February a Federalist senator wrote George Washington: "The legislature is much divided, and the parties in it as much embittered against each other as it is possible to conceive." [22] The consistent Federalist line, which Washington himself was taking, was that in a time of danger a factious group were opposing all measures of the government and seeking to undermine the Constitution. Some two months later, when in fact the tide had turned strongly in the administration's favor, Senator Theodore Sedgwick of Massachusetts wrote Rufus King in London that the session had been disagreeable and almost entirely unproductive. He blamed the House, which was almost evenly divided: there were, he said, "52 determined and rancorous Jacobins, and 54 who profess attachment to the government, or in other words, confidence in the Executive." The former, under the control of the Genevese Gallatin, were "a well organized and disciplined Corps, never going astray, or doing right even by mistake." Comment-

[22] James Ross of Pa., to Washington, Feb. 2, 1798, with Washington's reply of Feb. 12 (Fitzpatrick, XXXVI, 164 and note).

ing on the unpleasantness of the position of the Vice President, this High Federalist said: "More than once he has heard, in debates, and in terms which could not be mistaken, Philippics pronounced against the author of the letter to Mazzei. He is, I have no doubt, the very life and soul of the opposition." [23]

The Vice President, doomed to silent endurance in the Senate, was not in position to hear the reading of a garbled version of the now notorious letter in the House. One of the gentlemen of Connecticut, who were charged with the habitual use of hard language, made it a part of the record, saying that "nothing but treason and insurrection would be the consequence of such opinions." [24] This was in connection with the debate over the foreign intercourse bill which raged intermittently during a period of about six weeks, and in the course of which both the "whigs" and the "tories" took extreme positions. The former, solidly supporting the Nicholas amendment, which was aimed at cutting down the size of the diplomatic establishment and curbing executive patronage, advanced isolationist arguments such as Jefferson had found unpalatable when he himself was secretary of state.[25] Nicholas expressed the same sort of doubts about foreign ministers that Jefferson had once deplored, and even the judicious Gallatin was dubious about commercial treaties, the importance of which Jefferson had stressed and which he had labored to negotiate. The Vice President made no analysis of this particular bill and this amendment. He informed Madison that a motion had been made to reduce foreign intercourse to what it was before the extension of 1796, which probably accorded with his own present emphasis on economy and the reduction of executive power. He wrote this confidant that the debate would probably have good effects on the public mind, but that the advocates of the "reformation" expected to lose the question.[26] Regarding the attack on foreign intercourse, Gallatin wrote his wife: "We have made it violent because it is of importance that we should begin to assume that high tone which we must necessarily support in case of worse news from France, and because there is no other way to make any important impression upon public opinion." [27] Whether or not Jefferson shared this political judgment, there were other things which

[23] Sedgwick to King, Apr. 9, 1798 (King, II, 310–311). The figures he gave differed little from TJ's estimate of 51 to 55; he allowed for a few waverers.

[24] Joshua Coit, Feb. 28, 1798 (*Annals*, 5 Cong. 2 sess., pp. 1100–1101). Like the *Minerva* version of the Mazzei letter, from which this version derived, it contained a concluding passage not in the original and repeated other errors (see above, ch. XIX, note 28).

[25] See above, ch. I, with references in note 20.

[26] Jan. 24, 1798 (Ford, VII, 192).

[27] Jan. 19, 1798 (Adams, *Gallatin*, p. 189).

concerned him considerably more than this particular amendment — such as preventing the grant to private vessels of the right to arm, which would increase the likelihood of war in his opinion.

Gallatin's speech on foreign intercourse on March 1 has been described by his biographer as probably the best ever made on the side of the opposition in the period of Federalist rule, and also as "in effect a vigorous and eloquent defence" of the Mazzei letter, though this was barely mentioned.[28] The ablest of the Republican congressmen referred to the representation the day before — by Joshua Coit, who read the letter — that it was criminal to believe in the existence of a "Monarchico, Aristocratic Faction" wishing to impose on Americans the substance of the British government. Gallatin's own tone was far more temperate than that assumed by some on the other side, and his speech was unmarred by the arrogance which was so rife among the High Federalists. But it was a powerful attack on a system the extension of which would be, in his opinion, fatal to the country, and by the same token it was a stalwart defense of the right and duty of opposing that system. In his determination that it should go no farther he stood shoulder to shoulder with the Vice President, whose notable services to the cause of American freedom he implicitly extolled while modestly minimizing his own.

Shortly after this, the *Aurora*, referring to Congressman Coit's action, said that the Mazzei letter could stand on its own legs, since the facts mentioned in it were so obvious that they could be denied only by those who were uninformed or lacking in candor.[29] This assertion was followed by a far-fetched argument that the President of the United States was more of an absolute monarch than the King of England, and it was accompanied by aspersions on particular leaders, including Washington. That was not the reason why, a few days later, that distinguished patriot, finally convinced of Jefferson's perfidious designs by Clerk Nicholas of Albemarle County, wrote "finis" to their long-standing friendship.[30] But these things occurred about the same time in the same atmosphere of partisan rancor and the mistrust engendered by it.

The speech of Robert Goodloe Harper of South Carolina, the day after that of Gallatin, merits no encomium from historians, though they may cite it as an extreme sample of distortion.[31] In it he directly

28 Adams, *Gallatin*, pp. 197–198; the speech of Mar. 1, 1798 is in *Annals*, 5 Cong. I, 1118–1143, and was published as a pamphlet at the time (Philadelphia, 1798).

29 *Aurora*, Mar. 5, 1798.

30 To John Nicholas, Mar. 8, 1798 (Fitzpatrick, XXXVI, 182–184), apropos of the John Langhorne episode; see above, ch. XIX and note 49.

31 March 2, 1798 (*Annals*, 5 Cong., I, 1159–1200).

attacked an individual, attaching a footnote to the text so there could
be no possible doubt that he was speaking of the Vice President of
the United States. His explanation of the conflict over foreign policy
at least had the merit of simplicity. He charged that the "system" of
alliance with France and war against England was *imported* into the
United States by the French revolutionists by means of a missionary.
"The missionary arrived, who was to convert us to this new faith;
and this missionary was a citizen of our own, who was recalled from
public employment in that country, to fill a high official station here."
Then a French minister arrived to second his efforts.[32] This High Federalist overlooked a couple of decades of history, failing to mention
that the alliance dated from the American Revolution when war with
England was actually going on, and making no reference to the "spirit
of 1776." The incorrectness of his comments on the neutrality policy
of 1793 are scarcely forgivable, in view of the fact that so much of
the record had been made public, and there was no possible excuse
for the assertion that Jefferson had supported war while Hamilton
upheld neutrality. Not even the British said that at the time of Jefferson's retirement from office. Hamilton, of course, was depicted by this
speaker as the innocent victim of persecution by the press under Jefferson's direction. The invective which had flowed so copiously from
Hamilton's own pen was ignored altogether. This was a political tirade pure and simple. It deserves mention here only because it clearly
showed that the High Federalists regarded the Vice President as the
leader of the opposition, and that they would stickle at no misrepresentation in their effort to destroy him.

Early in the year 1798 unfavorable rumors about the mission to
France reached Philadelphia and these soon spread to Virginia. There
Madison analyzed the prospects more realistically than his more sanguine friend Jefferson could yet bring himself to do. Besides being
apprehensive about the spirit in which the negotiations would be conducted — on the American side and possibly on that of the French also
— he perceived the almost insuperable difficulties that were imposed
by the "insidious" Jay treaty. These could be resolved, he believed,
only by (1) dissolving the treaty, or (2) "stipulating with France that
she may plunder us as we have stipulated that Great Britain may
plunder us." Obviously doubting that either alternative would be accepted, he expected retaliatory action on the part of France, as indeed
Jefferson did in his less sanguine moments. Madison thought it less
likely that the United States would go directly to war than that it

[32] *Ibid.*, I, 1192.

would do so indirectly by using frigates as convoys, and so forth. His judgment that in either case the nation would be acting in defense of the British treaty, which had itself been adopted on the ground that it would prevent war, was sound enough in the light of the information then available, before word of further French provocations had been received, and the prognostications of this retired statesman were largely borne out by subsequent events.[33]

In the emotional atmosphere of the capital Jefferson indulged himself somewhat more in what a later generation would term wishful thinking. At this stage his conviction that the French would not make war on the United States may have been based in part on indirect word from their country. Writing Madison, he reported: "A letter is certainly received here by an individual from Talleyrand, which says our envoys have been heard, that their pretensions are high, that possibly no arrangement may take place, but that there will be no declaration of war by France." [34] He did not place much reliance in Talleyrand, however, and frankly stated that he was "entirely suspended" as to what was to be expected. That he did not anticipate a French attack on the United States is obvious from many other references, nonetheless, and in the light of history his judgment on this point was a sound one. It was shared by the British government. His confident references to the projected French invasion of England, which were several times repeated, now seem unrealistic because it never came off, and on other grounds they are much harder to justify. He was hopeful of this invasion, not because it might result in conquest — which he believed impossible — but because it would lead to the "republicanization" of that country and thus strengthen the cause of freedom by virtue of this example.[35] If this suggests that his inveterate fear of the British still blinded him to the imperialistic aims of the French, it shows, also, that the prime issue in his own mind was the preservation of the republican institutions and liberties of his own country. To this end his main concern was and continued to be the maintenance of peace.

The first official communication of news from France was on the very day that the Nicholas amendment to the foreign intercourse bill was defeated in the House by four votes. On March 5, Adams reported

[33] Madison to TJ, Jan. 21, Feb. 12, 1798 (MP, 20:79, 85).

[34] Jan. 24, 1798 (MP, 20:81; or Ford, VII, 192, where it is wrongly dated). This became a favorite reference with later writers of the Federalist tradition who sought to show "seditious" correspondence.

[35] TJ to TMR, Jan. 11, 1798 (LC, 17554), and to Peregrine Fitzhugh, Feb. 23, 1798 (Ford, VII, 210-211). In his letter of June 7, 1798 to Madison (Ford, VII, 268), he was still talking hopefully of this prospect.

to Congress that the first dispatches from the envoys had been received and were being deciphered. Because of its importance to the mercantile interest he immediately communicated the last dispatch, relating to a proposal of the Directory, certain of adoption, that neutral ships bearing English merchandise or commodities should be subject to seizure. That is, the flag would not cover the property; free ships would not make free goods. The members of Congress could also read, in the covering letter from the envoys, that the latter had no hope of being received by the French government or of accomplishing the objects of their mission.[36]

Jefferson, who had convinced himself that no news was good news, had written Madison only a few days earlier that the silence of the envoys was admitted to augur peace.[37] He now said that the French decree had struck the greatest alarm among the merchants that he had ever witnessed, and he foresaw as its probable result the driving of American vessels from the British trade. Despite the sensation created by the decree, however, he believed that among the merchants the sentiment against the arming of private vessels was still growing. He did not think that the "partizans of Republican government should despair."[38] The failure of the mission to France this stubborn optimist did not yet admit.

Adams reported that failure to Congress on March 19, saying that the dispatches had been considered and that he saw no hope that the objects of the mission could be accomplished, though everything that could be done had been done. Without revealing the dispatches he reiterated his former recommendations, urging upon Congress the prompt adoption of measures for the protection of commerce, the defense of exposed territory, and the provision of necessary military supplies and revenue. In other words, the rights of the nation were threatened and it should assume the posture of defense.[39] Jefferson referred to this as a war message, describing it as "insane" or at least "almost insane." He fully recognized its political effect: "Exultation on the one side, and a certainty of victory; while the other is petrified with astonishment."[40]

Believing that the supreme desideratum was to avoid everything warlike and gain time, he himself favored two actions: (1) since the

[36] A.S.P.F.R., II, 150–151.

[37] Mar. 2, 1798 (Ford, VII, 213).

[38] To Monroe, Mar. 8, 1798; to Madison, Mar. 15 (Ford, VII, 213–218).

[39] Mar. 19, 1798 (A.S.P.F.R., II, 152).

[40] To Madison, Mar. 21, 1798 (Ford, VII, 219). See also TJ to Monroe, Mar. 21, and to Edmund Pendleton, Apr. 2 (Ford, VII, 221–222, 227–230).

President had removed the executive prohibition of the arming of merchant vessels, Congress should impose one; (2) Congress should adjourn, and its members go home to consult their constituents. He also reported with apparent approval that the whigs would call for the papers. They did not take up his particular proposals. Instead, they offered what are known as the Sprigg Resolutions, which, while not unfavorable to limited defense measures, began with the statement that it was inexpedient to go to war with France.[41] Jefferson wrote Madison: "If we could but gain this season, we should be saved." [42] Believing that the pacific spirit was far greater in the country as a whole than in Congress, and viewing the approaching congressional elections with considerable confidence, he wrote Edmund Pendleton that the only source of anxiety was to avoid war at the present moment. If war should be forced on the country, the "tory element" would continue dominant and to them it would be left "to ride on the whirlwind and direct the storm" — a thing which in his opinion they alone desired to do. Continuing, he said: "The present period, therefore, of two or three weeks, is the most eventful ever known since that of 1775, and will decide whether the principles established by that contest are to prevail, or give way to those they subverted." [43]

That same day, the House by a large majority called for the papers. The Republicans, who took the initiative without realizing that they were loosing a boomerang, were joined by the Hamiltonians, who had good reason to surmise what was in the dispatches.[44] Adams submitted the famous XYZ Papers the next day.[45] By a surprising majority of more than three to one the House voted against their publication, but since the Senate promptly voted for it they were soon printed and widely distributed. Before they were officially released, reports of them got out. Jefferson regarded some of those that got into print as the "most artful misrepresentations," saying that they "produced such a shock on the republican mind" as had not been seen since the winning of independence.[46] His own reputation was involved. He wrote Monroe on the day Congress got the dispatches:

[41] The Sprigg Resolutions were offered Mar. 27; see Dauer, p. 146.

[42] Mar. 29, 1798 (Ford, VII, 225).

[43] Apr. 2, 1798 (Ford, VII, 229).

[44] TJ described this group as the Pinckney interest, from Thomas Pinckney who was now in Congress, but said that it was really the Hamilton party (to Madison, Apr. 5, 1798; Ford, VII, 230–231). Dauer, discussing this (p. 142), says that the vote was "significant in the highest degree." It was 65 to 27.

[45] Apr. 3, 1798. He communicated later dispatches on May 4. For both sets see A.S.P.F.R., II, 153–182.

[46] To Madison, Apr. 6, 1798 (Ford, VII, 236).

. . . At this moment my name is running through all the city as detected in a criminal correspondence with the French directory, & fixed upon me by the documents from our envoys now before the two houses. The detection of this by the publication of the papers, should they be published, will not relieve all the effects of the lie, and should they not be published, they may keep it up as long and as successfully as they did and do that of my being involved in Blount's conspiracy. . . .[47]

Full publication was far better from his point of view than "artful misrepresentation" or wild rumor, but the full story was certainly bad enough.

It now became a matter of common knowledge that the envoys had never been formally received, that they had had to deal with minor persons (publicly designated as X, Y, and Z), and that they had received proposals ranging from the impossible to the insulting. Specifically, these alphabetical emissaries proposed as a condition of the formal reception of the Americans and the beginning of actual negotiation: that they disavow certain passages in Adams's speech of May, 1797; that they provide a douceur of some £50,000 for the "pocket" of the Directory and ministers; that they offer a large loan to France. The most memorable sentence in these sensational papers was the American reply to a request for money: "No; no; not a sixpence." [48] To several letters to the Minister of Foreign Affairs the commissioners had received no answer. In later dispatches, submitted a month later, they included a full and powerful statement that John Marshall drew. Neither Congress nor the public had that at the moment, but they had enough to raise national indignation and national patriotism to a fever pitch. The Sprigg Resolutions were postponed, now that it appeared that the United States had been asked to buy peace with France, and the Republicans were placed in a desperate position.

Commenting on the XYZ revelations to his most important political correspondent as soon as he felt free to do so, Jefferson said that the "base propositions" for a bribe and the unworthy arguments to which the French agent resorted were "calculated to excite disgust and indignation in Americans generally," and to alienate Republicans in particular. The latter would naturally resent the presumption that they put attachment to France and hatred of the Federalists above their love of country. He rightly feared that "wavering characters" would "go over to the war measures so furiously pushed by the other party" in

[47] Apr. 5, 1798 (Ford, VII, 233).
[48] *A.S.P.F.R.*, II, 161.

order to "wipe off the imputation of being French partisans." [49] On analysis of the revelations as a whole, however, he concluded that they offered no additional motive for the United States to go to war. Therefore, in a time of patriotic excitement which verged on hysteria, he continued to be chiefly concerned to calm the war spirit and preserve the Republican opposition.

Jefferson entered into no public discussion of the XYZ dispatches, and Madison wisely disregarded the suggestion that he do so. Any attempt to make these disclosures seem less disagreeable than they first appeared would have unquestionably been attributed to political partisanship, as indeed it should have been in part, and designated as unpatriotic, even seditious. To have vied with the extremists on the other side in public expressions of patriotic devotion and denunciation of the French would have been wholly out of character for Jefferson. The author of the Declaration of Independence saw no need to resort to such devices in order to vindicate his patriotism, and he certainly had no reason to assert his love of country in private letters to intimates. In these, and presumably in conversation with fellow Republicans, he put the best face he could on the deeply embarrassing disclosures.[50] While in no sense condoning the solicitation of a bribe, he was disposed to blame this either on the "swindlers" into whose hands the envoys fell or on Talleyrand, the foreign minister, whom he described as a man "of most noted ill fame." Madison remarked on the stupidity of this action more pointedly than he did, but Jefferson was unwilling to attribute it to the French government. He said that knowledge of it by the Directory was not only unproved but improbable.[51] This, of course, was what he wanted to believe.

To this critic of the foreign policy of the administration the most significant revelation was that Adams's speech of the previous May was the first and major obstacle to successful negotiation. That, under the circumstances, it was an undiplomatic speech may be conceded, and Jefferson's own resentment of it was natural because of its reference to events connected with the leave-taking of his friend Monroe and its intimations that the French were working through the Republican party.[52] But it was not to be expected that the American envoys

[49] To Madison, Apr. 6, 1798 (Ford, VII, 235–238).

[50] He followed essentially the same line in his letters of Apr. 6, 12, 1798 to Madison and of Apr. 12 to Peter Carr (Ford, VII, 234–240), and also in that of Apr. 12 to TMR (LC, 17715).

[51] Ford, VII, 238. For Madison's comments, see his letter to TJ, Apr. 15, 1798 (Hunt, VI, 315).

[52] The particular passages in Adams's speech to which the French objected,

would disavow the words of the President who sent them, or would seize upon the alternative of a large loan to France. Jefferson himself did not say that they should have done either, but in trying to fix the responsibility for failure he indulged in oversimplification. On the American side the basic difficulty lay in Federalist policy as a whole from the spring of 1794 onward, as he and Madison often said. That policy made the maintenance of fair neutrality, with reference to France, virtually impossible. But the attempt to blame the recent failure on the American government, by stress on the tactical errors of the moment, was labored and injudicious. To Jefferson the danger of French dominance of American policy always seemed more remote than that of British dominance, and at this stage he had no sufficient reason to distinguish between the purposes of Adams and those of the High Federalists. His private utterances must be weighed against the violent public expressions on the other side in this time of intense emotionalism, but they do not do justice to the basic realism of his position. He was entirely correct in his frequently expressed conviction that nothing in the existing foreign situation gave sufficient grounds for war or for the disappearance of the party of opposition.

From his point of view the domestic outlook became much worse before it got any better. During the remaining weeks of the congressional session the sensations created by the late publication increased rather than diminished. A serious exodus of Republican legislators followed. He reported to Madison in late April that four from the Virginia delegation, including Nicholas and Giles, had gone home, that one was leaving, and another had gone over completely to the "war party." "In this state of things," he said, "they will carry what they please." [53] This statement essentially sums up the situation in which he and Gallatin now found themselves.

A couple of months after the XYZ exposé a Hamiltonian reported to Rufus King in London: "Gallatin continues to clog the wheels of government, but he has not sufficient strength to stop its motion. Without him the party would be completely scattered." Continuing, this writer said ironically: "He constantly preaches the duty of resisting all foreign attacks, and professes warm zeal for the constitution and country." [54] No more in Gallatin's eyes than in those of Jefferson

along with the speech of the President of the Executive Directory to which Adams objected, are given in *A.S.P.F.R.*, II, 160–161.

[53] To Madison, Apr. 26, 1798 (Ford, VII, 244). He said that Giles, Clopton, Cabell, and Nicholas had gone, that Clay was going, and that Parker had entirely defected.

[54] R. Troup to R. King, June 10, 1798 (King, II, 345).

did patriotic zeal require full support of all current proposals of legislation. Ostensibly the Vice President was only a spectator of the legislative scene, but there is little doubt that he approved the policy of the Republican faithfuls in the House and encouraged them in it. The whig party, he had said, "are willing to indulge the war-gentry with every reasonable measure of internal defence and preparation, but will oppose everything external." [55] He did not make clear just where the line between internal and external lay, but in fact the Republicans favored reliance on the militia rather than a provisional army and opposed the development of a navy. As things turned out, Congress went further in authorizing a military establishment than Adams himself recommended, and not as far as he desired in providing for the navy — reflecting the dominant influence of Hamilton behind the scenes. This early and important sign of a divergence between the Adams Federalists and the Hamiltonians does not appear to have been perceived at the time by Jefferson, who disagreed with both groups. Not that he could be described with any accuracy as a pacifist. If war should actually take place, he said privately, Americans must defend themselves. "If our house be on fire, without inquiring whether it was fired from within or without, we must try to extinguish it. In that, I have no doubt we shall act as one man." [56] This was as near as he came to flag-waving. But, believing that war would not come except by the action of the American government itself, he thought the measures being pressed by the High Federalists quite unnecessary and ruinously expensive.

At this time the distinction between Adams and the High Federalists, which had been so real in his mind a year earlier, was blurred by the intemperance of some of the President's utterances in answer to the patriotic addresses which were pouring in on him and most of which Jefferson believed to have been written in Philadelphia.[57] Both friends and foes recognized that Adams's ardent nature at times led him into verbal excesses. He contributed nothing to national unity when he spoke publicly of "a spirit of party which scruples not to go all lengths of profligacy, falsehood, and malignity in defaming our government." [58] Jefferson regarded the answers as more "thrasonic" than the addresses, and noted that the President's dire threats were di-

[55] To TMR, Apr. 12, 1798 (LC, 17715), also to Madison, Apr. 12 (Ford, VII, 237).
[56] To James Lewis, Jr., May 9, 1798 (Ford, VII, 250).
[57] A selection of these replies is in *Works*, IX, 182–236. Dauer (pp. 43–45) quotes violent expressions in others, drawn from the Federalist newspapers. As a rule the Republican papers did not print them.
[58] *Works*, IX, 182.

rected not only against the French but also against his fellow citizens. The High Federalists in general rejoiced at this vehemence, but Hamilton, now calmly confident of the triumph of his own ideas, thought that on occasion Adams went considerably beyond discretion.[59] Most of all, Jefferson personally resented what he regarded as an irrelevant and wholly unjustifiable reference to his friend Monroe as "a disgraced minister, recalled in displeasure for misconduct." [60] In order that the "disgraced minister" might gain a forum and re-establish himself, Jefferson suggested that he enter Congress from the Albemarle district in place of Cabell, but it turned out that Monroe did not take to the idea.

Shortly before Adams paid his compliments to Monroe a group of young men of Philadelphia addressed the President, delighting him by "their virtuous anxiety to preserve the honor and independence of their country." Some of them mounted the black or English cockade, and a fray ensued next day when men of a different persuasion appeared, wearing what was taken to be the tricolored cockade of France. According to Jefferson, this proved to be the old blue and red that was used early in the American Revolution. There was a certain significance in his report that it was now laid aside, though the black cockade was still common.[61]

Jefferson, conscious of his insulation, remained in Philadelphia long enough to witness, at some distance, the triumphal return of John Marshall in June. This lanky Virginian, who had hastened home in advance of his fellow envoys, was the hero of the hour. Time would show, also, that no other single person gained as much as he from the mission to France and the XYZ imbroglio.[62] Arriving unexpectedly in New York, he did not stay there long enough to receive much attention, but he was met some miles from Philadelphia by the Secretary of State and escorted into town by three corps of cavalry fully armed. The demonstration is said to have surpassed any that had been previ-

[59] To Wolcott, June 5, 1798 (*J.C.H.*, VI, 294–295).

[60] To the inhabitants of Lancaster County, Pa., May 8, 1798 (*Works*, IX, 190). For comments by TJ see his letters of May 17, 1798, to Madison, and May 21 to Monroe (Ford, VII, 254, 257).

[61] Adams replied to the address on May 7, 1798 (*Works*, IX, 187). TJ referred to the fray and the cockades in letters of May 10 and 17 to Madison (Ford, VII, 252–253).

[62] Beveridge, noting that Marshall received in cash above expenses three times his annual earnings at the bar, agrees that his appointment to the mission was a godsend, even though TJ said it, and refers to it as the turning point in his life. (*Marshall*, II, 211, 213.) The political results are written on the pages of history. Beveridge devotes a chapter to "The Triumphant Return" (II, ch. IX, see especially pp. 343–351).

ously received in the capital by any American except George Washington. Jefferson himself reported that great crowds gathered and that bells rang late into the night. To him it seemed that this was contrived as a show, but he was disposed to think that Marshall was not as "hot" as the party that had staged it. He understood that Marshall told Edward Livingston, who rode with him from New York, that in France they had no idea of a war with the United States.[63] He reported, however, that comments of a directly contrary nature were being circulated as from the returned envoy.

He himself called twice on Marshall, only to find him out. This act of politeness, which was politely acknowledged, had a particular purpose: he wanted to explain in person why, because of a previous engagement, he would be unable to dine in Marshall's company that day.[64] Apparently he was not referring to the banquet given the returned commissioner at Oeller's Hotel. He had no share in that historic celebration, at which a famous toast was drunk: "Millions for defence but not a cent for tribute." There were toasts to President Adams, to General Washington, to General Pinckney, and a final one to General Marshall — "The man whom his country delights to honor." There was also one to the American eagle, which was enjoined to disdain the crowing of the Gallic cock, but there was no toast to Elbridge Gerry, the envoy who had remained in France, and none to the Vice President.[65]

That gentleman, feeling more useless than ever in the chair of the Senate, where he now estimated the Federalist majority as three to one, had determined to go home before the end of the session. He delayed his departure several days, however, because of the state of affairs in Philadelphia. The week before Marshall's triumphant entry, Dr. George Logan, whom Jefferson regarded as the best farmer in Pennsylvania and who, besides that, was a leader in the Democratic Society and a Quaker in inheritance and spirit, set sail for Europe on a personal peace mission.[66] The Vice President, who wished that Logan had not slipped away so mysteriously on a trip he had long been planning, said that it was seized upon by the "war hawks" as a secret mission from the American Jacobins "to solicit an army from France,

---

[63] TJ to Madison, June 21, 1798 (Ford, VII, 272–273), describing the arrival; TJ to TMR, June 21 (LC, 17809).

[64] Beveridge, II, 346–347, quotes the "card" TJ left, dating it June 23, 1798, and gives Marshall's reply (which is in LC, 17542) without date.

[65] Beveridge describes the dinner (II, 348–350), giving toasts. TJ seems to have made no written reference to it at the time.

[66] June 13, 1798. The best account is F. B. Tolles, *George Logan of Philadelphia* (1953), ch. VIII.

instruct them as to their landing, etc." [67] Added to the public excitement engendered by the first vague reports of this singular undertaking was that created by the publication in the *Aurora*, about the same time, of the letter of Talleyrand to the American commissioners. This was a couple of days before Adams transmitted it to Congress.[68] Whether the actions of Benjamin Franklin Bache were owing chiefly to excess of partisan zeal or of journalistic enterprise, he played into the hands of those who wanted to perpetuate and accentuate the excitement. High Federalist sentinels, especially William Cobbett in *Porcupine's Gazette* and Robert Goodloe Harper in the House of Representatives, raised loud cries of alarm. The former warned the citizenry to be on guard lest the fire would be in their houses and the *couteau* at their throats, while the latter saw signs of criminal correspondence of the most treasonable variety. Dr. Logan was accused of an "infernal design," while the "French printer" was charged with being an agent of the Directory who had received Talleyrand's letter from the minister himself.[69] The alarmists could not hope to reach Talleyrand at the moment, but they hotly pursued the printer.

The details of that pursuit need concern us here only as they related to the Vice President, at whom the finger of High Federalist suspicion always pointed. In eager quest of treasonable correspondence, Secretary of the Treasury Wolcott betook himself to New York to interview William Lee, who, on his recent trip home from Paris, had served as courier for a number of people, according to the custom of travelers in those times. He delivered to Wolcott, and Wolcott sent on to Pickering, a number of communications, including a packet to Bache that bore the seal of the French Office of Foreign Affairs. When this was finally delivered to the editor of the *Aurora* on his demand it turned out to contain merely a couple of innocuous pamphlets sent him by a friend. Meanwhile, Bache had come up with an affidavit saying that he got Talleyrand's letter from a gentleman in Philadelphia.[70] Wolcott is said to have been even more anxious to get something on Jefferson than on Bache. Apparently he found nothing addressed to the Vice President that bore Talleyrand's official seal, but he did commandeer a

[67] To Madison, June 21, 1798 (Ford, VII, 273). For later developments, see below, p. 430.

[68] *Aurora*, June 16, 1798. On June 18 Adams transmitted Dispatch #8 from the commissioners, saying that this was received June 14. It included Talleyrand's letter of Mar. 18, and the reply of the envoys (*A.S.P.F.R.*, II, 188-199). Bache afterwards published the latter.

[69] Tolles, *Logan*, pp. 156-157, with citations.

[70] The Bache episode is well described by J. M. Smith in *Freedom's Fetters* (1956), pp. 193-198; Bache himself dealt with it and other things in his pamphlet *Truth Will Out!* (1798).

private letter. This was from Fulwar Skipwith, American consul general in Paris. It was published from the Wolcott papers half a century later, being then cited as one of those "surrendered to the Executive" by Lee which furnished "conclusive proofs of the agency of American Jacobins there [Paris] in instigating the measures of the Directory." [71] Jefferson had much to say about the tampering with his mail in this era, but at the time he does not appear to have been aware of this high-handed invasion of his private correspondence when the country was legally at peace.

Shortly before he went home Jefferson said: "Their system is professedly, to keep up an alarm." For that reason they kept Congress in session: to separate it would be "withdrawing the fire from under a boiling pot." [72] The pot was boiling even more furiously now than it had been two months earlier when he anticipated that the "war party" would pass a citizen bill, an alien bill, and a sedition bill.[73] Before he himself withdrew toward the end of June from a scene he regarded as delirious, Congress had passed two of the predicted measures. After his departure, besides abrogating the treaties with France by unilateral action, as he also expected, it passed the Sedition Act.[74] This last measure, destined to become notorious, bore out a penetrating though melancholy remark of Madison's: "Perhaps it is a universal truth that the loss of liberty of home is to be charged to provisions against danger real or pretended from abroad." [75]

[71] Skipwith to TJ, Mar. 17, 1798 (Gibbs, II, 158–161; see also pp. 68, 70, 72). Having found no indication that TJ ever got this letter and no other explanation regarding the presence of the recipient's copy in the papers of Wolcott, I see no choice but to assume that Wolcott took it. This judgment seems to run counter to the testimony of William Dunlap, who was present when Wolcott saw Lee, that when the former asked repeatedly if there were any letters for TJ the answer was invariably "No." (Smith, *Freedom's Fetters*, p. 195 and note 26, quoting *Diary of William Dunlap* [1930], I, 294, entry of June 20, 1798.) Perhaps Dunlap was referring to packets from Talleyrand. Wolcott appears to have made no use at the time of a letter which he had no right to take and which, while revealing Skipwith's critical attitude toward the American government, implicated TJ only by association.

[72] To Madison, June 21, 1798 (Ford, VII, 274).

[73] To Madison, Apr. 26, 1798 (Ford, VII, 244–245).

[74] Approved, July 14, 1798. The other measures which, along with this one, are collectively designated as the Alien and Sedition Acts were: the Naturalization Act, June 18; the Alien Act, June 25; and the unexceptionable Alien Enemies Act, July 6. They can be conveniently seen in Smith, *Freedom's Fetters*, pp. 435–442. TJ left Philadelphia June 27.

[75] To TJ, May 13, 1798 (MP, 20:112).

[XXIV]

Challenge to Freedom: The Alien and Sedition Acts

JUDGING from Jefferson's reception in one town on his trip homeward, opposition to the policy of the government was not deemed treasonable by the people of his own commonwealth. In Fredericksburg the local artillery company announced the arrival of the "virtuous and patriotic" Vice President of the United States by the discharge of sixteen rounds, and he was escorted into town by a "great concourse" of citizens, or so it was said. A number of Republicans gave him a dinner next day at which toasts were drunk to Elbridge Gerry, Madison, and Monroe, among others. No doubt there were local objectors, and political enemies of his elsewhere described his acceptance of the honor of a public dinner as an indiscretion, since the day happened to be Sunday. Weeks later a High Federalist reported with obvious satisfaction: "This fact has been trumpeted from one end of the continent to the other as an irrefragable proof of his contempt for the Christian religion and his devotion to the new religion of France. It has made an impression much to his prejudice in the Middle and Eastern States." [1] He and Madison probably did not discuss the question of Sabbath observance when, proceeding onward, he stopped for the night at Montpelier according to his custom. Very likely they talked about certain resolutions they soon had a hand in drafting, but at the moment there did not seem to be much that anybody could do, and certainly it was not a good time to forego the blessings of obscurity.

The older man arrived at Monticello on July 4. Not until his official duties took him back to the seat of government in mid-December did

[1] R. Troup to R. King, Oct. 2, 1798 (King, II, 432). Reference to criticisms of dinner in *Aurora*, Aug. 2, 1798; account of reception in *Aurora*, July 12, some days after the event.

he leave home. In this period of more than five months he was struggling to get a roof on his house, and judging from his Account Book he was also much occupied with his nail business. To his intense disappointment Maria could not make the visit he so anxiously awaited, but Martha and her children were there, taking cover where they could. In a real sense this was a domestic interlude. He wrote relatively few letters and these dealt largely with personal matters. The desperate holding operation of Gallatin and other Republicans in Congress went on until that body recessed two or three weeks after he left. John Adams then repaired to his own rural scene at Quincy, where his wife lay ill; and the President was not wholly aware of what his executive assistants were doing in his absence. The Vice President's most significant political activities before the legislative melee was resumed — those relating to the Kentucky and Virginia Resolutions — were wholly under cover. Knowing that every move of his was suspect, he did not make many. He wrote a few important political letters and may have done something more of which there is no record, but by and large this was for him a period of waiting.

The policy which he followed was in line with the suggestions of his friend Monroe, who believed as he himself did that there could be no important change in the present unfavorable political situation until the course of public events, foreign or domestic, should induce one. In Monroe's opinion, change in sentiment in the East, where it was most needed, would be impeded by new pressure from the South, and especially from Virginia. With wisdom which history was to demonstrate he said: "The more, therefore, that party [Federalist] is left to itself, the sooner will its ruin follow." [2] Equally sagacious was a comment in which he may well have been advising Jefferson how to conduct himself: "I am very much inclined to think that the patient must find out his own disorder, if not by himself yet that he must think so: that the physician must not appear, or if at all by no means as a prominent character." [3] To one who so often said that nature was the best physician for his grandchildren — a saying which was the more appropriate because of the existing state of medicine — this figure of speech could not have failed to be appealing. Recently he had written John Taylor of Caroline that the body politic was basically sound, that the people were substantially republican throughout the country. The present situation was "unnatural" and time would heal it. "A little

[2] To TJ, June 1798 from Richmond (S.M.H., III, 128–136; LC, 17820–17822). This seems to be the letter recorded by TJ as received June 10. Monroe was giving reasons why he did not want to return to Congress at this time.

[3] To TJ, June 16, 1798 (S.M.H., III, 127).

patience," he said, "and we shall see the reign of witches pass over, their spells dissolve, and the people, recovering their true sight, restore their government to its true principles." [4] More characteristic of him than the extravagant phrases he sometimes used in private was the extraordinary patience, coupled with tenacity, which marked his public conduct. He relied on nature, believing at this time, however, that the tax collector would soon remind the invalid of his unhappy state, and that somehow society must be kept aware of the dependence of its health on the fresh air of freedom.

He was in no position to do anything with respect to international relations. Several weeks before he came home he had concluded that war was inevitable, since the public mind had been artfully inflamed and irritations so multiplied as to shut the door of accommodation. Desiring peace with both of the major countries, despite great provocations and injuries from both, he would have preferred to sit the crisis out as other neutrals were doing. Since he had never believed that either of the contending powers wanted to provoke an armed conflict with the United States, he held that the choice had lain with his own country. With Great Britain it had chosen peace, with France war, and it was proceeding to actual hostilities.[5] In this summer of his own political impotence apparently he made no distinction between the President and the "war party." Before he left Philadelphia he heard the message in which Adams, besides informing Congress that the negotiations of the late envoys extraordinary to France were at an end, announced that he would never send another minister to that country without assurances that he would be "received, respected, and honored as the representative of a great, free, powerful, and independent nation." [6] Thus diplomatic relations remained suspended without any immediate prospect of their restoration. Jefferson was back at Monticello before the treaties with France were declared suspended, an action which he had anticipated. He had said privately that we should "haul off from Europe as soon as we can, and from all attachments to any portions of it." [7] Escape from these treaty obligations could hardly have been abhorrent to one who was advocating nonin-

---

[4] To John Taylor, June 4, 1798 (*Papers, MHS*, p. 63).

[5] His position was well stated in his letters to Archibald Stuart, June 8, 1798, and to Samuel Smith, Aug. 22, 1798 (Ford, VII, 269–271, 277–278). It should be noted that the latter was written several weeks after the attempt to secure a formal declaration of war had been defeated.

[6] June 21, 1798 (*Works*, IX, 159). TJ reported this to Madison that day (Ford, VII, 275).

[7] To John Taylor, June 4, 1798 (*Papers, MHS*, p. 64).

volvement, though the method and timing could not have been expected to meet the approval of a consummate diplomat who greatly feared alliance with the British.

There was no declaration of war, for all the talk of one. Soon after Jefferson got home, Senator Stevens Thomson Mason wrote him that the "Tory" leaders had fixed on July 4 for a formal declaration, but that, when some of the timid ones held back at a party meeting, it was concluded that a few more days of "high feeling" were needed. A House resolution for increasing the size of the provisional army was passed soon after that, the appointment of a committee of inquiry into the present situation with respect to France was in prospect, and a declaration of war was expected to follow on its recommendation. Mason also informed Jefferson that Washington was to be commander-in-chief of the army, assuming his acceptance.[8] Theodore Sedgwick, who favored a declaration, believed that every other Federalist in the Senate did but one. The war party could not swing the House, however. A resolution by John Allen of Connecticut, calling for the appointment of such a committee as Mason described, was introduced on July 5 and voted down next day without a roll call. Thus ended what has been described as "the most serious attempt in American history to declare war without a recommendation by the President." [9]

This was what Adams afterwards termed a half war, waged on the seas in protection of commerce by means of armed merchantmen and the incipient navy in which he took such pride but which Jefferson regarded as a piece of expensive futility. The maritime actions of the next two years represented the nearest approach to the "actual hostilities" which the Vice President expected. Had he been able to read the President's mind he would have found that Adams, no more anticipating a French invasion than he was, set little store by the provisional army, so dear to the heart of Hamilton, which he himself thought utterly unnecessary. If at this stage he did not distinguish between the aims of his old friend the President and his inveterate foe the former Secretary of the Treasury, that is not surprising, for Adams now was in high favor with the followers of Hamilton. Theodore Sedgwick wrote to Rufus King in England: "The President is daily rising in the opinion and affection of the well disposed; and in the same proportion *the second* is becoming more and more an object of abhorrence

[8] Mason to TJ, July 6, 1798 (LC, 17825–17826). This letter, which was actually out of date the day it was written, was not received by TJ until July 30, but he may have had reports from others at an earlier time.

[9] Dauer, p. 171, after an account of the move and its failure.

and detestation." [10] Another of Hamilton's supporters, crediting the President with all the ardor of youth along with the energies and firmness of middle age, predicted that if the country should survive this struggle his lustre would be comparable to that of Washington. At the same time this High Federalist reported that some "disorganizers" were being arrested for libeling the President and his Secretary of State. "It is determined," he said, "to try whether we have strength enough to cause the constituted authorities to be respected." No doubt the reference, in part, was to the indictment of Benjamin Franklin Bache at common law for seditious libel about the time that the Vice President left Philadelphia. [11] A little more than two weeks later Adams signed the Sedition Act, rounding out the program of domestic legislation whereby the dominant group, riding on the crest of the anti-French hysteria, sought to protect the country against supposed internal danger. It was against these repressive measures that Jefferson brought up his masked battery in the early autumn.

Of the four measures commonly included under the designation of the Alien and Sedition Acts, one only was contingent on a declaration of war. This was the Alien Enemies Act, authorizing the deportation of citizens or subjects of countries with which the United States was actually at war. It was voted and approved after Jefferson left Philadelphia and he took no exception to it. Although it commanded bipartisan support, it was in its final form essentially a Republican measure to which the extreme Federalists were indifferent. [12] There was no need to use it in this period, since war was not declared, but this justifiable measure, which was without limit of time, remained on the statute books.

None of the other acts could have been passed except under conditions of fear and patriotic hysteria. One perfervid anti-Gallican wrote George Washington that he looked upon war as necessary "to enable us to lay our hands on traitors." [13] Failing to get war, the extremists were nonetheless able to exploit war psychology for domestic political purposes. Politics was obvious in the Naturalization Act, which ex-

[10] Sedgwick to King, July 1, 1798 (King, II, 352–353).

[11] R. Troup to King, July 10, 1798 (King, II, 362–364). Bache was brought into federal court June 26, 1798, and paroled until June 29, when his trial was set for the October term and he was released on bail. He died of yellow fever in September (Smith, pp. 200–204).

[12] The legislative story is told in Smith, *Freedom's Fetters*, ch. 3. Discussion of this bill, which was recommitted at the instance of Gallatin, began after TJ went home and after the passage of the Alien or Alien Friends Act had given the High Federalists what they wanted.

[13] James Lloyd to Washington, July 4, 1798 (quoted by Smith, p. 110).

tended the requirement for the attainment of citizenship by immigrants from five to fourteen years, the maximum for the whole of American history. Rarely has nativism been manifested more arrogantly than it was by Harrison Gray Otis, Robert Goodloe Harper, and other High Federalists in connection with this measure, but the crux of the matter was that the immigrants, such as the "Wild Irish" against whom Otis declaimed, tended to vote Republican. This bill, which was passed while Jefferson was still in Philadelphia, was designed to diminish future accessions to that party. He said that a move to reduce the requirement of fourteen years to seven almost reached a tie vote in the Senate, in which case, seizing upon the rare opportunity to cast a vote, he would have broken it in favor of the lower figure.[14] Judging from earlier statements of his, he was not much disposed to encourage immigration, preferring to depend on the natural increase in population and to maintain homogeneity.[15] He once feared that most of the newcomers would bring with them the ideas of absolutist governments; and in his eagerness to forestall British influence in his own state he went so far as to suggest, only a year before this, that jury duty be reserved to natives or long-time citizens.[16] There is no need to suppose, however, that he regarded a long wait for citizenship as desirable in itself, and he had ample reason to dislike a measure that was deliberately designed to cut down his party's vote.[17]

Palpably political as the Naturalization Act was, the Alien or Alien Friends Act disturbed Jefferson far more deeply because of the arbitrary power it conferred on the President. This measure started in the Senate, and, besides hearing the discussion there, he could not have failed to be familiar with the debate in the House, which occurred before he left town. He described the bill as "a most detestable thing," and even after it had been modified beyond his expectations he said that it would place under "absolute government" all aliens not protected by treaties.[18] In a nutshell, the act authorized the President to

14 To Madison, June 14, 1798 (quoted by Smith, p. 33).

15 *Notes on Virginia*, Query VIII (Peden, pp. 84–85); see also *Jefferson the Virginian*, p. 385.

16 In connection with the Cabell case (Ford, VII, 163–164); see above, pp. 334–336.

17 The legislative history of the act is in Smith, ch. 2. The measure is severely criticized by S. E. Morison in *Harrison Gray Otis*, I, 109–111. TJ thought that the original purpose of the Federalists was to exclude Gallatin. This would have been impossible on constitutional grounds, and actually Gallatin was more responsible than any other single person for ridding the measure of its harsh retroactive features. TJ also reported that the bill was aimed at Callender, who eluded it by getting himself made a citizen before it was passed. To Madison, June 7, 1798 (Ford, VII, 267); see also Apr. 26, 1798 (Ford, VII, 245).

18 To Madison, May 31, June 7, 1798 (Ford, VII, 261, 266).

deport any alien he thought dangerous. As Edward Livingston of New York said in the House, exciting the suspicions of the President was the "new crime." One of the persons against whom Jefferson thought the law directed was the French philosopher Volney. Writing his son-in-law, he said: "It suffices for a man to be a philosopher, and to believe that human affairs are susceptible of improvement, and to look forward, rather than backward to the Gothic ages, for perfection, to mark him as an anarchist, disorganizer, atheist and enemy of the government."[19] Volney, erstwhile guest at Monticello, sailed off ahead of time with a boatload of French. Among them was Victor Marie du Pont, who had been named consul general but whose credentials Adams would not recognize. The President later signed a blank warrant to be used against this man's father, Jefferson's friend Pierre Samuel du Pont de Nemours, in case he should come to the United States, a thing which this founder of a famous family did not do as yet. Afterwards, Jefferson regarded Joseph Priestley, the English scientist and Unitarian clergyman, as a likely victim; and to him in due course he described the Alien Act as a "libel on legislation."[20] In fact, Adams overruled Pickering when the Secretary of State suggested Priestley's deportation, and actually the President deported nobody. That such would be the case Jefferson had no way of knowing at the outset, and it appeared to him that the law was directed at just the sort of persons he most wanted to come to America, men of science and learning. Though Hamilton objected to none of the arbitrary features of the act and believed that the mass of aliens should be obliged to leave the country, he originally wanted favor to be shown merchants and exceptions made of a few others whose demeanor had been irreproachable.[21] The Republicans in Congress opposed this bill primarily on constitutional grounds. There is no way of knowing whether Jefferson had any direct part in determining their policy, but in due course he virtually recapitulated their arguments.[22]

Anticipating a sedition law several months before the Act of July 14, 1798, Jefferson supposed that its main object would be the "suppression of the whig presses," especially that of Bache. Also, on the strength of one of Adams's intemperate public utterances he feared that the hand of "authority" might be employed against the circular letters of Republican congressmen to their constituents, and this despite the fact that Tory Congressmen wrote far more, and more out-

[19] To TMR, May 3, 1798 (LC, 17748). See also TJ to Madison, Apr. 26, and to Monroe, May 21, 1798 (Ford, VII, 245, 257).

[20] Mar. 21, 1801 (Ford, VIII, 22).

[21] To Pickering, June 7, 1798 (J.C.H., VI, 300).

[22] In the Kentucky Resolutions of 1798. For the debates, see Smith, ch. 5.

rageously.[23] He would have been warranted in adding that the *Gazette of the United States* and *Porcupine's Gazette* contained fully as many lies as the *Aurora*.[24] That extreme Federalists would have liked to punish Republican representatives for what they said outside Congress Hall, since they could not penalize them for what they said in it, and that in their effort to muzzle the press they were striking at the party, became abundantly evident in the subsequent debates and in expressions in the Federalist papers. During the summer the *Gazette of the United States* announced a slogan: "*He that is not for us, is against us.*"[25] A little later this same paper gave a definition on which, in fact, the dominant group proceeded: "It is patriotism to write in favor of our government — it is sedition to write against it."[26] This was another way of saying that the policies of those in power were sacrosanct.

Though Jefferson was not in town when the chief congressional debates on this topic occurred, he was still there when the first measures against sedition were introduced. Early in June he wrote Madison: "They have brought into the lower house a sedition bill, which among other enormities undertakes to make printing certain matters criminal, though one of the amendments to the Constitution has so expressly taken religion, printing presses, &c. out of their coercion. Indeed this bill and the alien bill both are so palpably in the teeth of the Constitution as to show they mean to pay no respect to it."[27] The shocking bill introduced in the Senate by James Lloyd, intemperate successor to Jefferson's moderate Federalist friend John Henry, now governor of Maryland, had its first reading the day before the Vice President went home. There was no need for him to describe it in writing to Madison, whom he was so soon to see, but no imagination is required to surmise what he thought of the first section of this measure. In it the French were designated as enemies of the United States though the country was technically at peace, treason was defined as giving aid and comfort to them, and the death penalty was prescribed for violation of this section of the bill. This measure was too harsh for Hamilton, and his objections to it have led to the com-

[23] To Madison, Apr. 26, May 3, 1798 (Ford, VII, 245, 247, 249).

[24] See the comments of Nathaniel W. Macon to that effect in the House (Smith, p. 124*n*.).

[25] July 7, 1798 (quoted by Smith, p. 15).

[26] Oct. 10, 1798 (quoted by Dauer, p. 165).

[27] June 7, 1798 (Ford, VII, 266-267). Presumably he was referring to the omnibus alien and sedition bill which was reported on June 4, and printed in the *Aurora* on June 6, along with the First Amendment (circumstances described in Smith, pp. 99-101). The House replaced this by the Senate Alien Bill and did nothing further about sedition until it received Lloyd's bill from the Senate on July 5.

mon mistake of attributing to him opposition to the bill which was finally passed.[28] The Federalist senators referred Lloyd's bill to a committee before Hamilton ever saw it. This was the day that Jefferson went home. On July 4, the day he got to Monticello, the Senate adopted a revised version, omitting the first two sections.

Both of the senators from Virginia promptly reported these events to the absent Vice President, though one letter was two weeks in transit and the other more than three. Henry Tazewell, who sent him a copy of the bill as passed, expressed his present opinion that it would pass the House and would be executed with "unrelenting fury." [29] Stevens Thomson Mason reported more fully, saying that there seemed to be "a particular solicitude" to pass the bill on Independence Day and that the noise outside considerably interfered with the senatorial debate. "The drums, trumpets and other martial music which surrounded us drowned out the voices of those who spoke on the question. The military parade so attracted the attention of the majority that much the greater part of them stood with their bodies out of the windows and could not be kept in order." This was no time for a calm appeal to reason. Attempts to gain a vote for adjournment and the postponement of the question failed. Despite the uproar, Mason got the drift of a speech by Senator Alexander Martin of North Carolina, who, after discoursing at length on the unconstitutionality of the bill, voted for it on the ground that "it was a lesser evil to violate the Constitution than to suffer the printers to abuse the government." By this action, however, he brought the North Carolina delegation "upon his back." [30] The author of the bill, taking it upon himself to inform George Washington of it, commented on it in different terms. He said that it "afforded much ground for declamation to the lovers of Liberty, or, in other words, the Jacobins." [31]

The Vice President, lover of liberty that he was and chief Jacobin that he was called, was not even an auditor of the declamation in the Senate, and it is uncertain when and how fully he was informed of what happened afterwards in the other chamber. The suggestion has been made by competent authority that the Sedition Act should logi-

[28] To Wolcott, June 29, 1798 (J.C.H., VI, 307). He thought such a bill might engender civil war and urged that it be not hurried through, saying: "Let us not establish a tyranny." For a general discussion of Lloyd's bill, see Smith, p. 107.

[29] Tazewell to TJ, July 5, 1798, received July 19 (LC, 17823).

[30] Mason to TJ, July 6, 1798 (LC, 17825), received July 30. It was in this same letter that Mason informed TJ of the plans of the "war party."

[31] Lloyd to Washington, July 4, 1798 (quoted by Smith, p. 110, from Washington Papers). In this letter he expressed the fear that the session would end without a declaration of war, which he looked upon as "necessary to enable us to lay our hands on traitors," and to defeat the machinations of the Directory.

cally be called the Lloyd-Harper Law; and, while Robert Goodloe Harper cannot escape being classed with James Lloyd as an extremist, the bill which the House amended and passed on July 10 by a majority of three was less illiberal than the one it had received from the Senate.[32] The fire of contemporary and subsequent objection was directed not against the first section, dealing with conspiracy, but against the second, dealing with false, scandalous, and malicious writings that were intended to defame the government, Congress, or the President and to bring them into contempt and disrepute. If the contention of the advocates of the measure that the federal courts already had common-law jurisdiction over seditious libel be accepted, along with Blackstone's definition of freedom of the press as freedom from restraint prior to publication, the law can be interpreted as one that regularized procedure and was not illiberal in its supporters' frame of reference. It set limits to fines and terms of imprisonment as the common law did not do. And it went beyond Fox's Libel Act of 1792 in Great Britian in permitting anyone charged with libel to give evidence of truth in his defense, the determination of both the law and the fact being left to the jury, under direction of the court.[33] These safeguards proved meaningless in practice, however, and regardless of questions of procedure and constitutionality the dominant group had obviously fashioned a political weapon against the opposition party which might be employed tyrannically against individuals. Odium has gathered round this intolerant partisan measure, progressively through the years, and only rarely have modern scholars defended it on its merits.

At the time no Federalist of any prominence objected to it except John Marshall. In the autumn of 1798, as a candidate for Congress, he stated that he would have opposed the Alien and Sedition Acts if he had been a member of that body — not on constitutional grounds but because he thought them useless and "calculated to create unnecessary discontents and jealousies." [34] The Federalist sage of Massachusetts, George Cabot, said condescendingly that Marshall should not be too

[32] The suggestion of the name is that of J. M. Smith (*Freedom's Fetters*, p. 151); he gives the legislative history in chs. 7–8, and the text of the Act on pp. 441–442. For Lloyd's bill, the Senate amendments, and the House amendments, see Dauer, *Adams Federalists*, Appendix IV.

[33] This line of interpretation is taken by L. W. Levy, in *Legacy of Suppression* (1960), esp. chs. 5, 6. See also M. D. Howe's review of Smith's *Freedom's Fetters* in *W. & M.*, Oct. 1956, pp. 573–576. For Smith's interpretation, which is at variance with this, see especially ch. 18. All these scholars condemn the Sedition Act as unfortunate and unwise.

[34] Beveridge, II, 389, citing Alexandria *Times and Virginia Advertiser*, Oct. 11, 1798. In ch. X, Marshall's biographer quotes many critical Federalist comments on his position.

severely condemned, since he had not yet learned his whole lesson, and that some allowance must also be made "for the influence of the atmosphere of Virginia which doubtless makes every one who breathes it visionary and, upon the subject of free government, incredibly credulous." [35] The air of Virginia did not have that effect on George Washington, who thought these laws necessary in view of the actions of the French and *their* party; he described the latter in the summer of 1798 as "the curse of this country." [36] The Ex-President was no alarmist about external dangers, believing a French invasion most unlikely, and he was no friend to tyranny, but he found criticisms of the constituted authorities by irresponsible journalists quite intolerable and on domestic questions at this stage he went along with the Hamiltonians.

Hamilton had objected to certain features of Lloyd's bill in the Senate, but later statements of his show that he favored a more drastic measure against sedition than the one on the statute books and more vigorous executive action against critics and aliens.[37] Hamilton did not originally propose the Alien and Sedition Laws, as Adams afterwards asserted, but they were the work of devoted followers of his. Neither did John Adams recommend them, but his wife was zealously for them and he signed them, regarding them as necessary. In later years he said that they were considered as war measures, "intended altogether against the advocates of the French and peace with France." [38] The Sedition Act was not contingent on war or suspended relations with France, however, and it was to remain in effect until the end of the term to which Adams was elected. That he apprehended "a hurricane of clamor" against these laws, and that this turned out to be even fiercer and more violent than he expected, may be conceded, just as a somewhat fuller understanding of the role of parties than that of Hamilton can be attributed to him. But Adams was by common consent a vain man with a high sense of his official prerogatives. Undoubtedly resenting the scurrilities to which he was subjected, he was not unwilling that the perpetrators of them should be punished.

[35] To R. King, Apr. 26, 1799 (King, III, 9).
[36] On the Alien and Sedition Acts, see his letter to Alexander Spotswood, Nov. 22, 1798 (Fitzpatrick, XXXVII, 23). He spoke with particular bitterness of the "French party" to Charles Carroll, Aug. 21, 1798 (*ibid.*, XXXVI, 384). Speaking of this letter and one of July 4 to Adams (XXXVI, 313), TJ in his own old age said that, over them "in devotion to his imperishable fame, we must forever weep as monuments of mortal decay" (Feb. 4, 1818 [Ford, I, 168]).
[37] His position is discussed at length by J. M. Smith, in "Alexander Hamilton, the Alien Law, and Seditious Libels," in *Review of Politics*, XVI (1954), 305-333.
[38] To the printers of the Boston *Patriot* (*Works*, IX, 291).

The violence of newspaper talk at that time, both on the part of editors and anonymous correspondents, cannot fail to impress the modern reader, even though he be inured to political invective. But the darts did not all fly in one direction: a very large number were aimed at the Vice President, who was not specifically mentioned in the Sedition Act and in fact was in an anomalous position, but who was nonetheless an official of the government whose patriotism might have been safely assumed. The political tricks of the day — name-calling, allegations of guilt by association, and the like — were so similar to those employed within present memory that twentieth-century demagogues of either the right or left would have felt very much at home, no doubt, if translated to the late eighteenth century. In the House, toward the end of the argument over the sedition bill, "Long John" Allen of Connecticut, who may be not inaptly termed a "radical of the right," referred to Jefferson as one who walked the streets arm-in-arm with Bache and was closeted with that "infamous printer" day and night. Allen was echoing charges in *Porcupine's Gazette* that on a certain day the Vice President had been "closeted" with Bache and two other Republican troublemakers of Philadelphia, Dr. Michael Leib and Dr. James Reynolds. Jefferson made no reference to Long John's innuendos in Congress Hall, which in fact were privileged, but he did reply to a letter from one of his well-wishers who sent him a clipping from Cobbett's sheet. His own letter, one of the very few he wrote that summer after the passing of the Sedition Act, is more important than the episode which occasioned it.[39]

In it he reiterated in striking language his consistent policy of *not* writing for the newspapers in defense of himself against attacks. "Were I to undertake to answer the calumnies of the newspapers," he said, "it would be more than all my own time and that of 20 aids could effect. For while I should be answering one, twenty new ones would be invented." The public would have to judge him from his actual conduct, but as occasion offered he gave to friends and political supporters factual statements for any private use they might care to make of them. In this instance the facts were that he was visited from time to time by Bache and Dr. Leib, though not by Dr. Reynolds. He was no more "closeted" with them than with anybody else, he said, but received them gladly because of their abilities and principles. He owed Bache further respect because of his grand-

[39] To Samuel Smith, congressman from Maryland, Aug. 22, 1798 (Ford, VII, 275-280). On John Allen and the episode in the House, see Smith, pp. 113-119, esp. p. 117.

father, Benjamin Franklin. He no more sought, even in private, to dissociate himself from the editor of the *Aurora* because of the latter's excesses than the Federalist leaders sought to dissociate themselves from William Cobbett, and lack of critical comments on these injudicious editors, in private at least, is regrettable on the one side as on the other. Whether or not Jefferson was as successful in maintaining tranquillity in the face of "calumny" as he implied, he was considerably more philosophical at this stage than either Washington or Adams, for the very reason that he set more store than they did on freedom of expression. He claimed that he harbored no resentment against those who, without any personal knowledge of him, hated him because of the representations of Porcupine and Fenno. "The only return I will ever make to them," he said, "will be to do them all the good I can, in spite of their teeth." To his enemies such words would have seemed pure cant, no doubt, but to his friends they were the expressions of a man of good will who fully recognized the sovereignty of the people.

As for his "principles," wishing them to be known he would speak of them freely to anybody. "They are the same I have acted on from the year 1775 to this day," he said, "and are the same, I am sure, with those of the great body of the American people." But he believed that the people were being deluded by the leaders of the dominant party. "I see the extent to which that delusion has been already carried, and I see there is no length to which it may not be pushed by a party in possession of the revenues and the legal authorities of the United States, for a short time indeed, but yet long enough to admit much particular mischief. There is no event, therefore, however atrocious, which may not be expected."

Though a long-range optimist, he believed that for a time anything could happen. He was undoubtedly aware of the common-law indictment of Bache. He did not refer to the arrest in July of John Daly Burk, the Irish editor of the New York *Time Piece*, who, besides being termed seditious because of utterances about President Adams, was an alien. The common-law action against Burk soon led to the desired result, the cessation of his paper. Jefferson must have heard of this during the summer, as perhaps he did of demonstrations against Congressman Edward Livingston in New York.[40] The arrest of Congressman Matthew Lyon of Vermont under the Sedition Act, because of publications of his in the course of his campaign for reelection when for a time he essayed the dangerous role of editor, did

[40] The Burk affair, which dragged on for a long time, is fully described by Smith, pp. 204–220. He eluded deportation.

not occur till fall. The full force of the Federalist attack on the press was not yet evident, but Jefferson was reading the signs aright when he quietly planned a counterattack in defense of freedom.

The issue raised by the repressive and intolerant legislation of the Federalist majority was a supreme challenge to him. This was not merely because he was the acknowledged leader of the party which the group in power sought to destroy by reducing it to silence, though that consideration alone would doubtless have been sufficient to arouse him. The watchword of his entire public career was freedom, and he had gained deserved and lasting fame as a champion of human rights against actual or potential tyranny. It has been argued on scholarly grounds that no "broad libertarian theory" of freedom of speech and the press emerged in the United States until 1798, when, under force of necessity, the Republicans invoked one.[41] But utterances of Jefferson's almost two decades before his party's protest against the Sedition Act pointed toward a very broad interpretation of freedom. In the preamble of his draft of the Bill for Establishing Religious Freedom appeared the assertion that "the opinions of men are not the object of civil government, nor under its jurisdiction." [42] This particular clause was deleted from the bill before its adoption, strongly suggesting that he was in advance of public opinion in this contention. The General Assembly of Virginia left in the bill his expression of faith in the triumph of truth under conditions of free argument and debate, "errors ceasing to be dangerous when it is permitted freely to contradict them." What the author of this immortal bill said here in a religious context he repeated in almost identical language a score of years later in the political context of his first presidential inaugural. In the *Notes on Virginia*, again in a religious context, he asserted that the operations of the mind, unlike the acts of the body, are not subject to the coercion of the laws. "The legitimate powers of government," he said, "extend to such acts only as are injurious to others." [43] To him freedom of thought was an absolute, and it may be assumed that he applied not merely to religious opinion but to all opinion this maxim: "Reason and free enquiry are the only effectual agents against error."

Convinced of the futility of coercion when directed against the mind, he undoubtedly believed that government ought to concern itself with overt acts rather than with words of supposedly dangerous

[41] L. W. Levy, *Legacy of Suppression*, p. viii and ch. 6.
[42] J.P., II, 546; see *Jefferson the Virginian*, p. 279.
[43] Query XVII, see esp. Peden, p. 159.

tendency, but it does not necessarily follow that at this stage, or indeed at any other, this experienced public servant regarded freedom of political expression as an absolute.[44] In the resolutions against the Alien and Sedition Acts which he drew in this period, he did not say that *all* government was powerless against the licentiousness of the press. He recognized the legal power of the states to abridge it without implying that this was unrightful. Before entering into the constitutional argument in which he denied that power to the federal government, we can and should point out that he believed the states, which were closer to the people, less likely to employ it tyrannically. If some of them should abuse it, the likelihood that all would do so seemed to him remote. After he himself had served as President and the Union had grown larger than it was when he was Vice President, he wrote to a European philosopher:

> . . . But the true barriers of our liberty in this country are our State governments; and the wisest conservative power ever contrived by man, is that of which our Revolution and present government found us possessed. Seventeen distinct States . . . can never be so fascinated by the arts of one man, as to submit voluntarily to his usurpation. Nor can they be constrained to it by any force he can possess.[45]

He resolutely opposed the Alien and Sedition Acts as a sincere champion of the highest practicable degree of human liberty in all fields. And, in seeking a weapon against them, he turned to state arsenals — seeing no other recourse and believing the states to be the best guardians of the human rights that were unquestionably imperiled.

[44] I am not yet disposed to agree with Levy (p. 283) that the treatise of Tunis Wortman, with its absolutist theses, is "the book that Jefferson did not write but should have."

[45] To Destutt de Tracy, Jan. 26, 1811 (Ford, IX, 308–310).

[XXV]

The Kentucky and Virginia Resolutions

IN HIS private protests against the Alien and Sedition Acts, in the years 1798 and 1799, Jefferson went further in his emphasis on the rights and powers of the states vis-à-vis the general government than he had ever done before or was ever to do again. During the American Revolution he was fully aware that the centrifugal tendencies of the time acutely endangered the success of the struggle for national independence; and during the period of the Confederation no one recognized more clearly that the powers of the states must be curtailed and the Union strengthened. His earliest critical comments on the Constitution of 1787 related, not to the reduction in the powers of the states, but to the lack of safeguards for individuals.[1] When these seemed to be provided in the Bill of Rights, and his fears that the President might become a monarch were allayed by his profound confidence in George Washington, he loyally supported the Constitution, believing that it provided a practicable equilibrium. He always held that the powers of the general government were and should be defined and limited, but the degree of liberalism or literalism with which he interpreted the constitutional instrument cannot be separated from the particular circumstances in which he found himself. The indubitable fact is that when he appeared, in his representations to George Washington, as a strict constructionist it was in opposition to the Hamiltonian system, which, as he believed, "flowed from principles adverse to liberty."[2] The constitutional arguments that he advanced throughout the decade were conditioned by his fear of potential tyranny, and time was to show that he took a less rigid position when that fear was relaxed;

---

[1] See *Jefferson and the Rights of Man*, p. 168.
[2] See, especially, *Jefferson and the Rights of Man*, ch. XX, dealing with the Bank of the United States and the question of its constitutionality, and his letter of Sept. 9, 1792, to Washington (Ford, VI, 102).

but his chief concern at all times was not to aggrandize state power for its own sake, but to safeguard the freedom of individuals.

This is not to deny that he had a strong sense of local attachment, a thing which was lacking in Hamilton. In facing the issues of the day, especially the economic issues, he was manifestly aware of the particular interests of Virginia and the states most resembling her, though to his mind these were also the interests of the agricultural population everywhere — that is, of a large majority of the American people. Before he went home in the summer of 1798 he wrote John Taylor of Caroline: "It is true that we are completely under the saddle of Massachusetts and Connecticut, and that they ride us very hard, cruelly insulting our feelings, as well as exhausting our strength and substance." [3] Perhaps the sectional conflict in the first decade of government under the Constitution has been insufficiently emphasized. But in this same letter he pointed out the cumulative folly of disunion to Taylor, who had said that "it was not unusual now to estimate the separate mass of Virginia and North Carolina, with a view to their separate existence." While by no means unaware of the geography of discontent, he laid much greater emphasis at this juncture on principles, and associated the dissensions and discords of the hour with parties, which, in his opinion, must exist in "every free and deliberating society." If, on the temporary superiority of one party, the other should resort to a "scission of the Union" he saw no hope that any federal government could exist. Indeed, the divisive spirit would not end its course until the Union had broken into its simplest units. This judgment differed little from that pronounced by Lincoln in his first inaugural that "the central idea of secession is the essence of anarchy." Jefferson preferred to endure existing ills rather than fly to others that might be confidently anticipated. "Seeing that we must have somebody to quarrel with," he said, "I had rather keep our New England associates for that purpose, than to see our bickerings transferred to others." [4]

Judging from this grimly humorous statement, he had recourse to the states in the present instance with no disunionist or sectionalist intent. He was merely seeking to apply what appeared to be the best available check on a federal government which was dominated in every department by men whom he regarded as unfriendly to individual rights and liberties.

In the Kentucky and Virginia Resolutions of this year, which Jefferson and Madison drafted behind the scenes, they denounced the

[3] June 4, 1798 (*Papers, MHS,* p. 62).
[4] *Ibid.,* p. 63.

Alien and Sedition Acts as unconstitutional infringements on human rights. The germ of these resolutions may perhaps be discerned in an earlier remark of Madison's. Writing Jefferson ten years before this, he said that even in the absence of specific constitutional guarantees of the rights of individuals, these were secured by "the limited powers of the federal government and *the jealousy of the subordinate governments.*" [5] Ironical though these may seem, even stronger statements to a like effect were made by Hamilton in *The Federalist*, at a time when he was trying to bring about the adoption of the Constitution and was wooing doubters.

> It may safely be received as an axiom of our political system [he said] that the State governments will, in all possible contingencies, afford complete security against the invasions of the public liberty by the national authority. . . . The legislatures . . . can discover the danger at a distance; and possessing all the organs of civil power, and the confidence of the people, they can at once adopt a regular plan of opposition, in which they can combine all the resources of the community. They can readily communicate with each other in the different States, and unite their common forces for the protection of their common liberty.

In another burst of prophecy he referred more specifically to the rights of individuals and went even further regarding possible state action:

> . . . the State legislatures, who will always be not only vigilant but suspicious and jealous guardians of the rights of the citizens against encroachments from the federal government, will constantly have their attention awake to the conduct of the national government, and will be ready enough, if anything improper appears, to sound the alarm to the people, and not only to be the voice, but if necessary, the ARM of discontent. [6]

We may safely assume that Hamilton afterwards regretted that he had said all this. Jefferson also had occasion to modify some of his earlier opinions. Arguing for a federal bill of rights before the adoption of one by Congress, he suggested that the judiciary might be relied on to uphold it. Even if he was thinking of state judges this idea

[5] To TJ, Oct. 17, 1788 (J.P., XIV, 18), italics added; referred to by Brant, *Madison*, III, 266–267.

[6] The quotations are from *The Federalist*, Nos. 28 and 26. Douglass Adair says that one of the reasons why Hamilton declined to have the authorship of individual numbers of these papers made known was that he did not want to reveal his responsibility for these sayings. Neither did Madison want to reveal his early advocacy of liberal construction (*W. & M.*, April, 1944, pp. 100–101).

could have been readily extended to the federal judiciary, of which at that time he had no fears.[7]

Madison took up the idea in Congress. Speaking in favor of a federal bill of rights, he said that "independent tribunals of justice" would consider themselves "in a peculiar manner" its guardians; they would be "an impenetrable bulwark against every assumption of power in the Legislative or Executive"; they would be "naturally led to resist every encroachment upon rights expressly stipulated for in the Constitution by the declaration of rights." Further security would lie in the state legislatures, which would "jealously and closely" watch the operations of the federal government, and would be able to resist every assumption of power more effectively than any power on earth could do. The state legislatures were, in his opinion, "sure guardians of the people's liberty." [8] But if he and Jefferson had been able to rely on the federal judiciary as the first line of defense of human rights, they would not have needed to fall back on the state legislatures.

In the summer of 1798 the part that the judicial branch of the government was to play in the enforcement of the Sedition Act was yet to be fully revealed, but the Republicans already had good reason to expect it to be highly partisan. In connection with the Cabell case, the year before this, Jefferson had warned that the federal grand jury was being perverted from a legal to a political institution, and Congressman Cabell himself had charged the judges with becoming a band of "political preachers." [9] In this case the only tangible result of Jefferson's private efforts was to secure from the House of Delegates of his state a condemnation of the action of a particular grand jury. After the passage of the Sedition Act, while facing and quietly combating what he regarded as a far greater usurpation of power by the federal legislature and executive, he nonetheless continued to harbor the hope that trial by jury could be preserved as "the true tribunal of the people" and would serve to protect "persecuted man." The procedure he proposed for the safeguarding of this was the popular election of jurors. Specifically, he suggested that they be elected in districts or precincts, and that assignment to grand juries or particular petit juries be made by lot thereafter. These ideas he embodied in a petition addressed to the General Assembly of his own commonwealth. He was not sure that he could reach federal juries through state law,

[7] To Madison, Mar. 15, 1789 (J.P., XIV, 659). He mentioned George Wythe, Edmund Pendleton, and John Blair, all from Virginia. Blair was appointed to the U. S. Supreme Court a few months later, serving until 1796.

[8] Speech of June 8, 1789 (Hunt, V, 385).

[9] See above, p. 335.

but, as he wrote Madison, he believed that if the people had the right of electing jurors in the state courts, Congress would either agree to conform federal courts to the same rule or be made odious in the eyes of the people generally.[10] Following the precedent he had set in the Cabell case, he had this petition presented in the name of certain inhabitants of Albemarle County, keeping himself out of sight. It was signed by a score of citizens and duly presented, but the state legislature was occupied with more important matters and did nothing about it.[11]

That this proposed democratization of the jury system would have promoted impartial justice is questionable, for it could hardly have failed to inject partisan considerations into the choice of jurors. In Virginia, where the Republicans were in the majority, it would doubtless have been to their advantage, but if elections were by districts they could have gained no monopoly; indeed, "persecuted man" would have lacked protection where, in Jefferson's opinion, he needed it most — that is, in Federalist districts. Furthermore, the need to shake off Federalist control of the courts was most obvious in the sphere which state action could have affected only by example. Therefore, these proposals now appear to be dubious even on political grounds.[12] They have some significance as a gesture of protest, however, and more in showing how the exigencies of the times were impelling Jefferson further in the democratic direction than he had ever gone before. Also, the episode suggests the extent of his local influence and the means by which he exercised it. Anything that he wanted done — in the presentation of ideas at least — he could get sympathetic fellow citizens to do while keeping himself in the background. The history of the Kentucky and Virginia Resolutions demonstrated the same thing on a larger scale.

The story of the drafting of these was a closely guarded secret for very many years and it cannot be told fully even now.[13] Not until he

[10] To Madison, Oct. 26, 1798 (Ford, VII, 287); undated petition, pp. 284-287. See also TJ to John Taylor, Nov. 26, 1798 (Ford, VII, 311-312).

[11] It is listed, under the date Dec. 24, 1798, in *Calendar of Legislative Petitions Arranged by Counties, Accomac-Bedford* (1908), p. 29, a publication of the Va. State Library. The brief description tallies with TJ's draft. It was signed by Th. Bell, Alex. Garrett, Thos. Carr, Jr., P. Scott, John Yeargain, C. Jouett, and 17 others. Apparently TJ also drew a bill, which was not presented. The reasons for the unavoidable postponement of this matter were stated by John Taylor in a letter of Feb. 15, 1799 (*J. P. Branch Hist. Papers*, II, 280); see also Madison to TJ, Feb. 14, 1800 (*Letters and Other Writings*, II, 156).

[12] Ammon, in his dissertation, "Republican Party in Virginia," pp. 174-176, emphasizes TJ's political motives in this move.

[13] It has been told best by Adrienne Koch and Harry Ammon in "The Virginia and Kentucky Resolutions: An Episode in Jefferson's and Madison's Defense of

had been several years in final retirement at Monticello was Jefferson's authorship of the Kentucky Resolutions made known, and little notice was paid it until his late seventies. Madison's authorship of the more moderate Virginia Resolutions came to public attention a little earlier, but he also was behind the curtain until the year that he became President.[14] In view of Jefferson's extreme distaste for anonymous communications to the newspapers, such as Hamilton indulged in and he avoided, his resort to secrecy in this instance and in that of the petitions which preceded it may seem inconsistent. He could have claimed, however, that he was dealing with basic issues, not personalities, and that these expressions were acceptable to the persons who presented them to the public. In any case, secrecy was a necessity under the present circumstances if he was disposed to criticize the existing government. As the avowed author of the Kentucky Resolutions, who would almost certainly have been blamed also for the Virginia Resolutions, the Vice President of the United States could have been charged with sedition and perhaps impeached for treason. In this period of hysteria almost anything could have happened, and he probably saw no real alternative between the course he followed and passivity in the face of what he regarded as a direct attack on the fundamentals of republican freedom.

He and Madison must have talked about that course when he stopped at Montpelier for the night on July 2, but seemingly they had no chance to talk about it again until late October, when Madison visited him, and there is no record of any letters between them in the interim. We may assume they were agreed that the Alien and Sedition Acts should be attacked on grounds of unconstitutionality by means of resolutions, and that, because of the gravity of the crisis, these should issue from state legislatures rather than local gatherings. Actually, there were meetings of protest in several Virginia counties, including Albemarle, in the late summer.[15] But, according to Wilson Cary Nicholas of Albemarle, an ardent Republican who shared Jefferson's confidence, these were not enough. He wrote his brother George in Kentucky: "I think everything depends upon the firmness of the

---

Civil Liberties" (*W. & M.*, April, 1948, pp. 147-176), and in Koch, *Jefferson and Madison*, ch. 7.

[14] John Taylor named Jefferson in 1814, but the information attracted little attention until 1821. He named Madison in 1809 (Koch & Ammon, p. 148).

[15] Ammon, "Republican Party in Virginia," pp. 176-177, speaks specifically of Powhatan, Albemarle, Goochland, and Prince Edward. An Albemarle petition, addressed to Congress and adopted *c.* Sept. 1, 1798, was printed in several newspapers, including the Richmond *Observatory* of Oct. 1. It may have been written by TJ.

state governments: town or county meetings will never produce the effect; the disease has gained too much strength to be destroyed by anything they can do; all that can be expected from them is to prepare the people to give their support to the state governments." [16] It had been rumored earlier that the Council of State had voted to summon the legislature of Virginia on September 3, which would have been a couple of months ahead of time and would have worked to the disadvantage of the Federalist members in the western part of the state, but that the Governor had refused to cooperate. The likelihood that the Virginia General Assembly would act in defense of freedom of speech was reported in Philadelphia by the *Aurora*. [17] It did not meet until the scheduled time, however, and meanwhile certain resolutions that originated at Monticello got into the hands of the legislators of Kentucky, who adopted them after some amending.

Jefferson drew these before October 4, when Wilson Cary Nicholas, to whom he had sent them, wrote him about them. Since John Breckinridge of Kentucky happened to be visiting Nicholas, that gentleman took the liberty of turning the resolutions over to him, on the assurance that the Kentucky legislature would adopt them and that Jefferson's connection with them would not be revealed. Indeed, anxious though Breckinridge was to pay his respects, he forebore visiting Monticello. Jefferson, who had entire confidence in Breckinridge, a former resident of the county, fully approved the action of Nicholas, saying that, although he had thought the resolutions should originate with North Carolina, recent changes in the political situation in that state suggested that they might not pass and that it was better they should come from Kentucky. Understanding that Nicholas was soon going to the neighborhood of Madison — from whom he said that he himself had no secrets — he expressed the wish that Madison be consulted about the resolutions. It is uncertain and even unlikely that that gentleman saw them before visiting Monticello a few weeks later, when they were on their way to Kentucky, though it may be presumed that he then saw a copy. Judging from later things he said, he would have liked to change them in certain particulars. [18]

[16] W. C. Nicholas to George Nicholas, Sept. 21, 1798 (Nicholas Papers, UVA), punctuation altered somewhat for purposes of clarity.

[17] *Aurora*, Aug. 6, 1798, under the heading IMPORTANT INFORMATION.

[18] This account of events, based chiefly on the letters of Nicholas to TJ, Oct. 4, 1798 (LC, 17877), and TJ to Nicholas, Oct. 5 (Ford, VII, 281–282) agrees with that of Koch & Ammon, but, as they point out, does not agree with TJ's own account in old age. In this he admitted that he might "misremember" certain circumstances, as in fact he did (to J. C. Breckinridge, Dec. 11, 1821 [Ford, VII, 290–291n.]).

The primary purpose of the resolutions that John Breckinridge carried to Kentucky from Albemarle County was to meet an immediate political situation.[19] Their author, maintaining the role of party leader while remaining anonymous, was seeking to focus attention on the Alien and Sedition Acts and make them the major issue of the hour. In attacking them as unconstitutional he was undoubtedly voicing his own conviction, but he was also following the line that the Republicans had taken in Congress. He was reaffirming their position. And if, in his effort to strengthen it, he went further than he had ever gone before in asserting the rights of states, this may be attributed to the fact that at no other time in his country's history as a nation had it seemed to him that human rights faced so dangerous a situation.

No valid objection could have been raised, then or thereafter, to his opening statement that the American states were not united "on the principle of unlimited submission to their government." And there was nothing startling at that time in his reference to the Constitution as a compact between states, for this view of it was widely held. He would have been on firmer ground, however, if he had distinguished between states as people and states as governments, and had said that he was referring to the former. This distinction was clear in the mind of Madison, who afterwards reminded Jefferson of it. The latter did not say, as Calhoun did later, that sovereignty was indivisible and remained with the states. The abstract question of sovereignty probably did not greatly interest him. He took the position which Madison well described a few months later: "The authority of constitutions over governments, and of the sovereignty of the people over constitutions, are truths which are at all times necessary to be kept in mind, and at no time, perhaps, more necessary than at present." [20] At this moment Jefferson would not have used the word "perhaps," and he was not setting forth his views so judiciously. But with him the essential truth was the sovereignty of the people, and the reality as he saw it was that the people lived in the several states and could express themselves most readily through state action. Regarding constitutions as shields against arbitrary power, he was disposed to interpret all of them strictly. In construing the federal Constitution strictly, however, he was pursuing no solitary course: he was quite in line with the Republican spokesmen in Congress.

[19] TJ's rough draft and fair copy in parallel columns are in Ford, VII, 289–309, preceded by a facsimile of resolutions moved by Breckinridge on Nov. 10, 1798. These were adopted that day by the House of Representatives of Kentucky, concurred in by the Senate Nov. 13, and approved by the Governor Nov. 16.

[20] In Madison's *Report* of 1800 (Hunt, VI, 352).

It would be difficult to determine who was most responsible for their adoption of strict construction as a weapon of defense. In point of time, perhaps Madison was, in arguing publicly against the constitutionality of the Bank of the United States before Jefferson did so privately for the benefit of George Washington. In view of Madison's previous constitutional position, there can be little doubt that he assumed this one in reaction against what he regarded as the excesses of Hamilton and his abuses of national power. The Republican leaders could have been in no doubt about Jefferson's current constitutional views, even though he expressed them only in private, but they would probably have taken the position they did anyway, since it was a natural one for opponents of "consolidation." They were strict constructionists by consensus. In his resolutions Jefferson virtually repeated their arguments against the objectionable laws, especially the Alien Act.

With respect to the Sedition Act, which he detested more and condemned first, he took the ground that this sort of definition of crime fell within none of the delegated powers and that this sort of action was specifically prohibited to Congress by the First Amendment. Though he did not say so here, he completely repudiated the doctrine that the federal courts already had common-law jurisdiction over seditious libel. He regarded the doctrine that the common law was in force in the federal courts without specific legislative action as an "audacious, barefaced, and sweeping pretension." [21] Also, in view of the fact that freedom of speech and the press are guarded against congressional action in the same amendment with freedom of religion, he held that whoever violated one of them threw down the sanctuary covering the others. It should be noted again, however, that he did not here deny to states the right to judge how far "the licentiousness of speech and of the press may be abridged without lessening their useful freedom." [22] This is certainly not to say that he set state rights above human rights, which he had striven so hard to safeguard in his own commonwealth. But, in a document designed for adoption by a state legislature, he was not warning against possible misuse of state power, and to him it was federal power that represented the clear and present danger.

In terms of constitutional theory the challenge of this political document lay in its assertions about the authority of a state to pass judgment on federal actions. In the first of his resolutions Jefferson categorically took the position that whenever the general government

[21] To Edmund Randolph, Aug. 18, 1799 (Ford, VII, 383–384).
[22] Ford, VII, 294.

assumed powers not delegated to it by the compact, its acts were "unauthoritative, void and of no force." He sounded as though he regarded this as automatic. But who had the right to determine that the general government had overstepped its proper bounds? As a practical man he was unwilling to concede this to the federal judiciary because of the obvious partisanship of the judges. Furthermore, on grounds of theory he thought it improper that the general government, or a branch of it, should be the exclusive or final judge of its own powers.[23] Denying that there was a "common judge," he concluded that each party to the compact had "an equal right to judge for itself, as well of infractions as of the mode and measure of redress."

He may have picked up this particular idea from John Taylor of Caroline. That fellow farmer and inveterate foe of "consolidation" wrote him early in the summer: "The right of the state governments to expound the Constitution might possibly be made the basis of a movement towards its amendment. If this is insufficient, the people in state conventions are incontrovertibly the contracting parties, and, possessing the infringing rights, may proceed by orderly steps to attain the object." [24] It should be noted that Taylor recognized state conventions as a higher authority than state governments. Jefferson made a similar distinction earlier, but he did not do so at this juncture.[25] One might assume from his draft that the rights he claimed could be exercised by a state legislature, even though he did not precisely say so. And in his first resolution he said they belonged to "each party" to the compact — that is, to each and every commonwealth rather than to all of them in their capacity as states.

Since the doctrine of judicial review was not established at this time, and there was no real consensus then or soon thereafter with regard to the nature of the Union, there was no impropriety in attempting to answer the perplexing question of how the constitutionality of federal actions could be fairly determined. But the doctrine which Jefferson was presenting here without express qualifications or safeguards could have paralyzed the general government if carried to its logical conclusion. It was not in character with the basic practicality he manifested when actually engaged in the conduct of the affairs of the Republic. Nor was it in accord with his recent counsel

23 Madison discussed this whole matter much more fully in his *Report* of 1800 (Hunt, VI, 351–352).

24 This letter of June 25, 1798 (*Branch Hist. Papers*, II, 271–276) was received by TJ on July 19, after he had visited Madison briefly and, presumably, before he submitted his resolutions to Nicholas.

25 See Madison's letter to him, Dec. 29, 1798 (Hunt, VI, 328*n.*).

to John Taylor against starting a divisive movement which might be expected to proceed to the last extreme.

His proposed resolutions were not presented in their entirety to the Kentucky legislature. Presumably, Breckinridge was responsible for the deletion of certain passages. Some deletion was in order anyway, since the draft was prolix and repetitious — a thing which could not often be said of his important papers. But the net result of the changes was to moderate it, as can readily be shown by referring to certain things that were left out. After saying that in cases of the abuse of delegated powers, a change in the members of the general government by the people was the "constitutional remedy," he made this assertion:

> where powers are assumed which have not been delegated, a nullification of the act is the rightful remedy: that every State has a natural right in cases not within the compact, . . . to nullify of their own authority all assumptions of power by others within their limits: that without this right they would be under the dominion, absolute and unlimited, of whosoever might exercise this right of judgment over them: . . .[26]

The distinction he appears to have made between a constitutional remedy and one based on natural right suggests that he really justified nullification under the sacred right of revolution. In that case, he would no more have had recourse to it for light and transient causes in 1798 than in 1776. By the same token, if he thought the threat of "absolute dominion" grave enough he would have recommended some sort of resistance whether it was constitutional or not. Things had not come to that pass, but in his desperate effort to find an ostensibly legal safeguard he had arrived at the opinion that the right lay with a single state, not only to decide when its basic liberties were invaded, but also to act in their defense. This he announced, not tentatively, but dogmatically with no suggestion of dangers which as an experienced public servant he might have been expected to perceive. Nevertheless, he wanted the commonwealth of Kentucky to say that, out of respect for its co-states, it was communicating with them — as was appropriate since they and they alone were parties to the compact. While he made no specific recommendation beyond the appointment of a committee to correspond with the several legislatures, his resolution expressed the hope that those bodies would take measures of their own to prevent these and other unauthorized acts from being exercised within their respective territories.

[26] In his eighth resolution (Ford, VII, 301).

As introduced and adopted, the Kentucky Resolutions of 1798 did not contain the term "nullification."[27] Furthermore, the specific actions they called for were relatively mild. These historic resolutions contained an injunction, which was not in Jefferson's original, to the senators and representatives of the state in Congress to seek a prompt repeal of the "unconstitutional and obnoxious acts." Also, they expressed the hope that other states, "recurring to their natural right in cases not made federal," would concur in declaring these acts void and of no force. But the Kentuckians sought concerted action with other states in effecting the repeal of these acts, clearly implying that they regarded their own action as insufficient. Jefferson took stronger ground, though this fact did not become generally known until his draft was published long after he was dead.[28]

If he objected to the changes in the paper he had drawn there is no record of his having said so. He seems to have concluded that, for the time at least, the government of Kentucky and the Republican party there had gone far enough. In a letter to Madison, after a paragraph about carpenters and the laying of floors at Monticello, he said:

> I enclose you a copy of the draught of the Kentucky resolves. I think we should distinctly affirm all the important principles they contain, so as to hold to that ground in future, and leave the matter in such a train as that we may not be committed absolutely to push the matter to extremities, & yet may be free to push as far as events will render prudent.[29]

Since he enclosed copies of both the resolutions that were introduced and those drafted by him, there is some doubt as to which he was referring to, but presumably he wanted Madison to avail himself of both of them while preparing resolutions for Virginia. He clearly indicated the changes, which Madison must have viewed with no small relief.

Jefferson's flexibility about tactics was also shown in a letter a little

[27] The Resolutions of 1799, which were the work of an unknown draftsman, did contain it. They are referred to hereafter.

[28] Resolution VIII as adopted, enjoining the senators and representatives, was not in TJ's draft. What was left of his own Resolution VIII was included in Resolution IX as adopted. To the best of my knowledge, his use of the word "nullification" in 1798 was not known at the time of the Nullification Controversy in South Carolina. His draft was published in the collection of his writings edited by H. A. Washington (1853), IX, 464–471. Randall, in 1857, published it in an appendix (III, 616–620), and discussed it in his text (II, 448–452). His factual account requires correction in the light of present knowledge.

[29] Nov. 17, 1798 (Ford, VII, 288). See Koch & Ammon, pp. 158–159, for discussion and information about enclosures.

later to John Taylor. In this he made his own current position somewhat clearer:

> . . . For the present, I should be for resolving the alien & sedition
> laws to be against the constitution & merely void, and for address-
> ing the other States to obtain similar declarations; and I would not
> do anything at this moment which should commit us further, but
> reserve ourselves to shape our future measures, or no measures,
> by the events which may happen.[30]

From these two letters it appears that, besides avoiding the term
"nullification," he was advocating no measures at present to prevent
the offensive acts from being carried into effect in Virginia. He was in
favor, however, of declaring these acts not merely unconstitutional but
also "void." On this point Madison disagreed with him.

Madison's Virginia Resolutions were introduced by John Taylor,
but, like Jefferson's Kentucky Resolutions, they passed first through
the hands of Wilson Cary Nicholas. He showed them to Jefferson before transmitting them. The latter now took it upon himself to suggest that the phraseology be so changed that Virginia would invite
the other states "to concur with this commonwealth in declaring, as it
does hereby declare, that the same acts are, and were ab initio, null,
void, and of no force or effect."[31] These words were substituted as
he desired, but, almost certainly at Madison's insistence, they were
stricken out before the final vote. In Madison's original language,
which was restored, the other states were urged to concur with the
commonwealth "in declaring, as it does hereby declare, that the acts
aforesaid are unconstitutional." At the same time confidence was expressed that necessary and proper steps would be taken by each, in
cooperation with Virginia, "in maintaining unimpaired the authorities,
rights, and liberties reserved to the States respectively, or to the people."[32]

By guarding his language Madison left himself in position to claim,
as afterwards he did claim, that the declaration of the legislature was
no assumption of judicial functions, but a justifiable expression of
opinion.[33] Jefferson's closest political friend did not believe that a
single state legislature could render an act of Congress null and void

[30] Nov. 26, 1798 (Ford, VII, 311).

[31] TJ to Nicholas, Nov. 29, 1798 (Ford, VII, 312–313). On this episode, see
Koch & Ammon, pp. 159–160; Brant, III, 462–463.

[32] The Virginia Resolutions, adopted by the House of Delegates on Dec. 21,
1798, and agreed to by the Senate on Dec. 24, are in Hunt, VI, 326–331. The
passage quoted is on p. 331.

[33] See, especially, his *Report* of 1800 (Hunt, VI, 402).

by saying so. He did believe and assert that federal powers were limited by "the plain sense and intention" of the Constitution, and "no further valid than they are authorized by the grants enumerated in the compact." Also, he said that in case of a "deliberate, palpable, and dangerous" exercise of ungranted powers, the states, as parties to the compact, "have the right and are in duty bound to interpose for arresting the progress of the evil, and for maintaining within their respective limits the authorities, rights, and liberties appertaining to them." But the term "interpose" could be variously interpreted and Madison spoke of "the states," not "a state."

The Virginia Resolutions were more moderate than those that emanated from Kentucky, even after Jefferson's draft of the latter had been amended. Because of their more restrained language they were less effective as an instrument of political propaganda, but they constituted a much firmer platform on which the Republican party could stand. Jefferson seems to have left no recorded comment on them after their passage, but in view of his present and subsequent relations with Madison, we may assume that he accepted without protest the rejection of his specific proposal, just as he did the amendments to the resolutions he drew for Kentucky. In both cases, wise counsel had prevailed over his initial impatience and he had been guarded against his own excess of zeal in defense of freedom. Without pressure and stimulus from him, Madison, who was trying to remain in retirement, might have been wholly silent. It is most unlikely that Jefferson could have persuaded him to do any more than he did, but it now seems a pity that Madison did not draft both papers. That is to take the long view. At the time Jefferson did not doubt that the legislatures of Kentucky and Virginia were pursuing the same objects. The common impression was that they were also proclaiming identical doctrines and resorting to the same methods, for Madison's fine distinctions were blurred and the two documents were lumped together in the public mind.

The nearest that Jefferson came to a formal statement of his own constitutional position, in the months immediately following the adoption of the Virginia Resolutions, was in what he himself described as a profession of his political faith. This was in a letter to Elbridge Gerry which is also important for other reasons. The passage most relevant to the constitutional question is as follows:

> I do then, with sincere zeal, wish an inviolable preservation of our present federal constitution, according to the true sense in which it was adopted by the States, that in which it was advo-

cated by its friends, & not that which its enemies apprehended, who therefore became its enemies; and I am opposed to the monarchising its features by the forms of its administration, with a view to conciliate a first transition to a President & Senate for life, & from that to a hereditary tenure of these offices, & thus to worm out the elective principle. I am for preserving to the States the powers not yielded by them to the Union, & to the legislature of the Union its constitutional share in the division of powers; and I am not for transferring all the powers of the States to the general government, & all those of that government to the Executive branch.[34]

This profession gives no clue to the means he would employ to preserve the Constitution as he was now interpreting it, and to safeguard the powers of the states as he understood them. Therefore, with respect to methods, which he wisely left indeterminate, one can read into it almost anything one likes. But there can be no possible doubt of his determination that strong protests should be made against current trends which, in his judgment, threatened to pervert the Constitution and "worm out the elective principle." Unquestionably, also, he was determined that the direction of the general government should be changed by force of public opinion. Repeatedly, during the next few months, he told persons of his own political persuasion that recourse to any other kind of force would be fatal.

[34] To Elbridge Gerry, Jan. 26, 1799 (Ford, VII, 327).

[XXVI]

The Aftermath of Protest

1799—1800

THE Kentucky and Virginia Resolutions, and the measures against which they protested, were by no means the only things in the public mind during the twelvemonth after their promulgation, but it seems desirable to carry their story on without much reference to other developments. In this period Jefferson spent relatively little time in Philadelphia. He left Monticello for that city on December 18, 1798, three days before the adoption of the Virginia Resolutions; but, since this session of Congress was the short one, he was away from home only a little more than two months on this trip, and he did not return to the seat of the federal government until the very end of 1799. We have a fuller record, however, of what he did there than of his activities during nearly ten months in Virginia.

Wherever he was, he was exceedingly careful about his letters. He observed to John Taylor that "the infidelities of the post office and the circumstances of the times" were against his writing freely and fully. "I know not which mortifies me most," he said, "that I should fear to write what I think, or my country bear such a state of things." [1] He told Monroe early in the year that, because of his suspicions of the post office, he would seldom write him. At the same time he counseled this friend always to examine the seal of his letters to see if they had been opened. He made similar excuses to others and issued the same warning to Madison.[2] Under these circumstances, it is not surprising that he did not mention the Kentucky and Virginia Resolutions even when writing Madison. He did not now need to bother about

[1] Nov. 26, 1798 (Ford, VII, 309).
[2] To Monroe, Jan. 23, 1799 (Ford, VII, 322); to Madison, Jan. 6, 1799 (Ford, VII, 318); to John Page, Jan. 24, 1799 (Ford, VII, 325); to Archibald Stuart, Feb. 13, 1799 (Ford, VII, 350).

them anyway, for they were to be transmitted to all the states and would thus give nationwide currency to the charges against the general government. In his own state the ground was well covered. The General Assembly ordered five thousand copies of its Resolutions printed and dispatched these to every county, along with a much more lengthy address to the people of the state which was also the work of Madison.[3] The Vice President could turn his attention to other means of calling attention to the issues of the day and the errors of the Federalists. The method he employed, that is, the promotion of public discussion by stimulating others and encouraging them to enter into it, probably was the only practical course open to him under existing circumstances, but it was also a congenial course to a highly sensitive man who personally liked privacy. While continuing to be immensely valuable to his party as a symbol he was serving it as a catalytic agent. This is clearly shown by the surviving record of what he did during his relatively brief stay in Philadelphia.

He was not immediately successful in his effort to get something more out of Madison, who did not take to the suggestion that he publish his notes on the debates in the Federal Convention. Jefferson believed that, in the revulsion of public opinion against the men in power which he expected, the Constitution would receive a different explanation from the one they were giving it, and that these debates, appearing at a critical moment, would have a decisive effect.[4] While such a publication would hardly have comforted Hamilton, whose extreme position with respect to centralization had found slight favor among the framers, it would not have been without embarrassment to Madison, whose emphasis had shifted. One wonders how fully Jefferson was informed about these debates. At any rate, Madison's notes on them, which are so precious to historians, were not published during his lifetime. Also, Jefferson vainly besought Madison to write regularly for the public on the issues of the hour and thus lessen the effect of his absence from Congress. He could send Jefferson what he wrote and Jefferson would get it published, keeping his name out of it altogether and thus sparing him the virulence of partisan counterattack. The channels of publication were not closed as yet, and obviously the discreet Vice President had access to them. "The engine is the press," he said. "Every man must lay his purse and his pen under contribution." [5]

---

[3] The *Address of the General Assembly*, dated Jan. 23, 1799, is in Hunt, VI, 332–340.
[4] To Madison, Jan. 16, 1799 (Ford, VII, 318).
[5] To Madison, Feb. 5, 1799 (Ford, VII, 344).

Among those he called upon, in this critical juncture, was Judge Edmund Pendleton. Early in the year a "patriarchal address" by this highly respected elder statesman to the people of his own Caroline County was running through the Republican newspapers in Virginia and elsewhere. Jefferson, delighted with the simple effectiveness of this plea for "republicanism," urged his old associate to write for a larger audience a recapitulation of the story of the erring administration. They could disperse from 10,000 to 20,000 copies of this throughout the United States, he said, with the help of congressmen who would soon be returning to their homes. Jefferson suggested specific things which might be mentioned in the statement and sent Pendleton documents on which to draw. When the Judge appeared reluctant, Jefferson renewed his "petition" to him, urging him to give the coup de grâce to the principles and practices that were ruining the country, and sending additional matter for his information. Somewhat to the surprise of his foster son, John Taylor, who had added his pressure to that of Jefferson, Pendleton prepared an address to the American citizens on the present state of their common country. While this did not reach Philadelphia soon enough to be dispersed according to Jefferson's plan, it was widely circulated in the newspapers under Pendleton's name, subjecting him to considerable Federalist abuse. It appeared as a pamphlet in Boston and was regarded by John Taylor as an antidote to arguments that were emanating from that stronghold of the administration.[6]

While doing what he could to provide the American people with the sort of political diet he wanted them to feed on, Jefferson gave special attention to the proper nourishment of the voters of Virginia.[7] Early in the year he sent to loyal supporters in the state copies of a pamphlet written by George Nicholas, brother of Wilson Cary Nicholas, in defense of the attitude of the citizens of Kentucky toward the general government. To his friend Archibald Stuart in the Valley, whom he so often consulted about his problems in marketing nails, he wrote: "These [pamphlets] I wish you to distribute, not to sound men who have no occasion for them, but to such as have been misled, are candid and will be open to the conviction of truth, and are of influence among their neighbors. It is the sick who need medicine, and not the well. Do not let my name appear in the matter." [8] Be-

[6] TJ to Pendleton, Jan. 29, Feb. 14, 1799 (Ford, VII, 336–339, 355–360); D. J. Mays, *Edmund Pendleton* (1952), II, 315–324.

[7] On this point see M. H. Woodfin, "Contemporary Opinion in Virginia of Thomas Jefferson," in Avery Craven, ed., *Essays in Honor of William E. Dodd* (1935), esp. p. 51.

[8] To Archibald Stuart, Feb. 13, 1799 (Ford, VII, 354). He said virtually the

sides making a strong case against the administration, Nicholas definitely denied the charge of seeking to destroy the Constitution and the Union. Jefferson was probably even more anxious than usual to keep his name out of the business because Nicholas made a complimentary reference to him. In this long pamphlet, however, the single statement which might have been expected to elicit most applause from critics of the general government in his commonwealth was the following:

> . . . If no other state in the union thinks as we do, Virginia, the ancient, the great, the powerful, the rich and the republican state of Virginia, still remains free and independent; . . .[9]

This was also calculated to arouse forebodings elsewhere, for his words could be interpreted as referring to something more than freedom of opinion.

Apparently Jefferson made no written reference at the time to the fears that were voiced in the replies of the other state legislatures to the Resolutions of Kentucky and Virginia. Most of these were made after he left Philadelphia for home on March 1, and his silence with respect to them makes it impossible to do more than guess just when he learned that the official replies from the states north of Virginia were uniformly unfavorable, and that the states to the southward did not respond at all. He probably anticipated and discounted the actions of the former, all of which were under Federalist control. If he was disappointed by the inaction of the latter, in which the Republicans were stronger, he gave no sign of it beyond his insistence in the summer that Virginia and Kentucky must continue to stand together.[10]

He must have been aware of the discussions in the Philadelphia papers.[11] Fenno and Cobbett made little reference to constitutional

---

same thing to Monroe when sending him a dozen copies on Feb. 11 (Ford, VII, 346). The pamphlet, entitled *A Letter from George Nicholas of Kentucky to His Friend in Virginia* (Lexington, 1798), is reprinted in *Filson Club Publications, No. 31* (Louisville, 1926), pp. 123-172.

[9] *Ibid.*, p. 160. The reference to TJ is on p. 155.

[10] The replies of seven states to Virginia are in Jonathan Elliot's *Debates in the Several State Conventions on the Adoption of the Federal Constitution* (1896), IV, 532-539. The others, to both Kentucky and Virginia, including the resolutions of Maryland, the first state to act, which were not communicated, and the protest of the minority in the last state, Vermont, are appended to F. M. Anderson's article "Contemporary Opinion of the Virginia and Kentucky Resolutions," in *A.H.R.*, V (1900), 45-63, 225-252. Counting New York, which addressed both states together, Kentucky got 4 replies to Virginia's 8. The dates of the various documents range from Dec. 28, 1798 to Nov. 5, 1799.

[11] Summarized by F. M. Anderson in *A.H.R.*, V, 236-237.

questions, but they had a great deal to say about resistance to the government. The latter described as "little short of high treason" the Address of the Virginia Assembly, in which the policy of the administration was discussed much more fully than in the Resolutions. At this stage the *Aurora* was restrained, doing little besides printing the documents along with numerous petitions against the obnoxious acts. Much impressed by the latter, Jefferson believed that sentiment in the middle states was swinging toward the position of Virginia. Like everybody else, he talked more about his own state than about Kentucky, which some Federalists designated as a satellite. He believed that the general government might venture to coerce Virginia if she were unsupported, and his desire that she gain support gave point to his insistence that she should avoid any show of force.

"Firmness on our part, but a passive firmness, is the true course," he wrote Madison. "Anything rash or threatening might check the favorable dispositions of these middle states, and rally them again around the measures which are ruining us." When urging Edmund Pendleton to take up his pen, he expressed fear that discontent with the government might lead to insurrection in Pennsylvania. "Nothing could be so fatal," he said. "Anything like force would check the progress of the public opinion and rally them round the government. This is not the kind of opposition the American people will permit. But keep away all show of force, and they will bear down the evil propensities of the government, by the constitutional means of election and petition." [12] In a mood of long-range optimism he was decrying overt rebellion and characteristically magnifying the appeal to reason.

The attitude of the congressional majority to petitions for repeal of the Alien and Sedition Acts did not commend itself to him, however. He described as scandalous the scene in the House in late February when the report of a committee rejecting them was taken up. Gallatin spoke on the Alien Act and John Nicholas on the Sedition Act, but the Federalists, who had determined in caucus to reply to no arguments, resorted at length to loud conversations, laughter, and coughing to drown them out. Edward Livingston wanted to speak, but was cut off, and the resolutions affirming the acts in question were adopted 52 to 48.[13] Perhaps the most surprising thing about this episode is that the Federalists were so high-handed and arrogant while, in fact, their margin was very small.

The mood of High Federalists leaders at the time is reflected in

---

[12] To Madison, Jan. 30, 1799; to Pendleton, Feb. 14, 1799 (Ford, VII, 341, 356).
[13] TJ to Madison, Feb. 26, 1799 (Ford, VII, 371). For the report, resolutions, and such debate as there was, see *Annals*, 5 Cong., III, 2985-3017.

private statements which would have accentuated Jefferson's fears of coercion if he had seen them. One of the most revealing of these is from Senator Theodore Sedgwick, who wrote Rufus King in England that he regretted the failure of the government to declare war on France immediately after the publication of the XYZ Dispatches. The domestic advantage of this would have been that "we should have superseded the necessity of alien and sedition laws — without them we might have hanged traitors and exported Frenchmen." As for recent actions in Virginia, he regarded the address of the General Assembly to the people as "little short of a declaration of war." [14] To this same Senator, from whom he seems to have had no secrets, Hamilton revealed the bellicose thought in his mind. With a professional army, rather than undependable militia, he would not hesitate "to subdue a *refractory and powerful state.*" Since Virginia had provided an obvious pretext, a force should be drawn towards her. Measures should then be taken "to act upon the laws and put Virginia to the test of resistance." [15]

Before he left Philadelphia for home, Jefferson concluded that the XYZ fever had abated and that the "system of alarm" was flagging. His hopes for republicanism and human liberty were still centered on the maintenance of peace, and their fluctuation reflected the course of foreign relations more closely, perhaps, than that of the domestic affairs we are considering here. Summing things up in a letter to General Kościuszko which was largely devoted to the personal concerns of this Polish friend of American independence, he said: "If we are forced into a war, we must give up political differences of opinion and unite as one man to defend our country, but whether at the close of such a war, we should be as free as we are now, God knows." If, however, peace should be maintained the spirit of the citizens, "rising with a strength and majesty" which showed the *"loveliness of freedom,"* would make the government in practice what it already was in principle, "a model for the protection of man in a state of *freedom and order.*" [16] Uncertain at the moment with respect to the course the government would pursue in foreign affairs, he was no doubt correct in assuming that the "system of alarm" based on the XYZ excitement was flagging. But in the spring of 1799 it had new fears to feed on and could take a more domestic direction.

[14] Sedgwick to King, Jan. 20, 1799 (King, II, 515–518).

[15] Feb. 22, 1799, quoted by Nathan Schachner, *Hamilton,* p. 387, from Sedgwick Papers, MHS.

[16] Feb. 21, 1799 (LC, 17993–17994). The latter italics are TJ's; the former have been added.

The actions of the government of Virginia were a boon to the Federalist alarmists. Charges that it had collected arms in Richmond in furtherance of its rebellious purposes were made in a public letter by Jefferson's troublesome neighbor John Nicholas, who had carried tales about him to George Washington.[17] A little later a Federalist leader in North Carolina, writing a Justice of the Supreme Court, described Virginia as the only state he despaired of, saying that recent visitors had reported that leaders of the "Jacobins" there were determined to overthrow the general government even at the risk of war and were talking boldly of secession.[18] Summing things up to Rufus King still later, Theodore Sedgwick reported that the government of Virginia had "displayed an anxiety to render its militia as formidable as possible, and to supply its arsenals and magazines," having imposed a tax on the citizens for this purpose.[19] These charges showed remarkable vitality, being revived after a couple of decades, but, since the specific actions referred to — especially the establishment of an armory — were authorized *before* the passage of the Alien and Sedition Acts, they can be readily explained on other grounds than those of meditated resistance.[20] Very likely there was belligerent talk by hotheads which alarmists could seize upon, but it does not follow that the most responsible leaders contemplated any overt act. During the winter and spring Jefferson left no possible doubt that he regarded the maintenance of peace and order as imperative.

Nevertheless, the disunionist trend which could be read into the actions of the majority in the legislature had an appreciable effect on public opinion within the state as well as outside of it. This was reflected in the congressional elections in the spring after Jefferson got home. The Federalists, electing eight of nineteen representatives, John Marshall among them, increased their delegation by four. During the autumn of 1798, when resentment of the Alien and Sedition Acts was so loud in the state, Marshall stated publicly that if he had been in Congress he certainly would have opposed the bills, regarding

[17] Koch and Ammon, p. 163, citing Richmond *Virginia Argus*, Mar. 29, 31, Apr. 2, 1799. The identification of him with Congressman John Nicholas, however, is erroneous. The letter of W. C. to George Nicholas, Sept. 21, 1798 (Nicholas Papers, UVA), speaking of the "defection" of J. Nicholas and of the wish that the latter would change his name for the sake of the family, must have referred to the cousin of these brothers, the other John Nicholas. For other references to this mixed identity, see above, ch. XIX, note 46.

[18] W. R. Davie to James Iredell, June 17, 1799, in the latter's *Life and Correspondence*, by G. J. McRee, II, 577–578.

[19] Nov. 15, 1799 (King, III, 148).

[20] P. G. Davidson disposed of them in "Virginia and the Alien and Sedition Laws," *A.H.R.*, XXXVI (Jan., 1931), 336–342. He did not know about the Nicholas letter, however.

them as useless and as "calculated to create unnecessary discontents and jealousies." [21] Federalist leaders elsewhere deplored this declaration. Sedgwick regarded it as a pitiful electioneering device, but the more sagacious George Cabot, while suggesting that allowance be made for the baneful air of Virginia, expressed confidence that, in Philadelphia, Marshall "would become a most powerful auxiliary to the cause of order and good government." [22] As a candidate the latter did not attack the Alien and Sedition Acts as unconstitutional, and the Address of the Federalist minority in the legislature, which was circulated at private expense, defended them against the charge.[23]

Marshall was elected by a very small majority after Patrick Henry had written a letter in his behalf.[24] Another victor was Light-Horse Harry Lee, who, in Jefferson's opinion, had poisoned Washington against him. He himself was unpleasantly surprised by these events but took comfort from the elections to the legislature, where the Republicans would be as strong as ever. But, since representation in the House of Delegates was on the basis of counties, the popular vote for congressmen probably represented public sentiment more accurately. Patrick Henry, now the darling of the Federalists, was elected to the General Assembly, but Jefferson observed that he would encounter such talents as he had not met before. Had he not died before the session began he would have had to cope with Madison, who had been persuaded to accept election. Jefferson did not doubt that the "cause of republicanism" would triumph in the long run. "Our citizens may be deceived for a while and have been deceived," he said; "but as long as the presses can be protected, we may trust to them for light; still more perhaps to the taxgatherers." [25] Another interpretation of these events was given by a much younger Republican, on whom Jefferson was to rely greatly in his last years. Joseph C. Cabell, while believing that the motives of the members of the last General Assembly in adopting their resolutions and addresses were perfectly pure, doubted if their measures were prudent and politic. During the preceding summer and fall, he said, the people "glowed with indignation" at the federal legislation and were determined to repel the injuries to their liberties. "But the handle that was made of the measures of the last Assembly has had its desired effect in alarming the people. The federalists have excited a belief that the legislature intended,

[21] Sept. 20, 1798 (Beveridge, II, 389, and App. III, pp. 574–577).
[22] Cabot to King, Apr. 26, 1799 (King, III, 9).
[23] The Federalists attributed this Address to Marshall, as Beveridge does (II, 402). Ammon, p. 199, attributes it to Light-Horse Harry Lee.
[24] Beveridge, II, 413–416.
[25] To Archibald Stuart, May 14, 1799 (Ford, VII, 378).

and that their measures led to, disunion. The people, fearing disunion as the worst of evils, have therefore thought it better, even at the risk of bad laws, to elect men who would never consent to a dissolution of the federal compact." [26]

What Jefferson regarded as the worst of evils was the coercion of opinion. To him this was a question that went beyond party or state or even the Union: it bore directly on the future progress and happiness of mankind. Along with his distrust of all rulers and fear of governmental power in any form went a profound faith in the limitless potentialities of unfettered intelligence. In this dark period, when his fears of tyranny — actual, potential, or imagined — were at their height, he voiced this faith strikingly in a letter to a college student who had sought counsel about his studies. To young William Green Munford he wrote:

> I am oné of those who think well of the human character generally. I consider man as formed for society, and endowed by nature with those dispositions which fit him for society. I believe also, with Condorcet, as mentioned in your letter, that his mind is perfectible to a degree of which we cannot as yet form any conception. . . .
> I join you therefore in branding as cowardly the idea that the human mind is incapable of further advances. This is precisely the doctrine that the present despots of the earth are inculcating, & their friends here re-echoing; & applying especially to religion & politics; . . . But thank heaven the American mind is already too much opened, to listen to these impostures; and while the art of printing is left to us science can never be retrograde. What is once acquired of real knowledge can never be lost. To preserve the freedom of the human mind then & freedom of the press, every spirit should be ready to devote itself to martyrdom, for as long as we may think as we will, & speak as we think, the condition of man will proceed in improvement.[27]

Thus spoke a prophet of progress who staked his ultimate hopes not on any particular form of political organization or government, but on the freedom of intelligence. Nonetheless, he was placing immediate reliance on his own party and on the states which alone had protested officially against federal coercion of opinion. And, while he

[26] Joseph C. Cabell to David Watson, June 7, 1799 (*Va. Mag.*, XXIX [1921]), 263–264.

[27] TJ to Munford, June 18, 1799 (recipient's copy, Teachers College, Columbia University; press copy, LC, by courtesy JP). This wonderful letter is partially printed in Koch & Ammon, pp. 151–152.

managed to keep out of public view during this summer at Monticello, he was consulted on crucial matters by political intimates and continued to serve as a catalyst. Specifically, the question was what the legislatures of Kentucky and Virginia should do at their approaching sessions. When Wilson Cary Nicholas, who was going to Kentucky, raised the question, Jefferson sent his letter to Madison along with a sketch of his own ideas about procedure. There was a degree of tentativeness in these, and he may have consciously overstated them, relying on Madison to suggest practical modifications as this sagacious friend so often did; but, as in no other letter he ever wrote, perhaps, he indicated the lengths to which he was willing to go, at last, in defense of freedom of opinion and the right of political opposition.[28]

Assuming agreement that the "principles" already set forth by the legislatures of Virginia and Kentucky were not to be yielded in silence, he roughly outlined the contents of another declaration. This "plan" Madison discussed with him at Monticello a few days later, talking him out of some of his expressions. He then embodied it in a letter to Nicholas, who had been unable to confer with them in person.[29] But for this letter, which Nicholas bore to Kentucky, it is entirely possible that the legislators there would have made no reply to the communications from the other states, for, as John Breckinridge afterwards reported, they were undisposed to make one at first. The communication of Jefferson's ideas to Breckinridge and possibly to others may well have provided the necessary impetus. The Kentucky Resolutions of 1799, adopted in November, accorded with his major purpose that this state should continue to act in concert with his own commonwealth, that the expressed doctrines of the Federalist majorities in the northern legislatures should not be silently acquiesced in, and that the principles proclaimed by the legislatures of Kentucky and Virginia should be reiterated. But he had stated that he intended to give only "a general idea of the complexion and topics" of such a declaration as might be drawn, and the hastily prepared resolutions of Kentucky were by no means an expansion of his current plan. They are most noted in history for their introduction of the word "nullification," which he had used in 1798 but was not now employing. Otherwise they are more conciliatory in tone than his letter to Nicho-

---

[28] To Madison, Aug. 23, 1799 (Rives Papers, LC). For this important letter we are indebted to Adrienne Koch; it is printed in her *Jefferson and Madison*, pp. 196–198, and in Koch and Ammon, pp. 165–166. Continued reference to these works may be assumed, even when there is no specific citation.

[29] To W. C. Nicholas, Sept. 5, 1799 (Ford, VII, 389–392).

las and considerably more moderate than his earlier letter to Madison.[30] Irrespective of the degree of influence he exercised in Kentucky at this juncture, however, these two private letters are of no little biographical interest as indicating the state of their author's own thinking at the time.

Jefferson's first suggestion to Nicholas was that answer be made to the "reasonings" in the replies of the states and in the report of the committee of the federal House of Representatives regarding the Alien and Sedition Acts. His final one was that something be said with respect to the "new pretensions" of federal common-law jurisdiction. The person who really carried out these suggestions was Madison in the able and moderate Report he soon drew for the General Assembly of Virginia. For his own part Jefferson gave no indication of any retreat in the area of constitutional interpretation except for his failure to mention nullification. What is more, he now referred to the right of secession — by implication in one recommendation and explicitly in another.

His idea was that the right should be reserved "to make this palpable violation of the federal compact [the Alien and Sedition Acts] the ground of doing in future whatever we might now rightfully do, should repetition . . . render it expedient." [31] Since Madison objected to the reservation, Jefferson told Nicholas that he readily receded from it, not merely because of deference, but also for this reason: "as we should never think of separation but for repeated and enormous violations, so these, when they occur, will be cause enough of themselves." Madison had objected to what he regarded as a threat of secession. Jefferson, while not renouncing the "right" — which, like many others at this stage of national history, he no doubt assumed — was brought to recognize that the likelihood of exercising it was so remote that there was no real point in mentioning it in a formal declaration.

He recommended to Nicholas that attachment to the Union and the Constitution be expressed in warm and conciliatory language,

[30] The Kentucky Resolutions of 1799 may be seen in Elliot's *Debates*, IV, 544-545, and elsewhere. John Breckinridge wrote TJ on Dec. 13, 1799: "It was at the opening of the session concluded on to make no reply [to the other legislatures], but on further reflection, lest no improper conclusions might be drawn from our silence, we hastily drew up the paper which I enclosed you" (LC, 18094-18095). He added that, while there was no dissenting voice in the House, there was considerable division in the Senate, particularly on the sentence declaring "*a nullification of those acts by the States to be the rightful remedy.*"

[31] The quotation is from the letter to Nicholas. In his more cumbersome original statement to Madison he implied that the "approbation or acquiescence of the several co-states" had compounded the injury and given further ground for independent action on the part of Kentucky and Virginia.

but with a qualifying statement: namely, that "we are willing to sacrifice to this [union] everything but the rights of self-government in those important points which we have never yielded, and in which alone we see liberty, safety, and happiness." He would have the legislators of the two states say that they were "not at all disposed to make every measure of error or of wrong a cause of scission," and that they relied on the good sense of the American people to rally with them around the true principles of the federal compact while there was yet time. In his letter to Madison, however, he had said something much more threatening: "But determined, were we to be disappointed in this, to sever ourselves from that union we so much value, rather than give up the rights of self government which we have reserved, and in which alone we see liberty, safety and happiness." He worked the final clause of this sentence into his letter to Nicholas, but after consulting Madison he left out the first part — in which he made explicit the threat which was implicit in the "reservation" his counselor objected to.

There appear to be no other recorded words of Jefferson which go so far in a disunionist direction. At that time, to be sure, there was nothing particularly startling in the *idea* that the Union was dissoluble, and threats against it were common, as they continued to be for a half century and more, until at length the concept of an indissoluble Union was fixed by predominant opinion and force of arms. Quite clearly, the author of the Declaration of Independence no more valued union for its own sake than he did government. He judged it, as he did every other manmade institution, by the ends it served. Fully recognizing its necessity during the struggle for independence, he had then striven to strengthen the centripetal against the centrifugal forces; and the desire to maintain the territorial integrity of the United States was central in his diplomacy. There can be no doubt that now, after a lifetime of devotion to the public weal, he was trying to preserve this Union by keeping it within what he regarded as its proper constitutional bounds. To him those who would pervert and exploit it were its greatest enemies.

Nonetheless, in view of what he had said to John Taylor about the futility of secession, and his repeated insistence that resistance to repressive governmental actions should take the form of appeals to reason, not to force — in view of these other calming words of his — it is surprising that he should have even tentatively suggested that any sort of reference to disunion should be included in a public document. It may be that developments of recent weeks — the contemptuous treatment of protests against the Alien and Sedition Acts by the

Federalist majority in Congress, the unfavorable replies of the northern states to the Kentucky and Virginia Resolutions, and the Federalist gains in his own state — had finally induced in this characteristically sanguine man a temporary mood of pessimism, even of desperation. At all events, but for the staying hand of Madison he would have had recourse to a threat which he had no real intention of backing by an overt act. His friend thought this gesture uncalled-for and it would unquestionably have been bad politics. Fortunately for him and his cause, the public knew nothing of the episode, just as the great body of his countrymen were unaware of what High Federalists were threatening behind the scenes. We ourselves have the additional advantage of being able to view it in the total context of what he did and said through all his years.

The public knew about the second set of Kentucky Resolutions, for they appeared in many papers; but, since they were blanketed by the news of the death of George Washington, little heed was paid them.[32] They were not transmitted to the other state legislatures, as the first set had been, hence they called for no response. Jefferson himself did not see a copy of them until the beginning of another year. After receiving one from John Breckinridge in January, 1800, he wrote: "I was glad to see the subject taken up and done with so much temper, firmness and propriety." [33] It is impossible to say what he thought of the reference to nullification, but it was not like him to criticize the actions of party leaders of whose general principles he approved.

With the formal response of his own commonwealth to the communications from other states Jefferson had nothing to do directly. It was the work of Madison as a member of the House of Delegates, and it took the form of a committee report which was adopted in January, 1800. After taking up the Virginia Resolutions of 1798 one by one and discussing them at length, Madison's Report ended with a resolution of adherence to them and a renewed protest against the Alien and Sedition Acts as "palpable and alarming infractions of the Constitution." [34] While yielding none of his devotion to human rights, Madison safeguarded his constitutional position by numerous carefully phrased qualifications and adopted a tone of becoming moderation. To do justice to this magnificent exposition of republicanism and a balanced government would be impossible here. Jefferson, now back in Phila-

[32] Anderson in *A.H.R.*, V, 242–243.
[33] To Breckinridge, Jan. 29, 1800 (Ford, VII, 416) replying to the letter of Dec. 13. A copy of the resolutions was sent him a little earlier.
[34] The Report on the Resolutions is in Hunt, VI, 341–406.

delphia, was informed by Madison of the course of events in Richmond, and very early in the year he received a copy of the Report as presented. In February he was complaining that he had not yet received a copy of it as passed.[35] He wanted it to be widely distributed, as eventually it was. Apparently he made no comment on what may be properly regarded as the classic statement of his party's constitutional position at this time, but he gave no sign that he objected to its moderation. It is said to have had an immediate and favorable effect in Virginia, but it seems to have been relatively little noted elsewhere.

To measure with any precision the political effects of this series of pronouncements is, of course, impossible. The initial response of the other state legislatures, or the lack of it, was hardly an index of public opinion, and other exceedingly important factors entered into later elections which went against the Federalists. The best available scholarly judgment is that, even among Republicans, the Kentucky and Virginia Resolutions were more acceptable as protests against the Alien and Sedition Acts than as interpretations of the relations between the states and the federal government.[36] That these acts were unconstitutional was a basic Republican tenet already, and it cannot be assumed that a majority of the American people at the time would have agreed that there was no authority higher than the United States Supreme Court. But the doctrine of the nullification of federal law by a single state appears to have been received with little favor outside Kentucky. Madison denied it, with Jefferson's silent acquiescence; and in his Report, while asserting that declarations by state legislatures were entirely proper, he expressly stated that these were but "expressions of opinion, unaccompanied with any other effect than what they may produce on opinion by inciting reflection." [37] In the end, therefore, this campaign which Jefferson had inspired boiled down to an appeal to public opinion against the offensive acts and the trend of the general government.

In any case such a campaign would have been viewed with contempt by those who were designating all criticism as illegitimate. But because of their constitutional implications these state documents might have been expected to alarm moderate men and give another handle to those who were charging the Republicans with being disorganizers and disunionists. It would appear, therefore, that certain of Jefferson's

[35] Various letters from Madison, Dec. 1799–Jan. 1800 (Hunt, VI, 342–347n.); TJ to Monroe, Feb. 6, 1800 (Ford, VII, 424).
[36] See, especially, Anderson in *A.H.R.*, V, 236–237.
[37] Hunt, VI, 402.

private recommendations marked a lapse from the political acumen which he generally manifested, and that on political grounds alone Madison was wise in moderating him. His conclusion by the spring of 1800 that the people of the middle states were almost rallied behind Virginia, and that the Republicans would soon have a majority in Congress, need not imply that he thought the Resolutions the main cause of this, but obviously he was glad that his state and Kentucky had taken the lead in combating the administration. This they did most conspicuously by their formal pronouncements. He did not cease to believe that the Constitution had been violated, and he looked forward to the time when a declaration of its principles could be drafted.[38] Just what this should contain he did not state, but he did say that it should be in the nature of a declaration of rights. We can safely assume that he would have wanted to emphasize human rights, whatever specific means he might have advocated for their protection.

This is not the place to consider the uses and abuses of the Virginia and Kentucky Resolutions by later decades and generations. It can surely be said, however, that to base a state-rights position on them without reference to human rights would be to disregard their central purpose. They must be viewed in no vacuum but in their own setting of time and circumstance. While their instigator was undoubtedly concerned to preserve his party and to check what he regarded as a trend toward consolidation, he was not seeking primarily to safeguard local interests, and certainly not vested interests, but the freedom of all men everywhere to think as they liked and speak as they thought. Emphasis should be laid not on the weapon he used, but on the ends he sought, and he should be recognized as a champion of rights which he deemed universal.

[38] To P. N. Nicholas, Apr. 7, 1800 (Ford, VII, 439-440).

[XXVII]

Adams *vs.* the High Federalists
1798–1799

DESPITE the Kentucky and Virginia Resolutions, the main political story during the months immediately following the passage of the Alien and Sedition Acts is that of the President and the Federalists, not that of the Vice President and the Republicans. As the unofficial leader of the unrecognized opposition Jefferson could do little more than communicate with sympathetic individuals and influence policy on the state and local level. Not only was national policy beyond his control; during much of the time he did not even have a close view of the course of national affairs. This can readily be seen by reference to the calendar. After his return home in July, 1798, he spent little more than two months in Philadelphia before the election year of 1800. Surprising though it may seem, Adams was away from the seat of government almost as long, for he took full advantage of the intervals between sessions of Congress. His wife was at Quincy in a precarious state of health, and he would not leave her until he had to. He described the summer of 1798 as the gloomiest he had ever spent, saying that the prospect of the coming winter in Philadelphia without his wife was even more dismal.[1]

A predominant impression of this period is one of impotence on the part of Jefferson and of increasing loneliness on that of Adams. The pity is that neither of these old friends could read the mind of the other. Neither the President nor the Vice President was unmindful of international affairs that summer and autumn, and Adams was beginning to be aware of domestic developments behind his back, but unquestionably his subordinates took advantage of his absence. We cannot be sure how soon or how fully Jefferson became aware of High

[1] To James McHenry, Oct. 22, 1798 (*Works*, VIII, 612–613).

Federalist machinations, but obviously it is less correct to say that he and his party were beginning to encompass the defeat of the men in power than that the latter were paving the way for their own downfall.

Years later John Quincy Adams said that the "first decisive symptom" of Federalist schism was the disagreement about the army.[2] Jefferson does not appear to have noted this during the second session of the Fifth Congress. He left a clear record of his own opposition to the increase of the military establishment but does not seem to have recognized, and certainly did not stress, the difference in emphasis between Adams and the Hamiltonians. The struggle over the rank of the highest officers in the future army, which has been often viewed as a bit of comic opera but which is supposed to have opened the eyes of Adams to the designs of Hamilton and his friends, occurred during the summer and autumn of 1798. Jefferson knew that after he left for home the Senate had confirmed the nomination of Washington as commander-in-chief, and no doubt he soon learned the names of the high officers who were confirmed a little later. The list included Hamilton, C. C. Pinckney, and Henry Knox as major generals, and he may have assumed that they were to rank in that order. The exchange of letters between Adams, Secretary of War McHenry, and Washington, showing that the President wanted both Knox and Pinckney to be ahead of Hamilton, and that he yielded to Washington's virtual ultimatum, was not made public. Since Knox was in financial difficulties which soon led to bankruptcy, and since Washington's judgment of Hamilton's superior abilities was unquestionably sound, the eventual outcome of this tussle behind the scenes may have been a relief to Adams.[3] But, while he was not fully informed of the intrigue of Pickering and McHenry, and probably did not know that at the moment Hamilton sounded less extreme than his supporters, the President had abundant reason to become aware of the magic of the new Major General's name in the highest circles. Unquestionably discomfited, he had good reason to wonder if he really had the authority of a President. He had already suffered discomfiture from the refusal of the Senate to confirm the nomination of his son-in-law, William S. Smith, to be brigadier general, which Washington had recommended. The reasons for this

[2] Quoted by Kurtz, *Presidency of John Adams*, p. 308. The importance of the disagreement is stressed in that book, see ch. 14.

[3] That it was a relief is the judgment of Bernard Knollenberg, whose paper "John Adams, Knox, and Washington," in *Procs. Amer. Antiquarian Soc.*, n.s. LVI (1947), pp. 207–238, esp. pp. 227–238, is the best account of the episode I have seen. It appears that Pickering concealed the fact that Hamilton had expressed his willingness to rank below Knox if necessary.

rejection were not made known to Adams at the time by Pickering, whose representations were responsible for it.[4]

One aspect of this affair would have been of great interest to Jefferson if he had known about it: on the original list of possible officers which Adams gave McHenry to communicate to Washington were the names of Gates, Muhlenberg, and Burr, all of whom were Republicans. Jefferson might have interpreted this as an attempt to win them over, but it was to the credit of Adams that he did not regard the army as the preserve of his own party.[5] By contrast, Washington listed only Federalists, and showed on numerous occasions that he now trusted no others. Learning that, in his own state, certain recent "brawlers" against measures of the government were seeking commissions, he gave McHenry this opinion: "that you could as soon scrub the blackamoor white, as to change the principles of a profest Democrat; and that he will leave nothing unattempted to overturn the Government of this country." Such a person, Washington believed, would be the first to defend the French in case of invasion.[6] Adams never went that far in his doubts of the patriotism of the Republicans.

After Jefferson got back to Philadelphia on Christmas Day, 1798, and resumed his role as reporter of national affairs to Madison and others, he had much to say about military proposals in Congress. In one calculation he figured that the various projected armies would add up to 44,000 men at least, though nobody pretended that there was any *real* danger of invasion.[7] A few weeks later, when summing things up to Edmund Pendleton, he voiced the suspicion which he had probably had all along, namely, that there was a design to use force "on the Constitution" — that is, on those who did not agree with the administration about its interpretation. He recognized that Hamilton would be the real general, Washington being commander only in name. Doubting that such an army under Hamilton could be disbanded, he rested his hopes on "the inability to raise anything but officers." [8] What he did not say and appears not to have perceived was that Adams regarded the military plans of the High Federalists as unrealistic. In the previous autumn the President had written Secretary McHenry from Quincy that they might find more than they had bargained for

---

[4] The circumstances are described in Adams, *Works*, VIII, 618–619*n.*, but the editor does not make clear just when Adams found out about Pickering's part in the business.

[5] Adams to McHenry, July 6, 1798 (*Works*, VIII, 574).

[6] Washington to the Secretary of War, Sept. 30, 1798 (Fitzpatrick, XXXVI, 474).

[7] Feb. 5, 1799 (Ford, VII, 342).

[8] To Pendleton, Apr. 22, 1799 (Ford, VII, 375–376).

if they had a great and costly army to maintain without an enemy to fight. "At present," he said, "there is no more prospect of seeing a French army here, than there is in Heaven." [9] Later events were to show that he was quite content that the American army should largely remain on paper.

The question of the uses of these projected military forces naturally arose in many minds. That certain Federalist extremists would have liked to have them as a threat against the political opposition, and would have welcomed the opportunity to use them as a weapon of suppression, can hardly be doubted in view of what they were writing each other. There are indications that Hamilton was more cautious than some of his most ardent supporters at this stage, but this champion of governmental power did not rely primarily on moral suasion. Outlining the domestic system he advocated in a letter to the Speaker of the House, he said that it would be wise to act on the hypothesis that the opponents of the government were resolved, if this should be practicable, "to make its existence a question of force." [10] His plan involved the erection of numerous nonmilitary "ramparts" — by extending the judiciary, increasing taxes, limiting the admission of new states, subdividing the great states, strengthening the laws against sedition — but military measures were an indispensable feature of it, and he might have been expected to have recourse to force.

An army would also have been most useful in connection with schemes of imperial expansion with which Hamilton and other High Federalists were flirting during the summer and autumn of 1798, when Adams was at Quincy and Jefferson at Monticello. The British submitted to Rufus King proposals of co-operation with the United States in pursuit of the plan of Francisco de Miranda to conquer Spanish territories in the New World, the assumption being that Louisiana and the Floridas would be the portion of the United States. King passed these on to Pickering and thus to Adams, who would have none of them, and had Miranda get in touch with Hamilton. In August, Hamilton wrote that he hoped the enterprise would be undertaken, saying that the American command would fall to him. He told Miranda, however, that he would not participate unless supported by the government of his own country. In his opinion, matters had not yet ripened sufficiently, but he hoped that winter would mature the project.[11] That

[9] Oct. 22, 1798 (*Works*, VIII, 613).

[10] To Jonathan Dayton, 1799 (J.C.H., VI, 383–388).

[11] Hamilton to King, and to Miranda, Aug. 22, 1798 (Lodge, VIII, 505–507). An admirable account of this episode is that of A. B. Darling, in *Our Rising Empire* (1940), pp. 316–328. For an excellent general discussion of High Federalist foreign policy, see Dauer, *Adams Federalists*, ch. XI.

they did not ripen was owing in part to the coldness of Adams. That autumn Hamilton in private spoke slightingly and rather condescendingly of the executive department, implying that it lacked the sort of energy in administration that he himself would have given it. Yet, while deploring delays and feebleness, he believed that the difficulties would be overcome. Writing Rufus King, he said: "I anticipate with you that this country will, ere long, assume an attitude correspondent with its great destinies — majestic, efficient and operative of great things. A noble career lies before it." [12] Actually, his dreams of power and glory for his country and himself were contingent on war with France, and the immovable obstacle in his path turned out to be John Adams.

At the opening of the third session of the Fifth Congress, in December, 1798, Congressman Harrison Gray Otis, chairman of the Committee on Defense, wrote Hamilton, asking his counsel. [13] The military bills that Otis introduced were those desired by the General, not by the President. To this influential Federalist congressman, the Inspector General of the Army outlined his program. He hoped that the President would be empowered to declare war in case a negotiation with France should not be on foot by August 1, or being on foot should terminate without an adjustment. He referred to the acquisition of the Floridas and Louisiana, and to the detachment of South America from Spain. He regretted that the preparation of an adequate military force was not proceeding more rapidly. "There is some sad nonsense on this subject in some good heads," he said charitably. "The reveries of some of the friends of the government are more injurious to it than the attacks of its declared enemies. When will men learn to profit by experience?" [14]

Certain comments of Adams on the General about this time could be applied to either the domestic or foreign policy of the latter. Writing Harrison Gray Otis, the President said: "This man is stark mad, or I am. He knows nothing of the character, the principles, the feelings, the opinions and prejudices of this nation. If Congress should adopt this system, it would produce an instantaneous insurrection of the whole nation from Georgia to New Hampshire." [15] By announcing his intention to reopen negotiations with the French, as Adams did before the end of the third session of the notorious Fifth Congress, he pointed

[12] Oct. 2, 1798 (Lodge, VIII, 511).

[13] Dec. 21, 1798 (Morison, *Harrison Gray Otis*, I, 158–160).

[14] To Otis, Jan. 26, 1799 (J.C.H., VI, 390–392); see also Dec. 27, 1798 (VI, 379–380).

[15] Adams to Otis, quoted by Morison, *Harrison Gray Otis*, I, 162, without precise date.

the way to both domestic and external peace, but at the same time he brought consternation to the advocates of a strong military establishment and to such as may have dreamed of imperialistic adventure.

Jefferson was disposed to believe almost anything that might be alleged against the "war party," but, judging from his extant correspondence, he was less informed of the particular designs and hopes of the High Federalist leaders than he was of the state of mind of the French officials. Oliver Wolcott, who commandeered the letter that Fulwar Skipwith, the American consul general in Paris, wrote Jefferson about the time of the XYZ exposure, claimed that there was "treasonable" correspondence between friends of France abroad and at home.[16] While properly refusing to concede that there was anything treasonable in the private exchange of views and information by individuals in two countries which were technically at peace, Jefferson himself had prudently refrained from writing friends in France since he had ceased being secretary of state — except only for William Short on his own affairs and James Monroe when there. He wanted the facts of the matter to be made known to his friends because of the frequent assertions in newspapers that he had given Dr. George Logan letters to Merlin, head of the Directory, and to Talleyrand.[17] The uproar over Logan, who was often referred to as "Jefferson's Envoy Extraordinary," reached its crescendo after this self-appointed peacemaker got back from France in November. The chorus of derision, led by Peter Porcupine, lasted into the congressional session.[18]

Dr. Logan promptly reported to the Secretary of State his impressions of the desire of the French for peace, but, according to Federalist report, Pickering dismissed him "with a flea in his ear." Washington, who happened to be in Philadelphia, gave the unofficial emissary a reluctant hearing and parted with him in some anger. After Adams finally got back from Quincy the President listened to him more attentively than the others but was noncommittal.[19] He took comfort from sympathetic local Republicans but did not report to Monticello. The congressional debates which ended with the passage of "Logan's Law," forbidding personal missions of this sort, happened to begin the

[16] Skipwith to TJ, Mar. 17, 1798 (Gibbs, II, 158–161); see above, pp. 378–379.

[17] He made the statement in a letter to Aaron Burr, Nov. 12, 1798 (LC, 17890) and elsewhere. I see no reason to doubt its correctness, though minor departures from his customary practice may possibly be discovered. As an example of the Federalist charge about Dr. Logan, see R. King to R. Troup, Sept. 16, 1798 (King, II, 415), and William Cobbett, *Porcupine's Works* (1801), IX, 283–285, giving an extract from *Porcupine's Gazette*, Oct., 1798.

[18] F. B. Tolles, *George Logan of Philadelphia* (1953), p. 173 and thereafter.

[19] *Ibid.*, pp. 174–180; Troup to King, Nov. 16, 1798 (King, II, 466).

day after Jefferson got back to Philadelphia and he was mentioned in them: Robert Goodloe Harper even threatened to read the Mazzei letter.[20] Soon after his own return the Vice President noted with pleasure that Dr. Logan had been elected to the legislature of Pennsylvania, and, after a bit, he visited his agricultural friend and political sympathizer at Stenton, where no doubt the opinions he already held about the French attitude were confirmed.[21] A few Americans in Paris had sent him letters which, unlike the one Wolcott commandeered, finally got through. One of these — from Joel Barlow, poet and critic of the "privileged orders" — also got out. Fortunately for Jefferson, this was addressed to Congressman Abraham Baldwin of Georgia, Barlow's brother-in-law, and, according to the writer, the bluntness was for Baldwin's eye. He sent a copy to Jefferson, however; and, after passing through the hands of Senator John Brown of Kentucky, who sent it under cover to Colonel Bell of Charlottesville in order to avoid "illiberal curiosity," it got to Monticello late in July, 1798.[22] This roundabout procedure suggests the difficulties in which Jefferson's relatively scanty transatlantic correspondence was involved.

Barlow's letter achieved considerable notoriety when Congressman Matthew Lyon of Vermont got hold of Baldwin's original and published it as a pamphlet. It was a major ground for Lyon's trial for sedition, resulting in his being fined one thousand dollars and sent to prison for four months — during which time he was triumphantly re-elected to Congress.[23] Described in Federalist circles as "an infamous libel on our government and eulogy on that of France," [24] it was unquestionably severe on Washington, Adams, and the late commission. Written about the time that the XYZ dispatches were sent to the United States, this long discussion of the "alarming misunderstanding" between the French and American governments was already out of date when Jefferson got it, but no doubt it strengthened his opinion that much fault lay on the American side and that Gerry had acted better than the other commissioners. A later and more moderate letter from Barlow to no less a person than George Washington, which was hastily trans-

[20] Tolles, ch. X; *Annals,* 5 Cong., 3 sess., pp. 2528–2531.

[21] To Madison, Jan. 3, 1799 (Ford, VII, 314); Account Book, Jan. 20, 1799, recording "vales" at Dr. Logan's.

[22] Barlow to Baldwin, Mar. 4, 1798, copy in letter of Mar. 12 to TJ (LC, 17619–17632, 17640); John Brown to TJ, June 29, 1798 (LC, 17818) — all received by TJ on July 26. A briefer letter of Mar. 26, 1798, from Barlow to TJ (LC, 17680), was to much the same effect.

[23] James Woodress, *A Yankee's Odyssey: The Life of Joel Barlow* (1958), pp. 195–196, saying that the letter, which Baldwin had used discreetly, was stolen, presumably by Lyon.

[24] R. Troup, Nov. 16, 1798 (King, II, 467).

mitted by him to no less a person than John Adams, was more influential on the course of events, despite the latter's immediate comment that not even Tom Paine was a more worthless fellow than its author.[25]

Comments on American mistakes did little good, but, before Jefferson got back to Philadelphia, he had received really encouraging news from overseas about the attitude of the high French officials. Nathaniel Cutting wrote him in duplicate, and the copy reached him at home in late November.[26] This American in Paris reported that the majority of the members of the Directory were emerging from the "cloud of error" in which they had been enveloped. He attributed the improvement of conditions especially to the following: Victor du Pont, late French consul at Charleston; Jefferson's friend General Kościuszko; Adet, the later minister, who had been "remarkably assiduous in his endeavours to promote a right understanding"; the indefatigable Joel Barlow; and Dr. George Logan, on whom so much ridicule was heaped. This observer said: "The present is, perhaps, the most favorable moment we can ever expect to adjust our differences, and to define our political relation with France."

The charge of "treasonable correspondence" would have been raised with fresh vehemence had the Federalist spokesmen known that Jefferson received a letter from Adet, who had sought to bring about his election as President in 1796, and they would have paid little heed if he had said that he did not answer it.[27] The main point of this was that the Directory wanted to remain at peace with the United States, the sentiments which attached them and the nation to the American people having triumphed over the "perfidious suggestions" of the secret friends of England. Since this was just what Jefferson wanted to believe, he may be assumed to have accepted the assurance.

At the same time he got another acceptable report, namely, that even those who avowed themselves "friends of order" and "supporters of government" believed that the trial of Congressman Matthew Lyon of Vermont had gone too far. Senator Stevens Thomson Mason wrote him: "If to a few such instances of political persecution there should be added just and reasonable overtures of peace on the part of France, I think the whole bubble of imposition and deception will be blown

[25] Barlow to Washington, Oct. 2, 1798 (*Writings of Washington*, Sparks edn., XI, 560–563); Washington to Adams, Feb. 1, 1799 (Fitzpatrick, XXXVII, 119–120); Adams to Washington, Feb. 19, 1799 (*Works*, VIII, 624).

[26] Cutting to TJ, Aug. 27, 1798; copy (LC, 17849–17850) received Nov. 22, original (LC, 17851–17852) received Jan. 2, 1799.

[27] Adet to TJ, July 27, 1798, received Nov. 29 (LC, 17839–17840). The latter part of the letter, including the signature, is missing, and it is very hard to read, but there is no doubt of its general drift.

up at once." [28] According to Federalist report, the "fountain of mischief" in the country — that is, the Vice President — remained in Virginia beyond the opening of Congress to aid in plotting "some diabolical plan against the federal government," but foreign affairs were by no means absent from his mind when he returned to Philadelphia on Christmas Day to take up his very restricted constitutional duties.

"This situation of Vice President," said a young British observer, "is rendered uneasy to him by the state of politics, as he presides over the Senate and they annoy him by their remarks frequently." [29] He was merely an onlooker on the actions of government, but his sight was keen and his hearing acute. He soon learned that Vans Murray, American minister at The Hague, who had been extremely suspicious of Dr. Logan, had made to his government the same sort of report — namely, that the French authorities were sincere in their overtures for reconciliation. Jefferson, who was confident that Elbridge Gerry's correspondence with Talleyrand would bear this out, suspected that this was being held back until war measures could be taken. When it was submitted to Congress, about the middle of January, it was accompanied by Pickering's critical commentary, but Jefferson did not change his opinion and soon thereafter he wrote Gerry. A month earlier he had received from the former envoy a letter which called for a reply, and Gerry had asked that this go by a private hand. Jefferson himself took the precaution of not signing it, and he prayed that the recipient burn the latter part of it, in which he answered a query about the vote on Gerry's appointment and gave other factual information involving persons who had criticized him.[30] This prayer he accompanied with a lamentation: "And did we ever expect to see the day, when, breathing nothing but sentiments of love to our country and its freedom and happiness, our correspondence must be as secret as if we were hatching its destruction!" That the latter construction would have been placed on the correspondence if it had come to light, Gerry recognized so clearly that he waited two years before resuming it.[31] By that time the presidential campaign was over and he could speak without being disloyal to Adams — whom actually he supported

[28] Nov. 23, 1798, received Nov. 29 (LC, 17894).

[29] D. M. Erskine, Jan. 1, 1799 (*W. & M.*, April, 1949, p. 281).

[30] Gerry to TJ, Nov. 12, 1798, received Dec. 28 (LC, 17889); TJ to Gerry, Jan. 26, 1799 (Ford, VII, 325-326). In TJ's own papers there is a draft of this letter, showing many alterations (LC, 17934-17935). Gerry did not burn any part of the recipient's copy.

[31] Gerry to TJ, Jan. 15, 1801, printed in *N.-Eng. Hist. & Genealog. Register*, XLIX (1895), 438-441.

for the first place while favoring Jefferson for the second. This was probably the most impelling reason for his delay. He was aware that Adams never questioned his sincerity or patriotism while he was being excoriated by the High Federalists and treated like a renegade in his own locality. George Cabot of Massachusetts wrote Rufus King in England that the President's disposition "to cover the follies and improprieties of his friend" threatened them with "new and mischievous schisms." [32] There was some desire on the part of the High Federalists, however, and a strong disposition on the part of Adams, to avoid a public controversy between Gerry and the other commissioners. While recognizing the naturalness of his friend's desire to defend himself against Pickering, the President advised him not even to do that. For these reasons, if for no other, Jefferson's suggestion that Gerry present his cause to the public evoked no response. [33]

Jefferson's references to the support of Gerry by Republicans, while he was being excoriated by Federalists, were designed, no doubt, to attach him to the Vice President's party. This letter was ingratiating in tone — too much so, perhaps, for the normal New England taste — but Gerry appreciated it. [34] And, while personally loyal to Adams, he was much closer to the Republicans than to the High Federalists in spirit, as his acceptance of nomination for governor by the former in 1800 was to show. Perhaps the chief historical significance of Jefferson's long letter lies in his statement of his own political views, which amounted to a platform for the election campaign which was soon to follow. His views on the XYZ affair and Gerry's part of it erred on the side of charity with respect to both the French officials and this commissioner, but in attributing to them a desire for peace he was much more realistic than the Hamiltonian Federalists. In the end John Adams, perhaps the most realistic of them all, stood much closer to Gerry and Jefferson than to those who castigated them.

Toward the close of the congressional session, Jefferson reported to Madison, Monroe, and other friends a great event — the "event of events" he called it — namely, the nomination of William Vans Mur-

[32] Nov. 16, 1798 (King, II, 468–469).
[33] W. C. Ford says, in a note to Gerry's letter of Jan. 15, 1801, to TJ, that Gerry sent Adams a long defense of his conduct on July 24, 1799. The editor did not know what happened to it.
[34] The description of it as a "wily, insinuating letter" by S. E. Morison (*New England Quarterly*, II [1929], p. 28) in his excellent article "Elbridge Gerry, Gentleman-Democrat," seems less than just in the light of the total circumstances, but TJ was not at his best when trying to be ingratiating.

ray, minister at The Hague, as minister to the French republic.[35] He described the circumstances: that overtures to Murray were made by Pichon, the French chargé at The Hague; that Talleyrand wrote approvingly to Pichon, giving further assurances; that the French foreign minister wanted Murray to transmit these views to his own government. Jefferson did not know that young John Quincy Adams, then serving his country in Prussia, had reinforced Murray's opinion of the sincerity of the French government. The suspicious Vice President believed at the time that the transmission of this information from Murray had been deliberately delayed until the "Feds" could complete their military measures. Perceiving, however, that the President's action was a shock to them in both houses, he correctly surmised that they were not informed in advance. The President had said that Murray should not go to France before unequivocal assurances had been received of his respectful treatment and the appointment of a minister of equal rank to negotiate with him. Jefferson was less than fair to Adams and showed little awareness of his political problems when he commented to Monroe: "You will perceive that this measure has been taken as grudgingly as tardily, just as the close of the session is approaching, and the French are to go through the ceremony of a second submission." [36] To this friend and others he also said, however, that the action silenced all arguments against French sincerity and rendered desperate all further efforts towards war.

Within a week he heard that, except perhaps for one Secretary, Adams had kept his purposes secret from his Cabinet, which would have opposed them. He wrote Madison: "Never did a party show a stronger mortification, and consequently, that war had been their object." [37] His own conjecture was that the Executive, "not meaning to meet the overture effectively," had kept it secret until the very end of the session; then the President, thinking further concealment unjustifiable if not impossible, made the nomination, "hoping that his friends in the Senate would take on their own shoulders the odium of rejecting it." It turned out, however, that no one, not even the Hamiltonians, would do that. His further conjecture was this: "The whole artillery of the phalanx, therefore, was played secretly on the President, and he was obliged himself to take a step which should parry the overture while it wears the face of acceding to it."

[35] To Madison, Pendleton, and Monroe on Feb. 19, 1799 (Ford, VII, 361–367). Adams's communication to the Senate was on the day before.
[36] Ford, VII, 366.
[37] Feb. 26, 1799 (Ford, VII, 370).

Later events were to prove that as an interpretation of Adams this was unjust, but with respect to the High Federalists it still seems correct. Yielding to them, Adams nominated two other envoys to serve with Murray, declaring that they should not depart until they had received assurances regarding their respectful reception. In Jefferson's opinion, this action would at least keep off from the dominant party the day of reconciliation, so hateful and fatal to them, and leave them more time for "new projects of provocation." At just this moment he described the "scandalous scene" in the House, when the report of the committee on the Alien and Sedition Acts was up for discussion and Republican spokesmen were drowned out.[38] When he left for home a few days later, he was of the opinion that the effect of the new nominations was "completely to parry the advances made by France towards a reconciliation." [39] While thoroughly pessimistic about national policy, he was convinced that a great change was taking place in the public mind, especially in the middle states.

Jefferson left Philadelphia on March 1, 1799, and did not return until the end of December. A few weeks after he got home he wrote a nonpolitical friend: "Every course of life doubtless has its difficulties; but in the stormy ocean of public life the billows are more furious, the blasts more deadly, than those which assail the bark moored in a retired port." [40] In his retired port — which was near no body of water except the little Rivanna River — his immediate difficulties were those of getting a roof on the north end of his house, seeing that the floors were laid in its many rooms, and making the place truly habitable.[41] The Randolphs were with him, waiting for their new house at Edgehill to be finished, and Maria was there by autumn — in a state which was most interesting to a parent, he said. That is, he expected to become a grandparent on her account before long. He was devoting himself to the circle of his nearest connections, which he described as "the only soil on which it is worth while to bestow much culture." [42]

During this period he was writing and receiving letters about the episode involving Chief Logan and Captain Cresap, which Luther Martin had advertised so extravagantly, and no doubt was preparing the appendix to the *Notes on Virginia* which he was to publish in 1800. He was encouraging Edmund Pendleton and others to write about public affairs in behalf of the sort of republicanism he believed in; he

[38] See above, ch. XXVI, note 13.
[39] To Bishop James Madison, Feb. 27, 1799 (Ford, VII, 372).
[40] To Charles Bellini, Apr. 24, 1799 (LC, 18024–18027).
[41] See above, ch. XV.
[42] To Maria, Jan. 1, 1799 (*Domestic Life*, p. 255).

was reflecting on the elections in Virginia; and in due course he gave thought to the legislatures of his state and Kentucky. His political activities, such as they were, appear to have been almost wholly local. He was in no position to learn what the executive officers of the government were doing or what the Federalist leaders were saying to each other. At the time these things were "behind the curtain." They had important effects upon his political career, but they bulk larger in history than in his biography.

Though he correctly surmised the consternation of the High Federalists when Adams manifested a determination to reopen negotiations with the French, he need not have realized what was going on in the mind of his old friend, who was now entering a period of extreme loneliness. If the squabble about the rank of the major generals opened the eyes of the President to the designs of Hamilton and his partisans, the events following the nomination of Vans Murray showed the Chief Executive that his constitutional authority in the conduct of foreign affairs was at stake.[43] Whether or not he threatened to resign when party representatives sought to dissuade him from his purpose, as the British minister reported, he would not have been out of character in doing so.[44] The High Federalists who made such a point of reporting developments to Rufus King in England showed unmistakably their vast dissatisfaction with the President. The comments of Hamilton's friend, Robert Troup, were particularly pertinent and pungent:

> . . . I am almost afraid to write to you about the State of our political affairs. We have experienced a sad reverse in the temper, ardor and zeal of our fellow citizens. The late nomination of the President for the purpose of renewing negotiations with France has given almost universal disgust. This measure, besides the intrinsic unfitness of it, was secret and without advice, which has also contributed to render it more disgusting. There certainly will be serious difficulties in supporting Mr. Adams at the next election if he should be a candidate.
>
> The army is progressing like a wounded snake. Last year its progress was obstructed by the President's retiring to Braintree [Quincy]. He is now there and likely to continue there during the whole season. All the measures of government are retarded by this kind of abdication. The only apology, in my opinion, for

---

[43] A full account of these events from Adams himself is in "Correspondence Originally Published in the Boston Patriot" (*Works*, IX, 241–266). Though dated 1809, this illuminating and moving account was based on contemporary documents and memoranda.

[44] Robert Liston to Grenville, Mar. 11, 1799, quoted by Dauer, p. 238, along with a letter of Adams, Mar. 29, 1799, to an unnamed person.

the present abdication is that Mrs. Adams was left sick last Fall at Braintree and that she has ever since continued there. . . .[45]

About the only good news this Hamiltonian had to report was that the insurrection in Pennsylvania against taxes, known to history as the Fries Rebellion, had been quelled. The ringleaders, whose conduct he viewed as dastardly, had been apprehended and imprisoned. Before Adams left Philadelphia, he issued a proclamation calling on the "insurgents" to disperse, and the High Federalists did not yet know that he would later pardon all these "traitors," against the advice of his Cabinet.[46] Soon after Troup wrote King, George Cabot gave the American minister in Great Britain the further information that, besides being jealous of Hamilton, the President was also jealous of Pickering, Wolcott, and many of their friends: shutting his ears to his "best real friends" he had opened them "to flatterers, to timeservers, and even to some Jacobins." [47] This supposed sage even suggested that, in order to avoid a *French* President, they might have to elect Washington again.

The anomaly and weakness of Adams's position was that, after asserting himself, he had quickly betaken himself to Quincy, again leaving the conduct of the government to the Secretaries of whom he was now reported to be jealous and certainly should have been suspicious. The charge that his administration was desultory, that he governed by "fits and starts," was not without warrant, though the prophecy that he would never recover from the wound he had inflicted on himself by making advances to the Directory was to be proved false.[48] While men like these thought that Hamilton had good reason to be disappointed and discontented, the ranking Major General gave sign that he had by no means relinquished his imperial designs. Urging military preparedness on McHenry, whose department he was in effect directing, he wrote some three months after Congress adjourned: "Besides eventual security against invasion, we ought certainly to look to the possession of the Floridas and Louisiana, and we ought to squint at South America." Over against this statement of policy we can now set the remark of Adams in later years that he would certainly have re-

[45] R. Troup to King, Apr. 19, 1799 (King, II, 596–597).

[46] Proclamation dated Mar. 12, 1799 (*Works*, IX, 174–176). For later developments, see Heads of Department to the President, May 20, 1800, and Adams to Charles Lee, May 21, 1800 (*Works*, IX, 59–61).

[47] Apr. 26, 1799 (King, III, 8).

[48] Troup to King, June 5, 1799 (King, III, 35).

signed and returned to his plow rather than go along with the Miranda business.[49]

Adams went to Quincy and his ailing wife only a little while after Jefferson went to Monticello to join his own nearest relations, and he remained away from Philadelphia almost as long. While on his farm he learned from Pickering in August, some six months after his original nomination of Murray, that Talleyrand had given assurances; and these he was willing to accept. This was not because he really trusted the French officials: he was not sure that their overtures were not "insidious and hostile at heart," and in his more suspicious moments he believed that they were designed to divide the American people. But, as he explained to Pickering, he no longer feared French diplomacy, believing that its magic was at an end in America, and he was determined to show a pacific and friendly disposition. The blame for conflict should not rest on him. "In this spirit I shall pursue the negotiation," he said, "and I expect the co-operation of the heads of departments."[50] He wanted commissions to be sent the appointees promptly, and their instructions to be put in proper form and dress. These had already been agreed on and were, in effect: (1) to gain full release from the French treaties; (2) to get compensation for French spoliations on American commerce.

It was after Adams had issued these instructions that all but one of the executive officers asked him to suspend the mission; and that the Secretary of the Navy, who had joined in this counsel but was loyal to him, urged him to come to the seat of government for personal as well as public reasons. That seat was now Trenton, whither the executive offices had been moved temporarily because of yellow fever in Philadelphia. The private reasons related to designs against Adams's re-election. Making light of these, Adams reluctantly left his wife, who was to join him in Philadelphia afterwards, and reached Trenton in the middle of October. There, grasping the nettle, he issued orders that the commissioners should forthwith depart.

The chief argument for suspending the mission was based on changes in the European situation. Recent French reverses had aroused fresh hopes of a Bourbon restoration. Hamilton, who was there on military business, remonstrated with the President. Adams said that the eloquence and vehemence of "the little man" wrought him to a high degree of heat and effervescence, but that his arguments revealed

[49] Hamilton to McHenry, June 27, 1799 (J.C.H., V, 283); Adams to James Lloyd, Mar. 30, 1815 (*Works*, X, 151).
[50] To Pickering, Aug. 6, 1799 (*Works*, IX, 10–12).

colossal ignorance of European affairs. Because Adams at last proved adamant the two American commissioners finally sailed to join Murray. They did not begin to negotiate until spring, however, and by that time the Directory had given way to the Consulate. Adams's later judgment on all this was sound: "Had Mr. Murray's nomination been approved, he would probably have finished the business long before, and obtained compensation for all spoliations." [51] As things turned out, all that the commissioners got was the renunciation of the treaties, and that only at the very end of the administration of Adams. The costly and unnecessary delay was no fault of his except that he countenanced it by not fully asserting himself sooner. He was more realistic than the Hamiltonians as a patriot and even as a politician. They never forgave him for disregarding them and the rift in the party widened thereafter, but at the court of public opinion he probably gained more in the next few months than he lost by his brave action.

Although Jefferson's sensitive ear picked up some rumors of Federalist dissension after he got back to Philadelphia late in 1799, he maintained a virtually impenetrable silence respecting the commission to France. While he was still at Monticello he became aware of late French misfortunes, which, in his opinion, would of themselves make the "consolidationers" more intolerant than ever at the next meeting of Congress.[52] It would have been more natural to assume that these misfortunes would cause the likelihood of war with France to seem even more remote, and thus would weaken the position of the "war party." After he got back to Philadelphia he learned of the "great revolution" in Paris, whereby a "dictatorial consulate" headed by Bonaparte was set up. These circumstances made him all the more ready to turn his back on Europe. The time to extol the French Republic had long since passed. He was now saying that whatever might happen in France, Americans by recognizing the will of the majority could maintain their own republicanism inviolate. He wrote his friend John Breckinridge of Kentucky: "Our vessel is moored at such a distance that should theirs blow up, ours is still safe, if we will but say so." [53] He still feared that, under the excuse of putting down domestic disorder, "our Buonaparte, surrounded by his comrades at arms" might "step in to give us political salvation in his own way." The reference to Hamilton was unmistakable, and if he had known all that was going on behind the curtain he should have found comfort in the thought

---

[51] Comment in 1809 (*Works*, IX, 256). The commissioners sailed on Nov. 3, 1799.

[52] To Charles Pinckney, Oct. 29, 1799 (Ford, VII, 398).

[53] Jan. 29, 1800 (Ford, VII, 417-418).

that Adams had cut the ground from beneath the feet of the potential American Bonaparte. Jefferson was hoping for general peace in Europe. He wrote his son-in-law: "We have great need of this event, that foreign affairs may no longer bear so heavily on ours." [54] His old friend Adams had made a powerful effort to relieve domestic affairs from the weight of foreign, and actually the foreign issue was no longer a valid one in American politics.

[54] Feb. 2, 1800 (Ford, VII, 422).

[XXVIII]

Personal and Parliamentary

1800

THE winter of 1799–1800 was Jefferson's last in Philadelphia, for the new federal city of Washington had become the seat of government by the next session of Congress. Leaving Monticello on December 21 with his own coachman and horses, and proceeding beyond Fredericksburg by stage, he arrived on December 28; following Monroe's advice he did not visit Madison en route, and he spent Christmas on the road.[1] Disregard of Christmas was nothing new for him: he had arrived on December 25 the year before. This devoted family man who so delighted in bestowing presents gave no sign of celebrating the day in any way; and there must have been those who believed that he carried anticeremonialism and secularism too far.

More immediately he was charged with deliberate avoidance of all ceremonies of respect to the memory of George Washington, who died a week before he left home and for whom Congress set aside December 26 as a day of formal mourning. He was not there when Light-Horse Harry Lee, whose election to Congress he had regretted, spoke the famous words: "first in war, first in peace and first in the hearts of his countrymen."[2] If the news of the passing of the nation's hero reached Monticello soon enough, as it probably did, presumably the Vice President could have started from home two or three days earlier. But in view of all that had been said in recent years about his relations with his old chief, this exceedingly sensitive man may have

---

[1] Details of journey from Account Book and letter to Maria, Jan. 17, 1800 (Ford, VII, 403–404); see also letter to Madison, Nov. 22, 1799 (Ford, VII, 400).

[2] The charge against TJ, coupled with a similar one against Burr, was made by R. Troup to R. King, Jan. 1, 1800 (King, III, 171). For an authoritative summary of the ceremonies and eulogies through Feb. 22, 1800, see Carroll & Ashworth, *George Washington*, VII, App. VII-3.

concluded that he would find these ceremonies embarrassing. If he had been there, some Federalist spokesman would almost certainly have described him as a hypocrite, and no doubt he was glad of a good excuse to be away.

During the two months that ended with Washington's birthday, some three hundred eulogies to him were delivered in 185 different towns. While grief for him was universal, the distribution of these eulogies reflected political sentiment to a notable degree. The New Englanders were easily the most vocal group, while the Virginians were relatively quiet.[3] The Republican reaction against the extravagance of some of these utterances was reflected in certain stanzas of Philip Freneau:

> No tongue can tell, no pen describe
> The phrenzy of a numerous tribe,
> Who, by distemper'd fancy led,
> Insult the memory of the dead.

> He was no god, ye flattering knaves,
> He own'd no world, he ruled no waves;
> But — and exalt it, if you can,
> He was the upright, Honest Man.

> This was his glory, this outshone
> Those attributes you doat upon:
> On this strong ground he took his stand,
> Such virtue saved a sinking land.[4]

Certain of Hamilton's comments on the death of Washington were more revealing than he realized. Besides saying that the news filled his heart with bitterness, he said: "Perhaps no man in this community has equal cause with myself to deplore the loss. I have been much indebted to the kindness of the General, and he was an *Aegis very essential to me*."[5] To more than one foe or critic of the colossus of Federalism it seemed that Hamilton had been shielded too long by the General's reputation. Jefferson himself had predicted that the "resuscitation" of the "republican spirit" of the country would be accelerated when this great name could no longer be evoked by anti-republicans.[6] He

---

[3] *Ibid.*, VII, 651, note 32. The lower South, except for Charleston, appears to have been least affected, and the middle states fell far behind New England.

[4] *Poems*, F. L. Pattee edn. (1902–1907), III, 235-237, apparently written early in 1800.

[5] To Tobias Lear, Jan. 2, 1800 (J.C.H., VI, 415); see also letters to R. King, Jan. 5, and Mrs. Washington, Jan. 12 (VI, 416, 418).

[6] Benjamin Rush to TJ, Mar. 12, 1801, recalling a conversation of a couple of

did not say that now; indeed, he said nothing in public and appears to have said nothing in private. Even a note to Mrs. Washington might have been misinterpreted. A year later, when circumstances brought him near her, he paid a visit to Mount Vernon, where she asked him particularly about his daughter Maria. And what he wrote a dozen years afterwards about the man with whom he had so long served remains until this day a "surpassing delineation" of Washington's character.[7] Meanwhile, as presiding officer of the Senate, he sat in a chair which was draped for a month in black.

Though the year 1800 was to prove exceedingly important in Jefferson's history and in that of his country, at its beginning he was largely immobilized as a political man and had virtually nothing to do in his official capacity. In the middle of January he reported that there was not enough business to occupy the Senate half an hour a day. Returning to Francis's Hotel, he lodged there until the middle of May, when the congressional session ended. He took into his service one Fortune Barnes, perhaps a body servant, and as spring approached he placed a horse at the Indian Queen. Toward the end of his stay he wrote his elder daughter: "Our scenes here can never be pleasant; but they have been less stormy, less painful than during the XYZ paroxysms."[8] But, more cautious than ever about his written words, he confined his political comments to such letters as could be borne by trusted friends or other wholly reliable messengers. Before picking up the story of party politics we may fittingly mention some of the things he turned his insatiable mind to, during this period of restriction, and some of his experiences as a human being.

On the personal side, he suffered considerable disquietude and some genuine grief. For one thing, he learned early in February of the death of Jupiter, his devoted coachman and companion of the road since student days. His own account of the circumstances, in a letter to his son-in-law, deserves quotation as an intimate document:

He [Jupiter] has fallen a victim to an imprudent perseverance in journeying. I was extremely against his coming to Fredsburg

years earlier in which TJ referred also to Patrick Henry (Butterfield, II, 832 and note 6).

[7] Carroll & Ashworth, VII, 653, use these words, referring to his letter of Jan. 2, 1814 to Dr. Walter Jones. TJ to Maria, Jan. 4, 1801 (Ford, VII, 478).

[8] To Martha, Apr. 22, 1800 (*Domestic Life*, p. 225). On Mar. 11, he made a memo. of a conversation with Mrs. Adams, showing that some degree of social relationship was maintained (Ford, I, 285).

with me & had engaged Davy Bowles, but Jupiter was so much disturbed at this that I yielded. At the end of the second day's journey I saw how much he was worsted, & pressed him to wait at Hyde's, a very excellent house, till the horses should return, & I got the promise of a servant from there. But he would not hear of it. At Fredericksburg again I engaged the tavernkeeper to take care of him till he should be quite well enough to proceed, and it seems that immediately on his arrival at home, he took another journey to my brother's where he died. I am sorry for him as well as sensible he leaves a void in my domestic administration which I cannot fill up.[9]

Perhaps the considerate master would have expressed himself even more strongly about the loss of this too-faithful slave had he not been borne down by an even more intimate sorrow. On the same day he learned from his other son-in-law, John Wayles Eppes, of the death of the first child of his daughter Maria. She left Monticello for Eppington about a month before he himself set out for Philadelphia, and at the family seat of her husband on the last day of the year she gave birth to a tiny daughter. The news did not reach her father for nearly three weeks, but, finding the first reports reassuring, he boasted that Maria had presented him with "the first fruits of a grandfather on her part." These honors proved fleeting, for the tiny infant quickly died, and the belated news from the young mother was disturbing. For weeks she suffered from an abscessed breast; she could not write her father, as young Eppes reported, since her arms were perfectly useless. Jefferson himself, while expressing the great anxiety he had suffered for her, said that her complaint had been longer than anything of the kind he had ever known. He spoke with some authority, having good reason, from his own wife's experience, to be aware of the tribulations of womankind in that century. Characteristically, he voiced his doubts about the medical treatment. "The system of physicking as subsidiary to the aid of surgery is very questionable," he wrote. "For every good effect it can produce, I am sure two bad ones will result."[10] By the opening of spring, however, Maria was more blooming than she had been for two years past. She and her husband were then at Mont Blanco, their own place, and were expecting a visit from her

[9] To TMR, Feb. 4, 1800 (LC, 18172). TJ's brother Randolph lived below the James, or Fluvanna.

[10] To TMR, Mar. 4, 1800 (LC, 18202). Other letters bearing on this episode are J. W. Eppes to TJ, Jan. 1, Feb. 7, 1800 (Edgehill Randolph Papers, UVA); TJ to Maria, Jan. 17, and to Martha, Jan. 21, 1800 (Ford, VII, 405-410); TJ to Angelica Church, Jan. 21, 1800 (MHS). He learned about the birth on Jan. 18.

father in May. He came that way when Congress recessed and took her with him for a few weeks' visit at Monticello.[11]

During this election year Jefferson and his Randolph son-in-law ran into financial difficulties for which they could partly blame the Federalist political doctors. He had felt impelled to return to the cultivation of tobacco, about the time he became vice president, in order to get cash for clothes and taxes.[12] In 1798 the high price of tobacco, which he reported as thirteen dollars per hundredweight, tempted him further. He thought the market would continue high, but unhappily it did not, and in 1799 he held his crop too long. He attributed the stagnation of the market to the suspension of commerce with France, the British monopoly of commerce, the consequent accumulation of tobacco in London, and the inability of the British to sell it in Europe under existing international conditions.[13] Resentment against the commercial policy of the administration played no inconsiderable part in determining the political alignment of his own state.[14] Early in 1800, in Philadelphia, he had to take seven dollars a hundred for his tobacco on long credit. Other tobacco he had let lie in New York, believing that the nonintercourse act would be allowed to expire and that the price would then rise. In March, however, after the law had been extended for another year, he sold for six dollars. Writing his son-in-law, he said: "and thus ends this tragedy by which we have both lost so much." [15]

This was not the whole of it. Randolph, falling behind on his payments on the mortgage on his Varina plantation, had obtained a temporary loan from a Richmond merchant and appealed to his ever-generous father-in-law for help. Jefferson was unable to assume this loan, but, by rallying all his resources, he paid off more than eighteen hundred dollars on it, which was some five hundred dollars less than Randolph asked for. The understanding was that he was to take over his son-in-law's tobacco crop when it came on the market and reimburse himself from it, as eventually he very largely did.[16] How-

---

[11] J. W. Eppes to TJ, Apr. 22, 1800 (Edgehill Randolph Papers, UVA); Account Book, May 15-29, 1800; TJ to Maria, July 4, 1800 (*Domestic Life*, p. 268), after her departure from Monticello.

[12] See above, p. 205.

[13] See especially his letter to George Jefferson, May 18, 1799 (*Farm Book*, pp. 271-272).

[14] This point, which seems to have escaped most writers, is made by W. E. Hemphill in *Virginia Cavalcade*, II, 10 (Spring, 1953).

[15] To TMR, Mar. 14, 1800 (*Farm Book*, p. 274). For other letters about this business, see pp. 269-275; see also TJ to TMR, Feb. 2, 1800 (Ford, VII, 423).

[16] Gaines, "Thomas Mann Randolph of Edgehill," p. 82, citing various letters; TJ to TMR, Mar. 7, 31, and May 7, 1800 (LC, 18209, 18233, 18277).

ever, these circumstances caused him to fall somewhat behind on certain payments on his own long-standing debts.[17] He maintained his own high credit, but these and other incidents show that he and his relatives and fellow Virginians were beset with financial trouble.

In this political interim, when there was little he could do in public affairs except to keep on waiting, Jefferson found other outlets for his energetic mind, bearing out the contemporary impression that he was a man of "very general knowledge" and displaying the intellectual enthusiasm for which he is still justly renowned. That he should have received books from scientists and literary men — such as *Thermo-metrical Navigation* from Jonathan Williams, grandnephew of Benjamin Franklin, and a work of the imagination from Charles Brockden Brown, reputedly the first American to make a profession of authorship — is not surprising. But his perceptive comments on these gifts went far beyond perfunctory acknowledgment and offer another clue to his hold on the loyalty of the intelligentsia.[18] With various persons on the frontier he carried on correspondence about Indian monuments and vocabularies. This was an aftermath to the inquiries he had been making relative to the appendix to his *Notes on Virginia* which he sent to the printer this year.[19] Perhaps his most illuminating correspondence of these months, however, was with two intellectuals from the Old World, Du Pont de Nemours and Joseph Priestley, at whom the Federalist extremists looked askance but whom he welcomed and encouraged.

While in Paris, he had known Du Pont, then a councillor of state, and had been aided by him in his efforts to gain commercial privileges for the struggling American republic.[20] Du Pont, who belonged to the Physiocratic school, commended himself to Jefferson by his emphasis on agriculture and his hostility to economic and intellectual barriers of all sorts. After numerous vicissitudes in revolutionary France he fell into danger because of his opposition to the Directory, and by French standards he was only a moderate reformer. He should have excited no alarm in America; and, after his arrival on January 1, 1800, at the

---

[17] To James Lyle, Mar. 17, 1800 (*Farm Book*, p. 275).

[18] He wrote both men on Jan. 15, 1800 (LC, 18130–18131). A good contemporary comment on his scholarly repute is that of D. M. Erskine (*W. & M.*, 3 ser., VI, 281).

[19] See above, ch. XXII.

[20] I have summed up their relationship in the introduction to *Correspondence between Thomas Jefferson and Pierre Samuel du Pont de Nemours* (1930) — hereafter designated as *Correspondence*. In quoting from this edn. I avail myself of the excellent translation of Du Pont's letters by Linwood Lehman. In the edn. of Gilbert Chinard (1931), they can be seen in the original.

head of a family party of about a dozen, he appears to have suffered no molestation. His major purpose was to repair his personal fortunes, but, apart from discouraging him against land speculation and warning him to be on his guard, Jefferson had nothing to do with this. We need not concern ourselves here with the commercial activities of his son Victor, which eventually proved unsuccessful, or with the extraordinarily successful venture of his son Eleuthère Irénée, who started the renowned powder works near Wilmington, Delaware. It is more important to note here that Adams had previously declined to grant Victor du Pont an exequatur as consul general of France, that the President had frowned upon the scientific mission which the elder Du Pont had originally coupled with his proposed expedition to America, and that the Vice President was the public man to whom the eminent Frenchman naturally turned as a sympathetic friend.[21]

Du Pont had written Jefferson hopefully: "I wish to die in a country in which liberty does not exist only in the laws, always more or less well, more or less badly, carried out; but chiefly in the fixed habits of the nation." It was as a friend of liberty that he was welcomed by Jefferson, after a voyage of ninety-five days, to a country whose language he could not speak.[22] Responding with enthusiasm, Du Pont sought Jefferson's counsel in Philadelphia. Before the Vice President left that city he in turn sought Du Pont's counsel. This was on the subject of education, and it was after he had approached Joseph Priestley to the same purpose. This expression of confidence was gratifying to both men, but no doubt it was specially appreciated by Dr. Priestley since that noted scientist and Unitarian clergyman had undeniably suffered persecution in America as well as England.

While Jefferson was in his first year of retirement from the office of secretary of state, Dr. Priestley landed in New York. This was several years after the clergyman's church and personal property in Birmingham had been destroyed by rioters in the name of the King and the Establishment. Encouraged by Thomas Cooper, a disillusioned reformer of Manchester who had made a prospecting trip to America and reported enthusiastically on his findings, he had decided to emigrate.[23] Though suspected by many of the clergy from the outset,

[21] Adams took the position in 1798 that there were already too many French philosophers in the country (*Works*, VIII, 596). Apparently he raised no objections in 1799, when Du Pont's purposes were ostensibly commercial.

[22] Du Pont to TJ, Aug. 27, 1799; TJ to Du Pont Jan. 17, 1800 (*Correspondence*, pp. 2–4).

[23] For a fuller account of these events, and the circumstances leading to them, see Dumas Malone, *Public Life of Thomas Cooper* (1926), pp. 30, 79–80, and elsewhere. This work is referred to hereafter as *Cooper*. Priestley landed on June 4, 1794.

Priestley, who had been for some years a foreign member of the American Philosophical Society and was regarded by Republicans as a refugee from a land of bondage, was well received at first. He had established himself in Northumberland, Pennsylvania, and by now he and Cooper were living in the same house; he himself regarded his library and "philosophical apparatus" as superior to anything of the kind in America. Priestley, who was never naturalized, sedulously avoided political controversy, desiring nothing more than to pursue his experiments and do his writing in peace. At first he enjoyed the favor of Adams, whom he had known in England and to whom he dedicated certain lectures he delivered in Philadelphia in 1796; according to New England standards these were considerably less than orthodox.[24] Almost immediately he became the target of William Cobbett (Peter Porcupine), who brought to the defense of Anglicanism and to attacks on republicanism powers of vituperation which no pamphleteer or editor on the other side, except possibly Callender, could match. Continually referring to Priestley as "the firebrand philosopher," he expressed the hope that he would see the "malignant old Tartuff of Northumberland begging his bread through the streets of Philadelphia, and ending his days in the poorhouse, without a friend to close his eyes." [25] In Republican circles it had been said that Priestley was one of the persons against whom the Alien Act was directed, but Adams prevented its employment against him, making light of his influence. Eventually, Priestley was goaded to make public response to the strictures of Cobbett, who had meanwhile found a target in Dr. Benjamin Rush. The Doctor won a famous libel suit against Cobbett, who left Philadelphia late in December 1799, and went back to England in the following June. Peter Porcupine had considerable ground for attacking Dr. Rush's practice of bleeding patients, but to the outward eye it certainly appeared that he and the High Federalists were against the intellectuals.

Jefferson became acquainted with Priestley in 1797 on his brief trip to Philadelphia for the inauguration. The clergyman, who was there for a few weeks doing some preaching, reported that Jefferson came to hear him and expressed the hope that the Vice President was not an unbeliever.[26] Their correspondence in 1800 began with a reference, not to religion, but to foreign commerce, which was much on Jefferson's mind at the time because of his own tribulations in mar-

[24] *Discourses relating to the Evidences of Revealed Religion.*
[25] Priestley quoted these particular expressions as being distressing to him (*Cooper*, p. 85).
[26] To T. Belsham, Mar. 14, 1797, in J. T. Rutt, *Life and Correspondence of Joseph Priestley* (1831), II, 373. See also comment of Apr. 23, 1803 (*ibid.*, p. 511).

keting tobacco. Priestley had sent him certain pamphlets written by him and Cooper. He had already seen these anyway — certainly those of Cooper, which were longer and which he soon distributed by the dozen in Virginia. "The papers of political arithmetic, both in your and Mr. Cooper's pamphlets, are the most precious gifts that can be made to us," he said; "for we are running navigation mad, and commerce mad, and navy mad, which is worst of all." [27] The position he was approving was that of *laissez faire*, with great emphasis on agriculture. Even more important in this context, however, was his expression of chagrin and mortification at the persecutions which "fanaticism and monarchy" had excited against this man of learning. A request for Priestley's counsel on the subject of higher education followed.

The thought of establishing a university on a broad and liberal plan had been in Jefferson's mind for a score of years, and, having failed in his original purpose of reconstituting the College of William and Mary, he was thinking of a future establishment in a more central and salubrious location. He had had some talk about the matter with Madison, as no doubt he had had also with Monroe, who was now governor of the state, but nothing came of this until many years later. The discussion he now entered into with Priestley, and soon with Du Pont, lay in the realm of theory. What he wanted of them chiefly was their ideas about the subjects which should be taught and the grouping of these among professors. Some of the ideas he himself expressed were to bear fruit later: "We should propose to draw from Europe the first characters of science," he said. He himself drew a hasty list of subjects, and in a supplementary letter to Priestley he went into the question of languages, saying some unforgettable things about his own love of the classics.[28] Some weeks later, he sought Du Pont's aid, stating his own wishes rather more succinctly.[29] His approach to the problem of the content of university education was critical and practical: he wanted to omit those branches of knowledge "no longer useful or valued," even though still generally kept up, and to introduce others "adapted to the real uses of life and the present state of things."

Priestley sent him some "Hints concerning Public Education" in May, when Du Pont was merely getting started.[30] These were brief and

[27] To Priestley, Jan. 18, 1800 (Ford, VII, 406). The discussion of education follows later in this letter.

[28] Jan. 27, 1800 (Ford, VII, 413–416).

[29] Apr. 12, 1800 (*Correspondence*, pp. 8–10).

[30] May 8, 1800 (LC, 18282–18283; printed by Chinard, *Jefferson and Du Pont*, pp. 16–18).

to the point, though not wholly agreeing with ideas already expressed by Jefferson. Priestley favored instruction in the field of religion and thought it unwise to have recourse to foreign countries for professors. Most helpful to Jefferson, probably, were his informed comments about mathematics and natural philosophy.

While Du Pont was beginning to busy himself on the work he had been charged with, his friend Jefferson, as president of the American Philosophical Society, informed him that he had been unanimously elected a member of that distinguished organization.[31] He had explicitly stated to the enthusiastic Frenchman that he did not expect a treatise on education from him, but toward the end of the summer, after much animated correspondence, he got one. In view of the extreme difficulty of making out Du Pont's handwriting he may have been overwhelmed by this; and, although he said he read it, he was slow in saying so. By autumn, Du Pont was talking of having the work translated — a purpose in which his friend discouraged him, saying that it would be easier to translate Homer. Eventually it was published in France, but not until the twentieth century did it appear in English. No doubt Jefferson was influenced by some of Du Pont's ideas when planning instruction for the University of Virginia years later, but at the moment this work did not fit into his purposes very well, since it laid prime emphasis on elementary schools, to which he was now devoting little attention, and called for a national rather than a state university as the apex of the pyramid.[32] Furthermore, his mind had inevitably turned to politics by the time he got it.

Since nothing immediate came out of Jefferson's correspondence on the subject of higher education with these two learned men, the whole of it may perhaps be dismissed as merely academic. But at least it shows that the leader of the Republican party was engaged in some elevated and long-range thinking during a considerable part of this furious election year.

At some time in the winter or spring one of the most notable of his portraits was painted by young Rembrandt Peale. Since the engravings of him which were so widely distributed in America and Europe during the next few years were based on this, it was the source of the visual image of Jefferson most impressed on the public mind at the

---

[31] TJ to Du Pont, May 12, 1800 (*Correspondence*, p. 15).

[32] *Sur l'éducation nationale dans les États-Unis d'Amérique* (2 edn., 1812); English translation by Bessie G. du Pont (1923). The most important letters relating to it are Du Pont to TJ, Aug. 24, Nov. 8, 1800; TJ to Du Pont, Dec. 12, 1800 (*Correspondence*, pp. 22–26). On the value of the plan, see P. A. Bruce, *Hist. of the Univ. of Va.* (1920), I, 63–65; and Chinard, *Jefferson and Du Pont*, pp. xcix–cii.

height of his national political prominence.[33] This is perhaps the strongest of all his portraits. As in others his coloring is high, but the hair is whiter than in the portrait of 1791 by Charles Willson Peale, showing scarcely a tinge of red. It is even whiter in the amusing portrait made of him in 1798 by his friend Tadeusz (Thaddeus) Kościuszko, which in fact seems to be that of a much older man. In profile, this emphasizes and exaggerates his upturned nose, but perhaps the most significant fact is that this Polish supporter of American independence, describing him as philosopher and patriot as well as friend, placed on his head a crown of laurel. No doubt this amateur artist regarded this portrait as a salute to liberty. He also saluted the cause of human freedom in a document. On May 5, 1798, when on the point of departure for the Old World, he drew a will in which he authorized Jefferson, in the absence of any other testamentary disposition of his American property, to use the whole of it to purchase, free, and educate Negro slaves.[34]

Perhaps the most striking thing about the portraits of Jefferson in this period is their variety. Even after allowance is made for the passing of time, the two Peales, father and son, depicted him differently: one caught him in a rather pensive mood, while the other saw him in full vigor. The contrast is even more striking between the near-caricature by his Polish admirer and the pen drawing made by the architect Benjamin Henry Latrobe about 1799. In this he is alert, perhaps a little cynical. What impressed Latrobe, no doubt, was not so much his strength or his idealism, but his intelligence. Being a half dozen men rolled into one, he presented no unvarying image to artists or anybody else; and it is fortunate that, neither then nor thereafter, did his lineaments become frozen.

Though Jefferson had referred to his post as a "tranquil and unoffending station" and saw no necessity to be in his chair in the Senate at the very beginning and the very end of every session, there is abundant evidence that as vice president he took his duties seriously. Regarding himself as a presiding officer pure and simple, he exercised his limited functions with greater care than his predecessor and left

[33] An authoritative account of this and the other portraits mentioned here, all of which are reproduced in the present volume, is in Alfred L. Bush, *The Life Portraits of Thomas Jefferson* (Charlottesville, 1962). The author has generously provided me with items from JP, Feb. 21–May 27, 1801, regarding a copy of it which TJ procured at a cost of $30 for an unnamed friend.

[34] Will filed in Albemarle County Courthouse. It was proved May 12, 1819, but TJ, who was 76, then declined "to take upon himself the burthen of the execution."

every successor his debtor. During a period when there were virtually no tie votes in the Senate for him to break, he had no influence
on legislation itself, but, as has been well said, no other American public man "left so enduring a mark on legislative procedure." This was
by means of the parliamentary manual he compiled during his term
and left to the Senate as a legacy. That it was cherished by his contemporaries and by posterity is amply demonstrated by the fact that
more than a century and a half after he left his chair it was still being
printed in the current *Senate Manual*, along with the Declaration of
Independence, Articles of Confederation, and Constitution.[35]

He recognized his responsibilities the more keenly because of the
rule of the Senate, adopted at the beginning of its first session, that
every question of order should be decided by the presiding officer
without debate. He could call for the sense of the body but did not
need to.[36] Jefferson said that this placed under the discretion of the
presiding officer "a very extensive field of decision, and one which,
irregularly exercised, would have a powerful effect on the proceedings and determinations of the House." [37] He was also aware, no
doubt, that there had been rather severe criticisms of the conduct of
his predecessor — the main ones relating to Adams's inconsistency and
proneness to enter extensively into the debates or otherwise express
himself.[38] The conduct of Jefferson, who was very conscious of
Adams's lack of system, was much more decorous and better ordered.
Perceiving that the presiding officer must necessarily recur "to some
known system of rules, that he may neither leave himself free to indulge caprice or passion, nor open to the imputation of them," he
found such a system in the rules of Parliament. He was also aware of
the need to safeguard minorities. In the opening section of his *Manual*,
he quoted as a maxim of the House of Commons that "nothing tended
more to throw power into the hands of administration and those who
acted with the majority . . . than a neglect of, or departure from the

[35] The comment is that of E. S. Brown in his article "Jefferson's Manual of Parliamentary Practice," *Michigan Alumnus: Quarterly Review, XLIV,* 148 (Feb. 20,
1943). The manual can be conveniently seen in L. & B., II, 333-450. It appears in the
Senate Manual of 1961; also, in large part, in the *Rules and Manual of the U. S.
House of Reps.* for 1961.
[36] Rule 16. On Apr. 16, 1789, the Senate adopted 19 rules as recommended by a
committee (*Annals,* 1 Cong., 1 sess., pp. 20-21). Additional rules were adopted
thereafter, bringing the total to *c.* 30 when TJ became vice president.
[37] Preface to his *Manual.* The present (1961) Senate Rule XX is that questions
of order are to be decided by the presiding officer without debate, *subject to an
appeal to the Senate.* Apparently this was adopted in 1884.
[38] The bitterly hostile *Journal of William Maclay* is the source commonly cited
in this connection, but there can be no doubt that Adams was an irregular presiding officer.

rules of proceeding; that these forms, as instituted by our ancestors, operated as a check, and control, on the actions of the majority; and that they were, in many instances, a shelter and protection to the minority, against the attempts of power." [39]

Jefferson's anti-British sentiments in international politics never precluded him from turning to English foundations of individual liberty or from drawing on accumulated English experience in the age-long struggle against tyranny. He was not the only American to recur to the precedents of his race when concerned with procedure in a deliberative body: that was the natural thing to do in colonial times. Nor can we credit him alone for the fact that the term "parliamentary law" came into universal use in his country after it became independent. But probably no other man did so much to check any tendency to repudiate it that may have sprung up and to expedite the trend toward its acceptance in the new nation. It was to his great credit that he went back to the prototype, not contenting himself with such modifications of the historic practices as had been made in particular American legislative bodies, including the Continental Congress and the existing House of Representatives. Their forms seemed to him so awkward and inconvenient that it was sometimes impossible to get at a true sense of the majority. While he availed himself of the experience of his own colony and commonwealth, he was not content until he went back to the original source. Considering "the law of proceedings in the Senate as composed of the precepts of the Constitution, the regulations of the Senate, and where these are silent, of the rules of Parliament," he collected and digested so much of them as were called for in ordinary practice, "collating the parliamentary with the senatorial rules" both where they agreed and where they varied. Thus he set up a standard for himself and deposited it with the Senate for possible future use. [40]

While minimizing the significance of what he did, he worked at it long and systematically. Before he assumed his post as presiding officer, realizing that he was rusty, he inquired of George Wythe if that old friend and mentor had any notes on the subject of parliamentary procedure. Wythe responded that he had made such notes thirty years before but did not know where they were and could not now rely on his memory. [41] Jefferson was therefore forced to depend on notes he himself had made in what he called a Commonplace Book, containing

[39] Section I, "The Importance of Adhering to Rules."
[40] Preface to *Manual*. This appeared in successive editions.
[41] To Wythe, Jan. 22, 1797 (Ford, VII, 110); from Wythe, Feb. 1, 1797 (LC, 17307).

many pages of references.[42] He made some sort of compilation within a year, for he referred certain notes to John Beckley, former clerk of the House of Representatives.[43] He turned to his task more actively early in 1800, obviously determined to complete it before the end of his term of office. Appealing again to Wythe, he gave him the fullest known account of his purposes.[44]

He had based his decisions on the parliamentary rules, he said, wholly rejecting those of the old Congress. He believed that this procedure had given entire satisfaction to the Senate; "in so much that we shall not only have a good system there, but probably, by the example of its effects, produce a conformity in the other branch." He had run into perplexities, however, to which he could find no clue in his own commonplace book. Regarding Wythe as "the only spark of parliamentary science now remaining," he sent him a list of queries, leaving a wide margin so that the old gentleman could write yes or no. Supplementing this letter a few weeks later, he said that he meant to deposit his manual with the Senate and was most anxious that it be correct.[45] Writing slowly with his left hand, Wythe replied to his "best friend" that his memory simply had not enabled him to answer the questions.[46] Thereupon, Jefferson sent them to Judge Edmund Pendleton. These were minute questions, to which no answers could be found in books. Pendleton answered them in the margins, and so, a little later, did George Wythe, saying: "Your solicitations are with me more cogent motives than with his slave are the mandates of a despot." He printed his left-handed letter, much as a child would do.[47] Jefferson had said that he meant to pursue this business in the summer of 1800 at Monticello, and presumably he largely finished it while the election campaign was being waged. Wythe's final words, besides being characteristic of that learned but charmingly modest jurist, were prophetic: "My language is didactic. Yet am I confident of nothing that I have written. I am persuaded the manual of your parliamentary praxis will be more chaste than any extant, and, if you can be per-

[42] Described by Randall as a "parliamentary pocket book" (II, 356); this is preserved in the Coolidge Collection, MHS.

[43] Beckley to TJ, Mar. 15, 1798 (LC, 17646), saying that he had penciled a few remarks and would look further into certain questions. Shortly before this TJ wrote Samuel Livermore, president pro tem of the Senate, Jan. 28, 1798 (LC, 17568), apparently giving some description of his compilation in what is now an illegible letter.

[44] Especially in his letter of Feb. 28, 1800 (Ford, VII, 426–428).

[45] Apr. 7, 1800 (Ford, VII, 428–429n.).

[46] To TJ, Apr. 10, 1800 (LC, 18254).

[47] Pendleton to TJ, June 17, 1800 (LC, 18305, 18470–18475); Wythe to TJ, Dec. 7, 1800 (LC, 18459–18460).

suaded to let it go forth, that it will be canonized in all the legislatures of America."

In one of his rare references to his *Manual* in later life, Jefferson described it as a mere compilation, into which nothing of his own entered but the arrangement and a few explanatory observations.[48] As he prepared it, it consisted of fifty-three sections in which the rules and practices peculiar to the Senate were printed in italics, and those of Parliament in Roman letters. The latter, in the form of quotation or paraphrase with citations of authorities, form the bulk of the work. Jefferson complained to Wythe that in Philadelphia he could find no book to aid him. His citations show, however, that he consulted practically all the main sources which a scholar might use, and obviously he did this in his own magnificent library at Monticello. The most important of these were *Precedents of Proceedings in the House of Commons* (1785), by John Hatsell, clerk of that body; and Architell Grey's ten-volume edition of *Debates in the House of Commons* (1667-1694), published in 1763.[49]

First published in Washington in 1801, Jefferson's *Manual* went through two further editions in 1812 and 1813; in these, minor factual details — such as the apportionment of representatives in the House — were added.[50] The text appears to have remained unaltered in the many later printings. Within half a century of the original publication there were no fewer than seventeen of these, two being in Spanish.[51] A count beyond that point would assuredly run into the hundreds. Though prepared for the Senate and best suited to that body, it came to be highly valued by the House of Representatives, where procedure was often notoriously disorderly in Jefferson's time. Less than a dozen years after his death the House passed a rule which is still in effect, namely, that the rules comprised in his *Manual* "shall govern the House in all cases to which they are applicable, and in which they are not inconsistent with the standing rules and orders of the House." [52] Many years later a committee that revised the rules of the House said that Jefferson's *Manual* was never specially valuable in

[48] To John W. Campbell, Sept. 3, 1809 (Ford, IX, 258).

[49] Sowerby, # # 2894, 2934. TJ said in 1812 that he had not seen the 3rd vol. of Hatsell. I have not checked the numerous other works he cited but have no doubt he owned virtually all of them.

[50] *A Manual of Parliamentary Practice for the Use of the Senate of the United States,* by Thomas Jefferson. Printed by Samuel Harrison Smith, Washington City, 1801.

[51] For this and much additional information, I am indebted to my friend and former pupil Russell W. Fridley, who prepared for me, some years ago, a study of Jefferson's *Manual.*

[52] Sept. 15, 1834; quoted in *Rules and Manual* for 1961, p. 115*n.*

the lower chamber, but the enduring judgment is that in certain parts of it "are to be found the foundations of some of the most important parts of the House's practice." [53] It has also been very influential in state legislatures. The Senate, besides continuing to reprint the *Manual*, currently attaches to its Standing Rules references to the corresponding sections in Jefferson's compilation.

Unquestionably, his influence on legislative procedure has been great and enduring. If he were to view the procedure of Congress today, however, he would probably be disturbed by one major departure from the recommendations he based on the time-honored practices of the House of Commons. He laid great emphasis on the committee of the whole house, as his party did in the 1790's. [54] The idea was that matters of general concern should be considered by the whole body in the first place, under conditions which permitted everybody to speak. Only after the sense of the meeting had been made manifest should an important measure be referred to a small special committee for the working out of details. His desire to guard the interests of minorities by means of ordered procedure was supplemented by his concern that the legislature serve the general good against particular interests. He wanted Congress to be a genuinely deliberative body, not a register of decisions reached by small groups working behind the curtain. In the House of Representatives, which had not formally approved his *Manual*, the period following the War of 1812 was marked by a decline in the importance of the committee of the whole and the rise of standing committees. [55] This trend may have increased legislative effectiveness, but these committees could be appointed by Speakers to serve special interests. Henry Clay packed the committee on manufactures with pro-tariff advocates. Nothing comparable to this specialization occurred in the House of Commons for a couple of generations, if indeed it ever did, and one may assume that Jefferson would approve of the present procedure in Parliament more than of the rigid system of standing committees in the American Congress today. [56] By the same token, he would no doubt be pleased to observe that the Senate, the body for which he prepared his manual, has preserved to a considerable degree the character of a deliberative body — regardless of the dangers of obstructionism.

He was looking backward, not forward, when he made his farewell

[53] *Ibid.*

[54] Section XII in the *Manual*. For calling my attention to this important matter I am indebted to Professor Donald G. Morgan of Mount Holyoke College.

[55] L. D. White, *The Jeffersonians* (1951), pp. 45, 55–56.

[56] On procedure in the House of Commons, see Ivor Jennings, *Parliament* (1957), pp. 268–282.

to the Senate on February 28, 1801. Then he graciously said that the "habits of order and decorum" which characterized the proceedings of that body had rendered the task of its presiding officer one of little difficulty. When, in their reply, the senators lamented the loss of the "intelligence, attention, and impartiality" with which he had presided, they did more than present an idle compliment.[57] Though often designated as a disorganizer in the reckless speech of political controversy, he had imparted order to the deliberations of the upper house in times of turbulence.

[57] Feb. 28, Mar. 2, 1801 (*Annals*, 6 Cong., pp. 753–754, 755–756).

[XXIX]

Politics and Libel

1800

SINCE the Federalists dominated all branches of the general government in 1800, the continuing struggle of the Republicans against them was waged more effectively on the state than the national level. Control of state governments was of crucial importance because the determination of the manner in which presidential electors should be chosen lay with the various legislatures. At this time there was no uniform practice, and as a rule the dominant political group in a particular state prescribed the method which promised to be to its own advantage.[1] A full story of the presidential election of 1800, therefore, would comprise accounts of the struggles over the control of the legislatures in all sixteen states, and the various actions with respect to the method of choosing electors. Since Jefferson himself played virtually no direct part in these local struggles, there would be no real point in attempting to describe them here even if it were practicable to do so. Reference may be made, however, to a few of them, beginning with his own commonwealth and Pennsylvania, a state which always bulked large in his political thinking and about whose affairs he was well informed because he was spending part of each year in Philadelphia.

In Virginia the Republicans consolidated their position during the winter of 1799–1800 at the session of the General Assembly. It was then that Madison, emerging from retirement to assume a dominant legislative role, presented the renowned Report which closed the cycle

---

[1] For precise information about the prescribed methods in the 16 states in 1796 and 1800 see the chart in C. O. Paullin, *Atlas of the Hist. Geography of the U. S.* (1932), p. 89. In 10 states choice lay with the legislatures in 1800, which was a larger number than in 1796. In this period the trend was away from popular choice, on a general ticket or by districts.

of the Kentucky and Virginia Resolutions by strongly reaffirming the opposition of the Assembly to the Alien and Sedition Acts and clarifying the constitutional position of the dominant party.[2] He and other persons in thorough sympathy with the universally recognized leader of that party were in full control of the situation. Jefferson's disciple James Monroe was now governor, and another neighbor and intimate friend, Wilson Cary Nicholas, was elected to the United States Senate after the death of Henry Tazewell. In the light of history the most important action of this Assembly was the adoption of Madison's Report, but in the immediate political situation the most significant thing it did was to change the election law. In 1796, when presidential electors were chosen in Virginia by districts, supporters of Jefferson carried all the districts but one. In later congressional elections, however, the Federalists made marked gains. The majority party now sought to assure itself of the entire electoral vote of the state by providing for the choice of electors on a general ticket, as is the rule in our own time. This was not an undemocratic move, such as provision for election by the legislature would have been, but it was clearly in the interest of the majority vis-à-vis the minority.

There is no reason to believe that the idea of changing the law was Jefferson's in the first place, but he expressed himself privately to Monroe, and through Monroe to Madison and other leaders, as favorable to it under existing political circumstances. He said that election by districts would be the best method if it were general throughout the country, but in view of the fact that ten states chose electors by means of the legislatures or on a general ticket, he thought it folly for the others not to do likewise. "In these ten states," he said, "the minority is entirely unrepresented."[3] Judging from the returns of the congressional elections, the Republicans would have gained considerably in the country as a whole if choice by districts had been universal — that is, if every state had had a law like the one in effect in Virginia in 1796. Their present action in that state seemed desirable on purely political grounds in view of the immediate local situation, but the vote on the general-ticket law was embarrassingly close and there were many objections to the change in procedure. Hitherto Virginians had voted *viva voce* for a single candidate whom they knew personally, rather than for a long list, and the change involved numerous practical difficulties. Before there was actual voting under the new law, the Republican organization devised means to relieve the in-

---

[2] See above, ch. XXVI, note 34.

[3] To Monroe, Jan. 12, 1800 (Ford, VII, 401). When the electors were actually chosen the number was even higher.

dividual voters by having written lists prepared in advance for distribution among the freeholders, who could deposit them after signing their names. Madison believed that since the avowed object of the change was to give Virginia "fair play," it would become popular after proper explanation. That it did become so may be questioned, but the least valid of the objections to it were raised by the Federalists, who conveniently disregarded the high-handed actions of their own party in other states.[4]

Writing Monroe, Jefferson added this observation to his comments on the proposal: "Perhaps it will be thought I ought in delicacy to be silent on this subject. But you, who know me, know that my private gratifications would be most indulged by that issue which should leave me most at home." Even with reference to political activities within his own state he generally was silent. His role was one of acquiescence in the judgment of his friends rather than that of organizer. These friends and supporters created an elaborate organization for this campaign before the legislators dispersed. To begin with, they adopted an impressive ticket of electors, drawn from all parts of the state. This included George Wythe, Edmund Pendleton, and James Madison. They set up a central committee of five in Richmond, under the chairmanship of Philip Norborne Nicholas, and a committee of the same number in each county. Informing Jefferson of these actions, Nicholas said that the objects of establishing the committees were "to communicate useful information to the people relative to the election; and to repel every effort which may be made to injure either the ticket in general or to remove any prejudice which may be attempted to be raised against any person on that ticket."[5] Correspondence between the general committee and the subcommittees was begun immediately and became increasingly important in the heat of the summer campaign.[6]

Jefferson explained his delay of nearly two months in acknowledging the letter from the man who was virtually his campaign manager

[4] Entire matter well discussed by Ammon, "Republican Party in Virginia," pp. 229–232. A circular, dated Aug. 9, 1800, giving a form of the Republican ticket with suggestions about the preparation of written lists in advance, is printed by Cunningham in *Jeffersonian Republicans*, p. 196.

[5] Nicholas to TJ, Feb. 2, 1800 (LC, 18171). Minutes of the meeting of Jan. 21, 1800, in which 93 members of the legislature were joined by others, are reproduced by W. E. Hemphill in *Virginia Cavalcade*, Summer 1952, pp. 28–29. At the meeting electors were chosen and the form of organization was decided on. This caucus met several times thereafter.

[6] For example, an address to the citizens of the state, dated July 7, 1800, appeared at regular intervals in the *Virginia Argus*. Cunningham (p. 194, note 82) gives eight dates, July 11–Oct. 24, 1800. My own reference is to the issue of Sept. 12.

in Virginia on the ground that he was waiting until he could send him certain pamphlets containing views which he was anxious to have generally distributed.[7] These were papers by Joseph Priestley's friend Thomas Cooper, on the subject of "political arithmetic," of which he sent eight dozen copies so that one or more might go to every county in the state. Cooper, who afterwards gained considerable note as an economist and advocate of *laissez-faire*, was attacking foreign commerce in a way which Jefferson would not have wholly liked while secretary of state, but which he now approved as a critic of the administration. He wanted the various committees to be agencies of information, which they unquestionably became, though some thought this particular item too heavy for the popular digestion.[8] Only to this degree does he appear to have co-operated directly with Nicholas's organization, and he left no doubt that he wanted his co-operation kept secret. At this stage there was no need for him to do anything for the Republican cause in his state, where things were going well. In the spring elections for the Assembly and Congress, his party made marked gains in Virginia.

Things were also going well in Pennsylvania. Before he returned to Philadelphia, soon after Christmas in 1799, the Republicans had gained a substantial victory in the fall elections in the state, after a campaign in which the Federalists considerably surpassed them in rancor. Judge Thomas McKean, who defeated United States Senator James Ross in the gubernatorial race, was a rather conservative Republican whose victory can be best explained as the result of rather more effective organization than that of his opponent and as a revulsion against the excesses of Federalist national policy.[9] His margin of victory was provided by the counties identified with the Fries Rebellion against federal taxes. Jefferson neither anticipated nor approved this particular revolt, but he had clearly foreseen the general reaction against taxation and repression. He viewed developments in Pennsylvania as a party man. When John Beckley, former clerk of the federal House of Representatives and an incessantly active Republican, made application to Governor McKean for an appointment, he supported it. McKean rewarded Beckley with the clerkship of two local courts, regarding these offices as roughly equivalent to the clerkship of which he had been "unjustly deprived." Jefferson had a high opinion of Beckley's competence, but he gave here one of the first signs of

[7] TJ to P. N. Nicholas, Apr. 7, 1800 (Ford, VII, 439).

[8] Ammon, p. 234, citing L. W. Tazewell to TJ, Mar. 29, 1800, from MHS.

[9] H. M. Tinkcom, *The Republicans and Federalists in Pennsylvania, 1790–1801* (1950), ch. XII.

his acceptance of the idea of a degree of spoilsmanship in politics. This is hardly to be wondered at since the Federalists proceeded on the assumption that only members of their persuasion were fit for office. He was amply repaid by Beckley, one of whose pamphlets in his behalf appeared in an edition of five thousand.[10]

The Federalists did not recover from their defeat in Pennsylvania, but by obstructive tactics in the legislature, where they retained control of the Senate, they threatened to rob the Republicans of the fruits of victory so far as the approaching presidential contest was concerned. They blocked the Republican attempt to pass an election law, with the result that there was no provision for the casting of the electoral vote of this state. The Republicans, therefore, could only bide their time until the fall elections of 1800, in which they hoped to gain control of both houses. Early in the year Jefferson himself recognized the possibility that Pennsylvania might be deprived of her vote in the presidential contest. This proved to be virtually the case, for the Republicans did not quite carry the state Senate in the fall, though they made gains there and were decisively victorious in other contests. To get ahead of the story, what finally happened was that, as a result of a legislative compromise, the Republican ticket got eight electoral votes and the Federalist seven, despite a clear Republican majority in the state.[11]

The notorious electoral count bill of Senator Ross arose directly out of the political situation in Pennsylvania. Sensing that there might well be a dispute about the vote of his state in the presidential contest, the recently defeated candidate for governor introduced into the United States Senate in January, 1800, a measure which would have assured Federalist victory there and elsewhere. It would have set up a committee of thirteen to pass on electoral returns, determining which votes should be counted or disallowed and who should be President — all this without the possibility of appeal from its decision. This committee would consist of six members elected by the House of Representatives, six by the Senate, and the Chief Justice — that is, it would have been dominated by the Federalists. Thus the issue would have been resolved quite simply in their favor.[12] Though this flagrantly partisan measure was passed by the Senate, and in amended

---

[10] TJ to McKean, Jan. 9, 1800; McKean to TJ, Mar. 7, 1800 (LC, 18163, 18210). On the circulation of Beckley's *Address to the People of the U. S.: with an Epitome and Vindication of the Public Life and Character of Thomas Jefferson*, see Cunningham, pp. 197-198.

[11] Tinkcom, ch. XIII; TJ to Madison, Mar. 4, 1800 (Ford, VII, 433-434).

[12] Jan. 23, 1800 (*Annals*, 6 Cong., 1 sess., pp. 29-32, giving the first debate).

form by the House, it died because of the intransigence of the extremists in the upper chamber.[13] Besides offering a striking example of arrogance and self-righteousness, this bill provided the occasion of a clash between the body over which Jefferson presided and William Duane of the *Aurora*, the Republican newspaperman the Federalists were most anxious to punish and silence. The Vice President was a firsthand witness of this affair, a thing which cannot be said of any of the trials under the Sedition Act.[14]

The Federalist executioners had been cheated of their prey when Benjamin Franklin Bache died of yellow fever in September, 1798, before he could be prosecuted for seditious libel. Duane, who succeeded him as editor of the *Aurora*, the most important single Republican paper, proved to be the most effective of the journalists of the opposition in this era and was supremely objectionable to the group in power for just that reason. Though the Ross bill was debated behind closed doors, Duane quickly got wind of it and denounced it. Then, receiving a copy of it from certain Republican senators, he published this in the *Aurora* with further caustic comments on senatorial conduct.[15] Some of his statements about what had happened were inaccurate but he correctly sensed the import of the measure.

This publication was regarded as a high breach of the privileges of the Senate by two-thirds of the members of that body — which in the opinion of at least Uriah Tracy of Connecticut could not be questioned by anybody at any time, anywhere. Despite the objections of the small Republican minority, who reminded their colleagues of severe criticisms of their actions which had been previously voiced by the Federalist *Gazette of the United States*, Duane was condemned by resolution without a hearing. He was then ordered to appear under a prescribed procedure which involved Jefferson.[16] When the culprit appeared, the presiding officer was to address him in specifically prescribed words, charging him with "false, scandalous, and malicious assertions" tending to defame the Senate and bring it into disrepute. Jefferson was to be spared from reading the Senate resolution of condemnation, since that task was committed to the clerk, but afterwards he was to ask if Duane had anything to say in excuse or extenuation. If there was no answer, the editor was to remain in custody

[13] TJ to Edward Livingston, Apr. 30, 1800, and to Madison, May 12, 1800 (Ford, VII, 443–444, 446–447).

[14] It is admirably described by J. M. Smith in *Freedom's Fetters*, pp. 288–306. My own account of it in *Cooper*, pp. 113–116, is more restricted.

[15] *Aurora*, Feb. 19, 1800.

[16] Form of proceedings, presented by Senator Dayton, Mar. 22, 1800 (*Annals*, 6 Cong., 1 sess., p. 117).

of the sergeant at arms until the Senate should reach a decision — that is, a sentence. When reached, this was to be pronounced by the presiding officer.

If the intolerant majority had in mind the embarrassment of Jefferson, as well as the punishment of Duane, their plans were circumvented by the ingenuity of the journalist and two Republicans whom he called into consultation — Alexander James Dallas and Thomas Cooper — and by Duane's subsequent elusiveness. The Federalist senators would undoubtedly have charged Jefferson with collusion had they known of the private letter in which Cooper informed him of the plan of campaign the trio had devised against the body over which he presided.[17] But, since this in no way affected the Vice President's official conduct, the chief purpose it served, no doubt, was to relieve his mind.

The upshot was that Duane, appearing before the Senate, requested that he be permitted to advise with counsel and withdrew. According to his plan, he then addressed letters to Dallas and Cooper, asking them to serve as counsel. This they both declined to do on the ground that the Senate had already prejudged the case and that they would only degrade themselves by appearing before the Senate under the limitations and restrictions that body had imposed. Duane submitted the entire correspondence to Jefferson as president of the Senate, with a statement that he declined to appear under the existing circumstances and that the Senate might proceed to do whatever it saw fit. All this he published in the *Aurora*.[18] The Senate then declared Duane guilty of contempt, though by a smaller majority than heretofore, and issued a warrant for his arrest. Jefferson signed this in his official capacity, but Duane absolved him of all blame for this formal action.[19]

Duane evaded the process server until after the adjournment of Congress, continuing to write for his paper all the while. After some weeks of hide and seek, a petition and remonstrance in his behalf from citizens of Philadelphia was presented by Senator William Bingham of Pennsylvania, who was himself quite out of sympathy with it. On the question whether or not it should be read, the vote was 12 to 12. Enjoying one of his rare opportunities to break a tie, Jefferson decided in the affirmative.[20] The Senate rejected the petition that it reconsider its action against Duane, but, apparently aware of its own impotence, it

[17] Cooper to TJ, presumably Mar. 23, 1800 (LC, 20951).

[18] Mar. 27, 1800.

[19] *Annals*, 6 Cong., 1 sess., pp. 121–124 (Mar. 26, 27, 1800); Duane in *Aurora*, Apr. 1, 1800.

[20] This is shown by the account in the *Aurora*, May 13, 1800, though not in the account in the *Annals* (May 10). Bingham voted against reading the petition.

requested the President to prosecute him under the Sedition Act.[21] This was the last action of the session, after the Vice President had excused himself to go home; Senator Tracy, who would tolerate no criticism, was in the chair. The criticism by Duane had no apparent effect, for, as Jefferson noted, the electoral count bill as passed by the Senate was more extreme than the one that appeared in the *Aurora*, since it extended the powers of the grand committee to "*all* subjects of enquiry." [22] Because of a succession of delays, however, nothing ever came of the prosecution of Duane, against whom proceedings were finally dropped after the former Vice President had become President. In this episode Jefferson consistently manifested respect for the Senate, though his sympathies lay elsewhere and his patience must have been sorely tried.

The Republicans rightly regarded the proceedings against Duane as more arbitrary and tyrannical than those in the federal courts under the Sedition Act, but all these proceedings were similar in purpose. It is noteworthy that a large proportion of the sedition trials did not occur until 1800, when the war danger which had provided the original occasion and excuse for repressive measures had receded. The timing of the trials was in part accidental, for the mills of justice (or injustice) ground slowly, but it became increasingly obvious that these were in fact political trials in a crucial election year. Their object, as Jefferson had perceived from the beginning, was the silencing of the opposition press.[23] During the course of the actual trials his recorded comments on them were few. He gave them blanket condemnation, regarding the men convicted in them as victims of political persecution. No doubt he was informed of the various individual trials during what he described as a reign of witches, but the two that came closest to him were those of Thomas Cooper and James Thomson Callender. The former, which was a direct consequence of Cooper's activities in behalf of Duane although the charges were based on things he had said about John Adams some months earlier, occurred in Philadelphia. The latter took place in Virginia, where Callender had sought refuge but where Justice Samuel Chase sought to provide the Republican gentry with an object lesson in federal authority.

The names of Duane, Cooper, and Callender were frequently con-

---

[21] May 14, 1800 (*Annals*, 6 Cong., 1 sess., p. 184).

[22] To L. W. Tazewell, Apr. 10, 1800, quoted by Smith, p. 300, note 70, from MHS.

[23] An excellent summary of the enforcement of the Sedition Act is given in Smith, *Freedom's Fetters*, ch. IX. He treats individual cases afterward. According to his estimate, there were at least 14 indictments under the Act and 3 at common law.

joined in the Federalist newspapers of the time, especially in Philadelphia. They were often castigated as "foreign emissaries." Cooper was English while Callender was Scottish, and both of them could be properly regarded as refugees. Duane's case was much disputed, for although born in the province of New York he had grown up in Ireland and spent years in various parts of the British Empire. The Federalists made no bones about designating him as an Irishman of dubious American patriotism. A more important allegation was that these three "emissaries" took their orders from Jefferson as "Chief Juggler."

The case was thus presented in a communication to a Federalist paper:

> With respect to the organization of their political plan, it commenced by a subdivision of their business in detail, into three Grand Departments. Callender takes the southern, Duane the eastern, and Cooper, with Priestley for his aid major, has the whole of the Jacobin interest of the western country under his immediate controul; all the doings of these three *chiefs of division*, are subject to the controul of the Chief Juggler and his select council.[24]

The charge that Jefferson directed the Republican editors and pamphleteers followed the line that Hamilton had laid down at the time of Freneau, but neither at that time nor at any other in this decade is it borne out by available records, and, in fact, he would have been out of character had he done so. He was not that sort of party leader. He encouraged the Republican press and at times urged particular persons, like James Madison and Edmund Pendleton, to write on specified topics. Upon occasion he provided information on request, but he would have done this for anybody, and there is no suggestion that he was responsible for the leakage of any official information. This advocate of the freedom of the press left the party writers to their devices, and if he erred he did so in trusting them too much.

This year marked the beginning of an intellectual friendship between him and Thomas Cooper, then of Northumberland, Pennsylvania, which lasted the rest of his life. Though Jefferson tended to overrate the abilities of Priestley's friend, Cooper was a man of impressive learning whose contributions to campaign literature were of an unusually high order.[25] Though an inveterate controversialist, he served only temporarily as a journalist — relieving the editor of the *Sunbury and Northumberland Gazette* for a few months in 1799. In

[24] A Federal Republican, in Philadelphia *Gazette*, Mar. 12, 1800.
[25] I have discussed these in *Cooper*, pp. 92–110.

the volume of *Political Essays* which he published soon thereafter he declared himself to be in America as he had been in England "a decided opposer of political restrictions on the liberty of the press, and a sincere friend to those first principles of republican government, the sovereignty of the people and the responsibility of their servants." [26] His discussion of freedom of the press was broadly philosophical, and this, with his economic philosophy of *laissez-faire*, showed him to be a man after Jefferson's own heart. In the election campaign of 1799 in Pennsylvania his services were comparable to those of Duane.

Tried on the charge of seditious libel in April, 1800, Cooper was sentenced on May 1 to pay a fine of four hundred dollars and spend six months in jail.[27] The specific remarks about John Adams which led to his conviction were drawn from a handbill he had published the previous autumn. Some of these remarks were extravagant, but the statement of Justice Samuel Chase that this was the boldest attempt he had known "to poison the minds of the people" was much more so. Quite obviously, Cooper was punished because he had made himself conspicuous in the Duane affair and was politically objectionable to the ruling group. When Chase voiced the suspicion that his fine would be paid by his party, Cooper repudiated the suggestion, saying that he was no party writer but spoke out of his own convictions. His later career was not wholly consistent, but the sincerity of this statement need not be doubted. By the same token, he sought no aid from Jefferson or anybody else, willingly accepting martyrdom for the cause. This was not the most ludicrous of the sedition cases — that honor belongs to the case of Luther Baldwin of New Jersey, who in a state of inebriation expressed the wish that a cannon shot, fired in salute to Adams, had struck the President's posterior.[28] It may not have been the most cruel, though Cooper's wife died while he was in prison. But, most clearly of them all, it was an attack on the freedom of intelligence.

Ironically, the case of James Thomson Callender, the needy hack writer who, as time was to show, was willing to blacken anybody's reputation, touched Jefferson more directly. In the summer of 1798, in fear of the Sedition Act and perhaps because of other troubles, Callender had quitted Philadelphia. Jefferson's old landlord, the merchant Thomas Leiper, promised to take care of Callender's four children, and Senator Stevens Thomson Mason offered him safe lodging in Virginia. Accordingly, he walked all the way to Mason's place, Raspberry

---

[26] *Political Essays* (1799), preface. A 2nd edn. appeared early in 1800.
[27] Account of trial in *Cooper*, ch. IV, and Smith, ch. XIV.
[28] Smith, pp. 270–274.

Plain in Loudoun County.[29] Leiper advised him not to come back, and he was sick of even the Republicans, he said, since so many of them had treated him badly. He also said that the aristocracy of his present neighborhood, "one of the vilest in America," had incessantly abused him and Mason. The plight of this hunted and impoverished creature who had no weapon but his pen was sad indeed, and when informed of it Jefferson sent him fifty dollars. That is, he asked Mason to draw on his agent in Richmond, George Jefferson, for that amount, keeping Callender's name out of the business. It was a humane act and no doubt this excessively generous man would have reproached himself if he had not done something of the sort. Like the two others who had specially befriended Callender, he was fully aware that the journalist had brought trouble on himself because of his attacks on the Federalists. In a letter which he wrote before he got the money, and which Jefferson received after he had ordered the money sent, Callender implied that the "assistant writer" of a party was entitled to support.[30] Jefferson would have been wise to challenge that statement for the record, but at a time when he was inordinately careful about his letters he obviously avoided writing this dubious character unless he had to.

While he was still enjoying the hospitality of Senator Mason and had the use of a good library, Callender, whose health had improved, formulated plans for other writing which would itself bring in money while stimulating the sale of the works he had already published. He would give his readers "such a tornado as no government ever got before." [31] Jefferson made no response to this prophecy, but by the summer of 1799, when Callender had found employment on the Richmond *Examiner*, there was promise of its fulfillment. Callender wrote Jefferson late in August, saying that he was to be a subscriber to his (Callender's) next volume, though there is no record of Jefferson's having said so, and reminding him that the fashion in Virginia was to pay for such things in advance. At the same time he dilated on the dangers to which he was subjected.[32] Actually there was an organized attempt to run him out of town. Replying from Monticello, Jefferson said that his agent in Richmond would give him fifty dollars on account of the

[29] Virtually the entire correspondence between TJ and Callender in this period was published by W. C. Ford in *N.-Eng. Hist. and Geneal. Register*, Vol. 50 (1896), pp. 321-333, 445-458; Vol. 51 (1897), pp. 19-24. Unless otherwise indicated, reference is to this collection, letters being cited by dates. Smith covers Callender and his trial admirably in ch. XV.

[30] Callender to TJ, Oct. 26, 1798. His first letter from Raspberry Plain was dated Sept. 22. TJ gave instructions to Mason on Oct. 11 (Ford, VII, 282).

[31] To TJ, Nov. 19, 1798.

[32] Callender to TJ, Aug. 10, 1799. On the threat to Callender, see Smith, p. 338, note 18.

book he was about to publish. He was to send two or three copies when it came out and hold the rest until Jefferson called for them. Reporting that the violence meditated against Callender had aroused indignation in his own part of the country, Jefferson reassured him by saying that Virginia had always been noted for lawful conduct and good order.[33]

Jefferson had put his latest gift in the guise of payment for copies of a publication. This turned out to be *The Prospect Before Us*, on the basis of which its author was afterwards convicted of seditious libel.[34] Jefferson saw this work, presumably in page proof, during the autumn of 1799 — at just the time that his spirits were at their lowest point with respect to public prospects. He gave Callender at a very late date certain information which he could legitimately have given anybody, but there is no indication that he influenced the contents of the volume. Here as elsewhere Callender said precisely what he wanted to. Just how many pages Jefferson had seen when he expressed himself about the work is uncertain — perhaps sixteen, though Callender sent him upwards of a hundred eventually. At any rate he left these words on record: "Such papers cannot fail to produce the best effect. They inform the thinking part of the nation; and these again, supported by the taxgatherers as their vouchers, set the people to rights." [35] He commended nothing specifically and he had not seen the whole work, but he said enough to permit the author to associate the acknowledged leader of the Republican party with this publication if he chose to. Callender, who had considerable recourse to the bottle in later years, may then have deteriorated further, but if he was "a poor creature, . . . hypochondriac, drunken, penniless and unprincipled," as Jefferson said toward the end of his own life, he himself was blind and exceedingly gullible in not realizing this sooner.[36]

The facts do not support the later Federalist claim that he hired Callender to calumniate Hamilton and Adams: that is a gross distortion. But his later justification of his own conduct, after Callender had indeed shown "base ingratitude" by publishing far more scandalous false charges against him than that writer ever made against John Adams, leaves something to be desired.[37] Like most mortals he was not beyond rationalization and self-deception. His actions, as we

---

[33] TJ to Callender, Sept. 6, 1799 (Ford, VII, 392).

[34] Extracts from the correspondence bearing on the work can be conveniently seen in Sowerby, III, 421–427. The first volume sold for a dollar.

[35] Oct. 6, 1799 (Ford, VII, 395).

[36] To Robert Richardson, Apr. 20, 1824 (Sowerby, III, 427).

[37] To Monroe, July 15, 1802 (Ford, VIII, 164–166); to Abigail Adams, July 22, 1804 (*A.-J. Letters*, I, 275).

have reported them thus far, do not bear out the later statement that, while still considering Callender a proper object of benevolence, "no man wished more to see his pen stopped." This sounds like an after-thought. The simplest explanation of the matter is that he did not want the attacks on Adams's public acts stopped, since he essentially agreed with these, despite the vehemence of Callender's language. He was warranted in saying that he no more sanctioned the "calumnies and falsehoods" against Adams than, as he supposed, Adams sanctioned the far more numerous ones hurled by Peter Porcupine and others against him, but he needed to allow for the influence of political excitement on anybody's judgment. He probably regarded some degree of personal attack, as distinguished from attack on public policy, as inescapable in view of the way the game was being played. Actually, the particular comments of Callender's about Adams which led to his trial and conviction could have been matched in the writings of Peter Porcupine and others, not to speak of a letter Alexander Hamilton was to write ere long. As for the praise lavished on him himself by Callender at this stage, Jefferson would not have been in character if he had not found this embarrassing.

In the full sense Callender's trial for sedition in Richmond in May and June, 1800, before Justice Samuel Chase, was political. A copy of his latest work with marked passages was given Chase by the Federalist bulldog Luther Martin when the Justice was on circuit, and he had determined to punish the author before he got to Richmond, where he also expected to put the Virginia lawyers in their place. Haranguing the grand jury, he struck a left-handed blow at Jefferson by asserting that he would allow no atheist to give testimony. The alleged atheist himself said that, coming from Chase, the calumny would have less effect than from any other man in the country. Early in the year Monroe had predicted to Jefferson that an attempt would be made to carry the Sedition Law into Virginia as an electioneering trick. The Governor now hoped that the people would behave with dignity and was determined to prevent any public protest against Callender's arrest. He inquired of his friend, however, if it would not be proper for him to employ counsel to give the accused man legitimate defense. Jefferson's reply appears to be his only recorded comment on this trial at the time. "I think it essentially just and necessary that Callender should be substantially defended," he said. "Whether in the first stage by public interference [that is, by state-appointed counsel], or by private contributors, may be a question." [38] In view of the condemna-

[38] May 26, 1800 (Ford, VII, 448). The promptness of his reply was made possible by the fact that he was visiting at Eppington.

tion of the Sedition Act by the General Assembly, he regarded this case as a challenge to the state, but at the same time he wanted respect to be shown the Union.

Actually, the procedure that was followed was private: subscriptions were sought and lawyers volunteered their services. Among these, however, were Philip Norborne Nicholas, recently appointed attorney general of the state; William Wirt, clerk of the House of Delegates; and Monroe's son-in-law, George Hay. They proved useless, for Chase contradicted and overruled them so persistently that they withdrew. The presiding judge was the central figure in these proceedings, not the accused. Republicans believed that they had sufficient political reason to support Callender against him from the start, and, before he got through, Virginians in general regarded him as insulting to their state. Callender, who was sentenced to a nine months' imprisonment and fine of two hundred dollars after a trial in which he was virtually defenseless, had more friends in jail than when at liberty. He served the Republican cause more effectively as a victim than as a writer.

While incarcerated he wrote a second part of the *Prospect*. He sent Jefferson sheets of this, saying he flattered himself that "although neither the style nor matter could be exactly conformable" to Jefferson's "ideas or taste, yet that upon the whole, they would not be disagreeable." [39] Jefferson did not acknowledge receipt of them or answer any of the numerous letters Callender wrote him in the fall and winter. But he instructed his agent in Richmond to take fifty dollars to the prisoner on the understanding that two copies of the proposed work would be sent him when published and further copies on convenience. He was again cloaking his charity in the guise of a purchase and was being as secretive as possible about the entire transaction. In view of past actions, political realities, and Callender's plight it would doubtless have been difficult to do otherwise. [40] It is hard to excape the impression that he had let himself become the victim of a species of blackmail. He did not destroy the documents, however, and for any mistakes of heart and head he may have made in dealing with this unfortunate and unscrupulous journalist time was to exact superabundant retribution.

[39] To TJ, Oct. 11, 1800.

[40] To George Jefferson, Oct. 24, 1800; from George Jefferson, Nov. 3, 1800; to George Jefferson, Nov. 7, 1800; from George Jefferson, Jan. 12, 1801 (all MHS). Later developments, relating to Callender's fine, his unsuccessful application for office, and his slanderous attacks on Jefferson, belong in the story of the latter's presidency, even though some of the documents antedate his inauguration.

ii

Before Callender was brought to trial in Richmond there were important political developments elsewhere which were distinctly encouraging to the Republicans. Jefferson, who thought the presidential contest hinged on the middle states, recognized the crucial importance of the election of members of the New York legislature, which chose the presidential electors on joint ballot. Despite the Federalist assertion that the victory of their foes would cause the music of the hammers on the wharves and the hum of busy industry to cease, while the temple of the Most High was being "profaned by the impious orgies of the Goddess of Reason," the party which Aaron Burr marshalled swept the city elections in New York City on May 1 sufficiently to ensure a majority in the legislature.[41] Jefferson got the news about the time that he heard of party victories in his own state, and when the intelligence reached the Federalist Senate that body, in no mood for business, quickly adjourned. These events brought gloom to every Tory countenance, according to Republican Edward Livingston. Also, they bore out the earlier comment of Governor John Jay that some were persuaded that George Washington had been taken away from *evil to come*.

They occasioned the extraordinary suggestion of Hamilton that Jay call into session the existing legislature, which had a Federalist majority, with a view to changing the law so that presidential electors would be chosen by districts. In such times of extraordinary peril it would not do to be overscrupulous, he said. Instead, every legal and constitutional step should be taken "to prevent an atheist in religion, and a fanatic in politics, from getting possession of the helm of state." [42] Jay wisely declined to adopt for party purposes so unbecoming a measure, and an immediate consequence of this election was to boost the political stock of Burr, who was credited on every hand with the result. Gallatin's father-in-law, James Nicholson, attributed the miraculous issue to "the intervention of a Supreme Power and our friend Burr the agent." [43]

By this time the Republican congressional leaders had already decided on sound political grounds that Jefferson's running mate should

---

[41] Good brief account in S. I. Pomerantz, *New York, An American City, 1783–1803* (1938), pp. 126–130.

[42] To Jay, May 7, 1800 (Lodge, VIII, 549–551). Also, E. Livingston to TJ, received May 3 (LC, 18297); Jay to Rev. Dr. Morse, Oct. 24, 1800 (*Correspondence and Public Papers*, IV, 266–267).

[43] Nicholson to Gallatin from N. Y., May 6, 1800 (Adams, *Gallatin*, p. 241).

be a New Yorker. Gallatin, who had been delegated to make the necessary local inquiries, asked Nicholson to see George Clinton and Burr. The net result was the report that the former declined and that the latter, who was approved by all whom Nicholson talked with, could probably be induced to stand if assured of fair treatment in the southern states, where he had received such indifferent support four years before. At the same time Mrs. Gallatin, then in New York, wrote her husband: "Burr says he has no confidence in the Virginians; they once deceived him, and they are not to be trusted." [44] Burr was undisposed to give up the certainty of being elected governor for the uncertainty of becoming vice president, and some of his friends thought the chief state office more important anyway. His name "must not be played the fool with," said Nicholson, and the business of the last election must be smoothed over.

At a very large meeting of Republicans — that is, a caucus — on the night of May 11, it was unanimously agreed to support Burr for vice president.[45] There never had been any question about the candidate for President. In a memorandum of a conversation with Burr shortly before the latter was replaced on the Republican ticket in 1804 by George Clinton, Jefferson said that Burr claimed he had accepted the nomination in 1800 to promote Jefferson's fame and advancement and from a desire to be with him, "whose company and conversation had always been fascinating to him." Jefferson did not swallow that, and on his own part he now said that he had distrusted the man from the time he had first observed him as a senator.[46] If this was not an afterthought he cloaked his distrust during his years as leader of the opposition, when he established and maintained friendly political relations with the useful New Yorker. There is no reason to doubt his statement that there never was any intimacy between them, much as Burr may have enjoyed his conversation. Nor need it be doubted that he played a wholly passive role in the matter of Burr's nomination. He shared the determination of his own friends, however, that his running mate should get a full vote in Virginia as an evidence of good faith, bringing some personal influence to bear for that end. Under his benign leadership the Republicans really closed ranks in this campaign. "The Jacobins appear to be completely organized throughout the United

---

[44] Nicholson to Gallatin, May 7, 1800, and Mrs. Gallatin to her husband, May 7 (ibid., pp. 242–243). A fuller account, prepared by Nicholson in 1803, is in A.H.R., VIII, 511–513 (April, 1903).

[45] Gallatin to his wife, May 12, 1800 (ibid., p. 243). No proceedings of this or of the Federalist caucus were published. The standard account is in F. W. Dallinger, Nominations for Elective Office in the U. S. (1916 edn.), pp. 14–16.

[46] Memo. of Jan. 26, 1804 (Ford, I, 301–304).

States," lamented a High Federalist.[47] These "base plotters against the peace, safety and felicity" of the country acted in unison, he said, seeking to introduce into the state governments "unprincipled tools" of faction, and to assure the election to the chief office of "the great arch priest of Jacobinism and infidelity." To this purpose Burr had already proved himself an invaluable accessory.

Writing his son-in-law a few days before the Republicans decided on their second man, Jefferson, after saying that the Federalists did not conceal their despair because of the results of the election in New York, reported that they had held a caucus and determined on some "hocus-pocus maneuvers." That is, they were running Charles Cotesworth Pinckney to draw off votes in South Carolina, and possibly in North Carolina. A week later he commented that they were not without hope of giving Pinckney preference over Adams, reporting at the same time the resignation of McHenry, the dismissal of Pickering, and the succession of John Marshall to the latter's post as secretary of state.[48] His recorded contemporary references to these events are sparse, but they show that he perceived the dissension in the other camp and the purposes the High Federalists so fully expressed in private correspondence which naturally he did not see.[49]

They named Adams by force of political necessity, but the ultras preferred Pinckney, who was not himself a party to this intrigue. Their feelings were acerbated further when Adams cleared his Cabinet of two of his secret enemies and assumed at this late date undisputed command of his own official household. Hamilton had written Theodore Sedgwick: "To support *Adams* and *Pinckney* equally is the only thing that can possibly save us from the fangs of *Jefferson*." After receiving further information, he wrote that he would never more be responsible for Adams by direct support, even though the result would be the election of Jefferson. He was sure the government would sink under either man, but if they had to have an enemy at the head of it he preferred an open one. If convinced that Pinckney would be supported equally with Adams in the East, he would go along, but otherwise he would pursue Pinckney as his "single object."[50] Adams suspected as much, no doubt, and among the ultras he

[47] T. Parsons to John Jay, May 5, 1800 (Jay, *Correspondence and Public Papers,* IV, 269).

[48] To TMR, May 7, 14, 1800 (LC, 18277, 18215).

[49] These matters are discussed in detail by Dauer, ch. 16; Kurtz, ch. 17; and by other writers.

[50] Hamilton to Sedgwick, May 4, 1800; Sedgwick to Hamilton, May 7; Hamilton to Sedgwick, May 10 (J.C.H., VI, 436-438, 441-442).

was reported to have said that he would sooner serve as vice president under Jefferson than to be indebted to "*such a being* as Hamilton," whom he did not hesitate to call a bastard and as much an alien as Gallatin.[51]

These references to "billingsgate language" were made on hearsay by prejudiced reporters, but this feud was destined to surpass the one between Jefferson and the former Secretary of the Treasury. Rumors were also current in these same circles of a coalition between Jefferson and Adams, though the former appears to have made no reference to them and the latter denied them.[52] The real cause of complaint on the part of the High Federalists was that Adams, while critical of them, acted "as if he did not hate nor dread Jefferson." At times, indeed, he and the good lady his wife spoke of him with much regard, affecting indignation at the charge of irreligion against him and making no mention of his "wild philosophy and gimcrackery in politics." [53] Under existing political conditions, it is hard to see how any coalition between these two old friends could possibly have been effected, and neither could now have been expected to consent to serve under the other, but developing circumstances had blurred the issue between them. As things turned out, they were both against Hamilton and what he stood for.

The caucuses and John Adams's housecleaning took place at the very end of the congressional session — the last to be held in Philadelphia. In the middle of May, Jefferson, who had had many painful experiences in this place in the last three years, along with some delightful associations with men of learning, made his final departure in an optimistic state of mind. Even the news from abroad was good, for word had come that the American envoys to France had been favorably received and he believed that a settlement could not be avoided. He and one of his sons-in-law had some financial troubles, because of the state of the tobacco market, but he was going to see Maria and her husband, to visit the Eppes family and his Sister Bolling, and take his younger daughter back with him to Monticello where he was above the storms of politics.

Originally he planned to go by the Eastern Shore, a route he had never taken, proceeding up the south side of the James to Eppington.

---

[51] Pickering to Rufus King, June 26, 1800 (King, III, 262).

[52] In later years Pickering revived talk of this, but the resulting correspondence of the year 1811 between Adams, Benjamin Stoddert, and Samuel and Robert Smith of Md. (Adams, *Works*, X, 3–9) revealed only a shadowy episode which, in my opinion, can be dismissed from consideration.

[53] Fisher Ames to R. King, Aug. 26, Sept. 24, 1800 (King, III, 296–297, 304–306).

Then he would go straight home, missing Richmond altogether. He wanted to avoid ceremony everywhere and to keep his name out of the papers. In the end he did go by Richmond, where he stayed with James Monroe, but he seems to have been spared distasteful ceremony. It was while he was at Eppington that Governor Monroe asked his advice about the defense of the wretched Callender.[54] He got home toward the end of May and there, by July 4, he harvested the best wheat crop he had ever had. Not until the end of October, when he visited Poplar Forest, did he leave the county, and not until the last week in November of this election year did he set out for the new Federal City of Washington.

During these months he gave himself to the rural employments which always attracted him so much, and when at his writing desk he was considerably occupied, no doubt, with the manual of parliamentary practice which he was putting into final shape. He received letters from supporters in various parts of the country and kept in constant touch with the course of political affairs, but he maintained the policy of engaging in a minimum of political correspondence — assuming the attitude of passivity which, in his opinion, propriety required while he was being subjected to the free discussion of his countrymen. It is impossible to determine just how much of this discussion he was aware of, but it certainly should not be supposed that he read all, or even a substantial part, of the pamphlets and papers to which modern students of this age have access. The chances are that he read relatively few of them. Some things unquestionably came to his personal attention, however — such as the report of his death which got out before the Fourth of July.[55]

Oddly enough, this report was communicated to a friendly paper by a writer who referred to its subject as "the man in whom is centered the feelings and happiness of the American people," and who was himself convinced of its falsity.[56] The form in which it was circulated in the press thereafter, and the degree of credence given to it, depended largely on the politics of the particular newspapers. Supposedly the report was brought to Baltimore in the first place by three gentlemen from Winchester, who were said to have learned from a man from Charlottesville that Jefferson had died at Monticello after

[54] TJ to Monroe, Mar. 26, Apr. 13, 1800 (LC, 18230–18231, 18256); Monroe to TJ, Apr. 23, May 25, 1800 (S.M.H., III, 173–174, 179–180); TJ to TMR, May 7, 14, 1800 (LC, 18277, 18215). His various stopping places are shown in his Account Book.

[55] This interesting minor episode is well described by Charles Warren in *Odd Byways of American History* (1942), ch. VII.

[56] *Baltimore American*, June 30, 1800, quoted by Warren, p. 129.

an illness of forty-eight hours. It was taken up by papers in Philadelphia and New York and then in New England at a time when Virginia papers were taking no note of it or were actually denying it. The rumor ran faster than the denials, and the *Aurora* quickly scented ulterior Federalist designs. Duane's paper described this as "a fabrication intended to damp the festivity of the 4th of July and prevent the author of the Declaration of Independence from being the universal toast" of that festival. Indeed, the *Aurora* claimed that the Federalists had shown marked indifference to the celebration in Philadelphia this year, while the Republicans rejoiced in it as usual. One Republican, charging the Federalists with exulting over the false report, said: "When lions fall, asses bray." That is, "the asses of aristocracy, fearing the paws of this republican lion, reported his death — because they wished him so!" [57]

This may be regarded an extreme and unwarranted assertion, but in the Federalist papers there was a notable absence of expressions of regret, though the conjunction of this report with the celebrations of American independence would certainly have led one to expect them even if good manners alone did not. Meanwhile, Du Pont de Nemours, after several days of "indescribable unhappiness," congratulated Jefferson and the United States on the falsity of the news. Other prominent supporters and friends, while disposed to believe that the report was political in origin, wondered if he had suffered any indisposition. Replying to Du Pont, he said: "I am much indebted to my enemies for proving, by their recitals of my death, that I have friends. . . . I have never enjoyed better nor more uninterrupted health." [58]

Since Jefferson was the living symbol of Republicanism and the rallying center of his party, his reputation as well as his life was precious to his partisans, and it was actively defended by them. He himself played no more direct part in the furious battle of words in the summer and autumn of 1800 than he did in matters of local organization, and for that reason we need not describe it in detail. The principles and policies which his supporters proclaimed were those he had set forth bit by bit, and sometimes in summarized form, in

[57] *Aurora*, July 3, 7, 1800, quoted by Warren.

[58] Du Pont to TJ, July 6, 1800, and TJ to Du Pont, July 26 (*Correspondence*, pp. 17–18); Elijah Griffith to TJ, July 8, 1800 (LC, 18315); S. T. Mason to TJ, July 11 (LC, 18317–18318). Warren cites (p. 132) a newspaper item attributing the rise of the report to the fact that a slave named Thomas Jefferson had died at Monticello. I have found no such slave listed in the *Farm Book* and doubt the use of the surname by any slave still in TJ's possession.

private letters.[59] He had never ceased talking about the "spirit of 1776," and he must have liked the language of the dignified address to the citizens of his own state which was printed so many times by the committee of which Philip Norborne Nicholas was chairman. Among other things this said: "As a friend of liberty, we believe Jefferson second to no man, and the experience of no man has afforded better lessons for its preservation." Therefore, the committee offered him to the affections of his fellow countrymen as the ablest guardian of their "peace, freedom, and constitution." [60] To this he himself would probably have added some reference to economy. But the party principles had been largely arrived at by consensus during the years of opposition, and he made no public pronouncement until his first inaugural, when he expressed essentially the same ideas in more moving language.

The verbal campaign of 1800 in the country as a whole, falling far below the level of the official Virginia address, surpassed that of 1796 in both quantity and scurrility. It has been estimated that upwards of a hundred pamphlets were issued on one side or the other, and there were far more communications to the newspapers, a large majority of which supported the party in power.[61] Whether the Federalist pot or the Republican kettle was the blacker, one would hesitate to say, but at least the opposition could attack the actual policies of the administration, while their opponents were emphasizing vague fears and dread future dangers. And it seems safe to say that the charges hurled against Jefferson, who was shielded by no sedition law, were more reckless than those against Adams and much less relevant. Indeed, it may be claimed that the personal attacks on the chief Republican were the most vicious in any presidential campaign on record.[62] One may doubt if a more distorted picture of a candidate for the first office has ever been presented by his foes. Many of these attacks were mere repetitions or elaborations of what had been said four years earlier. Many followed the line that Hamilton had laid down for his supporters in 1792, when, writing as CATULLUS, he attacked his colleague in Washington's official family as an intriguing incendiary and secret

[59] Most notably, perhaps, in his letter of Jan. 26, 1799, to Elbridge Gerry (Ford, VII, 327–329). Cunningham, after quoting the most pertinent part of this, reprints from the *Aurora* a contrasting list of Federal policies and Republican promises, designating the latter and TJ's letter as in effect a party platform (pp. 211–214).

[60] *Virginia Argus*, Sept. 12, 1800, and other dates.

[61] The estimate is that of C. O. Lerche, Jr., in his excellent article "Jefferson and the Election of 1800: A Case Study in the Political Smear," in *W. & M.*, Oct. 1948, pp. 467–491. A more journalistic treatment is Coley Taylor and Samuel Middlebrook, *The Eagle Screams* (1936), ch. III.

[62] So Charles Warren says in *Odd Byways in American History*, p. 127.

enemy of the Constitution. But, to a greater extent than previously, Jefferson was assailed on religious grounds.

Though the main themes were the old ones, with increased emphasis on his "infidelity," there were minor ones which were played up in particular localities. Thus in South Carolina, where until now the Federalists had been stronger than in any other southern state, his liberal views on slavery were brought up against him. Evidence was drawn from his *Notes on Virginia*, where he described his vain early attempt to start gradual emancipation in his state, and from a kindly letter to a Negro almanac maker which had long been in print. He had gladly recognized and been encouraged by the achievements of Benjamin Banneker, giving them more praise in fact than he afterwards thought warranted.[63] Ironically, the slave revolt in Virginia that goes by the name of Gabriel was put down in the late summer of this year by Jefferson's friend the Governor, who wrote him several times about it, as Callender did from the Richmond jail. His advice to Monroe was on the side of mercy to the insurrectionists. At the summer's end he thought there had been hangings enough and was inclined to favor deportation of the remaining rebels, but there were more executions after he wrote, including that of the ringleader. One High Federalist, a close friend of Hamilton, sarcastically remarked that the Virginians were beginning to feel "the happy effects of liberty and equality," but Jefferson, fully aware of the extreme difficulties and dangers of the situation which slavery had created, wrote his friend Benjamin Rush, "We are truly to be pitied." [64]

Charges of personal immorality against Jefferson, who was in fact one of the most moral of men, appear to have entered into the campaign of 1800, especially the whispering campaign, but not until Callender turned on him in mad fury when he was President were these widely and gleefully publicized. Reflections on his financial integrity were nothing new, for the Federalists had long been asserting that his political attitude and that of his fellow planters was owing to their British debts, and unjust allegations of improper financial practice on his part had been made before. In the light of his heroic efforts during

[63] W. S. Jenkins, *Pro-Slavery Thought in the Old South* (1935), pp. 61–62, referring to *Address to the Citizens of South Carolina, by a Federalist* (Charleston, 1800). See also TJ to Banneker, Aug. 30, 1791 (Ford, V, 377–378), the letter which was printed, and TJ to Joel Barlow, Oct. 8, 1809 (Ford, IX, 261).

[64] A sympathetic account of the Gabriel insurrection is in Herbert Aptheker, *American Negro Slave Revolts* (1943), pp. 219–223. Gabriel himself was captured on Sept. 25 and hanged on Oct. 7. TJ wrote Monroe on Sept. 20, 1800 (Ford, VII, 457–458) and made the comment to Rush in his famous letter of Sept. 23 (Ford, VII, 461). Robert Troup spoke of the matter to King on Oct. 1 (King, III, 316).

a quarter of a century to meet his inherited obligations honorably, and in view of his excessive personal generosity, these could not have failed to gall him when called to his attention. This summer he received a report that the Reverend Cotton Mather Smith, whose very name suggested the implacable New England clergy, had charged him with obtaining his property by fraud and robbery, and, more particularly, with defrauding a widow and her children as the executor of an estate. To his well-meaning informant he replied that every tittle of the tale was fable. Then, after demonstrating this in some detail, he suggested that if Mr. Smith regarded the precepts of the gospel as applicable to preachers as well as others, he might well repent and make some acknowledgment of his own error. Jefferson wrote this private letter for the satisfaction of his correspondent and others whom that gentleman might choose to speak to, but as usual he urged that under no circumstances was it to get into the papers.[65]

In the last of the letters signed BURLEIGH and originally published in Connecticut, the author asked a question: "Do you believe in the strangest of all paradoxes — that a spendthrift, a libertine, or an atheist is qualified to make your laws and govern you and your posterity?" [66] The charge of atheism was the one most pressed in this campaign: it was not only made in the public press; it was hurled from pulpits in various places, most of all probably in Connecticut. As the story goes, the time was approaching when Bibles were to be hidden in New England's wells. The long-lived conflict which the dominant clergy of that region and certain other wearers of the cloth waged against this apostle of religious freedom cannot be conveniently or appropriately treated here. We are chiefly concerned with its immediate political significance and with Jefferson's own reaction to it.

The attitude of his clerical foes can be partly explained on grounds of misunderstanding, for he made no effort to clarify his own position or make his personal religious opinions known. On the contrary, he regarded this as a wholly private matter which was nobody's business but his. Actually, he was a deist, not an atheist. His general position might well have been compared to that of John Adams, who discussed religious questions with him at great length and with utter candor in later years and who, even in the heat of a campaign, was critical of his clerical persecutors. In religion as in economics Jefferson was an advocate of *laissez-faire*. His ideas had been carried into effect in Vir-

[65] To Uriah McGregory of Derby, Conn., Aug. 13, 1800 (*Domestic Life*, pp. 269-270), replying to a letter of July 19, received Aug. 7.

[66] Quoted by Warren, p. 128, from N. Y. *Commercial Advertiser*, Oct. 9, 1800. This noted attack by BURLEIGH, first published in the *Connecticut Courant*, appeared in the N. Y. paper in 15 numbers, beginning July 11.

ginia to a greater extent than elsewhere, and the example of revolutionary France, which his opponents so often held up as a terrible warning of things to come, was in fact quite irrelevant. But no theological absolutist could have been expected to like his views, and an entrenched clerical body, like that in New England where the alliance of church and state was still so strong, not unnaturally feared him. One at least of his public critics said that he objected to him solely because of his "disbelief" in the Scriptures and his deism, but we may safely assume that the overwhelming majority of those who raised the religious issue against him were also Federalists on other grounds.[67] They probably would not have supported him if he had had the simple faith and piety of Robert E. Lee.

One of his most notable clerical critics, the Reverend John M. Mason of New York, said that while his infidelity had long been undisputed, proof of it was at ready hand. "Happily for truth and for us," he said, "Mr. Jefferson has *written;* he has *printed.*" [68] But the detaching of single phrases or passages from the *Notes on Virginia,* without regard to their total context, seems less a pursuit of truth than of another objective. The obvious object of all this was to discredit the man and scare voters from his side. Exaggeration is to be expected in a political campaign, but the invocation of God in behalf of the Federalists is a striking example of the conjunction of self-righteousness with arrogance which they so often effected. The final words of Burleigh were: "GREAT GOD OF COMPASSION AND JUSTICE, SHIELD MY COUNTRY FROM DESTRUCTION."

Noting that Jefferson had been fiercely attacked on religious grounds, Hamilton's friend Robert Troup, more realistic at the moment than most of his High Federalist fellows, expressed doubt that anything said on that subject would deprive the Republican leader of a single vote.[69] He attributed this presumable failure to the irrevocable determination of Jefferson's supporters, but it might be attributed to public reaction against excess.

Jefferson's own reaction to these attacks has proved far more memorable than they have. It was not made known to the public but was revealed in what has come to be regarded as one of the most notable of his private letters. This he addressed affectionately to Dr. Benjamin

[67] The reference is to the author of *Serious Questions on the Election of a President* (New York, 1800); see Lerche, p. 472. In the *Virginia Argus,* Sept. 8, 1800, this emphasis on the religious issue in disregard of others was objected to.

[68] Quoted by Lerche, p. 473, from *The Voice of Warning, to Christians, on the Ensuing Election* (New York, 1800).

[69] R. Troup to R. King, Sept. 14, 1800 (King, III, 299–300).

Rush.[70] It is a sign of his intimacy with this friend that he was willing to discuss religion with him. He had promised him a letter on Christianity, he said, and would send it some day. He believed that his view of the subject ought to displease neither the rational Christian nor deist, and that it "would reconcile many to a character they have too hastily rejected." He doubted if it would reconcile him to the irritable tribe of clergy who were in arms against him — on grounds of their own interest, as he was convinced. He believed that certain groups of them wanted an establishment of their particular form of Christianity. The real danger may have been considerably less than he had thought, but, since freedom of the press had been so successfully attacked, there had surely been grounds to fear for freedom of religion. With renewed confidence he now said: "The returning good sense of our country threatens abortion to their hopes, and they believe that any portion of power confided to me will be exerted in opposition to their schemes. And they believe truly. For *I have sworn upon the altar of God eternal hostility against every form of tyranny over the mind of man.*" [71]

That was all they had to fear from him, he said, but that was enough to cause them to print lying pamphlets. Time has largely relegated those pamphlets to oblivion, while painting in bold letters on the walls of his national monument what is perhaps the most characteristic of all his single utterances. He spoke as a champion of the freedom of the human spirit, not as the leader of a party, and at the moment nobody heard him except Dr. Rush. But his record already spoke for itself to anyone who would listen.

[70] J. P. Boyd, in "Mr. Jefferson to Dr. Rush With Affection" (*Library of Congress: Quarterly Journal of Current Acquisitions*, Vol. I, No. 1, Oct.–Dec. 1943) presented for the first time the full and authentic text of the famous letter of Sept. 23, 1800, with perceptive comments.

[71] Italics inserted.

[XXX]

The Ordeal of Victory

LATE in the summer of 1800 or early in the autumn, at Monticello, the master of the place penned some notes and comments on his life and his achievements thus far. In his fifty-eighth year Jefferson had a generation of public service to look back on, but ordinarily he was much too busy to waste his cherished time in retrospection. He had been drawn to the subject, he said, by something he had seen in a Richmond paper. There he had seen extracts from the widely circulated pamphlet, written by John Beckley under a pseudonym, which contained an epitome of his life.[1] It also contained a characterization and injunction which his supporters could set over against current Federalist caricatures and fears:

> *Jefferson*, mild, amiable, and philanthropic, refined in manners as enlightened in mind, the philosopher of the world, whose name adds lustre to our national character, and as a legislator and statesman stands second to no man's — *Jefferson still lives*. On him then concentrate your present views and your future hopes.

He himself made no comment on this passage, but he noted certain minor inaccuracies in the account of his life, and in correcting these he denied himself some credit that had been claimed for him. Then, having set the record straight, he drew up his private list of services that he deemed most worthy of remembrance.[2] He said that he had sometimes asked himself if his country was the better for his having lived and was not sure it was. He had been the instrument of doing certain things, but they would have been done by others — done as

[1] *Virginia Argus*, Sept. 2, 1800. The pamphlet was *An Address to the People of the U. S.*, dated Pennsylvania, July, 1800. (See above, ch. XXIX, note 10.)

[2] LC, 219:39161. This part of the memo. is in Ford, VII, 475–477, with the conjectural date of 1800; and in L. & B., I, 256–259, without date, as an Appendix to his Autobiography of old age.

well, if not better. In the case of the most important of them we may well doubt this.

Those who did not really know him would probably have found his list surprising, both for what he put in and what he left out. It began with something which was scarcely remembered even in his own locality — his successful efforts as a very young man to improve the navigation of the little Rivanna River, which had ever since carried to market his and his neighbors' produce. It included the Declaration of Independence, which of course everybody knew about, and certain measures of the Virginia legislature, resulting from his proposals in the years immediately thereafter. Among these was the act for religious freedom, and also, at the very end of the list, the act for the more general diffusion of knowledge. This he mentioned with hesitation since it was passed in emasculated form and little had come of it. Obviously he most valued his services to freedom, to enlightenment, and to human well-being. Among the latter he listed the sending of olive plants and upland rice to South Carolina and Georgia when he was in France. This lover of the land did not yet know how small the result of these actions would be when he laid down what he regarded as a general truth: "The greatest service which can be rendered any country is to add a useful plant to its culture; especially a bread grain; next in value to bread is oil." This apostle of light and liberty who never ceased trying to be useful said nothing else about his diplomatic mission to France. He made no mention of his arduous labors as secretary of state, or of any offices at all, or of anything he had done as party leader. At the moment, nonetheless, this party leader stood on the threshold of victory, facing the likelihood of election to the first office in the Republic.

Though a long-range optimist who was rather too trustful of human nature, he was not disposed, in a particular political situation, to be more sanguine than the observable facts warranted his being. In counting up votes beforehand he did not let his hopes sway his judgment, as some of his leading supporters were prone to do. Before he left Philadelphia, however, he had sensed a change in spirit. Describing it some weeks later, he said: "The arrogance of the proud hath ceased, and the patient and meek look up." [3] Growing confidence in the success of his party was reflected in his correspondence during the months he remained at home — that is, until late November. This correspondence was out of balance, for he got many more letters than he sent; during October and November he wrote hardly any. Since he got them from all directions, however, he was able to feel the

[3] To Pierce Butler, Aug. 11, 1800 (Ford, VII, 449).

political pulse of the country. By the end of the summer if not earlier he was confident that the Republicans would carry the congressional elections, and before he went to Washington he had good reason to believe that they would have a majority of the electors.

Perhaps the nearest he came to prescribing for the body politic was in his correspondence with a supporter of his in Connecticut, where, in his opinion, that body was suffering the greatest ills. Nothing could have pleased him more than the report he had early in the summer from Gideon Granger that a "mighty revolution in opinion" had taken place in New England within a year. He himself could not believe that this would have an appreciable effect until another election, except for the picking up of a few congressmen here and there, but with a view to the future he set forth his "principles of government" to Granger at some length, as he had done to Elbridge Gerry previously and not without effect. The former envoy, while remaining loyal to Adams, accepted the Republican nomination for governor of Massachusetts in 1800 and gave the Federalists a good scare. As Jefferson described Republican principles to Granger, they called for a very simple and inexpensive organization of the general government: "a few plain duties to be performed by a few servants." But even if the Republicans gained control, such a government would be uneasy if confronted by the opposition of the whole body of New England.[4] The penetration of this bastion of Federalism was important in his strategy then and afterwards.

Toward the end of his stay at home he learned from this Gideon of Connecticut that its Federalist walls had withstood such trumpet blasts as the little Republican band had sounded. "We have been defeated, but *not conquered*," wrote Granger. Indeed, they had increased and were increasing, despite the powerful combination of officialdom, the Congregational clergy, and the bar against them. "We suffer much from an unceasing persecution and constant operation of the system of terror," he said, adding that he himself had been hissed, called a Jacobin, and pronounced "the friend of the Atheist." But even in Connecticut the Republicans had formed a party. "We took our ground," said this reporter, "planted our standard and shouted boldly. It resounded through half New England, and aroused many from their torpor. Our force was not equal to the contest, but those who have advanced cannot retire." He calculated that they had the support of a

---

[4] His letter of Aug. 13, 1800, to Granger (Ford, VII, 450–453), though much shorter and less concerned with foreign affairs, may be compared to that of Jan. 26, 1799 to Gerry (Ford, VII, 325–336). It was in reply to a letter of June 4, 1800, from Granger (LC, 18298–18299).

third of the people in Connecticut, that the situation was somewhat worse in New Hampshire and slightly better in Massachusetts, that Vermont had become doubtful, and that Rhode Island had been "republicanized." [5]

This report on New England had less significance at the moment than it did later, when President Jefferson appointed its maker postmaster general and sought in other ways to warm and foster the leaven of Republicanism in the region of his most unyielding foes. So far as the present presidential contest was concerned, he had eliminated New England from consideration. But Burr, the only one of the four principals who did any overt electioneering, visited New England and spread favorable reports of prospects in Rhode Island which entered into later charges that he and his lieutenants engaged in deception and intrigue. In private he planted the idea that, although electors of this state would support Adams, Jefferson would pick up a vote or votes there while he himself would get none.[6] He did not mention this or his own acquiescence in it, as a mark to his credit, when he sent word to Madison and Jefferson of the supposedly favorable situation in Rhode Island, but the fact that he took occasion at the same time to express doubts about the sincerity of southern support of him is not without significance. He did this through the agency of Joseph Alston, who visited Montpelier and Monticello in October on his return to South Carolina after a northern trip, bearing letters of introduction which did not designate him as the prospective husband of Burr's daughter Theodosia. The one to Jefferson merely referred him to the bearer for information about domestic politics. Young Alston also brought Madison a letter from David Gelston, political lieutenant of Burr, who expressed graver doubts of southern integrity than he did. The net result of all this was to strengthen Madison's determination that Burr be fully supported in the South, a determination which was shared by Jefferson. They wanted to make sure that he would not be left behind and lose the vice presidency.[7]

While these leaders were manifesting such concern about Burr and the maintenance of a united party front, not realizing the full danger

[5] Granger to TJ, Oct. 18, 1800, from New Haven (LC, 18424–18425), received Nov. 7.

[6] Brant, Madison, IV, 23, citing Burr to Robt. Livingston, Sept. 24, 1800, from N.-Y. Hist. Soc. It was afterwards alleged that report of this was spread in the South.

[7] Burr to TJ, Oct. 9, 1800, introducing Alston (LC, 18407); Madison to TJ, Oct. 21 (Hunt, VI, 409–410). Brant quotes from Gelston's letter of Oct. 8 to Madison, in Rives Papers. The Rhode Island report was severely condemned in the bitterly hostile pamphlet of James Cheetham, A View of the Political Conduct of Aaron Burr (New York, 1802), pp. 47–48.

of the situation, dissension had been increasing in the upper circles of Federalism. This can be most clearly perceived in the correspondence of Hamilton and his political intimates, which Jefferson and Madison did not see, but it burst into the open in October through the agency of Burr. He got hold of a copy of the letter of Hamilton concerning the public conduct and character of John Adams which the author was having printed to circulate among his friends. The result was that extracts from it soon appeared in the *Aurora* and other Republican papers and that Hamilton, to prevent its unauthorized use, proceeded to have it copyrighted and published as a pamphlet. He believed it would do good. He had written his friend Wolcott: "I hope from it two advantages — the promoting of Mr. Pinckney's election and the vindication of ourselves." [8]

Since he condemned recent actions of Adams in the realm of foreign policy which have gained the approval of posterity, his letter cannot be well described in terms of vindication. And, as for his references to the "disgusting egotism, the distempered jealousy and the ungovernable indiscretion of Mr. Adams's temper," it may be claimed that in castigating the President he unwittingly characterized himself. At all events, the "Colossus of Federalism" attacked the President with a violence entirely comparable to that of the Republican journalists and pamphleteers whom the party in power had sought to silence as dangerous enemies of the government. The Republican press naturally made the most of his bitter outburst, and one of the victims of the Sedition Act publicized Federalist inconsistency by means of a dramatic gesture. Thomas Cooper, having served his prison term for saying things about the President which were much less damning, sought to determine "whether *Republicanism* is to be the victim of a law, which *Aristocracy* can break through with impunity." That is, he threatened to institute a prosecution of Hamilton, well knowing that his efforts would come to naught but hoping they would be noted in the papers, as they were. Hamilton was contemptuous of this gesture.[9]

Presumably Jefferson saw extracts from Hamilton's sensational letter in a Richmond paper early in November, and the whole pamphlet in Washington in December, but if he commented on it at the time he does not appear to have done so in writing.[10] Even the High

[8] Hamilton to Wolcott, Sept. 26, 1800 (Lodge, VIII, 563). With his letters of Aug. 1 and Oct. 1, 1800, to Adams, it is in Lodge, VI, 391–446. For good general comment, see J. C. Miller, *Alexander Hamilton: Portrait in Paradox* (N. Y., 1959), pp. 520–524.

[9] Described in *Cooper*, pp. 138–145.

[10] Extracts from it, copied from the *Aurora* of Oct. 22, appeared in *Virginia Argus*, Nov. 4, 1800. A copy of the copyrighted edn. of the pamphlet was in his

Federalists disapproved of it, regarding it as injurious to the party and believing that it would lessen Hamilton's influence, as unquestionably it did.[11] Noah Webster was in arms against him. Madison afterwards believed that, although "its recoil has perhaps more deeply wounded the author than the object it was discharged at," it was injurious to the standing of Adams. One of Hamilton's intimate friends said, after the election, that in his opinion it did not alter a single vote, though some people believed that it had an adverse effect on Federalist fortunes in South Carolina.[12] The Federalists in Pinckney's home state were probably looking for an excuse, however, and no judgment on the effect of the pamphlet on the election can rise above conjecture. It was probably slight at so late a date.

This was no national campaign in the modern sense: it was a series of local contests in a number of which the outcome was determined by what had happened months before, such as the Republican victory in the elections to the New York legislature in the previous spring. What was called "election day" — December 3, 1800 — was the day set for the electors to cast their votes in their respective states. These electors were themselves chosen in a confusing diversity of ways and on various days in the month of November. The slowness with which reports came in prolonged uncertainty, but, in the presidential contest, the issue had narrowed to a very few states before Jefferson set out for Washington. Summing things up for his son-in-law after he got there, he said the issue lay with South Carolina. His reports from that crucial state had been belated, but just before he left home he got a letter from Senator Charles Pinckney, who was leading the Republicans there despite the fact that he was a cousin of Charles Cotesworth Pinckney, and who now was confident of a decided majority in the legislature, which would choose the electors.[13] Besides having this important information, Jefferson was well aware of the gratifying outcome in his own state, though only in the extent of the Republican victory could this have been surprising.

If one may judge from election returns, the Squire of Monticello

---

library (Sowerby #3237, without comment from him). He wrote TMR on Nov. 30 that he would try to get one for him.

[11] See, esp. Troup to King, Nov. 9, 1800 (King, III, 330–331).

[12] Madison to TJ, Jan. 10, 1801 (Hunt, VI, 411–412); R. Troup to R. King, Dec. 31, 1800 (King, III, 359).

[13] Pinckney's long letter, written on three different dates, Oct. 12, 16, and 26, is printed with other documents under the heading "South Carolina in the Presidential Election of 1800," in *A.H.R.*, IV, 111–129 (Oct., 1898). In order to safeguard this important letter, Pinckney sent it under cover to Madison. TJ listed it as received at Monticello, Nov. 24, but it may have been delivered at Montpelier, where he spent that night.

was never a prophet without honor in his home country. From the time he was first chosen as a burgess for the County of Albemarle he never suffered defeat at the Virginia polls; indeed, he was rarely opposed. The victory in his state in 1800 was that of a party and not merely of a man, but the fact that newspaper returns of the vote for electors were under the headings "Adams" and "Jefferson" rather than "Federal" and "Republican" suggests a tendency to personalize the contest.[14] Pinckney and Burr seem to have been little considered at this stage, though supporters of the administration liked to refer to themselves as "Washingtonians." They grumbled about the "unprincipled mode of election" — that is, on a general ticket rather than by districts — ignoring the change in Adams's Massachusetts from choice by districts to choice by the legislature.[15] They did not fail to note that the Republican party had an active central committee and that the election officials were appointed by Governor James Monroe. Unquestionably these factors entered importantly into Republican success, but the freeholders voiced their disapprobation of the administration and their confidence in their fellow Virginian in language that was unmistakable.

The electors pledged to him got more than three-fourths of all the votes cast, while the rival ticket got none whatever in five counties. In only five did the self-designated Washingtonians gain impressive majorities: two on the Eastern Shore, one in the Valley, and two in the region beyond the Alleghenies. The Jeffersonians carried all the rest in this, the largest American state.[16] Jefferson's troublesome neighbor, the John Nicholas who was clerk of the county, said that the day the electors cast their votes should be a day of mourning, but as he himself set out for Washington on November 24 and talked things over with Madison that night he was well assured that his own people were behind him.[17] Also, the likelihood that a majority of the electors of the nation would vote for him seemed sufficient to warrant his broaching the subject of appointments, including that of Madison as secretary of state. When he and his servant Davy proceeded northward from Montpelier he did not yet realize that he was approaching the scene of another contest, and that for two months and more he

14 *Virginia Argus*, various dates in November, 1800.

15 T. Evans to Leven Powell, Oct. 30, 1800 (*Branch Hist. Papers*, I, 54).

16 An interesting account of the election by W. E. Hemphill, containing statistics and followed by an admirable map, is in *Virginia Cavalcade*, spring 1953, pp. 8-13. A list of the electors, as certified by the Governor, and returns by counties appeared in *Virginia Argus*, Nov. 21, 1800.

17 John Nicholas to W. C. Nicholas, from Charlottesville, Dec. 3, 1800 (Edgehill-Randolph Papers, UVA).

THE ORDEAL OF VICTORY

was to remain in doubt of his election as President of the United States. He was going to have to draw further on his huge reservoir of patience before his ordeal was over.

On November 28, 1800, the following item appeared in the *National Intelligencer*, newly established in the new federal city by Samuel Harrison Smith:

> Last evening arrived in Washington, THOMAS JEFFERSON, Vice President of the United States, and took up his lodgings in Messrs Conrad and McMunn's apartments.

No partisanship need be read into this, but the Vice President promptly subscribed to Smith's paper for himself and his son-in-law, John W. Eppes, and shortly arranged with this friendly journalist for the printing of his *Manual of Parliamentary Practice*. He had timed his journey so as to arrive after the address of the President to the joint session of Congress, for his presence might have occasioned embarrassment on both sides. A veritable morass lay between the boxlike Executive Mansion, where the Adamses were now living in some discomfort, and Capitol Hill, on which for some weeks at least Jefferson's life must center. There was a causeway of sorts known as Pennsylvania Avenue, but he saw no immediate need to communicate with the occupant of the unfinished house at the other end.

The boarding-house of Conrad and McMunn, often referred to as Conrad's, was on the south side of the Hill at the corner of New Jersey Avenue and C Street within easy reach of the Capitol — that is, the North or Senate Wing, the only part of the projected structure that was finished. The house belonged to Thomas Law, a prominent local proprietary. It was one of the seven or eight boarding-houses which, with a few shops, clustered around what there was of the Capitol. Built on a slope, it commanded an extended view in the rear. Margaret Bayard Smith, wife of the journalist and herself a warm admirer of Jefferson from early Washington days, thought he went to this particular house because of this wooded view. But arrangements seem to have been made for him and a group of congressmen by one of them, some months in advance, and no doubt he supposed he would have to take any place he could get. No one should have been slower than he to complain of the limitations of the raw federal city, for, next to the first President himself, he had played a larger part than any other statesman in making it a reality.[18] If Washington was its father, he might perhaps be called its uncle, and he lavished

[18] See *Jefferson and the Rights of Man*, ch. XXII.

solicitude on it in later years. At the moment it must have seemed like a naturally beautiful but wild and undeveloped waif. The federal city promised much but as yet had delivered very little.

In fact, he was pleased with his accommodations, public and private, finding them better than he had expected. He was relatively fortunate in his quarters. By contrast with Albert Gallatin, who on arriving at this same house some six weeks later reported to his wife that he had to share a room with another congressman, the Vice President had a parlor or reception room as well as a bedroom. By that time there were from twenty-four to thirty at the common table, including two Nicholases from Virginia, Senator Langdon of New Hampshire, Samuel Smith of Maryland, and Abraham Baldwin of Georgia. To his enemies it seemed, no doubt, that he was living with a "knot of Jacobins," just as he had done in Philadelphia. Whether or not he took a low seat at this table in the spirit of equality, as Mrs. Smith was to say in her reminiscences, he was among political friends. He greatly needed them during the three months he was at Conrad's.[19]

He had been there two weeks when he received confirmation of the success of his party in the political contest. Meanwhile, he repaired regularly to the North Wing of the Capitol, where he presided over the Senate. That body was housed in some elegance, as things went in the new city, but it did nothing in particular during the remainder of this last month and year of the eighteenth century. There was little he himself could do but wait for news from the outlying regions of the country. On December 12 the *National Intelligencer* lived up to its name by making an important report under the heading SPLENDID INTELLIGENCE. This was that the legislature of South Carolina, by a substantial majority, had chosen the Republican ticket of electors. Added to this factual statement was an editorial deduction: "Mr. Jefferson may, therefore, be considered as our future President." Until further information was received, however, the only certainty was that neither John Adams nor Charles Cotesworth Pinckney could be so considered.

Returns had not yet come in from the most remote states, but there could now be little doubt that Federalist electors had been chosen in all New England, despite Burr's prognostications about Rhode Island. The legislature of New Jersey had elected 7 Federalists, while in Pennsylvania the Republican House of Representatives, finally recog-

[19] M. B. Smith, *The First Forty Years of Washington Society* (1906), pp. 9–12, based on memory; Gallatin to his wife, Jan. 15, 1801 (Adams, *Gallatin*, pp. 252–253); W. B. Bryan, *Hist. of the National Capital*, I (1914), ch. XIV, esp. 342–343, 379; TJ to TMR, Nov. 30, 1800 (*Papers, MHS*, p. 79).

nizing that the Federalist majority of 2 in the upper house was adamant, and not wanting the state to be out of the election altogether, had accepted the compromise whereby 8 Republicans and 7 Federalists were chosen. In Maryland, where choice was by districts, the electors were evenly divided; and in North Carolina, under the same procedure, the Republicans got 8 and the Federalists 4. Everybody expected Georgia, Kentucky, and Tennessee to be Republican. Therefore, the Federalists could count on 65 electoral votes at the maximum, and the Republicans were sure of 73. The failure of the earlier hopes of the latter for New Jersey and the disappointing outcome in Pennsylvania, which Governor McKean took occasion to explain to Jefferson in a private letter, were now of no consequence.[20] The margin of his party in the electoral vote was small, but it was larger than that of the Federalists in 1796. Furthermore, when the returns of the congressional elections finally came in, the tally in the federal House of Representatives was 65 to 41. This was really a better index of popular opinion. Beyond any doubt the Federalists had lost their grip on the country and the opposition had become the majority party.[21]

Reports of the voting of the electors themselves, when they met in their respective states on the appointed day, were still incomplete. As things turned out, Hamilton's hopes that C. C. Pinckney would run ahead of Adams were not realized. On the contrary, one of the electors in Rhode Island voted for Adams and John Jay, with the result that the final count was Adams 65, Pinckney 64. Something of the sort should have happened on the Republican side, and for a time Jefferson supposed it had. On the same day that Samuel Harrison Smith's paper published its "splendid intelligence," he received private word from South Carolina that one of the electors there would cast his ballot for George Clinton instead of Burr, with the result that the latter would have 7 votes to Jefferson's 8. "You will easily discover why the one vote is varied," said his informant.[22] If the unnamed elector had done what was expected of him he would have spared his country two months of unnecessary uncertainty.

At the moment Jefferson, besides being sure of the victory of his party, was reassured with respect to himself by this bit of inside in-

[20] McKean wrote TJ, rather apologetically, Dec. 15, 1800 (LC, 18496).

[21] The results, with respect to both electors and representatives in Congress, can be conveniently seen in the table in Dauer, *Adams Federalists*, p. 257. It should be noted that not all of the congressional elections were held at this time. In New Jersey, where the Republicans made a clean sweep, they were held a few weeks later.

[22] Peter Freneau to TJ, Dec. 2, 1800 (LC, 18461, received Dec. 12). This editor wrote in the absence of Charles Pinckney, who had managed the local campaign, and at his request.

formation. Finding that a reliable messenger to New York was available, he took occasion to dispatch thither two important letters which he would have hesitated to write a few days later. One of these was to Robert R. Livingston, to whom he as the presumable President-elect offered the post of secretary of the navy. He may have expected the declination he afterwards got: he admitted that Livingston was not nautical by profession, saying at the same time, however, that Republicanism was rare in the country's most nautical region — that is, John Adams's New England. He may have taken this polite method of informing Livingston that he would not be appointed secretary of state and of implying that Madison would be.[23] At any rate, he concerned himself for a brief time with future presidential appointments, a subject he had discussed with Madison on his trip to Washington.

Of greater historical import is the letter he wrote the next day to Aaron Burr.[24] In this, after informing his running mate of the certainty of a Republican electoral majority, he said that, although he had not heard precisely how the South Carolina electors had voted, he had learned sufficiently what they were expected to do. He passed on the report that one of them would withhold his vote from Burr and the further report, presumably picked up in Congress or at Conrad's, that an elector in Tennessee and another in Georgia would do likewise. Admitting no doubt that he himself would stand first, he assured Burr that he would be four or five votes ahead of Adams. While acknowledging that he himself could speak with no certainty about the amount of withholding, he said that this matter should not have been left to hazard. The truth was that he was now finding out that this was precisely what had happened while he himself had been pursuing a policy of passivity. Whether Burr and his lieutenants had been equally passive, under this system which so lent itself to intrigue, is a question which cannot be answered categorically. Jefferson voiced no suspicions of his running mate at this time, and in this particular matter seems never to have done so. Madison appears to have kept his to himself for many years, but he wrote Jefferson toward the end of the latter's life that the tie of 1800 resulted from "false assurances dispatched at the critical moment to the electors of one state, that the votes of another would be different from what they proved to be." These assurances he attributed to one of Burr's henchmen.[25]

23 This is the opinion of Brant (*James Madison: Secretary of State*, p. 27). TJ's letter of Dec. 14, 1800 is in Ford, VII, 462–466. Livingston was afterwards appointed minister to France.

24 Dec. 15, 1800 (Ford, VII, 466–468).

25 Madison to TJ, Jan. 14, 1824 (quoted by Brant, *Madison, Sec. of State*, p. 26); see *ibid.*, ch. II, on the entire matter.

While he may have harbored no suspicions, Jefferson could scarcely have been unaware of Burr's repute for craftiness, and in his own adroit letter of congratulation he was sounding him out — just in case a tie might eventuate. He invited reassurance from Burr when he said: "I understand several of the high-flying Federalists have expressed their hope that the two Republican tickets may be equal, and their determination in that case to prevent a choice by the H of R (which they are strong enough to do) and let the government devolve on a President of the Senate." He meant a President pro tempore, selected by the Federalist majority from their own number; and the constitutional provision which, as he had heard, some of the high-flyers were seeking to nullify was the one requiring the House, voting by states, to choose between the two persons who had an equal vote and both of whom had an electoral majority.

He was not certain that he and Burr were tied until nearly the end of the month, when the last returns were received in Washington. Ironically, they came in official form to him as the presiding officer of the Senate and he reported their arrival to the Secretary of State, John Marshall.[26] Within a few days of his letter to the other successful candidate, however, he concluded that their parity in the electoral vote was probable. The chief fear that he voiced soon thereafter to Madison and a few other intimates, in behalf of his Republican brethren in Congress as well as himself, differed only in detail from the one he had expressed to Burr. He now made reference to a scheme whereby the Chief Justice or Secretary of State should assume the presidential office if the House could reach no decision. Two or three weeks later the *Aurora* publicized what it described as a "conspiracy" to designate the Chief Justice, claiming that it was hatched in the home of Justice Chase in Baltimore.[27]

On the Federalist side Senator Gouverneur Morris, writing to Hamilton in December, had reported the proposal to prevent an election and throw the government into the hands of a President of the Senate. Certain members of his party had gone to the point of casting about for a person, he said. He thought this a wild measure and believed it had been given up. Hamilton himself regarded such a policy as "most dangerous and unbecoming" even if it should succeed, which he was sure it could not do.[28] The impracticality of the

[26] TJ to Sec. of State, Dec. 28, 1800 (LC, 18543). Complete returns were in *National Intelligencer*, Dec. 29.

[27] *Aurora*, Jan. 10, 1801. TJ reported successive rumors to Madison, Dec. 19, 26, 1800 (Ford, VII, 470, 473).

[28] Morris to Hamilton, Dec. 19, 1800 (J.C.H., VI, 493-494); Hamilton to Morris, Jan. 9, 1801 (J.C.H., VI, 508).

various proposals calling for the succession of some designated official may have been tacitly recognized by the Federalists in Congress before the month of January had run its course, but Jefferson himself still believed that a large portion of them intended to prevent an election if they could.[29] Meanwhile, rumors of Federalist designs created alarm of varying degree throughout the country. In Virginia, the report was that power would be committed by legislative act to John Marshall or somebody else until another election. Governor Monroe wrote Jefferson that he himself could not believe the other party bold and wicked enough to entertain such an idea seriously, but that the report had created a "strong sensation" in the state and had led to talk of counteraction by the Assembly. "If that party [Federalist] wish to disorganize," he said, "*that* is the way to do it. If the union could be broken, that would do it.[30]

The danger of disregard of the constitutional provisions applicable to this case was exaggerated, no doubt. But Jefferson was wholly realistic when he predicted that the Federalists would make all they could of the embarrassing outcome of the electoral vote, so that, as he had told Monroe, "after the most energetic efforts, crowned with success, we remain in the hands of our enemies by want of foresight in the original arrangement."[31] The only thing for him and his party to do was to press for a decision by the House, which might conceivably result in Burr's election. Writing a trusted friend, he said there might be a reversal of what had been understood to be the wishes of the people as to the President and Vice President, though the Constitution did not permit a designation of either office.[32] He himself recognized that this was a grave fault in the existing electoral system. But, deeply disappointed though he must have been, he appears to have gone no further than this in referring to his personal claims, and the evil he feared was from the Federalists.

Among the reassuring letters he received from leaders of his own party was one from the man whom he had regarded as the candidate for the second office. Written two days before Christmas, this reached him on the first day of the new year. Burr apprehended no embarrassment if the votes for them should be equal. "My personal friends are perfectly informed of my wishes on the subject and can never think of diverting a single vote from you," he said. If the matter came

29 To Thomas McKean, Feb. 2, 1801 (Ford, VII, 486). H. H. Brackenridge on Jan. 30 reported to TJ alleged comments of Senator James Ross, implying that the "usurpation" was abandoned (LC, 18650–18651).

30 To TJ, Jan. 6, 1801 (S.M.H., III, 254).

31 Dec. 20, 1800 (LC, 18511).

32 To John Breckinridge, Dec. 18, 1800 (Ford, VII, 469).

before the House he did not doubt Jefferson's having the vote of at least nine states. Continuing, he said: "As far forth as my knowledge extends, it is the unanimous determination of the Republicans of every grade to support your administration with unremitted zeal." For himself he stated that his whole time and attention would be unceasingly employed to render Jefferson's administration grateful and honorable to the country and to him. To this he was impelled, he said, "as well by the highest sense of duty as by the most devoted personal attachment." [33]

The day before Jefferson read these reassuring words, General Samuel Smith of Maryland, one of his fellow lodgers at Conrad's, gave to the press an extract from a letter of an earlier date which he had had from Burr. In this the other Republican candidate said that in the unlikely event of his having an equal number of votes with Jefferson, everyone who knew him must know that he would "utterly disclaim all competition." Saying that it would be an insult to suspect that he would consent to be an instrument in "counteracting the wishes and expectations" of the country, he constituted Smith his proxy to declare these sentiments if the occasion should require.[34] Very early in the new year Jefferson wrote Maria that at first the Federalists were confident they could "debauch Colonel Burr from his good faith by offering him their vote to be President" and had seriously proposed it to him. "His conduct has been honorable and decisive, and greatly embarrasses them," said Maria's father.[35]

Apparently he did not surmise, as he might have after checking the dates, that Burr may have supposed, at the time he wrote Smith, that he was behind Jefferson in the vote. A few days later, James A. Bayard wrote Hamilton from Washington that the letter was there "understood to have proceeded, either from a false calculation as to the result of the electoral votes, or was intended as a cover to blind his own party." Theodore Sedgwick reported that Burr was displeased at its publication.[36] Burr may still have thought that he had actually been elected Vice President when in his letter to Jefferson he spoke of "your administration." At any rate, Samuel Smith received a different sort of response from him after the facts of the election were

[33] Burr to TJ, Dec. 23, 1800 (LC, 18525), received Jan. 1, 1801.

[34] Dec. 16, 1800, published in *National Intelligencer,* Dec. 31; crucial passage quoted from *Washington Federalist* of same date by J. S. Pancake, in "Aaron Burr: Would-Be Usurper" (*W. & M.,* Apr. 1951, p. 205). This article and the treatment of Irving Brant (*op. cit.,* ch. II) are the most damning accounts I have seen of Burr's part in this highly controversial episode.

[35] Jan. 4, 1801 (Ford, VII, 478).

[36] Bayard to Hamilton, Jan. 7, 1801 (J.C.H., VI, 506); Sedgwick to Hamilton, Jan. 10 (J.C.H., VI, 513).

known. Then he said that he had not deigned to reply to a question propounded to him by one Republican, namely, whether he, if chosen President, would engage to resign. This suggestion was "unreasonable, unnecessary, and impertinent," he said, but if he had made a reply it would have been that as at present advised he would not. Smith interviewed him in Philadelphia after that, gaining the impression that Burr's position was that if the House could not elect Jefferson it should elect him.[37]

In attempting to judge Burr's response to these unprecedented circumstances, one should resist the temptation to read backward from later events.[38] On the basis of contemporary records alone, however, it seems indisputable that he was unwilling to make an explicit renunciation of the presidential office once he saw a chance to gain it. Such abnegation may be more than could have been expected of an exceedingly ambitious man; but if he had reiterated in January what he said to Smith in mid-December, he would not only have served the party which had supported him for the second office; he might have saved himself from certain ills that befell him afterwards. What is more, he would undoubtedly have served his country.

In that case the comment of the *National Intelligencer* on the election — which would have been appropriate to virtually all subsequent national elections if only the party names were changed — would have had a meaning which subsequent events threatened to invalidate. On December 15, 1800, this paper said:

> The storm, which has so long raged in the political world, has at length subsided. Parties have tried their strength, and victory has crowned with success, in the Presidential election, the efforts of the REPUBLICANS.
>
> To *Republicans* it must be a cause of sincere felicitation that their country has surmounted, without any other agitation than that of the public sentiment, the choice of their first magistrate.
>
> The example is auspicious to the destinies of the world. . . .

One of the most unfortunate consequences of the unnecessary uncertainty about the presidency was the blurring of the significance of the election. A change in government had been enjoined and the right

---

[37] Pancake quotes Burr to Smith, Dec. 29, 1800, from a copy in Smith-Carter MSS, UVA, stating that the original is not available. Brant's opinion that Smith's visit to Burr was on Jan. 4, 1801, is borne out by B. Hichborn to TJ, Jan. 5, 1801 (LC, 18589). See also TJ's memo. of Jan. 2, 1804 (Ford, I, 301).

[38] The treatment of him by Morton Borden in *The Federalism of James A. Bayard* (1955), ch. VII, is notably objective. The account by Nathan Schachner, in *Aaron Burr* (1937), ch. XIV, written before some of the present information was available, now seems too favorable.

of political opposition unmistakably affirmed. But the party in power, far from admitting this, seized upon the opportunity to deny it in effect and to do everything they could to nullify it. Emboldened by the unexpected tie, they put off what they regarded as the evil day as long as possible, thus making the transition from one administration to another, and from one party to the other, all the more difficult. Burr could have denied himself to the Federalists, who would then have had no constitutional alternative to the unquestionable leader of the victors.

Since the election law prescribed that the certificates of the electors' vote were to be opened on the second Wednesday in February, no legal action with respect to the tie could be taken before then. The prolongation of the uncertainty until that time, which was only about three weeks before March 4, the date for the beginning of a new administration, was unfortunate for the country. It must have been exceedingly trying for Jefferson, though it would not have been like him to say so. He started the new year and century by ferrying across the Potomac at Georgetown, proceeding to Alexandria, where he lodged, and riding to Mount Vernon to call on Mrs. Washington. He hired a horse at a cost of three dollars for this journey. She and Mrs. Lawrence Lewis — that is, Nelly Custis — inquired especially about Maria, whom they well remembered from earlier journeys.[39] The Senate attended to some important business after he resumed his chair: it approved the convention with France, after some amendment; it passed the judiciary act, seeking to solidify Federalist control of one branch of the government now that the other two seemed lost; and it confirmed the nomination of John Marshall as Chief Justice. But the total amount of business was small, the sessions were generally short, and the presiding officer was little more than an observer anyway. The House of Representatives met in the Senate wing during this session in a room on the back which was much too small.[40] On it must devolve the crucial question.

The decision of the Federalists in the House to support Burr, which appears to have been reached at a caucus before the middle of January, was not owing to the influence of the members of the party regarded by posterity as the most eminent. Honest John Adams, grieving over the death of his son Charles more than over the outcome of the election, was not entering into this matter. He left some sarcastic comments on one of the candidates, however. "Mr. Burr's good for-

[39] TJ to Maria, Jan. 4, 1801 (Ford, VII, 478); Account Book, Jan. 1-3, 1801.
[40] The House later moved to a temporary building known as the "Oven."

tune surpasses all ordinary rules, and exceeds that of Bonaparte," he said. "All the old patriots, all the splendid talents, the long experience, both of federalists and antifederalists, must be subjected to the humiliation of seeing this dexterous gentleman rise, like a balloon, filled with inflammable air, over their heads. . . . What a discouragement to all virtuous exertion, and what an encouragement to party intrigue, and corruption!" [41]

Adams was addressing a friend who could not have influenced the ensuing contest, but Hamilton wrote repeatedly to men who could. Sounding the alarm at the moment a tie seemed likely, he said categorically: "Jefferson is to be preferred. He is by far not so dangerous a man; and he has pretensions to character." On the other hand, he saw nothing in Burr's favor and now gave him a designation which was destined to endure — namely, "the Catiline of America." Strongly as Hamilton argued against Burr, he let his own partisanship lead him to an unfortunate qualification: "Yet it may be well enough to throw out a lure for him, in order to tempt him to start for the plate, and then lay the foundation of dissension between the two chiefs." [42] Probably Burr would have been approached by some Federalist in any case, and as a matter of fact this divisive strategy did not work. There is no sufficient reason to believe that Burr responded affirmatively to such advances, and the Federalists themselves afterwards condemned him for his unwillingness to commit himself to their policies. The sins he committed, if any, were those of omission. Furthermore, there was no outward sign of any breach between him and Jefferson before the voting began in the House of Representatives. The older man, who made such a point of party unity, went out of his way to expose what he interpreted as an attempt to sow tares between them. In reply he got an emotional letter from Burr, containing a reference to the "malignant spirit of slander and intrigue," though this did not come until after the casting of the last ballot. [43]

Hamilton's extensive correspondence with respect to Burr and Jefferson, consisting of letters to and from leaders of his own party, casts a flood of light on the motives of the latter in this episode and contains characterizations of the two principals on which writers of history have never ceased to draw. [44] Hamilton kept insisting that his posi-

[41] To Elbridge Gerry, Dec. 30, 1800 (*Works*, IX, 577–578). His son Charles died under unusually sad circumstances in late November.

[42] Hamilton to Wolcott, Dec. 16, 1800 (J.C.H., VI, 486). He said the letter might be communicated to Marshall and Sedgwick.

[43] TJ to Burr, Feb. 1, 1801 (Ford, VII, 485–486); from Burr, Feb. 12, 1801 (LC, 18726), received Feb. 20.

[44] The letters in J.C.H., VI, 486–524, almost without exception, relate to this

THE ORDEAL OF VICTORY

tion was based on public, not personal, considerations. For him to contribute to Jefferson's "disappointment and mortification" would be "only to retaliate for unequivocal proofs of enmity," he said; if there was a person in the world he ought to hate it was Jefferson. In view of what happened later it is hard to credit his statement that he had "always been personally well" with Burr, but that is what he said.[45] In the oft-quoted characterization of his former colleague and inveterate antagonist to James A. Bayard he described Jefferson as "a contemptible hypocrite," among other things. At the same time, he denied the contention of John Marshall that Jefferson was an enemy to the power of the executive, and the frequent allegation that he was a dangerous revolutionary. To Hamilton's mind a true estimate of his character warranted "the expectation of a temporizing rather than a violent system." He added that there was "no fair reason to suppose him capable of being corrupted." [46] In this and other characterizations Hamilton drew a caricature of his eternal rival, as he had so often done before. Nonetheless, he pointed out features and expressions which more judicious observers would do well to note. While denouncing Burr, he was in his own immoderate way appealing to his party to take a moderate stand toward Jefferson. It was with him, rather than with Burr, that an understanding should be sought. To his own mind no understanding with Burr could possibly mean anything.[47]

Hamilton's comments on the lack of principle and the lust for power of the man he called Catiline were matched by many which he received from Federalists in Washington, who showed no disposition to argue the case on the ground of Burr's intrinsic merits. Yet Jefferson's alleged demerits had been displayed by the party press far more widely and for a much longer time. The image of him which the High Federalists had sought to fix in the public mind was a very bad likeness in the eyes of those who really knew him, but he was properly recognized on all hands as the supreme symbol and chosen leader of the opposition. All the more reason that he should be in the first office, after his party had gained a majority in the country — that is what we can say now and what some Federalist leaders said then. Gouverneur Morris was one of them, but he was in the Senate, not the House. Others were more shortsighted, and sheer hatred of

topic. Among the writers or recipients were Wolcott, H. G. Otis, Sedgwick, James Gunn, Gouverneur Morris, James A. Bayard, John Marshall, and John Rutledge, Jr.

[45] J.C.H., VI, 499, 501.

[46] To Bayard, Jan. 16, 1801 (Lodge, VIII, 581–582). This letter is misplaced in J.C.H.

[47] To Wolcott, Dec. 17, 1800 (J.C.H., VI, 487, 489).

Jefferson was an important factor in this business. Along with this was the desire on the part of many to punish Virginia, a state which they claimed was overambitious and which had unquestionably been the seat and center of opposition to the policies of the federal government from the moment there had been any that was worthy of the name. But the basic reason for the Federalist decision, in disregard of Hamilton, was avowedly partisan: they thought that they as a political group had less to fear from Burr and more to gain. They ventured to believe that, supported by them, he would have to come over to their side. Some allowance must be made for the fact that the contrast between him and Jefferson was much less clear and sharp to them at the time than it now is to those who view the two, but the men most responsible for this decision offer one of the most flagrant American examples of putting the interests of party above those of country. Before the bar of history their position is unenviable.

Meanwhile, the Republicans had been forming their lines and counting their states. This question had to be decided by the existing Congress, in which the Federalists had a majority, but fortunately for Jefferson the vote was to be by states. He was making his count also: at first he was confident of only seven states but before long he and his fellows felt sure of eight, which was one less than the required majority. Until almost the appointed day he believed that one or another of a half dozen moderate men who could shift one state's vote would swing over and give him nine, but one crucial man, presumably James A. Bayard, the only congressman from Delaware, went the other way, making the other side sure of six states, with two divided.[48] The alignment was clear: Jefferson would be supported by the states with a Republican majority, Burr by those with a Federalist. His hold on his own party was unweakened. Many of his enemies knew this and others soon found it out.

The joint session of the two houses was held on February 11, as the law prescribed.[49] The certificates of the electors of the sixteen states were then opened by Jefferson himself in his capacity as presiding officer, and after the tellers had arrived at the figures everybody knew already, he declared the result of the vote. The Senate then declared that the remaining duties devolved on the House. Whereupon the more numerous body repaired to its smaller chamber and began to vote according to elaborate rules which had been adopted two days

[48] To Thos. McKean, Feb. 2, and to Tench Coxe, Feb. 11, 1801 (Ford, VII, 486, 488).

[49] *Annals*, 6 Cong., 2 sess., pp. 743–744.

earlier.[50] Though the doors were closed to others, seats were provided for the President and senators. No mention was made of the Vice President, who could hardly have been happy there.

One of the rules that the House had adopted was that they would not adjourn until after they had made an election. Whether or not they violated this is largely a question of semantics. They were not in continuous session during the six days they balloted — in fact, Sunday intervened — but they went to the limit of their endurance. The Senate met regularly in the meantime with Jefferson in the chair, but it did virtually no business. Monroe had informed him that if "any plan of usurpation" should be attempted in the federal town, he would convene the General Assembly of Virginia without delay.[51] Members of the delegation from the state sent him reports of the balloting day by day, though the letters did not reach him as promptly as they should have and he suspected that they were held up on purpose.[52] While the Governor was in a suspicious state of mind, young Randolph, Jefferson's son-in-law, became much alarmed. When visiting in Bedford County he learned that part of the arms and military stores had been removed from a federal arsenal there. Also, he understood that others would be. Suspecting a design of "disarming the state in order to secure an usurpation," he excitedly wrote Monroe. Incidentally he remarked that power was the first passion of Hamilton's soul and that he himself feared him the more because of his declaration in favor of Jefferson.[53] At the moment, in fact, Hamilton was deeply chagrined, believing that his efforts against Burr had been wholly wasted.

Jefferson himself had received letters respecting possible actions in case the government should be without an executive head because of the failure of the congressmen to reach a decision. These are now of little more than academic interest, since the threatened abyss did not open, but they reflect the desperation in many minds.[54] Meanwhile, there was much shrieking in the Federalist press, notably in the Philadelphia *Gazette of the United States*. This paper charged "the bold and imperious partisans of Mr. Jefferson" with the purpose of marching on Washington and dethroning as an usurper any officer what-

[50] Feb. 9 (*ibid.*, pp. 1009–1011).

[51] Monroe to TJ, Jan. 27, 1801 (S.M.H., III, 257).

[52] Letters from various members, Feb. 11–17, 1801, are in vol. 6 of his Papers (LC). He wrote Mason and Nicholas on Feb. 18, inquiring about the delay (6:1073).

[53] TMR to Monroe, Feb. 14, 1801 (Monroe Papers, 6:1053–1055).

[54] Among the most interesting of these is one from Judge H. H. Brackenridge, in Pittsburgh, Jan. 19, 1801, received Jan. 30 (LC, 18645–18649a).

ever who might be designated to administer the government in the event of nonagreement in the House. The agitated editor asked: "Are they then ripe for civil war, and ready to imbrue their hands in kindred blood?" He added that Massachusetts had 70,000 men under arms, while the Jeffersonians could command loyalty in only the states of Virginia and Pennsylvania.[55] Whether or not civil war might have ensued, the country faced the peril of anarchy if the deadlock should not be broken before March 4. It lasted until February 17, when the situation became precisely what it should have been two months before.

The House balloted nineteen times on February 11 and again after midnight.[56] It balloted thirty-five times during five days, with no change except a few indecisive ones within state delegations. The tally always stood eight states for Jefferson and six for Burr, two being divided and therefore not voting. This looked like the meeting of an irresistible force and an immovable object. The immovable object never did give way, but it finally crumbled at the edges sufficiently to permit passage by and over it. On the thirty-sixth ballot the Federalists in the two divided states of Vermont and Maryland abstained, giving the vote of these to Jefferson, who thus had ten. Delaware and South Carolina also abstained, being recorded as not voting. The other four New England states, by supporting Burr to the bitter end, suggested that they belonged to the Old Guard which preferred death to surrender.

The breaking of the deadlock was directly attributable to the actions of Bayard of Delaware, who had long said that as the sole representative of his state he had the election in his hands and who found himself "encircled by all the doubtful votes." His entirely credible explanation was that, since it was "perfectly ascertained" that Burr's election was impossible, he concluded that the only remaining object of supporting him was "to exclude Jefferson at the expense of the Constitution." When he announced to his fellow Federalists his unwillingness to pursue such an object he aroused prodigious clamor and received vehement reproaches. Nonetheless, after two caucuses he might have gained general acquiescence but for one Connecticut congressman. The final actions could be interpreted as meaning that, while everybody except the New Englanders had given up Burr, nobody had accepted Jefferson. His colleague, Robert Goodloe Harper, reversed Bayard's emphasis in his own report to his constituents: he

55 *Gazette of the U. S.*, Feb. 16, 1801.
56 For all the balloting, see *Annals*, 6 Cong., 2 sess., 1022–1030. It was reported promptly in *National Intelligencer*.

charged the Republicans with an inflexible determination "to risk the Constitution and the Union" rather than give Jefferson up, thus laying the blame on them and attributing to his own party the higher patriotism.[57]

Perhaps Bayard was influenced by Hamilton to some extent and got from him the idea of seeking some sort of guarantees from Jefferson. Whether he received them or not, through the agency of Samuel Smith of Maryland, was afterwards a disputed question. It seems sufficient to say here that, while Smith probably assured Bayard that Jefferson would not disturb the fiscal structure or make unreasonable removals of Federalists from office, which could have been assumed from his record and recent conversation of Conrad's, there is no evidence that he made any sort of deal.[58] Jefferson believed, as his friends did, that the vast body of Federalists around the country approved the outcome of this contest. And few will now question the calm statement of the *National Intelligencer* that the voice of the people had prevailed.[59] The President-elect got words of cheer from men whose approval he valued more than that of the diehards in Congress. His friend Du Pont de Nemours, addressing him as "the greatest man in [the] greatest place of the United States," wrote him thus: "You never had but one *Vice*. I compliment your Country and both Hemispheres that you have at last lost it." [60] He himself seems to have said little even in private, and what he wanted to say in public he wisely reserved for the inaugural address he would soon be delivering.[61]

Maintaining his dignity and keeping his hands clean, he had survived another ordeal and become more than the leader of the opposition. As a public man, he had been forced by circumstances to be almost wholly on the defensive during the decade he had just lived through. It was much easier, therefore, to see what the country had been saved from than what it had been brought to. He and his party had shown that the spirit of 1776 was by no means dead, that the fruits

---

[57] See especially J. A. Bayard to Samuel Bayard, Feb. 22, 1801, in his correspondence in *A.H.A. Report for 1913*, II, 131–132. His correspondence for this entire period (*ibid.*, II, 116–132) is an invaluable source. Harper's letters to his constituents follow in the same collection.

[58] This question is admirably discussed by Borden, ch. VII. He does not credit Bayard's final actions to Hamilton's influence.

[59] Feb. 18, 1801.

[60] Feb. 20, 1810, as translated in *Correspondence*, p. 30. What Du Pont actually wrote was this: "Vous n'avez jamais eu qu'*un Vice*. Je fais mon compliment à Votre Patrie et aux deux Mondes de ce qu'enfin vous l'avez perdu."

[61] Because of the importance of the events of these weeks as a prologue to the presidency which Jefferson assumed so soon after the decision of Congress, I expect to describe and discuss them further in the next volume of this work.

of the American Revolution need not be lost, that on the political front at least the counter-revolution was checked. They had administered a deserved rebuke to the arrogance and intolerance of High Federalism, and he had kept his record clear as a true friend of liberty — going too far, if anything, in recommending weapons with which to defend it. He had said much, too much in fact, about what he and his party would *not* do in office. There was little likelihood that he would be reckless or destructive, but no one could yet say whether or not he could unify the country after these bitterly divisive years. Many might wonder whether he would be a leader or a presiding officer. As he received congratulations in the North Wing and greeted visitors in his reception room at Conrad's there could be little doubt that an era had ended. But it remained to be seen what sort of era he would start in a new city and a new century.

Acknowledgments

IN VIEW of the fact that aid rendered me in connection with earlier volumes of this series is reflected in the present book, some repetition of previous acknowledgments is in order. It is only fitting that I again make mention of the grant made to me by the Rockefeller Foundation at an early stage of this undertaking. During the life of that grant some of the materials in the present volume were collected, just as some of those collected while it was in process will be used hereafter. In the interim between the appearance of *Jefferson and the Rights of Man* and my retirement from the faculty of Columbia, I had two sabbatical leaves from that University and I now take occasion to express my appreciation of these. The Guggenheim Foundation granted me a fellowship on each of the two years, enabling me to start this volume in the first — though not to get very far with it — and, in the second, to gain a firsthand acquaintance with Palladian architecture in Europe. To that liberal Foundation and most particularly to its General Secretary, Henry Allen Moe, I now return thanks. I hope the benefits of these architectural experiences are reflected to some degree in the present volume and that they will be in later ones.

My sense of indebtedness to the Thomas Jefferson Memorial Foundation is suggested by the dedication of this book to my colleagues on its Board of Directors. They have supported the professorial chair at the University of Virginia which I have been privileged to occupy, first as a visitor and then as a resident, under conditions enabling me to devote myself to Jeffersonian scholarship to a degree which had previously been impossible. They are in no sense responsible for any faults which may be found in this book, but they can hardly escape the charge of being in a special sense its sponsors. I hope it will serve in some measure to justify their faith.

While the materials on which this volume is based were collected over a considerable number of years in a variety of places, all of the writing, except for what was done during summers in my study on Cape Cod, was done in the Alderman Library of the University of

Virginia. No one could ask for better facilities or a more congenial atmosphere than Mr. Jefferson's University has provided. My admiration and affection for the Alderman Library, which I have known so intimately and so long, and for its staff, some of whom I have known as long, have been voiced so many times that I need not express them here. Since I should have to name a score of persons if I once got started I shall content myself with giving the staff a blanket endorsement and general vote of thanks. I have denied the allegation that I sleep at the library, but in a real sense I have written this entire book at home.

Other repositories, especially the Massachusetts Historical Society, have helped me generously, but the one that I have drawn upon most heavily is the Library of Congress, which in its historic origins is Jeffersonian. Without singling out individuals, I want to thank all the officials and attendants in the Division of Manuscripts and the Rare Book Room.

In working on this volume, as on the others, I have had at all times the friendly cooperation of Julian P. Boyd, editor of *The Papers of Thomas Jefferson*, and of his staff at Princeton. Besides giving me the benefit of his learning in connection with numerous specific questions, he read and commented on one of the toughest of my chapters. Alfred L. Bush of that staff has helped me greatly in the matter of Jeffersonian portraiture, a subject on which he speaks with full authority.

I hope I have sufficiently recognized my indebtedness to the written works of other scholars by my references to these in the notes and bibliography, and I trust that if I omitted somebody I may be pardoned. Below I list a few of the many people to whom I am indebted in a more personal way for help and counsel.

James A. Bear, Jr., Curator of Monticello, for making available the construction files and other materials in his office in Jefferson's house, for providing illustrations, for reading several chapters of this book, and for helping me in many other ways.

Harold Jefferson Coolidge, for letting me keep for an inordinately long time a rare and valuable book of his, which was very useful in the preparation of this volume.

Noble E. Cunningham, authority on the organization of the Jeffersonian Republicans, for voluntary suggestions and generous replies to my own questions.

Russell W. Fridley, Director of the Minnesota Historical Society, for preparing for me, years ago when in my seminar at Columbia, a study of Jefferson's *Manual of Parliamentary Practice* which I have recently found very useful.

W. Edwin Hemphill, for sending me, when he was the editor of *Virginia Cavalcade*, interesting and important materials about the election of 1800 in the state.

Mrs. Marjorie M. Keith, for research assistance in newspapers which has been valuable in connection with the present volume as well as its predecessor.

Jerry W. Knudson, my student and friend, for valuable newspaper items, especially in 1800–1801.

Adrienne Koch of the University of California at Berkeley, for reading the troublesome chapters dealing with the Kentucky and Virginia Resolutions, and giving her wise counsel about them and other matters.

Mrs. Audrey Hadow Michie, for intelligent secretarial assistance ending with her marriage, an event which was regrettable for this though for no other reason.

Professor Donald G. Morgan of Mount Holyoke College, for letting me see in manuscript his study of the responsibility of Congress for considering constitutional questions and for valuable suggestions regarding Jefferson's constitutional position and ideas about procedure — with special reference to his *Manual of Parliamentary Practice*.

Frederick D. Nichols, friend, colleague, and authority on Jeffersonian architecture, for reading the chapters dealing with that subject in this book, and for giving me his friendly counsel on numerous occasions.

Mrs. Marjorie H. Payne, secretary, for copying most of these chapters, for checking innumerable references, and for seeing me through the last throes of this volume.

Mrs. Mercedes Renzulli, for valuable secretarial assistance at an earlier time and a very considerable amount of copying.

Archibald F. Robertson, Jr., student and friend, for seminar papers on the Sedition trials and other legal topics which proved most helpful.

James Morton Smith, authority on the Alien and Sedition Acts, for counsel and suggestions.

Finally, I want to thank my publishers, Little, Brown and Company, for their vast patience with a slow-moving author and their skill and celerity once they received his belated copy. And, for yet another time, I do public penance to my wife and family for my absorption in a work which must have seemed endless and which, I fear, made me appear neglectful.

List of Symbols and Short Titles[1] Most Frequently Used in Footnotes

A.H.R.	*American Historical Review.*
A.S.P.F.R.	*American State Papers, Foreign Relations*, ed. by Lowrie and Clark. References here to Vols. I–II (1832).
Account Book	Jefferson's informal account books, in various repositories. Cited by date only.
Adams, *Works*	*Works of John Adams*, ed. by C. F. Adams.
A.-J. Letters	*Adams-Jefferson Letters*, ed. by L. J. Cappon.
Annals	*Annals of Congress.*
Bixby	*Thomas Jefferson Correspondence Printed from the Originals in the Collections of William K. Bixby.*
Brant	*James Madison*, by Irving Brant. Referred to by volume number, chiefly to Vol. III, *Father of the Constitution, 1787–1800.*
C.F.M.	"Correspondence of the French Ministers to the U. S., 1791–1797," *Ann. Report A.H.A. 1903*, Vol. II.
D.A.B.	*Dictionary of American Biography.*
Domestic Life	*Domestic Life of Thomas Jefferson*, by Sarah N. Randolph.
Farm Book	*Thomas Jefferson's Farm Book*, ed. by E. M. Betts.
Fitzpatrick	*Writings of George Washington*, ed. by J. C. Fitzpatrick.

[1] Repositories are designated by roman capitals run together, the names of editors and authors are in roman type, and the abbreviated titles of printed works are in italics. Further details about these works, and about others frequently used but more easily identified from the references in the notes, are in the Select Critical Bibliography which follows. To avoid excess of italics in the lists, long titles are printed there in roman except in cases where a magazine or other work is italicized to distinguish it from an article in it.

Ford
: *Writings of Thomas Jefferson*, ed. by P. L. Ford (10 vols.).

Garden Book
: *Thomas Jefferson's Garden Book*, annotated by E. M. Betts.

Gibbs
: *Memoirs of the Administrations of Washington and John Adams*, ed. from the Papers of Oliver Wolcott by George Gibbs.

HEH
: Henry E. Huntington Library. Unless otherwise indicated, references are to the Jefferson manuscripts.

HP
: Papers of Alexander Hamilton, Library of Congress.

Hunt
: *Writings of James Madison*, ed. by Gaillard Hunt.

I.B.M.
: "Instructions to the British Ministers to the U. S., 1791–1812," *Ann. Report A.H.A. 1936*, Vol. III.

J.C.H.
: *Works of Alexander Hamilton*, ed. by J. C. Hamilton.

J.P.
: *Papers of Thomas Jefferson*, ed. by Julian P. Boyd (Princeton, 1950–   ).

JP
: Jefferson Office in Princeton University Library and files for the Boyd edn.

Jenkins
: *Jefferson's Germantown Letters*, ed. by C. F. Jenkins.

King
: *Life and Correspondence of Rufus King*, ed. by C. R. King.

L. & B.
: *Writings of Thomas Jefferson*, ed. by Lipscomb & Bergh.

LC
: Library of Congress. Unless otherwise indicated the references are to the Jefferson Papers there.

Lodge
: *Works of Alexander Hamilton*, ed. by H. C. Lodge (10 vols.).

MHS
: Massachusetts Historical Society. Unless otherwise indicated the references are to the Jefferson Papers in the Coolidge Collection.

MP
: Papers of James Madison, Library of Congress.

Papers, MHS
: *Jefferson Papers, Collections Massachusetts Historical Society*, 7 ser., I.

Randall
: *Life of Thomas Jefferson*, by H. S. Randall.

S.M.H.
: *Writings of James Monroe*, ed. by S. M. Hamilton.

Sowerby
: *Catalogue of the Library of Thomas Jefferson*, compiled by E. M. Sowerby (5 vols.).

UVA
: Alderman Library, University of Virginia. Unless otherwise indicated the references are to the Jefferson manuscripts.

VSL
: Virginia State Library.

Va. Mag.
: *Virginia Magazine of History and Biography.*

W. & M.
: *William and Mary Quarterly Historical Magazine.*

Select Critical Bibliography

A. *Manuscripts*

AS IN the two earlier volumes of this work, I have drawn chiefly on Jefferson's papers in the Library of Congress (LC), the Massachusetts Historical Society (MHS), and the Alderman Library, University of Virginia (UVA). Since his papers bulk largest in years when he was in office, they are rather less numerous in this period, which extends from late 1792 to early 1801, than in the one covered in *Jefferson and the Rights of Man*. For the year 1793, his last as secretary of state, they seem interminable, but he was in retirement for more than three years after that and had little official business as vice president. In the Library of Congress, for the present period, the documents are chiefly in Volumes 79–109. I have cited them, as heretofore, by dates and folio numbers. They are so well indexed in the card catalogues of the Division of Manuscripts in that great repository that nobody need have any difficulty in finding them. Documents in the Massachusetts Historical Society and the Alderman Library are referred to here by date only. Other supplementary collections at the University of Virginia, such as the Edgehill-Randolph Papers which are important for his family, are referred to by name in the notes, as are those elsewhere.

Photostat copies of Jefferson's Account Books, which are in various repositories, are available at both the Library of Congress and the Alderman Library. The original of the one covering the present period is in the New York Public Library. I have in my own study a photostat copy of this invaluable record and have made it my constant companion. Along with it I have used a photostat of his Index to Letters (LC), written and received. Knowledge of the precise dates at which he received particular communications is often exceedingly important; I have given a number of these dates in the notes.

The Construction File in the office of the Curator of Monticello, James A. Bear, Jr., consisting of copies of extracts from papers bearing on Jefferson's building operations, is not a collection of original documents, but it is exceedingly useful. The same may be said of the copies of his correspondence with his two daughters which are in the same office.

For this volume as for its predecessor, the most useful of the manuscript papers of Jefferson's contemporaries are those of James Madison in the Library of Congress, especially those in Volumes 17–22. I have made greater use than heretofore of the Papers of James Monroe in the same repository, though I do not find that his handwriting has become any easier to read. I have also made considerable use of the Hamilton Papers in the Library of Congress. As the notes indicate, I have drawn on other manuscript collections there and elsewhere, but as a rule I have found the printed writings of Jefferson's other contemporaries more than I could fully utilize. The most important of these are listed below under Contemporary Writings.

B. *Jefferson's Published Papers*

The following work, containing letters to Jefferson as well as those from him and other important materials, has superseded all other printed collections as far as it has proceeded:

The Papers of Thomas Jefferson. Julian P. Boyd, ed. (Princeton, Princeton University Press, 1950–   ).

Of the fifty-odd projected volumes, sixteen have been published at this writing. Unfortunately, these lack several years of reaching the beginning of the period in which the present book falls, but I have used some of them to excellent advantage in connection with the background of certain episodes. As this great edition catches up with me, reference to it should be facilitated by the chronological form of citation I have used. In the meantime, I continue to refer curious readers to older and less adequate editions, citing printed sources for their convenience whenever I can. As in my earlier volumes, I have referred chiefly to the two following collections:

The Writings of Thomas Jefferson. Paul Leicester Ford, ed. (10 vols., New York, 1892–1899). Since this is better than any of the other large collections prior to the Boyd edition, I cite it in preference to them, calling attention to inaccuracies that I have perceived when these seem worth mentioning.

The Writings of Thomas Jefferson. A. A. Lipscomb and A. E. Bergh, eds. (20 vols., Washington, 1903). More extensive than Ford but less accurate in text.

The following smaller collections, containing letters to Jefferson as well as from him, have value that goes beyond their size.

The Jefferson Papers. Collections of the Massachusetts Historical Society, 7 ser., I (Boston, 1900).

Thomas Jefferson Correspondence. Printed from the Originals in the Collections of William Bixby. With notes by W. C. Ford (Boston, 1916).

The Letters of Lafayette and Jefferson. Introduction and notes by Gilbert Chinard (Baltimore, The Johns Hopkins Press, 1929).

Volney et L'Amérique, d'après des documents inédits et sa correspondance avec Jefferson, par Gilbert Chinard (Baltimore, The Johns Hopkins Press, 1923).

The Adams-Jefferson Letters: The Complete Correspondence between Thomas Jefferson and John and Abigail Adams. Lester J. Cappon, ed. Vol. I, 1777-1804 (Chapel Hill, published for the Institute of Early American History and Culture at Williamsburg, Virginia, by the University of North Carolina Press, 1959).

Jefferson's Germantown Letters Together with Other Papers Relating to His Stay in Germantown During the Month of November, 1793. By Charles Francis Jenkins. (Philadelphia, William J. Campbell, 1906).

Thomas Jefferson and James Thomson Callender. By W. C. Ford. (Originally in *New England Historical and Genealogical Register*, vols. 50, 51 [1869-1897]; published separately, 1897).

Correspondence between Thomas Jefferson and Pierre Samuel du Pont de Nemours, 1798-1817. Dumas Malone, ed., translations by Linwood Lehman (Boston and New York, Houghton Mifflin Co., 1930).

Correspondence of Jefferson and Du Pont de Nemours, with an introduction on Jefferson and the Physiocrats, by Gilbert Chinard (Baltimore, The Johns Hopkins Press, 1931). Here Du Pont's letters are in their original French.

Glimpses of the Past. Correspondence of Thomas Jefferson, 1788-1826. Missouri Historical Society, Vol. III, April-June, 1936 (St. Louis, 1936). Chiefly in the year 1801 and thereafter.

The two following works, edited by Edwin M. Betts, are invaluable:

Thomas Jefferson's Garden Book, 1766-1824, with relevant extracts from his other writings (Philadelphia, American Philosophical Society, 1944). The extracts are more important than the entries in these years.

Thomas Jefferson's Farm Book, with commentary and relevant extracts from other writings (Published for the American Philosophical Society by Princeton University Press, 1953). Indispensable for Jefferson's agricultural activities in this period.

The personal letters in Henry S. Randall's *Life of Thomas Jefferson* (3 vols., 1858), a work of enduring merit in itself, impart to it something of the character of a source book. Sarah N. Randolph's *Domestic Life of Thomas Jefferson* (New York, 1871) has a good deal of the same material.

Besides containing all that anyone could ask about his books, E. Millicent Sowerby's *Catalogue of the Library of Thomas Jefferson* (5 vols., The Library of Congress, Washington, 1952–1959) gives rich and pertinent comments that he made on them.

In the bibliography of an earlier volume, I stated that full and precise details about the literary history of the only real book Jefferson ever published could be had from Coolie Verner's *A Further Checklist of the Separate Editions of Jefferson's Notes on the State of Virginia* (Bibliographical Society of the University of Virginia, Charlottesville, 1950). During this period, the following additions to that history were made:

Notes on the State of Virginia. By Thomas Jefferson. Second American Edition. (Philadelphia: Printed for Mathew Carey, No. 118, Market-Street. November 12, 1794.)

An Appendix to the Notes of Virginia Relative to the Murder of Logan's Family (Philadelphia: Printed by Samuel H. Smith, 1800). A second edition was issued immediately after the first in order to include a declaration of John Sappington.

In the bibliography of *Jefferson and the Rights of Man* (p. 497) I commented on the contemporary memoranda known as the "Anas." I have continued to use these for what they were, that is, as notes of the moment. Notably full for his last year as secretary of state, they are much more sparse during his vice presidency, and they were discontinued during his retirement.

The two works listed below contain original materials of the first importance which cannot be described as writings but may be classified under Jefferson's papers:

Thomas Jefferson Architect. Original Designs in the Collection of Thomas Jefferson Coolidge, Junior. With an Essay and Notes by Fiske Kimball. (Boston, printed for private distribution, 1916.) A classic work.

Thomas Jefferson's Architectural Drawings. Compiled and with Commentary and a Check List by Frederick Doveton Nichols. (Boston, Massachusetts Historical Society; Charlottesville, Thomas Jefferson Memorial Foundation and University of Virginia Press. Revised and enlarged second edition. Copyright, 1961.) Supplements Kimball's work and brings it up to date.

C. *Official and Semi-Official Collections*

American State Papers. Selected and Edited, under the Authority of Congress, by Walter Lowrie and Matthew St. Clair Clarke.

> Class I. Foreign Relations. Vols. I, II (1832) are indispensable for this period (referred to as *A.S.P.F.R.*).

> Class III. Finance. Vol. I (1832) is important for the attack on Hamilton in 1792–1793.

Annals of Congress, 2 through 6 Congress, 1793–1801 (1849–1851). Important, despite the dubious reporting of the debates.

Journal of the Executive Proceedings of the Senate of the United States, Vol. I, 1789–1805 (1828).

Correspondence of the French Ministers to the United States, 1791–1797, ed. by Frederick J. Turner (referred to as *C.F.M.*): Annual Report of the American Historical Association for the Year 1903, Vol. II (1904).

Instructions to the British Ministers to the United States, 1791–1813, ed. by Bernard Mayo (*I.B.M.*): Annual Report of the American Historical Association for the Year 1936, Vol. III (1941). Very illuminating.

Treaties and Other International Acts of the United States of America, ed. by Hunter Miller, Vol. II, 1776–1818 (1931).

Francis Wharton, State Trials of the United States during the Administrations of Washington and Adams (1849). Of special value in connection with the Sedition trials.

D. *Contemporary Writings*

1. CORRESPONDENCE AND OTHER PAPERS

ADAMS, ABIGAIL. Letters of Mrs. Adams, the Wife of John Adams, ed. by C. F. Adams (4th edn., Boston, 1848).

———. New Letters of Abigail Adams, 1788–1801, ed. by Stewart Mitchell (Boston, Houghton Mifflin Co., 1947).

ADAMS, JOHN. Works, ed. by C. F. Adams. 10 vols. (Boston, 1856).

———. Correspondence between the Hon. John Adams and the Late William Cunningham (1823). Bears on events dealt with in this volume.

AMES, FISHER. Works, with a Selection from His Speeches and Correspondence, ed. by Seth Ames. 2 vols. (Boston, 1854).

BAYARD, JAMES A. Papers, 1796–1815, ed. by Elizabeth Donnan, Annual Report of the American Historical Association for the Year 1913, Vol. II (Washington, 1915). This valuable collection includes letters of Congressman Robert Goodloe Harper to his constituents.

BURR, AARON. Memoirs of Aaron Burr with Miscellaneous Selections from his Correspondence, by Matthew L. Davis. 2 vols. (New York, 1836–1837).

CABOT, GEORGE. Life and Letters, by Henry Cabot Lodge (Boston, 1878). Contains many letters.

GALLATIN, ALBERT. Writings, ed. by Henry Adams. Vol. I (Philadelphia, 1879). Contains very few items prior to Jefferson's inauguration. The *Life* by Adams is a better source because of the letters in it.

GIBBS, GEORGE. See Wolcott, Oliver.

HAMILTON, ALEXANDER. Works, ed. by John C. Hamilton. 7 vols. (New York, 1850–1851). I have used this (referring to it as J.C.H.) almost interchangeably with the Lodge edn. Neither is at all adequate.

HAMILTON, ALEXANDER. Works, ed. by Henry Cabot Lodge. 9 vols. (New York, 1885–1886). Difficult to use because of the topical arrangement and marred by extreme partisanship, but a present necessity.

HARPER, ROBERT GOODLOE. See Bayard, James A.

JAY, JOHN. Correspondence and Public Papers, ed. by Henry P. Johnston. 4 vols. (New York, 1890–1892).

JONES, JOSEPH. Letters to Madison (1788–1802), in *Proceedings Massachusetts Historical Society*, XV (1902), 122–161.

KING, RUFUS. Life and Correspondence, ed. by Charles R. King. Vols. I–III (New York, 1894–1896) cover this period, and, because of the letters to King from so many leaders of his party, they are an invaluable source for High Federalist opinion.

MADISON, JAMES. Writings, ed. by Gaillard Hunt. 9 vols. (New York, 1900–1910). This edn. requires much supplementation but is indispensable.

———. Letters and Other Writings, published by order of Congress. 4 vols. (1894). Contains some letters not in Hunt.

MONROE, JAMES. Writings, ed. by S. M. Hamilton (referred to as S.M.H.). 7 vols. (New York, 1898–1903).

OTTO, LOUIS-GUILLAUME. "Considérations sur la conduite du Gouvernement américain envers la France, depuis le commencement de la Révolution jusqu'en 1797" (*Bulletin de l'Institut Français de Washington*, No. XVI, December, 1943, pp. 9–37).

PAINE, THOMAS. Complete Writings, ed. by Philip S. Foner. 2 vols. (New York, Citadel Press, 1945).

———. Writings, ed. by Moncure D. Conway. Vol. III (New York, 1895).

PINCKNEY, CHARLES. Letters to Jefferson and Madison, 1800–1801, in *American Historical Review*, IV, 113–129 (October, 1898).

POWELL, LEVEN. Correspondence Relating to the Election of 1800, in *John P. Branch Papers of Randolph-Macon College*, I (1901), 54–63, 242–251.

PRIESTLEY, JOSEPH. Life and Correspondence, by John T. Rutt (1831).

RUSH, BENJAMIN. Autobiography. His "Travels through Life" together with his Commonplace Book for 1789–1813, ed. by George W. Corner (Published for the American Philosophical Society by Princeton University Press, 1948).

———. Letters, ed. by L. H. Butterfield. Vol. II (Published for the American Philosophical Society by Princeton University Press, 1951).

SMITH, MARGARET BAYARD. The First Forty Years of Washington Society, ed. by Gaillard Hunt (New York, Scribner's, 1906). Because of its contemporary letters, an important source for Jefferson's presidency, but relatively unimportant before that.

South Carolina Federalists. Correspondence, 1789–1797, in *American Historical Review*, XIV, 776–790 (July, 1909).

TAYLOR, JOHN. Letters, May 11, 1793 — April 19, 1823, in *John P. Branch Historical Papers of Randolph-Macon College*, II (June, 1908), 253–353.

WASHINGTON, GEORGE. Writings, ed. by J. C. Fitzpatrick. 39 vols. (Washington, Government Printing Office, 1931–1941). Vols. XXXII–XXXVII, covering this period, have been invaluable.

———. Washington's Farewell Address, ed. by Victor H. Paltsits (New York, New York Public Library, 1935). A richly documented and moving story of the composition of the address.

WOLCOTT, OLIVER. Memoirs of the Administrations of Washington and John Adams, ed. from the papers of Oliver Wolcott by George Gibbs. 2 vols. (New York, 1946). Comparable to King as a source of High Federalist opinion.

2. TRAVELS

DAVIS, JOHN. Travels of Four Years and a Half in the United States of America; during 1798, 1799, 1800, 1801, 1802 (New York, 1803). More important for the later years than the earlier ones.

ERSKINE, D. M. Letters from America, 1798–1799, ed. by Patricia Holbert Menk, in *William and Mary Quarterly*, April, 1949, pp. 251–284. Contains some interesting references to Jefferson and considerable comment on the Philadelphia scene.

LA ROCHEFOUCAULD LIANCOURT, FRANÇOIS A. F., DUC DE. Travels through the United States of North America. 2 vols. (London, 1799). Contains an account of a visit to Monticello.

MICHAUX, ANDRÉ. Portions of the Journal of André Michaux . . . 1785 to 1796, with introduction and notes by C. S. Sargent, in *Proceedings American Philosophical Society*, XXVI (1889). Journal in French.

———. Journal of Travels into Kentucky, in R. G. Thwaites, *Early Western Travels* (Cleveland, A. H. Clark Co., 1904). Translated from the above.

MOREAU DE ST. MÉRY. Moreau de St. Méry's American Journey (1793–

1798), trans. and ed. by Kenneth and Anna M. Roberts (New York, Doubleday & Co., 1947).

WANSEY, HENRY. An Excursion to the States of North America, in the summer of 1794 (2nd edn., Salisbury, 1798).

WELD, ISAAC, JR. Travels through the States of North America . . . during the Years 1795, 1796, and 1797 (2nd edn., London, 1799). Contains the account of a visit to Monticello.

E. *Newspapers and Contemporary Pamphlets*

Newspapers are exceedingly important in this period, although when reading them one must make large allowance for their partisan extravagance and their scurrility. As the notes show, I have dipped into many of them. Owing to their custom of copying one another freely and their tendency to follow the line of their party, though with individual divergences and varying excesses, there would be no point in anybody's reading all of them, except for purposes of entertainment, even if he could. It is wise as well as necessary to follow a selective procedure and to use representative papers. Partisanship was the rule rather than the exception, but this varied considerably in degree; in a surprising number of cases it did not preclude the printing of communications on both sides of the political argument. Only in the last years of this period did editorial comment amount to much, and even then it was limited to a relatively small number of publishers, as the men in charge of newspapers were generally called.

Even in the last years of the century, newspapers supporting the party of the administration outnumbered those favoring the party of opposition two or three to one. On the Federalist side, I have chiefly used the following:

Philadelphia *Gazette of the United States*, published by John Fenno until his death late in 1798, and successively thereafter by John Ward Fenno and Caleb P. Wayne. This paper, which was favored with government printing and received considerable financial aid from Hamilton and his friends, faithfully followed the party line as laid down by the "Colossus of Federalism."

Philadelphia *Porcupine's Gazette*, published by William Cobbett from Mar. 4, 1797 to Oct. 26, 1799. Extracts from this were afterwards published in William Cobbett, *Porcupine's Works*, Vols. IX, X (London, 1801). This brilliant journalist, who attacked Joseph Priestley so bitterly, had a marked individuality. In power of invective he was unmatched among the Federalist newspapermen.

Among other important administration papers may be mentioned the Boston *Columbian Centinel* and Noah Webster's New York *Commercial Advertiser*, successor to the *Minerva*. When the test came, Webster was for Adams, against Hamilton. The Georgetown *Washington Federalist* has importance as an administration journal in 1800–1801. For information about the publishers of these and other papers, and the available files, reference should be made to the invaluable work of Clarence S. Brigham, *History and Bibliography of American Newspapers, 1690–1820* (2 vols., American Antiquarian Society, Worcester, 1947).

Of the outnumbered Republican papers I have chiefly made use of the following:

Philadelphia *National Gazette*, published by Philip Freneau until its discontinuance after Oct. 26, 1793. In 1793 its position was extreme in comparison with that of Jefferson.

Philadelphia *Aurora*, and it predecessor, the *General Advertiser*. Published by Benjamin Franklin Bache until his death in September, 1798, and after that by William Duane, this was the major opposition paper throughout almost all of this period.

Washington *National Intelligencer*, established by Samuel Harrison Smith Oct. 31, 1800, and of great importance from that time on.

Richmond *Virginia Argus*, especially for the campaign of 1800.

Other important Republican papers were the Boston *Independent Chronicle*, published until May, 1799, by Thomas Adams; New York *Argus*, published successively by Thomas Greenleaf and David Frothingham; and toward the end of the century, Richmond *Examiner* of Meriwether Jones, the paper with which Callender was connected for a time.

At various points in the text reference has been made to Jefferson's relations with the party press. He sought to encourage Republican papers, making some financial contributions to them as other leaders did, but he did not send communications to them and appears to have made no effort to direct their policies. When the facts all come out, I think it will appear that Hamilton, besides contributing numerous communications and considerably more money to publishers, had a much greater direct influence on their policy. Of Jefferson's emphasis on the importance of the press, however, there can be no doubt whatever.

The brief list of pamphlets, and of communications to newspapers that afterwards appeared as pamphlets, which I give below is merely suggestive. In rough chronological order, the following emanated from the Republican side:

JOHN TAYLOR. An Examination of the Late Proceedings in Congress, respecting the Official Conduct of the Secretary of the Treasury (1793).

GEORGE NICHOLAS. A Letter from George Nicholas of Kentucky, to His Friend in Virginia, Justifying the Conduct of the Citizens of

Kentucky (Lexington, 1798). Relating to the Kentucky Resolutions.

JOHN BECKLEY. Address to the People of the United States, with an Epitome and Vindication of the Public Life and Character of Thomas Jefferson (Pennsylvania, 1800). This pamphlet, published under a pseudonym, was widely reprinted, especially the epitome of Jefferson's life.

CHARLES PINCKNEY. A series of papers, signed A REPUBLICAN, appearing in Charleston *City Gazette*, August–October, 1800, and widely reprinted.

On the other side, mention may be made of:

WILLIAM LOUGHTON SMITH. The Pretensions of Thomas Jefferson to the Presidency Examined; and the Charges against John Adams Refuted (two parts, October–November, 1796). This was replied to in part by Tench Coxe, in a pamphlet called "The Federalist."

BURLEIGH. A series of 15 letters, originally published in *Connecticut Courant*, and appearing in New York *Commercial Advertiser*, July–October, 1800, which included a violent attack on Jefferson.

JOHN M. MASON. The Voice of Warning to Christians, on the Election of a President of the United States of America (New York, 1800). One of the most noted of the clerical pamphlets against Jefferson.

The list could be extended to great length but the lines of argument can be readily perceived from the foregoing. The notorious pamphlets of James Thomson Callender are mentioned and sufficiently described in the text and notes, so we need not recur to that unpleasant subject. Nor do we need to refer here to the much more significant contributions of Madison, Monroe, Gallatin, Thomas Cooper, and others, since these are readily accessible or have already been sufficiently described.

F. *Secondary Works and Articles*[1]

ADAMS, HENRY. The Life of Albert Gallatin (Philadelphia, 1879).

ADAMS, JOHN QUINCY. Parties in the United States (New York, Greenberg, 1941).

AMMON, HARRY. "The Formation of the Republican Party in Virginia, 1789–1796," *Journal of Southern History*, XIX (August, 1953), pp. 283–310.

———. The Republican Party in Virginia, 1789 to 1824 (Doctoral dissertation, University of Virginia, 1948).

ANDERSON, DICE R. William Branch Giles: A Study in the Politics of Virginia and the Nation from 1790 to 1830 (Menasha, Wisconsin, George Banta Publishing Company, 1914).

---

[1] This very select list contains the titles of indispensable works and others to which I am specially indebted.

——. "Edmund Randolph," in Bemis, ed., *American Secretaries of State*, ed. by S. F. Bemis, vol. II (New York, Knopf, 1927), pp. 97–159.

ANDERSON, FRANK M. "Contemporary Opinion of the Virginia and Kentucky Resolutions," *American Historical Review*, V, 45–64, 225–253 (October, 1899; January, 1900).

BALDWIN, LELAND D. Whiskey Rebels; The Story of a Frontier Uprising (University of Pittsburgh Press, 1939).

BEARD, CHARLES A. Economic Origins of Jeffersonian Democracy (New York, Macmillan, 1915).

BEMIS, SAMUEL FLAGG. Jay's Treaty. A Study in Commerce and Diplomacy (New York, Macmillan, 1924).

——. Pinckney's Treaty. A Study of America's Advantage from Europe's Distress (Baltimore, The Johns Hopkins Press, 1926).

——. "Thomas Jefferson," in *American Secretaries of State and their Diplomacy*, ed. by S. F. Bemis, Vol. II (New York, Knopf, 1927).

——. "Washington's Farewell Address: A Foreign Policy of Independence," *American Historical Review*, XXXIX (January, 1934), pp. 250–268.

BEVERIDGE, ALBERT J. The Life of John Marshall. Vol. II (Boston and New York, Houghton Mifflin Co., 1916). Reflects Marshall's unfriendly view of Jefferson and his party.

BORDEN, MORTON. The Federalism of James A. Bayard (New York, Columbia University Press, 1955).

BOWERS, CLAUDE G. Jefferson and Hamilton (Boston and New York, Houghton Mifflin Co., 1925). Still interesting but exaggerates Jefferson's role as party leader and views him uncritically.

BOWMAN, ALBERT HALL. The Struggle for Neutrality. A History of the Diplomatic Relations between the United States and France, 1790–1801 (Doctoral dissertation, Columbia University, 1953).

BRANT, IRVING. "Edmund Randolph, Not Guilty!" *William and Mary Quarterly*, 3 ser., VII (April, 1950), pp. 179–198.

——. James Madison: Father of the Constitution, 1787–1800 (1950).

——. James Madison: Secretary of State, 1801–1809 (Indianapolis and New York, Bobbs-Merrill, 1953).

BURT, A. L. The United States, Great Britain, and British North America (New Haven, Yale University Press, 1940).

BUSH, ALFRED L. The Life Portraits of Thomas Jefferson. Catalogue of an exhibition at the University of Virginia Museum of Fine Arts, April 12 through 26, 1962 (Charlottesville, Thomas Jefferson Memorial Foundation, 1962). Supplementing Kimball's study, this is the latest authoritative word on the subject.

CARROLL, JOHN ALEXANDER, and MARY WELLS ASHWORTH. George Washington, Vol. 7, completing the biography by Douglas Southall Freeman (New York, Charles Scribner's Sons, 1957).

CHARLES, JOSEPH. The Origins of the American Party System; Three Essays (Williamsburg, Institute of Early American History and Culture, 1956).

CHILDS, FRANCES. "The Hauterive Journal," *New-York Historical Society Quarterly*, XXXIII (April, 1949), pp. 69–86.

CRESSON, W. P. James Monroe (Chapel Hill, University of North Carolina Press, 1946).

CUNNINGHAM, NOBLE E., JR. The Jeffersonian Republicans: The Formation of Party Organization, 1789–1801 (University of North Carolina Press, for Institute of Early American History and Culture at Williamsburg, 1957).

———. "John Beckley: An Early American Party Manager," *William and Mary Quarterly* (January, 1956), pp. 41–52.

DARLING, ARTHUR B. Our Rising Empire (New Haven, Yale University Press, 1940).

DAUER, MANNING J. The Adams Federalists (Baltimore, The Johns Hopkins Press, 1953).

———. "The Two John Nicholases, Their Relationship to Washington and Jefferson," *American Historical Review*, XLV (January, 1940), pp. 338–354.

DAVIDSON, PHILIP G. "Virginia and the Alien and Sedition Laws," *American Historical Review*, XXXVI (January, 1931), pp. 336–342.

DE CONDE, ALEXANDER. "Washington's Farewell, the French Alliance, and the Election of 1796," *Mississippi Valley Historical Review*, XLIII (March, 1957), pp. 641–658.

DUMBAULD, EDWARD. Thomas Jefferson: American Tourist (Norman, University of Oklahoma Press, 1946). Useful for this, as for earlier periods.

GAINES, WILLIAM H., JR. Thomas Mann Randolph of Edgehill (Doctoral dissertation, University of Virginia, 1950).

GARLICK, RICHARD CECIL, JR. Philip Mazzei, Friend of Jefferson, His Life and Letters (The Johns Hopkins Studies in Romance Literatures and Languages, extra vol. VII, Baltimore, The Johns Hopkins Press, 1933).

HARASZTI, ZOLTÁN. John Adams and the Prophets of Progress (Cambridge, Harvard University Press, 1952).

KIMBALL, FISKE. Thomas Jefferson, Architect (Boston, 1916).

———. "The Life Portraits of Jefferson and Their Replicas," *Proceedings of the American Philosophical Society*, Vol. 88, No. 6 (December, 1944), pp. 497–534.

KNOLLENBERG, BERNHARD. "John Adams, Knox, and Washington," *Proceedings American Antiquarian Society*, N.S. LVI (Worcester, 1947), pp. 207–238. Dealing with the seniority squabble.

KOCH, ADRIENNE. Jefferson and Madison: The Great Collaboration (New York, Knopf, 1950).

Koch, Adrienne, and Harry Ammon. "The Virginia and Kentucky Resolutions: An Episode in Jefferson's and Madison's Defense of Civil Liberties," *William and Mary Quarterly* (April, 1948), pp. 145–176.

Kurtz, Stephen G. The Presidency of John Adams. The Collapse of Federalism, 1795–1800 (Philadelphia, University of Pennsylvania Press, 1957).

Lerche, Charles O., Jr. "Jefferson and the Election of 1800: A Case Study in the Political Smear," *William and Mary Quarterly* (October, 1948), pp. 467–491.

Levy, Leonard W. Legacy of Suppression: Freedom of Speech and Press in Early American History (Cambridge, Belknap Press, 1960).

Link, Eugene Perry. Democratic-Republican Societies, 1790–1800 (New York, Columbia University Press, 1942).

McCarrell, David K. The Formation of the Jeffersonian Party in Virginia (Doctoral dissertation, Duke University, 1937).

Malone, Dumas. The Public Life of Thomas Cooper, 1783–1839 (New Haven, Yale University Press, 1926. Reprint, Columbia, University of South Carolina Press, 1961).

Marsh, Philip. "Hamilton and Monroe," *Mississippi Valley Historical Review*, XXXIV (December, 1947), pp. 459–468.

———. "John Beckley, Mystery Man of the Early Jeffersonians," *Pennsylvania Magazine of History and Biography* (January, 1948), pp. 54–69.

Martin, Edwin T. Thomas Jefferson: Scientist (New York, Henry Schuman, 1952).

Mayer, Brantz. Tah-gah-jute, or Logan and Cresap (Albany, 1867).

Miller, John C. Alexander Hamilton: Portrait in Paradox (New York, Harper & Bros., 1959).

———. Crisis in Freedom: The Alien and Sedition Acts (Boston, Little, Brown and Company, 1951).

Morison, S. E. "Elbridge Gerry, Gentleman-Democrat," *New England Quarterly*, II (January, 1929), pp. 6–33.

———. The Life and Letters of Harrison Gray Otis. Vol. I. (Boston, Houghton Mifflin Co., 1913).

Mott, Frank L. Jefferson and the Press (Baton Rouge, Louisiana State University Press, 1943).

Palmer, Robert R. The Age of the Democratic Revolution (Princeton, Princeton University Press, 1959).

———. "Reflections on the French Revolution," *Political Science Quarterly*, LXVII (March, 1952), pp. 64–80.

Powell, J. H. Bring Out Your Dead: The Great Plague of Yellow Fever in Philadelphia in 1793 (Philadelphia, University of Pennsylvania Press, 1949).

Schachner, Nathan. Aaron Burr, A Biography (New York, F. A. Stokes Company, 1937).

————. Alexander Hamilton (New York, Appleton-Century, 1946).

SETSER, VERNON G. The Commercial Reciprocity Policy of the United States, 1774–1829 (Philadelphia, University of Pennsylvania Press, 1937).

SIMMS, HENRY H. Life of John Taylor (Richmond, William Byrd Press, 1932).

SMITH, JAMES MORTON. Freedom's Fetters; The Alien and Sedition Laws and American Civil Liberties (Ithaca, Cornell University Press, 1956).

STEWART, DONALD H. Jeffersonian Journalism. Newspaper Propaganda and the Development of the Democratic-Republican Party, 1789–1801 (Doctoral dissertation, Columbia University, 1950).

THOMAS, CHARLES MARION. American Neutrality in 1793. A Study in Cabinet Government (New York, Columbia University Press, 1931).

TINKCOM, HARRY MARLIN. Republicans and Federalists in Pennsylvania, 1790–1801 (Harrisburg, Pennsylvania, Pennsylvania Historical and Museum Commission, 1950).

TOLLES, FREDERICK B. George Logan of Philadelphia (New York, Oxford University Press, 1953).

WALTERS, RAYMOND, JR. Alexander James Dallas: Lawyer-Politician-Financier, 1759–1817 (Philadelphia, University of Pennsylvania Press, 1943).

————. Albert Gallatin. Jeffersonian Financier and Diplomat (New York, Macmillan, 1957).

WHITE, LEONARD D. The Federalists. A Study in Administrative History (New York, Macmillan, 1948).

WOODFIN, MAUDE HOWLETT. Citizen Genet and His Mission (Doctoral dissertation, University of Chicago, 1928).

————. "Contemporary Opinion in Virginia of Thomas Jefferson," in Essays in Honor of William E. Dodd, ed. by Avery Craven (Chicago, University of Chicago Press, 1935).

WOODRESS, JAMES. A Yankee's Odyssey: The Life of Joel Barlow (Philadelphia and New York, J. B. Lippincott Company, 1958).

Long Notes on the Attack on Hamilton

(Ch. II, note 18). TJ's comments on Hamilton's report of Jan. 3, 1793, (*Am. State Papers, Finance*, I, 180–183) and the tables made by him out of the figures he drew from it, are in LC, 16478–16480, in the form of a press copy. The original of this document, except for the very last part where a page seems to be missing, is in MP, Vol. 15, showing that at some time it was given or sent to Madison. The document, which has neither title nor date, is printed by Ford (VI, 165–168) under the heading "Mal-Administration of the Treasury," supplied by the editor, and with the conjectured date, Feb. 7, 1793. Internal evidence leads to the opinion that it was written in the period between Jan. 4 and Feb. 4, that is, the dates at which two of Hamilton's reports were received by the House, and probably before Jan. 18, when Hamilton submitted a statement in response to the Senate resolution of Jan. 15, 1793 (See Ford, VI, 165, 176 and note). A similar but not identical document is printed in J. C. Hamilton's edn. of his father's *Works* IV, 334–337) with the title "Jefferson to Washington," and the tables seem jumbled. The title appears to have been imposed by the editor, who does not say where he got the document.

(Ch. II, note 44). In the attempt to show that TJ's conduct in this whole episode was hypocritical and deliberately deceptive, passages from a letter of his to Hamilton, on Mar. 27, 1793 (Ford, VI, 208–209), have been quoted (Schachner, *Hamilton*, p. 314). This letter was in response to Hamilton's request for his view of the "destination" of a loan of three million florins made previous to the acts of Aug. 4, 12, 1790, when it was proposed to include it under those acts. His reply was based on a memo. made at the time (Aug. 26, 1790). The particular passages are:

(1) The subject however not being within my department, and therefore having no occasion afterwards to pay attention to it, it went out of my mind altogether, till the late enquiries brought it forward again.

He may very well have forgotten the precise circumstances until the matter came up in Congress. The allegation of hypocrisy here is based on the assumption that the entire movement in Congress was instigated by him.

> (2) [After having stated the view he took in 1790] I did not take it up then as a Volunteer, nor should now have taken the trouble of recurring to it, but at your request; as it is one in which I am not particularly concerned, which I never had either the time or inclination to investigate, & on which my opinion is of no importance.

This might have been strictly true with respect to this particular episode, and such investigation as TJ engaged in during this fight appears to have been on the basis of Hamilton's published reports. To say that he was "not particularly concerned," and that his opinion was of no importance, was to engage in elaborate irony or sarcasm.

In other words, the episode does not seem to mean much, one way or the other.

For TJ's opinion of Aug. 26, 1790, on fiscal policy, referred to by me on p. 527 as a memo., see *J.P.*, XVII, 425–430, which appeared (1965) after this book was first printed. In his extensive note the Editor emphasizes the official character of this paper, which was drafted at Washington's request, and minimizes the "depreciatory comment" with which TJ's letter of Mar. 27, 1793, to Hamilton closed. The Editor regards the latter letter as a challenge to Hamilton to ask Washington for a statement supporting his position. Thus this episode, which I seem to have underplayed, bears directly on Hamilton's later attempt to clear himself before a congressional committee (see p. 181, above). Also, in the light of the extended treatment of the episode now available, TJ appears to have been more fully informed of the situation in 1790 than my account of events of the winter of 1792–1793 may have led readers to suppose (see p. 20, above). — AUTHOR.

Long Note on Jefferson's Debts*

THE Wayles inheritance and the debt that went with it are described in an appendix in *Jefferson the Virginian*, pp. 441–444. There were numerous gaps in the record when I wrote that account, and these may never be wholly filled. The documents in *J.P.*, XV, 643–646, from old court records, especially the formal agreement of Feb. 7, 1790, between TJ, Francis Eppes, and Henry Skipwith on the one hand, and Richard Hanson representing Farell & Jones on the other, constitute a valuable addition to the fragmentary and widely scattered source material. The illuminating editorial note is most helpful to anyone trying to understand these complicated transactions. TJ used the spelling "Farrell" instead of "Farell," and I perpetuated that easy mistake. It now appears that no interest was charged on this debt for the period of the war, 1775–1783, a point on which I was originally in doubt.

The mortgage on TJ's slaves, which is referred to in Ch. X of the text, covered his debt to Henderson, McCaul & Co., and a number of other obligations, including the smaller one to Nicholas and Jacob Van Staphorst of Amsterdam, with whom he appears to have become acquainted on his visit to that city with John Adams in 1788. Among documents bearing on this transaction are a deed between him and this firm, dated Nov. 21, 1796 (LC, 17247), mortgaging 150 slaves and conveying them to various creditors; and bonds to the bankers for their loans. From the endorsement on one of these papers, it appears that the latter were finally paid off June 7, 1818 (LC, 17331–17333; see also 17340, 17506, and Account Book, Mar. 26, 1797). His account with Henderson, McCaul & Co., 1790–1798, is in Edgehill-Randolph Papers (UVA).

A monograph on Jefferson's financial history is still needed, and until one is written no doubt we shall remain uncertain about a number of details. Meanwhile, the main outline is clear enough for the period under consideration. To the references in Appendix II of *Jefferson the*

* Referred to in ch. X, note 35.

Virginian and those already given in the present volume, the following may be added: TJ to Francis Eppes, Mar. 11, 1792 (LC, 12450–12451), summarizing provisions for the payment of his bonds to Hanson; TJ to Richard Hanson, Sept. 25, 1792 (MHS), giving power of attorney for the collection of bonds to him; TJ to James Lyle, July 29, 1792, and Lyle to TJ, Aug. 11, 1792, and Dec. 14, 1794 (MHS), about arrangements with Henderson, McCaul & Co.; TJ to James Brown, Dec. 20, 1792, and to Francis Eppes, Apr. 7, 1793, (MHS), Aug. 1, 1796 (LC, 17192) regarding the case of Cary's executor; TJ to Mr. Clarke, Aug. 5, 1794 (MHS), regarding suits against people in debt to him.

Index

Index

of collectors of customs to enforce neutrality, 84; laments personal sacrifices in public office, 88; progressively disillusioned with Genet, 96–8, 101–03, 114; denies right of French to arm and man privateers in American ports, 77, 100, 102; connection with Michaux expedition, 104–109; urges Madison to answer Hamilton's PACIFICUS papers, 110; actions in connection with *Little Democrat*, 114–18; in connection with Genet's recall, 122–26, 128–29, 144, 148; recommends that Republicans support neutrality and repudiate Genet, 134–35; services in Germantown, 147–52; final services in Philadelphia, 152–62

Relations to public affairs during retirement (1794–1797), xvii; informed of developments by Madison, 180–81, 246, 255, 259; of French affairs by Monroe, 186–87, 260; continued suspicions of Hamilton's financial operations, 181–82, 255–56; increasingly anti-British, 183, 260; declines appointto Spain, 187–88; disturbed by administration's interpretation of Whiskey Rebellion and attack on democratic societies, 189–91; hopes to see Madison President, 191; says (1795) that for him matter is "forever closed," 193; has nothing to do with public questions, 245; disapproves of Jay's Treaty, 245, 247–49, 254; writes Adet, 249–50; privately supports constitutional position of Republicans in House, 251–52, 256–57; nonparticipant in Presidential election (1796), 273; "nominated" by Republican congressional leaders, 274–75; attitude to Adams, 275–76, 289–94; attacked and defended in campaign, 277, 279–83; elected Vice President, 290; prefers second office, 291–92

Vice President: inauguration, 296–97; regards functions as purely legislative, 300; compiles manual of parliamentary procedure, 317–18, 453–56; official duties light, 360; annoying remarks against, in Senate, 433; farewell to Senate, 457–58

Leader of the Opposition, xvii–xix; notes war fever, 301; learns of publication of Mazzei letter, 302; pursues policy of silence about this, 303–05;

breach with Washington, 308–11; turns against Adams, 316; seeks to influence moderates and hearten faithful, 319; avoids publicity, 320; object of newspaper attacks, 322; conciliates Burr and re-forms inner circle of leaders, 323–24; attitude in Reynolds affair, 327–28; insinuation of Hamilton against, 329–30; draws paper in Cabell case, 335; procedure in protection of individual rights (1797), 336–37; accepts Monroe's defense of conduct in France, 337–38; attacked by Luther Martin, 320, 346–50; services in XYZ Congress, 359, 361; characterizes parties, 364–65; attacked in House, 366–68; seeks peace, 369, 415; favors independent foreign policy, 313–14, 369, 382, 441; charged with correspondence with Directory, 371–72; with contempt for Christian religion, 380; declines to answer "calumnies," 391–92; sees supreme challenge in Alien and Sedition Acts, 393; advocates popular election of jurors, 398–99; drafts Kentucky Resolutions, 402; flexible in tactics, 407–08, 409; opposes recourse to force, 409, 414; stimulates public discussion, 411; distributes literature, 412, 462; influences policy on only state and local level (1798–1799), 425; discusses military proposals of Federalists, 427; learns of state of mind of French officials, 430–32; interprets Adams's reopening of negotiations, 434–36; approves change in Virginia election law, 460; improperly charged with directing Republican writers, 466–67; gives financial help to Callender, 332–33, 469, 470–71, 472; attitude to Burr as running mate, 474; attacks on (1800), 479–82; own view of public services, 484–85; strongly supported in Virginia, 489–90; learns of party success in election, 492; writes R. R. Livingston, 494; correspondence with Burr (1800–1801), 494–95, 496–97, 500; elected President by House of Representatives, 504–05

Papers
(*see* Bibliography)

Opinion (1793) on applicability of treaties with France, 76–79; letter to Morris regarding conduct of Genet,